Production and Operations Management

Theory and Practice

Dipak Kumar Bhattacharyya

Professor

Xavier Institute of Management, Bhubaneshwar

Universities Press

UNIVERSITIES PRESS (INDIA) PRIVATE LIMITED

Registered Office
3-6-747/1/A & 3-6-754/1, Himayatnagar, Hyderabad 500 029 (A.P.), India
email: info@universitiespress.com, www.universitiespress.com

Distributed by
Orient Blackswan Private Limited

Registered Office
3-6-752 Himayatnagar, Hyderabad 500 029 (A.P.), India

Other Offices
Bengaluru / Bhopal / Bhubaneshwar / Chandigarh / Chennai / Ernakulam / Guwahati / Hyderabad / Jaipur / Kolkata / Lucknow / Mumbai / New Delhi / Noida / Patna

ISBN 978 81 7371 776 5

Typeset in Iowan Old Style 10.5 by
OSDATA, Hyderabad 500 049

Printed in India by
Indcom Press, Chennai 600 042

Published by
Universities Press (India) Private Limited
3-6-747/1/A & 3-6-754/1, Himayatnagar, Hyderabad 500 029 (A.P.), India

Preface

The impetus for writing this book dates back to the early 1980s, when I worked for the *Indian Ordnance Factories*. I started my career there on the shop floor. Placed at the heart of production, I became closely involved with the training and development of workers. During this period, I developed an interest in the intricacies of the Production and Operations function.

Thereafter, in the 1990s, I taught Production and Operations Management as a subject at several business schools in the country. I felt then that a textbook, covering all aspects of this branch of management, was necessary and I looked for an opportunity to write such a book. Universities Press has now given me the opportunity to do so.

In writing this book, I have used my own experiences as a teacher, researcher and practitioner, and have kept in view the requirements of management students.

Production and Operations Management is compulsory reading for MBA students as it is a core subject. However, students often find it a challenging subject, given its engineering orientation. To enhance their understanding, practical examples from industry have been used to explain theory, making it pleasant reading for students.

Each chapter has been carefully crafted, to be in tune with industry requirements, thereby enabling students to become up-to-date in the theories and practices of the subject.

The special features of this book are:

- The language is lucid
- There is limited use of technical jargon
- Case studies have been added
- Explanation of theories with practices from industry have been given as examples
- Numerical examples have been included
- Discussion of contemporary areas have been added
- Adequate examples and illustrations have been provided
- General and Critical Review Questions have been appended at the end of each chapter.

The book is divided into 18 chapters. It conforms to the syllabus requirements of most national and international MBA/PGDBM programmes.

Emerging areas discussed in this book are: Ethical Issues in Production and Operations, Six Sigma Practices, Production and Operations Management Research, and International Production and Operations Management.

Chapter 1 introduces the Production and Operations Management function. It defines the concepts and characteristics and explains the transformation process model. It also highlights the manufacturing plant, the role and functions of the production and operations manager, outlines recent trends and takes up strategic issues for discussion.

Chapter 2 introduces Production Planning and Control, explaining the concepts involved, production planning functions, aggregate planning, master production schedule, capacity requirements planning, material requirements planning, manufacturing requirements planning II, forecasting tools and techniques and decision making.

Chapter 3 is unique, as it discusses New Product Planning and Development, and covers concepts, processes, product and service life cycle analysis, process selection and break-even analysis.

Chapter 4 highlights Facilities Planning, Layout and Location Analysis; it introduces various tools and techniques, models, flowcharting and location analysis.

Chapter 5 covers Scheduling and Sequencing Techniques, both in production and in service operations, introducing various tools and techniques; it discusses the use of Gantt Charts, Johnson's Rule and Queueing Theory.

Chapter 6 explains Work Study and Work Measurement Techniques, detailing the concepts of job information, job analysis, job description, job evaluation, job pricing, work study and method study, work measurement techniques, ergonomics and machine design, motion economy and work sampling for work simplification.

Chapter 7 focusses on Network Analysis and Project Management, introducing the concepts of float, PERT/CPM networks, crashing of project time, project life cycle analysis, project planning and the duties and responsibilities of project managers.

Chapter 8 covers Maintenance Management, highlighting total productive maintenance and overall equipment effectiveness (OEE) strategies, best practice maintenance, spare parts planning and maintenance and reliability.

Chapter 9 introduces Quality Management Practices and discusses its influence on organizational improvement. ISO standards and quality systems management, Six Sigma and innovation and creativity, employee empowerment, quality of work life, quality circles, quality function deployment, and statistical process control are covered in this chapter.

Chapter 10 covers the application of Six Sigma in production and operations management functions. It also highlights quick response manufacturing and lean practices, and Six Sigma and HR strategies.

Chapter 11 combines Cross-cultural Aspects and the various models of excellence with BPR and TQM. Lean Practices, Toyota Production System, and Quick Response Manufacturing practices have been discussed from a cross-cultural perspective.

Chapter 12 covers the strategic interface of Human Resource Management with Production and Operations Management functions.

Chapter 13 elaborates on Productivity, Incentives and Production and Operations Management, introducing various measurement tools and techniques.

Chapter 14 is dedicated to the Materials Management and Inventory Control functions, highlighting various tools and techniques.

Chapter 15 introduces Supply Chain Management, its processes, strategies, the decision making involved, and models.

Chapter 16 is a new area. It covers Ethics, Corporate Social Responsibility, Environment Management and related issues.

Chapter 17 is a discussion of various Production and Operations Management Research issues, with details on the use of various tools and techniques.

Chapter 18 is about International Production and Operations Management.

The book covers new areas, which are essential, but absent in competing textbooks. I welcome feedback and critical evaluation of this book from readers. I can be contacted at: dkbhattacharyya@yahoo.co.in.

Dipak Kumar Bhattacharyya
Bhubaneswar

Acknowledgements

I sincerely acknowledge the support and help I have received from my students, and colleagues who are part of the faculty at the Xavier Institute of Management, Bhubaneshwar (XIMB) and those at the Camellia Business Schools.

My thanks to Father P.T. Joseph, Director, XIMB, students and colleagues at XIMB and Professor Sanjoy Bhattacharyya, Director, NITTR, Kolkata. Mr. N.R. Datta, Mr Partha Pal and Mr Sumit Shome of the Camellia Group and Professor S. Banerjea of the University of Calcutta have also been a source of support.

Thanks are also due to my friends and my family, especially my wife and children. Finally, I acknowledge with gratitude the team at Universities Press and thank them for their cooperation and help in bringing out this book within such a short time frame.

Contents

To

Sutapa, Sudip and Topodeep,

for relentlessly supporting my writing pursuits.

CHAPTER 1
Introduction to Production and Operations Management

LEARNING OBJECTIVES

After reading this chapter, you will be able to understand:

- The Definition and Concept of Production and Operations Management
- Production Characteristics
- Transformation Process Model
- Process Perspective of Operations
- Production System
- Manufacturing Plant
- Role and Functions of a Production and Operations Manager
- Recent Trends in Production and Operations Management
- Strategic Issues in Production and Operations Management

Opening Vignette

SKF and Quality Management across Countries

SKF, the international giant in the manufacture of bearings, has production facilities in four countries. Although country-specific cultures differ, the company follows uniform quality management systems across its production centres. In production and operations, quality management is a fundamental area of concern for any organization. Although it is the endeavour of every organization to create a culture of its own, because of the incongruity between organizational and national culture, often, quality suffers. *SKF* is headquartered in Sweden, with manufacturing units in London, Germany, France and Italy. In order to retain its global market leadership, the company successfully implemented quality management practices, addressing country-specific cultural issues, without compromising quality systems requirements. To do this, *SKF* initially identified commonality in the quality precepts of these countries. Customer-centricity as the prime driver of quality could be identified as a possible area of quality in all these four countries, despite other differences. This common driver ultimately helped *SKF* implement uniform quality management systems at its manufacturing facilities in all four countries.

1.1 INTRODUCTION

An aspiring manager has to understand the basic framework of production and operations management. Such understanding becomes more relevant when the subject is discussed in the organizational and managerial context. Over the years, the production and operations management function has changed, and it now encompasses value-added activities, be it in manufacturing or in the rendering of services. The basic premise of production and operations management is the **transformation process model** – the process of conversion of inputs to outputs. While studying the transformation process model, we will discuss the various aspects of operations systems and their management, including focus on suppliers and customers, and the external environmental forces that encompass the production and operations functions.

Every day, whether it is in an organization or in our personal lives, we make use of various products and services. All these products and services, before reaching the end users, undergo various processes of transformation. Production and operations management helps us study how goods and services are produced and through value adding supply chain management reach the end users.

Every organization is engaged in value addition activities, either in the form of production of goods and/or services. To perform these activities, the organization procures resources, and through the process of transformation converts such resources to output, and finally, distributes the products or services (outputs) to the end users. The entire cycle is classified as the production and operations management cycle. Depending on the size of the organization (in terms of volume of activities), operations functions are either integrated with other functions (for small-scale units) or managed by a dedicated team of employees, who have specialized in these activities. Production and operations management is now an important functional area, and it has to be customer-centric. Although the main organizational pursuit is to gain profitability, growth and competitiveness, today, ensuring value for money to customers is accorded overriding priority.

1.2 DEFINITION AND CONCEPTS

Production and operations management is now being studied as an independent specialization with an inter-disciplinary approach. Production is generally assigned to those with a technical or engineering background, however, management inputs and knowledge can improve functioning, as timely delivery, cost effectiveness, productivity and quality are increasingly vital for an organization to gain a competitive edge. Production management is used for the manufacturing set-up, whereas Operations management is a broader concept, covering not only traditional manufacturing, but also processes, programmes, plants and people.

In the past, the production function was strictly engineering based, as it focussed on manufacturing functions and processes. But today, production covers services as well; any value addition activity is deemed production. Under the new definition, production is not only the traditional manufacturing process of converting inputs to outputs, it encompasses all operational activities that assist this manufacturing process and also the provision of services. In this book, we will consider the terms, 'production' and 'operations', to mean one and the same thing.

Production management covers all the processes and decisions made during manufacturing, which ensure that the output is cost effective, meets delivery schedules, adheres to quality control and achieves customer satisfaction.

In this context, we can define the production and operations management functions as those that involve designing, managing and improving the systems to create value-added goods and services, matching customer needs and expectations. And in this process, it makes use of financial and human resources to transform inputs to outputs to deliver the same to customers. This is why effective production and operations management is critical to organizational success.

Even though the terms production and operations management have been used interchangeably in this book, we find many authors delineate the concepts first and then use them, integrating the two, thereby keeping pace with modern corporate practice. Without stretching the debate, we can define operations management as the managing of the conversion of inputs into intended outputs, which may be either tangible (goods) or intangible (services).

Therefore, operations functions have some basic elements. There is a (i) transformation and conversion process, which utilizes (ii) some inputs to produce some (iii) intended outputs. But this is a more classical way of defining the concept. Because of its strategic focus and integration with an enterprise-wide decision support systems (DSS), the modern approach also integrates information feedback into the model. Modern organizations being extremely customer focussed and quality and cost conscious, DSS is used to ensure efficiency in operations management.

Adam and Ebert (1995), while explaining the concept of production and operations management have pointed out that in the process of transformation or conversion, unplanned or uncontrollable influences may cause more deviation in actual output than envisaged. Such influences may be both exogenous and endogenous. Exogenous factors, being external to the organization, may not always be controllable. However, good organizations through scenario planning can reduce the adverse effects of such factors. Endogenous factors are, however, controllable. To ensure checks and balances in the production and operations management functions, we require a 'feedback loop' to provide key information, in order to ensure control over operations by suitable intervention.

While explaining the basic framework of production and operations management, Muhlemann, Oakland and Lockyer (1994) warned that production and operations management functions are interdependent, hence, separating the two may destroy conceptual clarity. Even though the distinction between manufacturing and service operations is difficult to describe, based on Adam and Ebert's definition (1995), we can differentiate between the two on the following counts:

1. Nature of output may be either tangible or intangible. Manufacturing operations are identified by tangible output, while service operations are identifiable by intangible output.
2. Consumption pattern, in the case of manufacturing or tangible output continues over a time period, but for service operations or when output is intangible, we find that customers consume the same immediately.
3. Nature of job for manufacturing is more technology intensive and the usage of labour as an input is relatively less. But for service operations, we find more use of labour than equipment.
4. The degree of customer contact in manufacturing is relatively less compared to service operations. This is because even though conversion in manufacturing is essentially done for customers, their physical presence at the conversion site is not tenable. However, services are rendered directly to the customers, so in service operations there is a higher degree of customer contact. Customers' participation in manufacturing operations is relatively low.
5. Performance measurement for manufacturing is quantitative, while for service operations it is qualitative.

However, the distinction between manufacturing and services on the above counts may not always be feasible given the changing technology and management styles and philosophy. For example, in the process of making organizations increasingly customer focussed and to retain their competitive edge, we find an increasing trend to customize output using flexible or job-shop type manufacturing facilities. In management strategy also, we find that overriding priority is accorded to customers, whose feedback is used for effecting change. Six Sigma approach leads to a customer-centric process that recreates a new process rather than repair the existing process in organizations, both for improving the bottom line and enhancing customer satisfaction (by giving them increased value for money). The Customer Operations Performance Centre (COPC) approach meant primarily for IT-enabled service (ITeS) operations – a joint product of *Dell, Microsoft* and *American Express* – also emphasizes customer/client satisfaction.

The actual differences between manufacturing and services are becoming narrower, hence, attributing production to manufacturing and operations to services would be the historic approach. Using the term 'operations' more holistically to encompass both manufacturing and services is the right approach. However, using the term 'Production and Operations' (POM) would be a better choice, as it is a more inclusive term and includes both manufacturing and services.

A better definition of POM would therefore be that it is a value-added process of transformation of inputs into goods and services of the desired quality by the optimum utilization of resources at minimum cost. The elements of definition would, therefore, be:

1. Optimum utilization of resources
2. Achieving the desired quality in goods and services
3. Achieving cost efficiency in the transformation process
4. Value-added activity.

Value addition is ensured by the process of alteration, transportation, storage and inspection. Alteration is a process of change effected in the state of inputs; it is physical in nature for manufacturing and psychological in nature in the case of services. Transportation is the movement of goods and services from one place to another. Like alteration, transportation also adds value from the customer's point of view, when output is made available at different locations with better logistic support. ATMs for banks are an obvious example of value-added banking services for customers. Similarly, supply or distribution chains to make available the output of a manufacturing process to different locations, add value from the customers' point of view. Storage also adds value to customers, as organizations ensuring storing of output in a protected environment make sure that it is available over a period of time. Physical output with a long shelf life is stored by organizations to make the same available to customers when they require it. Similarly, service output in the form of data and information may be made available by a service provider through their data warehouse, which a customer can utilize over a period of time. Inspection processes add value to outputs when organizations ensure verification of outputs to conform to quality standards.

These apart, recent developments in POM, like making POM systems efficient and compatible with the environment, are also offering new opportunities to organizations. Effluent Treatment Plants (ETP) not only reduce harmful by-products but also provide opportunities to organizations to maximize their gains by waste re-cycling, generating energy (for example, a sintering plant for steel manufacturing unit), using recycled water for cooling towers, etc.

IFB Agro produces rectified spirit using industrial molasses. Rectified spirit is the core raw material for the liquor industry, so excise duties are levied on its production and its price is controlled by the Government. The company could hardly generate a surplus, and was almost on the brink of closure. At this juncture, the Pollution Control Department issued a stricture that unless the company installed an Effluent Treatment Plant (ETP), they would have to close down their operations. Processing of industrial molasses leads to high carbon deposition, causing environmental hazards. However, it was pointed out that installing an ETP would help the company to open a new profit centre, through the production of dry ice. This was a business opportunity envisaged by a consultant to the company. Production and operations managers have to envisage such opportunities to make their organizations viable, and to sustain themselves in a competitive environment.

Achieving zero defects through the Six Sigma approach to sustain competitive advantage is yet another new development in POM. Six Sigma suggests recreating an error-free measurable process through innovation.

1.3 DIFFERENCES BETWEEN MANUFACTURING AND SERVICES

Although rendering of services also forms part of production and operations management, manufacturing and service operations are characteristically different. Some of the distinguishing features of manufacturing and service operations are:

- Nature of output
- Nature of job
- Nature of quality assurance
- Nature of performance measurement

These differences are listed in the following table:

Table 1.1 *Differences between Manufacturing and Services*

Characteristic	Manufacturing	Services
Nature of Output	Physical or Tangible	Abstract or Intangible
Degree of contact with customers	Less	Frequent
Work Process	Capital Intensive	Labour Intensive
Output Variety	Uniform	Not Uniform
Quality Assurance Issues	Standardized	More customer-centric
Performance Measurement	Standardized	More subjective
Degree of customization	Less	More

1.4 HISTORICAL PROCESS OF DEVELOPMENT OF POM FUNCTIONS

Human endeavour, in manufacturing goods and rendering of services, is age old. Even before the coming of industrialization, we observe its presence, if not for trade purposes, then for survival. We find that the function has changed drastically over time, starting with home-centred production and going on to factory-centred mass production. We can classify these into three stages – craft manufacturing, mass production and production in the modern period. All these stages are, however, in the post-industrialization era.

During the stage of craft manufacturing, skilled workers used to produce a variety of goods, to meet the requirements of customers. In this phase, the owners of the means of labour and the means of capital were one and the same. Over the years, the transfer of skill from masters to apprentices and journeymen took place, and later, it was controlled by guilds. The crafts manufacturing process used to be managed by skilled workers, either from their homes or from small workshops. As the volume of production in this era was small and market reach was limited to the surrounding area, management of the production function was dependent on the individual, and depended largely on individual ingenuity.

Mass production began in the 19th century. Characteristically, mass production is the bulk production of goods with less variety, and by its nature, requires a specialized method of manufacturing. The focus of mass production was to gain cost competitiveness by producing the same nature of goods in bulk. As a result, customers had fewer choices to get products and services specific to their requirements, although customers did get the benefit of reasonable pricing. Mass production was possible because of the standardization of production facilities. Side by side, F.W. Taylor's (1911) scientific management principles facilitated job redesigning and process simplification, resulting in higher rates of production. By job breakdown analysis, division of labour – a specialized group of people to perform tasks of a similar nature – was made possible (Kanigel, 1999). Along with Taylor, Henry Ford's contribution was also exemplary. Ford introduced the assembly line system of production, which requires a worker or a group of workers to perform specific tasks at specific work stations, as the job moves from one work station to another. Ford's assembly line concept facilitated the production of standardized products in large volumes, with decreasing costs, leading to economies of scale.

In the modern period, production systems started from the 1970's primarily to deal with market fragmentation, reduced product life cycles, increased competition, globalization, and the need to present customers with greater choice. Side-by-side, Japanese production techniques, particularly just-in-time (JIT) manufacturing, lean manufacturing, innovations in technology like flexible manufacturing systems (FMS), direct numeric control (DNC), computer numeric control (CNC) , cellular manufacturing, etc. set the pace of modern manufacturing systems. All these were further strengthened with total quality management (TQM), quality circles (QC), total employee involvement (TEI), Six Sigma practices, etc. We will discuss these tools and techniques and their applications in production and operations management with examples, in subsequent chapters.

Like mass production, modern production systems is not an isolated approach, rather it is the confluence of multiple approaches. Some of these approaches are flexible specialization, lean production, agile manufacturing, etc. Flexible specialization, pioneered by Piore and Sabel (1984), suggest focussing on separate parts of the value-adding process and to achieve a collaborative effect within networks in order to produce products. It requires well-developed networks, effective collaboration processes, and long-term sustainable relationships between firms. Womack et al (1990) developed lean production systems, emulating the practices of *Toyota*'s production system. The primary focus of lean production is to eliminate waste, efficient inventory management, cycle time reduction and cost minimization. Mass customization (Pine et al, 1993) combines bulk production, adapting to individual customer requirements. With the latest technology, mass customization is now possible, resulting in cost efficiency. With agile manufacturing (Kidd, 1994), modern organizations are now able to switch from one product mix to another, depending on changing market needs.

The above historical sketch makes it clear that with modern technology, we are able to produce in bulk, even addressing changing customer requirements.

1.5 MODELS FOR PRODUCTION/OPERATIONS

The objective of any production/operations systems is to add value to output (goods or services), following a framework of activities. Sample production/operations systems can be expressed mathematically as under:

$$Y = f(c_1, c_2, c_3, \cdots\cdots c_n)$$

Where '*Y*' is the output and $c_1, c_2, c_3, \cdots\cdots c_n$ are the inputs. The type of production/operations system would again depend on a number of factors. Broadly, however, it depends on the nature of products/services and the type of production. While the nature of products/services may be anything like chemical, pharmaceutical, textile, electronic, banking, telecommunication, BPO/HRO and so on, the type of production/operations may be engineering, process, extraction, cognitive, etc.

To determine the outcomes of the proposed courses of action in POM, we use different models. A model is defined as a replica or abstraction of important characteristics of a process. It explains the inter-relationships between various factors of the POM process. By using simulation models we can understand the problems, if any, in a given POM system. In POM, we generally use the following types of models:

(i) Verbal/written/descriptive/physical models: All these models are categorized under one group because of their approach to explain a situation by scaling it down to a manageable size. Verbal/written/descriptive models explain a situation in words, while physical models explain a situation using a physical replica, duly scaling down a machine or a structure. Physical models are also known as iconic models.

(ii) Schematic models are represented by charts, graphics, maps of routings, network diagrams, etc.

(iii) Mathematical models show the functional relationships among different variables using mathematical symbols and equations. In POM, we use two types of mathematical models:

1. (a) Optimization models, which help to analyse problems and suggest solutions and

   (b) Heuristics models, which are established decision-making procedures to solve a problem.

In linear programming, we try to achieve the best and most feasible solution within some given constraints. This is one example of an optimization model, which we use in POM. Another example of an optimization model can be a simple equation like:

$$TC = F + vN$$

Here we assume that total cost (TC) is the function of fixed (F) and variable unit cost (vN).

Heuristic model is a rule of thumb (for example, a set of steps) which we use in POM for finding the solution to a problem, which may not, however, be optimal. For line balancing, that is, the assessment of total work to be done or performed on a line, duly breaking down the tasks and assigning the tasks to work stations, we use heuristic models. Here, we apply a set of rules systematically as an algorithm.

Using various models, we can control the variables in production/operations systems, understand the cost implications and make the best trade-offs with regard to costs. Throughout the book, we have used various models for explaining POM systems.

Usually in a POM systems model, we find the following:

Inputs: These are used in production and include raw materials, spare parts, other consumable items, energy, information, know-how (knowledge, technology, etc.), plans, programmes or schedules. Thus, inputs may be either physical or abstract.

Process: Once all the inputs are available, the second stage of production is the processing of inputs, through a series of operations. The number of these operations varies with the nature of the output. Each step of the operation is entrusted to a separate group, which has specialized knowledge of that job. Processing takes place using labour services with plant, equipment and machinery.

Output: These can be in either in the physical or the abstract form. At the processing stage, operations are monitored to ensure quality, cost effectiveness and adherence to delivery schedules.

Other features that are also important in a production system are storage, transportation and management information systems (MIS), since these are vital to any effective production model.

Storage relates to the storing of input materials, semi-processed materials (also called work in progress, where the production process involves more than one stage) and for finished goods, that is, the output.

Transportation refers to the transport of semi-processed goods from one shop to another, within the organization or factory, for different stages of operation. This is done by using battery-operated trucks, forklifts etc.

Management information systems (MIS) link all the physical activities through a feedback mechanism. It helps control the system and prevents deviations from the programme. MIS is also the basis of managerial decisions.

In this book, the terms 'production' and 'operations management' are used interchangeably; however, other authors have explained the concepts separately and have then integrated them, in keeping with current corporate practice. To put it simply, *operations management is the management of the conversion of inputs into intended output, which may be tangible goods or intangible services.*

The primary role of operations management functions, that is, creating and delivering goods and services, meeting customer satisfaction, is amply clear. Therefore, a suitable model of transformation can help us analyze operations management. Primarily, operations have three components – inputs, transformation processes and outputs. The basic thrust of the operations management function is to provide systematic direction and control of processes to transform inputs into finished goods or services for customers. This basic model of transformation (Fig. 1.1) is equally applicable, both in manufacturing and in service organizations.

All inputs are not directly used in transforming or creating goods and services. Some are used, and some go into the process of creation. From this perspective, input resources can be classified as either transformed resources or transforming resources. Transformed resources are used to produce goods and services. Transforming resources on the other hand are those that are used to perform the process of transformation.

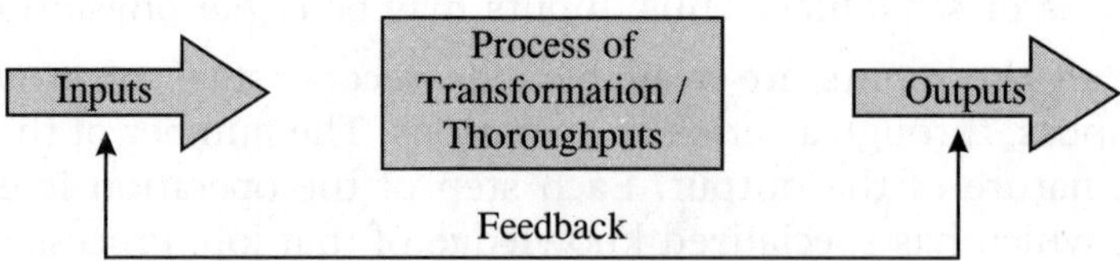

Figure 1.1 *The transformation model*

Inputs may be in the form of materials, information and knowledge. Transforming resources include human resources, facilities like buildings, machinery and equipment – these are sometimes referred to as 'capital'.
Outputs The transformation processes produce both goods and services. The goods and services that are finally produced are the output.

In the process of transformation, it is also important for the operations management function to ensure minimization of the environmental impact of waste over the life cycle of their products, up to the point of final disposal, protecting the health and safety of employees and of the local community and adopting ethical behaviour in relation to the social impact of transformation processes, both locally and globally.

1.5.1 Transformation processes

The transformation process uses inputs to add value to products, to match the needs of the customers. Where the inputs are raw materials, the transformation processes include:

- Changes in the physical characteristics of materials or customers
- Changes in the location of materials and information
- Changes in the ownership of materials
- Information storage or accommodation of materials
- Changes in the purpose or form of information based on customer expectations
- Changes in the physiological or psychological state of customers, etc.

An organization may transform all the inputs on its own, or it may involve the services of multiple vendors or services providers for some parts of the jobs

One useful way of categorizing different types of transformation is as follows:

- Manufacture – the physical creation of products (for example, cars)
- Transport – the movement of materials or customers (for example, a taxi service)
- Supply – change in ownership of goods (for example, in retailing)
- Service – the treatment of customers or the storage of materials (for example, hospital wards, warehouses).

Several transformations are usually required to produce goods or services. The overall transformation can be described as the macro operation, and the more detailed transformations within this macro operation are known as the micro operations. For example, the macro operation in a tea manufacturing plant is making tea. The micro operations include (Fig. 1.2):

- Withering of tea leaves after plucking
- CTC operation (crush, tear and curling of withered leafs using the CTC machine)
- Fermenting (spreading the CTC leaves on a fermenting bay to allow fermentation and in order to get a coppery colour

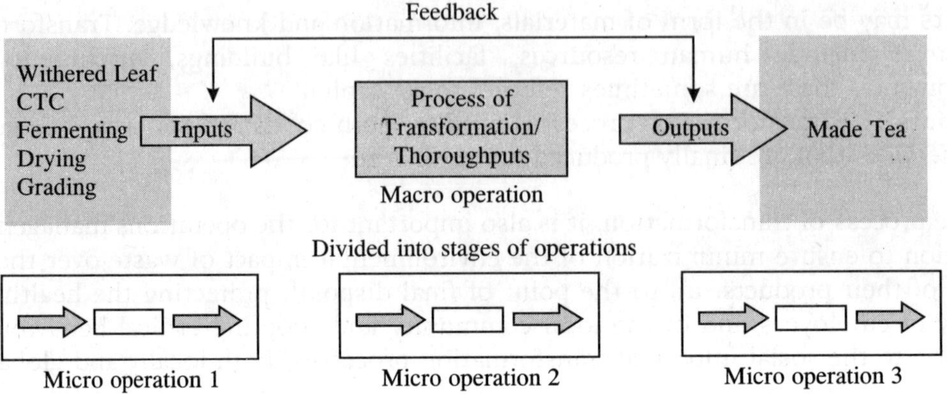

Figure 1.2 *Macro and micro operations*

- Drying the fermented leaves
- Spreading the dried leaves
- Grading
- Stacking the made tea into bins and packaging

Feedback in the transformation model is used to ensure control in the operations system. Based on feedback, we adjust the inputs and the transformation processes to achieve the desired output. Feedback is essential for operations managers. It can come from both internal and external sources. Internal sources include testing, evaluation and continuously improving goods and services; external sources include those who supply products or services to the end-customers, as well as feedback from the customers themselves.

For *IFB Agro*, the proper fermenting of industrial molasses is essential to get a better yield of rectified spirit. Imported yeast plays a crucial role in the process of fermentation. The company makes use of yeast imported from Australia. Yeast grows on successive breeding. The breeding time of yeast depends on the specific condition of the molasses discharged in the process of production. Industrial molasses is sourced by the company from different countries, and the quality varies widely. The yeast count that each tonne of molasses discharged has is highly subjective. During the process of manufacturing, the operations managers collect feedback from the control switches, and accordingly vary the yeast count to ensure proper fermentation of the molasses.

1.5.2 The Boundary of the Operations System

The transformation model in Figure 1.1 explains operations from different dimensions, and based on the model we can tackle the analysis and designing of operations in different types of organizations.

The model helps in the identification of the boundaries of the system of operations for reaching the produced goods and services to the customers. As may be seen in Figure 1.3, the model encompasses three boundaries:

- Suppliers
- Customers
- The environment.

Vendors or suppliers provide inputs to any system of operations. Suppliers may provide inputs like raw materials, sub-assemblies, or semi-finished components, assemblies or any services. In the transformation process model, customers are construed as being the users of output; so, they are external to the organization. Hence, the transformation process boundary can be considered as the boundary of the organization itself.

Again, we can consider operations both from macro and micro perspectives. Macro operations consist of many micro operations or sub-systems. Operations activities from the organization perspectives as a whole are considered as macro operations. From this perspective, final assembly, being a separate function, can be defined as a micro operation. Thus, operations serve the need of both internal and external customers.

Environmental issues affect the operations activities of the organization. Such issues may be functional, in other words, they may be internal or external. Functional environmental issues encompass policies, resource allocation, goals and objectives, and constraints. External environmental issues are social, political, legal and economic conditions. Change in any of the environmental constructs brings change in the operations functions.

Organizations may be insular in their operations activities with a closed system approach, they may adopt this approach to get rid of environmental disturbances (Thompson, 1967). Such insularity in operations requires the operations function to lose contact with external customers and vendors, and focus only on the

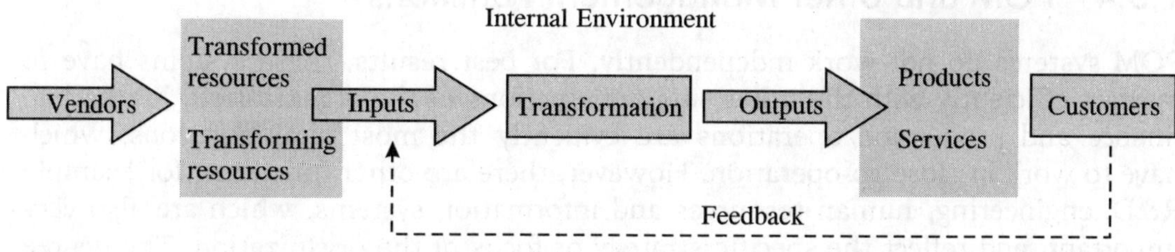

Figure 1.3 *The operations boundary*

transformation process. But such inflexibility may force the operations system to lose its competitiveness. This is why an open systems approach to operations is considered to be the best. Various research studies have authenticated that an open systems approach to operations increases communication with customers and suppliers, which helps build operations capabilities to cope with environmental changes effectively. Obviously, for these reasons, operations management has to activate the interfaces between the organization, and the external customers and suppliers.

1.5.3 Process Perspective of Operations Management

The overall process of transformation consists of a series of micro-processes. Proper management of such sub-processes influences overall organizational performance. David Garvin (1998) has focussed on the importance of considering the work processes for achieving performance improvement in organizations.

Basic work process approach considers work as a series of chains of activities, irrespective of the functions and the nature of activities. In operations management, we find two types of processes – processes that facilitate production and delivery of goods and services, and processes which do not directly transform the goods and services, but are necessary to manage the overall processes of transformation, or for that matter the business of the organization. Hence, in organizations, we can have two types of processes – operations processes and administrative processes. Operational processes are concerned with product development, production and logistics management. Administrative processes, on the other hand, are those that help in strategic planning, budgeting and performance measurement. Both processes undergo several aligned and inter-dependent activities, which together facilitate the final transformation.

The work processes approach, apart from managing the process of production, also focusses on redesigning and recreating the processes for achievement of performance excellence through quality improvement, cost minimization and cycle time reduction.

1.5.4 POM and other Management Functions

POM systems do not work independently. For best results, these systems have to interact efficiently with the other support functions of the organization. Marketing, finance and production/operations are evidently the most vital functions, which have to work in close co-operation. However, there are other functions, for example R&D, engineering, human resources and information systems, which are also very important, and reflect the specific strategy or focus of the organization. The degree of inter-dependence between the different functions varies from organization to organization.

It may be noted that with enterprise-wide decision support systems (DSS), other management functions can also help by providing vital inputs to make decisions. For example, bench-marking with competitors is possible through data collection, which helps the organization to compare its performance in terms of cost, quality and market share, vis-a-vis their competitors. Also, bench-making helps the organization to understand the need for outsourcing of non-core activities and the need for developing an integrated supply chain management. For example, human resource information systems (HIRS) provide details of HR costs, which are important cost inputs for POM.

1.6 THE ROLE OF THE OPERATIONS MANAGER

In very simplistic terms, we see each and every activity of the organization as a function of operations management. From this perspective, operations management is the responsibility of every manager, as managers in the transformation process add value to the output. It is because of this that production and operations management is taught as a core subject in MBA programmes. However, such a holistic definition of operations management is not accepted by all, and like other functional management specialists, in operations management, we also have specialists or professionals, who are trained to manage this function professionally.

Operations managers thus manage the activities aligned with the process of production of goods and services. As this process is considered from a broader perspective, we can delineate it into two parts: the direct activities and indirect activities. The direct activities of the operations managers encompass framing of operations strategy design, control of operations activities, improvement of operations performance, etc. The indirect activities, on the other hand, extend to interaction and coordination with other functional areas of the organization, like marketing, sales, finance, human resource management, research and development, etc.

1.6.1 Functions of a Production and Operations Manager

Although the functions of a Production and Operations Manager will vary with the nature of the product, the main functions will cover most of the following:

1. Production Planning and Control: Once the orders are booked from the customers, the Marketing or Sales Department will send these to the Production Planning and Control Department. The Production Manager has to plan for the actual production of these orders, in keeping with customer specifications and maintain correct delivery.
2. Production: Another important function is to ensure production as per the production plan.

3. Inspection: A final inspection for quality control is essential after the production process. With increasing emphasis on quality control and in order to reduce rejection, some organizations also conduct receiving or inward inspection of raw materials and components as well as in-process inspection.
4. Engineering: An emphasis on R&D greatly helps the production process by providing innovation in product design and by designing tools, jigs and fixtures. Some large organizations have independent tool rooms/departments.
5. Industrial Engineering: Another important function of a Production Manager is to monitor the optimal use of resources (both human and material), by conducting periodic work studies. This may be done either by method study to examine the best method of doing a job or by work measurement technique, which measures the time required for doing different jobs.
6. Maintenance: Periodical maintenance of plant and machinery is essential to minimize machine down time and subsequent loss of production. In the past, the emphasis was on breakdown maintenance, that is, only to attend to machinery that was not working, but the emphasis today is on total productive maintenance or ongoing maintenance to prevent breakdowns.
7. Inter-departmental co-ordination: A Production Manager has to work in close co-operation with other departments. The Production plan has to be decided with the Sales Department; the Personnel Department has to provide manpower and the requisite training, and procurement of raw materials is done with the help of the Materials Department.

The Operations Manager's role and responsibilities encompass the following functions:

1. **Managing human resources** In operation activities, employees are engaged by the organization. Such employees need to work under the direction of an operations manager. Hence, the operations manager, despite being engaged in a line function has to perform human resource management functions like motivation, performance management, training and development, managing employee discipline and so on. In many large-scale manufacturing units, the human resource management team works with the operations managers.

2. **Cost management** Operations management process requires incurring of costs of producing goods and services, in the form of acquiring inputs or resources, process costs involved in transforming inputs into outputs, and the costs associated with the delivery of goods to the customers, and percentage share of operations costs toward total costs of the organization itself. Operations costs are the most significant cost factor for the organizations. Hence, efficient cost management is also a significant area of responsibility for operations managers.

3. **Decision making** Operations managers, in the process of performing their role, need to take various decisions like designing the operations system, managing the operations system, improving the operations system, etc. These require the operations managers to take decisions regarding the processes by which goods and services are produced, decisions on quantity and quality of goods or services, decisions on assessing material (inventory) requirements, and decisions pertaining to the management of human resources.

1.6.2 Production Systems

Production Systems in an organization vary according to the nature of the product or existing production facilities. These systems can be divided into two kinds – continuous or intermittent. The continuous system is possible where facilities are standardized, for example, in assembly lines or in continuous flow chemical operations. The intermittent system is more flexible and can accommodate a wide variety of products in different sizes, for example, in job shop type machine shops, fabrication units or batch type chemical operations. Intermittent type of production is often called customized production systems. Both, continuous and intermittent systems have advantages and disadvantages.

1.7 MANUFACTURING PLANT

For every production and operations manager, an understanding of the technical details on the manufacturing plant, location, factory buildings, service facilities, layout, handling of materials, manufacturing processes, etc. is necessary.

Location: Proximity to source of raw materials or markets, transport and communication facilities, availability of power and fuel are some of the factors that determine the location of the plant. The practice is to assign weights to each cost factor and then compute the relative advantages or cost ratios of different locations. This is called Dimensional Analysis. The decision of either buying or renting a plant location will be made on the basis of opportunity cost.

Decisions with regard to the factory building itself will depend on the process of manufacture – whether single-storey or multi-storey will depend on factors such as floor load, vibration, noise, natural light, ventilation, utilization of space etc.

Service facilities include plant utilities and employees services. Some plant utilities like safety, pollution/effluent treatment and control, and most employee facilities are required to be provided by statute. However, in the interests of efficient management and increased employee motivation, many organizations provide facilities beyond those required by law.

The layout of the factory depends on the type of production system in operation. For example, in a job-shop or a functional organization, it is appropriate to have a process type of layout as opposed to a product type layout that is used in the case of assembly line production. Another factor is layout by fixed position, which is used for heavy items or those difficult to move, for example, shipbuilding. Batch type of layout is preferred for multi-product processing systems.

The placing and positioning of materials to assist their movement or storage is called material handling and it is another important function of production management.

A vital function of production management is production planning and control, which covers a wide spectrum of activities to achieve the objectives of the production department.

1.8 RECENT TRENDS IN PRODUCTION AND OPERATIONS MANAGEMENT FUNCTIONS

Over the years, production and operations management functions have significantly changed. Some of these factors have already been highlighted in the introductory discussions. Here again, we need to recapitulate those factors as under:

1. Global Competition
2. Customer-centric approach to production
3. Quality consciousness
4. Rapid expansion of advanced technologies
5. Continued growth of the service sector
6. Scarcity of operations resources
7. Social responsibility issues

The scope of production and operations management today includes decision making about the design, planning and management of the many factors that affect operations. Decisions include what products to produce, how large a facility to build, where to locate the facility with respect to customers and suppliers, what techniques and equipment to use to make the goods or to provide the services, how many units to produce next month, how employees should be trained, and what methods to use to enhance product quality.

1.9 PRODUCTION AND OPERATIONS STRATEGY

Given the complexities of today's business, what holds good today may not hold good tomorrow! What makes one succeed may not be a role model for others! Like every core function of an organization, POM has some important functional strategies.

Every organization should have a strategy, which reflects its vision, mission, goals and objectives and also provides the basis for performance measurement. A well defined strategy integrates all organizational components and provides direction for an action plan to achieve the intended goals and objectives. It also reflects on competitive advantages, which an organization should exploit to gain an edge over its competitors.

Functional strategies in POM guide decisions on all important aspects of POM, both in the short-term and in the long-term. While short-term strategies focus on the organization's basic POM systems to achieve optimum balance between inputs and output, emphasizing location, facilities and process planning; long-term strategies of POM stress the planning and control aspect. Aligning POM functions with market demand, inventory holding or extent of sub-contracting or outsourcing is a part of long-term strategies.

1.9.1 Devising Production and Operations Strategies

For devising a production plan, a company has many options. For example, to manage fluctuations in demand, the operations manager can adopt the following strategies:

- Manage inventory to absorb demand fluctuations.
- Ensure flexible manpower, matching demand (tenure track recruitment, outsourcing, etc. could be the option).
- Ensure resource flexibility to meet higher demand.
- Make effective use of job sub-contracting. Use part-time workers
- Practice backordering, that is, advance order booking to provide service or product at a later time period.

Broadly, we find the use of two types of production and operations strategy – level production strategy and chase demand strategy. Level production strategy ensures a consistent rate of production throughout the year, building finished inventory in low-demand periods, and using such finished inventory in high demand periods. Organizations of this type vary widely in their inventory holding, but their other resources (including manpower) remain constant.

On the other hand, companies that follow chase demand strategy in production and operations management keep low or zero inventories, that is, the product is manufactured to the extent that demand for it is met. Obviously, in such organizations, manpower and other resource requirements vary widely. It requires effective lean management practices.

Depending on the specific production needs, companies follow either pure strategy or mixed strategy. Pure strategy indicates the use of a single production strategy to meet the customers' demand. On the other hand, mixed strategy indicates use of a strategy-mix, that is, the combination of several strategies for production planning, to meet the demand of customers.

Thus, level production strategy follows production at a constant rate, and maintains inventory of finished goods to meet the demand of the market. Chase demand production strategy varies the rate of production depending on the fluctuations in market demand, maintaining minimum finished inventory. In both cases, depending on the specific requirements, companies maintain resources (inputs), under stretch, or over stretch production, sub-contract jobs, etc. Some companies follow a backordering strategy of pre-booking orders, when customers are ready to wait for products and services.

Operations strategy is drawn based on the policies and plans for effective utilization of production resources. It supports a company's long-term competitive strategy. Typical operations strategy considers all the critical aspects of manufacturing processes like capacity, facilities, technology, vendor development, workforce skill development, quality, etc. However, the basic focus of operations strategies is on cost, quality, speed of delivery and flexibility. To successfully compete in the market, every company needs to focus on lowering its cost of production. Although quality is increasingly gaining importance in product sell, use of cost as a primary determinant of purchase is still evident. Strategically, therefore, companies need to manage their cost. As part of operations strategy, companies enforce quality, both in their products and in their processes. With innovative quality management practices, companies can ensure conformance to quality, meeting both the specifications and customers' expectations. Like cost and quality, companies also develop their supply chain for speed of delivery. Likewise, flexibility is also strategically important; this requires companies to build their capabilities to offer a wide product range, keeping pace with the changing needs of the customers.

Problems on Strategic Choice of Production Plan

A confectionary major recently introduced celebration chocolate packs to make it a habit for Indians to gift this pack, rather than traditional Indian sweets, in the festive seasons to friends and relatives. The demand for celebration chocolate packs reaches a peak during festive seasons, but it is very poor at other times. Based on their past performance, the company has made available their sales data for four quarters. Analyze their sales trend and formulate a level production plan and a chase demand production plan:

Quarters	Sales Forecast (in Packs)
Quarter – 1	80,000
Quarter – 2	50,000
Quarter – 3	1,20,000
Quarter – 4	1,50,000

In addition, the company has made available the following data:

- Manpower hiring cost - Rs. 100 per worker
- Manpower firing cost - Rs. 500 per worker
- Inventory carrying cost - Rs. 0.50 per pack of chocolate
- Production rate per worker - 1000 packs per quarter
- Manpower at the beginning - 1000

Solution

Confectionary Company
Level Production Plan

Quarter	*Sales Forecast*	*PP*	*Inv*	*Man power Need*	*Man power Hired*	*Man power Fired*	*Inv carrying cost*	*Hiring Cost*	*Firing Cost*
1	80000	100000	20000	100	0	0	10000	0	0
2	50000	100000	70000	100	0	0	35000	0	0
3	120000	100000	50000	100	0	0	25000	0	0
4	150000	100000	0	100	0	0	0	0	0
Total	400000						*Total Cost:*		70000

Confectionary Company
Level Production Plan

Quarter	*Sales Forecast*	*PP*	*Inv*	*Man power Need*	*Man power Hired*	*Man power Fired*	*Inv carrying cost*	*Hiring Cost*	*Firing Cost*
1	80000	80000	0	80	0	20	0	0	10000
2	50000	50000	0	50	0	30	0	0	15000
3	120000	120000	0	120	70	0	0	7000	0
4	150000	150000	0	150	30	0	0	3000	0
Total	400000						*Total Cost:*		35000

From the above computation tables, it is clear that the chase demand production plan is a lower cost choice. Comparing these two tables, it is clear that inventory carrying cost is higher for the level production plan, although the hiring and firing costs of manpower are not. We find the opposite happening in the case of the chase demand production plan..

The level production volume is decided taking the quarterly average demand figure. Similarly, the inventory figure has been calculated considering the previous inventory + production – sales for the month.

1.9.2 Operations Strategy Factors

From the operations manager's point of view, it is important to study the following factors while adopting an operations strategy.

1. The number, type, size and location of operations facilities.
2. Type of equipment that will be utilized (focussed and specific or general-purpose and flexible, automated or principally manual).
3. Make or buy decision.
4. Organization structure – whether it is suitable to accomplish and coordinate all the necessary efforts.
5. Workforce selection, employment security, compensation methods and management style.
6. The information systems that will be used to collect, to analyze and distribute information on production, purchasing, inventory, quality, personnel, etc.
7. Production planning, scheduling and control, systems and inventory policy.
8. The quality control and improvement methods that will be used.
9. Productivity improvement methods – machine/manpower.

1.9.3 Operational Control Systems

Strategic controls are useful to top management in monitoring and steering the basic strategic direction of the company. But operation managers also need to control methods appropriate to their level of strategy implementation. The primary concern at the operating level is the allocation and use of the company's resources. Operational control systems guide, monitor and evaluate progress in meeting the annual objectives. Usually, the following steps are taken for operational control:

1. Set standards of performance
2. Measure actual performance
3. Identify deviations from standards
4. Initiate corrective action or adjustment.

SUMMARY

1. The terms, production management and operations management are used interchangeably in organizations, which prove they are one and the same, despite theoretical differences.
2. Production and operations management is concerned with the management of the resources and processes to produce goods or services, and to deliver the same to the customers.
3. The production and operations function is basically a transformation process which converts resource inputs to outputs in the form of goods and services.

4. The ambit and scope of production and operations management functions, not only encompass the activities related to direct process of transformation, but is also extended to various other associated activities, which indirectly facilitate the process.
5. The role and the functions of Production and Operations Managers, therefore, extend to various areas like shop floor management, production planning and control, material handling, quality control, supply chain management, etc.
6. Production and operations management functions are now strategically important, as they facilitate the achievement of quality and cost competitiveness – two major drivers to derive sustainable competitive advantages.

KEY WORDS

Location Proximity to source of raw materials or markets, transport and communication facilities, availability of power and fuel are some of the factors that determine the location of the plant.

Production Systems Production systems in an organization can be divided into two types – continuous or intermittent. The continuous type is possible where facilities are standardized, for example, in assembly lines or in continuous flow chemical operations. Intermittent type is more flexible and can accommodate a wide variety of products in different sizes, for example, job-shop type machine shops, fabrication units or batch type chemical operations. Intermittent type of production is often called a customized production system.

Agile manufacturing With agile technology, modern organizations can now switch from one product mix to another, depending on changing market needs

Heuristics Models These models are some established decision-making procedures used to solve a problem. Heuristic model is a rule of thumb (for example, a set of steps) which we use in POM for finding a solution to a problem, which may not, however, be optimal.

Operational control systems It guides, monitors and evaluates progress in meeting annual objectives. Operational control is enforced by setting standards of performance, measuring actual performance, identifying deviations from standards and by initiating corrective action.

Management Information System (MIS) It links all physical activities through an efficient feedback mechanism and thus helps in enforcing control and/or in correcting deviation from the plan. It also provides the basis for managerial decisions.

GENERAL REVIEW QUESTIONS

1. Is production management different from operations management? Do you think the principles of production and operations management can also be made applicable to the service industry?
2. Develop a transformation process model to illustrate the production function of any hypothetical FMCG (Fast Moving Consumer Goods) company. (Hint: Collect the inputs on the soap manufacturing process or toothpaste manufacturing process from company websites).
3. Discuss why production and operations management functions are strategically significant?
4. What are the recent trends in the production and operations management functions?
5. Short notes
   (a) DSS
   (b) Assembly line
   (c) Job shop
   (d) Lean production
   (e) Production systems

CRITICAL REVIEW QUESTIONS

1. In many service organizations, Chief Operating Officers (COO) are appointed to manage the operations. Visit any such service organization, say a BPO unit, and study the functions and roles of the COO.
2. You have been appointed as the Production and Operations Manager of a cement manufacturing unit. After a thorough study of the cement manufacturing process, develop some strategic roles that can benefit your unit in terms of achievement of production target, quality and cost effectiveness.

REFERENCES

1. Adam, E. E and Ebert, R.J. 1982. *Production and Operations Management* (2nd ed). London: Prentice Hall.
2. Garvin, D. A. 1998. The Processes of Organization and Management. *Sloan Management Review,* Cambridge; Summer, pp.35–37
3. Kanigel, R. 1997. *The one best way: Frederick Winslow Taylor and the enigma of efficiency*. New York: Viking.
4. Kidd, P.T. 1994. *Agile Manufacturing: Forging New Frontiers*. Reading, MA: Addison-Wesley.
5. A Muhlemann, J Oakland and K Lockyer, 1992. *Productions and Operations Management*. Macmillan.

6. Pine, B.J.H, Voctor, B. And Boyton, A. 1993. Making Mass customisation work. *Harvard Business Review*, Vol. 71, Issue 5, pp. 108–118
7. Piore, M. J. and Sabel, C. F. 1984. *The Second Industrial Divide: Prospects for Prosperity*, New York: Basic Books.
8. Taylor, Frederick Winslow. 1911. *The Principles of Scientific Management*. New York, NY, USA and London, UK: Harper and Brothers

ADDITIONAL REFERENCES

1. Atwater, B. and Gagne, M.L. 1997. The Theory of Constraints versus Contribution, Margin Analysis for Product Mix Decisions. *Journal of Cost Accounting*, Vol. 6, No.15
2. Bard, J. F., Srinivasan, K., and Tirupati, D. 1999. An Optimization Approach to Capacity Expansion in Semiconductor Manufacturing Facilities. *International Journal of Production Research*, Vol. 37, No. 15, 3359–3382.
3. Chase, R. B., and D. A. Garvin. 1989. The Service Factory. *Harvard Business Review* 67, no. 4, 61–69.
4. Chase, R., Jacobs, R. and Aquilano, N. 2005. *Operations Management for Competitive Advantage,* 11th ed. New York: McGraw-Hill.
5. Cohen, M.A. 1997. *Manufacturing Automation*. Chicago: Irwin.
6. Garvin, David A. 1988. *Managing Quality*. New York: Free Press
7. Hayes, Robert H., Gary P. Pisano, and David M. Upton. 1996. *Strategic Operations: Competing through Capabilities*. New York: Free Press.
8. Holthaus, O. and Rajendran, C. 1997. Efficient Dispatching Rules for Scheduling in a Job Shop. *International Journal of Production Economics,* Vol. 48, No. 10, 2857–2870.
9. Konz, Stephen. 1983. *Work Design: Industrial Ergonomics,* 2nd ed. New York: John Wiley & Sons.
10. Nicholas, John M. 1998. *Competitive Manufacturing Management*. Boston: Irwin/McGraw-Hill
11. Ohno, T. 1995. *Toyota Production System: Beyond Large-scale Production*. New York: Productivity Press.
12. Richard, B., Chase, Nicholas, J., Aquilano, and F. Robert, Jacobs. 2002. *Operations Management for Competitive Advantage*. New Delhi: Tata McGraw-Hill Publishing Company Limited.

CASE STUDY

You have taken over as the Production Manager of a Company. The General Manager of the company has asked you to write a few points on the company's present management system, within the scope of your function. After due examination of the company's production and operation systems, you submitted the following observations:

The production process is the traditional one of conversion of inputs into desired output. There is no Production Planning and Control Department, and planning is undertaken by those in charge of the shop floor, based on job orders received from the Production Manager. It is the Production Manager's responsibility to monitor the progress of production and plan the production activities efficiently, to achieve quantitative targets.

The Maintenance Department of the factory attends to break down problems, and hence, there is always a chance of loss of production. Production Manager always attends to job-orders in the order of their receipt.

After reading your comments, the General Manager asks you for suggestions to implement changes in the system. Clarify the above points, with special reference to the need for modern production management systems.

APPENDIX-I

Job Description of Manager – Operations

The company is a domain-focussed IT services partner of India's famous technology company, specializing in the financial services, insurance and healthcare segments.

Tentative Job Descriptions:

1. Data Center management
2. Server management – system administration including backup/restore management, Patch
3. Management and anti-virus management
4. Network management (LAN/WAN) database management (Oracle/MS SQL)
5. Vendor management
6. Validation management as per client SOPs
7. Change management and incident management as per client SOPs
8. First-level scientific applications call support

Desired Profile

1. The candidate should have *eight* to *ten* years of IT experience with *three* to *five* years as a team lead/operations manager.
2. The candidate should have experience in team management with the team size of more than 10 members.
3. The candidate should be capable of handling the technical calls escalated to him.
4. The candidate should be willing to work as a team player in resolving technical issues and be able to drive the team for routine activities.
5. Coordination with other teams of IT across the organization.
6. Good communication skills, written and verbal.

Experience

10–12 years

Industry Type

IT-software/software services

Education

UG–Any Graduate–Any Specialization,
PG–Any PG Course–Any Specialization

CHAPTER 2

Production Planning and Control

LEARNING OBJECTIVES

After reading this chapter, you will be able to understand:

- Production Planning and Control – Concept and Differences
- Production Planning Functions
- Aggregate Planning
- Master Production Schedule
- Capacity Requirements Planning
- Material Requirements Planning
- Manufacturing Requirements Planning - II
- Forecasting Tools and Techniques
- Decision Making

Opening Vignette

Production Planning at Wallow

From a single production facility for manufacturing cricket bats, *Wallow* has diversified into manufacturing an array of products, based on carefully developed plans with specific goals. Their first long-range plan (covering five years) focussed on achieving 20% sales from a diversified product-mix (other than cricket bats). Subsequent five-year plans focussed on further diversification, expanding into other products or areas. But this initiative did not lead to success. In fact, the company experienced serious difficulties. Problems largely occurred due to wrong supply of items, which lead to defects in output, unrealistic estimation of market demand and the holding or stockpiling of a huge inventory of near-obsolete products.

To ease the situation, the company reorganized the planning process under a central planning department. Their long-range (strategic) plan now outlines the major directions and goals for the company, to keep pace with the changing environment. Medium-range (tactical) plans, of a maximum duration of 3 years (subject to annual revision), focus on the allocation of various resources and facilities and address short-term issues to amplify long-range plans and goals. These efforts are strengthened with contingency plans to fight against adverse situations. Short-range plans focus on maximum utilization of resources to obtain results. This way, the company could turn around.

2.1 INTRODUCTION

Every organization has to develop plans and strategies to realize its objectives. In a dynamic business environment, effective planning helps the organization to prepare for any eventuality, so that the organization is able to design appropriate systems to produce goods and services, in keeping with customer requirements. The production and operations function is the key driver for organizational success, so it requires planning to manage the key elements of activities with a focus on encountering future eventualities.

Production planning helps an organization to plan the effective utilization of organizational resources, through effective design of the production system. It also helps in effecting a change in the systems, in tune with changing requirements. Modern organizations, to sustain themselves, may have to scale down their activities in line with lean management practices. At the same time, production capacity may have to be increased to keep pace with demand. Such scaling down and up can be effective only when production plans are in place.

Even though the functions of POM require meeting the day-to-day challenges of operations, like resource allocation, manpower deployment, machine maintenance, inventory management, quality checks, etc., some POM decisions require long-range planning. Such long-range plans facilitate decisions about facilities, technological change, etc. However, the time horizon for long-range planning differs from organization to organization. For example, an FMCG (fast moving consumer goods) company may consider a one-year span as its long-range plan horizon, while an aircraft manufacturer may consider 8 to 10 years as its long-range plan horizon. Medium-range production plans are normally of one year duration. With a medium-range production plan, organizations may not be able to effect changes in the facilities, but they can determine manpower requirements and their training needs to perform the tasks of operations, vendor identification and development, effect improvements in product quality and in delivery schedules, inventory planning, etc. Short-range production plans are drawn based on scheduling techniques; such plans are basically concerned with aspects like job allocation to machines or reducing the idle time on machines.

2.2 DEFINITION AND CONCEPTS

Production or operations managers are required to forecast future events which have the potential to affect their activities. Such forecasting may either be a long-run estimate or a short-run estimate of demand. From the production managers' point of view, forecasting is important for planning, scheduling and controlling the system to achieve efficient output of goods and services.

Planning of the system is done by the production managers by forecasting aggregate demand and it helps to design or redesign processes to keep pace with demand. For example, what should be the degree of automation (semi-automated or fully automated), types of production facilities (assembly line, job-shop or intermittent), etc. can be assessed through aggregate demand analysis. Similarly, using long-run estimates, capacity planning is also done to decide about the expansion of capacity.

Scheduling of the system is done to ensure the best use of the existing conversion process. It requires a short-run demand estimate. Scheduling of a job can be more effective once we are able to forecast demand accurately. Similarly, optimum manpower requirement, rate of production, etc. can also be assessed using forecasting techniques. Demand forecasting is also necessary to control the system as it helps to control inventory, production, manpower and total costs.

However, demand forecasts alone may not always be effective in planning and controlling operational decisions. Some organizations also use technological and economic forecasts along with demand forecasts for achieving accuracy in their decisions. Such forecasts are usually done by retaining experts.

To secure and execute orders to the customers' satisfaction are the two primary objectives of a manufacturing organization. Production planning and control by definition is the management of the process of executing orders. This process includes planning, scheduling, dispatching, loading, progressing and controlling.

1. Planning involves deciding how the production is to be carried out.
2. Scheduling assists in creating a timetable and in routing production tasks.
3. Dispatching gives the authority to start the work by obtaining the required tools, materials and items for production.
4. Work timetables for loading frames are created for an operator or machine according to the plan. This is also a control function, which ensures that plan objectives are met by the production department.
5. Progressing involves the movement of goods and is considered an important construct for the production planning and control function.

In Chapter 1, we discussed the basics of the production management function, clearly identifying Production planning and control as a vital element of the entire process. The scope of Production planning and control goes far beyond the activities of the production department.

Once the product is designed, the production manager has to put together plans for manufacturing the product. To manufacture the end product from the part prints (classified drawings for complicated products which involve several sub-assemblies or parts, for example, the manufacture of an armoured tank for war), product prototype or drawing, the production manager has to develop and follow a streamlined process of sequence of operations. These include the selection of tools and equipment for manufacturing processes to attain the desired quality level and plans to achieve economy in operations. This function is also known as process engineering.

Process engineering differs from product engineering. As a product engineer, the production manager develops experimental designs and models, to test their utility, before making the part prints of the product.

Production planning can be defined as a systematic way of determining manufacturing methods for a product so as to achieve both economy and customer satisfaction. It broadly covers identifying, devising and specifying tools, equipment and processes to convert raw material into the finished product.

The functions of Product planning are to:

- determine the manufacturing process
- decide the sequence of operations
- ascertain the requirements of equipment, tools and gauges
- outline norms for implementing changes in the process, tooling or equipment, when drawings or part prints need to be altered
- assist in product design development

On the basis of the above mentioned functions, the following are the contents (scope) of a production plan:

1. Identify and state the purpose of production: This should include the item's name and code of the product; the quantity, volume or lot sizes; the raw material specifications, etc.
2. Sequential list of operations: This should include cycle time for completing the production process
3. List of technical specifications, for the different manufacturing stages as well as for quality control
4. List of equipment, machines, tools, gauges, jigs, dies, fixtures, etc. required for the different stages of production
5. List of specifications to be followed to achieve optimum performance standard, for example, the cycle time, set-up time, output level, etc.

2.3 STEPS IN PRODUCTION PLANNING

Careful planning and adherence to procedure can help Production managers resolve problems that are likely to be encountered. These steps are as follows:

Step 1: Clear definition of the requirements and conditions of the production process

Step 2: Allow for continuous improvement in the production process
Step 3: Create a list of all the basic operations in the process
Step 4: Determine the most economical and efficient manufacturing methods
Step 5: Create a detailed list of all the equipment required
Step 6: Decide the sequence of operations
Step 7: Identify the gauging requirements

Production planning and Process planning are terms used to define the same function in different organizations. Similarly, organizations also tend to use Production planning and Production control interchangeably. Yet, there is a small difference as Production control involves the execution of the Production plan. This can be better understood once we define the objectives of Production control.

2.3.1 Objectives of Production Control

The objectives of Production control are to

1. Submit good delivery dates to customers
2. Achieve on-time deliveries
3. Make optimum use of manpower and machinery
4. Ensure Work-in-Progress (WIP) remains at minimal levels
5. Eliminate production delays and changes in the production plan
6. Build a database for proper planning

2.3.2 Functions of Production Control

From the objectives listed above, we can also derive the possible functions for Production control, which are:

1. **Basic Planning** for developing policy decisions, stock holding, delivery periods for customers, etc.
2. **Pre-production planning** that includes capacity planning and controls the receiving of orders
3. **Ordering** of make-and-buy items including direct ordering, requirements planning and stock control
4. **Manufacturing Control**, including:
   (a) Shop load analysis
   (b) Shortage control
   (c) Avoidance of potential delays
   (d) Production scheduling

(e) Maintenancc of progress records

5. **Inventory Management** and **Store Keeping**

Organizations that offer competitive delivery dates to their customers are bound to attract more business and record healthy growth. When making such offers, organizations have to take into consideration the sequence of activities associated with manufacturing and delivering the product. This production chart then needs to be matched with the quoted delivery period. To avoid making unrealistic commitments on delivery dates, there is a need to balance factory capacity with load. This is done through order intake control. Balancing factory capacity with load is not possible in isolation. Systematic capacity planning is done to forecast the volume of business and adjust factory capacity with the projected load.

But the task does not end here. Continuous and systematic efforts need to be maintained to ensure on-time deliveries. Some reasons for not meeting delivery dates could be:

- insufficient manufacturing capacity
- scarcity or non-availability of materials, tools, fixtures, etc.
- inadequate specifications or instructions
- unforeseen circumstances, for example, breakdown of machinery, absenteeism, labour problems, quality issues, etc.
- production sequence not meeting plan requirements

Ordering, which involves decisions on make-or-buy requirements, planning and stock control, is the function that ensures material availability at the right time. In cases where confirmed orders for the manufacture of specific products in specific quantities are received, the direct ordering technique is used. For situations in which the same material is used for the manufacture of goods for different customers, the requirements planning technique is used. This is followed by an assessment of the future demand for the same material. Analyzing historical demand trends and taking averages helps to maintain stock control. To reduce the frequency of stock-outs, the storage control procedure proves efficient in stock control. This involves a regular check on the availability of materials, a few hours or days before they are issued from the store. This technique also helps in balancing the stock and work-in-progress.

The Shop Load Analysis Technique proves useful in making optimum use of plant and manpower. The load on each section when balanced with capacity helps us to identify underload and overload situations. As a result, plant and manpower resources can be redeployed to balance the distribution of load and ensure optimum utility.

Pre-emptive action has to be taken to reduce possible delays caused by unforeseen circumstances like machine breakdown, labour unrest or rejection. Routine preventive maintenance makes provisions for delays caused by absenteeism or rejection. It also helps in identifying the reasons for the delay and the measures that could alleviate the problem.

Frequent absenteeism can be tackled by boosting the morale of workers; proper production scheduling can reduce production delays.

The last important function of Production control is that of maintaining MIS records, gathering data and building a historical database. This could form the basis of future organizational and production planning successes.

To sum up, the basic functions of Production control can be broadly classified as:

(i) Planning
(ii) Scheduling
(iii) Routing
(iv) Dispatching and Progress control

2.3.2.1 *Routing*

The final Production plan for a plant is fine-tuned at different stages. Routing specifies which work stations are involved in the manufacture of different products, product parts or sub-assemblies. This is a very crucial part of capacity planning. It is routing that makes product traceability possible, if required, which by fixing responsibility, can contribute to product quality. A routing sheet (See Exhibit) is extensively used for product traceability in ISO documentation.

Exhibit

A route sheet for a tea blender that markets packaged tea under a brand name and gets supplies both from its own gardens and from the auction market could typically be:

Lot No.	Description	Grade	Qty. (in Kgs.)	Source
SJ 1000	Good	BOP	1000	P-1
SJ 1005	Fair	BPSM	500	P-4
SJ 1002	Bad	PD	250	P-1
SJ 1003	Good	CD	500	P-2
SJ 1001	Poor	SBP	300	P-3
SJ 1004	Good	D-1	400	P-4
AR 1006	Good	OF-1	500	TT-1
AR 1008	Fair	BOP	500	WM-2

2.3.2.2 *Dispatching*

Dispatching documents help the front-line supervisors to understand the order position and the priority, that is, the tentative guideline for sequencing the orders. Most organizations prepare daily dispatch lists. However, in cases where orders are taken on a weekly basis, dispatching can also be done on a weekly basis. In such cases, midweek revisions may be necessary. Simple dispatch list information, apart from priority information, lists information on the date, the plant, the work station, quantity of orders and capacity requirements.

Manufacturing begins from the dispatching phase of Production planning and control, when the job and material orders are released. These orders put into action the operations of the Master Production Schedule (MPS). For jobs that comprise several individual parts, orders are dispatched in the form of job cards. Dispatch can either be centralized or decentralized, as per the organizational structure, and involves:

- Checking material availability
- Ensuring all drawings, part lists, material lists specifications, process instructions and production aids are readily available
- Acquiring quality control instructions for inspections, checking schedules, etc.

The main activities involved in Dispatch are as follows:

- Work assignment to machine and shop floor
- To assign responsibility for the issue of materials, tools, gauges and fixtures to Stores and other departments
- To distribute forms to gather information on production, cost data, payroll, etc.
- To allocate responsibility for progress monitoring and change control authority in unforeseen circumstances

While the primary objective of the Production control department is to achieve organizational efficiency in production, by planning and scheduling operations, it also has the responsibility of intermediate and long-range planning. This kind of planning is closely related to demand forecasting, adjustments in production capacity, manpower requirements, timing of investments, new production facilities, hiring sub-contractors, etc. It cannot be planned for individual product lines and has to follow an integrated approach for the organization as a whole. This is known as aggregate planning.

2.4 AGGREGATE PLANNING

Aggregate planning works to make the optimum use of organizational resources to meet demand forecasts. It focusses on the collective levels of capacity and demand of an organization and plans quantity and timing of output for medium and long-term periods.

While preparing an aggregate plan for an organization, the following objectives need to be met:

1. To provide levels of output, inventory and backlogs in keeping with the organization's comprehensive business plans
2. To balance resources with load for optimized capacity utilization
3. To maintain a consistent approach to manpower utilization in keeping with organizational policy on hiring, overtime, layoffs, etc.

Organizations use different approaches when they make aggregate plans, varying the manpower deployed, the inventory levels or sub-contracting. Each approach has its inherent advantages and disadvantages.

2.4.1 Steps to be followed in Aggregate Planning

Step 1 Decide on the level of aggregation that is required. Is it required across all product lines (for organizations with multiple product lines) or only for one?

Step 2 Take into account the kind of capacity available, demand for the products, timing of investment, manpower requirement (including layoffs, specialization and flexibility for cross-sectional jobs), etc.

Step 3 Determine the measures to be taken with regard to production and capacity. These could be computing the requirement of man-hours, direct labour costs, number of units (weight or volume) produced, value of production (or capacity), etc.

So in effect, aggregate planning is the means of balancing capacity management with demand management. Changing manpower, varied working hours (overtime or time reduction), need for subcontracting (to off-load jobs), new equipment requirements, etc. are some factors that need to be taken into account for effective capacity management. The factors that affect demand management are new product launches, sales promotional activity, pricing, etc.

Aggregate plans that are made taking into account controllable variables, such as employment, idle time, overtime, part-time, plant capacity, inventories, sub-contracting, back-orders (where customers are willing to wait for delivery), etc. are those that have adopted pure strategies to account for fluctuations in demand and the uncertainties of the production process.

2.4.2 Aggregate Planning Methods

As mentioned earlier, methods for aggregate planning differ across organizations. Yet, one constant is that top management always provides the basic guidelines to work on. Effective aggregate plans usually follow the guidelines mentioned below:

1. Consult organizational policy on controllable variables
2. Apply proper forecasting technique as the basis for the plan
3. Determine the correct units of capacity
4. Maintain a stable workforce
5. Manage inventories efficiently
6. Build flexibility into the plan to adapt to future changes
7. Evaluate and check plans at regular intervals

Aggregate production planning is done to estimate the resource capacity over an intermediate time span, say six months to one year. We call it an aggregate production plan, as here we focus on all the products, rather than on an individual one. Some of the important features of aggregate planning are:

- matching of market demand to resource availability
- plan for an intermediate time horizon

- evaluate capacity in general terms
- develop optimum resource allocation.

2.4.3 Master Production Schedule (MPS)

To put it simply, the MPS further breaks down the aggregate plan in terms of specific items to be produced at different time periods. If the aggregate plan specifies the number of motors to be produced each month, the MPS details the different types and sizes of motors to be produced in different months. The MPS therefore controls the production activities after the formal production plan is made, setting down the requirements for capacity and materials.

Type, volume and component lead times of products govern the time intervals specified in an MPS. This can vary from one week to several months. Once the MPS is finalized, it is updated from time to time keeping pace with the progress or changes, if any, in the production schedule. This needs to be done frequently, adjusting to changes required, to avoid affecting the MPS.

2.4.3.1 Functions of MPS

1. To convert aggregate plans into specific end items
2. To assess alternative schedules
3. To finalize material requirements
4. To determine capacity requirements
5. To focus priorities
6. To optimally utilize available capacity

2.4.4 MPS Methods

1. Start from an aggregate plan
2. Identify and schedule common modules wherever possible
3. Load facilities realistically
4. Ensure timely release of orders
5. Closely monitor inventories
6. Be agile in rescheduling as and when required

Thus, the MPS is a formal production plan of finished products to meet on-time demand, in keeping with the capacity of the organization. It expresses what the company wants to manufacture, how much and at what time. MPS follows the framework in Fig. 2.1.

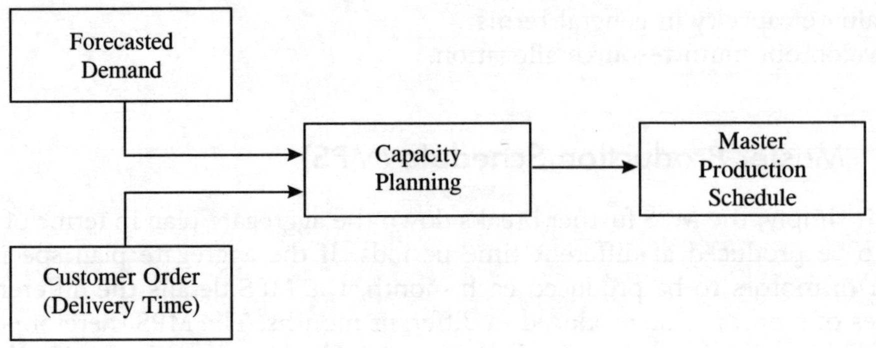

Figure 2.1 *Master Production Schedule Framework*

The Material Requirement Planning (MRP) process starts with the MPS. The time span and the planning horizon are the two key considerations in setting up the MPS. The time span depends on the specific production plan, which may be daily, weekly or monthly. The planning horizon indicates the extent of stretching the plan forward, that is, the scope or the spread of the plan. Exploding, Netting and Offsetting are the three distinct steps involved in MRP.

Step 1 Exploding indicates uses of the Bill of Materials (BOM), that is, the detailed lists of required components for every item of manufacture.

Step 2 Netting is the final determination of requirements, subtracting gross requirements from stock availability.

Step 3 Offsetting determines the starting time of manufacture of the finished products, keeping in view the lead time of operation.

A typical MPS can be illustrated as under:

Code	WEEKS								
TV	1	2	3	4	5	6	7	8	9
GR			400	600		800	300		

Note TV is the product code and GR indicates the gross requirements in specific weeks.

Along with this MPS, we require an Inventory Master File. Let us assume we had 550 TVs in stock, and the security stock of TVs is a minimum of 50 items. The initial stock is indicated by A, security stock by SS, net requirements as NR. NR is calculated as follows:

1. If the availability is more than 0, NR = GR – A + SS
2. If the availability is equal to 0, NR = GR.

Code	WEEKS								
TV	1	2	3	4	5	6	7	8	9
GR			400	600		800	300		
A	550	550	550	150	0	0	0	0	0
SS	50	50	50	50	50	50	50	50	50
NR	0	0	0	500	0	800	300	0	0

Net Requirements of the MRP:

Week 1 Gross requirements are invalid, the availability is 550 units, the security stock is 50, and therefore, if we do not have gross requirements, there is also no Net Requirement.

GR = 0

A= 550, SS = 50

NR = 0

Week 2 the same as week 1, so we have an availability of 550 units and the security stock is 50 units.

Week 3 The gross requirement is 400 units, but we have an availability of 550 from the last week, so we can satisfy the 400 units with the 550 available and we make sure that we have 50 units for the security stock.

$NR = GR - A + SS; NR = 400 - 550 + 50; NR = -100$

It is important to realize that the result is negative, which means we do not need to make more SS, because there are 150 available. 550 – 400 = 150

Week 4 We need to make 600 SS, but we only have 150 units that were left from the weeks before, so the net requirements are:

$NR = GR - A + SS; NR = 600 - 150 + 50; NR = 500$

We have to make 500 SS during the 4th week; we ensure that the Security Stock has 50 units.

Week 5 The GR are invalid, we do not need to fabricate more because the NR are also invalid.

Week 6 The Gross Requirements are 800 units, the availability is invalid so,

$NR = GR, NR = 800$

We have to fabricate 800 units during the 6th week, and our security stock is 50 units.

Week 7 The same as in the week 6, our net requirements are 300 units,

$NR = GR, NR = 300$

2.5 CAPACITY AND MATERIAL REQUIREMENT PLANNING

The Material Requirement Planning (MRP) Technique makes it easier to decide the quantity and timing for procuring materials as per the Master Production Schedule (MPS). While Capacity Requirement Planning (CRP) helps in determining the capacity requirements of machines and manpower to achieve the objectives set by MPS and MRP. The technique that integrates all managerial functions such as finance, marketing, personnel and engineering with Production Planning and Control is MRP-II. These days, with the help of computers, these techniques are used more effectively and efficiently. Nowadays, Enterprise Resource Planning or ERP software is widely used in organizations across the globe.

2.5.1 Capacity Planning

Capacity is defined as the ability of the machine to produce. The capacity of a factory is determined by aggregating machine capacity. Characteristically, in production and operations management, we can have potential capacity, immediate capacity, or effective capacity.

1. Potential capacity indicates the degree to which the top management can stretch the capacity, depending on the requirements. Hence, potential capacity is considered as the strategic level decision of the organization.
2. Immediate capacity indicates the production capacity that can be made available as on date, that is, immediately after the production plans have been made.
3. Effective capacity is the productive capacity actually used by the organization.

Capacity planning is done to estimate the requirements of machines and manpower so as to achieve production targets. It helps to determine capacity and to adjust capacity to match resource availability, to cope with demand fluctuation. With a stable demand pattern, the task of capacity planning become easier, while with fluctuating demand, the task becomes complicated due to the efforts required for optimal utilization of available resources or new resource acquisition, as the case may be. Excess capacity will minimize productivity; while under-capacity will strain customer services and the long-term growth and profitability of the organization. For effective capacity planning, production and operations managers need to consider factors like machine standards, production cycle time, labour productivity, multiplicity of shifts, plant efficiency, scheduling delays, maintenance problems, power failure, absenteeism, other eventual manufacturing problems like improper design, inherent process bottlenecks, unavoidable rejection, etc. In addition, capacity planning decisions also consider the scope of job sub-contracting, make-or-buy decisions, manpower inventory, manpower planning, etc. The whole exercise ultimately helps to compute the available machine and man-hours, to match the production target.

For better comprehension, we can list the following factors:

1) **Identify items to be manufactured for the present and in the near future:**

   This identification process is quite simple, as the company's order booking position clearly spells out these details. However, more dynamic production and operation managers may even keep in view the market sentiments and the perspective plan documents of the organization.

2) **Determination of Standard Output Information**:

   Standard output rate for each job or operation can be made available from machine literature, which indicates the cycle time for each job unit. But this may not be always correct, as it is done based on pre-determined motion–time standards. Many organizations, which have considered machine literatures' mandated cycle time as the standard time for compensation planning, are now experiencing difficulties and labour unrest arising from improper job co-relation. Therefore, the standard output rate has to be determined by evaluating the organization-specific standard time, duly carrying out a time study. The Route Sheet or Process Sheet can, to a great extent, supplement efforts but may not, by itself, convey the correct position.

3) **Determining Quantity to be manufactured**:

   This is also another important factor for capacity planning.

4) **Labour efficiency rate determination**:

   This can be determined along with standard output rate determination, by carrying out a time study. The selection of qualified workers (as sample), deciding the performance rate are some of the important issues involved in this process.

5) **Plant Efficiency Factor**:

   Determination of plant and machine efficiency, duly considering the idle time is also important for effective capacity planning. Machine idle time increases for scheduling delays, break-down, preventive maintenance, production change-over (which increases set-up time), etc. Work sampling studies can make this process simple. However, the actual rate of efficiency varies from machine to machine, and from organization to organization.

6) **Multiplicity of Shifts**:

   This is also another important decision to be made while planning capacity. However, such a decision cannot be taken without adequate economic analysis. Ideally, two–shift work is better than single or three-shift work due to obvious productivity and cost constraints.

7) **Scope of Sub-contracting**

Sub-contracting means job off-loading to established vendors. Conventionally, low technology jobs are sub-contracted by companies to reap a cost advantage. However, this decision is also taken after careful cost–benefit analysis. A decision to sub-contract also depends, to a great extent, on organizational policies.

2.5.2 Objectives of Capacity Planning

Important objectives of capacity planning are to:

1. Satisfy future demand for the products.
2. Assess the optimal capacity.
3. Optimize the initial investment to reduce the volume of break-even quantity.
4. Build capacities to pursue the long-term objectives of the company.

Some important considerations for capacity planning are issues involved in products and services, process factors, operational issues, supply chain issues, break-even level, etc.

2.5.3 Process of Capacity Measurement

For an organization engaged in the manufacture of a single product or homogenous products, capacity measurement is relatively simple, as it can be measured in terms of the number of units produced per unit of time, say daily, weekly, monthly or annually. For example, a scooter manufacturer's capacity can be understood in terms of the number of scooters produced in a month. While, for a shoe manufacturer, such measurement can be done in terms of the number of pairs produced in a month. But for organizations engaged in the manufacture of multiple products, capacity measurement in terms of definable units per unit time becomes difficult because of the sharing of common manufacturing facilities. In such cases, capacity may be defined in terms of available labour hours or machine hours. For example, for a job-shop or intermittent type production system, capacity can be measured in terms of labour or machine hours.

2.5.4 Different Types of Capacity

Capacity limits the capability of the organization. Although such capability limitations can be overcome to some extent by introducing multi-shifts or by sub-contracting, by and large, such capacity can be quantitatively described as follows:

1. **Licensed Capacity**: This denotes the actual capacity licensed by the concerned Government Authorities. Before starting actual production, the required capacity has to be declared by the organization, Government authorities will vouch for the veracity of this capacity, after due inspection of available facilities in the organization. In reality, a particular organization may obtain higher licensed capacity, keeping future expansion requirements in view.
2. **Installed Capacity**: It represents capacity in terms of machines actually installed. Machines procured for installation have some defined capacity, as provided in their printed literature. The sum of such capacity gives the total installed capacity. Installed capacity may not be exactly at the same level as licensed capacity.
3. **Rated Capacity**: This denotes the actual performance efficiency of the machines, which can be understood after a trial run. Obviously, the highest production rate becomes the benchmark. But deciding the capacity rate based on one of time highest achievement may not be always correct. It is necessary to assume the average of the performance rate of machines over a time period, for a more effective rating decision.

Capacity Planning at *Sonajuli Tea Estate*

Capacity is measured in terms of units of work. Time and the machine capacity are two major constraints in capacity management. Operationally, capacity is generally known as the highest quantity of work in a given time frame.

Sonajuli Tea Estate has made available the following information on grading and packing per Kg of 'made tea' in a day.

Sl.No.	Job Description	Standard Time Required Per Kg (in minutes)	Average Qty. required per month
1	Arranging the made tea on a wire mesh	2	1300
2	Running of machine 2	1300	
3	Storing the graded tea in aluminum bins	3	1300
4	Packing the graded tea in packets of various sizes	5	1300

For all the above operations, the use of wire meshes is compulsory as it helps in more accurate grading through subsequent machine runs. Based on the above information, estimate the requirement of wire meshes and manpower, assuming a labour efficiency rate of 75% and a plant efficiency rate of 80%. Assume a particular wire mesh can be run for 100 hours a month, as it requires thorough clearing every week. The nature of job does not warrant multi-shift working and one operator can operate two machines.

Solution

1. Compute the total hours required by multiplying standard time per Kg. (in hours) by the average monthly requirement. Since Standard time per Kg is given in minutes, to arrive at total working hours, it should be divided by 60.
2. Since labour efficiency is 75%, running of wire meshes (the equipment), is restricted to the extent of 75%, and thus, the above value has to be divided by 0.75 to arrive at the adjusted equipment running hours.
3. Similarly, to arrive at capacity hours at 80% utilization of the wire meshes, adjusted equipment running hours has to be divided by 0.80.
4. Finally, the requirement of wire meshes (the machine), is decided by dividing the adjusted capacity in hours by the available hours per machine, which is 100 hours per month, as indicated above.

Therefore, the number of operators required would be two, as the net requirement of wire meshes is four and one operator can operate two wire meshes/machines.

Capacity measurement types can be classified as output or input measures for product and process focusses respectively. For example, we compute the capacity utilization rate as follows:

$$\text{Utilization} = \frac{\text{Actual output}}{\text{Design capacity}}$$

Capacity efficiency rate is determined by:

$$\text{Efficiency} = \frac{\text{Actual output}}{\text{Effective capacity}}$$

Effective capacity is determined as:

Effective Capacity = Design Capacity (maximum output rate) – Allowances (e.g. personal time, maintenance, and scrap)

Table 2.1 *Calculation of machine and manpower requirements*

Sl. No.	Job description	Standard time/Kg in (in minutes)	Average requirement per month (in Kg)	Total hours required for given quantity	Equipment running hours at 75% labour machine shift	Capacity hours at 80% utilisation	Machine requirement on single shift
1.	Arranging the made tea on wire mesh	2	1300	43.33	57.77	72.22	0.72
2.	Running of machine	2	1300	43.33	57.77	72.22	0.72
3.	Storing of graded tea in Aluminum bins	3	1300	65	86.66	108.33	1.08
4.	Putting the graded tea in tea packets	5	1300	108.33	144.44	180.55	1.81

Total requirement of the wire meshes = 4.33

Net requirement of wire meshes = 4

We also compute capacity cushion, using this formula:

Capacity cushion = 1 – Utilization

Capacity cushion indicates the amount of reserved capacity, which provides the company with a buffer to suddenly increase capacity, as may be required due to demand fluctuation.

Some of the important formulae for assessing capacity requirements are:

1. For one type of product

$$M = \frac{Dp}{N(1 - C)}$$

where, D = number of units (customers) forecast per year

p = processing time (in hours per unit or customer)

N = total number of hours per year during which the process operates

C = desired capacity cushion rate (%)

2. More than one type of product: n types of products:

$$M = \frac{[Dp + (D/Q)s]_{product1} + [Dp + (D/Q)s]_{product2} + \ldots + [Dp + (D/Q)s]_{productn}}{N(1 - C)}$$

Q = number of units in each lot s = setup time (in hours) per lot

Note Always round up the fractional part for the number of machines required.

2.6 MATERIALS REQUIREMENT PLANNING (MRP)

MRP is a scientific technique for planning and scheduling material requirements for production. It combines inventory control with production planning under dependent demand conditions, utilizing inputs from a Master Production Schedule (MPS), Bills of Materials (BOM) and Inventory Status Report (ISR). MPS as explained earlier expresses the aggregate plan in terms of specific items. BOM expresses how the end product is to be manufactured, duly detailing all sub-component or sub-assembly items, their sequence and quantity, work centres performing the respective job sequence, etc. ISR on the other hand, provides detailed information on the inventory status of each item. Such a status report also contains information on safety, stock level, procurement lead time, vendor rating details, etc.

MRP, therefore, is basically a planning tool for effective inventory management and production scheduling. With Manufacturing Resource Planning (MRP-II), it has now become more effective and purposive. With information technology support, MRP can now play an effective role. MRP ensures optimization of production plans based on master production schedules, sales forecasts, inventory status, open orders and bills of material. Effective MRP is a proactive approach to manage inventory levels and the flow of materials, so it can reduce the outflow of cash and increase profitability. Some of the benefits of MRP are:

1. Effective inventory management leading to optimum inventory holding
2. Improved supply chain and distribution network
3. Improved customer services
4. Improved productivity
5. Effective job scheduling
6. Production cost minimization
7. Lead time reduction
8. Quality improvement
9. Quality cost minimization due to less scrap arising and minimum rework cases.
10. Overall efficiency leading to enhancement of the company's competitive position.

However, MRP has to make use of the following elements to optimize the level of inventory and purchases, and production schedules.

- Master Production Schedule (MPS)
- Bill of Materials (BOM)
- Information on lead times
- Scrap arising rate
- Lot size policies
- Safety stock requirements

Thus, with MRP, we can plan the production of the right materials at the right place and at the right time. In production and operations management, MRP plays a significant role, as it can effectively manage inventory and enforce production control. Thus, it not only manages the cost, but through improved quality and services, also enhances customer satisfaction. MRP helps in reducing inventory and lead time (both for production and delivery), giving more realistic and achievable delivery schedules to customers, and finally, increases efficiency.

Table 2.2 *MRP Report for a single item*

Item Code : XLM 2169 Seat Cushion
Lead Time : Two Weeks
Report Date : 0 week

Particulars	Week Nos.							
	1	2	3	4	5	6	7	8
Gross requirements				200				250
Scheduled Receipts								
Available on hand (at the end of the week)	25	25	25	25				
Net requirement					175			250
Planned order Release (beginning of the week)		175				250		

2.7 MANUFACTURING RESOURCE PLANNING (MRP-II)

We have seen that Material Requirements Planning (MRP) only helps in Scientific Production Planning, synchronizing input information from MPS, BOM and ISR. MRP-II on the other hand, synchronizes all aspects of the business plan, duly coordinating all functional areas of business, like Marketing, Materials Manufacturing, Finance and Personnel. The process helps to integrate business plans with the production plan, using a closed–loop MRP.

To overcome the shortcomings of MRP, MRP-II has been introduced, which like MRP makes use of BOM and MPS, and follows the same three steps. Some of the added features of MRP-II are, however, as follows:

- Use of Feedback: MRP-II being more technology enabled makes use of feedback from the shop floor to track the progress of work, using a closed feedback loop.
- Resource Scheduling: MRP-II draws detailed resource scheduling plans based on shop floor reports. This obviously ensures better control over the operations in terms of optimization of resource utilization.
- Incorporation of Batching Rules: This is done using standard software packages. Depending on the company's specific policies, batching orders can be either lot-for-lot, economic batch quantity (EBQ), and plant period cover. Lot-for-lot indicates the making of batches in line with orders. EBQ is decided based on cost minimization principles, balancing the set up cost against the cost of stock. Part period cover indicates the making of batches based on the period of demand.

Standard software is now available for MRP-II. These MRP-II suites are capable of performing all the tasks mentioned above, and can help in efficient production planning, controlling and scheduling.

2.7.1 Closed-loop MRP

Material requirements planning is useful, but due to the problems that are faced by the organization after implementation of MRP and the lack of awareness of other related production and business functions, organizations begin to shift towards a closedloop MRP system (Fig. 2.2). The diagram below shows a much wider data horizon that has now opened up for organizations, which have started using better information technology to upgrade their MRP system.

MRP-II using an MPS in a closedloop feedback system (Fig. 2.3) performs strategic production planning, control and scheduling, based on organizational capacity, supply chain systems, design work and cash flow. It means MRP-II facilitates the planning of resources like labour, machinery, tools, space and materials. It can extend support to design engineering, and can effectively help in deciding the replacement and re-designing of tools, which are used as production aids. A typical framework of MRP-II is reproduced in Fig. 2.3

The main advantage of MRP-II is that it lowers in-process inventories significantly, and quickly tracks material requirements, depending on the demand. However, because of system complexity and problems in implementation, many organizations avoid its usage.

2.8 FORECASTING

Forecasting is defined either as an estimate or inference of a future event. A forecast may not always be an accurate estimate or inference as it is always based on past trends. However, it provides an effective basis for planning the various operations and activities of an organization. From the production manager's point of view, forecasting is important for planning, scheduling and controlling the system to achieve efficient results.

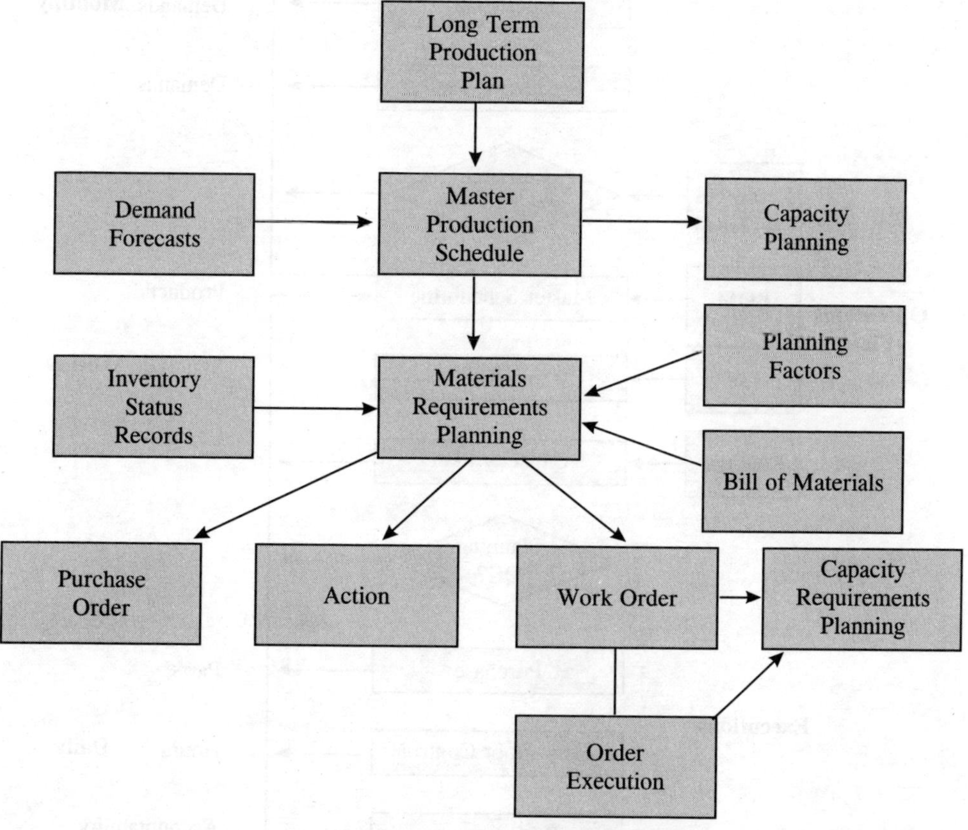

Figure 2.2 *Closed-loop MRP*

2.8.1 Steps in Forecasting

The following basic steps are required for effective forecasting:

Step 1 Identify the objectives for which forecasting is done. For example, from the manager's point of view, forecasting objectives may be reducing the queuing problem of customers by enhancing the number of service counters, initiating changes in the design of a product or measuring customer's response pattern.

Step 2 Determine the time period of forecast, which may be long-run or short-run. Depending on the time period, managerial decisions and actions may vary. To illustrate, if an organization requires extra manpower for a period less than one-year, instead of direct recruitment, they may avail of the services of an outsourcing agency (that makes people available on hire).

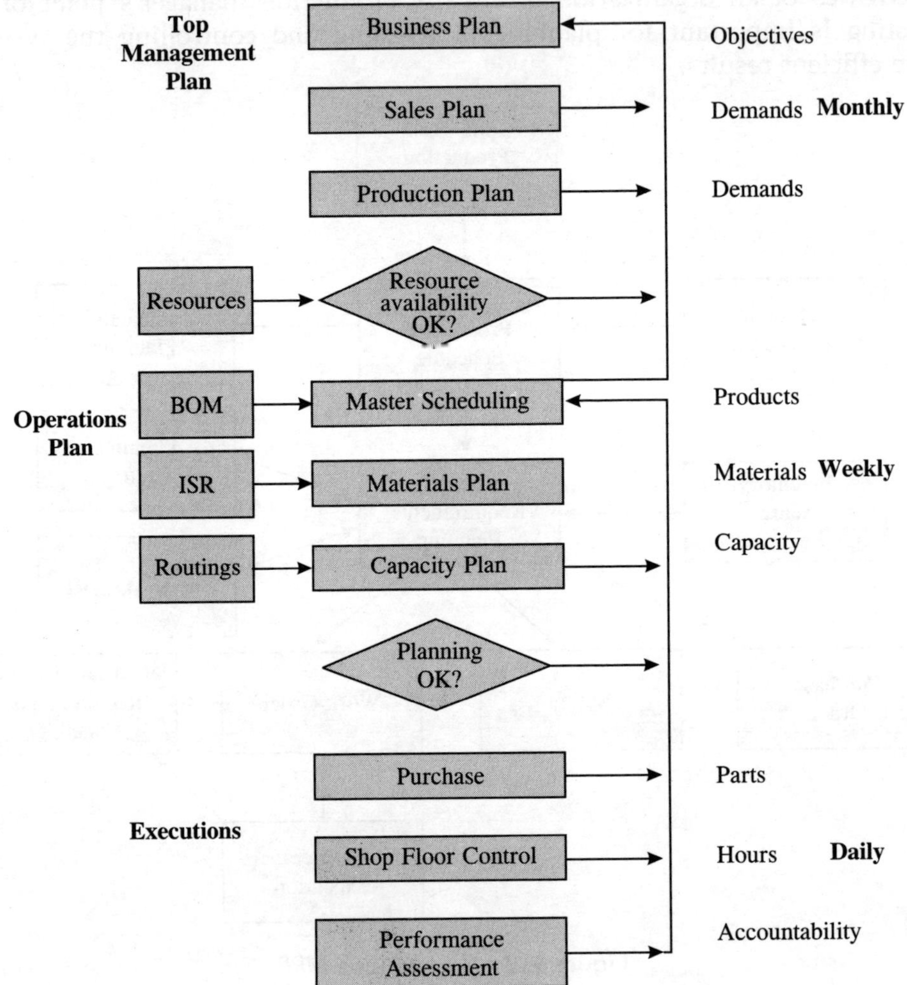

Figure 2.3 *MRP –II Closed loop Feedback system*

Step 3 Select the right forecasting method in line with the objectives and time frame. For example, the annual sales forecast (for an existing organization) is better done using Time Series Analysis, while the Delphi Technique or Market Research Methods are best applied where collective opinions are required to be assessed.

Step 4 Collect the required data and information that matches the selected forecasting method. For time series analysis, past data is collected, while for market research, primary data are collected by conducting a survey.

Step 5 Implement results for managerial decisions (planning and control),

Step 6 Periodically evaluate forecasting, by assessing the degree of error and reliability and revise.

2.8.2 Types of Forecasting

Forecasting techniques are broadly of three types. These are qualitative or judgmental, time–series and cause–effect models. Depending on the type chosen, different techniques are adopted. Qualitative forecasts involve the collection of opinions and preferences, which are quantified using different statistical tools. The Delphi Method, the Nominal Group Technique and Market Research are widely used qualitative techniques.

Quantitative forecasts are divided into Time Series Analysis and Cause–effect Models. Time Series Analysis uses historical data to calculate the average of past demand; the results thus obtained (average) are used as forecasts. Last Period Demand, Simple Average, Moving Average, Exponential Smoothing, Trend Projections are popularly used techniques under Time Series Analysis.

Table 2.3 *Types of Forecasting and Techniques used*

Forecast Type	Techniques used
Qualitative Model	Delphi Technique Nominal Group Method Market Research Method
Quantitative Model	Time Series Analysis Last Period Method Simple Average Method Moving Average Method Exponential Smoothing Trend Projections
Cause–effect Model	Correlation Regression Method Econometric Method Input–Output Analysis End-use Analysis

Forecasting, using cause–effect models are done by using correlation regression or econometric techniques. Correlation Regression Technique shows cause–effect relationship between an organizations's past sales data and the market or economic forces that caused the changes (either negative or positive) in the demand pattern. Econometric models are used to forecast economic conditions. We use such a technique when the principles of consumption theory are used to forecast the demand pattern. Similarly, Input–Output Analysis and End-use Analysis are some other sophisticated quantitative models.

The different forecasting models discussed above may be listed as in table 2.3.

2.8.2.1 *Time Series Analysis*

Employment data over a time period (time series) are used under this method as the basis for a manpower forecast. However, merely projecting the past into the future, without considering endogenous and exogenous changes, will increase forecasting errors, which may result either in the under forecasting or in the over forecasting of manpower requirements.

When we record employment levels over a time period, we observe the following five distinct elements in it.

1. **Trend:** Fluctuations in the level of employment over a time period.
2. **Cyclical Effects**: Change in employment in relation to some particular event, like economic liberalization in India or WTO resolutions.
3. **Seasonality:** Seasonal fluctuations that occur more than once in a given time period, like requirements of additional staff for maintenance; for example, in an electricity service provider in the summer and rainy season, than in winter.
4. **Step:** This is a sudden change in the employment level due to factors like the economic environment or increased market share or procurement of some new machines.
5. **Random Fluctuations:** These are fluctuations in the employment level which are random in nature; such fluctuations do not follow any obvious pattern. We can address this problem by following a moving average method.

2.8.2.2 *Moving Average Method*

In this method, the average combined employment level data for the recent past is considered as the forecast for the employment level for the next period. This technique is useful to guard against random fluctuations. However, it requires careful selection of time periods, which may be a 6-period, 10-period, 12-period moving average. If the time periods chosen are too few, we may get wide variability in our forecast. Therefore, considering more time periods, we get better results. Whatever time period we select for our forecast, it is necessary to continue to use the same number of periods for our computations. After each period elapses, the figure for the oldest period is dropped and the figure for the newest period is added for subsequent computations of manpower requirements.

Example

Godrej Healthcare Division

The following is the manpower data for *Godrej's* healthcare division for the last six years:

Year	Manpower Level/Data (in nos.)
1995	500
1996	600
1997	800
1998	1000
1999	1100
2000	1300

You have been asked to forecast their manpower requirements in 2001 using a 6-period moving average

Solution

$$F_m = \frac{500 + 600 + 800 + 1000 + 1100 + 1300}{6} = 5300/6 = 883 \text{ nos.}$$

If we are asked to use a 4-period moving average to forecast manpower for 2001, then we have to take the data from 1997 and compute the forecasted manpower as under:

$$F_m = \frac{800 + 1000 + 1100 + 1300}{4} = 4200/4 = 1050 \text{ nos.}$$

From the above variation in results, the danger of considering lesser time periods in manpower forecasting is clear.

For achieving better results, weights may be assigned for different time periods at the discretion of the analyst. For example, the manpower levels in 1995, 1996 and 1997 may be less relevant, hence, for these years weights may assigned as 1 each. For 1998, the weight may be 2, for 1999 weight may be 3, for 2000, the weight may be 4. Now, the manpower forecast for 2001, will be :

$$F_m = \frac{1(500) + 1(600) + 1(800) + 2(1000) + 3(1100) + 4(1300)}{\sum w, i.e., 12}$$

$$= \frac{500 + 600 + 800 + 2000 + 3300 + 5200}{12} = 12400/12 = 1033 \text{ nos.}$$

2.8.2.3 *Exponential Smoothing*

In the moving average method, we need to carry forward a large volume of historical data. The need for past records can be eliminated by adopting this method; it removes random errors by giving exponentially decreasing weights to historical data.

Such a weight factor is indicated by alpha ($\propto$), which is a smoothing constant, a non-linear decimal value which lies between 0 and 1. The formula for the exponential smoothing model is:

$$F_m = F_t + \propto (A_{t-1} - F_{t-1})$$

where,

F_m = Forecasted manpower

F_{t-1} = Forecasted demand for the previous period

$\propto$ = Smoothing constant

A_{t-1} = Actual manpower required for the previous period

Example:

Assume that the forecasted manpower requirement for an organization is 500, while the actual requirement is 480. Considering an alpha value of 0.4 (which the company feels would produce the best results), compute the manpower requirement for the current period.

Solution

500 + 0.4(480500) = 492 nos.

Double exponential smoothing can also be done to get a further cushion.

2.8.2.4 *Regression Analysis*

Regression analysis is used as a forecasting tool to statistically understand the average relationship between the dependent and independent variables. In simple regression analysis we find one independent variable, while in multiple regressions, we observe the involvement of two or more variables. Simple linear regression analysis is done based on least-squares method – the assumption of $Y = a + bX$ relationship. The least-squares method estimates the values of the parameter in the regression equation. In least-squares, we compute the difference between the observed value and the estimated value, to define the error, which is symbolically indicated as u.

$$u = YY'$$

where, Y = observed value of the dependent variable

Y' = estimated value based on $Y' = a + bX$.

The least squares criterion requires that the line of best fit be such that the sum of the squares of the errors (or the vertical distance in Figure 2.4 from the observed data points to the line) is a minimum, that is,

Minimum: $\sum u^2 = \sum(Ya - bX)^2$

We can indicate it using the following figure:

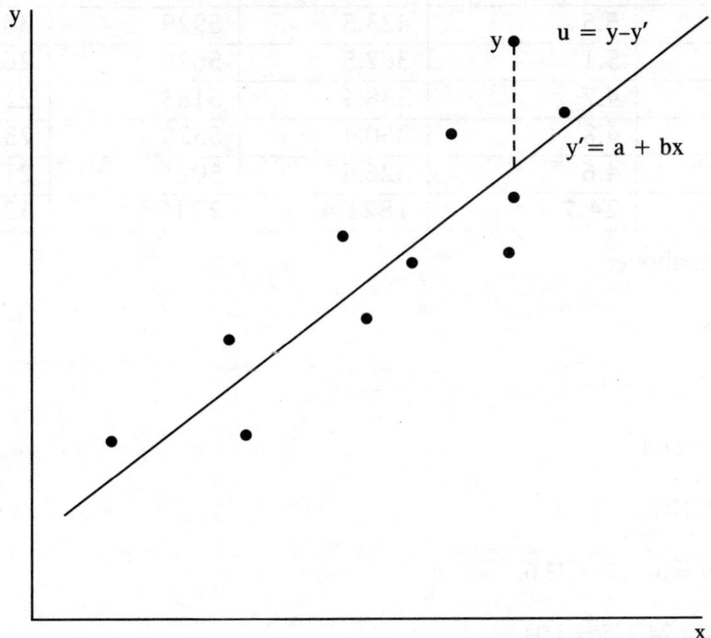

Figure 2.4 *Regression analysis*

We can fit this into the following normal equations:

$$\sum Y = na + b\sum X$$

$$\sum XY = a\sum X + b\sum X^2$$

Solving the equations for b and a yields

$$b = (n\sum XY(\sum X)(\sum Y))/n\sum X^2(\sum X)^2$$

$$a = YbX$$

$\sum Y/n$ and $X = \sum X/n$

Example

To illustrate the computations of b and a, we will refer to the data below. All the sums required are computed and shown below.

Computed Sums				
Advertising X (in thousands)	Sales Y (in millions)	XY	X^2	Y^2
77	5.5	423.5	5929	30.25
75	5.1	382.5	5625	26.01
72	4.7	338.4	5184	22.09
73	4.8	350.4	5329	23.04
71	4.6	326.6	5041	21.16
368	**24.7**	**1821.4**	**27108**	**122.55**

From the table above:

$$\sum X = 368;$$

$$\sum Y = 24.7;$$

$$\sum XY = 1,821.4;$$

$$\sum X^2 = 27,108$$

$$X = \sum X/n = 368/5 = 73.6;$$

$$Y = \sum Y/n = 24.7/5 = 4.94.$$

Substituting these values into the formula for b first:

$$b = \frac{n\sum XY - (\sum X)(\sum Y)}{n\sum X^2 - (\sum X)^2} = \frac{(5)(1,821.4) - (368)(24.7)}{(5)(27,108) - (368)^2} = \frac{17.4}{116} = 0.15$$

$$a = \overline{Y} - b\overline{X} = 4.94 - (0.15)(73.6) = -6.10$$

Thus, $Y' = -6.10 + 0.15X$

Note that $\sum Y^2$ is not used here, but is computed for r and r-squared (r^2).

Regression statistics requires finding the correlation coefficient (r) and the coefficient of determination ($r1.^2$), standard error of the estimate ($S2._e$) and prediction confidence interval. Among these, correlation coefficient is the most popular. Correlation coefficient (r) measures the degree of correlation between Y and X.

2.8.2.5 *Trend Analysis through Correlation Regression Methods*

A Production manager, analyzing customer feedback, observed that customers often alleged that the quality of the company's products was poor, and hence, they were generally reluctant to go in for repeat orders. The company could provide marketwise data with the breakup of equality failure (X) and the drop in customers (Y).

Market Areas	Quality Failure Reports (X)	No. of customers Reluctant to give Repeat orders (Y)
Kolkata	4	16
Chennai	6	29
Delhi	10	43
Mumbai	5	20
Jaipur	1	3
Bhopal	2	4
Pune	3	6
Total	31	121

- Find out whether the two variables are related.
- Show the magnitude of the relationship on a scale of 0.0 to 1.0.
- What is the direction of the relationship? Is it positive or negative?

Scatter plotting of the data shows the following trend:

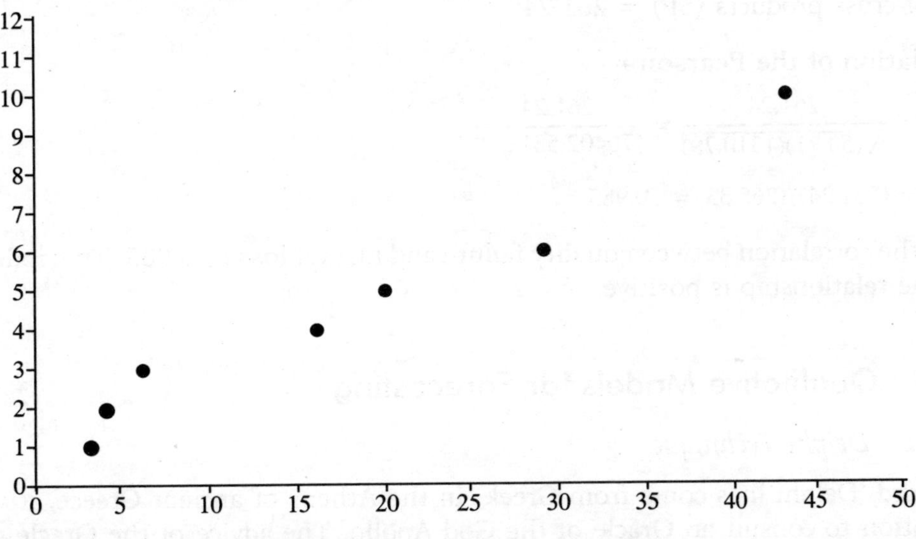

Figure 2.5 *Scatter plotting of data*

2.8.2.6 *Pearson Product-Moment Correlation Coefficient*

Karl Pearson (1857–1936), a British mathematician and statistician also developed the Chi-Square Test

$$r = \frac{\Sigma(X - X)(Y - Y)}{\sqrt{\Sigma(X - X)^2 \Sigma(Y - Y)^2}}$$

Incidence of Quality failure (X) and market loss (Y)

City	**X**	**Y**	**(X – X) ^{2}**	**(Y – Y) ^{2}**	**(X – X) (Y - Y)**
Kolkata	4	16	0.1849	1.6641	0.5547
Chennai	6	29	2.4649	137.124	18.4789
Delhi	10	43	31.0249	661.004	143.2047
Mumbai	5	20	0.3249	5.7100	1.5447
Jaipur	1	3	11.7649	204.204	49.0147
Bhopal	2	4	5.9049	176.624	32.2947
Pune	3	6	2.0449	127.464	16.1447
Total	31	121	53.7143	1310.794	261.2371

Mean of number of quality failures and withdrawal from the market is:

$X = 4.43$ and $Y = 17.2$

Sum of squared deviations in quality failure = 53.71

Sum of squared deviations in market loss = 1310.79

Sum of cross products (SP) = 261.24

Calculation of the Pearson r

$$r = \frac{261.24}{\sqrt{(53.71)(1310.79)}} = \frac{261.24}{[70402.53]\sqrt{}}$$

$$r = (261.24)/(265.33) = +0.985$$

Thus, the correlation between quality failure and market loss is: 0.985. This indicates that the relationship is positive.

2.8.3 Qualitative Models for Forecasting

2.8.3.1 *Delphi Technique*

The word 'Delphi' has come from Greek. In the Athens of ancient Greece, it was a convention to consult an Oracle of the God Apollo. The advice of the Oracle could only be interpreted by a priest.

In modern times, this method is essentially a group process to achieve a consensus forecast. It calls for the selection of a panel of experts, either from within or outside the organization, whose comments are crystallized from a series of questionnaire responses and then used as the basis for forecast. A series of questionnaires are prepared from the responses received from a prior set of questions in a sequencing manner. At every stage, information obtained from the previous questionnaire is shared among participating members, without disclosing the majority opinion, this may otherwise lead to peer-group influence on minority opinion.

The Delphi Technique procedure is as follows:

1. To start with, it requires the selection of a coordinator and a panel of experts, drawn from both, within and outside the organization.
2. The coordinator circulates questions in writing to each expert.
3. The experts write and send in their observations.
4. The coordinator edits and summarizes these observations, without disclosing the majority opinion in his summary.
5. On the basis of his summary, the coordinator then develops a new set of questionnaires and circulates those among the experts.
6. Experts then answer the new set of questions.
7. The coordinator repeats the process until he sees a consensus of opinion among the experts.

The success of the process depends on the following factors:

1. Experts should be so chosen that they have the requisite knowledge and skills to provide the best answers.
2. Questions should be relevant to the objective.
3. Criteria for evaluating responses should be consistent, unbiased and befitting the objectives.

Although no universal set of criteria for evaluating responses exist, it is often considered necessary to follow the guidelines mentioned below:

(a) Consider the assessment made by the experts in terms of their knowledge in the area.
(b) Consider the assessment in terms of feasibility, objectives, time and resource requirements.
(c) Consider the assessment in terms of desirability.
(d) Consider the assessment in terms of extraneous factors.

2.8.3.2 Nominal Group Method

Like the Delphi Method, the Nominal Group Method also involves a panel of experts. However, the major difference between the two is that while under the Delphi

Technique, experts are not allowed to discuss among themselves, for assessing the questions, under the Nominal Group Method, experts are given the opportunity to discuss among themselves. Under this method, the coordinator assumes the role of a facilitator, allowing the experts to sit together to discuss their ideas and records of such discussions are made on a flip chart. After these round table discussions on ideas, experts are asked to rank their ideas according to their perceived priority. The group consensus is then derived mathematically in terms of individual rankings. The process, therefore, affords creativity and facilitates scientific group consensus, unlike consensus by qualification (as the coordinator ultimately decides the best course of action) under the Delphi Technique.

2.8.4 Market Research

This qualitative method of forecasting is used to develop a model for consumer buying behaviour. From published secondary source data, factors like market size, population size, its biographical characteristics, income distribution pattern, past sales data, product groups, competitive advantages are synthesized to develop the desired consumer behaviour model. To supplement this observation, often surveys are conducted, interviewing target population (samples) and administering structured questionnaires. These supplementary efforts concretize judgment and make the forecast more effective. This technique is usually employed by organizations to forecast new product sales or sales of established products in new markets or for long-range market forecasts.

2.8.5 Tracking Signal for Tracking Forecasting Errors

An automatic monitoring mechanism to keep track of the accuracy of forecasting models is known as a tracking signal (TS). It is the ratio of cumulative forecasting error to the mean absolute deviation (MAD). Cumulative forecasting error or running sum of forecasting error (RSFE) is indicated by:

$$\sum_{t=1}^{n} (At - Ft)$$

where, At = Actual demand for period 't' and

Ft = Forecasted demand for period '*t*'

$$\text{Therefore, Tracking Signal (TS)} = \frac{\text{RSFE}}{\text{MAD}} = \sum_{t=1}^{n} (At - Ft) \div MAD$$

Tracking Signal is recalculated every time there is availability of actual demand data and the forecasting is updated. TS should be fairly small; only then can we say that the forecasting is accurate or near accurate. If a TS moves outside some pre-established range, we call it 'tripping of signal'. Every time a signal trips, we adjust our forecasting method. Usually, the limit of the TS is taken to vary between 3 and 8. Let us now illustrate TS with an example of actual demand data, forecasted demand data and the rcsultant value of TS. Let us assume up to period 5, we have made an initial estimate of the MAD to test the accuracy of our forecasting model. For each subsequent period, we have computed the TS value to understand whether it is within the accepted range of 3 to 8.

Period Demand	Actual Demand (A_t)	Forecasted (A_t–F_t) (F_t)	Errors	Sum of errors	MAD	TS $\frac{\Sigma(A_t - F_t)}{MAD}$
1	125	132	–7	–	–	–
2.	144	139	+5	–	–	–
3.	133	136	–3	–	–	–
4.	130	134	–4	–	–	–
5.	137	136	+1	-	4.00	–
6.	143	141	+2	+2	3.67	+0.54
7.	137	140	–3	–1	3.57	– 0.28
8.	138	141	–3	–4	3.50	– 1.14
9.	133	139	–6	–10	3.78	– 2.65
10.	131	136	–5	–15	4.30	– 3.49
11.	130	134	–4	–19	3.91	– 4.86

In this case, our TS is less than the limit of 3 to 8 up to a period 9. In periods 10 and 11, it undershoots the limit. As of now, the forecasting model is considered to be functioning well. However, if the trend persists in subsequent periods, we may have to re-assess our forecasting model. Using a tracking control chart, we can plot the data to explain the situation.

2.9 DECISING MAKING

Decision making is the process of selecting a course of action from a number of alternatives. Like planning, decision making is also all-pervasive. Like forecasting, decision making is also an important part of planning. Policy documents help in taking managerial decisions. But these are decisions of a routine nature, which we also call operational decisions. Strategic or important decisions, obviously, are taken considering different alternatives. In order to be a successful manager, one has to necessarily develop decision-making skills. The decision-making process is similar to strategic planning, which we have explained earlier. It involves:

1. Diagnosing, defining and identifying the source of the problem
2. Information gathering and analysis of the facts required to solve the problem
3. Developing and evaluating alternative solutions to the problem
4. Choosing the best decision alternatives

5. Communicating the decisions and implementing them.

The forecasting tools, explained earlier, help us in decision making. The Decision Tree, which is probably the most important tool for evaluating decision making, is explained here.

2.9.1 Decision Tree

A decision tree is a graphic representation of the sequence of decisions required to determine the expected values of an alternative course of action. Each decision alternative is weighed by developing a pay-off matrix, which depicts the probable value of each of the decision alternatives by quantifying the various outcomes and probabilities of their occurrence. Probability is the degree of likelihood that a particular event will occur. It varies from zero (no chance of occurring) to one (certain of occurring). Outcomes are quantified in terms of Expected Value (EV). It is the sum of values of the expected outcomes multiplied by their respective probabilities. To illustrate: suppose a manager expects 0.20 probability of earning Rs. 60,000/- from a business, 0.40 probability of earning Rs. 30,000/- from the business again and 0.30 probability of losing Rs. 20,000/- from the business. Such assumptions are based on his past experience or from the analysis of general trends in the industry. We can compute his EV as under:

$$\begin{aligned} EV &= 0.20(60{,}000) + 0.40(30{,}000) - 0.30\ (-20{,}000) \\ &= (12{,}000 + 12{,}000) - 6{,}000 \\ &= 24{,}000 - 6{,}000 \\ &= 18{,}000 \end{aligned}$$

Likewise, the manager can now compare the expected value of Rs. 18,000/- with other alternatives and decide on the best alternative, based on the higher expected value. Let us now analyze the following pay-off matrix:

		High Sales (probability = 0.60)	**Low Sales (probability = 0.40)**
Investment Alternative 1	Company-A	+ 30,000	– 15,000
Investment Alternative 2	Company-B	+ 70,000	– 30,000
Investment Alternative 3	Company-C	+ 40,000	– 10,000

From the above pay-off matrix, we have to first compute the expected value company-wise for each decision alternative, and then we can represent the same in the form of a Decision Tree.

EV for Companies is as under:

Company – A (Investment Alternative-1)	0.60(30,000)+0.40(–15,000) = 12,000
Company – B (Investment Alternative-2)	0.60(70,000)+0.40(–30,000) = 30,000
Company – C (Investment Alternative-3)	0.60(40,000)+0.40 (–10,000) = 20,000

It is seen from the above that investment in Company – B, i.e., investment alternative 2 is the best option. Now, we are representing the observations in the form of a Decision Tree.

Apart from the pay-off matrix and decision tree, queuing models and distribution models, inventory models and game theory are also used as decision tools. The queuing model helps us to reduce waiting time to ensure better service to customers. The distribution model helps us determine a cost-effective way of distributing products and services. Inventory models help us to determine the optimum inventory level for both inputs (raw materials and spares/components) and output (finished goods). Game theory helps us measure the decision outcomes under different situations of uncertainty. These apart, all the forecasting tools discussed earlier in the chapter are also used as important managerial tools. The Delphi Technique and the Nominal Group Technique are examples of group decision making. These apart, group decisions are taken by forming various committees.

2.10 MANAGEMENT INFORMATION SYSTEMS (MIS) AND DECISION SUPPORT SYSTEMS (DSS)

MIS is a system that gathers comprehensive data, organizes and summarizes it in a form that adds value to managerial decision making. It is computer-based information system for more effective planning, decision making and control. A typical MIS has four major components: data gathering, data entry, data transformation and information utilization. Most organizations keep a centralized database, which can be used for a wide variety of applications. DSS is an interactive computer system, which is easily accessible and operated by people, who need not be computer savvy. DSS helps them to plan and make decisions. A typical DSS consists of the following elements:

1. An MIS to support several ways of accessing and summarizing data

2. It is a sophisticated database that allows information to be accessed in various ways.
3. It is a user-friendly interface which enables the user to use simple commands (rather than complicated computer terms), while communicating with the DSS.
4. The database for DSS contains both internal and external information, which helps the manager to relate to and benchmark (compare) his decisions.
5. The response time for DSS is rapid, which makes the system more effective than conventional MIS.

2.11 SCENARIO PLANNING FOR PRODUCTION AND OPERATIONS MANAGEMENT

Scenarios are the alternative views of the future. From the organization's point of view, scenario planning helps in identifying a strategic-fit, pending some future developments. Scenario plans reflect on future situations within a certain frame of reference. Based on some stories we plot the scenarios, and make such scenarios the basis for framing plans and strategies. Like other managers, production and operations managers can also make use of scenario plans to forecast proposed change initiatives, reflecting on future situations, like technological change, change in the manufacturing process, capacity building, manpower skill development, inventory planning, etc. To explore these scenarios, managers have to think about uncertain aspects to unfold any eventual happenings that might cause harm to the organization.

Globalization has increased the market scope on the one hand, but on the other, it has also been responsible for business discontinuities due to changes in the business environment, new emerging technologies, etc. For production and operations managers, such effects may require changes in the production process, product-mix, technology, scaling the production volume up and down, and so on. Through scenario plans, production managers can explore such eventualities, and accordingly, pre-develop certain shared understanding or commitment for strategic interventions to bring future changes.

Scenario plans, therefore, effectively prepare the organization to face market turbulence. With prior plans and programmes, pre-conceiving various scenarios, managers can take effective decisions when needed. Ringland (1998) and Schwartz (1991) have identified that organizations worldwide are developing scenario plans to respond to unforeseen change situations. According to Schwartz, these are future contingencies, for which organizations are able to determine their future directions with contingency plans. According to Wack (1985), scenario planning involves the development of three or four different plots along with the associated narratives to illustrate the major driving forces for change and critical uncertainties in the environment.

Thus, scenario planning is a creative strategic planning method. The key driving forces for the scenario plans are changing social, technical, economic, environmental, educational, political and aesthetic (STEEEPA) trends.

Globally, we find that *Shell* and *Siemens AG* have made extensive use of scenario plans. *Shell* as an organization has made the most extensive use of scenario planning since 1973, primarily to cope with the oil crisis sparked by the Organization of Petroleum Exporting Countries (OPEC). *Shell*'s strategy was to cope with the environmental turbulence, often sparked by non-compromising OPEC members, who never reached an agreement on collective price rises or on production strategy. Such a non-comprising attitude on the part of OPEC members often caused operational discontinuities in petroleum, oil and lubricants (POL) companies worldwide. Peter Drucker (1954) said "the greatest danger in times of turbulence is not the turbulence – it is to act with yesterday's logic." Drucker's argument also emphasizes the need for strategic forecasting, making use of scenario plans to cope with organizational change.

Effective scenario plans require informed assumptions. Use of brainstorming, application of the Delphi technique and focus group interviews are some of the common techniques used to arrive at informed assumptions. To draw a framework of informed assumptions, managers can make extensive use of their intuition or can follow a structured pattern, more in the form of a flow chart. Likewise, we need to act at each step to finally draw the scenario and make use of the scenario for framing the strategies for the future of the organization. These steps are also known as *Shell*'s model of Scenario Planning.

Both the Delphi technique and the nominal group method help in drawing up scenario plans, and depending on the issues and the time constraints, organizations choose the appropriate method to minimize the risk of forecasting based on scenario plans.

2.12 LIMITATIONS OF PLANNING

Even though planning is the all-pervasive, primary function of management, planning is subject to certain limitations. Without proper understanding of such limitations, planning may become a futile exercise. We have listed some limitations of planning, an understanding of which may improve the efficiency of planning.

1. **Planning Premises may be wrong**
   Planning premises are the basis and framework for decisions. Understanding the planning premises with absolute accuracy is not possible. Hence, there always exists some margin of error, which obviously vitiates the plans. Difficulty in assessing the premises for planning is therefore the most important limitation.
2. **Rapidity of Change**
   Every organization operates in a certain internal and external environment. The

environment cannot always be stable. The extent of change in the internal and external environment, therefore, creates a situation of instability, making the planning job extremely difficult.

3. **Time and Cost Constraints**
   Every organization has to plan within given time and cost constraints. Such constraints go against the efficiency of planning. In a situation of crisis, an organization may even have to take decisions on a war-footing, which is literally, without planning. Non-availability of time and resources may compel the organization to come out with the best of business plans.

4. **Planning may limit New Ideas**
   New ideas or innovativeness in planning may not be possible because of the traditional mind-set of people. The vision and philosophy of the organization and its people, if not progressive, may limit the planning initiative of the management.

   Similarly, procedural and policy rigidities also come in the way of planning. Procedures, rules and policies, once documented, are difficult to change. Such inflexibility obviously affects planning.

5. **Capital Investment Constraints**

   Capital sunk in the business, both in the form of equipment and employees (investment in training), often limit the planning initiative, keeping pace with environmental changes. Managers are quite often compelled to set their planning premises, keeping in mind the capital investment, which cannot be foregone.

6. **Non control over External Factors**

   Some external factors may seriously impede the planning. These include sudden changes in government policies, union pressures on wage hike, war and international policies (like WTO, EEC, ASEAN resolutions).

   Despite such limitations, organizations cannot get away without planning. Every manager has to systematically plan to achieve the desired results.

2.13 PRODUCTION-RELATED FORMS

To enforce proper production management and control, many organizations make use of computer-generated production reports and forms. Some production-related computer-generated forms are shown in Figs. 2.6 and 2.7.

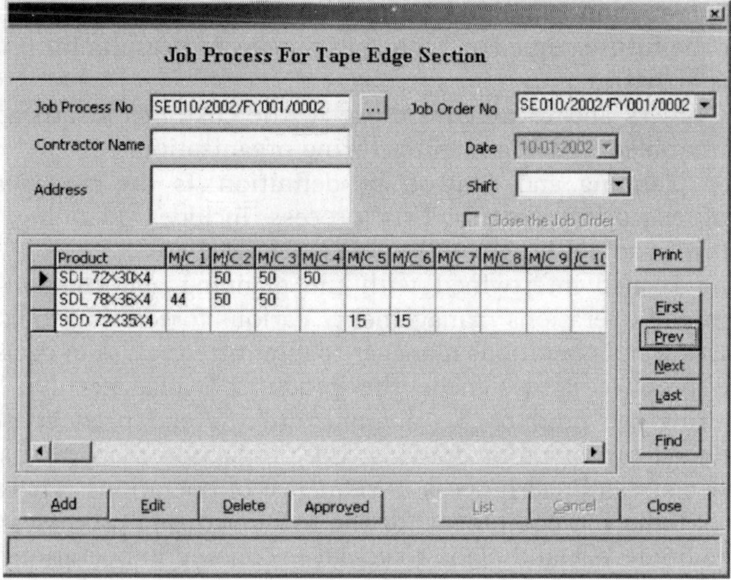

Figure 2.6 *Computer generated form for job process in the tape edge section*

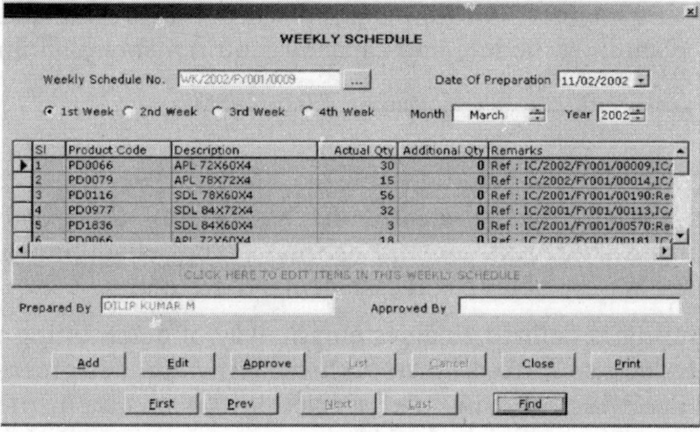

Figure 2.7 *Computer-generated form for weekly schedule*

SUMMARY

1. In this chapter, the processes involved in the formulation of production plans using various techniques have been discussed, so that organizations through effective production plans, can efficiently manage their operations.

2. Through production planning, an operations manager projects a course of action for the future, aimed at achieving the desired results for production and operations activities.
3. To secure orders and to execute those to the customer's satisfaction are the two primary objectives of a manufacturing organization.
4. Production planning and control, by definition, is the management of the process of executing orders. This process includes Planning, Scheduling, Dispatching, Loading, Progressing and Controlling.
5. Forecasting is also intertwined with the planning and control functions of production and operations management. Various forecasting tools are used by the production and operations manager to minimize the risk of decisional errors.
6. Once the product is designed, the production manager has to plan for manufacturing the product. To manufacture the end product from the part prints, product prototype or drawing, the production manager has to develop and follow a streamlined process of sequence of operations. These include the selection of tools and equipment for the manufacturing processes to attain the desired quality levels, and plans to achieve economy in operations.
7. Production Planning and Process Planning are terms used to define the same function in different organizations.
8. Similarly, organizations also tend to use the terms, Production planning and Production control interchangeably. Apart from production planning and control, in this chapter, we have also discussed aggregate planning, master production planning schedule and capacity requirements planning.

KEY WORDS

Scheduling is a system used to ensure the best use of the existing conversion process. It requires a short-run demand estimate. The scheduling of a job can be more effective once we are able to forecast demand accurately.

Production Planning is defined as a systematic way of determining manufacturing methods for a product, so as to achieve both economy and customer satisfaction. It broadly covers identifying, devising and specifying tools, equipment and processes to convert raw material into finished products.

Shop Load Analysis The Shop Load Analysis Technique proves useful in getting optimum use of plant and manpower. The load on each section when balanced with capacity, helps us to identify under- and overload situations. As a result, plant and manpower resources can be redeployed to balance the distribution of load and ensure optimum utility.

Routing specifies the work stations involved in the manufacture of various products, product parts or sub-assemblies. This is a very crucial part of capacity planning. It is routing that makes product traceability possible, if required, which by fixing responsibility also contributes to product quality. The routing sheet is extensively used for product traceability in ISO documentation.

Aggregate Planning works to make the optimum use of organizational resources to meet demand forecasts. It focusses on the collective levels of capacity and demand of an organization, plans quantity and timing of output for medium and long-term periods.

Master Production Schedule MPS further breaks down the aggregate plan in terms of specific items to be produced in different time periods. If the aggregate plan specifies the number of motors to be produced each month, the MPS details the different types and sizes of motors to be produced in different months. The MPS, therefore, controls production activities after the formal production plans are made, setting down the requirements for capacity and materials.

Capacity Planning This is done to estimate the requirements of machines and manpower, so as to achieve production targets. It helps to determine capacity and to adjust capacity to match resource availability, to cope with demand fluctuations. With a stable demand pattern, the task of capacity planning becomes easier, while with fluctuating demand, the task becomes complicated due to the efforts required for optimal utilization of available resources or new resource acquisition, as the case may be.

Materials Requirements Planning MRP is a scientific technique for planning and scheduling material requirements for production. It combines inventory control with production planning under a dependent demand condition, utilizing inputs from a Master Production Schedule (MPS), Bills of Materials (BOM) and Inventory Status Report (ISR).

GENERAL REVIEW QUESTIONS

1. Define Production Planning. Explain its functions and scope.
2. What are the steps involved in a production plan? How is a production plan different from production control?
3. What is routing? Using a route sheet how we can establish product traceability?
4. What is aggregate planning? What objectives can we achieve by using an aggregate plan?
5. Explain the term, capacity planning. What factors should we consider in a capacity plan?
6. Explain the important qualitative and quantitative decision-making tools.
7. In what way do MAD, MSE or Bias analysis help us to evaluate a forecast? Which of these do you feel is more effective?
8. *ABC Corporation* has experienced steady growth in annual sales in its seven year history. The firm has traditionally used a three-year moving average to predict

sales for the coming year. The newly appointed CEO of the company feels that a simple three year moving average is too unrealistic and results in extremely poor sales forecasts. Because inaccuracies in the forecast may affect many important managerial decisions, the CEO of the organization has asked you to determine the best time-series technique for estimating sales by comparing:

(a) A weighted 7-year moving average using the following weights: 0.1, 0.1, 0.2, 0.2, 2, 3, 3 respectively, from the oldest to the most recent year.
(b) A simple exponential smoothing model using an alpha of 0.35.

9. Assume a 1997 sales forecast of Rs. 305,000 and forecast for subsequent years based on annual sales of previous years.
Which forecasting method (3-year moving average, 7-year moving average, or exponential) would you recommend for this historical data)? Give reasons for your choice.

Annual Sales and Forecast Data

Year	Sales (in Rupees)
1997	305,000
1998	328,000
1999	345,000
2000	370,000
2001	
2002	387,000
2003	404,000
2004	405,000

10. Short Notes
(a) Ordering
(b) Installed capacity
(c) Rated capacity
(d) MRP-II

CRITICAL REVIEW QUESTIONS

1. A consumer electronics company follows a level production strategy to manufacture TV sets. When the accumulation of finished inventory crosses the Rs. 100-crore mark, the company stops production and goes in for plant maintenance, rendering the entire outsourced employees jobless. The company wages a price war to dispose of their manufactured stock with a price discount. As a production and operations manager, identify possible areas of risk in such a production strategy.

REFERENCES

1. Drucker, Peter. 1954. *The Principles of Management*. New York: Harper Collins.
2. Ringland, Gill. 1998. *Scenario planning: Managing for the future*, Chichester; New York: Wiley.
3. Peter Schwartz. 1991. *The Art of the Long View Planning for the Future in an Uncertain World.* New York: Doubleday.
4. Wack, Pierre. 1985. Scenarios: Uncharted water ahead. *Harvard Business Review* 63(5), pp. 73–89

ADDITIONAL REFERENCES

1. Blackstone, J. H. 1989. *Capacity Management*. Cincinnati: South-Western Publishing.
2. Ernest Dale. 1965. *Management Theory and Practice*, New York: McGraw Hill Book.
3. Joseph L. Massie. 1987. *Essentials of Management*. New Delhi: Prentice Hall.
4. Koontz H. 1961. The Management Theory Jungle. *Academy of Management Journal*, 4(3), pp. 174–188
5. Konz, Stephen. 1983. *Work Design: Industrial Ergonomics*, 2nd ed. New York: John Wiley & Sons
6. Richard, B., Chase, Nicholas, J., Aquilano, and F. Robert, Jacobs. 2002. *Operations Management for Competitive Advantage*. New Delhi: Tata McGraw-Hill Publishing Company Limited.
7. Sule, D. R. 1988. *Manufacturing Facilities: Location, Planning, and Design*. Boston: PWS-Kent Publishing.

CASE STUDY

Effective production planning alone cannot guarantee success. It requires control, re-visiting the planning premises and the systematic monitoring of employee activities. A more effective way, however, is nurturing a culture of performance through shared understanding. To ensure successful institutionalization of performance culture, a medium-scale steel manufacturer, focussed on the following issues:

1. Defining the purpose and results based on accountability.
2. Discarding existing job descriptions systems.
3. Developing shared business objectives.

4. KRAs-based performance targets.
5. Implementing performance management systems based on balanced score cards.
6. Helping employees to back-track and ascertain how their contributions help achieve the overall objectives of the organization.
7. Re-designing the work systems to create a compelling culture of performance.

Discussion Question

With the above approach, the company could achieve success in their production and operations management functions. As an aspiring operations manager, do you think this approach will work?

CHAPTER 3

New Product Planning and Development

LEARNING OBJECTIVES

After reading this chapter, you will be able to understand:

- New Product Planning and Development
- New Production Development and Selection Process
- Product or Service Life Cycle Analysis
- Process Selection
- Break-even Analysis

Opening Vignette

New Service Design of 'Never Say No ' Bank

Globally, we observe the importance of service organizations, and the service sector as a whole, playing a crucial role in the national income in many countries, including India. To stimulate growth in the service industry, the service sector has to focus on continuous development and innovation through new quality service design. To facilitate this process, the concept of service engineering has emerged. Many companies are now embracing this service engineering concept for the design and development of new services.

Service engineering framework deals with idea generation with regard to the launch of new services in the market. 'Never Say No' Bank is a new generation retail bank in India The bank focusses on high net-worth customers, the minimum deposit in their savings account is Rs one lakh, which is not at all competitive, compared to public sector banks which require a minimum deposit of Rs. 1,000/-. However, the bank's customer base has grown very strong, within just a year of its entry into the banking industry. The uniqueness of the bank's savings account is that it offers service at the customer's door-step. Both withdrawal and deposit collection are done at the customer's premises. Further, the bank offers its savings account customers benefits similar to those offered for a current account – there is no restriction on the number of withdrawals and deposits, and the customer enjoys the interest offered by a savings bank account. Most branches of the bank are strategically located near *bazaar* areas. The bank was able to do this by following the service engineering model:

- Customer demand survey
- Specific analysis of value chain and services
- Modelling new services by integrating the proof of concept, proof of services and proof of business

Many new generation private sector retail banks are replicating the model of 'Never Say No' Bank.

3.1 INTRODUCTION

In most organizations, new product planning and development are taken care of by the marketing department. After assessing market opportunities, the marketing department, suggests new product development, either by eliminating their existing products, or with the purpose of adding to the product-mix to gain an edge over competitors. Often, the existing product-mix requires improvement based on market feedback. But the marketing department alone cannot facilitate the process of new product development; it requires extensive support and co-operation from the engineering and the technical divisions of the company. Wherever separate research and development wings exist, companies need to pilot-test such new product ideas and develop prototypes to judge feasibility of production. The marketing department, therefore, plays the role of product selection, to match market requirements. New product planning and development not only involves introducing an altogether new product-mix, it also requires improving existing products by the addition/deletion of product features in keeping with the changes in demand. Some companies prefer to improve their newly introduced products after market testing and feedback analysis. Irrespective of the nature and scope of new product development initiatives, production and operations managers play a significant role, as they take these new products through multiple phases of production, fitment trial, duly mapping its technical feasibility, matching it with workers' skills.

The process of new product selection involves the following activities:

1. Introduction of new products and
2. Improvement of existing products

Some of the reasons for new product development by organizations are:

1. To combat sluggishness in the growth rate of the organization

2. To replace short-lived products
3. To optimally utilize the existing surplus capacities of the organization in terms of available physical facilities, managerial expertise and workmen skills
4. To re-deploy manpower rendered surplus due to organizational restructuring after technological changes
5. To effectively use the surplus funds and increased borrowing power of the organization
6. To enhance the image of the organization and to improve market visibility with a new product range
7. To meet the new requirements of customers.

Improvement of existing products, on the other hand, is done for the following reasons:

1. To give existing products a new look
2. Utilize existing equipment and manpower
3. To satisfy the immediate needs of the customer
4. To increase sales by providing new advantages like more functionality, maintainability, multiple utility satisfaction, etc.
5. Increase market share
6. Develop brand loyalty
7. Achieve economies of scale by producing in bulk
8. Cost efficiency

The first four are short-term objectives and the others are long-term objectives for the improvement of existing products.

From the point of view of strategy, new products and service planning are initiated for the following reasons:

1. Companies feel compelled to develop new products and services, because globally, we observe the trend of failure of new products and services to the alarming extent of 90%. Even the *Life Insurance Corporation* of India has had to withdraw from many insurance schemes, for one reason or the other.
2. With the launching of new products and services, companies can increase their sales revenue substantially, at least for the short-run. Hence, companies can step up their rate of growth. However, its perpetuity depends on a continuous effort to scale up the value addition features of new products and services.
3. Through new product development, companies try to create a niche in the market, to stay ahead of competition.
4. Companies can integrate customers' expectations through new product development.
5. Companies through effective new product development can also enjoy the benefits of being cost effective. Today, many pharmaceutical companies offer over-the-counter (without prescription) products at premium prices, to push

their items as FMCG products. Notice how much less we pay for a new pack of antacid or a calcium tablet, against its original price, if it is offered in the conventional style.

3.2 STEPS FOR NEW PRODUCT DEVELOPMENT

New products and services planning and development requires the organization to follow a series of steps. Companies need to follow such steps before ideas mature and result in the development and launch of a new product or service. Although such steps vary widely with the nature of the products and services, and also depending on specific organizational strategies, some of the common steps are:

1. **Generating ideas** Each new product or service starts with an idea. Companies at the outset consider this aspect, encouraging their employees to generate new ideas. Generating ideas with cross-functional inputs become more effective. For example, the marketing department can come up with an excellent idea about new products, but the operations department may find it infeasible from a technical perspective, for example, it may not be possible to produce with the given technology or human resource availability. Similarly, the materials department may feel the constraint of raw material availability. However, such constraints need not deter the generation of ideas at the outset. Rather, more and more ideas should be generated. Out of 100 ideas, one or two may ultimately click and lead to the designing of a successful new product.
2. **Screening for new ideas** At this stage, we eliminate those ideas that are infeasible, either for technical, commercial, operational, marketing or financial reasons. We may discard some ideas for their mismatch with the business focus of the company. Organizations also consider different categories of risk in executing such ideas. Such risks may be strategic, market or internal risks. Strategic risks are understood in terms of the degree of mismatch of the new product idea with the company's strategic intent. Market risks are measured in terms of the degree of gap between the new product idea and the market demand. Internal risks may be mainly budgetary constraints, etc. Based on such risk assessment, companies may discard many new ideas, and shortlist only those which are more feasible.
3. **Project Planning** After screening the initial idea, companies do the project planning to further assess the efficacy of the new ideas, which are analyzed in terms of production, marketing, financial and competitive factors. Project planning also requires preparing the development budget and undertaking marketing and technical research. All these enable the understanding of alternative product and service features. Also, companies can settle for go or no-go decisions.
4. **Product Development** After finalizing the project plan, and settling on the idea, companies initiate new product development. Such an initiative facilitates

understanding of the engineering, manufacturing, finance and marketing implications of the new products. Each aspect of the manufacturing and marketing, like design, tooling requirements, marketing test plan, etc., are finalized.

5. **Test Marketing** A test marketing trial of new products and services, usually through a controlled experiment, confined to a limited geographical area, helps in framing strategies for the successful launch of the new product or services. Along with test marketing, companies also carry out a trial run of production.
6. **Commercialization** This is the final stage of development, which facilitates the formal launch. Along with this stage of commercialization, organization structure is also decided, along with the marketing strategy. Equal emphasis is given to design, costs, quality control and inventory management issues.

3.3 NEW SERVICE DEVELOPMENT DESIGN

Service design starts with the beginning of service. To design high-quality service, customers' needs and expectations must be considered and reflected in the design process for each service element. The objective of service design is to retain customers and to address their needs. From a business perspective, service design is expected to increase customer loyalty and satisfaction as well as profit margins and overall business reputation. Therefore, service providers should optimally distribute limited resources to design service systems that address customer needs as well as to upgrade organizational service productivity. Organizations use various service design development methods and tools. Some of the tools are service blueprinting (Baum, 1989), functional analysis (Berkley, 1996), structured analysis and design technique (Congram and Epelman, 1995), quality function development (Ermer and Kniper, 1998), and root cause analysis (Duffy, 2000).

Quality function deployment (QFD) translates customer needs into specific quality development, and in the process achieves service effectiveness. Most of these techniques have been discussed in this book. Here, we are concerned with the total service experience and engineering methodology. It is the methodology used in the transformation process involved in the development of new services from the stage of generating ideas to market testing before market launch. It systematically organizes the process from creative ideas to innovation (to translate creativity into actions), to explain the important concepts and working steps explicitly, to provide the service developer with a comprehensive process and tool for reference. Like the stages in new product development, service testing is done, involving the real-life users of services, and based on the results, services are adjusted. Internationally, we observe that companies like *IBM, General Electric* and *Hewlett-Packard* have strategically designed their service products to create niches, and by doing so, have created a competitive market for these services.

3.4 NEW PRODUCT SELECTION OR DEVELOPMENT PROCESS

This is a complex process, which begins with idea generation and continues till commercialization. The process requires co-ordination between various departments. It can be broken up into the following stages:

1. **Exploration** New ideas are sought from the sales force, as they are in constant direct contact with customers. The analysis of customer needs also takes into account competitors' products and services. Consultants, shareholders, management employees, study of foreign markets and products, trade journals, R & D laboratories, other research reports, etc. help in generating new ideas. Companies need to examine such ideas in the context of technical feasibility and market potential.
2. **Screening** Guesswork or hunches may often work, but are certainly not reliable while selecting the best new ideas. To ensure a more scientific and less risky selection process, it is necessary to keep in mind all possible quantitative as well as qualitative information. Keeping in mind the organizational objectives and available facilities, the following points must be considered while selecting an idea:
    - Market potential
    - Technical feasibility of the Idea
    - Does the idea fall under any intellectual property rights or patent regulations?
    - Raw material supply position – at present and in the future
    - Do existing production facilities and resource availability remain suitable for commercialization of the new idea?
    - The level of investment required and can the company generate this amount from internal sources?
    - If borrowing is a must, then the cost of borrowing has to be considered.
    - Does profitability projection analysis suggest adequate return on investment?

Profitability Projection Study can be made using the following formulae:

(i) $$PVI = \frac{CTS \times CCS \times AV \times /L}{TPC}$$

Where, PVI = Project value index

CTS = Chances of technical success, calculated on a rating scale, which may be arbitrary, say 0 to 10

CCS = Chances for commercial success, on a scale, say 0 to 10

AV = Annual volume of total sales in units
P = Profit per unit
L = Life of product (in years)
TPC = Total project cost

However, a more simple approach, as under, may be considered to arrive at net probable return per rupee:

(ii) $I = (PN/C)$,

where I = Index of relative worth
P = Overall probability of commercial attainment of goal
N = Estimated net return for an arbitrary five-year period
C = Estimated future cost

In addition, Point System and Graphs can also supplement the profitability projection analysis of a new product.

3. **Business Analysis** At this stage, technical and economic factors, like man hours, cash flow, inventory holding etc. are analysed to evaluate commercial feasibility. This will ultimately facilitate the budgeting process.
4. **Development** A working model is developed at this stage to evaluate the practicability of the new idea, by studying the acceptability of customers to the working model. Most companies use a Product Life Cycle Model at this stage.
5. **Testing** Redesigning of the working model into a production prototype and testing the market before bulk production.
6. **Commercialization** At the final stage of new product planning, decisions have to be made whether to make or buy the components. Factors like production methods, distribution networks, integration with mainstream activities, mission and vision of the company, envisaged sales volume and profitability have to be meticulously studied at this stage.

3.5 PRODUCT/SERVICE LIFE CYCLE ANALYSIS

This analysis covers the pattern of demand throughout a product's life span. It similarly identifies the patterns and stages of the useful life span of a process (Fig. 3.1). This concept, which is commonly used in marketing management literature states that a product is supposed to go through a number of stages, as shown below:

1. **Stage 1: Introductory/launching stage** This is the introductory or launching stage when the product/service has to win a place in the market and prove its worth. Sometimes, this stage is broken into two stages – product development and testing, and introduction. Here, however, this is taken as one stage.

2. **Stage 2: Rapid development stage** Once the product/service has general acceptability, it passes on to this stage of rapid development. At this point, manufacturing and distribution systems need to be streamlined through method study, work measurement, value engineering, ergonomic or human engineering techniques with suitable changes in technology, if required. At this point, when the demand for the product/service peaks, it calls for an increase in output volume by the organization.
3. **Stage 3: Steady stage** This is called the steady stage. During the rapid development phase, competitors try to capture market share by introducing similar products/services. Because of this, the growth rate of the product/service slows down. This is also termed the established stage.
4. **Stage 4: Declining/phase-out stage** At this point, the demand for the original product/service dies out or disappears, either due to changes in customer taste or due to technological breakthrough.

The different stages in a product/service life cycle can be shown using the following figure:

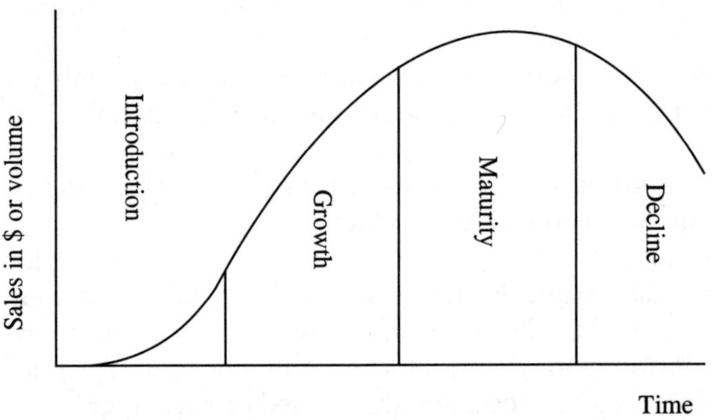

Figure 3.1 *Stages in the product/services life cycle*

3.6 PROCESS SELECTION

The manufacturing process involves converting inputs into outputs and adding value to the products. It is the most important part of the production/operation function, and the appropriate process selection involves getting the desired output and quality, while maintaining cost efficiency. That is why appropriate process selection is such a vital strategy decision. Once a process is selected and implemented, it is difficult to change it due to the obvious cost implications. The choice of process will depend on various factors, but two basic objectives are of paramount importance – meeting specification requirements and achieving cost effectiveness.

3.6.1 Factors that influence Process Selection

The factors that influence process selection are

- **Volume and Variety** If the degree of repetitiveness is high, then a continuous production process is indicated, to ensure higher output volume at a higher speed. However, organizations that produce a wide variety of items would require multi-skilled workers, general-purpose machines and complex production planning and control systems. Here, job-shop type (intermittent) or batch type of production is more suitable.
- **Capacity of the Plant** The choice between job-shop type and mass production also depends upon the projected sales or output volume. Fixed costs are high in the continuous process and variable costs are high for job-shop type process.
- **Flexibility** This allows an organisation to satisfy the varied needs of the customer. When the flexibility of production is high, then, the process has to be an intermittent manufacturing process.
- **Lead Time** Faster deliveries, to a great extent, allow an organization to remain a market leader, whereas delays eventually cause a decrease in the market share. To ensure adherence to delivery schedules, batch production process should be selected where there is a variety of products, and mass production where there is uniformity.
- **Economy of Scale** It is important to have optimum utilization of machine and manpower to achieve cost efficiency in the production process. This is an aspect that has to be considered while selecting a manufacturing process.
- **Environment** Environmental issues are increasingly being considered, while selecting a manufacturing process. For example, plastic moulded butts are replacing wooden rifle butts and the cold swaging process is in use for metal forming as it is more environment-friendly.

No single criterion is sufficient to decide the selection of the process. Various manufacturing processes will be discussed in detail later.

In addition to the above factors, organizations may also use cost–benefit analysis and break-even analysis to choose a given process.

3.6.2 Cost–Benefit Analysis

Under cost–benefit analysis, cost estimates are prepared for each of the alternative processes and the least-cost alternative is chosen. The following costs are considered:

1. Cost of materials
2. Cost of unavoidable rejection (UAR)
3. Cost of scrap arising
4. Tooling cost
5. Processing cost

3.6.3 Break-even Analysis

Break-even analysis technique is widely used in production and operations management. Break-even analysis categorises production costs into variable and fixed costs. Variable costs change with the volume of production, while fixed costs remain unchanged. Total variable and fixed costs are compared with the sales revenue to determine at which level of sales volume, sales value or production, the business makes neither a profit nor a loss, that is, the break-even point.

Break-even analysis, therefore, suggests preparing cost estimates for different available alternatives. Obviously, for a given quantity 'N', the least cost alternative is selected. For determining the value of 'N', we use the following formula:

$$N = \frac{F_2 - F_1}{V_1 - V_2}$$

Where,

N = Quantity, cost for which is same for both the machines
F_1 = Annual fixed cost for the first machine
F_2 = Annual fixed cost for the second machine
V_1 = Variable cost per 'N' unit for the first machine
V_2 = Variable cost per 'N' unit for the second machine

If quantity to be manufactured is less than 'N', then obviously, the process with lower fixed cost is selected, or else when quantity to be produced is more than 'N', its break-even quantity, the process with the lower variable cost is selected.

Let us illustrate break-even analysis using the following example:

Problem

The turning or machining job of a given component in a manufacturing process can be done using either a centre lathe or a turret lathe. The firm has received an order for 1000 numbers from an ordnance factory, for meeting an urgent requirement of spares for the *Bofors* gun. There is no chance of repeat orders, as the original supplier abroad has agreed to supply the spares in future due to an improvement in the diplomatic relationship. Different cost break-ups (in rupees) for the two machines are given in the following table:

Table 3.1 *Cost details*

Cost Details	Centre Lathe	Turret Lathe
Tooling up cost	300	600
Labour cost per hour	3	3
Depreciation and other miscellaneous expenditure per hour	12	18

Set up time for the centre lathe is 30 minutes, while for the turret lathe it is 100 minutes; the cycle time for processing a component is 15 minutes and 10 minutes respectively.

Suggest up to how many units of the centre lathe would be preferred over the turret lathe? Also suggest for 1000 Nos., which lathe is more suitable?

Solution

Since, we have not been given the procurement cost for these two machines; fixed cost would be set-up cost and tooling cost of the machine. Assuming that the machining is to be done in one lot, fixed cost would be calculated as follows:

Centre lathe (F1) = set-up time * {labour cost + depreciation (in hours)}+ tooling cost
= 30/60 * 15 + 300 = Rs. 307.5

Turret lathe (F2) = 100/60 * 21 + 600 = Rs. 635

Variable cost would be, similarly, computed as under:

Centre lathe (V1) = cycle time (in hours) * {labour cost +depreciation per hour}
$= 15/60 \times (3 + 12) = Rs.3.75$

Turret lathe (V2) $= 10/60 \times (3 + 18) = Rs.3.5$

Applying the formula, therefore, we get the break-even quantity as under:

$(635 - 307.5)/(3.75 - 3.5) = 372.5/0.25 = 1310$ nos.

Since the break-up quantity is higher than the required quantity of 1000 nos., we could prefer the centre lathe to the turret lathe, as fixed cost for the centre lathe is considerably lower than the turret lathe.

3.6.3.1 Break-even Chart

The break-even chart (Fig. 3.2) is a graphical representation of costs at various levels, with the change in sales and volume of activity (say, production). At the break-even point, the company neither makes a profit nor incurs a loss. The graph indicates the intersection point 'P' at which level, total income (sales and revenues) just recoups the total costs (fixed and variable). Using this approach, we can define a break-even point as follows:

Let us now explain the graph. The QA point represents income variation with respect to the changing level of production. OB is the fixed cost, which remains unchanged despite the change in the production volume. BC is the variable costs, which changes with respect to the change in production volume. At a low level of output, the total cost (fixed + variable) is more, due to which the company suffers a loss. However, with the increase in the volume of production, income exceeds the total costs, and the company can earn a profit. The point of intersection, P, indicates total costs are exactly equal to income, that is, the stage of no loss–no profit.

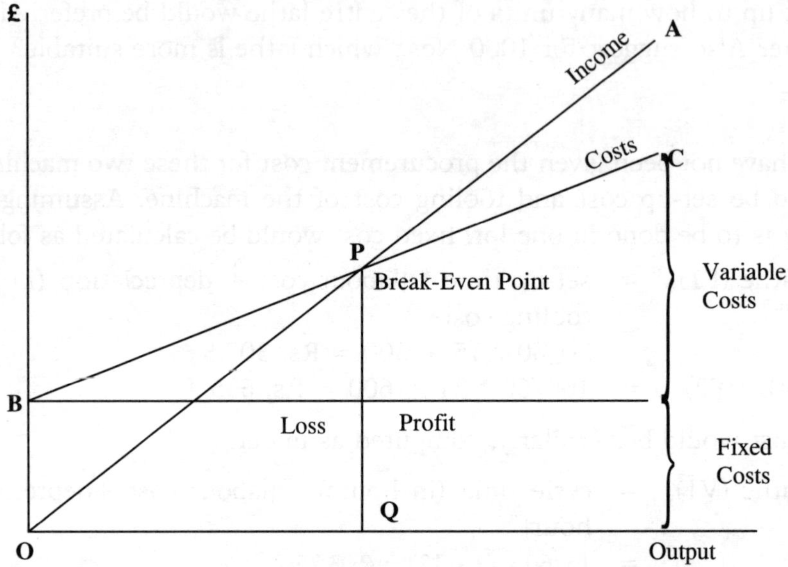

Figure 3.2 *Break-even chart*

In a competitive market, companies always go in for innovative new products and services design to survive. Life cycles of products and services are becoming shorter and shorter. Customers expect new value addition to the products and services, or some altogether newly designed products and services. Companies need to understand that customers' demands for the products and services are based on four perceived values. These are utility value, cost value, exchange value and esteemed value. Hence, customers do not buy products and services for utility value alone. For example, buying a holiday package, or joining a holiday club for future services need not depend on its utility value alone. The perceived value in terms of esteem often sensitizes our need for many products and services. Membership of a prestigious club or buying a costly car can be categorized under this.

Through new products and services development, companies also consolidate their competitive growth strategy. Also, such pursuit must be continuous. Products and services selling well must not be construed as a perpetual situation. 'Lifebouy' soap manufactured by *Hindustan Unilever* (HUL) which earned nearly 40% of *HUL*'s revenue had to face the brunt of competition, which compelled the company to reposition this brand through multiple brand repositioning and brand extension strategies. Today, we observe a similar strategy being adopted in the case of *HUL*'s toothpaste 'Pepsodent'. *Colgate Palmolive* also follows the same strategy for their toothpaste and other products.

SUMMARY

1. Although new product planning and new product development is considered more relevant to the marketing management function, the production and operations department plays a crucial role in translating their plans into new products and services.
2. Through systematic product/service life cycle analysis, organizations periodically identify the scope of developing new products and services, to remain competitive in the market.
3. Once the new product and service is identified for development, the production department has to consider the process duly studying the volume and variety, capacity of the plant, flexibility, lead time, economy of scale, environment etc.
4. Finally, before implementation, or streamlining production of the new product, organizations are also required to perform cost–benefit analysis and break-even analysis.

KEY WORDS

Fixed Costs are those which do not directly relate to the level of production. Examples of fixed costs are rent and rates, depreciation, research and development, marketing costs, administration costs, etc.

Variable Costs vary directly with the level of output. Such costs are categorised as output-related and revenue-related costs. Output-related costs are raw materials, direct labour, fuel, etc. Revenue-related costs are commissions, etc. Again, variable costs can be classified into direct variable costs and indirect variable costs. Direct variable costs can be directly attributed to production. Indirect variable costs, on the other hand, cannot be directly attributed, as it changes with production volume.

Semi-variable costs Some fixed costs change with the scale and complexity of business. With more people on the pay roll, an organization may be required to maintain an independent HR department. Costs incurred are variable and partly fixed.

Process Selection The manufacturing process that converts inputs into outputs, adding value to the products. It is the most important part of the production management function, as it produces the desired output, maintaining quality and cost efficiency.

Business Analysis At this stage, technical and economic factors, like man-hours, cash flow, inventory holding etc. are analysed to evaluate commercial feasibility. This will ultimately facilitate the budgeting process.

Commercialization It is the final stage of new product planning. Decisions like make or buy, methods of production, distribution networks, integration of the new product with the normal activities of the organization, etc. are taken at this point.

GENERAL REVIEW QUESTIONS

1. Explain product selection. How does it differ from process selection?
2. Explain the main stages in the selection of a new product.
3. Prepare the product life cycle of a hypothetical branded washing powder.
4. What are the factors that govern process selection?
5. How do cost–benefit analysis and break-even analysis assist in deciding the selection of a process?
6. Short notes
   (a) Service life cycle
   (b) Profitability projection analysis
   (c) Phase-out stage
   (d) Flexible process
   (e) Lead time

CRITICAL REVIEW QUESTIONS

1. An automobile manufacturing company enjoys 30% market share for its branded passenger car. The company observed that the sales volume had remained stagnant for quite some time. As a production manager of the company, consider whether the company should go in for new product development or should it opt for product improvement. Justify your answer

REFERENCES

1. Baum, S. 1989. *Putting quality circles to work: A practical strategy for boosting productivity and profits*. New York: McGraw-Hill.
2. Berkley, B.J. 1996. Designing services with function analysis. *Hospitality Research Journal*, 20(1), 73–100.
3. Congram, C., Epelman, M. 1995. How to describe your service: an invitation to the structured analysis and design technique. *International Journal of Service Industry Management*, 6(2), 6–23.
4. Duffy, J.A. 2000. Service recovery, in *New service development: Creating memorable experience*, Fitzsimmons, J., Fitzsimmons and Mona J. Fitzsimmons. (Eds.), Thousand Oaks, CA: Sage.
5. Ermer, D. S. and Kniper, M. K. 1998. Delighting the customer: Quality function development for quality service design. *Total Quality Management*, 9(4/5), 86–91.

ADDITIONAL REFERENCES

1. Adam, E. E and Ebert, R.J. 1982. *Production and Operations Management*, 2nd ed. London: Prentice Hall.

2. Bruce, M. and Bessant, J. 2002. *Design in Business: Strategic innovation through design*. London: Pearson Education
3. Cooper, R. G. 1993. *Winning at New Product: Accelerating the Process from Idea to Launch*. Canada: Addison-Wesley Publishing Company Inc.
4. Clark, K. B., and T. Fujimoto. 1991. *Product Development Performance*. Boston: Harvard Business School Press
5. Clark, K.B. and Wheelwright, S.C. 1995.*The Product Development Challenge: Competing Through Speed, Quality, and Creativity*. Boston, MA: Harvard Business School Press.
6. Fitzsimmons, J.A. and Fitzsimmons, M.J. 2000. *New Service Development: Creating Memorable Experiences*. London: Sage.
7. Makridakis, S., Wheelwright, S.C. and Hyndman, R. 1998. *Forecasting: Methods and Applications* (3rd Ed.), London: John Wiley and Sons.
8. Richard, B., Chase, Nicholas, J., Aquilano, and F. Robert, Jacobs. 2002. *Operations Management for Competitive Advantage*. New Delhi: Tata McGraw-Hill Publishing Company Limited.
9. Schmenner, R.W. 1995. *Service Operations Management*. Prentice Hall, Englewood Cliffs, M.J.
10. Wheelwright, Steven C., and Kim B. Clark. 1995. *Leading Product Development*. New York: Free Press
11. Bullinger, H. J., Fahnrich, K. P., Meiren, T. 2003. Service engineering-methodica development of new service products. *International Journal of Production Economics*, 85, 275–287.
12. Franceschini, F. and Terzago, M. 1998. An application of quality function deployment to industrial training courses. *International Journal of Quality and Reliability Management*, 15(7), 753–768.

CASE STUDY

New Product Development of *Vitro India*

Every organization goes in for new product development to create a niche in the market and to gain sustainability. Any new product development is preceded by designing, keeping in view the customers' preferences. Apart from the look and feel of the product, designing involves detailing of the product architecture, with materials and process requirements. Like designing, the development aspect requires identification of market opportunities. Finally, before the commercialisation of the production of new products, it requires pilot testing and inspection, to eliminate any eventual problems in the products. Despite all these processes, new product development is essential, primarily for shortening of the product life cycles, and to meet the changing expectations of the customers.

Market globalization has increased the market reach of companies, and has at the same time, made customers more demanding.

Vitro India is a renowned brand name in the Indian sports industry. It manufactures sports goods, its *Walkers* for domestic use are targeted at those who cannot afford morning or evening walks due to work pressure. *Vitro's Walkers* are already a brand name in the Indian market, and sell well. *Vitro*'s market survey indicated that the new generation of IT sector executives require a tougher walker than the one they now offer in the market. The speed of the existing walkers can be adjusted to a moderate level, depending on the requirements of the users. The new generation IT executives, often in their late twenties, require the walkers' motors to move faster, at 25 km per hour. *Vitro*'s *Ultra* model, the new generation walker for youngsters was a roaring success. *Ultra,* developed with Austrian technology moves at a minimum speed of 25 km per hour and depending on the capability of the users, the motor can be moved up to a speed of 60 km per hour.

IT executives get their health regularly checked up by their attending physicians in the companies. One such health report indicated that over walking has caused serious damage to the ligament of some *Ultra* users. This information caused a significant drop in the sales of the *Ultra.*

Discussion Question

As an operations manager of the company, you are required to identify possible lapses in the new product development of *Vitro.*

CHAPTER 4

Facilities Planning, Layout and Location Analysis

LEARNING OBJECTIVES

After reading this chapter, you will be able to understand:

- The Concept of Facilities Planning
- Various Tools, Techniques and Models used for Layout Planning
- Layout Decisions and its Techniques
- Flowcharting
- Various Types of Layout
- Location Analysis
- Various Tools, Techniques and Models for Location Analysis

Opening Vignette

BMW's location decision

BMW, the world-renowned automobile manufacturer had to take strategic decisions about the location of their new plant for producing a new series of models. Due to insufficient facilities at their existing plant to produce the new models, BMW initially decided to locate their plant at a new site. However, on leveraging their past experience, the company decided to start-up at one of its existing plants, at the Regensburg plant in Germany. The reasons for choosing the Regensburg plant for the new start-up, were attributed by the company to that facility's track record of high quality standards, its flexibility to shift production from one model to another and the agility of the production team there. The company believed their decision to start a new model in an existing plant would help save a substantial amount of time and would facilitate skill development of new recruits.

The Regensburg plant is spread over two square kilometres, it is well connected with roadways, train lines and an airport. Existing human resources are well trained and understand the mechanism of production. Accessibility to local markets, cost effectiveness and a congenial political climate are some other important determinants that influenced this decision.

Facilities planning requires the physical arrangement of the facilities of the manufacturing plant or service organization, and also suitable decisions on plant location. In this chapter, we will discuss plant layout and plant location issues. Effective facilities planning helps the organization to achieve cost efficiency and improve performance and productivity, which leads to increased profitability. Facilities planning issues are discussed at the outset, followed by locational decision analysis.

4.1 PLANT LAYOUT

Plant layout is the physical arrangement of all the production facilities, and employees' services in a plant. Appropriate layout is essential in achieving production efficiency. An efficient plant layout can ensure smooth and rapid flow of materials, right from the stage of receipt of raw materials to the end product. Thus, layout is the technique of arranging machines, processes and plant services within the factory or the manufacturing centre to achieve cost effective quality production. It requires direct workflow.

We can define layout as the physical arrangement of machines, equipment and all other supportive facilities to production within a factory, to ensure easy and cost effective flow of materials, right from the receipt of raw materials to various stages of production, and finally the output. Riggs (1970) has defined layout as an economical, physical arrangement to achieve the desired quantity and quality of output. From a similar perspective, we can define plant layout. Accordingly, we can define layout as the process of space allocation and physical arrangement of machines and equipment with minimum costs of operation.

Layout decision is important as it has an impact on the process of production, like optimization of relationship among output, floor area and manufacturing process, minimization of material-handling time and cost, flexibility of operations, easy flow of materials, economic use of land and building, effective manpower utilization, and improved quality of work-life for workers. Ease of flow of materials through different stages of production is most important as this can ultimately help in achieving labour efficiency, ensuring proper supervision and control. Also, this can help in the optimization of space utilization and can provide opportunities for future expansion.

From the above discussions therefore, it is clear that effective plant layout can help in achieving objectives like efficient floor space utilization, uninterrupted flow of materials from one shop floor to another with minimum material handling costs, provision for adequate production capacity (including future expansion), efficient utilization of manpower with minimum safety and security hazards, minimum maintenance problems, maximization of machine capacity utilization and overall improvement of productivity.

4.2 DETERMINANTS OF LAYOUT

Depending on the nature of the organization, plant layout decisions are taken. Some of the important determinants of plant layout can be listed as under:

4.2.1 Product

Whether it is production of goods or rendering of services, layout decisions are influenced by the nature of the product. For production, the design of product, quality standards, production for stockpiling of finished inventory, or production against order, volume of production, size and dimension of produced materials, etc. are important areas of consideration. For example, production of steel bars, whether for stockpiling for future sales, or for immediate execution of customers' orders, requires layout which can make available adequate space to accommodate the finished items on the shop floor for subsequent movement to stores or warehouses. Most steel plants maintain their warehouses in different locations to cater to market needs. For economizing on the cost of transportation to warehouses, steel plants always try to send full wagon loads of produced items, till such time, produced items require some space on the shop floor itself. On the countrary, layout for a factory which produces automobiles will require a different set of arrangements, as in this case, the finally assembled car or vehicle has to be rolled out from the assembly shop for road trial and subsequent shipment to the distributors.

4.2.2 Production process

Like product or service type, the particular process of production used is also important for determining the nature and type of layout. Along with the process, the particular type of technology used for production, the nature and types of input materials and the way the produced materials or services are provided to the end users, etc. are also considered to determine the layout. For example, the process of production of 'made tea' requires normalization of temperature before grading. This is done by spreading the made tea on the production floor, before taking the same through grading and subsequently to the stock bins. Hence, along with the drying section, adequate space should be available to facilitate the process. Similarly, some produced items require delivery to the customers with temperature conditioning, like soft drinks, life saving drugs, processed meat, etc. As the process of production is stretched to the customers' end, this aspect also deserves consideration in determining the layout.

4.2.3 Volume of Production

Production volume also affects the current layout and capacity utilisation. If through machine run, companies can churn huge numbers of products, the aisle or the gangway space should be large enough to accommodate the output for further shifting to stocks or to other shop floors, when the output is input for other shops. On the other hand, when the production volume is less, it requires less aisle space.

4.3 TYPES OF LAYOUT

For manufacturing units, we usually observe four types of plant layout:
(a) Product or line layout
(b) Process or functional layout
(c) Fixed position or location layout
(d) Combined or group layout.

4.3.1 Product or line layout

This type of layout is very common, and it requires the arrangement of machines and equipments, in line with with the sequence of operations. Under this, machines and equipments are arranged in one line depending upon the sequence of operations. Sequence of operations depends on the specific requirement of production of the products. For example, production of any standardised item in an assembly line, requires following stage-wise production at each work-station, where non-completion of one stage cannot allow performing the operations in subsequent stages. Movement of materials from one stage of production to another is facilitated in this type of layout without any backtracking or deviation. Because of this, the system does not permit correcting any deviation in the previous stage(s) in a subsequent stage of operations, and the quality ultimately falls. For example, products with manufacturing defects are sold in the market as 'seconds with price discount. We have seen VIP 'seconds shops' sell VIP briefcases even at 40% discount. Despite such price deviation, the company benefits, as defective items do not have any other alternative salvage value.

Production process being standardized, this type of layout requires grouping of machines in one sequence. As a result, input materials fed in the first machine automatically move to other machines, and the process continues, till the line of machines churn out the final output. For example, industrial molasses charged in the pit move to the process of fermentation and ultimately churns out rectified spirit, i.e., the end product or the output of *IFB Agro*. The output of one machine becomes the input of the next, e.g. in a paper mill, bamboo is fed into the machine at one end and paper comes out at the other end. The raw material moves very fast from one workstation to other stations with minimum work in progress storage and material handling.

In product or line layout, grouping of machines is done in such a way that all the machine tools and other items are available along with the machines, without any provision for backtracking. Characteristically in such a production process, quality checking and even the packaging (if required depending on the nature of products), are integrated with the line or array of machines.

This type of layout is also known as a line processing layout, as here people and equipments are arranged in order of the sequence of production.

Product or line layout is very common in manufacturing organizations. A typical product layout is illustrated in Fig. 4.1 below:

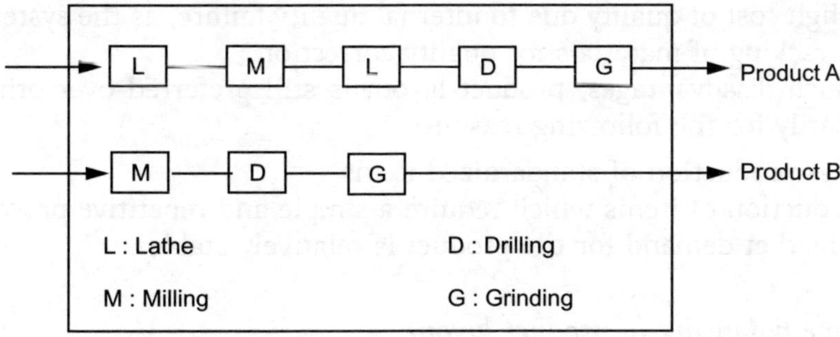

Figure 4.1 *A Product Layout*

The advantages of this type of layout are:

- Lower material handling cost due to use of straight line conveyors, mono rails, etc. for movement of materials and in-process goods
- Lower labour costs due to job commonality; tasks performed at each workstation are simple and can be done even by unskilled labour
- Substantially lower work-in-process and inventory costs
- Low cost of material handling, due to straight and short route
- Production control is simple, as jobs are routed through a fixed path and monitored by controlling the flow of materials and sub-assemblies to the line, lowering supervision cost
- Allows for optimum utilization of plant, equipment and processes
- Production scheduling is simple as only one or few products are to be made or assembled
- Less or zero congestion in the work process

- Enhance cost competitiveness for the organization, as per unit cost of production using this method become much lower.

Disadvantages of this type of layout can be listed as under:

- Zero or less flexibility of operations ultimately weakens the company's market competitiveness, as the company cannot provide a wide variety of items. The company fails to customize the products.
- Due to monotonous nature of job, workers often feel demotivated.
- Initial investment in machines and equipments in this type of layout is quite high, which many companies cannot afford.
- As the process of operations is inter-dependent, any clog at any stage can halt the entire process.

To reduce the machine down time, this type of layout requires companies to maintain maintenance back up. This again involves huge investment. For example, keeping an inventory of airplane engines is very expensive, but to ensure customer service when the engines fail, to ensure flying operations, companies need to maintain such costly inventory. High cost of quality due to internal quality failure, as the system does not permit backtracking of materials for quality correction.

Despite such disadvantages, product layout is still preferred over other types of layout, primarily for the following reasons:

- For mass production of standardized items
- For production of items which require a simple and repetitive process
- When market demand for the product is relatively stable

4.3.1.1 Line balancing in product layout

To eliminate the defects of product layout, line balancing technique can be used. This technique ensures smooth flow of materials, reduces idle time both for the machines and workers, and optimizes the cost. We can define line balancing as the equality of output at different stages like sequencing of a line. When outputs are equal, we assume a perfect balance in the layout. But when outputs are not equal across the departments, we assume defects in the layout, as unequal output results in an increase in ideal time. Thus, line balancing ensures distribution of workloads evenly through the process of sub-division of activities or tasks in such a way that all work stations get equal amount of work in terms of time requirement of job performance. It ensures optimization of labour and resources.

While using line balancing technique for layout, we require the following input information:

- Maximum cycle time requirements for performing the designated tasks of the line.
- The length of the longest elemental task that indicates the minimum possible cycle time.

Some of the mathematical equations used in line balancing are indicated below:

- Daily capacity of a line: Calculated by dividing the daily operating time by the cycle time of line.

$$\text{Output} = \frac{OT}{CT}$$

OT = operating time per day and CT = cycle time.

- Work stations requirement: This calculation helps us to allocate the specified rate of output to each workstation.

$$N = \frac{Dx \sum t}{OT}$$

N = minimum number of stations,

D = desired output rate,

$\sum t$ = sum of task times, and

OT = operating time.

- The cycle time requirement: This is calculated to understand what should be the desired level of output.

$$CT = \frac{OT}{D}$$

OT = operating time per day and

D = desired output rate.

- Percentage of idle time: This is computed workstation-wise, using the ratio of idle time per cycle to total available time per cycle, i.e., N x CT.

4.3.1.2 Line balancing problem

Let us assume a product can be divided into five basic tasks, with the cycle time required for each element of task along with the precedence relationships as under:

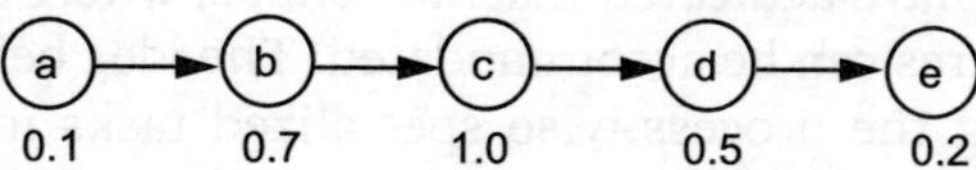

Assuming availability of 480 minutes in each line, with cycle time requirement of one minute per element of work output, determine the minimum number of workstations required.

Solution

With the output requirement of 480 units, using the following formula we can determine the workstation requirement as under:

$$N = \frac{Dx \sum t}{OT}$$

= (480 units per day × 2.5 minutes per unit, aggregating the total time requirement of work elements). 480 minutes per day per station = 2.5 work stations, which we round up to 3 work stations.

Now we have combined the five job element tasks in 3 work stations with the cycle time of 1 minute. The revised assignments would be as under:

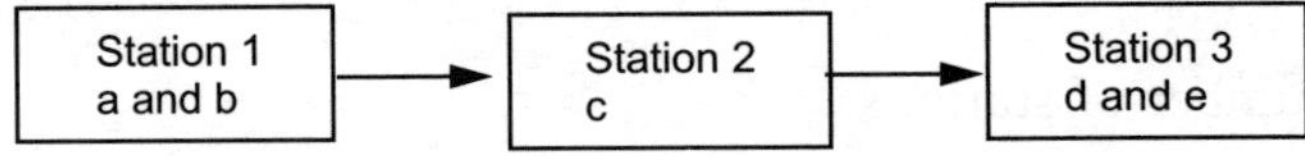

Computation of idle times for the above assignments would therefore be as under:

Table. 4.1 *Computation of idle time*

Work Station	Work Station Time	Work Station idle time
1	0,8(0,1 + 0,7)	0.2(1–0.8)
2	1.0	0 (1–1)
3	0.7(0.5 + 0.2)	0.3 (1 – 0.7)
	Total	0.5

Hence, the idle time percentage is the idle time per cycle, i.e., $N \times CT = 0.5/3 = 16.66\%$.

4.3.2 Process Layout

Process layout is also known as functional layout. This type of layout requires the arrangement of similar type of machines together at one place. For example, machining jobs are done for surface finish of cast materials, using lathe machines, which may be either conventional or a computer numeric control(CNC) machining centre. A company may have dedicated machine shops, where all such lathe machines or CNC-machining centres can be accommodated. The idea behind this type of layout is to ensure performing the process-wise specialized tasks in one shop. In process layouts, we also observe batch processing layouts, when a large number of identical items are processed as a group following the same production sequence

This is why in many organizations, we see arrangement of departments process wise, like drilling department, milling department, welding department, etc. The concept of process shops has emerged from our age-old division of production systems based on specialized skills. This is why we can also call it handicraft method of production. Workers who are attached to such process shops are specialized in their nature of work. Characteristically in such a layout, similar machines are arranged in dedicated process shops; hence, we cannot get any general purpose machines in such shops. We can illustrate a process layout or a process shop (Fig. 4.2) as under:

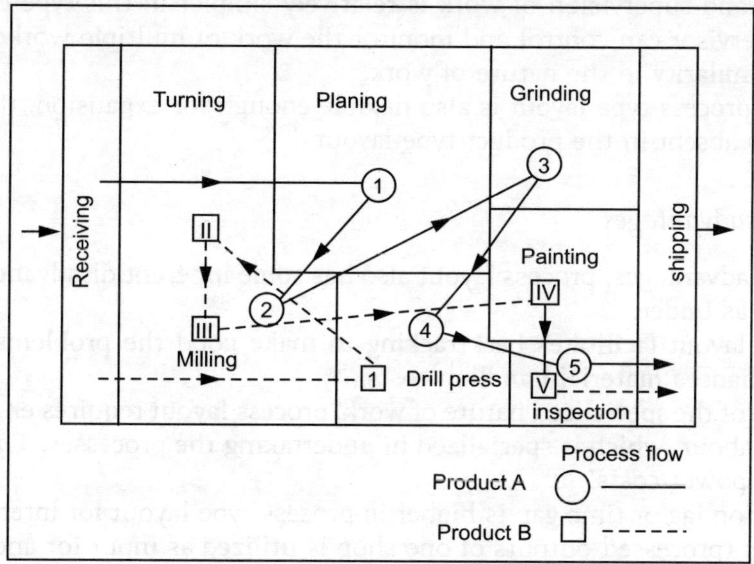

Figure 4.2 *A process layout*

While following the process layout, machines arrangements are done in such a way, that distance between the departments are as short as possible, and movement of materials from one shop to another can be done at ease. For example, after machining of a material, it may require coating and painting, and this calls for arranging the coating and painting division close to the machining shops. In a steel plant, twisting and coiling department has to be arranged close to the sheet metal division, as the output needs to be properly coiled for shipment. In a tea processing unit, close to the CTC operation, we need to arrange the fermenting bays, etc. Even in retail malls, cash counters need to be centrally placed, so that customers require less movement to make payment of bills after their purchase. This also minimizes the queue.

Advantages and disadvantages of process layout can be summarized as under:

4.3.2.1 Advantages

- Process layout can substantially reduce the initial investment in machines and equipment, compared to a highly specialized dedicated product type layout.
- This type of layout optimizes machine utilization, as processes for every product can be undertaken in such process shops.
- Product customization does not interfere with this type of layout, as processes are by and large common.

- The overhead costs for this type of layout are lower than the product type layout, as the same machines can be utilized to perform the processes of all products.
- Unlike product type layout, in a process type layout, breakdown of one or two machines cannot bring the process of production to a grinding halt.
- Control and supervision of work is relatively simpler in this type of layout, as one supervisor can control and monitor the work of multiple workers, because of the similarity in the nature of work.
- Finally, process type layout is also flexible enough for expansion, the scope for which is absent in the product type layout.

4.3.2.2 Disadvantages

Despite such advantages, process layout also has some inherent disadvantages. These can be listed as under:

- Process layout facilitates backtracking to make good the problems of quality. This enhances material handling costs.
- Because of the specialized nature of work, process layout requires engagement of skilled labour, which is specialized in undertaking the processes. This enhances the manpower costs.
- Production lag or time gap is higher in process type layout for interdependence of shops (processed outputs of one shop is utilized as input for another shop). Such time lag causes loss of production time and thus enhances the costs.
- In process layout, work in progress (WIP) inventory holding is higher, requiring more storage space and liquidity problems (as money gets blocked for the period of stockpiling or storage).
- In process layout, bad workmanship can be attributed to the problem of quality; hence, it is also prone to enhancement of the cost of production.

Despite such problems, process layout is adopted when products need frequent customization, keeping pace with the changing requirements of the customers. Even minimal product customization requires thorough change in the design, which is obviously not possible in a product type layout. Therefore, when job-shop type of work is essential, process layout is the only option. Often, companies due to a resource crunch opt for a process or functional layout, as a standardized assembly-line for product type layout is very expensive. For light and heavy engineering products, jewelley, fabrication work and similar jobs, a process type layout is more effective.

4.3.2.3 CRAFT Model of Process Layout

Computerized Relative Allocation of Facilities Technique (CRAFT) is a relatively new technology-enabled layout model developed by Francis and White (1974). CRAFT is an interactive graph, and it demonstrates different types of process layout with details of costs for movement of inventory. To illustrate, let us assume with a CRAFT solver we are trying to assess the best process layout plan of a manufacturing organization.

A steel manufacturing unit produces six products in 10 different departments. All these products have different routings and demands. In this hypothetical situation, changing the demands, we can see how the process layouts change. Accordingly, we can modify the layout, as the model recalculating the cost of transportation (for obvious change in the transportation distance) for each product, suggests the best possible process layout.

Apart from the CRAFT model, we have several other types of computerized layout methods, which are either based on constructive or improvement type algorithms. CRAFT makes use of improvement type algorithms. On the contrary, Automated Layout Design Programme (ALDEP), and Computerized Relationship Layout Planning (CORELAP) make use of a constructive type algorithm.

A computerized worksheet for the CRAFT model of process layout is reproduced (Figs. 4.3 and 4.4) below. Using the click button on the options dialog, we can examine various process layout options, and select the most cost effective one.

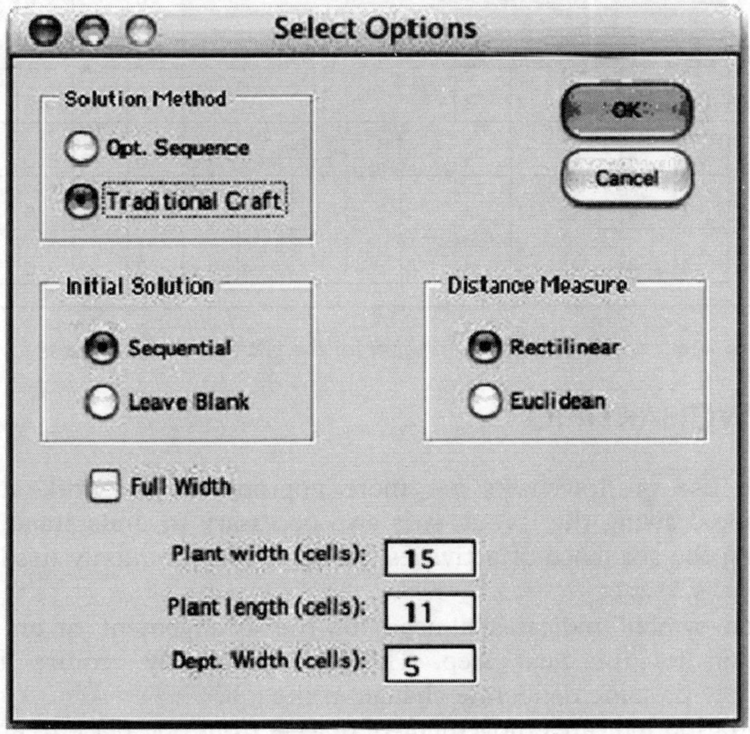

Figure 4.3 *Computerized worksheet for a CRAFT model process layout*

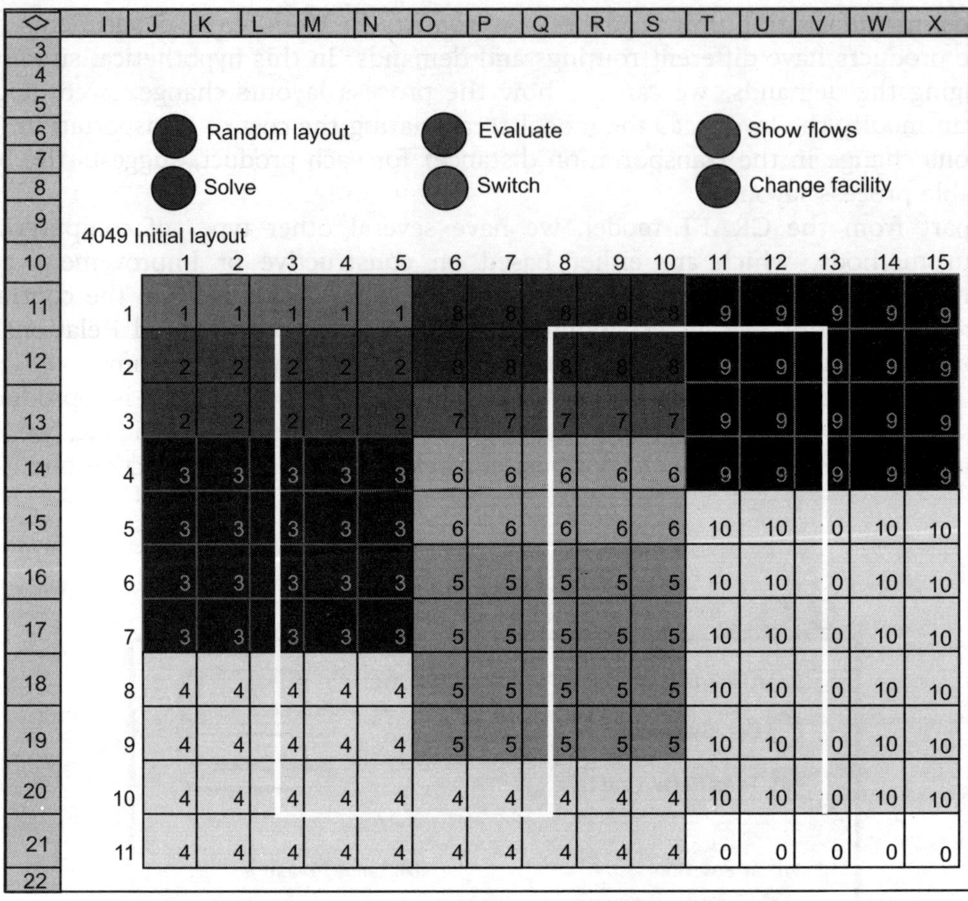

	1	2	3	4	5	6	7	8	9	10	11	12	13	14	15
1	1	1	1	1	1	8	8	8	8	8	9	9	9	9	9
2	2	2	2	2	2	8	8	8	8	8	9	9	9	9	9
3	2	2	2	2	2	7	7	7	7	7	9	9	9	9	9
4	3	3	3	3	3	6	6	6	6	6	9	9	9	9	9
5	3	3	3	3	3	6	6	6	6	6	10	10	0	10	10
6	3	3	3	3	3	5	5	5	5	5	10	10	0	10	10
7	3	3	3	3	3	5	5	5	5	5	10	10	0	10	10
8	4	4	4	4	4	5	5	5	5	5	10	10	0	10	10
9	4	4	4	4	4	5	5	5	5	5	10	10	0	10	10
10	4	4	4	4	4	4	4	4	4	4	10	10	0	10	10
11	4	4	4	4	4	4	4	4	4	4	0	0	0	0	0

Figure 4.4 *Computerized worksheet for the CRAFT model process layput*

4.4 FLOWCHARTING

Although the use of flowcharts are more appropriate for work simplification exercises, while drawing the layout, it is also necessary to understand the process of flowcharting the sequence of activities. Some of the commonly used symbols in flowcharts (Fig. 4.5) are:

1. Operation symbol indicates a need for the arrangement of an object, and preparation for the next step. The next step may require assembly or disassembly or some deliberate change in the job.
2. Transportation indicates movement of objects from one place to another.
3. Inspection is the process of verification of quality, quantity, attributes, features or characteristics of an object.
4. Delay indicates putting an object in the waiting line for the next phase of action.
5. Storage is keeping of an object protected against unauthorized removal.

Subsequently, some more additional symbols of doing the work have been added, of which three are for value added work, and the fourth one is to represent destruction or termination. Three value-added symbols are the Do symbol for manufacturing processes and the Originate and Add/Alter symbols for information processes. These symbols are presented below (Fig. 4.6.):

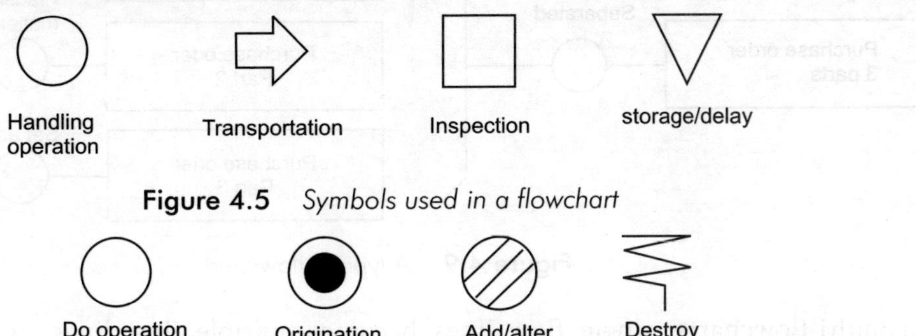

Figure 4.5 *Symbols used in a flowchart*

Figure 4.6 *Flowchart symbols to denote value addition.*

These apart, there are number of other symbols, which we commonly use in process flowcharts. Flowcharting helps us in breaking down the work into individual items with the indication of nature of item-wise processing involved. Flowcharts flow from left to right. A flowchart with the use of the above symbols is presented (Fig. 4.7.) below:

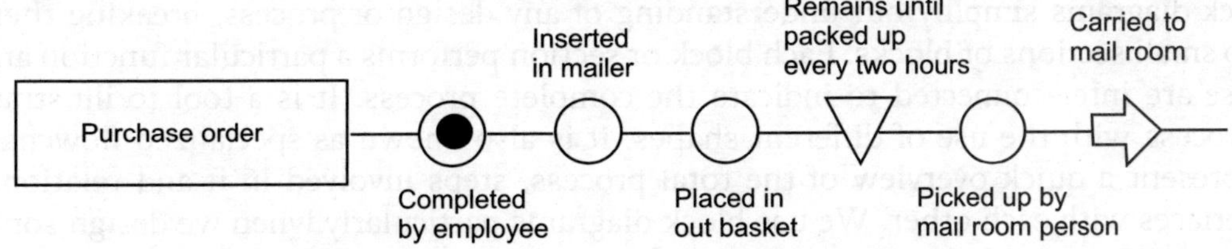

Figure 4.7 *Flowchart using symbols*

To indicate information processing using a flowchart, the relationship between the items is displayed with the vee-shape lines (Fig. 4.8)as under:

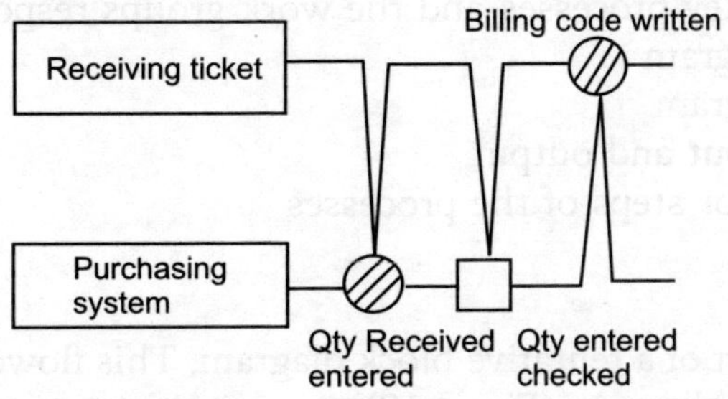

Figure 4.8 *Information processing shown using a flowchart*

Relationships between the items link them together as a single process (Fig. 4.9).

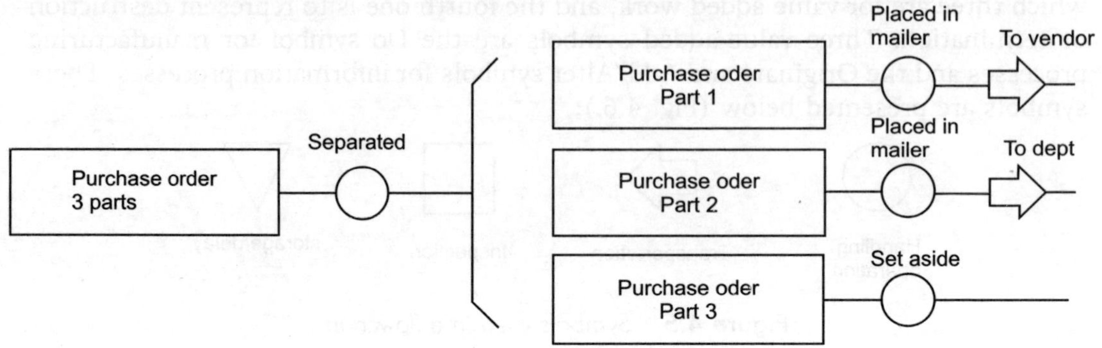

Figure 4.9 *A typical flowchart*

In multi-flowcharts, single flow lines become multiple flow lines. It also breaks down the work into individual elements. Every horizontal line in a multi-flow chart indicates different items.

4.4.1 Block Diagrams

Block diagrams simplify our understanding of any design or process, breaking them into small sections or blocks. Each block or section performs a particular function and these are inter-connected to indicate the complete process. It is a tool to illustrate a process with the use of different shapes. It is also known as specialized flowchart to present a quick overview of the total process, steps involved in it and relational interfaces with each other. We use block diagrams particularly when we design some new processes, to help operations people understand the differences. Some of the essential elements of a block diagram can be listed as under:

- Identification of a process
- Identification of key processes and the work groups responsible for the same
- Outlining the diagram
- Labelling the diagram
- Indicating the input and output
- Definition of major steps of the processes
- Authentication

Let us see the flowchart of a tentative block diagram. This flowchart explains various components of a block diagram (Fig. 4.10).

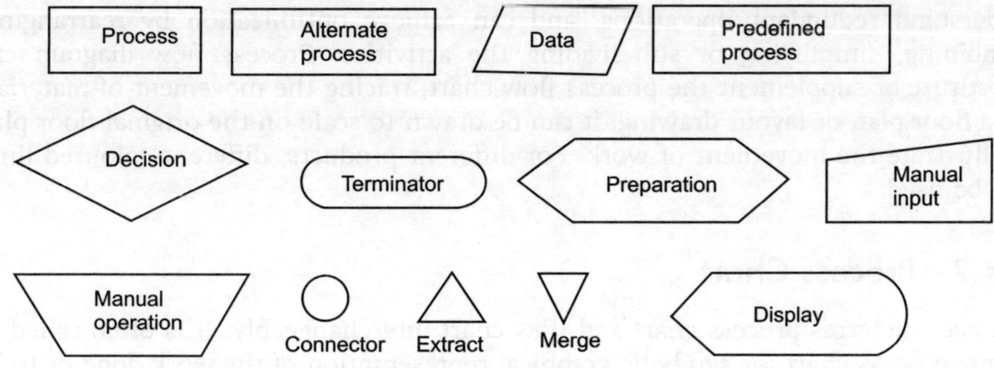

Figure 4.10 *Components of a block diagram or flowchart*

Based on the inputs above, we can draw the block diagram as in Fig. 4.11

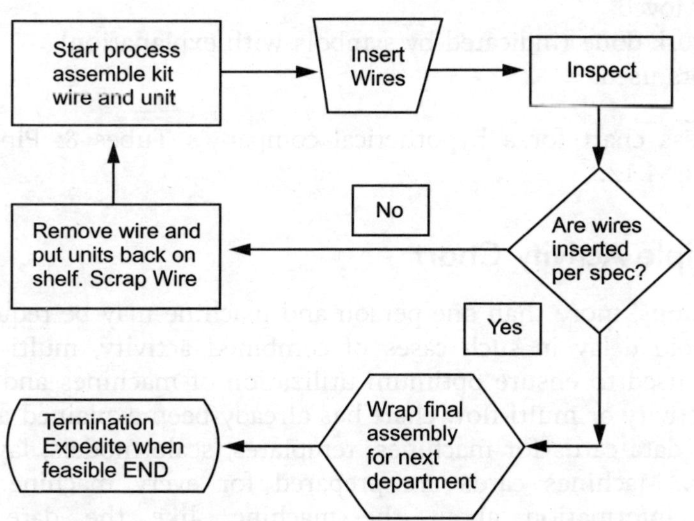

Figure 4.11 *A block diagram*

Thus, we can sum up block diagram as the composition of different shapes and lines that explains the components of a programme, process, or system that relate to one another.

For facility planning, operations and production managers make use of several charts and diagrams to summarize and analyze the production process and procedure. These are operation process chart and flow process chart, etc. Operation process charts sub-divide the process to indicate in flow lines the sequence of activities or operations involved in a manufacturing cycle. Flow process charts are the graphical summary of all the activities involved in a shop floor. Using this chart, we can understand redundant operations, and can achieve optimization by rearranging, combining, simplifying or sub-dividing the activities. Process flow diagram can substitute or supplement the process flow chart, tracing the movement of materials on a floor plan or layout drawing; it can be drawn to scale on the original floor plan to illustrate the movement of work. For different products, different coloured lines can be used.

4.4.2 Process Chart

We use the terms process chart and flow chart interchangeably. It is often called as a flow process chart for symbolic graphical representation of the work done or to be done on a product, while it passes through several stages of a process. In a typical process chart, the following information is made available:

- Quantity
- Distance Moved
- Type of work done (indicated by symbols with explanation)
- Equipments used

A typical process chart for a hypothetical company's Tubes & Pipes Division is presented in Fig. 4.12.

4.4.3 Multiple Activity Chart

In some operations, more than one person and machine may be required for doing the job. To avoid delay in such cases of combined activity, multi-activity charts (Fig. 4.12) are used to ensure optimum utilization of machines and manpower. A typical multi-activity or multi-flow chart has already been explained above.

These apart, data cards for machines, templates, scale models, layout drawings, etc., also help. Machines cards are prepared for every machine to document all the basic information about the machine, like the date of purchase and installation, capacity of the machine, power requirements, environmental conditioning requirements, etc.

Templates are machine drawings, with requirements for tools outlined, on a sheet of paper. Templates eliminate unnecessary handling, with a visual picture of the proposed or existing plans or layouts. Scale models are two-dimensional templates, primarily used in layout engineering. Layout drawings detail the complete layout, covering machines, equipments, storage and office areas.

A process chart can be in the form of an outline or flow diagram. An outline process chart gives a bird's eye view of the process, concentrating only on the operations and inspections. A flow process chart provides detailed information, using all the symbols discussed above. A two-handed process chart documents the activities that involve use of both the hands of the worker. It is also known as a SIMO (simultaneous fine micro analysis) chart. It makes use of 'therbligs', developed by the American industrial psychologists, Frank and Lillian Gilbreth, for the detailed analysis of human motions (The term 'threblig' was formed by reversing their name, Gilbreth). A flow diagram shows the relative position of the machines and equipments. A string diagram uses continuous string or thread to mark the path. A cycle graph studies the path of movement. A chronocycle graph, in addition to the path of movement, also shows the direction and speed of the movement.

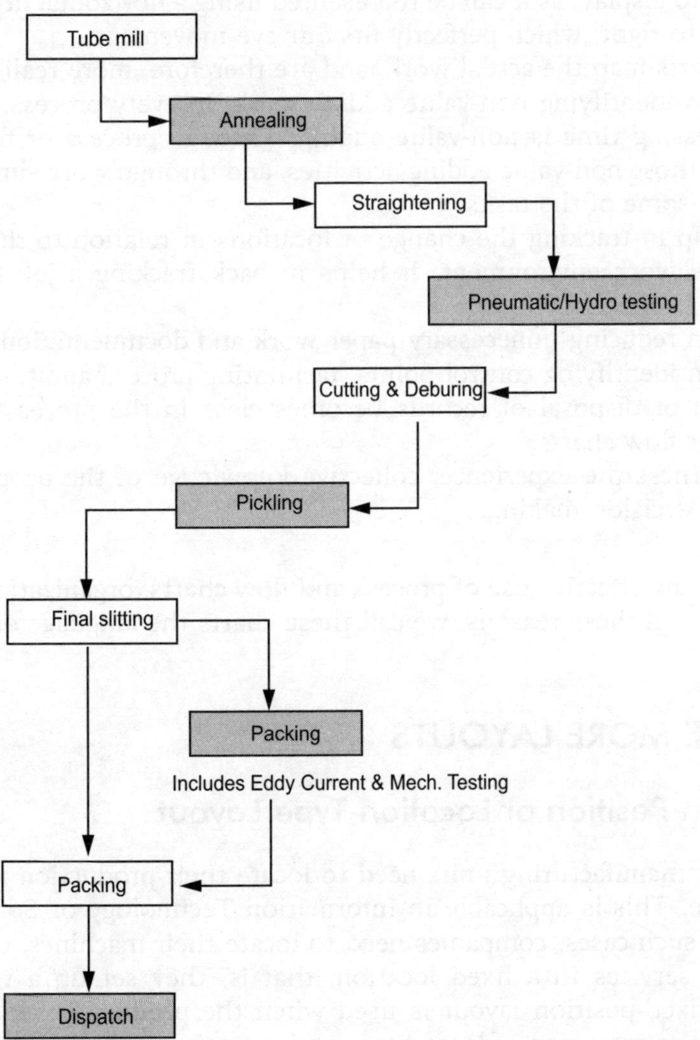

Figure 4.12 *A typical process chart*

4.4.4 Benefits of Process Charts and Flow Charts

The primary benefit of these charts is that it does not require us to get into the details. Managers can get an overview of the process, and accordingly, take important decisions. Some other benefits can be listed as under:

1. It helps in recording the facts sequentially; thereby, it helps reduce the confusion.
2. It is easy to display, as it can be represented using a horizontal flow of processes from left to right, which perfectly fits our eye movement.
3. These charts map the actual work, and are therefore, more realistic.
4. It helps in identifying non-value adding work. In every process, about 95% of the processing time is non-value adding. Through process or flow charts, we can trace those non-value adding activities, and through work simplification can eliminate some of the tasks.
5. It can help in tracking the change of locations in relation to the activities. In a real life work environment, it helps in back tracking a job for re-work, if required.
6. It helps in reducing unnecessary paper work and documentation.
7. It helps in identifying control points, facilitating process audit.
8. Retention or disposal of records becomes clear in the process of developing process or flow charts.
9. It can harness the experience, collective knowledge of the people, facilitating informed decision making.

Therefore, making effective use of process and flow charts, organizations can benefit immensely. For all these reasons, we call these charts the language of the process.

4.5 SOME MORE LAYOUTS

4.5.1 Fixed Position or Location Type Layout

In many cases, manufacturing units need to locate their production facilities at the customer's site. This is applicable in Information Technology or Software support companies. In such cases, companies need to locate their machines, equipment and other support services in a fixed location, that is, they set up a work center in one place. A fixed-position layout is used when the product is very bulky, heavy or fragile. For the execution of large construction projects, shipbuilding and aircraft manufacturing, a fixed position layout is more suitable.

A typical fixed position layout is illustrated in Fig. 4.13 below:

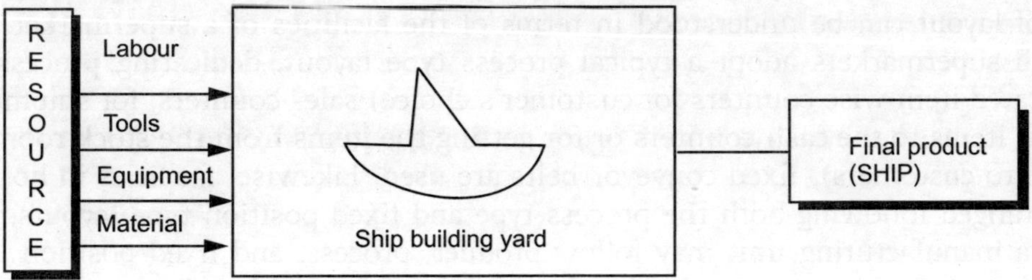

Figure 4.13 *A fixed layout position*

Advantages and Disadvantages of a Fixed Position Layout

Advantages

Some of the advantages of the fixed position layout are:

- This type of layout substantially saves time and cost of execution of customer's orders.
- The cost of distribution or delivery to customers is substantially less, as the job is executed at the customer's mandated sites.
- Based on customer requirements, this type of layout can significantly change the job design and the sequence of operations, due to its inherent flexibility.
- This type of layout is more effective for executing several projects for the same customer simultaneously; it also helps in economizing cost and for ensuring fixed availability of resources.

Disadvantages

The fixed position layout also has some inherent drawbacks. These are:

- Capital investment for projects of this type is quite high, as machines and equipments need to be dedicated to execute customer-specific orders.
- Space requirement for accommodating plant and machineries, and other support services at the customer's site is quite high, which often compels the customers to discourage such layouts, fearing conflicts with their available space.
- Despite such problems, for manufacturing complexities and delivery in terms of uncharted customer specifications, this type of layout is often preferred over others.

4.5.2 Combined, Mixed or Hybrid Layouts

For improving competitive edge in terms of increased market share, many organizations follow the combination approach, through consolidation of various types of layouts. For the compelling needs of the customers, large organizations make their facilities flexible enough for adopting this layout type. The concept of this type of layout can be understood in terms of the facilities of a supermarket. Even though supermarkets adopt a typical process type layout, dedicating process-wise (dedicated item-wise counters for customer's choice) sales counters, for shipment of bought items to the cash counters or for getting the items from the stock room (not visible to customers), fixed conveyor belts are used. Likewise, facilities in hospitals are arranged following both the process type and fixed position type layouts, while a pizza manufacturing unit may follow product, process, and fixed position layout simultaneously. Now, most pizza outlets follow a competitive time cycle for pizza delivery. This requires them to pre-manufacture the pizza base, following the product type layout. Pizzas are ordered by the customers with different toppings (or top-up). Such work requires process type layout, say vegetarian, chicken, with cheese, etc. Delivery of the finally produced pizza to customers waiting at the counter can be facilitated by a conveyor belt from the kitchen to the delivery counter, that is, a fixed position layout. Such an approach significantly reduces the cycle time for delivery of the pizza.

4.5.3 Cellular Manufacturing (CM) Layout

This type of layout requires the grouping of machines into different cells. The Operations manager takes a decision on grouping based on work requirements. Work that is similar in nature is put into one cell. A cellular layout ensures fast processing of jobs, reduced material handling costs, less work-in-process inventory and reduced setup time.

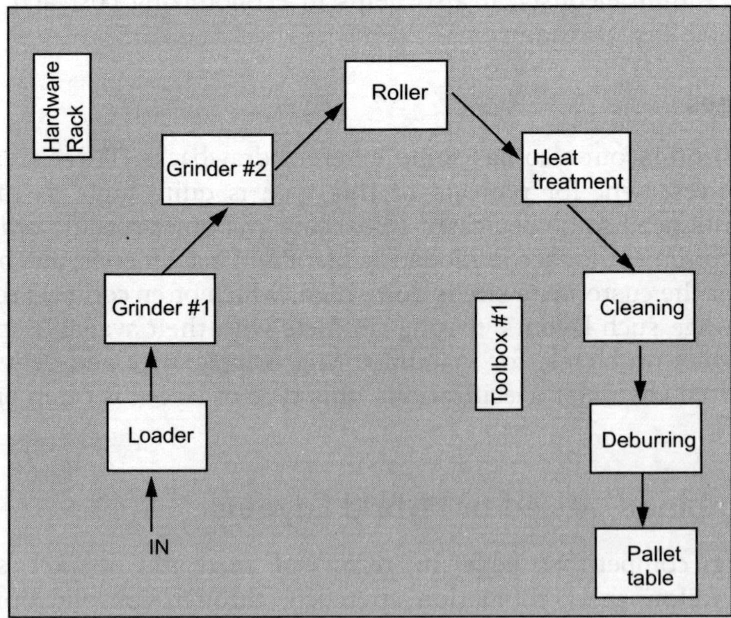

Figure 4.14 *A cellular layout*

However, by using this layout, companies cannot manufacture items in bulk. Only when the variety of products is limited, and the volumes are moderate, such a layout may be effective. A typical example of a cellular layout is illustrated in Fig. 4.14.

4.5.4 Systematic Layout Planning

Richard Muther (1973) developed the concept of systematic layout planning using the principles of nearness priorities, other than the cost of transportation. This method uses a half matrix type grid (Fig. 4.15) to show the relative importance of

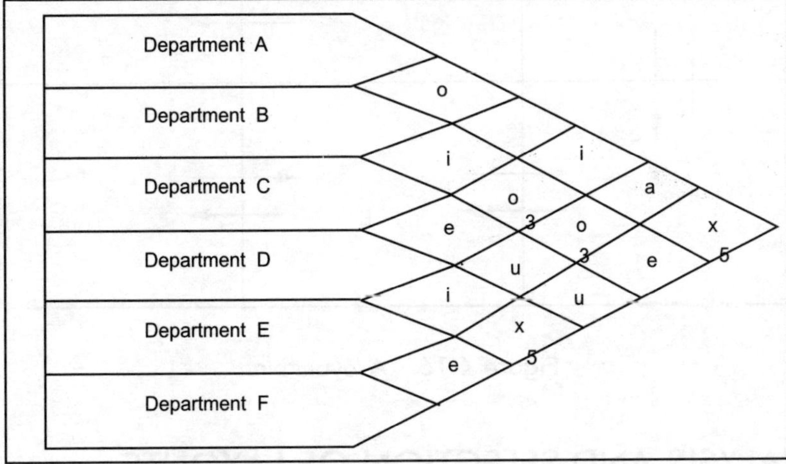

Figure 4.15 *Using a half-matrix grid in systematic layout planning*

distance from one department to another. The typical diamond-shaped boxes on the right side of the figure depict the desired relationships between two intersecting departments.

Letters *a*, *e*, *i*, *o*, or *x* depict the desired relationship and the numbers indicate the reason for the relationship. Let us interpret the figure using the following tabular information:

Table 4.2 *Half-matrix grid table*

Nearness Code	Importance	Possible reason code	Detailed reasons
A	Absolute necessity	1	Similar equipment
E	Extreme Importance	2	Common manpower
I	Important	3	Easy workflow
O	Moderately important	4	Easy communication and supervision
U	Not important	5	Unsafe
X	Not desirable		

Again referring to the figure, we can understand that *'a'* in the matrix indicates absolute necessity of putting E and A departments close to each other. Likewise *'e'* indicates that department F must be close to departments E and B, while department C should be near department D. So also, *'x'* indicates the preferable location of department F, it should be close to departments D and A.

Accordingly, the following layout plan (Fig. 4.16) can be made:

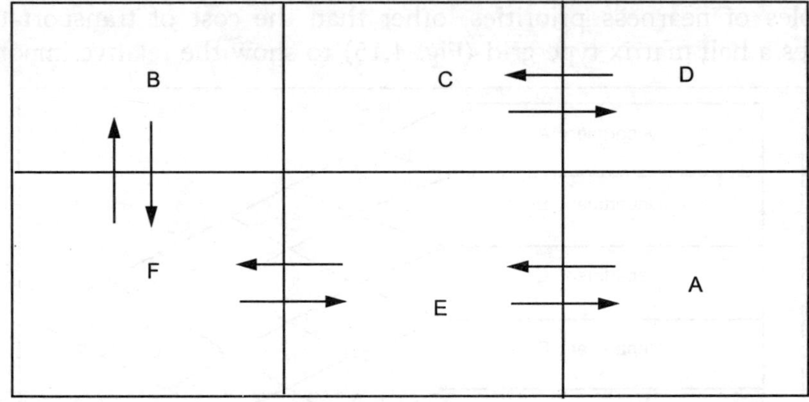

Figure 4.16 *A layout plan*

4.6 ANALYSIS AND SELECTION OF LAYOUTS

Apart from the reasons cited against each type of layout, organizations select a layout based on the cost burden of material handling and the effectiveness of the workers. Material handling costs for different types of layout are different. Again, such costs vary with the nature of the product and services. Again, the performance effectiveness of workers depends on the type of layout. In a product type layout, workers or groups of workers perform one type of job, within a time bound schedule; hence, although such specialized job(s) can get a higher rate of performance, often workers feel bored by repetitive functions. On the other hand, in a process type layout, workers have the flexibility of multi-tasking; hence, can get the benefit of job enrichment and also job enlargement.

In product type or line layout, material flow time gets significantly reduced, resulting in minimization of cycle time for production or processing. In services, such cycle time reduction can also ensure on-time customer services. Using some numeric examples, we can explain this better.

4.6.1 Procedure for Layout

The basic steps to be considered when making an effective layout plan are:

- Study the material requirements list and decide on 'make' or 'buy' items
- Decide on items to be stocked and manufactured after studying the output targets
- Create operation-planning sheets giving details on production routing, manpower requirements, equipment requirements and processing times
- Decide on the space required for each workstation
- Determine storage requirements and develop a stock policy
- Prepare charts and diagrams
- Decide on gangways for movement
- Prepare layout drawings

4.6.2 Layout Tools

A variety of charts and diagrams are used as layout tools to explain the process, which may include labour operation, materials movement, storage, inspection, etc. Two-dimensional scales may be used for indicating the location of facilities like storage areas, aisles, machine space requirement, etc. For explaining the process in three dimension, small-scale replicas and models can also be arranged.

Operation Process Charts graphically detail the operations step-by-step, duly identifying the points at which materials are introduced into the process, the time for each operation and inspection activity, etc. This, however, does not take into consideration other activities like transportation, storage, etc. Two symbols are used in these charts; these are a small circle, to indicate operations and an equal-sized square, to indicate inspection activity.

Operation Process Charts have restricted use as analysis tools, since they have inherent definitional limitations.

Flow Process Charts To avoid the above limitation, Flow Process Charts, offering more information on productive (operation and inspection) and non-productive (transportation, storage, etc.) activities, have been introduced by the American Society of Mechanical Engineers (ASME). These charts show the relationship between processes and equipment, flow of materials or in-process items, movement of workers, location of facilities, etc.

In addition to Operation Process Charts, Route Cards are also used to indicate the sequence of operations and the work centres involved. A typical route card lists lead times in each work centre, standard times for set-up and run, materials, tolerances, tools, etc.

4.6.3 Important criteria for a good layout

Some of the important criteria for a good layout are:

- **Flexibility**: The layout must be flexible enough to keep pace with changing production requirements, and to match the changing tastes and preferences of the customers. Market volatility often requires companies to alter or modify the layout quickly. With flexibility, this task becomes easier.

- **Co-ordination**: Irrespective of the type of layout, the entry and the exit points must be convenient enough for the issue and receipt of materials. This will enhance coordination and can make the process healthy.
- **Maximization of space volumes**: From the organizational point of view, a layout must have adequate space availability.
- **Maximization of volume**: The layout should be such that it can facilitate the highest level of availability of space, making use of racks, modern lifting devices, etc.
- **Visibility**: Layouts should also ensure visibility.
- **Increased accessibility**: It should ensure quick and timely access to most important services or facilities departments like stores, maintenance, canteen, etc.
- **Minimum movements**: This can be ensured by reducing the distance from one shop floor to another. This can also ensure reduction in material handling costs.
- **Better arrangement of physical facilities**: Absence of such facilities like lighting, heat, noise, makes the layout a source of discomfort. Hence, in a layout, such physical facilities have to be ensured.

In addition, safety, security, efficient process flow, etc. are also considered as important criteria for an effective layout. Operations managers, for effective layout decisions, also depend on certain inputs like the nature of output, estimated demand for products or services, number of operations involved in the production process, process-wise and also work centre-wise requirements of space, present availability of space, etc. Thus, a good layout can benefit an organization as it would result in substantial cost minimization through the reduction of movement of goods and materials, in reducing the cycle time for manufacturing, simplifying the process of supervision and control, making the system adaptable to change, motivating employees, and finally, by improving the quality of products and services.

4.6.4 Facilities Decisions

The facilities available in an organization decide its capacity or the productive capability. This is also known as capacity planning. It is a very crucial decision for the Operations Manager, as capacity planning tends to optimize scarce resource utilization, bearing in mind customer demand, time availability, cost efficiency, etc. Facilities or capacity decisions being strategic in nature are usually taken at the highest corporate level. However, the Operations Manager also plays a crucial role in supplementing such decisions by using different tools like economies of scale, location planning, break-even analysis, linear programming models, etc.

4.7 STEPS INVOLVED IN FACILITIES PLANNING

The steps usually followed in Facilities Planning are:

Step 1 – Measuring Facility Capacity: This helps to define the maximum rate of output of an operation in terms of measurable units per output time period. The nature of the product or services will dictate the measurable unit to be used. For a Business School, it may be the number of students graduating per year; while for a Steel plant, it would be the quantity of steel produced per year. Here again, there is a difference between Peak Capacity and Sustained Capacity. Peak Capacity can be sustained only for a short duration with overtime, additional workers, tough performance monitoring, etc. whereas Sustained Capacity can be maintained for a longer duration

Step 2 – Demand Forecast: Short and long-term demand can be forecast using the time series model or even by adopting some qualitative methods. Qualitative Methods include the Delphi Techniques (developed by a panel of experts duly answering a series of questions in successive rounds), Market Surveys, etc. But for long-range demand forecasting, a mixed approach, consisting of both the qualitative and quantitative methods are usually adopted.

Step 3 – Determining Capacity Needs: Facility needs are assessed at this stage, based on demand forecasts; also, the degree of management risk is taken into account.

Step 4 – Development and Evaluation of Alternatives: This step ensures a cost-effective decision, considering various alternatives. For example, whether a Business School should be located in an NCR region or in New Delhi can be decided based on the respective score values (illustrated later), of both these sites

Step 5 – Decision on Capacities or Facilities: After weighing all the factors involved, the final decision is taken, considering the objective of the organization as a whole rather than focussing on mere operational advantage

4.8 TOOLS FOR FACILITIES PLANNING

Like layout plans, we use various tools for facilities planning.

1. Economies of Scale: As the simple economic logic of reducing cost by increasing capacities may not hold good unless weighed in relation to volume, capacity and nature of process, this can partly supplement the decision of facilities or capacities.

2. Location Planning: A decision on the appropriate location for a facility depends on several variables. The Operations Manager has to consider cost, profitability, availability of infrastructure facilities, etc. The following example can clarify the concept.

EXAMPLE

Table 4.3 *Computation of Location of Store*

Weighted variables or factors	Kalyani (S1)	Salt lake (S2)
Transportation Costs 50	8	12
Cost of Electricity 20	10	6
Tax Advantages 15	8	10
Labour Costs 10	11	9
Proximity to market 5	10	6

Based on the above score factors of two different locations, we can compute the aggregate value, and accordingly decide the right location.

$$S1 = (50 \times 8) + (20 \times 10) + (15 \times 8) + (10 \times 11) + (5 \times 10) = 880$$

$$S2 = (50 \times 12) + (20 \times 6) + (15 \times 10) + (10 \times 9) + (5 \times 6) = 990$$

The location with the highest score value is Salt Lake, which should be preferred rather than Kalyani.

3. Break-even Analysis: This analysis depicts the relationships between volume of output, cost and revenues. It is a very commonly used tool.
4. Linear Programming Models: This model helps in taking decisions after clearly setting out the decisional objectives, within the given resource constraints. It is like break-even analysis.

4.9 PLANT LOCATION

In any organization, aspects like the technical, financial, economic factors and the market study of a business plan no doubt play a crucial role. However, the location of business and the layout (the arrangement of physical facilities) are also strategically important.

Plant location indicates the choice of region and the selection of a particular site for setting up the plant or the business of the organization. Such a decision is taken, duly considering the cost and benefits aspect of different alternative sites. This decision is strategic as an effective location can reduce the costs and enhance profitability. It is also strategic, as plant location cannot be changed once it is in place. Optimization of plant location, therefore, is extremely important.

Against the backdrop of the above discussion, we can define an ideal location as one where the cost of the product can be kept to a minimum, and simultaneously, the largest market share can be achieved. Thus, optimum location ensures minimum unit cost of production and distribution, and maximum market reach, and a consequential enhancement of market share.

From Chapter-1, we understand that an effective transformation system requires not only the conversion of inputs to outputs, but also the process of transfer of products and services to the customers. In this context, a decision regarding plant location is crucial, as with proper location, companies can reach their products and services to the customer, incurring minimum costs and maximum value addition (due to less loss in transit, or due to deterioration of the product's features in shipment).

Thus, plant location means the establishment of the plant at a particular place, keeping all the above issues in mind. Decisions on plant location require the evaluation of various factors like geographic areas, demography, economic landscape, infrastructure availability, distance from raw material sources and market, etc. All these factors are weighed to take the final decision on location.

Demographic analysis involves the study of the population of the proposed location in terms of number, age-mix, per capita income, education and occupation pattern. Economic factors, among others, consider the comparative costs of different sites, both in terms of cost of establishment and cost of operations. Proximity to market is also considered and compared between different alternative sites. Competitive analysis helps in judging the relative brunt of competition and for assessing market potential. At times, companies also consider the need for traffic analysis of the proposed site, to assess the possible impact on the market for flying customers or customers whose arrival is time dependent. This is particularly important for the location a of petrol pump, a restaurant, an ATM, etc.

4.10 LOCATION ANALYSIS

The fundamental objective of location analysis is to maximize profits by minimizing the total cost of production associated with the production process. Total costs are the summation of fixed costs and operational costs. Fixed costs are expenditure on land, building, machines and other equipments. Operational costs are the expenditure incurred on inputs, process of transformation and for final distribution of output, etc. Some of the other factors considered for plant location are:

- Availability of amenities: A location which provides good external amenities is often more attractive than one which is more remote.
- Availability of transport: It is important that good transport facilities are readily available.
- Availability of inputs: A location near main suppliers will help to reduce costs and permit staff to meet suppliers easily to discuss quality, technical or delivery problems.
- Availability of services, suitability of land and climate are some other factors considered while deciding plant location. Thus, location analysis is a dynamic

process to analyse and compare the appropriateness or otherwise of alternative sites to select the best site for a given plant, or manufacturing or service facility.

4.10.1 Location evaluation methods

Location evaluation is done based on ranking the various weighted factors. The process of assigning weights to the factors is explained below:

1. Draw the list of various possible factors and their potential influence on your location decisions.
2. Understand the importance of such identified factors, and accordingly, assign weights against each factor, using a defined scale, for example, most important is 1, and so on.
3. Based on your assigned weights rank each factor.
4. Multiply your ranking with the respective weight factors.
5. Total the scores for each location, and then make the comparative analysis.

Depending on the nature of activities involved, like manufacturing, service, warehouses, stockyard (for steel plant), etc. the location decision changes. Setting up a heavy engineering unit, obviously has a huge space requirement, so the preferred location would be in a place, where land is available and the costs are relatively cheaper. Automobile, cement, steel plants, oil refineries, bulk chemical plants, etc. are examples of units which require space. However, such decisions also consider other factors like transportation costs, cost of construction, raw material availability, labour cost and availability, waste disposal systems, proximity to market, etc. On the other hand, for a light industry, the location decisions are different. Because of technological sophistication, light engineering units often prefer locating their units close to the city where there is availability of skilled workers, who otherwise may not agree to move to distant places. Moreover in cities, such units, being less polluting, do not face major restrictions from the pollution control authorities. For locating warehouses and distribution centres, favourable environmental conditions, availability of public utility services, security, transport facilities and costs, and proximity to market are some of the determining factors. A retail outlet on the other hand, first considers the probable footfalls in a particular location, and their consumption propensity, along with buying capacity.

In many cases, the Government provides incentives for locating units in some designated sites. Such policies are given to eliminate regional imbalances in economic development and growth. Such incentives may be in the form of a tax moratorium, relaxation in government regulations, soft interest loans, power subsidy, etc. In India, several Export Processing Zones (EPZs) have been developed to encourage entrepreneurs to set up their units. Such EPZs provides multiple benefits. Despite the availability of incentives, business units decide on their location based on their own internal economic considerations.

Example

A proposed manufacturer of heavy duty trucks shortlisted three possible sites for locating their new unit. The manufacturer is entering the Indian market for the first time. After scoring the factors, the company made available the following information. Based on your analysis, suggest which could be the best possible site for the company (scores are from 1 to 100).

Location Factor	Weight	Site-A	Site-B	Site-C
Labour Availability	0.30	80	65	90
Availability of Vendors	0.20	100	91	75
Proximity to Market	0.15	60	95	72
Rail Connectivity	0.15	75	80	80
Road Connectivity	0.10	65	90	95
Air Connectivity	0.05	85	92	65
Environmental Factors	0.05	50	65	90

Identify the best locational choice for the manufacturer.

Solution

Multiply the weight for each factor by the respective site score. Sum up the weighted scores, and find out the best site based on comparative ratings. Using the table above, your calculation will show that Site-C is the best choice as it has the highest score value.

4.10.1.1 Center-of-Gravity Technique

This technique of locational analysis is used when bases of multiple customers and suppliers exist in more than one geographic location. In such cases, companies decide to locate their units centrally, so that services to the customers at different locations can be catered to; so also, services from the suppliers can be availed of. Obviously, in such decisions, the cost of transportation gets the overriding priority. The center-of-gravity technique requires the use of a mathematical equation to finally decide a location. The primary considerations of this technique are location at the centre of the geographic area, value of weighted factors, grid-map of the area, and finally, the solution to the equations on the centre of gravity.

Center of Gravity:

$$x = \frac{\sum_{i=1}^{n} x_i W_i}{\sum_{i=1}^{n} W_i} \qquad y = \frac{\sum_{i=1}^{n} y_i W_i}{\sum_{i=1}^{n} W_i}$$

$x = i = 1$ $y = i = 1$

where,

x, y = coordinates of the new facility at the center of gravity

x_i, y_i = coordinates of existing facility i

W_i = annual weight shipped from facility i.

The above equation is presented in the figure (Fig. 4.17) below using the grid approach method:

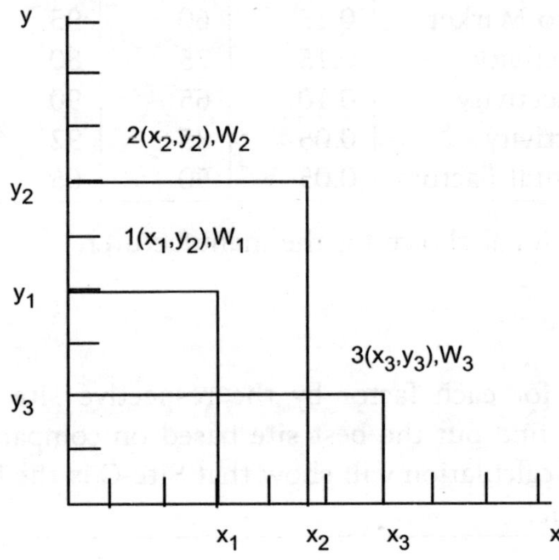

Figure 4.17 *Grid approach method*

Example

A food mart is part of a well-known international chain, which makes the need for visits to bazaars redundant for retail buyers. The company maintains toll-free numbers for customers to book their orders for free home delivery within a stipulated time of 30 minutes. The food mart chain serves both cooked food items and vegetables, and other non-cooked provision items at 10% less than the market price. The food mart also sells over the counter to customers who visit. However, analysis of their past business history indicates that such visiting customers only account for 10% of the company's business revenue, the remaining 90% comes from their specialized home delivery services.

The food mart's decisional dilemmas on location are based on the following:

1. As a core philosophy, the company believes and ensures on-time delivery to its customers, that is, within 30 minutes of order booking.
2. The company supplies cooked items in a ready-to-eat condition, that is, hot and warm, which they ensure through specialized packaging and 15 minutes cycle time for delivery after the cooking to meet the deadline of delivery within 30 minutes of order booking. To ensure this, the company operates multiple mobile supply vans which operate round the clock. Such vans are equipped with a system for warming the food. Customers' orders are routed through these 'Food Mobile' vans for on-time delivery.
3. The vendors of the company are dispersed in four different locations – A, B, C, D.
4. Such vendors transport full truckloads of items for every food mart of the company on a weekly basis, on an average as under:

A – 75
B – 105
C – 135
D – 60

5. A typical topography of the vendors' point of locations, indicate the following:

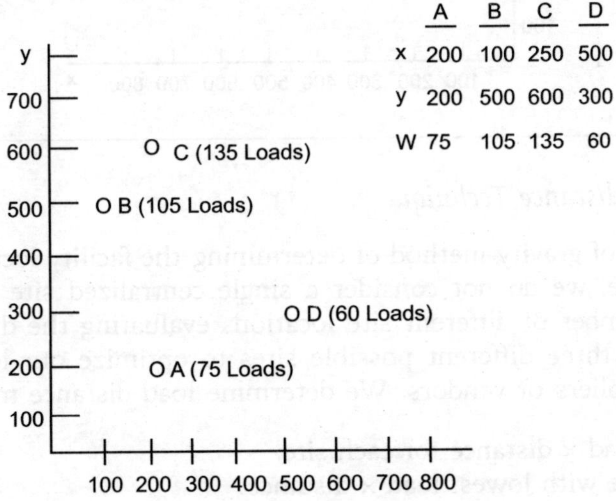

Based on the above input information compute the centre of gravity to ascertain the ideal location of the proposed food mart.

$$x = \frac{\sum_{i=1}^{n} x_i W_i}{\sum_{i=1}^{n} W_i} = \frac{(200)(75) + (100)(105) + (250)(135) + (500)(60)}{75 + 105 + 135 + 60} = 238$$

$$y = \frac{\sum_{i=1}^{n} y_i W_i}{\sum_{i=1}^{n} W_i} = \frac{(200)(75) + (500)(105) + (600)(135) + (300)(60)}{75 + 105 + 135 + 60} = 444$$

Based on the above analysis, the company must choose their location site, using the grid map, that correspond to 238, 444, as shown in the figure.

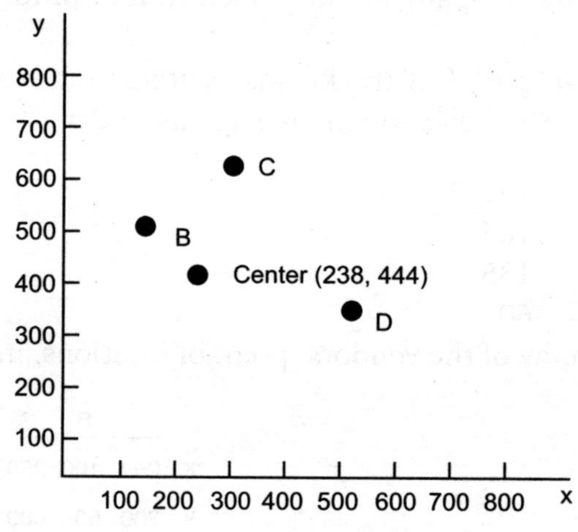

4.10.1.2 *Load–distance Technique*

Unlike the centre of gravity method of determining the facility location, in the load distance technique, we do not consider a single centralized site location. Rather, we consider a number of different site locations evaluating the distance and load. We may evaluate three different possible sites to optimize our location, between four different suppliers or vendors. We determine load distance method as per the methods below:

- Determine load × distance for each site.
- Select the site with lowest load × distance.
- Find out distance on the basis of actual mileage or straight-line on x, y coordinates. Following the above method, we can use the equation below to find out the optimum location site using the load–distance method:

$$\text{LD} = \sum_{i=1}^{n} l_i d_i$$

where,

LD = the load–distance value.

l_i = load in terms of weight, number of trips, or units being shipped from the proposed site to location i.

d_i = the distance between the proposed site and location i.

$$d_i = \sqrt{(x_1 - x)^2 + (y_i - y)^2}$$

where, (x, y) = coordinates of proposed site (x_i, y_i) = coordinates of existing facility

Now find out the distances for site 1 based on the weighted loads as under:

LD (site 1) = (75)(161.2) + (105)(412.3) + (135)(434.2) + (60)(184.4)

LD (site 1) = 125,063

Likewise, find out the LD score for the other site as well. Select the site with the lowest LD score

Example

Let us take the example of Food Mart earlier, and assume that the company is evaluating three possible sites for locating its shop. The x, y-coordinates for the three sites are:

Site	X	Y
1	360	180
2	420	450
3	250	400

Consider again the weight factors for each vendor, shown earlier.

	Vendors			
	A	B	C	D
X	200	100	250	500
Y	200	500	600	300
Wt	75	105	135	60

Find out the load distance for these three sites.

Solution

Compute the distances for site 1 to each of the four suppliers as under:

$$\text{Site 1: } d_A = \sqrt{(xA - x1)^2 + (yA - y1)^2}$$

$$= \sqrt{(200 - 360)^2 + (200 - 180)^2} = 1612$$

$$\text{Site 1: } d_B = \sqrt{(xB - x1)^2 + (yB - y1)^2}$$

$$= \sqrt{(100 - 360)^2 + (500 - 180)^2} = 412.3$$

$$\text{Site 1: } d_C = \sqrt{(xc - x1)^2 + (yc - y1)^2}$$

$$= \sqrt{(250 - 360)^2 + (600 - 180)^2} = 434.2$$

$$\text{Site 1: } d_D = \sqrt{(xD - x1)^2 + (yD - y1)^2}$$

$$= \sqrt{(500 - 360)^2 + (300 - 180)^2} = 184.4$$

4.10.1.3 *Brown Gibson Model*

The Brown and Gibson (1972) Model is a multi-attribute location decision-making technique. This model considers both the objective and subjective factors in a location decision. The model can be mathematically represented as under:

$$Mi = Ci \times [D \times Oi + (1 - D) \times S\,i]$$

Where,

M = Measure for an alternative '*i*'

C = Critical Factor Measure which could either be 0 or 1 for an alternative '*i*'

O = Objective Factor Measure vary between 0 and 1, the total however adds to 1.

S = Subjective Factor Measure which vary between 0 and 1 with total add back to 1.

D = Objective Factor Decision Weight assigned with value ranging between 0 and 1.

Example

Let us assume a Boiler manufacturing company sells about 200 units of boilers every year. The company pays Rs. 20 per unit per year for its storage space. Using the Brown Gibson Model, and assuming an ordering cost of Rs. 35 per order, determine the economic ordering quantity that can justify your storage space and layout. Assume that interest cost annually is close to 10% per year and the total cost of one unit is Rs. 100.

Solution

We use the EOQ formula, $EOQ = (2RC_o/C_h)^{0.5}$

Here R = 200 units, C_o = Rs. 35 and the holding cost Ch = Rs. 30 per unit per year. This is calculated by Rs. 20 (direct storage cost per unit per year) + Rs. 100 × 0.10 (this term indicates the interest lost if one unit remains in stock for one year).

Hence, $EOQ = (2RC_o/C_h)^{0.5} = (2 \times 200 \times 35/30)^{0.5} = 21.602$ units, i.e., 22 units. Thus, with an EOQ of 22 units, the company can justify the existing storage space and the layout in general.

SUMMARY

1. This chapter discusses facilities planning and its importance in the layout and locational decisions of organizations.
2. Layout is the physical arrangement of all the production facilities, and employees' services, and is essential in achieving production efficiency. An efficient plant layout can ensure smooth and rapid flow of materials, right from the stage of receipt of raw materials to the end product.
3. Layout decisions depend on types of products and processes, and the volume of production. We can have various types of layout, like product or line layout, process layout, fixed position layout, hybrid or mixed layout, cellular layout, etc. Systematic layout planning requires consideration of the principle of nearness, apart from the material handling costs.
4. For effective layout, we make use of various layout tools like operation process charts, flow process charts, route cards, etc. Some criteria for good layout are flexibility, coordination, maximisation of space volumes, visibility, increased accessibility, minimum movements, better arrangement of physical facilities.
5. Decisions on facilities planning are supplemented by tools like economies of scale, location planning, break-even analysis, linear programming models, etc. Some of the steps involved in facilities planning are measurement of

facility capacity, demand forecast, determining capacity needs, evaluation of alternatives, and finally, the decisions.

6. Location indicates the choice of region and the selection of a particular site for setting up the plant or the business of the organization. A decision on location is taken considering the cost and benefits aspect of different sites.
7. Companies through location analysis and evaluation decide the appropriate site for locating their units. Some of the models for location analysis are centre of gravity technique, load distance technique and the Brown Gibson Model.

KEY WORDS

Line Balancing It ensures even distribution of workloads through the process of sub-division of activities or tasks so that all work stations get an equal amount of work in terms of time requirement of job performance. It ensures optimization of labour and resources.

Multiple-activity Chart In some operations, more than one person and machine may be required for doing the job. To avoid delay in such cases, multi-activity charts are used to ensure optimum utilization of machines and manpower.

SIMO Chart Two-handed process chart documents the activities that involve use of both the hands of the worker. It is also known as a SIMO (simultaneous fine micro analysis) chart.

Operation Process Chart It graphically details the operations step-by-step, duly identifying the points at which materials are introduced into the process, the time for each operation and inspection activity, etc.

Flow Process Charts These charts offer more information on productive (operation and inspection) and non-productive (transportation, storage, etc.) activities.

Center-of-Gravity Technique This technique of location analysis is taken when multiple customers and supplier bases exist in more than one geographic location. In such cases, companies decide to locate their units centrally, so that services to customers at different locations can be catered to, as also, services from the suppliers can be availed of.

Load–Distance Technique In this technique, we consider a number of different site locations evaluating the distance and load.

Brown Gibson Model This model is effective in multi-attribute location decision making. The model considers both the objective and subjective factors in location decisions.

GENERAL REVIEW QUESTIONS

1. Explain the significance of plant location and layout.
2. What are the factors that deserve the attention of a production and operations manager in finalizing plant location?
3. From a business perspective, describe the importance of location factors for a retail mall.
4. Using at least two models, discuss the process of location analysis.
5. In framing the layout of restaurant, what are the factors you feel deserve our attention?
6. What are the advantages and disadvantages of a fixed position layout?
7. Explain the difference between product layout and process layout.
8. What is a hybrid layout? How is this type of layout better than other types of layout for the customer service department of a multi-product electronics company?
9. Explain the procedure of systematic layout planning (SLP) with the help of a diagram.
10. What are the major issues to be considered while deciding on the location of a plant? Explain.
11. What are the basic differences between an Operation process chart and a Flow process chart?
12. Short notes
    (a) Line Balancing
    (b) Flowchart
    (c) Block Diagrams
    (d) Multi-activity Chart
    (e) Cellular Manufacturing (CM) Layout
    (f) Centre of Gravity
    (g) Brown Gibson Model

CRITICAL REVIEW QUESTION

1. You have recently joined an upcoming sponge iron plant as CEO. The company wants you to suggest a possible location. Apart from the economic issues, elaborate on the other factors you must consider and why? (Hints: Study the sponge iron plant requirements from website materials).

REFERENCES

1. Brown, P. A., and Gibon, D. F. 1972. A Quantified Model for Facility Site Selection Application to Multi Plant Location Problem. *AIIE Transactikons,* Vol. 4. Issue 1, pp. 1–10.

2. Francis, R. L., and White, J. A. 1974. *Facility layout and location*. Englewood Cliffs, N. J: Prentice-Hall,
3. James, L., Riggs. 1970. *Production Systems: Planning*, Analysis and Control. New York: Wiley.
4. Muther, R. 1973. *Systematic Layout Planning*. Boston: Cahners Books.

ADDITIONAL REFERENCES

1. Florence. P. Sargent. 1984. *Investment, Location and Size of plant*. London:Cambridge University Press.
2. Buffa Elwood S.(no date). *Operations Management*. New Delhi:Wiley Eastern,
3. Read Ruddel R. 1978. Plant Layout—*Factors, Principles and Techniques*. Illinois: Richard D. Irwin.
4. Shubin, John A. and H. Madeheim. 1986. *Plant Layout*. New Delhi:Prentice Hall of India.
5. Muther, R. 1973. *Systematic Layout Planning*. Boston:Cahners Books,
6. Vollman, Thomas E., Christopher E. Nugent, and Robert L. Zarter. 1968. A Computerized Model for Office Layout. *The Journal of Industrial Engineering*, X1X: 312--327.
7. Quarterman. EE. 1997. *Facilities & Workplace Design*.Norcross, Georgia: Engineering and Management Press.
8. Skinner, Wickham. 1974. The Focused Factory. *Harvard Business Review*, May–June
9. Phillips, Edward J. 1997. *Manufacturing Plant Layout: Fundamentals and Fine Points of Optimum Facility Design*. Dearborn, Michigan, USA: Society of Manufacturing Engineers,
10. Richard Francis. 1991. *Facility Layout and Location: An Analytical Approach*. New Delhi: Prentice-Hall of India

CASE STUDY

Retail India's location decision

The retail industry is booming in our country. Many large and medium sized business houses have now made their foray into the retail sector. The most important criteria for the success of the retail industry is its location and the second most important factor is the layout, to exert a compelling pressure on people to step in and buy. Theoretically, we observe that retail outlets make use of models like a circular trade area, spatial interaction or gravity and location allocation.

Retail India is now a household name. The company has presence in all metropolitan cities. As part of its strategy it chooses those location sites, which are at the centre of gravity, to facilitate an uninterrupted flow of material, and also to increase the number of footfalls. The company believes that such a strategy has helped them grow. Although due to business compulsions, the company has always waged price wars, reducing their cost of inventory holding, the company still believes the location factor plays a crucial role.

Retail India has now introduced a new retail vertical, known as a 'community store', both in the existing cities where their mega marts exist, and in new places. Community stores are a tenth of the size of the mega mart, requiring only 1000 sq.ft. floor area. Community stores are located in new housing colonies, where the local market is more than a kilometer away. Housing colonies develop contiguously in certain specific sites, so that the cost of infrastructure development can be shared among the promoting companies. Apart from free home delivery, the community stores provide a 24-seater bus facility, free of cost every week for those wanting to shop at their mega marts. Such a spoke-and-hub model of business helped the company consolidate its growth in community stores.

Discussion Question: Based on the inputs in the case study, analyse the location strategies of two retail companies in India. Identify their uniqueness.

Chapter 5

Scheduling and Sequencing of Production

LEARNING OBJECTIVES

After reading this chapter, you will be able to understand:

- The Concept and Usefulness of Scheduling
- History of Production Scheduling
- Scheduling and Sequencing
- Scheduling of Service Operations
- Various Tools and Techniques for Sequencing
- Use of Gantt Charts, Johnson Rule, etc. for Scheduling
- Application of Queuing Theory for Scheduling

Opening Vignette

Scheduling of Production and Ordnance Factories

Manual job scheduling is an age-old practice in Indian Ordnance Factories. Each Ordnance factory has an independent planning section. The planning section's personnel visit the shop floor to collect data on a daily basis and feed it into the computer to analyze the degree of conformance to order requirements. Production targets are assigned to each job floor after analysis of order booking positions from the Army and other civil agencies. Managers arrive at the job allocation plan, keeping in view the in-built machine capacity. Ordnance factories produce items only against orders, as stockpiling of strategically important defence items such as finished inventory is not permissible. Of late, ordnance factories are making use of computerized systems for job scheduling. However, in the case of 'critical' jobs, where workmanship of a high order is required, the task of job scheduling is still done manually; computerized systems only supplement this process.

5.1 INTRODUCTION

The production schedule emanates from the production plan. We have already discussed Production Planning and Control in Chapter 2. In this chapter, we will focus on production scheduling. Production scheduling per se is a plan framed for the operators to perform their jobs to produce goods within a given time frame. Based on orders from the customers for different types of items, the marketing department analyzes these orders and places a job order on the production and operations department. The Production department first performs an analysis to work out the pacing of jobs, or job sequencing, to optimize resources, with minimum machine idle time, after taking their customers' delivery commitment into consideration. The process of scheduling helps at this stage. Scheduling jobs involve taking into consideration the due (delivery) dates to avoid late completion of jobs. Also, the production department takes into account factors such as throughput time and the utilization of machines at different work centres. Using various scheduling techniques, production managers decide on the best option, depending on the varying needs of the sales and marketing department. Thus, the production schedule is also a plan that authorizes production personnel to manufacture, balancing all the requirements. This task is also executed by the production planning and control department.

Scheduling for the operations function (both manufacturing and services), relates to the use of equipment and facilities, it encompasses utilization of manpower and receipt of materials. It is the final stage in the process of transformation before getting the actual output. Operations managers take scheduling decisions within the constraints of a long-term plan. Through scheduling, organizations make tradeoffs among conflicting goals for efficient utilization of labour and equipment, lead time, inventory levels and processing time.

The terms, production planning and scheduling, are often used interchangeably. However, the two are different. The production plan considers aggregate data for a medium range timeframe. Production plans consider several stages of production to optimize the total cost of production. Production scheduling on the other hand, considers information on single stage production facilities for a short timeframe. Hence, production schedules are drawn within the ambit of production plans, and often considered within a single framework. Because of such interaction between the production plan and production schedule, often we find the use of common models or sequencing rules. Production schedules are plans for job processing. They aim to minimize the operations costs, controlling the release of jobs to the work centres (shop floor), and honouring the delivery commitment to the customers. Balancing job priorities and the capacity, production scheduling determines the time required for job performance.

There are fundamental differences between production planning and production scheduling. Planning models often utilize aggregate data and cover multiple stages in a medium-range timeframe, in an effort to minimize total costs. Scheduling models use detailed information, usually for a single stage or facility over a short-term horizon, in an effort to complete jobs in a timely manner.

Despite these differences, planning and scheduling often have to be incorporated into a single framework, information has to be shared, and there has to be extensive interaction. They may also interact with other models such as forecasting models or facility location models.

In organizations, production scheduling is done using Gantt charts or computer-based scheduling tools. IBM's Logistics Management System (LMS) is one such known computer-based scheduling tool which helps improve on-time delivery, with a realistic production schedule.

5.2 COMPONENTS OF PRODUCTION SCHEDULING

While developing a production schedule, the production planning and control department considers the following aspects:

1. **Available capacity** Organizations have an in-built capacity to produce items in terms of machines, equipment, other infrastructural support and manpower. Such capacity is pre-determined and drawn up in a master schedule plan, also known as a capacity requirements plan. This is reinforced by the resource requirements plan, known as aggregate planning (See Chapter-2).
2. **Infinite Job Loading Capacity** This capacity is calculated based on the requirements of various work centres, irrespective of the capacity available to perform the job.
3. **Finite Job Loading Capacity** This capacity is considered as a constraint for job loading (as a particular work centre cannot execute jobs in excess of its available capacity). It helps in assigning priorities to balance the job load within the given constraints.
4. **Drum-Buffer-Rope (DBR)** This method helps us understand both scheduling constraints and the constraints of managing operations (internal constraints). In other words, we call this method capacity-constrained resource planning.
5. **Forward Scheduling** This scheduling technique considers a known start date, computes the job completion date, considering all the operations involved in the process. Accordingly, this technique identifies the earliest possible start dates for the operations.
6. **Backward Scheduling** This technique considers the due (or delivery) dates of the orders, and works backwards to understand the required start date and/or due dates for each operation.

5.3 HISTORY OF PRODUCTION SCHEDULING

Production scheduling has a rich history. F.W. Taylor (1911) is acknowledged as the founding father of the production scheduling concept with his idea of setting up a planning office for effective manufacturing. Such separation of planning and execution was the beginning of scheduling, which has now become critical for every manufacturing organization. Based on Taylor's idea, we now consider production scheduling as a distinct decision-making process to share information, make plans and respond to unexpected events.

Henry Gantt (Alford, 1934), worked with Taylor in companies like *Midvale Steel Company, Simonds Rolling Machine Company* and *Bethlehem Steel*. Gantt's seminal work 'Work, Wages and Profits' (1916) discusses scheduling in the job shop manufacturing process. He emphasized the need to coordinate activities on the shop floor. With an innovative chart, Gantt helped managers to visualize the planned and the actual production, graphically. It is more like a control chart, as the visualization helps managers understand the deviation from plans, and accordingly, develop a suitable action plan. The Gantt chart is explained in detail later on in this chapter.

Another pioneering work is credited to S.M. Johnson (1954). He helped analyse the properties of an optimal solution to a scheduling problem. Johnson's algorithm can be applied to two-stage, and even scheduling problems that had three or more stages. Johnson viewed scheduling as an optimization problem to generate optimal production schedules.

Thus, analyzing the history of production scheduling, we observe three different dimensions – the organizational (Taylor), the decision-making (Gantt) and the problem-solving dimensions (Johnson).

5.4 SCHEDULING OF SERVICE OPERATIONS

So far, our discussions have centred on the scheduling of production or manufacturing jobs. But production and operations management from a broader perspective also considers the rendering of services. For example, when we visit a restaurant, we get a service. In a restaurant, unless the orders are served on time, there may be queuing problems, customers may feel unhappy, and ultimately, it may result in a loss for the company. Similarly, in banks, unless cycle time for services is minimized, banks may lose customers.

Services by nature are intangible, and such intangibility creates the problem of service inventory. In banks, customers' arrival is time independent, causing a queuing problem. Since service demands are time independent or random, the problem of scheduling is more complex. Customers become restless and demand real-time services. This requires the company to provision for manpower and other resources, using various mathematical models, of which queuing theory is the most prominent.

Queuing theory estimates arrival rates and service rates to determine an optimum manpower plan. Restaurants, hospitals, clubs and public utility services often build their service capabilities by engaging people on call basis, and even develop employees through cross-training. Multi-skilled and cross-trained employees can undertake services of different verticals, and thereby help minimize queuing.

Service scheduling becomes complicated when it requires coordination between resources. A good example is hospital services. We know that in most hospitals, doctors work as consultants. The arrival of patients in any hospital is also time independent. The immediate need for surgery requires coordination between the operation theaters with regard to availability, surgeon availability, availability of operation theater assistants, etc. This complicates the process of service scheduling. Although hospitals try to minimize delay and optimize scheduling through prior appointments and reservations, often, they may be required to refuse admission to patients due to their inability to cope with the problem of service scheduling.

5.5 TOOLS AND TECHNIQUES FOR SCHEDULING

5.5.1 Batch Production Scheduling

This is related to the planning and scheduling of production under the batch manufacturing process. Operationally, production scheduling is more relevant for product line or assembly line production; however, this technique can be used in batch processing when the capacity is finite. In batch production, a job is construed as a set of identical parts; hence, it has to be processed as a whole. This therefore, requires the processing of batch production jobs in full, before sequencing or scheduling other jobs. For a typical job, it may be necessary to partition a batch into several smaller batches for ease of processing. This typical problem arises when smaller batches need to be processed independently on multiple machines. This can facilitate a reduction in the average batch flow time. Similarly, in batch scheduling, we are also required to perform a batch overlapping function, this involves transferring a job from one machine to another machine, to complete the total operations involved in the job.

5.5.2 Assignment or Job Loading

After scheduling we do the actual job loading, assigning jobs to work centers and to various machines at these work centers. For loading a job only on to one machine, we do not encounter any problem. But when we need to load the jobs on multiple machines encompassing several work centres, we have to solve complicated job assignment problems. There are two approaches to job loading – infinite loading and finite loading.

Infinite job loading technique is only relevant when we need not consider the capacity constraints of the work centre (as sufficient capacity is available). In such a case, we consider simple priority rules, also known as *vertical loading*. On the contrary, finite loading needs to consider capacity constraints and processing time requirements and balance the conflict, by ensuring that process time does not exceed capacity. The order of job allocation in finite loading systems requires adherence to the highest priority, and then moving on to the job with the next highest priority and so on. This is why finite loading is called *horizontal job loading*. With finite loading, the scheduler loads or allocates the job in order of priority considering the work load at all the work centres. Accordingly, the job that is next highest in terms of priority is allocated or loaded. This process is referred to as horizontal loading.

Under this technique, the following steps are suggested to determine the optimal cost of assigning various job loads on to the machine:

1. From the given job–machine combination matrix, a revised matrix has to be prepared by allowing for the subtraction of the smallest figure from all figures in the column. This has to be done for each column.
2. The next stage requires performing row subtraction in a similar manner, as explained above – the smallest number in any row is subtracted from all the figures in that row. Accordingly, a revised matrix is developed.
3. At this stage, a further revised matrix is prepared to determine the minimum number of lines needed to cover all zeros.
4. If the minimum number of lines are not equal to rows or columns (at this stage), then this will not lead to an optimal solution, as many machines will remain idle. In that case, some production lines may become redundant. Lines refer to the array of machines on the shop floor, and usually in each line, some operation or the other is carried out. In such cases, where it becomes necessary to make some lines redundant, a revised matrix must be prepared.
5. To further revise the matrix (in case of the situation explained in step-4), we have to add the smallest uncovered number of the earlier matrix to the numbers at the intersection of the covering lines and subtract it from other uncovered numbers, leaving other numbers as it is.
6. Finally, based on the revised matrix above, we can assign the jobs to machines, starting first with those where rows and columns have only one zero.

We will now explain all these steps using the following illustration:

Example 1

X & Co. has won an order for four jobs which can be executed using any of their four available machines. However, the manufacturing cost is different for different job–machine combinations. The following matrix depicts the problem faced by the company. We have to find the best option to assign jobs to the machines to achieve cost effectiveness.

MATRIX-A

Jobs	Machines			
	1	2	3	4
W	8	4	7	14
X	15	12	9	3
Y	9	18	12	16
Z	10	20	15	5

Solution

1. Following Step-1, we get the revised Matrix as under:

MATRIX-B

Jobs	Machines			
	1	2	3	4
W	0	0	0	11
X	7	8	2	0
Y	1	14	5	13
Z	2	16	8	2

2. Following Step-2, we get the revised Matrix as under:

MATRIX-C

Jobs	Machines			
	1	2	3	4
W	0	0	0	11
X	7	8	2	0
Y	0	13	4	12
Z	0	14	6	0

Following Step-3, we can determine the minimum number of lines required to cover all zeros; the results indicate that the minimum number of lines required is 3, which means that, we have to make one line redundant and make the corresponding machine idle, this will outweigh the benefits of cost effectiveness (that we aspire to achieve).

Looking at Matrix-C itself, we can verify that we can make one line, that is, one array of machines redundant, reducing the number of lines required from four to three. However, the number of jobs being four, this is not an optimal solution. We, therefore, need to draw a revised Matrix-D, following the subsequent steps.

Following Step-5, therefore, we can draw revised a matrix as follows:

MATRIX-D

Jobs	Machines			
	1	2	3	4
W	2	0	0	13
X	(7)	6	0	0
Y	0	11	2	(12)
Z	0	(12)	4	0

It can be seen from the above Matrix-D that rounded numbers, in this case, 7 and 12 have not been changed; neither has the smallest number been added (they are not falling under an intersection), nor has the smallest number been subtracted (as it is not uncovered).

After this, we make the final assignment, following Step-6. As explained, we start selecting a job–machine combination, looking at the Matrix-D, allocating the first job to that line/machine, where the rows and columns have only one zero. Row 'Y' and Column 1 have only one zero, hence job 'Y' is assigned to Machine-1. Thereafter, job 'W' is assigned to Machine-2; job 'Z' can be assigned to Machine-4 and job 'X' to Machine-3. Therefore, our final job–machine combination would be as under:

MATRIX-E

Jobs	Machines
W	2
X	3
Y	1
Z	4

5.5.3 Index Method

This method is applied to finite job loading. It is called finite because job loading is done according to the capacity of the machine. Under the Index Method, the lowest time or cost required by a particular job–machine combination is taken as the base and the indices for the others are prepared based on the base variation. While doing such allocation, the job with the lowest index is done first followed by the job that is next lowest and so on. However, such allocation has to be done within the capacity of the machine, which should not be exceeded under any circumstance.

For example, we can illustrate the index method of job loading by slightly modifying the earlier example as shown:

Example 2

Suppose X & Co. has now indicated the capacity of the individual machines (considering other job loads) in terms of hours available as follows:

Jobs	Machines			
	1	2	3	4
W	8	4	7	14
X	15	12	9	3
Y	9	18	12	16
Z	10	20	15	5
Hours available in each Machine	14	15	13	10

Solution

We have solved this problem as under:

Jobs	1		2		3		4	
	Hours	Index	Hours	Index	Hours	Index	Hours	Index
W	8	2.00	4	1.00	7	1.75	14	3.50
X	15	5.00	12	4.00	9	3.00	3	1.00
Y	9	1.00	18	2.00	12	1.33	16	1.77
Z	10	2.00	20	4.00	15	3.00	5	1.00
Hours available	14		15		13		10	
Hours allocated	9		4		0		(5+3) = 8	

As you can see from the matrix, Job 'Y' has the lowest index in Line 1, and it is within the capacity of the machine, hence it is allocated there. The next job 'W' is therefore allocated to Line 2 and 'Z' to Line 4. Line 3 will remain idle. The table shows that the company can bag further orders to feed Line 3 and to utilize the surplus capacities of the other lines, as well.

5.6 SEQUENCING

Sequencing is the process of determining the order of job processing. Sequencing considers job processing at different work centers, and also at individual level work stations. To meet the pressing needs of the customers, often, work centres may be overloaded, for obvious volume and length of job orders. This makes the process of sequencing complicated. At this stage, companies need to consider the tradeoff between the cost of waiting and the cost of idle time at different work centres. Such a trade off is done using different sequencing rules, based on which job loading is prioritized.

5.6.1 Sequencing Rules

Sequencing determines the order of job processing. Sequencing covers job allocation, both for the work centres and at the individual machine level. Various priority rules for job sequencing can be drawn from the pioneering work of Volkmann, Berry, Whybark and Jacobs (2005) as follows:

1. **Random (R)** Choose jobs in the queue with equal probability, and use the same as a benchmark to compare with other rules.
2. **First come first served (FCFS)** This rule demands the processing of jobs in the order of their arrival.
3. **Shortest processing time (SPT)** This rule requires processing of jobs which have the shortest processing time requirement. Obviously, it helps reduce the work-in-process inventory, and the average job lateness.
4. **Earliest due date (EDD)** As per this rule, jobs with the earliest due dates are processed first. This rule is more customer friendly as job lateness can be avoided substantially.
5. **Critical ratio (CR)** This rule calculates the priority index using the formula: due date – now/lead time remaining. It is more suitable for job scheduling and is widely used.
6. **Least work remaining (LWR)** This rule is as extension of the SPT method. The basis of this rule is to schedule jobs as per the remaining processing time. As a result, with less remaining work in the process, production scheduling is done earlier.
7. **Fewest operations remaining (FOR)** This rule, like SPT, requires job sequencing based on the number of operations remaining for the jobs. When fewer operations remain, the job is scheduled.
8. **Slack time (ST)** This rule is more like EDD, and it utilizes the slack variable. Slack is determined by subtracting the sum of setup and processing times from the remaining time till the due date.
9. **Slack time per operation (ST/O)** In this method, slack time is divided by the number of remaining operations till job completion, and job scheduling is done for those cases with the smallest values.
10. **Next queue (NQ)** The NQ method considers queues at each succeeding work center, according to which jobs move. Jobs with the smallest queue are processed first.
11. **Least setup (LSU)** This rule requires the processing of those jobs first which have minimum changeover time on a given machine.

Sequencing rules assume that job sequencing is independent of the setup time and setup costs. Operationally, however, this may not always be the case, as jobs that require similar setups can reduce setup time when sequenced back to back.

Thus, the setup time and processing times are deterministic and not variable; there will be no interruptions in processing if the set of jobs is known, no new jobs arrive after processing begins, and no jobs are cancelled.

The choice of which rule is most appropriate depends on the average job lateness and the average number of jobs in the system. Least job lateness will ensure customer satisfaction, optimum utilization of machines, reduced slack time, etc. The above rules enable an organization to choose the best option for job sequencing which causes least job lateness or slack time. Let us study the following example to understand the sequencing method:

Example 3

X & Co. has indicated process time for four jobs with their respective due dates as follows:

Jobs	Process Time (in days)	Due Date (in days from now)
W	5	12
X	6	18
Y	7	21
Z	10	14

Let us prioritize these jobs following different rules of job sequencing.

Solution

As a first step, it is necessary to compute the following:

i. Total completion time
ii. Average completion time
iii. Average number of jobs in the system
iv. Average job lateness

Solution 1 (MINPRT/SOT)

Job Order sequence	Process time	Flow time/Cumulative process time	Due Date	Job Lateness
W	5	5	12	0
X	6	11	18	0
Y	7	18	21	3
Z	10	28	14	14
Total	28	62		17

1. **Total completion time** 28 days is the total of process time to complete all jobs
2. **Average completion time** The average time or days that jobs remain in the system. This is calculated by dividing the Total Flow Time by the number of jobs in the system, in this case, 62 divided by 4 = 15.5
3. **Average number of jobs in the system** This is calculated by dividing Total Flow Time by Total Process Time, here that means 62/28=2.21
4. **Average job lateness** Obtained by dividing Total Job Lateness by Total number of jobs in the system. Therefore, in this system, 17/4=4.25

Solution -2 (FCFS)

If we follow the FCFS (First Come First Served) Method for this problem, we will get the same result as above. Thus, Total Completion Time, Average Completion Time, Average Number of jobs in the system and Average Job Lateness under the FCFS rules are the same as those obtained under the MINPRT/SOT rule.

Solution -3 (LPT)

Job Order/ Sequence	Process Time	Flow Time/ Cumulative Process Time	Due Date	Job Lateness
Z	10	10	14	0
Y	7	17	21	0
X	6	23	18	5
W	5	28	12	16
Total	28	78		21

1. **Total Completion Time:** 28 days
2. **Average Completion Time:** 78/4, i.e. 19.5
3. **Average No. of Jobs in the System:** 78/28, i.e. 2.78
4. **Average Job Lateness:** 21/4 = 5.25

Solution - 4 (DD)

Job Order/ Sequence	Process Time	Flow Time/ Cumulative Process Time	Due Date	Job Lateness
W	5	5	12	0
Z	10	15	14	1
X	6	21	18	3
Y	7	28	21	7
Total	28	69		11

1. **Total Completion Time:** 28 days
2. **Average Completion Time:** 69/4= 17.5 days
3. **Average Number of Jobs in the System:** 69/28 = 2.46 Nos.
4. **Average Job Lateness:** 11/4 = 2.75 days

Solution - 5 (DS/RO)

According to this method, it is necessary to indicate separately the number of operations against each job. There may be a number of operations for any given job. For example, for manufacturing a Ball point pen, the operations involved would be:

1. Put Polymer dust in the dice to get the body
2. Fix metal parts like holding pins etc. on the cover
3. Insert refill into body
4. Emboss brand name/logo
5. Pack the final product

The rules discussed earlier are static but this rule is dynamic. In our hypothetical problem, let us assume the number of operations involved in each job is as follows:

Job W	2
Job X	3
Job Y	2
Job Z	4

As stated earlier, if the number of operations are not specified, it is assumed to be one. Given the above number of operations, we shall now solve the problem. First, the job sequences have to be ranked in order of minimum slack time or DS/RO ratio and the jobs re-arranged according to the computed values.

Job sequence	Processing time	Desired delivery date	DS/RO ratio	Rank
W	5	12	3.5	2
X	6	18	4	3
Y	7	21	7	4
Z	10	14	1	1

Now as per the rank (given in the last column), we have to arrange the job sequence and compute the earlier details, these are Average Completion Time, Average Job Lateness, etc.

Job sequence	Processing times	Flow Time/cumulative processing time	Due Date	Job Lateness
Z	10	10	14	0
W	5	15	12	3
X	6	21	18	3
Y	7	28	21	7
Total	28	74		13

Total Completion Time = 28 days

Average Completion Time = 74/4 = 18.5 days

Average Number of Jobs in the System = 74/28 = 2.64

Average Job Lateness = 13/4 = 3.25 days

We can now compare different job sequences using the different prioritization rules and decide which is better under the given situation:

Sequencing/Priority Rules	Total Time	Average Completion times	Average No. of Jobs in the System	Average Job Lateness
MINPRT	28	15.5	2.21	4.25
FCFS	28	15.5	2.21	4.25
LPT	28	19.5	2.78	5.25
DD	28	17.25	2.46	2.75
DS/RO	28	18.5	2.64	4.25

One criterion is not sufficient to compare the different rules; therefore we have to consider all the resultant figures under the various sequencing rules. However, importance is given to two criteria – Average job lateness and the Average number of jobs in the system. Accordingly, therefore, the DD method is considered more efficient than the other methods, in the above example.

5.7 JOHNSON'S RULE FOR SCHEDULING

S.M. Johnson developed this sequencing process which helps to minimize the idle time of different work centres by optimum job allocation. This is applied where a number of jobs have to be processed through different work centres. The basic principles of this sequencing system are as follows:

Step 1 Listing respective time requirement of each job at each workstation.

Step 2 We need to consider the job with the shortest processing time. If this job is meant for the first workstation, it can be scheduled first. However, if the job with the shortest processing time is meant for workstation 2, we will schedule it last. If two or more jobs of work centres 1 or 2 have the same processing time, an arbitrary decision needs to be taken.

Step 3 Once the first and last jobs have been identified under step 2, and they have been allocated, we do not consider these jobs further.

Step 4 Positions are assigned to all the other jobs following the same logic explained in steps 2 and 3.

We shall explain this rule through an example where there are two work centres.

Example 4

X and Co. is engaged in casting and machining of different groups of jobs. Casting operations are carried out in Work Centre 1 and machining in Work Centre 2; these two operations complete the entire job. We are going to schedule the jobs, allocating them between the two Work Centres, so as to minimize idle time as much as possible. The following information provides data on time required at each Work Centre for all the job groups:

Job Title	Casting (Work Centre-1 - in days)	Machining (Work Centre-2 in days)
A	6	7
B	8	8
C	16	2
D	7	3

Solution

Step 1 Listing of all the jobs with their respective time requirements at different work centres, as done above.

Steps 2,to 4 We see from the table that job 'C' in Work Centre 2 has the lowest processing time. Therefore, according to Johnson's Rule, it will be assigned last. Similarly, Job 'D' has the second lowest processing time, hence it will be assigned second last. Job 'A' in Work Centre 1 has the third shortest processing time and is therefore scheduled first. The sequencing position will therefore look like this: *A?DC*

Since there is only job left, i.e. 'B', this will be assigned next to 'A'. The final scheduling would therefore be:

Position of Sequencing	• 1	2	3	4
Jobs assigned	A	B	D	C

The sequential times for two work centres would be as below:

Work Centre 1	6	8	7	16
Work Centre 2	7	8	3	2

Using a Gantt chart, we can illustrate the Johnson's algorithm as follows:

Work Centre-1A			B		D			C		
	6				8		7		16	
Work Centre-2	Idle Hours	A	Idle Hours	B	D		Idle Hours	C	Idle Hours	
	6	7	1	8	3		4	2	14	

5.7.1 More Examples of Johnson's Rule for Scheduling Jobs through Two Work Centers

Steps

1. From the list of unscheduled jobs, select the job with the shortest processing time in either work center.
2. If the shortest time is at the first work center, perform those jobs that are first in the schedule, otherwise, take up the job that is last in the schedule.
3. Remove the job assigned in Step 2 from the list of unscheduled jobs.
4. Repeat steps 1, 2 and 3 filling in the schedule from the front and the back until all jobs have been scheduled.

Example 5

A company produces different types of ball pens using two machines. Time requirements for producing the ball pens as per orders are as under:

Ball Pens	Machine-1	Machine-2
A	4	2
B	3	5
C	5	1
D	7	3
E	8	6

Questions

1. Determine the order of tasks using Johnson's Rule.
2. Determine the time requirement for doing all the jobs.
3. Calculate how many hours Machine-1 will remain idle?
4. Calculate how many hours Machine-2 will remain idle?

Answers

1. B-E-D-A-C
2. 28
3. 1
4. 11

Example 6

Your company needs to perform seven tasks using two work centres. Time requirement in hours for each task at the two work centres is presented below:

Tasks	Work Centre-1	Work Centre-II
A	2.58	3.47
B	1.66	5.84
C	2.71	2.41
D	5.52	1.99
E	3.38	7.62
F	5.22	1.73
G	2.89	1.11

Questions

1. Determine the sequence of tasks
2. Determine the time requirement to complete all tasks at both the work centres
3. Determine the total idle hours for work centre-I
4. Determine the total idle hours for work centre-II

Answers

a. B-A-E-C-D-F-G

b. 25.83

c. 1.87

d. 1.66

5.8 GANTT CHARTS

The Gantt chart, named after its inventor, Henry Gantt (1917), is a very effective scheduling tool, which can help managers to enforce control over job loading and scheduling, balancing the plan and the actual results on the shop floor. The chart facilitates tracking of the present state of production, and accordingly, helps in scheduling the jobs that are in the queue. Although we find different types of Gantt charts, for scheduling, we commonly use the load chart and the schedule chart. *Load charts* display the loading and idle times for machines or departments. This chart, therefore, explains which jobs are to be scheduled to start, and which job is expected to be finished, and where we expect the idle time to occur. A *schedule chart*, on the other hand, is used to monitor job progress. In a schedule chart, the vertical axis shows the orders or jobs in progress, while the horizontal axis represents time. We can also find Gantt charts in the form of records charts, which track the actual time spent on delays, etc.

Gantt Charts have to be updated at regular intervals, for instance, when commencement of the work is delayed, or when work continues beyond its time schedule or if the progress of work is not as per the actual plan. If unforeseen eventualities occur, corrective action may have to be taken and this will also need corresponding changes in the Gantt chart.

Thus, in the form of a matrix, a Gantt chart lists, on the vertical axis, all the tasks to be performed. Each row contains a single task identification which usually consists of a number and name. The horizontal axis of the chart indicates the estimated time requirements, requirements of skill and persons who are assigned for the job. Along with this information, the chart in the other column shows the time duration for the project.

The horizontal bars for the jobs show both the estimated start and end time, and actual start and end time in different colours (for distinction). This facilitates comparison.

Variants of this method include a lower chart which shows personnel allocations on a person-by-person basis. For this section, the vertical axis contains the number of people assigned to the project, and the columns indicating task duration are left blank, as is the column indicating the person assigned. The graphics consists of the same bar notation as in the upper chart which indicates that the person is working on a task. The value of this lower chart is evident when it shows slack time for the project personnel, that is, times when they are not actually working on any project.

The advantages and disadvantages of Gantt Charts are discussed below:

Advantages

1. This is a simple and very inexpensive method and can be developed even by supervisory staff with some amount of training.
2. These charts clearly show the decided time and work schedule for each job.

3. Monitoring and control is easier and can be done within a minimum time frame and at the lowest cost.
4. These charts can be changed and updated quickly at a lower cost.
5. There is no need to develop customized Gantt Chart Boards as standard Chart Boards are available in the market.

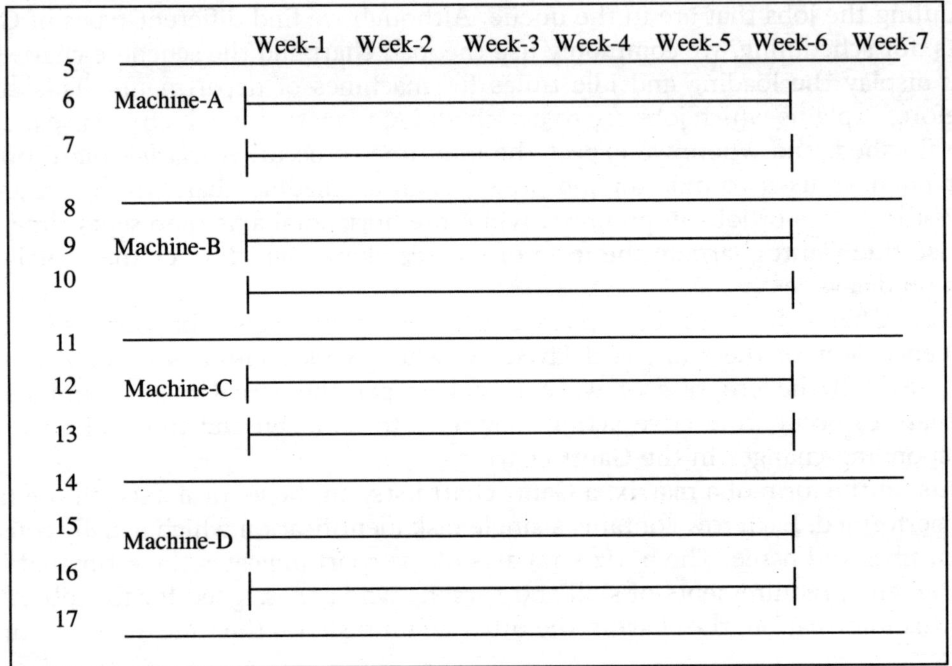

Figure 5.1 *Gantt load chart*

Disadvantages

1. They do not show job inter-relationships and interdependencies.
2. Cost implications cannot be shown.
3. With these charts, it is not possible to depict other alternatives for project completion.
4. The shape and form of Gantt charts can differ according to the nature of the requirement. Fig. 5.1 is a very simple Gantt Load Chart.

The above chart shows that Machine-A has been loaded till week 5 for a given job, and Machine-B has been loaded till the first half of the 4th week and so on.

With computer support, Gantt Charts (Fig. 5.2) can now be generated using software. One such computer generated Gantt chart drawn using Excel is presented in Fig. 5.2.

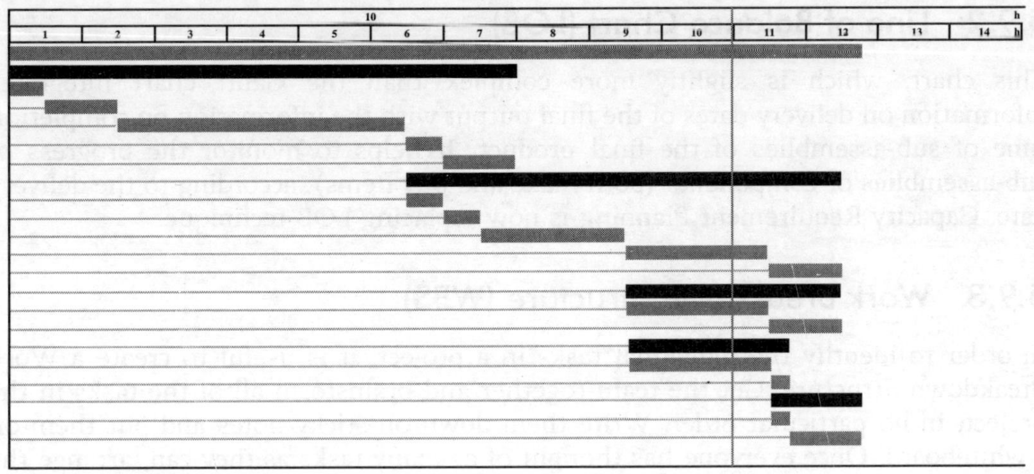

Figure 5.2 *Gantt chart generated using Excel*

The horizontal bar graph on the chart represents the time requirement for the activity. This is called an occupancy style Gantt chart.

5.9 MORE SCHEDULING TOOLS AND TECHNIQUES

5.9.1 Dispatching

Another common technique for job sequencing is dispatching or the dispatch list. In this method, the jobs are ranked and relative priorities are given which are based either on Due Date or on the Critical Ratio. The Due Date (of delivery) has been explained above, Critical Ratio is computed by dividing Time Remaining by Work Remaining, as shown below:

$$\text{Critical Ratio (CR)} = \frac{\text{Time remaining (TR)}}{\text{Work remaining (WR)}}$$

A CR equal to 1 means that the job is on schedule, a CR of less than 1 indicates that the job is behind schedule and a CR of more than 1 is indicative of slack time.

The Production Planning Department prepares a dispatch list based on relative priority, and work responsibility is assigned to those in charge of various shop floors. Traditionally, such persons are called either Dispatchers or Planners; it is their responsibility to visit the shop floor to collect data on work progress according to the Dispatch list and also give the prepared Dispatch list to those in charge of the shop floor. Because of increasing reliance on computerized Management Information Systems (MIS), they are now becoming redundant.

5.9.2 Line of Balance Chart (LOB)

This chart, which is slightly more complex than the Gantt chart integrates information on delivery dates of the final output with the information on completion time of sub-assemblies of the final product. It helps to monitor the progress of sub-assemblies or components (both make and buy items), according to the delivery date. Capacity Requirement Planning is now replacing LOB technique.

5.9.3 Work Breakdown Structure (WBS)

In order to identify the individual tasks in a project, it is useful to create a Work Breakdown Structure. Get the team together and brainstorm all of the tasks in the project, in no particular order. Write them down on sticky notes and put them on a whiteboard. Once everyone has thought of as many tasks as they can, arrange the sticky notes into groups under the major areas of activity.

A detailed project plan is developed based on the understanding of tasks, and the time requirement. Also it considers the resource requirement, and allocation of jobs to workers. All these we do, using the work breakdown structure. A tentative work breakdown table can be drawn as under:

WBS number	Task Description
1.0	Project initiation
1.1	Draft project plan
2.0	Analysis phase
2.1	Plan user interviews
2.2	Schedule user interviews
3.0	Examination and test
4.0	Design
5.0	Test
6.0	Implementation
7.0	Post implementation review

5.9.4 Milestone Charts

Milestones charts help us to sequence our jobs in logical order, keeping pace with resource constraints. To develop this chart, we need to understand the priorities of our operations. It is used particularly in mapping the project life cycle to facilitate our understanding of project-centric milestones, that is, different levels of achievement in terms of project deliverables. This chart is also used as a reporting tool to top management. In job scheduling, this chart helps in documenting the important events of activities to enable us to conform to the deadlines. Obviously, because of its importance, in many important operational activities, that is, this chart can also be used in machine installation, production changeover, execution of orders, etc.

5.10 QUEUING THEORY

Queuing theory is applied for service scheduling, although it can be equally important for arriving at production job scheduling decisions. In any situation, where there is competition for limited resources, the problem of queuing is bound to occur. For example in a restaurant, we need to queue up or wait for the services; jobs are queued up for processing through machines. Using queuing theory, we can understand the queuing phenomenon and optimize our systems to manage the queue. With fewer queues, we can increase customer spread and gain in terms of productive use of resources.

To solve the queuing problem, first, we have to design the queuing system, balancing the customers' services and optimization of our available resources. Accordingly, using the work breakdown structure (WBS), we understand various sub-systems or entities of queuing for different activities.

The following information helps us solve queuing problems:

- Process of arrival of customers; say single arrival, arrival in groups, etc.
- Probability distribution of arrival time
- Finite or infinite population

The process of arrival may be constant, that is, the time interval between successive arrivals could be the same, or random. Customers' arrival at random shows a typical *Poisson distribution pattern*, this is a situation where customers' arrival is time independent, or exponentially distributed. Also, we see cases of scheduled arrivals, batch arrivals, etc.

The mechanism of services – the distribution of service time, availability of number of servers (separate or parallel), etc. need to be considered.

Similar considerations of queuing characteristics – first-in-first-out (FIFO), last-in-first-out (LIFO), first-come-first-served (FCFS), random, etc. is essential to solve queuing problems.

Queuing problems can be solved using analytic methods, like the use of formulae, and computer-based simulation. For example, to solve queuing problems for a busy airport, computer-based simulation is the right choice. However, to solve the queuing problem in a restaurant, we can use analytic methods.

The following symbols are used in solving problems using the analytic queuing model:

$Q(t)$	Length of Q at time t
$A(t)$	Cumulative arrivals of customers to form the queue at time t
$D(t)$	Cumulative departures of customers from the queue at time t
μ	The maximum possible service rate
$\mu(t)$	The rate of service at time t
$\lambda(t)$	Arrival rate at time t

For application of queuing models, we consider four major types of flow as follows:

Types of Flow	**Importance**
t_0	The point at which $\lambda(t)$ equals the maximum rate of service μ
t_1	At this point $\lambda(t)$ is maximum
t_2	At this point $\lambda(t)$ is decreased to μ
t_3	This is the final point where queue problem gets resolved, i.e., $\mu(t) = \lambda(t)$

A queue graph is quadratic for its obvious two times differentiation attributes at or near t_1.

Therefore, a queuing equation is as follows:

$$\lambda(t) = \lambda(t) = \beta(t - t_1)^2$$

Where constant is represented by:

$$\beta = -\frac{1}{2}\frac{d^2\lambda(t)}{dt^2}|_{t=t_1}$$

For small $t - t_1$; $t_0 < t < t_3$, i.e., t_0 and t_2 can be estimated by substitution as under:

$$\mu = \lambda(t_0)$$

$$= \lambda(t_1) - \beta(t_0 - t_1)^2$$

$$t_0 = t_1 - \left(\frac{\lambda(t_1) - \mu}{\beta}\right)^2$$

$$t_2 = t_1 + \left(\frac{\lambda(t_1) - \mu}{\beta}\right)^2$$

The queue length is:

$$Q(t) = A(t) - D(t)$$

$$= \int_{t_0}^{t} [\lambda(t) - \mu(t)]dt$$

Using the substitutions, we can derive the substitution as under:

$$Q(t) = \int_{t_0}^{t} [\lambda(t) - \mu(t)]dt$$

$$= \beta(t - t_0)^2 \left(\frac{t_2 - t_0}{2} - \frac{t - t_0}{3} \right)$$

5.10.1 Problems on Queuing

A fast food centre in the heart of a business hub faces queuing problem during lunch hours, while at other times, such queuing is almost absent. The shop does not like to lose customers, and has asked you to suggest the optimum number of service boys to be employed, based on the data of average number of customers during lunch hours; this would include factors like the queue length, idle time of the service boys as a percentage of their total working time. The shop owner is prepared to employ up to five service boys.

To help in your decision making, the following information has been made available by the shop owner:

- Mean time taken by the service boys to serve an order is 2 minutes, and the standard deviation is 5/4 minutes.
- Because of the space availability, the fast food centre can accommodate any number of customers inside the shop.
- Arrival of customers follows a Poisson distribution pattern with a mean of 25 per hour.
- The shop follows the first-come-first-served principle of customers' service.

Solution

We can solve this problem using the steps below:

1. Calculate Lq and W as under:

   $$r = \frac{\lambda}{\mu} = \frac{25}{30} = \frac{5}{6}$$

   $$p = \frac{\lambda}{c\mu} = \frac{r}{c} = \frac{5}{6c}$$

   Lq is the average length of queue

   W is the percentage of service boys remaining idle.

2. Calculate p_0 (p represents number of orders per hour), L_q, and W to assess the idle time using the equation below:

   $$p_0 \left(\sum_{n=0}^{c-1} \frac{r^n}{n!} + \frac{r^c}{c!(1-p)} \right)^{-1}$$

$$L_q = \frac{r^c p p_0}{c!(1-p)^2} = \frac{5^{c+1} p_0}{6^{c+1} c! c \left(1 - \frac{5}{6c}\right)^2}$$

$$w = \frac{1}{\mu} + \frac{L_q}{\lambda} = \frac{1}{30} + \frac{L_q}{25}$$

$$\text{Idle time} = 1 - p = 1 - \frac{5}{6c}$$

3. Get the results of these equations to arrive at the number of service boys to be engaged to optimize resources.

Answer

Solving all the five equations, we can come to the conclusion that 1 or 2 service boys will be enough to ensure customer services without much of a queuing problem. Using standard computer programmes, such decisional problems can be solved quickly.

SUMMARY

1. Scheduling is a decision-making function which has high strategic significance in terms of cost minimization, customer satisfaction and resource optimization in manufacturing and service industries.
2. Apart from production and services, scheduling is also applied to procurement, supply chain management, information processing and communication.
3. The scheduling function makes use of mathematical optimization techniques or heuristic methods to allocate limited resources to the processing of tasks either related to production or services, or in areas like procurement or supply chain management.
4. Production scheduling has a rich history. F.W. Taylor (1911), Henry Gantt (1916), and S.M. Johnson (1954) are the major contributors to the concept of production scheduling. F.W. Taylor introduced the concept of planning for effective manufacturing, and viewed it as a decision-making process. Henry Gantt discussed the role of scheduling in the job shop manufacturing process, and introduced a chart named after him. S.M. Johnson introduced the principles of optimal solution of scheduling problems through mathematical algorithms.
5. Scheduling of service operations is also important for restaurants, banks, customer service centres, hospitals and various public utility services. Job scheduling also helps in batch production, in job loading, sequencing, Gantt charts, dispatching, Line of Balance Chart (LOB), Work Breakdown Structure (WBS), Milestone Charts.
6. Queuing theory is important for production and also for taking services-related job scheduling decisions. Using queuing theory, we can understand the queuing phenomenon and optimize our systems to manage the queue. With fewer

queues we can increase customer spread and gain in terms of productive use of resources.

KEY WORDS

Drum-Buffer-Rope (DBR) This method helps us understand both the scheduling constraints and the constraints of managing operations (internal constraints). In other words, we call this method, capacity-constrained resource planning.

Index Method This method is applied to finite job loading cases. It is called finite because job loading is done according to the capacity of the machine. Under the Index Method, the lowest time or cost required by a particular job–machine combination is taken as the base, and the indices for the others are prepared based on the base variation.

Dynamic Slack/Remaining Operation (DS/RO) or Minimum Slack per Operation Method (MINSOP) In DS/RO, we first calculate Dynamic Slack (DS), which is the difference between Due Time and Processing Time and then divide this DS by the Remaining Operation (RO). Unless specified, it will be assumed that RO is one. The final scheduling of the job is done as per the ranking of DS/RO. Jobs with the lowest value are attended to first, a similar ranking is given in the order of the next lowest and so on

Johnson's Rule S.M. Johnson developed this sequencing process which helps to minimize the idle time of different work centres by optimum job allocation. This is applied where a number of jobs have to be processed through different work centres.

Milestone Charts Milestones mark significant events in the life of a project, usually critical activities which must be achieved on time to avoid delay in the project. Milestones should be truly significant and reasonable in terms of deadlines (avoid using intermediate stages).

Work Breakdown Structure (WBS) In order to identify the individual tasks in a project, it is useful to create a Work Breakdown Structure. Get the team together and brainstorm all of the tasks in the project, in no particular order. Write them down on sticky notes and put them on a whiteboard. Once everyone has thought of as many tasks as they can, arrange the sticky notes into groups under the major areas of activity.

Batch Production Scheduling This type of scheduling performs planning and scheduling of production in the batch manufacturing process when the capacity is finite. In batch production, a job is construed as a set of identical parts; hence, it needs to be processed as a whole. This therefore requires processing of batch production jobs in full, before sequencing or scheduling other jobs.

Sequencing is the process of determining the order of job processing. Sequencing considers job processing at different work centers, and also at individual level work stations.

GENERAL REVIEW QUESTIONS

1. Explain job loading and the steps involved. Does it differ from the Index Method? Illustrate your answer with some examples.
2. What are the different rules of job sequencing? In your opinion, which rule is the best and why do you consider this the best?
3. When should the Johnson's Rule be applied?
4. Explain the advantages and disadvantages of Gantt charts. Are dispatching and LOB better alternatives than Gantt charts?
5. Explain the history of production scheduling.
6. Describe how Queuing theory can help in production scheduling.
7. What are the components of production scheduling?
8. Short notes

   (a) Forward scheduling
   (b) Backward scheduling
   (c) Critical ratio
   (d) Job lateness
   (e) Due date
   (f) Sequencing

CRITICAL REVIEW QUESTIONS

1. A bank has approached you to help them develop a detailed document listing cycle time requirement for different types of customer services. As an acknowledged job scheduler, explain what are the steps and methods you will follow for developing this document.
2. A departmental store has fifty different product display counters under one roof. Each counter displays similar products. The store often observes that in some counters, queuing by customers is an acute problem, while customers hardly visit some other product counters. An effective layout plan creates compelling pressure on customers to visit the stores. Each product centre is manned by three salespersons. The store observed that their inventory holding is significantly low in more than 50% of the product display counters, while in another 50%, inventory holding is medium to high. The store wants your suggestion to manage the queuing problem.

REFERENCES

1. Alford, Leon P. 1934. *Henry Laurence Gantt: Leader in Industry*, New York: ASME.
2. Gantt, Henry L. 1916. *Work, Wages, and Profits*, 2nd ed. New York: Engineering Magazine Co., Reprinted 1973. Easton, Maryland: Hive Publishing Company.
3. Gantt, Henry L. 1919. *Organizing for Work*. New York: Harcourt, Brace, and Howe. Reprinted 1973. Easton, Maryland: Hive Publishing Company.
4. Johnson, S.M. 1954. Optimal two-and three-stage production schedules with setup times included. *Naval Research Logistics Quarterly*, Volume 1, pages 61–68
5. Taylor, Frederick W. 1911. *Shop Management*. New York: Harper and Bros.
6. Volkmann, Thomas E., William L. Berry, Clay D. Whybark, and F. Robert Jacobs. 2005. *Manufacturing Planning and Control for Supply Chain Management*, 5th ed. New York: Irwin McGraw-Hill.

ADDITIONAL REFERENCES

1. Cohen, M.A. 1997. *Manufacturing Automation*. Chicago: Irwin.
2. Konz. Stephen. 1983. *Work Design: Industrial Ergonomics*, 2nd edition New York: John Wiley & Sons.
3. Richard, B., Chase, Nicholas, J., Aquilano, and F. Robert, Jacobs. 2002. *Operations Management for Competitive Advantage*. New Delhi: Tata McGraw-Hill Publishing Company Limited.
4. Schmenner, R.W. 1995. *Service Operations Management*. Englewood Cliffs, M.J: Prentice Hall.
5. Brucker, Peter. 2004. *Scheduling Algorithms*, Fourth Edition. Berlin: Springer-Verlag.
6. Clark, Wallace. 1942. *The Gantt Chart, a Working Tool of Management*, second edition. London: Sir Isaac Pitman & Sons, Ltd.
7. Herrmann, Jeffrey W. 2006. A History of Production Scheduling, in *Handbook of Production Scheduling*. New York: Springer
8. McKay, Kenneth N., and Vincent C.S. Wiers. 2006. The human factor in planning and scheduling, in *Handbook of Production Scheduling*, J.W. Herrmann, ed., New York: Springer.
9. Pinedo, Michael, and Xiuli Chao. 1999. *Operations Scheduling with Applications in Manufacturing and Services*. Boston: Irwin McGraw Hill.
10. Thompson, C. Bertrand. 1974. *The Taylor System of Scientific Management*. Easton, Maryland: Hive Publishing Company. (Reprint of the 1917 edition published by A.W. Shaw Co., Chicago.)
11. Pinedo, Michael L. 2005. *Planning and Scheduling in Manufacturing and Services*. New York: Springer.
12. Morse, P. M. 1958. *Queues, Inventories and Maintenance*. New York: John Wiley & Sons.

13. Newel, G. F. 1971. *Applications of Queueing Theory* (Ch. 6). London: Chapman and Hall.

CASE STUDY

Opt for indigenous systems: lessons from a multinational glass manufacturer

A multinational glass manufacturing company, specialized in the production of tempered glass for agriculture and marine use, follows a just-in-time production plan. The company runs its production only on demand; as specialized glass is not a standard saleable item in the market. A just-in-time production plan for such value-added production of specialized glass based on customer demand cannot be controlled manually. It requires computer support for the correct management of activities, including the procurement of materials and supply chain. Realizing this, the company decided to use ERP (enterprise resource planning) modules to substitute their existing manual for production planning and job scheduling systems.

The company hired the services of a noted software developer for customizing the ERP systems for their production planning functions. The ERP vendors after a series of meetings with the planning department of the company could not come to the sign-off stage, causing delays in implementation. Meanwhile, the company decided to continue with their existing practices. With recent technology upgradation, the company's process of manufacturing of tempered glass items has become more complicated. The Company also entered into contracts with the Army, Navy and Air Force to supply items as per their mandated specifications and standards. With the existing market, further addition of value-added demand from the country's security forces, literally dragged the company to an alarming position in terms of the production planning and controlling function. Huge inventory holding scaled down profitability due to the rise in cost. Also, the company utterly failed in the area of manpower planning, as idle hours for some sections of workers increased, while for others, job pressure started mounting. While the company tried to address the problem through quick job redeployment and relocation, the result was not at all encouraging.

To overcome the problem, the company devised their own computerized systems. After pilot testing the same, the company started using the systems with great success.

Discussion Question

List the lessons from the experience of this glass manufacturer. Also, critically comment why this company faced such a problem?

Chapter 6
Work Study and Work Measurement

LEARNING OBJECTIVES

After reading this chapter, you will be able to understand:

- Definitions and Concepts of Work Study and Work Measurement
- Concepts of Job Information, Job Analysis, Job Description, Job Evaluation and Job Pricing
- Work Study and Method Study
- Work Measurement Techniques
- Time Study
- Ergonomics and its Relation to Human Engineering and Machine Design
- Motion Economy and Value Analysis
- Work Sampling and Work Simplification

Opening Vignette

For efficient supply chain and logistics management, a large consumer goods manufacturer carried out a time-and-motion study for validating their costs. Over several months, the company observed that their delivery costs to the customers were increasing. The company until then had used the market-validated Predetermined Motion Time Standards (PMTS) as the basis to price their services. However, over the years, it had significantly improved its systems – it had introduced direct order booking to the warehouses and computer-generated delivery schedules within minutes, etc. With the alarming rise in shipment costs, the company decided to economize on the cost of labour, by developing their own time standards. For this purpose, the company retained the services of professional industrial engineers and had made 300 observations in 30 of its warehouses across the country. The industrial engineers used stop watches to record the time taken for loading and unloading operations up to $1/10^{th}$ of a second. Based on such time records, the company was able to develop time standards for each qualified worker to load or unload at least 300 packets of less than 20 kg weight in an 8-hour work shift. The existing cycle time requirement per loading or unloading, as per the company's records, was 1.25 minutes. Workers received a relaxation allowance of 10% of their total working hours, and a lunch break of an hour.

The workers union resented this change in work flow, and demanded a corresponding increase in wages. The company subsequently educated the workers and drew them into the process of time standards determination to make them understand that the existing change was meant for technology-enabled systems, it was not meant to cause physical exertion. In fact, with the new technology, it was pointed that they were getting more recess time. The process began to work well after a sustained workers education programme.

6.1 INTRODUCTION

Scientific work measurement is an essential prerequisite for successful production and operations management practices. After production planning, layout and location analysis, and job scheduling, companies need to measure work to understand its relative worth, and to scientifically draw up a compensation plan. For production and operations management, work measurement requires effective information and documentation with regard to job analysis, job description and job evaluation. All these processes help in identifying job requirements and suitably describing jobs and job-families, skill sets, skill mapping and developing skill inventories. These are also critical inputs to make decisions about manpower requirements to meet present and future needs. At the outset, we must understand the meaning and context of job analysis, job description and job evaluation. Subsequently, we will relate these to production and operations management issues.

Time-and-motion studies are the most critical inputs for effective work measurement. Without a standard time, companies cannot decide worker's compensation scientifically, and workers cannot assess the expectations of the organization from them. Globally, it is estimated that 12% of total cost is from direct labour. The remaining cost comes from materials (43%) and overheads (45%). However, for the service sector, the direct labour cost is much higher. Developing time standards for each job, and making workers match such standards, is what we seek to achieve through effective work measurement systems. For better cost management, we have to standardize every activity of the organization.

For effective work measurement, we have to consider various inputs through job information, job analysis, job description, job evaluation and then arrive at job pricing.

6.2 JOB INFORMATION

Job information facilitates job evaluation for compensation, in designing and in disseminating information to employees about their duties and responsibilities. Imperfect knowledge due to inadequate job information about their duties and responsibilities also affects the performance of employees and therefore, the overall organizational productivity. In setting performance standards and establishing job objectives, job information is essential both in qualitative and quantitative terms. This also helps in performance appraisal as it is done against set standards, and so, is more scientific.

6.2.1 Objectives of Job Information

The objectives of job information are as follows:

1. The first objective of job information is to communicate duties and responsibilities attached to a job to the employees for their clear understanding. This also helps employees to understand organizational expectations.
2. Another objective of job information is organizational analysis. It helps in work flow analysis with respect to a job and also helps in the identification of redundant work elements in a job, and thus, facilitates job restructuring.
3. Job information also helps in analysing the scope for internal hiring and the requirements of external hiring for staffing various positions in the organization.

Job information provides critical inputs for many human resource management related decisions like

1. promotion
2. transfer/relocation
3. redundancy and
4. compensation designing

6.3 JOB ANALYSIS

A job is a group of essentially similar activities or tasks performed by a person or a group of persons. These activities or tasks together become a job. Job analysis is the process of gathering information about the job and evaluating such information in terms of what is necessary and relevant. Essentially, job analysis involves three issues:

a) nature of the job
b) area of analysis and
c) methods of analysis.

Job analysis can be done based on the organizational manual, time-study reports, former job descriptions, and method studies.

The nature of job information for job analysis depends upon a number of considerations such as:

1. whether the analysis is required for evaluation purposes or for other purposes as well
2. what job level is to be analyzed
3. what type of evaluation plan is to be used and
4. the job knowledge held by the analysts who are going to conduct the evaluation.

6.3.1 Fundamental Purpose of the Job

1. Work elements in the job. It requires the study of specific tasks, areas of responsibility and examples of work.
2. General importance of each job element and its relationship to the total operation. How it is integrated with the total job.
3. Approximate time spent on each task or specific area of responsibility.
4. Scope of the job and its impact on the operation.
5. Inherent authority (not only formal delegation but also latitude of action), and formal or informal audits of work.
6. Working relationships (including supervision).
7. Specific methods, equipment or techniques required for the job.
8. Job climate, including objectives and work environment.
9. Job conditions like physical effort, hazards, discomfort, chasing of deadlines, travel requirement, creativity and innovation required, etc.

6.4 METHODS OF ANALYSIS

Job information can be obtained in various ways, either by a staff analyst or by the individual line manager. Because of functional proximity, it is always better to involve the line managers in compiling job information. One relatively simple and inexpensive method of analysis is collecting job information through the questionnaire–response survey. Direct observation of work performed is another important method job analysis. Observation of work is essential to understand the job role. However, it is more costly and time consuming.

6.4.1 Job Questionnaire

A job questionnaire is a special tool for consolidating job information. It is a printed form, in which essential information about the job may be listed, either by the employee or by his supervisors.

6.4.1.1 *Advantages*

The major advantage of the job questionnaire is that:

1. it uses the knowledge of those who are proximate to the job.
2. In addition, it gives each employee an opportunity to participate and contribute by giving responses to the questionnaire, which facilitates immediate compilation of job information.
3. Another important advantage of the job questionnaire is that compiled information can be used as job descriptions. This, therefore, eliminates the requirement of further writing of job descriptions.
4. Moreover, by using a job questionnaire, organizations also get the benefit of communicating up-to-date job information to their employees.

6.4.1.2 *Disadvantages*

However, the major disadvantages associated with the job questionnaire are that

1. its success depends on the understanding and writing ability of individual employees and supervisors. Inconsistencies may arise in the response pattern for this reason. Such inconsistencies in the response pattern may multiply further when a greater cross-section of employees participates in the questionnaire response/survey.
2. In addition, compiling job information from a questionnaire–response survey may suffer from the problem of exaggeration.

Problems of information quality are inherent in the job questionnaire approach.

6.4.1.3 *Solution*

To eliminate such problems inherent in compiling information through a job questionnaire, it is always better to compile information through a combination of direct observation and job questionnaire. This approach may be time consuming and could involve a huge cost, but it is more scientific, as it eliminates the chance of error by accounting for differences in the perception arising from the gap between what they perceive and what they do.

6.4.2 Job Description

Compiled job information and analysis are translated into job descriptions. Job descriptions are written records of job duties and responsibilities and provide a factual basis for job evaluation. Job descriptions are recorded on a standard form, in a uniform manner. In terms of format, the job descriptions should first name the job, using the title which accurately summarizes the duties assigned. While naming a job, it is always better to consider the job family.

At the operations management level, job descriptions may be limited to a listing of specific duties performed, equipment used and procedures followed. The broader the use of the job description information and the higher the functional level, the longer the job description. Therefore, for operational positions, the job description may be about one page; while for those in higher levels of management, it may run to several pages.

Today's organizations are dynamic and every now and then require restructuring, which also necessitates the re-designing of jobs. Therefore, it is widely believed that showing a job description to employees may cause controversy, and in future, employees may resist doing work which is not specifically listed in their job descriptions. However, if job descriptions are well developed, there is nothing wrong in sharing them with the employees, as they spell out the list of duties employees are expected to perform. To eliminate the problem, an all inclusive statement like: 'in addition to the listed duties and responsibilities, your superior may ask you to perform other tasks from time to time' can be included.

By sharing job descriptions with employees, organizations can make their job evaluation process participative and avoid any dissonance on job evaluation results. This is also important, as organizations also have to deal with employee dissatisfaction about job pricing. Communication of job descriptions enhances acceptance of the same, as employees are not left with any doubts about their duties and responsibilities. Such communication with the employees should be an on-going exercise, as it also helps employees understand the changes, if any, in their job duties and responsibilities.

6.4.2.1 Management and the Use of Job Description

Job descriptions help in getting things done through people, and help management to accomplish the following objectives:

1. Efficient organization of jobs
2. Proper recruitment or staffing
3. Assigning jobs to people by communicating to them their duties and responsibilities and by setting job standards
4. Performance review
5. Improving performance through appraisal and training.
6. Rewarding employees

Therefore, job descriptions play a very critical role in key management activities. However, it is very important for the manager to ensure that job descriptions are correct, and whatever jobs have been assigned, are essential. He/she must ensure that only essential tasks have been grouped into jobs. Since job descriptions have interconnectivity, it has to be aligned to recruitment, performance appraisal, training needs, and promotion, transfer and relocation decisions. From the employees' point of view, it should also show them what is expected of them and indicate how to do the work assigned.

By listing the assigned duties in a job description, a manager can determine reasonable performance standards. Identification of such performance standards facilitates benchmarking of the performance of an employee against the best performer.

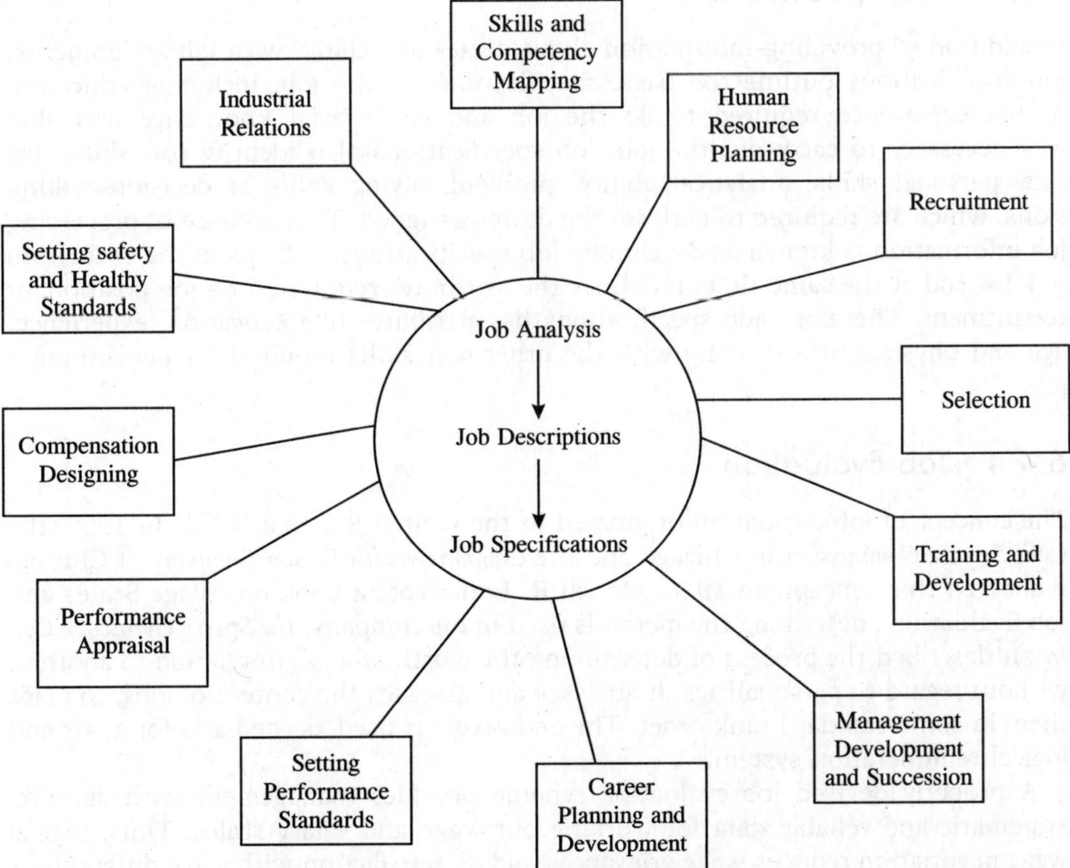

Figure 6.1 *Job analysis: a central peripheral relational model*

Job descriptions also facilitate proper manpower utilization. By periodically reviewing the listed duties, a manager can identify those jobs that are time consuming, but require a lower skill-set. He can reassign such jobs, accordingly, to lower-paid employees. In addition, the manager can also study jobs in terms of workload and determine man-hours required. For low technology and low-skill jobs, he may decide to off-load the job to sub-contractors. Therefore, it has tremendous implications for effective human resource management in an organization. We may also call this an instrument for proper rightsizing of employees in an organization.

Finally, job descriptions, as a basic management tool, also influence operating procedures by identifying duplication of work, indicating scientific workflow, suggesting better allocation of jobs and by pointing out possible job bottlenecks.

A central peripheral relational model of job analysis is given in Fig. 6.1.

6.4.3 Job Specifications

In addition to providing information about duties associated with job assignments, job specifications outline the basic specifications of the job, including education or the experience required to do the job and the special knowledge and skill sets necessary to carry out the job. Job specifications also identify soft skills like inter-personal skills, analytical ability, problem-solving skills or decision-making skills, which are required to perform the duties assigned. This exercise of processing job information is known as developing job specifications. It helps in the evaluation of jobs, and at the same time, it defines the attributes required for a job position, at recruitment. Therefore, job specifications list attributes like education, experience, age and physical fitness along with the other soft skills required for performing a job.

6.4.4 Job Evaluation

The concept of job evaluation originated in the United States in 1971. In 1909, the *Civil Service Commission* in Chicago and the *Commonwealth Edison Company* of Chicago pioneered this concept. In 1926, Merrill R. Lott wrote a book on 'Wage Scales and Job Evaluation', describing the methods used in his company, *the Sperry Gyroscope Co., Inc*. It described the process of determining the worth of a job in relation to another, without regard to personalities. It analyses and assesses the content of jobs, to place them in some standard rank order. The end result is used as the basis for a fair and logical remuneration system.

A properly devised job evaluation scheme provides management with definite, systematic and reliable data for working out wage and salary scales. Thus, logical wage negotiation reduces wage grievances and dissatisfaction with wage differentials and ensures fair treatment for each employee. It also provides a logical basis for promotion. A survey by the *British Institute of Management* indicated the following reasons for its use:

- To reduce layout turnover (Layout turnover indicates the flow of time within the operating systems. Increased layout turnover time indicates loss of production).
- To increase output
- To improve morale

- To reducc loss of timc due to wage negotiation and disputes
- To reduce complaints regarding wages
- To reduce wage and salary anomalies.

6.4.4.1 *Steps in Job Evaluation*

- Thorough examination of the job (job assessment)
- Preparation of job description (recording its characteristics to suit assessment of the method)
- Preparation of job analysis to set out the requirements of the job under various headings
- Comparison of one job with another
- Arrangement of jobs in a progression
- Relating the progression of jobs to a money scale

6.4.4.2 *Types of Job Evaluation Schemes*

There are four basic types of job evaluation. These are:

1. **Ranking** This is a simple system to judge each job as a whole, to understand its relative worth by ranking one whole job against another job. To start with, a job description is prepared in a narrative form, stating duties, responsibilities and qualifications required for the job. Jobs are then ranked in order of relative difficulty or value to the company and grade levels are then defined and wage levels are finalized. One of the disadvantages of this method is that the degree of difference between jobs cannot be indicated. Ranking, therefore, may be incorrect and unduly influenced. The relative value of the employees (currently occupying these jobs) may be ranked, rather than the jobs. The methods may be adequate for the easily-defined jobs of a small number of workmen, but it is impracticable for complicated jobs involving a large number of workmen.

2. **Classification** This is different from ranking, as in this case, grade and wage levels are pre-determined before jobs are ranked and descriptions are written defining the type of job which should fall into each group. In this method, usually a committee allocates jobs to each group using job descriptions. The system is simple, but suffers from a limitation similar to that of the Ranking System. The limitation is that the degree of difference between jobs cannot be indicated.

3. **Points Rating** Under this system, to achieve a higher level of accuracy, rather than evaluating the job as a whole, each job is broken down into its component factors or characteristics, and then evaluated separately. A narrative job description is prepared and supplemented by a statement of the various requirements (present in the job). Characteristics like experience and training,

mental and physical effort common to the jobs are selected and a point value for each characteristic or factor is determined. Factors are defined objectively and points are given to each factor based on its estimated importance. Consolidated point values are finally converted into money terms.

4. **Factor Comparison** This method is also similar to the Points Rating System as here too, each job is broken into factors. The only difference is that here, five factors are used; these are mental requirements, skill requirements, physical requirements, responsibility and working conditions. After arriving at job descriptions, key jobs are judged and related to one another. The jobs are considered one by one and reviewed to understand how much of the current wage rate for the job is paid for by each factor. Key jobs are arranged in a scale, in order of their value for each factor.

The remaining jobs are compared with the key job factors and a comparative money value is determined for each factor in each individual job. The total of the factor values so determined for each job represents its rate. This is a complex system; however, a higher degree of accuracy can be attained through this.

6.4.4.3 Limitations of Job Evaluation

Job evaluation alone cannot establish a wage scale. For wage fixation, we need to take into cognizance, statutory requirements like the Minimum Wages Act, 1948. Similarly, other factors of wage fixation like the capacity to pay, inter-industry wage variation, inter-regional wage variation and the collective bargaining agreement, if any, also need to be given importance. Job evaluation is highly subjective (being based on a judgmental estimate). Similarly, it cannot take into account the cyclical nature of the market value of various occupations. For example, finance jobs were highly priced in the market at one point of time (now IT and marketing have taken its place). However, with the failure of NBFCs, finance jobs are not that highly priced in the market, at least at this point of time, even though there has been no material change in the job profile of finance professionals in the interim. Despite such limitations, the job evaluation technique is considered very useful.

6.4.5 Job Design

Jobs undergo constant modification, because of the impact of mechanization and automation. Some jobs become redundant, while others are created and still others are altered in content. This necessitates different types of education, experience and other attributes. Also for effecting job design, the organization has to respect the unions, who otherwise may stall the move on one ground or the other.

While designing a job, management must also be concerned with the practical considerations regarding the quantity and quality of available personnel (both within the organization and in the labour market). Factors like personality conflicts and friction, problems of human relations, boredom or obsessive thinking have to be taken care of.

Thus, the factors, which are likely to affect job design, can be enumerated as follows:

1. Job specialization and repetitive operations
2. Changing technology
3. Labour union policies
4. Abilities of present personnel
5. Adequate availability of potential personnel
6. Interaction among jobs with the system and
7. Psychological and social needs that can be met by the job.

6.4.6 Job Assessment

At this stage, information about each job is made available to the assessors. Every job, whether manual or not, is closely observed and inspected in actual operation by the assessors. If required, assessors question the operators and their supervisors to collect further details about the job, to clear doubts if any. To keep pace with the changing job content, due to technological changes, it is necessary to make a periodic re-assessment of the job, keeping in view the old job description.

6.4.7 Pricing Job Value

The purpose of job evaluation is to establish the relative job value within the organization, in terms of points or rankings and in terms of pay levels. The next step is to translate these data into a pay structure through job co-relation. This involves deciding the pay grades, and then, developing a pay range for each grade.

6.4.7.1 Steps in Job Pricing

The initial process of pricing the job and fitting it into a pay structure calls for translating the points into different job grades. Thereafter, jobs have to be grouped as per different pay grades and then related to comparable jobs in other companies. However, this may not be possible for jobs which are unique in nature. When jobs are properly grouped, it is not difficult to price each such job group. After pricing each job group, pay structure can be developed on the mathematical principle that 'things which are equal to the same things are equal to each other'.

Based on the survey reports of other companies, base salaries for each pay grade are established, considering the average paid by the companies surveyed.

The next step in job pricing is to develop pay ranges around the base salaries. Once this is developed, individual compensation based on performance and other considerations can be worked out. Different pay ranges enable an organization to adopt a flexible approach (within the range) in hiring new employees, taking labour market flexibility into cognizance.

Illustration

To illustrate, for a manufacturing organization, a Machinist may have a pay grade ranging between Rs. 5000 to Rs 10,000 per month. This pay grade can be broken into different ranges, like, Machinist Grade-I – Rs.8000 to Rs 10,000/- per month, Machinist Grade-II – Rs. 6000 to Rs 8000 per month, Machinist Grade-III – Rs. 5000 to Rs 6000 per month.

6.4.7.2 Other Methods of Job Assessment

There are various other methods of job assessment for pricing a job value, which is essential for compensation designing. At the same time, such methods ensure job simplification and humanization of jobs. Even though some of these methods do not directly contribute to job pricing, these are still useful for achieving productivity and efficiency.

6.5 WORK STUDY

Literally, it implies 'the study of human work'. British Standard 3138:1969 defines Work Study as "A management service based on those techniques, particularly Method Study and Work Measurement, which are used in the examination of human work in all its contexts, and which lead to the systematic investigation of all the resources and factors which affect the efficiency and economy of the situation being reviewed, in order to effect improvement."

Thus, it is a generic term for two inter-dependent techniques, that is, Method Study and Work Measurement. In the British Standard, Method Study has been defined as "....the systematic recording and critical examination of the factors and resources involved in existing and proposed ways of doing work, as means of developing and applying easier and more effective methods and reducing costs." Method Study, therefore, is concerned with the way in which the work is done. Work Measurement on the other hand has been defined by the British Standards as "the application of techniques designed to establish the time for a qualified worker to carry out a specified job at a defined level of performance."

Contextual analysis of the agreed definition of Work Study given by the British Standards Institute enables us to define the subject as a procedure for understanding and determining the truth about the activities of the people, plant and machineries, identifying the factors which affect their efficiency, and achieving economy through their optimum utilization. Most productivity improvement techniques involve major capital expenditure in plant or equipment. Work Study being a management technique, on the other hand, ensures productivity by using existing resources. In Work Study, the human element is emphasized and importance is given to the operation rather than to the technical process. This, therefore, assists management in the following, which are actually its primary objectives:

- effective use of plant and equipment.
- effective use of human effort.
- evaluation of human work.

6.5.1 Human Context of Work Study

If work study techniques are not properly applied, they are likely to encounter resistance at all levels. Therefore, it is important to understand human reactions and design the programme investigation and implementation accordingly. Most of the unions by now are aware that work study provides benefits to the workers by eliminating drudgery, frustration and an unhealthy working environment. It also gives an opportunity to the workers to increase their earnings (at the micro level, and for the nation as a whole at the macro level).

However, to satisfy the unions, the following points have to be considered:

1. Workers should be consulted before the introduction of any scheme, which is likely to affect their interest, in one way or the other.
2. There should be a definite policy for those workers who will become redundant after implementation of the recommendations of the work study team.
3. The procedure to deal with the changes in the method of work and for the measurement of work should be laid down and communicated to the workers.

The International Labour Organization (ILO) has emphasized the importance of such sharing of information with the workers, in a resolution concerning consultation and cooperation between employers and workers at the level of the undertaking in its 35th session at Geneva in 1952.

6.6 METHOD STUDY

Method study is a productivity improvement step, which helps to produce the same output using fewer resources or enables more production with a proportionately less increase in the inputs. Thus, it reduces, if not eliminates, waste. Method Study ensures creativity, innovativeness, optimal decision-making power, good organizational practices and better communication. It is essential to keep the following factors in mind while carrying out a method study:

1. Economic considerations
2. Technical considerations
3. Human reactions

6.6.1 Role of Method Study

Summarizing the above discussions, we can, therefore enunciate the role of method study as follows:

1. To appraise the purpose and objectives of the organization
2. To assess the tasks of the organization
3. To evaluate the communication and control structure of the organization
4. To optimize the use of resources of the organization
5. To improve the procedures, methods and processes of the organization
6. To ensure individual and group effectiveness, and at the same time, satisfaction of work in the organization.

6.6.2 Importance and Objective of Method Study

The objective of the Method Study is to find better ways of doing things and to contribute to improved efficiency by eliminating unnecessary work, avoidable delays and other forms of waste. Through systematic recording, analysis and critical examination of the methods and movements involved in the performance of existing or proposed ways of doing work, it achieves the above-stated objectives. However, the importance or objectives of the Method Study would be clearer once we review the contributions that flow from its role. The contributions of the Method Study are:

1. Reorientation of corporate objectives and mission
2. Review of plans and programmes
3. Evaluation of tasks, targets and available resources
4. Balancing the structure of the organization
5. Introduction of a good communication system in the organization
6. Better design of plants and equipment
7. Simplification of processes and methods
8. Standardization of products and procedures
9. Improvement of work flow
10. Planning and control of work
11. Managing resources, inventory control and replacement of plants and machinery
12. Quality and cost control
13. Improving the layout of the shop floor
14. Betterment of working environment and working conditions
15. Optimum utilization of resources
16. Higher standards of safety, security and health
17. Performance satisfaction.

6.6.3 Basic Procedure, Steps, Process or Mechanism of Method Study

Method Study technique is flexible enough to accommodate different situations, however, a simple framework for its application in any given circumstance may be designed as follows:

Simple Framework for the Application of the Method Study Technique

Select	:	the work to be studied
Record	:	all the relevant facts of the present (or proposed) method
Examine	:	facts critically and in sequence
Develop	:	the most practical, economic and effective methods, with due regard to all contingent circumstances
Install	:	that method as standard practice
Maintain	:	that standard practice by regular routine checks

Even though we have indicated five basic steps in a particular order, in an actual study, it does not necessarily follow that sequence or pattern. Selection of the subject of study may be preceded by a study of the possibility of data collection. Similarly, preliminary critical examination (pilot study) may be needed in order to identify problem areas. During a pilot study, there may be a need for more detailed data. Or, it may be revealed during preliminary critical examination that the real problem is something other than the selected one. Thus, sticking to a rigid procedure of analysis may often mar the prospect of getting a productive solution.

In the Method Study, there should not be any veil of secrecy. Discussion, exchange of views and efforts at mutual understanding are part of method study. There are several undefined stages. Before implementation, the final plan has to be discussed with all concerned. Similarly, installing the new system has to be preceded by a plan to familiarize all concerned through reorientation programmes.

After installation, the system has to be maintained to ensure that this becomes the accepted standard.

The steps of Method Study, therefore, may be enumerated as follows:

- Initial data collection
- Preliminary/pilot survey and assessment
- Identification of problem areas
- Collection and assembly of data concerning the factors
- Determining their inter-connection
- Finalizing the subjects for study
- Defining the problems/subject for study
- Assessment of their impact/reaction
- Evolving alternatives
- Deciding optimal solutions

- Testing the solutions
- Preparation of the report
- Presentation of recommendations
- Decision on implementation
- Preparation for implementation
- Installation of the newly evolved system
- Maintenance of the newly installed system
- Evaluation of improvements achieved

6.6.4 Detailed Procedures – Steps

Procedures/steps in detail in any method study investigation may be enumerated as follows:

1. **Selection of the job:** Once the Method Study idea is conceived, the first step is the orientation and determination of objectives. The problem must be defined. The method study investigator faces the following types of problems and is normally required to solve them:
   - Bottlenecks, which disrupt the smooth flow of materials or processes.
   - Products which may be required to be produced economically by the application of cost reducing techniques.
   - Economic utilization of space, including land and buildings.
   - Economic utilization of labour, material and plant
   - Elimination of idle time or non-value adding time caused due to problems of flow, queues and congestion.

   While selecting the subjects for study, it is essential to keep in mind that the ultimate objective of the method study is to improve achievements by raising the level of productivity and increasing satisfaction at work. Second, the term 'select' should not be taken in a narrow sense, that is, to choose from among others, it must include a preliminary survey, which enables the investigator to decide on the continuity of the study. Similarly, select does not necessarily mean just selection of the job but also selection of the appropriate techniques to achieve the end-result.

2. **Record the Facts:** Before discarding the existing method or procedure, adequate facts about the present system must be collected. This is required to prepare an objective record of the way the job is carried out. To eliminate the change of bias, this record is not compiled from second-hand accounts or on the manager's version as to how he thinks the job is done or an operator's description of how the job is done, but based on direct observation by the concerned investigator.

3. **Critically Examine the Facts:** This is an important stage of the method study. Information collected is scrutinized and each part of the job is critically examined to determine whether any part may be:

- eliminated altogether
- combined with any other part of the job
- changed in sequence
- simplified to reduce the content of the work involved.

For effective examination of the facts, the following questions are generally asked:

- What is done and why?
- What it does and what does that person do?
- Where is it done and why there?
- When is it done and why then?
- How is it done and why this way?

By rearranging, simplifying, combining, eliminating or modifying the facts or records, a basis is obtained for an improved method.

4. **Develop a New Method:** Alternatives selected are used to reshape and develop the new method, layout or procedure. These may require test runs to determine their feasibility. Tests of this nature may be preferably carried out at a place, away from the work site, if possible. To ease the problems of acceptance for the new method in the department, it is good to involve the department. The end-result must be an improved method and must be acceptable to the departmental staff and workers. It must meet all their practical requirements and technical specifications.

5. **Install the Method:** To install the method, a decision must be taken on
   (a) ordering of new plants or material (if any)
   (b) phasing in changes in the production process
   (c) deciding the extent of redeployment
   (d) training
   (e) introducing new documentation procedures
   (f) setting new quality standards and test procedures. It is good to have a detailed time table for effecting such changes. The end-product of the installation stage is that the new method is in operation at the work site, the line management is in complete control, and finally, that all members of the department are fully conversant with the method.

6. **Maintain the Method:** Methods, after implementation, tend to change slowly due to small alterations made by the operators or supervisors. A reference standard (job instruction sheet) is needed against which the job can be compared to detect any alterations. Similarly, a corresponding document for an incentive scheme, which also contains details of the standard time for each job, called a job specification, is prepared. With these data, changes in method can be detected. If changes are considered to be useful, the instruction sheet can be amended to incorporate them and if they are thought undesirable, they can be removed through line management.

6.7 WORK MEASUREMENT

ILO defines Work Measurement as "the application of techniques designed to establish the work content of a specified task by determining the time required for carrying it out at a defined standard of performance by a qualified worker." Conventionally, it is known as Time Study, which is primarily carried out to determine the standard time taken to perform a specific task. A time standard is used for planning and scheduling work, for cost estimations, or for labour cost control, or it may serve as the basis for a wage incentive plan. It has wide applications in deciding a wage incentive plan.

6.7.1 Techniques of Work Measurement

There are different techniques of Work Measurement. However, the following are the principal ones:

- Time Study
- Ratio–delay Study (Statistical Sampling Technique)
- Synthesis from Standard Data
- Pre-determined Motion Time Standard
- Analytic Estimating.

Of these, only the Time Study Technique is widely used, as the others are complicated in nature. We will discuss Time Study in detail, and will define the other techniques.

6.8 TIME STUDY

The ILO defines Time Study as "a technique for determining as accurately as possible from a limited number of observations, the time necessary to carry out a given activity at a defined standard of performance." For carrying out a Time Study, equipment like a stopwatch, study board, pencils, slide-rule, etc. are required. The stopwatches are of different types:

1. Stopwatches which record one minute per revolution by intervals of 1/5 of a second, with a small hand recording 30 minutes
2. Stopwatches which record one minute per revolution, calibrated to 1/100th of a minute, with a small hand recording 30 minutes
3. Decimal-hour Stopwatches which record 1/100ths of an hour per revolution, graduated in 1/1000ths of an hour and a small hand recording up to one hour in 100 divisions.

In very simplistic terms, time study sets the correct time requirements to perform various jobs. The idea was pioneered by F.W. Taylor (1911), and is considered the most effective technique and means of work measurement. We can define time study as defining employee productivity standards, describing the steps involved to perform each part of a task, the sequence of movements of employees in performing the tasks, and the time requirement for each task.

Time study takes into account the unavoidable delays, fatigue and other work-related bottlenecks due to exogenous factors. Many 'time wasters' are not taken into account in a time study, for example, searching for tools, etc., as we assume that the workplace design is good enough to accommodate the work without any interruptions or work stoppages. Companies develop their manpower plan based on the time requirements of a job. After Taylor, it was Frank and Lillian Gilbreth who finally gave shape to the concept of time-and-motion studies and helped put it into practice.

6.8.1 Steps in Time Study

The following steps are necessary for carrying out a Time Study for the measurement of work:

- To collect and complete all available information about the job, and the surrounding conditions and also those attributes of the operators, which are likely to affect the work.
- To record the details of the method and also to break down different operations into their elements.
- To record the time taken by the operators to perform the operation (element-wise), measuring preferably with a timing device like a stopwatch.
- To assess the working speed of the operators and comparing the same with a pre-determined normal speed.
- To convert the observed time to normal time.
- To decide the rate of allowances which may be given over and above the normal time of the operation
- To determine the allowed time for operation.

6.9 OTHER TECHNIQUES OF WORK MEASUREMENT

6.9.1 Ratio-delay technique

Since carrying out a time study for each job is a time consuming task, a statistical technique called a ratio-delay study is often carried out. Ratio-delay is a sampling technique. Instead of going in for a complete job production study, using ratio-delay techniques, a sufficiently large number of readings are taken at random intervals. Like all other sampling techniques, in this method too, there are bound to be some errors. However, the cost of such a study being less, many organizations, which have the expertise may prefer this method. Moreover, in this method, rating is not done, and time is recorded directly using a stopwatch, so it does not encounter resistance from the workers.

6.9.2 Synthesis Technique

Many organizations cannot conduct their own time study to set the time standards due to time and resource constrains. In order to follow a time standard, they synthesize from published standard data on time requirements. Nowadays, most technology vendors provide standard cycle time requirement for a job, based on their own studies. These apart, at the international level, standard occupation specific time study data are available. Synthesizing time standards based on such data help companies to approximate the standard time requirement for jobs, to a great extent. However, this runs the risk of inherent errors, due to non-commonality of level of skill, technology, work process, and the overall work culture and environments, which may be organization-specific, across countries.

6.9.3 Pre-determined Motion Time Standards

This technique is also used as the basis for setting time standards. Some organizations, instead of going in for a thorough time study, again and again, maintain that their previous time study records hold good even for the future. This may result in time and cost saving, but again, it runs the risk of error due to the time lag. Standard time requirements may vary simply due to changes in the work processes, or due to technological changes in the interim.

6.9.4 Analytical Estimating

In some work, because of its nature, it is difficult to develop time standards through a time study. Maintenance, tool room jobs, research and development work, software development, etc. are typical examples of such jobs. Broadly, in any job that involves innovation and creativity, these problems are faced. To avoid such problems, analytic estimating technique is used. The technique relies more on the experience of time study specialists, who also make use of data synthesis from a standard data table.

Analytical estimation is difficult in nature and it is not always a fool-proof method as job measurement is difficult if the job is creative in nature.

6.10 CONCEPT AND DEFINITION OF ERGONOMICS

'Ergonomics' is derived from the Greek words 'ergon', meaning work and 'enomos', meaning laws. It is the study of the effects of a work system on workers and it aims at fitting the work to the men to increase their efficiency, comfort and satisfaction.

The ILO defines ergonomics as "the application of human biological sciences in conjunction with engineering to the worker and his working environment, so as to obtain maximum satisfaction for the work which, at the same time, enhances productivity."

A contextual analysis of the ILO definition provides a more meaningful basis for understanding ergonomics. An ergonomist, for effective accomplishment of work, tries to integrate the work system (which broadly includes the tasks, working equipment, working conditions and working space), with the capabilities and requirements of work. In this process, he tries to ensure job satisfaction for the workers, which, inter alia, increases their productivity.

Ergonomics can be applied in all schemes of human activity, be it in offices, factories, shops, ships, air and even in space. Some of the areas where ergonomics has been successfully applied are:

- Design of equipment, power and hand tools
- Design of displays and warning systems
- Design of furniture, seats, rests and steps for operators
- Design of tools, jigs and fixtures
- Plant layout
- Improvement in working conditions and environments
- Computation of relaxation allowances for workers
- Selection, training and placement of personnel
- Motivation of workers.

However, for better understanding, the areas of ergonomic investigation of a work system may be grouped as follows:

1. **Human Characteristics**
   Health, physique, anthropometric data, personal background, education, training, experience, age, sex, intelligence, aptitude, reaction time, interest, personality characteristics, temperament, attitude towards work, motivation, etc.
2. **Work**
   Physical loads, perceptual loads, mental loads, displays and warning systems, controls, compatibility of inputs and outputs.
3. **Working Conditions**
   Working conditions encompass workplace layout, postures, motion and movements, fatigue, monotony and relaxation allowances, comfort, safety and health, working hours and shift work conditions.
4. **Environment**
   Illumination, ventilation, temperature and humidity, colour dynamics, fumes, dust, odour and smoke, landscape, scenery and garden, cleanliness and sanitation.

Many alternative terms like human engineering, human factors in engineering, engineering psychology, applied experimental psychology, applied and human engineering research, man–machine system analysis, etc., are used to designate the discipline.

This subject was developed during World War II through the coordinated efforts of physiologists, psychologists and design engineers. Its earliest application can be traced to Frederick Winslow Taylor (1856–1915). Taylor's experiments were mainly to arrive at the optimum design of equipment for specific types of work and to train workers to suit them for each type of task.

Frank Bunker Gilbreth (1869–1924) and his wife Lillian, elaborated the principles of motion economy and introduced the idea of rest pauses and spacing out of work to reduce fatigue and eliminate stress. Since then, with the advancement of experimental physiology, psychology and method study, the subject delved deeper into the human make-up for better and scientific understanding of the effects of working conditions and environment on the human body and mind.

6.10.1 Impact of Ergonomics on Work Study

Work study, which aims at scientific analysis of a work system to increase productivity and satisfaction at work, is dependent on ergonomics for research data on many facets of human reaction to a given work situation. Such input information makes the task of the work study practitioner more scientific and result-oriented. Such input information/data mostly relates to the following areas:

- Limits of sustained physical endurance, normal speeds of movement and optimum method of handling of controls.
- Receptivity to sensory inputs and time required for perception of deviations.
- Reaction time for motion output and time required for evaluation and decision making.
- Anthropometric data to guide the design and layout of equipment, work place and furniture.
- Effects of different types of environmental conditions on the human being in order to generate improvements.
- Effects of working conditions so as to raise the standards of comfort, safety and health.
- Qualitative and quantitative analysis of factors contributing to industrial fatigue for computations of 'relaxation allowances'

6.10.2 Ergonomics and Management

Ergonomics is a discipline available to management from the planning and design stage of a work system. In the organization and control of human effort directed to specific ends, management needs to have an appreciation of the human factors involved in a work system. Ergonomics also has an important influence on the work situation and managerial performance. The aim is to eliminate all perceptual and mental loading that may arise from the perusal and evaluation of reports on the normal activities of the organization, thereby highlighting only the deviations from the equilibrium state. This will permit more effective application of managerial talent to really important problems over a wide span. In other words, ergonomics can help in increasing the productivity of managerial brain power. This single improvement, by itself, without any changes in the methods on the shop floor will lead to a spectacular increase in the overall productivity of an organization.

6.10.3 Working Areas

The working area of an operator may be categorized into three groups: Normal, Immediate and Maximum working areas.

1. The normal working area is one that can be reached by the operator using any movement up to, and inclusive of, class 3 movements (see Table 6.1). This area is bound by the two arcs made by the fingers, using the elbow as the pivot.
2. The immediate working area is the surface immediately in front of the operator where the two arcs of the normal working area overlap.
3. The maximum working area is one that can be reached by the operator using any movement up to and inclusive of class 4 movements. This area is bound by the two arcs made by the fingers, with the shoulders as the pivot.

The space between the normal and the maximum working areas is accessible through class 4 movements. Anything beyond the maximum working area may be reached only through a class 5 movement, including body bending or stretching.

The immediate working area is most suitable for bi-manual operation. If the various equipment, materials and tools are replaced within the normal working area, they can be reached without using the upper arm and shoulder muscles. It is not desirable to place anything outside the maximum working area. The field of vision should also be taken into account while considering working areas. The normal cone of vision, without head movement, is restricted. Covering the whole perimeter of the normal working area would impose undue eye strain, and sometimes involve excessive head movements. Due care must, therefore, be taken to position all the materials well within the workman's cone of vision. In the case of inspection, as much of the work as possible, must take place directly in front of the operator. For better understanding, classes of movements can be grouped under the following five categories, based on the pivots around which the body parts move:

Table 6.1 *Categorization of body movements*

Class	Pivot	Body Member Movement
1.	Knuckle (finger joint)	Finger(s)
2.	Wrist	Hand and Fingers
3.	Elbow	Forearm, hand and fingers
4.	Shoulder	Upper arm, forearm, hand and fingers
5.	Trunk (body apart from limbs)	Torso, upper arm, forearm, hand and fingers

A similar classification is available for the movements of corresponding parts of the leg. For economy of motion, the movement should be of the lowest classification possible, compatible with the normal capacity of the body part affected.

6.10.4 Motion Economy

Motion economy is the process of minimizing the physical and perceptual loads imposed on people engaged in any type of work; whether it is in the office, the shop floor, the kitchen or at the driving wheel. It leads to better design of equipment, jigs and fixtures, hand tools, furniture and labour-saving devices. Also, it facilitates better layout of offices, warehouses, plants and operating areas like the office desk, work bench, aircraft, cockpit and crew compartments of armoured vehicles. Application of the principles of motion economy eliminates or minimizes wasteful and fatiguing movements and increases the productivity of the workers. It tries to minimize movements in respect of:

- Number of movements
- Length of movements
- Classification
- Number of parts of body used
- Necessity for control
- Muscular force
- Complexity of movements
- Distances between eye fixation
- Time required for eye fixation.

For achieving motion economy, the following principles have been evolved by different specialists:

- Principle of Minimum Movement
- Principle of Natural Movement
- Principle of Simultaneous Movement
- Principle of Rhythmic Movement
- Principle of Habitual Movement
- Principle of Continuous Movement

Simultaneous movements reduce fatigue and increase the rate of output. More fatigue is caused when only one hand is working and the other is idle. Simultaneous movements include the movements of the feet, while both the hands are operating as in driving a car. Application of this principle leads to the better design of jigs, fixtures and the duplication of tools, so that both hands work at similar tasks simultaneously.

The principle of symmetrical movements should be applied in conjunction with simultaneous movements. Proper balance is achieved only when the movement of one hand is the 'mirror image' of the movement of the other. Symmetry in movements promotes ease and speed, and eliminates fumbling. When movements of the hands are asymmetrical, there is a tendency on the part of the operators to interpolate additional, but non-productive, movements in order to achieve balance.

Rhythm is the regular repetition of a movement pattern. It often incorporates the accentuation of a specific part of a cycle. Rhythm contributes to speed, eliminates fumbling, and reduces fatigue. Examples of rhythmic movements are rowing, hammering at the smithy and drawing water from a well, using a see-saw lift.

The pattern of movements should be so designed as to facilitate habituation. When a cycle of activities is performed habitually, the movements are executed almost as a reflex action. Habitual movements eliminate hesitation, and increase speed of performance. Rhythm helps speed habit formation. Tools, materials, displays and controls must always be located in the same position. The pattern must be standardized for similar types of panels, work places and equipment. Continuous movements which are smooth and curved are superior to jerky straight line movements which involve sudden changes of direction and loss of momentum. Materials, tools and jigs must be so positioned as to incorporate smooth, curved and continuous movements, and eliminate undue changes of direction.

The above principles should be treated merely as guides, and not as rigid rules. Quite often, one principle may be in conflict with another, and a proper evaluation of all the principles in their totality, would be needed for optimization. Conditions differ from job to job. It may sometimes be necessary to compromise the principle of minimum movements in order to distribute the physical load over the various muscles equitably, or to give due weightage to the principle of continuous movement. It is, therefore, essential that the principles are applied with flexibility.

6.10.5 Human Engineering

Method study seeks to determine the effective combination of man, machine and the working environment. In doing so, it is necessary to determine which functions are better performed by man and which functions are better performed by machines. Both man and machine can surpass each other in certain ways. The question of economy again influences the man–machine combination. The term, human engineering, is more appropriately used to solve man–machine problems in design, operation and maintenance of plants and machineries, and in fact, it broadly comes under the purview of ergonomics. It is, therefore, not appropriate to designate human engineering as an independent discipline, separating it from ergonomics. However, to understand the context and meaning of human engineering, it is considered necessary to define it in line with Ernest J. McCormick. He defined it as the mechanism for "the adaptation of human tasks and working environment to the sensory, perceptual, mental, physical, and other attributes of people. This adaptation for human use applies to such functions as the design of equipment, instruments, man–machine systems, and consumer products, and to the development of optimum work methods and work environment."

6.10.6 Human Engineering and Machine Design

The designer of the machine should know how the human being functions, his body dimensions, his physical limitations and also the conditions under which a person performs perfectly. For performing a task, a person normally does the following:

1. receives the information (through different sense organs);
2. makes decisions (acting on perceived information);
3. takes action (which results from decision).

Thus, the basic control cycle for the human being consists of these three parts – sense, decide and act. Power to reason inductively, exercise judgment, develop concepts and create methods are unique to human beings, while the quick performance of repetitive routine tasks, the power to perform rapid computations, apply great force, the simultaneous performance of many different functions etc. are characteristic features of machines.

The designer of the machine, therefore, is required to consider all the above details before developing a better designed machine for productive use. Most Computer Numerically Controlled (CNC) Machining Centres developed by large industrial organizations in India are not performing well, as these have been designed without taking the human factor into consideration. In fact, sophisticated machining centers, whenever introduced, have lead to industrial relations problems, as it adversely affects workers' pay packets.

Since a badly-designed machine may be responsible for the poor performance of workers, the application of ergonomics/human engineering techniques is necessary to design machines. Modern machines are ergonomically designed to prevent stress and fatigue of the workers, to make them work at ease, and at the same time, to achieve an increased rate of production. We find the application of human engineering/ergonomic techniques even in designing consumer products, kitchen gadgets, furniture, etc. Recently, *Blow Plast Ltd.*, under technical collaboration with *Klober* of Germany, ergonomically designed office-chairs.

6.11 VALUE ANALYSIS

Henry Erlicher of *General Electric Company* in 1947, drawing lessons from World War II, observed that the substitution of materials (as manufacturers were then compelled to go in for such substitution to deal with shortages of original materials), often led to cost reduction and better functionality. This prompted further research into alternative materials and processes. L.D. Miles, another top executive of the company, was directed by him to go into the details which were later called Value Analysis. By 1949, this approach in a more institutionalized form was used in the *General Electric Company* and gradually in the US Department of Defence. By 1970, the Value Engineering concept had received international attention. Value

Engineering is an organized, creative technique to analyse the functions of a product or service or a system to achieve the required functions at the lowest cost ensuring its performance, reliability and maintainability. It is also known as Value Analysis or Value Management.

Literally, value is the worth of an article/product/service. In terms of cost and function, value is determined. Value of a product can be improved by:

1. Improving function (keeping cost constant)
2. Reducing cost (keeping function constant)
3. Both by improving function as well as by reducing cost.

An industrial product has different types of value, which may be classified as follows:

1. **Use Value** These are the properties and qualities which are useful and which enable the accomplishment of the purported work. Use value may be either for primary use, secondary use or for auxiliary use.
2. **Esteem Value** Aesthetic features or properties which attract a customer to own it.
3. **Cost Value** The cost required to produce the item.
4. **Exchange Value** The properties which enable the owner to exchange it for anything else, if he so desires, in future.

However, for all practical purposes, industrial situations are primarily concerned with use value and esteem value only.

Value Analysis, therefore, can be defined as a "method of search, a systematic procedure resulting in the orderly utilization of alternative materials and processes. It focuses engineering, manufacturing and purchasing with attention on one objective that of obtaining equivalent or even better performance for lower cost."

6.11.1 Steps in Value Analysis

The following are the steps in Value Analysis:

- Collection of facts and information about the product
- Get the details of the cost break-up
- Determine the function
- Think creatively
- Compare and evaluate the alternatives.

To succeed at each step, it is necessary to take the following line of action:

- Eliminate the redundant parts
- Initiate action on the use of cheaper substitutes without impairing the use value
- Standardize parts
- Develop alternative methods
- Re-design, if necessary.

Advantages

The following are the advantages stemming from Value Analysis:

- Lowering of cost
- Better quality of product
- Increased efficiency
- High level of morale and team spirit
- Increased customer satisfaction
- Optimum resource utilization
- Improved methods of production
- Increased job satisfaction and motivation to workers through the use of their creative ability.

The term, Value Analysis, has now been replaced by Value Engineering in corporate circles. In most organizations, Value Engineering practices are followed forming Value Engineering teams of workers (a small group activity like Quality Circles, etc.). This provides workers with the opportunity to derive creative satisfaction and also to fulfill their intrinsic needs. At the same time, the organization also gets active participation from the workers.

6.12 WORK SAMPLING

Work sampling or random sampling or activity sampling, is a work measurement technique to collect data on the activities of a group of workers at discrete time intervals. To carry out a time-and-motion study, organizations often face resistance, as workers are sensitive to such efforts. An unobtrusive method of data collection through work sampling is either periodic or random. Also, work sampling is a particularly useful technique whenever time study data collection is not possible, or is cost prohibitive, or even encounters resistance from workers and trade unions.

The method involves the recording of observations on workers (in a group), or machine activities. Consolidating such observations, statistical approximation is made and an overall percentage of occurrences of observed samples holds good for the population of workers and machines. Work sampling also helps us to estimate the delay allowances in performing a job. It can also be used to estimate the normal time. The technique, therefore, requires the random observation of workers while they perform the task to determine the proportion of time workers actually work and the time they idle. When they are idle, we try to assess the reasons for their idleness and come out with a possible action plan to solve the problem of idleness.

Like time-and-motion studies, work sampling also helps in creating standard times for performance (Tippets, 1934). This method is more suitable for examining group activities or in cases where an individual worker performs more than one activity. Basically, it is an arithmetical method to compute the period of time used by workers in group activities.

Although characteristically both the work sampling and time-and-motion studies techniques have a common purpose of setting time standards, the two are different in terms of their data collection method, types of observation, and scope of application in production and operations management related decision making. Work-sampling technique requires data collection at definite time intervals, five times every hour. Intervals between observations may be either fixed or random. Percentage of observations is related to an activity, to approximate the time spent on it. In the time-and-motion study, observers record the exact time spent on each activity. Hence, time-and-motion study is a more labour intensive method of data collection for obvious one-to-one observation. While in work sampling, paper and a pencil are used, in a time-and-motion study we use instruments, like stop watches, etc.

Work sampling results may be wrong, as these are prone to suffer from systematic bias, wrong selection of samples, which in a time-and-motion study is minimum.

6.13 WORK SIMPLIFICATION

For industrial management, we make use of several management tools, of which, the work simplification process, time-and-motion studies, method studies, ergonomics and human engineering, value analysis are of prime importance. This chapter has introduced all these concepts, keeping organizational practices in view.

Work simplification increases the effectiveness and efficiency of organizations, focussing on people and tools for continuous improvement. Frank and Lillian Gilbreth in 1921, at the annual general meeting of the American Society of Mechanical Engineers (ASME) presented the concept of Process Charts. Subsequently, the work simplification concept was developed in 1932, by Allan Mogensen with an established set of five symbols, encompassing every aspect of the work environment, for use in operation and flow process charts. Theoretically, work simplification is the organized application of common sense to organize and study work.

Mogensen used the participative approach for getting the best results through work simplification. His assumption was that proximity to the job makes a person more knowledgeable than others; hence he/she can suggest the best way of doing the job. For its obvious simplicity, the work simplification process received wide acceptance from organizations. Unlike other improvement techniques, work simplification places more stress on the human element. It does not consider people, products and information as inputs and outputs; rather it considers people as valuable resources, the reservoir of organizational knowledge and memory, which ensures continuous improvement through the process of work simplification. With human resources and the process charts, work simplification becomes more result oriented. Mogensen considered the process chart to be the lifeblood of an organization.

From its limited focus on application in a manufacturing work environment, the work simplification process was extended to an office environment by Ben S. Graham (1958). This revolutionized the concept of work simplification, as in office work, it could simplify paperwork, and significantly reduce the time loss and decision-making time for getting better performance results. In the *Standard Register Company*, Graham, introducing the horizontal process flowchart to accommodate the flow of multiple information, could significantly reduce the paperwork through the work simplification process. While extending the concept and application of the work simplification process to an office environment, Graham introduced two value-added steps to information processing; these are Origination and Add/Alter. Origination helps us trace the creation of a record. Add/Alter; on the other hand, represents the addition or change of information in records or sets of papers. Some internationally acclaimed organizations that have made use of the work simplification process are *Texas Instruments, Proctor and Gamble, Ford,* etc.

Operationally, the work simplification process makes effective use of organizational memory, to achieve improvement. In the process of leveraging organizational memory, it recognizes people, whose involvement makes the process faster and more acceptable. Ultimately, work simplification helps in achieving operational efficiency, gaining complete control over activities.

Given the complexity of today's work processes, and the technological intensity of these processes, work simplification, as an organizational improvement tool is getting less attention from industry. However, its base knowledge, can be a good precursor for modern improvement tools, like total quality management, Six Sigma and lean management. Even in the application of Kaizen or value stream mapping, supply chain management or the documentation for the ISO certification process, prior knowledge of work simplification helps significantly.

6.13.1 Work Simplification through Flowcharting

The time-and-motion study, popularized by Maynard, Stegmerten and Lowry (1927), paved the way for the work simplification approach. Mogenson (1932) used the concepts of motion study for work simplification. Flowcharting is used as an important tool for work simplification. With *Microsoft*'s software 'Visio', flowcharting (Fig. 6.2) can be done more effectively. Some of the important steps for work simplification are listed below:

- Identification of the job/activity that needs improvement
- Review why the jobs/activities are used – asking questions like:
    - The necessity and purpose of the jobs/activities
    - Time frame for doing the jobs/activities
    - Possible best way of doing the jobs/activities
    - The place where the jobs/activities need to be done, etc.
- Perform work breakdown analysis to get the details of the jobs/activities
- List the details for accomplishment of the jobs/activities
- Identify tools and equipment to be used to perform the jobs/activities
- List the nature of body movements necessary to accomplish the jobs/activities

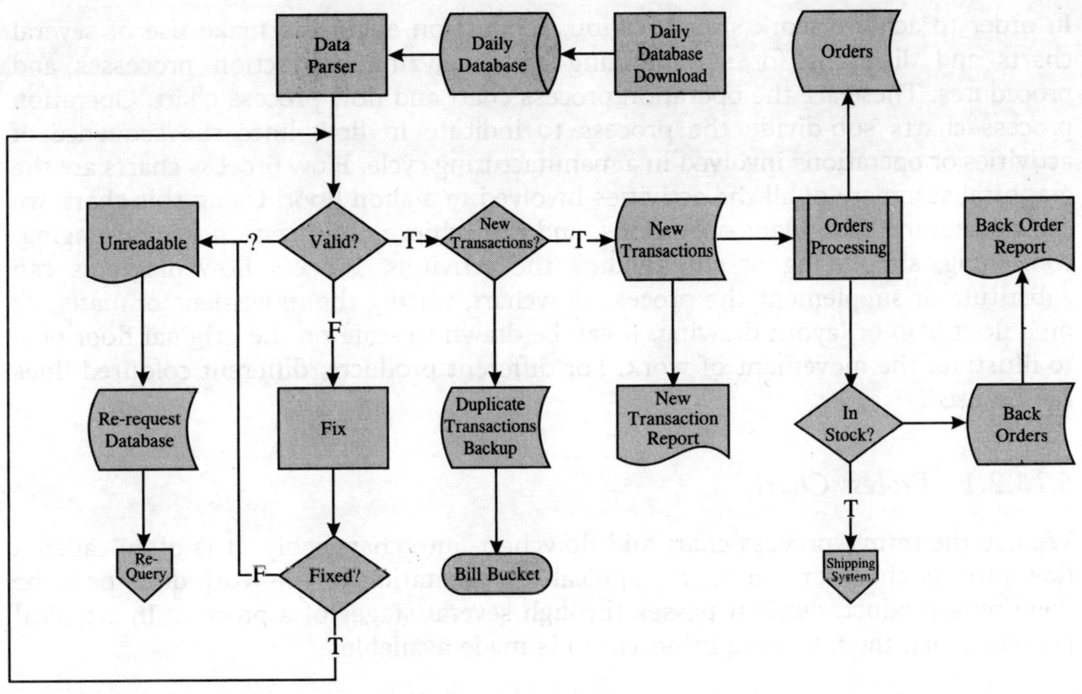

Figure 6.2 *'Visio' flowcharting*

Likewise, after following the above steps for work simplification, organizations develop new methods of performing jobs, focussing on the following aspects:

- Elimination of unnecessary details
- Combining the motions and activities
- Rearranging the sequence of jobs/activities
- Simplifying the necessary details
- Applying the new method
- Rearranging tools and equipment
- Readjusting working heights and work areas
- Setting up work stations
- Discarding unnecessary items.

In work simplification, process charting is done using some meaningful symbols for the doing of work, moving work from one location to another, checking the work and indicating that nothing has happened. These symbols are used in all work processes/work situations. We have discussed these symbols in chapter 7.

6.13.2 Charts and Diagrams for Work Simplification

In order to achieve work simplification, production engineers make use of several charts and diagrams for summarizing and analyzing production processes and procedures. These are the operation process chart and flow process chart. Operation process charts sub-divide the process to indicate in flow lines the sequence of activities or operations involved in a manufacturing cycle. Flow process charts are the graphical summary of all the activities involved in a shop floor. Using this chart, we can understand redundant operations, and can achieve optimization by rearranging, combining, simplifying or sub-dividing the activities. Process flow diagrams can substitute or supplement the process flowchart, tracing the movement of materials on a floor plan or layout drawing; it can be drawn to scale on the original floor plan to illustrate the movement of work. For different products, different coloured lines can be used.

6.13.2.1 Process Chart

We use the terms, process chart and flowchart, interchangeably. It is often called a flow process chart for symbolic graphical representation of the work done or to be done on a product, while it passes through several stages of a process. In a typical process chart, the following information is made available:

1. Quantity
2. Distance Moved
3. Type of work done (indicated by symbols with explanation)
4. Equipments used

6.13.2.2 Multiple Activity Chart

In some operations, more than one person and machine may be required for doing the job. To avoid delay in such combined activities, multi-activity charts are used to ensure optimum utilization of machines and manpower.

These apart, data card for machines, templates, scale models, layout drawings, etc., also help in the work simplification process. Machines cards are prepared for every machine to document all the basic information about the machine, like the date of purchase and installation, capacity of the machine, power requirements, environmental conditioning requirements, etc. Templates are machine drawings with tools requirement on a sheet of paper. Templates eliminate unnecessary handling with a visual picture of the proposed or existing plans or layouts. Scale models are two-dimensional templates, primarily used in layout engineering. Layout drawings detail the complete layout, covering machines, equipment, storage and office areas.

Process charts can be in the form of an outline or flow. Outline process charts give a bird's eye view of the process, concentrating only on the operations and inspections. A flow process chart provides detailed information, using all the symbols discussed above. A two-handed process chart documents the activities that involve use of both the hands of the worker. It is also known as a SIMO chart. SIMO stands for simultaneous fine micro analysis. It makes use of 'threbligs' (Chapter 4) for detailed analysis of human motions. A flow diagram shows the relative position of the machines and equipments. String diagrams use a continuous string or thread to mark the path of movement. Cycle graphs study the path of movement. A chronocycle graph, in addition to the path of movement, also shows the direction and speed of the movement.

6.13.3 Benefits of Process Charts and Flowcharts

The primary benefit of these charts is that it does not require us to get into the details. Managers can get an overview of the process, and accordingly take important decisions. Some other benefits are:

- It helps in recording the real events sequentially; thereby it helps reduce confusion.
- It is easy to display as it can be represented to show a horizontal flow of processes from left to right, which fits the worker's eye movement perfectly.
- These charts map the actual work, and are therefore more realistic.
- It helps in identifying non-value adding work.

In every process, about 95% of the processing time is non-value adding. Through process or flowcharts, we can trace those non-value adding activities and through work simplification can eliminate some of these tasks.

- It can help in tracking the change of locations in relation to the activities. In a real-life work environment, it helps in back tracking a job for re-work, if required.
- It helps in reducing unnecessary paper work and documentation.
- It helps in identifying the control points and facilitates process audits.
- Retention or disposal of records becomes clear in the process of developing process or flowcharts.
- It can harness the experience and collective knowledge of all those involved, facilitating an informed decision making process.

Therefore, by making effective use of process and flowcharts, organizations benefit immensely. For all these reasons, we call these charts the language of the process.

6.13.4 Problems on Time Study

Time Study is a Work Measurement Technique that is widely used in industry to decide standard time and then to compare the time taken by the workmen. Though it basically helps in pricing a job, it is also used for other purposes like deciding training requirements, payment of incentives and rewards, etc. Try the following problem to understand its computational details.

Problem

Set the standard time for manufacturing ball point pens based on the following activity details. You have observed the ongoing job for 100 hours and have seen that within this period 1000 ball point pens have been manufactured. Assume that while performing the job, workmen get a personal time allowance of 10%. Compute Standard Time for manufacturing a single ball point pen.

Activity	Rate (Per cent)	No. of times jobs observed
A	120	200
B	90	300
C	80	500
D	70	100
	Idle Time	200
	Total Observed Time	= 1300

Solution

To solve this problem, at the outset, it is necessary to compute Average Cycle Time, dividing observed period by No. of ball point pens produced, i.e., 100 Hours/1000 ball point pens = 1/10 of an hour, or 6 minutes.

Thus, 6 minutes on an average is taken for manufacturing a ball point pen.

Now, we have to compute distribution of time, activity-wise, using this formula:

Average Cycle Time × (Observed Time/Total Time) × Rating

Average Cycle Time has already been computed, which is 6 minutes.

Observed Time is the activity-specific time, already shown in the problem.

Total time is total observed time. Rating is the perceived rate of efficiency of the observer given in the problem.

i. Time taken for Activity 'A'

$6 \times (200/1300) \times (120/100) \quad = \quad 1.1$

ii. Time Taken for Activity 'B'

$6 \times (300/1300) \times (90/100) \quad = 1.2$

iii. Time Taken for Activity 'C'

$6 \times (500/1300) \times (80/100) \quad = \quad 1.8$

iv. Time Taken for Activity 'D'

$6 \times (100/1300) \times (70/100)$	=	0.3
Total Normal Time	=	4.4

Now, we have to compute Standard Time using this formula:

(Total Activity-wise Time or Normal Time/ {1 – Personal Fraction Time})

Time Study Questions and Answers Standard time is defined as the allowable time for an average worker to manufacture a product or to render service under normal conditions, with due consideration of workers' personal fraction time, fatigue, etc. To calculate standard time, at the outset, we need to consider the normal time, using the formula as under:

$$T_n = T_0 \times R$$

T_0 = observed time, that is, the recorded observations of the worker, while he/she performs the task.

R = performance rating, or the pace of working.

To the normal time, we have to add the time allowances, like personal fraction time, fatigue allowances or any other unavoidable delays. This makes our formula:

$$T_s = T_n \times (1 + A_{pfd})$$

Here A_{pfd} denotes time percentage given as allowances for personal fraction time, fatigue allowances, or any other unavoidable delays.

The performance rate or the pace of work is decided by the rater, based on his/her expertise. The factors usually considered during the process of rating are skill, effort, condition and consistency.

For calculation of standard time, we use the formula as under:

$$ST = (NT)(1 - AF)$$

Where ST = Standard Time
NT = Normal Time
AF = Allowance Factor

Problems and Solutions

1. One of your workers performs a drilling operation on a component, which takes about 10 minutes. This worker does the task at 110% rate of performance (pace). Your company provides 15% time as fatigue allowance. Calculate the normal time and the standard time.

Solution

Normal time = (total times)(%working on this task)(rating)/(number of units produced)

= (10)(1.00)(1.10)/1 = 11 minutes

$$\text{Standard times} = \frac{\text{Total Normal time}}{\text{1–Allowance factor}} = \frac{11}{1 - 0.15} = \frac{11}{0.85} = 12.9$$

2. A.K. Singh, an editor at *Vikas Publishing House*, takes three hours and 25 minutes to edit a chapter. Singh performs at 95% rate of efficiency (work space), and his personal time fraction allowance is 8%. Calculate the normal, and also the standard time for editing a chapter.

Solution

Normal time=(total time)(%working on this task)(rating)/(number of units produced)

= (205 minutes)(1.00)(0.95)/1 = 194.75 minutes

$$\text{Standard time} = \frac{\text{Total normal time}}{\text{1–Allowance factor}} = \frac{194.75}{1 - 0.08} = \frac{194.75}{0.92} = 211.68 \text{ minutes}$$

Moulding and packaging are two operations performed by workers in preparing a plastic toy. The company allows 15% time as personal fraction time and fatigue allowance. The workers at a moulding machine are rated at a 110% level of efficiency, in contrast to the level of efficiency of packers at 80%. The company follows the batch production process, and could make available batch-wise observed time as in the table below:

	Observed Time (in minutes)			
Tasks	1	2	3	4
Moulding	26	30	29	31
Packaging	45	50	35	30

Calculate the normal and standard times for the tasks.

Solutions

For Moulding:

Average for the actual moulding cycle = 29 minutes per batch

Normal time = (total times)(%working)(rating)/number of units produced)

=(29)(1.00)(1.10)/1 = 31.9 minutes per batch

Standard time= (normal time)/(1–Allowance)

=31.90/(1 – 0.15) = 37.5 munutes per batch

For Packaging:

Average actual packaging time = 40 minutes

Normal time = (total times) (%working) (rating)/number of units produced)

=(40)(1.00)(0.80) = 32 minutes per batch

Standard time= (normal time)/(1–Allowance)

=(32)/(1 – 0.15) = 37.6 munutes per batch

Problem 4:

A 40-hour period time study of a toy manufacturers indicated that an individual worker performs in general at 85% efficiency and produces 12 toys. The worker's idle time and personal time fraction are 10% and 12% respectively. Calculate the normal and standard time for the activity.

Average actual time = 40 hours

Normal times= (total times) (% working) (rating)/(number of units produced)

= (40 hrs)(0.90)(0.85)/(12) = 2.55 hours per part

Standard time)/(1–Allowance)

= 2.55/0.88 = 2.90 hours per part

Problem 5:

From a sample of 75 observations, the toy manufacturer could compute an average cycle time of 15 minutes with a standard deviation of 2 minutes. Determine whether the same was large enough to conclude with 99% confidence that the standard time is within 5% of the true value.

To find the number of samples required:

$$n = \left(\frac{z\sigma}{h = \bar{x}}\right)^2$$ where h is the accuracy desired and z is the confidence level

$$n = \left(\frac{2.575 * 2}{0.05 * 15}\right)^2 = \left(\frac{5.15}{0.75}\right)^2 = 47.15 \text{ or } 48 \text{ samples}$$

Therefore, the sample size of 75 is sufficient.

Problem 6:

You are an expert brought in to measure the work. Your company has assigned you to determine the standard time for manufacturing one unit of product X. You have observed the job for 10 hours and could collect the following information:

No. of units produced	=	350
Idle time	=	15%
Performance rating	=	120%
Allowances	=	10%

Calculate the standard time for one unit of the work.

Ans:

Observed time in minutes	=	600(10 × 60)
Less 15% idle time	=	90
	=	510

Normalized time = time taken × performance rating = 500 × 12/0100 = 612 minutes.

Standard time = Normalized time + Allowances = 612 + 1/9th (1 – allowances) of normalized time, i.e., 510 + 68 = 680 minutes.

680 minutes is the standard time for 350 units, for one unit, the standard time would be 680/350 = 1.943 minutes, roughly 1 minute 57 seconds, i.e., 3 seconds short of 2 minutes.

Problem 7:

A company has already established the standard time for some element of a job as 20 seconds. You, as an expert, could observe the performance ratings of workers as 100%, 125% and 80%. Calculate the observed timings with three different performance ratings.

Solution

With 100% performance rating, the observed time = 20/1 = 20 seconds.

With 125% performance rating, the observed time is 20/1.25 = 16 seconds.

With 80% performance rating, the observed time is 20/0.8 = 25 seconds.

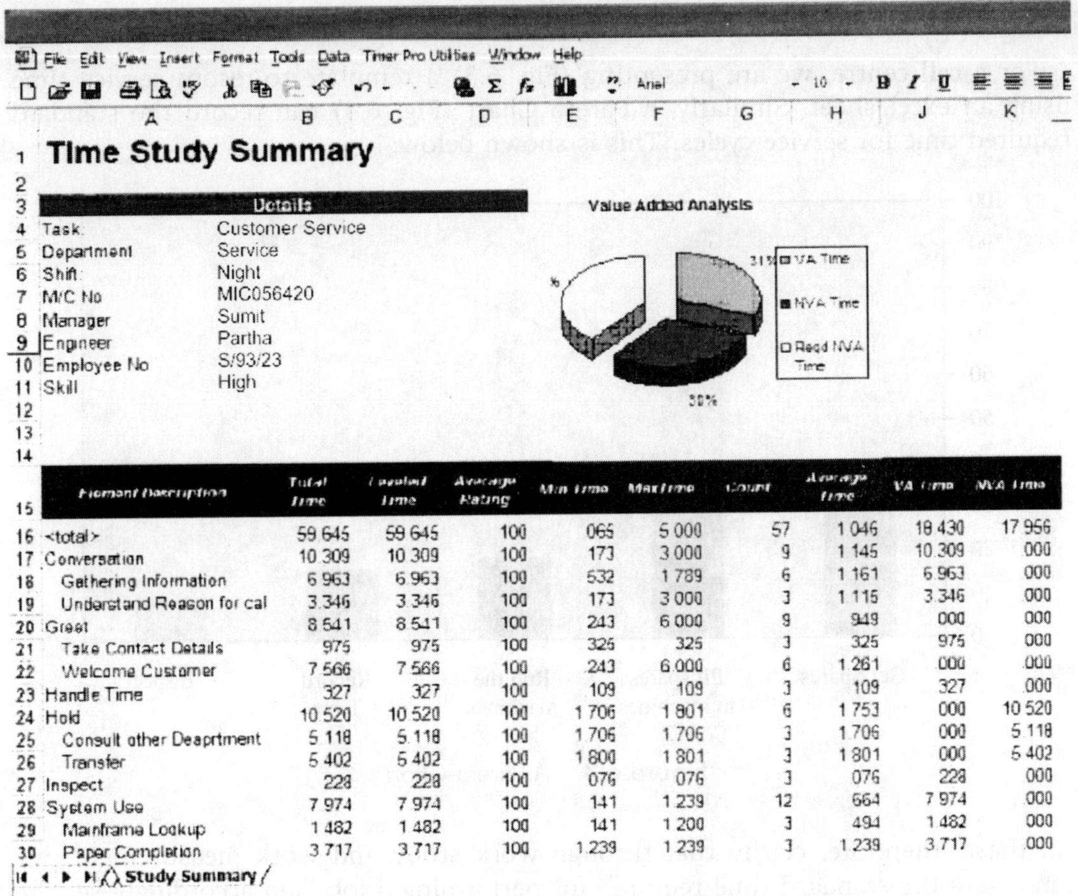

Time Study Summary

Details	
Task	Customer Service
Department	Service
Shift	Night
M/C No	MIC056420
Manager	Sumit
Engineer	Partha
Employee No	S/93/23
Skill	High

Element Description	Total Time	Leveled Time	Average Rating	Min Time	Max Time	Count	Average Time	VA Time	NVA Time
<total>	59 645	59 645	100	065	5 000	57	1 046	18 430	17 956
Conversation	10.309	10.309	100	173	3 000	9	1 145	10.309	.000
Gathering Information	6 963	6 963	100	532	1 789	6	1 161	6 963	000
Understand Reason for cal	3.346	3 346	100	173	3 000	3	1 115	3.346	.000
Greet	8 541	8 541	100	243	6 000	9	949	000	000
Take Contact Details	975	975	100	325	325	3	325	975	000
Welcome Customer	7 566	7 566	100	243	6.000	6	1.261	.000	.000
Handle Time	327	327	100	109	109	3	109	327	.000
Hold	10.520	10.520	100	1 706	1 801	6	1 753	000	10 520
Consult other Deaprtment	5 118	5.118	100	1.706	1.706	3	1.706	000	5 118
Transfer	5 402	5 402	100	1 800	1 801	3	1 801	000	5 402
Inspect	228	228	100	076	076	3	076	228	000
System Use	7 974	7 974	100	141	1 239	12	664	7 974	.000
Mainframe Lookup	1 482	1 482	100	141	1 200	3	494	1 482	000
Paper Completion	3 717	3.717	100	1.239	1 239	3	1.239	3.717	.000

Study Summary

Figure 6.3 *Time study sheet recording service time at a call centre*

6.13.5 Time-and-Motion Study for Service Jobs

It is evident that time-and-motion study plays a pivotal role in manufacturing to effect positive change in the performance level of workers, both in terms of quality and optimization of resource capacity. However, nowadays, time-and-motion studies are also used in the service industry to improve the service cycle time. Service jobs, even though intangible in nature, can be recorded using tools like stop watches, video cameras, etc. Using the same standard formula, we can calculate the service standard time. The formula for computing the standard time is as follows:

$$ST = (NT)(1 - AF)$$

Where ST: Standard Time

NT: Normal Time

AF: Allowance Factor

For a call centre, we are presenting (Fig. 6.3) a template to record service time using an excel sheet. Similarly, a Pareto Chart (Fig. 6.4) can record the standard required time for service cycles. This is shown below:

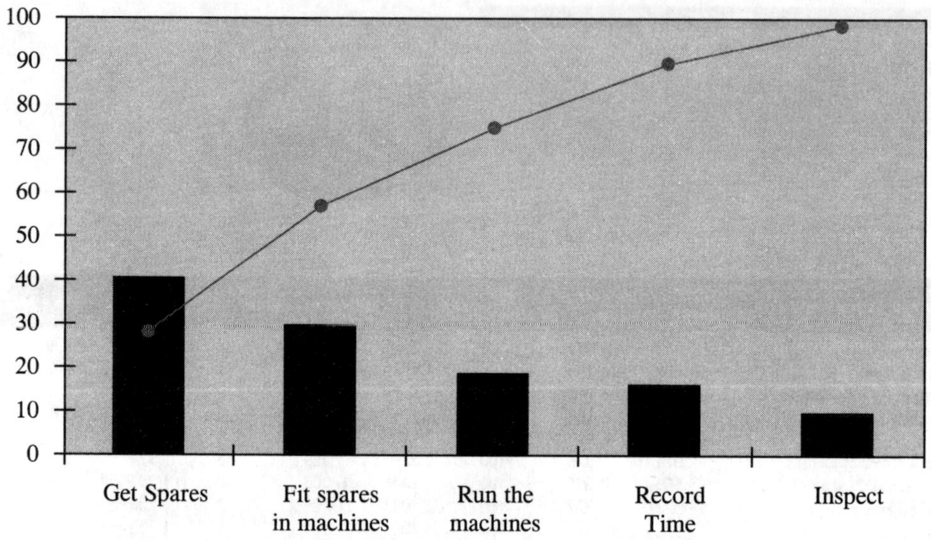

Figure 6.4 *A Pareto Chart*

All these, therefore, clarify that through work study and work measurement, we can assess the standard time required for performing a job, and accordingly set the performance standards for workers, and decide their compensation.

SUMMARY

1. For production and operations management, work measurement requires effective information and documentation on job analysis, job description and job evaluation. All these processes help in identifying job requirements and suitably describing jobs and job-families, skill sets, skill mapping and developing skill inventories. These are also critical inputs to make decisions regarding manpower requirement to meet present and future needs.
2. Time-and-motion studies are the most critical inputs for effective work measurement. Without a standard time, companies cannot decide workers' compensation scientifically, and workers also cannot assess the expectations of the organization from them. For effective work measurement, we need to consider various inputs through job information, job analysis, job description, job evaluation and then job pricing.

3. Other methods of job assessment for pricing a job value are work study. This is carried out through method study and work measurement, and it can bring positive change to the organization. Time study is the most important work measurement technique. Both method study and time study require certain well-defined steps. Organizations standardize their activities based on method study and time study.
4. Ergonomics, motion economy, human engineering, value analysis, work sampling, and work simplification, etc. are some other techniques of work measurement explained in this chapter.

KEY WORDS

Method Study It is a productivity improvement step. Method Study helps to produce the same output using fewer resources or produce more with proportionately less inputs. It reduces, if not eliminates waste. Method Study ensures creativity, innovativeness, optimal decision-making power, good organizational practices and better communication.

Motion Economy The process of minimizing the physical and perceptual loads imposed on people engaged in any type of work is known as motion economy. It could be in the office, the shop floor, the kitchen or at the driving wheel. This science leads to better design of equipment, jigs and fixtures, hand tools, furniture and labour-saving devices. It also facilitates better layout of offices, warehouses, plants and operating areas like the office desk, work bench, aircraft, cockpit and crew compartments of armoured fighting vehicles, etc. The application of the principles of motion economy eliminates or minimizes wasteful and fatiguing movements and increases the productivity of workers.

Human Engineering Method Study seeks to determine the most efficient combination of man, machine and the working environment. It is necessary to determine which functions are better performed by man and which functions are better performed by machines. Both man and machine surpass each other in different ways. Economy again influences the man–machine combination. The term, human engineering, is more appropriately used to solve these man–machine problems in the design, operation and maintenance of plants and machinery. In fact, it is not appropriate to treat this science as an independent discipline as it is, broadly, under the purview of ergonomics.

Value Engineering It is an organized creative technique to analyse the functions of a product, service or a system to achieve the required functions at the lowest cost, ensuring its performance reliability and maintainability. This is also known as Value Analysis or Value Management.

GENERAL REVIEW QUESTIONS

1. Define Work Study. What are its important objectives? How do trade unions react to Work Study Programmes? In what way can you combat such reactions?
2. What are the important roles of Method Study? Identify the important contributions of Method Study and discuss at least five such contributions in detail.
3. Discuss in detail the steps involved in a Method Study Programme.
4. Define Work Measurement. What are its different techniques? Discuss at least three techniques elaborately.
5. What are the steps involved in a Time Study Programme? How does it help in the Work Measurement Programme in an industrial unit?
6. What is Ergonomics? How does it help to increase productivity? Discuss with examples.
7. What are the basic principles of Motion Economy? Discuss these principles in relation to a work area with which you are familiar.
8. Explain how Human Engineering techniques influence Machine Design. Select an advertisement of a furniture item and discuss its ergonomic features.
9. What are the steps involved in Value Analysis? What course of action would you suggest for a successful Value Analysis Study? Elaborate your answer.
10. Explain the concept of work sampling. Do you think work sampling is a better technique than time study? Justify your answer.
11. Short notes
    (a) Job Questionnaire
    (b) Ranking
    (c) Points Rating
    (d) Factor Comparison
    (e) Motion Economy
    (f) Use Value
    (g) Process Chart

CRITICAL REVIEW QUESTION

1. You have been appointed as an analyst for work sampling jobs. Your company manufactures sophisticated electronics items. Workers are divided into small groups and perform well-defined and structured tasks in different work stations. Draw up a work sampling plan with suitable justification

REFERENCES

1. Allan H. Mogensen. 1932. *Common Sense Applied to Motion and Time Study*. New York: McGraw-Hill Book Company Inc.

2. Brisley, C. L. 1971. "Work Sampling." In *Industrial Engineering Handbook*. H. B. Maynard ed. New York: McGraw Hill.
3. Cohen, M.A. 1997. *Manufacturing Automation.* Chicago: Irwin..
4. Tippet, L.H.C. 1927. *Random Sampling Numbers: Traces for Computers, XV.* Cambridge, Massachusetts: Harvard University Press.

ADDITIONAL REFERENCES

1. Adler, Paul S. 1993. Time-and-Motion Regained. *Harvard Business Review.* Boston: Jan/Feb, Vol.71, Issue. 1, pp. 97–108.
2. Konz, Stephen. 1983. Work Design: Industrial Ergonomics, 2nd edition. New York: John Wiley & Sons.
3. Lott, Merrill R. 1926. *Wage Scales and Job Evaluation: Scientific Determination of Wage Rates on the Basis of Services Rendered.* New York: Ronald Press.
4. Richard, B., Chase, Nicholas, J., Aquilano, and F. Robert, Jacobs. 2002. *Operations Management for Competitive Advantage*. New Delhi: Tata McGraw-Hill Publishing Company Limited.
5. Schmenner, R.W. 1995. *Service Operations Management*. Englewood Cliffs, M.J: Prentice Hall.
6. Lowry, S.M., Maynard, H.B., and Stegemerten, G.J. 1927. *Time and Motion Study and formulas for wage incentives.* New York: McGraw-Hill

CASE STUDY

Ergonomically designed machines – the case of *Orient India*

Orient is a noted manufacturer of berge wood furniture, which is popular in Germany and Italy; as a result, it exports almost 90% of its manufactured furniture items to these two countries. *Orient* gets a tremendous cost advantage by sourcing berge wood at very competitive rates from the northeastern states of India, where the local people use it as firewood.

Italy is famous for furniture design. Most of *Orient's* designers are trained in Italy after they graduate from institutions like the National Institute of Design. Furniture designing is a very high profile job with a good pay package. Some of *Orient*'s designers are paid as much as its Directors.

Orient recently introduced assembly lines for furniture manufacturing, replacing their age-old job shop type manufacturing systems. It had to take this decision to switch over to batch production. The company's workers are highly skilled and competent enough to manufacture any furniture item with high accuracy and precision. Workers use their creative instincts to shape furniture as per the design.

At times, workers' inputs are used by the designers of the company. Along with the assembly line, simultaneous change to the CNC machining centres was introduced, which were capable enough to perform the tasks as per the programmed design. The company trained its workers on the new systems of production and on CNC machine operation. To the workers, initially, it was fascinating. However, when they began using the new method of production, they started resenting the changes and requested the company go back to the earlier work process. Workers argued that such fragmentation of job content, in an assembly line with the back-up of CNC machining centres, reduced their job to a routine, repetitive one, which they felt was an insult to their skill and craftsmanship. Many *Orient* workers are carpenters by profession. Carpenters in India are traditionally viewed as respected members of society.

Discussion Question

Experts retained by the company attributed this to an ergonomic problem, namely, the lack of man–machine interface. Do you agree? Justify your answer.

CHAPTER 7

Network Analysis and Project Management

LEARNING OBJECTIVES

After reading this chapter, you will be able to understand:

- Definitions, Concepts and Different Forms of Network Analysis
- Definitions and Concepts of Float
- PERT/CPM Networks
- Process and Rules of Drawing Network Diagrams
- Crashing a Project Time Requirement
- Definitions, Concepts and Management of a Project
- Project life cycle and its Analysis
- Project Planning
- Duties and Responsibilities of Project Managers

Opening Vignette

Project Management in Software Development

In 2000, a group of young entrepreneurs started a software development centre at Hyderabad. The company which is now famous for its innovative software solutions, and is applauded world-wide, wanted to highlight its global presence through extensive marketing. This resulted in huge order booking globally. All software projects are time bound and require the company to develop the software and implement the same at the customers' premises, following a time-bound schedule. Delay in project implementation adversely affects the business of the company, due to the penalty levied by the customer and in terms of customer dissatisfaction. The company is well recognized for its quality customer services, but inordinate delays, at times, made the customers impatient, and in some cases, customers have even cancelled their orders when project completion time had been overshot. To counter such an adverse situation, the company developed a project control mechanism. The newly-developed project control mechanism helped the company to understand factors such as the trade-off between the project duration and its cost, identification of the critical path of a project for early completion, and activity-wise time–cost relationship.

To successfully implement the newly-developed project control mechanism, the company trained all its project managers, and even the team members to understand this and self-assess the problem of project delay and its consequential effects. The control mechanism provides signals when a project gets delayed beyond seven days. By referring to this project control mechanism, however, it is possible for team members to understand the possible delay, even on an hourly basis. The company is now able to manage its projects on time, and even in some cases, completes projects ahead of schedule

7.1 INTRODUCTION

A project is a one-time activity to achieve some defined goals. It is different from a programme, which is an ongoing process; for example, inventory management programme, new product development programme, etc. From this perspective, a project is a sub-set of a programme, as a programme per se manages several projects at one point of time. Project management is a carefully crafted series of organized activities for the successful completion of a project.

Successful project management requires a project plan. Companies often consider this requirement redundant and directly engage in project activities; which often lead to multiple complications in project execution. Project planning is, therefore, a prerequisite for successful project management.

Successful management of a project requires the effective services of a project manager, who manages the project. The job of a project manager requires specialized knowledge and skill. The project manager has to be responsible for everything related to the project.

A project life cycle follows certain basic sequential actions like start, plan, do and finish. For production and operations management, we usually observe different phases a of project life cycle such as initiation, planning, implementation and commissioning. However, for a service project (like a software project), such phases change to inception, elaboration, construction and transition.

It is done by describing each segment or linkage of the system in terms of other components or activities of the system. Thus, it makes explicit the total system and the inter-relationships among the parts. A network is illustrated by a flowchart or diagram. The flow of materials and/or information is measured as volume, specifications or time.

7.2 DIFFERENT FORMS OF NETWORK ANALYSIS

There are different forms of Network Analysis, which may be simple or complex, may be generalized or may be exclusively designed for specific types of projects. PERT/PEP and CPM are the most widely-used techniques used in Network Analysis.

7.2.1 Critical Path Method (CPM)

This technique is used for planning, scheduling, estimating and controlling engineering and construction. This method was used by *Du Pont* in 1959 to schedule plant maintenance shutdowns during changeovers. The lessons learned through this application, were later used for planning purposes, building and construction, especially in large construction projects.

The key tool in this technique of planning, scheduling and controlling complex construction jobs is a diagram using arrows to represent specific jobs. Such line diagrams clarify the relationships of every task to every other task; this cannot be done using bar charts. *Critical jobs* are those jobs which relate to one another (from start to finish of a project), each depending upon the completion of the one before it. Total project time, therefore, is the summation of the time to be taken up by a critical job. There may be more than one critical job in a project.

A simple form of a CPM diagram illustrates the jobs to be performed to finish a project (in order of sequence), timing and costs. Once all these elements are specified, both the total time and total cost of the project can be determined by adding the different sub-elements. The consequences of various managerial decisions can be predicted by simulating their impact.

7.2.2 PERT/PEP Technique

The PERT/PEP Technique is based on critical path scheduling. However, there is a fundamental difference between PERT/PEP and critical-path scheduling. The PERT/PEP technique is applicable where there is no established system for doing the task, and therefore, no exact basis for estimating the required time to complete each task. Critical path scheduling, on the other hand, is usually applied to jobs which are established or have been done before and where it is possible to predict performance accurately. Consequently, more sophisticated mathematical models must be used in the PERT/PEP technique.

PERT may, therefore, be defined as follows:

PERT is a statistical technique that is diagnostic and prognostic; it is used to quantify knowledge about the uncertainties faced in completing intellectual and physical activities, essential for timely achievement of programme deadlines. It is a technique for focussing management's attention on danger signals that require remedial decisions, and on areas of effort which have trade-offs in terms of time, resources or technical performance, which might improve capability to meet major deadlines.

The PERT technique is, therefore, based on the concept that in any programme, there are three variables:

(i) time
(ii) resources (HR, facilities, funds)
(iii) performance specifications.

Any one of these may vary within the limits established for such a programme, while holding the other two constant. For example, holding time and performance constant, the requirements for resources may be determined.

It is, therefore, clear that both PERT and CPM have similarities in terms of concepts and methodology. We use these techniques in project scheduling problems. However, we use PERT in analyzing project scheduling, where completion time is not certain, and CPM, where activity durations are known with certainty. In essence, therefore, PERT is probabilistic in nature and more appropriately used in R&D Projects, while CPM is a deterministic technique, which finds application more appropriately in construction projects.

7.2.3 Graphical Evaluation Review Technique (GERT)

Graphical Evaluation Review Technique (GERT) is known as a stochastic network analysis technique. It is based on probabilistic treatment of network logic and activity duration estimation. GERT helps us establish a logical relationship between project activities. The GERT technique was first introduced by Pritsker (1966). Although GERT can eliminate the inherent defects of PERT/CPM, identifying activities that need not be performed, it is not used widely because of its complexity.

7.3 BENEFITS OF NETWORK ANALYSIS

Some of the benefits of network analysis can be enumerated as follows:

1. It helps reappraise existing systems and identify duplication and overlapping that may detract from the effectiveness of the system design.
2. It helps management to evaluate the sub-systems and their inter-connecting networks continuously, consistent with the over-all objectives of the system.
3. It allows an evaluation of the impact of various sub-system changes on other sub-systems and/or the total system. A change in type of output or a change in scheduling in a particular sub-system can affect operations in other areas. This effect can be determined in units of time, money, facilities or other resources.
4. It encourages introspection of an existing system or provides the framework for visualizing the make-up of a proposed system.

7.4 DEFECTS OF NETWORK ANALYSIS

Despite the importance and benefits of network analysis, it has some inherent defects also:

1. It provides no guarantee for effective system design, as variations in performance could always occur.
2. There always exists the danger of assuming relationships among segments which do not exist, ignoring important relationships which should be considered, or weighing existing relationships improperly.
3. It requires constant follow-up as the relationship between the segments may change with time.

7.5 DEFINITION AND CONCEPT OF FLOAT

A float is defined as the available time to delay an activity without, however, delaying the date of completion of a project. It means any possible delay in some activity or activities will not increase the duration of the project. However, it is important to understand that only non-critical activities can be delayed. Delaying critical activities can ultimately delay the completion time of the entire project. The term 'float' can also be defined as slack, cushion, margin, excess time or flexibility. We can calculate floats based on two types of networks, these are the Activity-On-Node (AON) and the Activity-on-Arrow (AOA). Both the methods, however, will give similar results.

We have three types of floats: independent, free and total. An independent float indicates that an activity can be started late and finished early. Because of this, results from this type of float often become negative. Free float on the other hand is a normal float, and it explains which activity cam be delayed, without, however, delaying a successive activity or activities. Some of the characteristics of a free float, are: when we have more than one succeeding activity, the minimum of the floats must be construed as free, and it is always less than or equal to the total float. Therefore, in all critical activities, free float is always zero. Total float shows which activities can be delayed from its early start without delaying completion of the project. In a free float, when we delay one activity, we have to start succeeding activities on time. When we have more succeeding activities, we have to consider the minimum. For critical activities, both the total float and the free float are always zero.

For both the AON and AOA methods of calculation of floats, we follow different formulae. For AON, the formulae are:

Independent Float (IF)	=	EF – LS
Free Float (FF)	=	G (ES) – D (EF)
Total Float (TF)	=	D (LF) – D (EF)

where,

ES stands for earliest start
LS stands for latest start
EF stands for earliest finish and
LF stands for latest finish
G stands for early start of successor activities
D stands for early finish of existing activity

For calculation of float under the AOA method, we use the following formulae:

Independent float (IF) = EF – LS
Free Float (FF) = G (ES) –D (EF)
Total float = D (LF)– D (EF)

Formulae are:

1. $IF(i, j) = EF(j) - ES(i) - D(i, j)$
2. $FF(i, j) = EF(j) - ES(i) - D(i, j)$, (If there is more than one activity, the minimum thereof)
3. $TF(i, j) = LF(j) - ES(i) - D(i, j)$ (If there is more than one activity, the minimum thereof)

Apart from all the floats mentioned, we have the interference float, which is indicated as the difference between total float and independent float.

Let us understand the interference float, using a simple example:

XIMB Bhubaneswar has organized an international conference at their campus, where they are expecting nearly 2000 experts from across the country and from abroad. The conference is scheduled for 15th to 19th July, 2012. The institute has to arrange for the travel of delegates by air. Bhubaneswar has a small airport with limited flying operations. The institute has to arrange for special flights to arrive from 14th July onwards, and for departure, from 20th July onwards. Bhubaneswar is a city of temples, and has a lot of sightseeing opportunities. Expecting some delegates to leave immediately after the conference, from 20th July, 2012 onwards, depending on flight availability, and that some guests would opt for sightseeing, we can calculate the floats as under:

Suppose a delegate decides to delay his/her journey for shopping and sightseeing for a day; this one day is called independent float. Any time beyond this (minus the actual conference timing), would be considered as the total float time. Interference float is the scope to modify the sightseeing time, depending on the priority of the delegates.

Thus, for a project, consideration of floats helps us decide which activity has to be given priority, and which has to be rescheduled. Floats, therefore, help us manage the project with resource optimization by manipulating the time requirement of non-critical tasks.

7.6 PERT/CPM NETWORKS

A project is a set of activities or jobs (tasks or operations) that are performed in a certain sequence, determined logically or technologically. Initially, therefore, it is necessary to determine all specific activities that comprise the project and their inter-dependent relationships. We can illustrate this with the following example:

Let us assume that a new CNC machine has been procured from abroad and it now requires installation. The activity starts with the procurement of manpower (both internally and from the firm from which the machine has been procured), doing grouting and foundation work, doing electrical work, installing the machine, training the operators, and finally, the trial run. The various activities required to be performed can be then distributed, time-wise as below (Table 7.1):

Table 7.1 *List of activities with precedence relationships for installing a CNC Machine*

Activity Code	Job Description	Job Duration (in days)	Immediate Predecessor(s)
A	Procurement of manpower	2	-
B	Grouting of Foundation	5	A
C	Electrical Work	1	A
D	Installing the Machine	1	B
E	Train the Operators	6	C
F	Trial Run	1	D, E

The immediate predecessors for a particular activity indicate that those activities are required to be completed before the starting of this job. Once the activities comprising a project and their inter-relationships are identified, we can graphically portray it by a network or arrow diagram. We can depict the network as in Fig. 7.1 below:

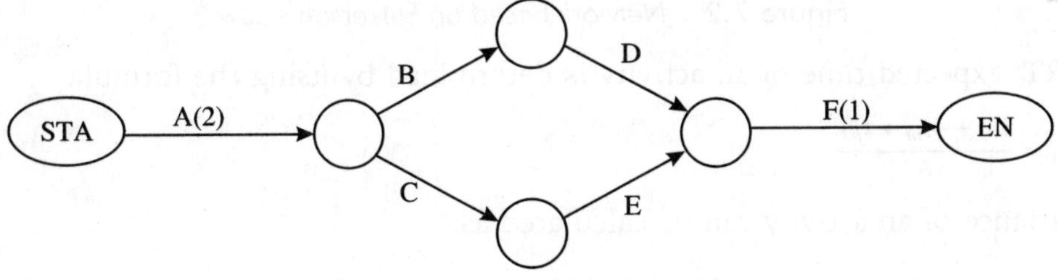

Figure 7.1 *A network diagram*

We define a network as a logical graphical representation of the activities in a project. A network demonstrates the logical sequence of depicting interrelationships among the various activities and events of a project. Activities are physical and an identifiable part of a project, and are represented by an arrow in a network diagram. The 'start of an activity' is represented by the head of an arrow, while the end is indicated by the tail of an arrow.

In a network, an event indicates accomplishment of some task. The beginning and ending of an activity are represented by events (initial and terminal), and indicated as a node. We indicate nodes by a circle, and number it using the Fulkerson's Rule.

In line with Fulkerson's Rule we follow the steps as under to number the nodes, which help us to correctly draw the network diagram.

- Number the initial arrow as 1. Initial arrow has no incoming arrows. It can only have outgoing arrows.
- Represent each activity by a single arrow.
- Maintain precedence relationships among the activities.
- If required, include dummy activities to maintain precedence relationships.
- Avoid looping among activities.
- Create nodes from the initial node (at least more than 1), and number them consecutively.
- Repeat the process to reach the final node, where all arrows come in.

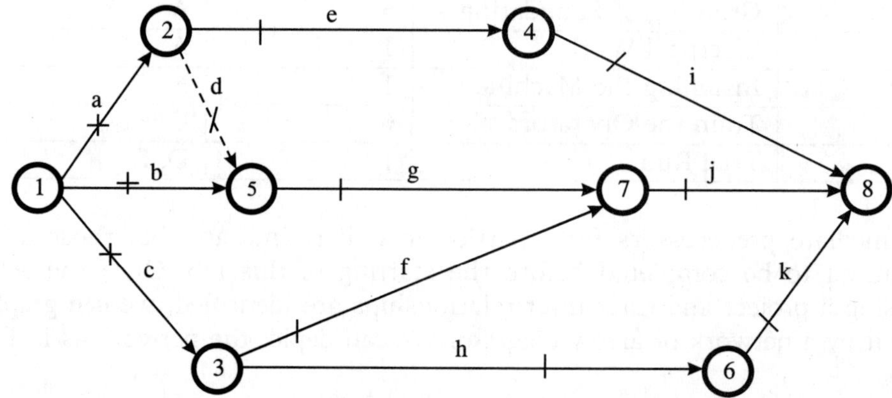

Figure 7.2 *Network based on Fulkerson's Law*

In PERT, expected time of an activity is determined by using the formula:

$$t_0 = \frac{(t_0 + 4t_m + t_p)}{6}$$

The variance of an activity can be calculated as:

$$\sigma^2 = \left[\frac{(t_p - t_0)}{6}\right]^2$$

Process and rules of drawing the diagram Notice we have only a single start and end event in the diagram. Time requirement in the diagram flows from left to right and so also the numbering sequence. Each event has been given a unique number; hence, activities have a unique label, that is, head and tail event numbers. Some of the rules of network construction are:

1. Each defined activity is represented by a single arrow. Thus, a single activity cannot be represented twice in the network.
2. Before undertaking a particular activity, all activities, preceding it, should be completed first.
3. Events are identified by numbers, and hence, duplication of event numbers must be avoided.
4. All networks should have one initial and one terminal node.
5. There may be a situation where more than one activity needs to be simultaneously completed. We call this a situation of merge event. Similarly, a burst event is one where more than one activity needs to be simultaneously initiated.
6. Parallel activities, without having intervening relationships, are prohibited.
7. It may be necessary to incorporate a dummy activity, when two or more activities have identical predecessor and successor activities.

Rules regarding dummy activities In a network, we are required to use dummy activities, in cases where two or more parallel activities have the same head or tail events, or else, network construction will remain incomplete. Dummy activity does not require time or resources and it is indicated by dotted lines.

7.7 NETWORK DIAGRAM SYMBOLS

Some of the common symbols used in the network diagram are indicated (in Fig. 7.3) below:

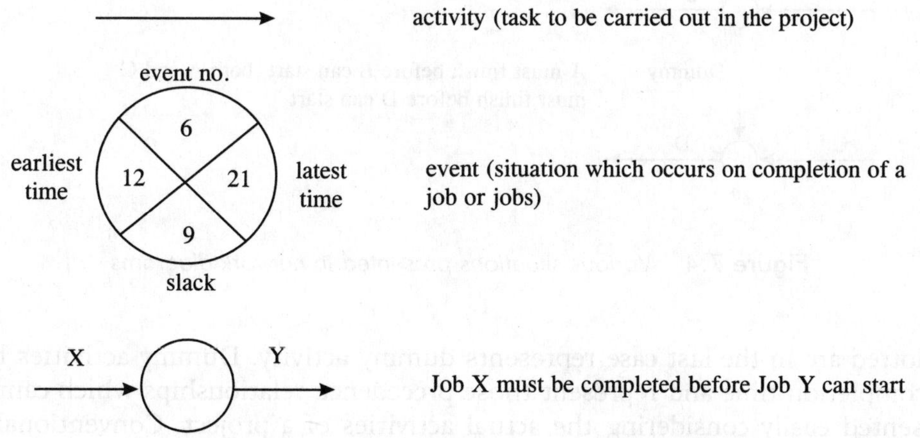

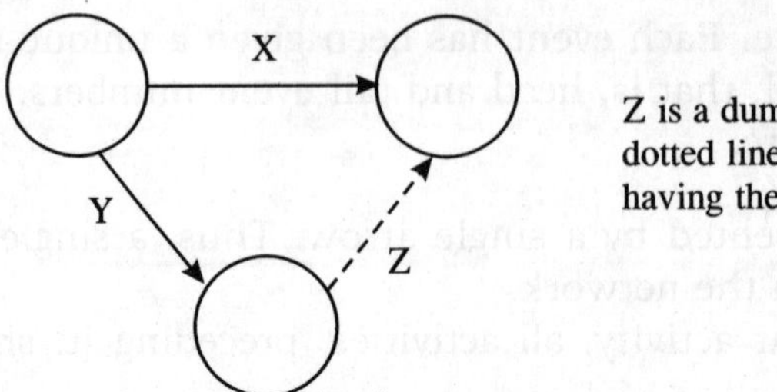

Figure 7.3 *Common symbols used in network diagrams*

Some of the situations that we face while constructing network diagrams can be presented as follows (Fig. 7.4).

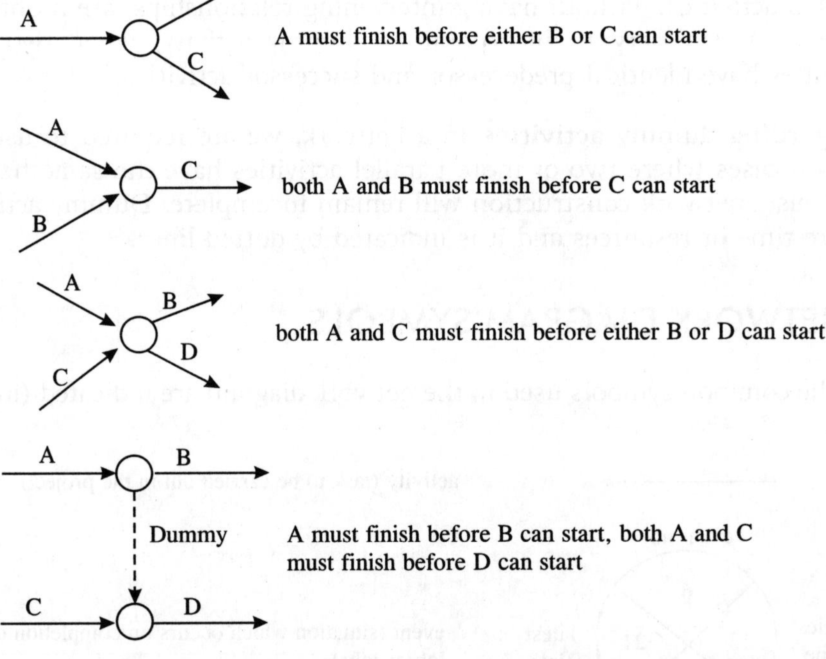

Figure 7.4 *Various situations presented in network diagrams*

The dotted arc in the last case represents dummy activity. Dummy activities have a zero completion time and represent those precedence relationships which cannot be represented easily considering the actual activities of a project. Conventionally we show dummies as dotted arcs in network diagrams.

7.8 PROGRAMME EVALUATION AND REVIEW TECHNIQUE (PERT)

We have so far discussed the methodology of scheduling times of different activities, critical path and the project length, assuming activity times are known and constant. Usually, activity times are known and constant. But this assumption does not hold good for PERT, as there is every possibility of completing a job before the expected time or there may be some unplanned delay. Thus, instead of having a single estimate, there may be three estimates for an activity

(a) **Optimistic Time (a)** This is the shortest time a particular activity can take to be completed and is therefore an ideal estimate.

(b) **Most Likely Time (m)** This is the modal time, which is expected to be taken to complete a job and is based on past records.

(c) **Pessimistic Time (b)** This is the longest time an activity can take and it occurs with a probability of less than one per cent. This, therefore, is the worst time estimate, for any eventuality.

With these three time estimates, a single expected time to complete a project is determined with the following weighted average formula:

$$t = \frac{a + 4m + b}{6}$$

Where, t = expected time of the activity

a = optimistic time

m = most likely, or modal time

b = pessimistic time.

The standard deviation, of the completion time of an activity is calculated as follows:

$$\sigma = \frac{b - a}{6}$$

$$\text{Variance} = \sigma = \frac{(b - a)}{6}$$

7.9 CRITICAL PATH CALCULATION

Based on the critical path calculation guidelines given above, let us now solve the given problem.

Task	Dependent on	Duration
A	-	3
B	-	6
C	-	3
D	A	5
E	C	2
F	B,D,E	6
G	A	9

Calculation of Earliest Time:

Let us first draw the diagram as follows:

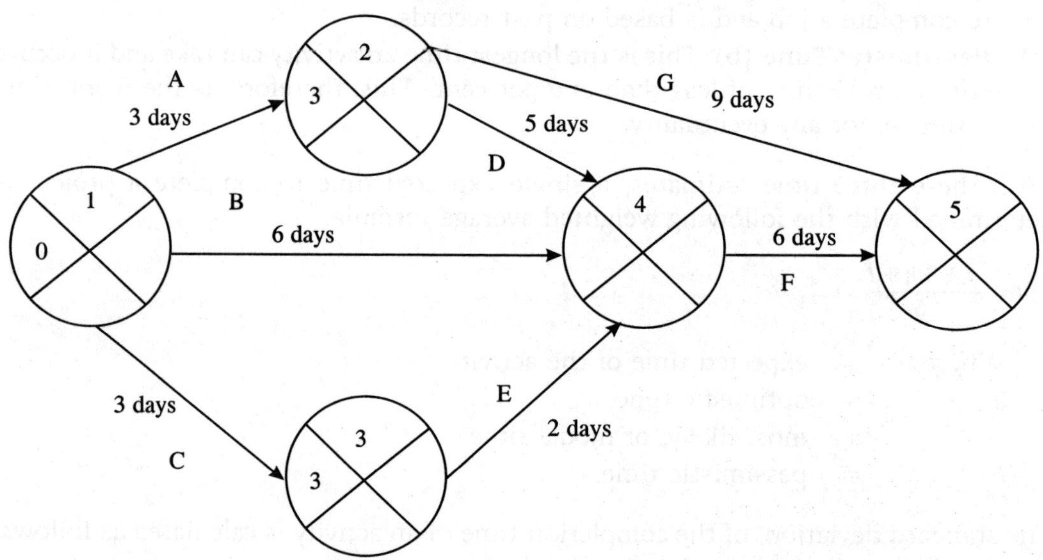

Figure 7.5 *Network diagram to calculate the earliest time*

Let us now calculate the earliest time, both for events 4 and 5.

Solution to Calculation of Earliest Start Time for Event 4:

Activity	Preceding ET	Duration	Calculated ET
$2 \rightarrow 4$	3	5	8
$1 \rightarrow 4$	0	6	6
$3 \rightarrow 4$	3	2	5

So the earliest start time for event 4 is day 8.

Solution to Calculation of Earliest Start Time for Event 5:

This solution builds on the previous one – the earliest start time for event 4 was day 8 therefore

Activity	Preceding ET	Duration	Calculated ET
2 → 5	3	9	12
4 → 5	8	6	14

So, the earliest start time for event 5 is day 14 (by this time all the preceding activities will have been completed).

Calculation of Latest Time

Let us once again redraw the diagram as under:

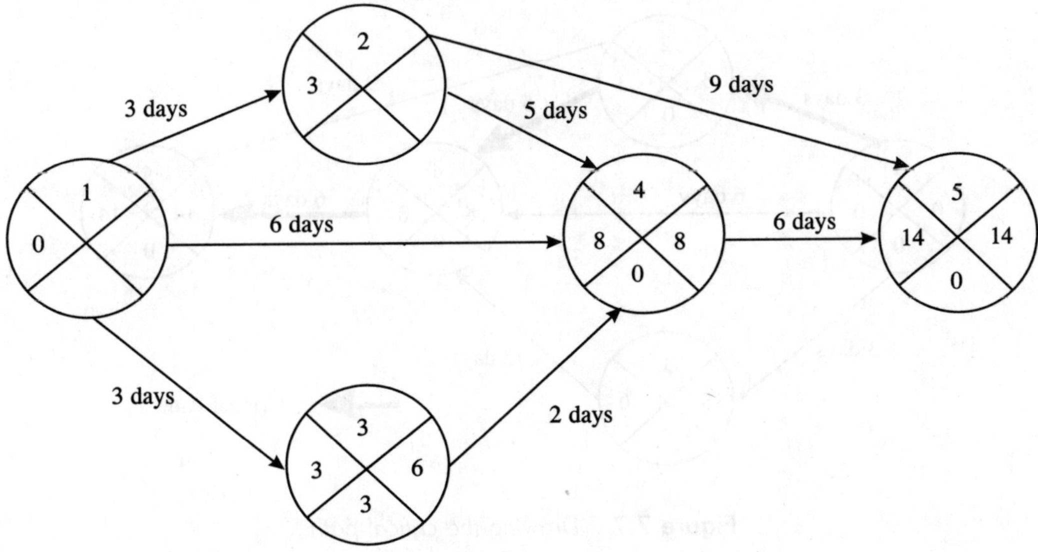

Figure 7.6 *Network diagram used to calculate the latest time.*

Based on Fig. 7.6, let us now calculate the latest time of events 2 and 1. Solution to Calculation of Latest Start Time for Event 2

Activity	Preceding ET	–Duration	= Calculated ET
2 → 4	8	5	3
2 → 5	14	9	5

So, the latest start time for event 2 is day 3 (by this time, the minimum amount of remaining time is left to complete subsequent tasks).

Solution to Calculation of Latest Start Time for Event 1:

This solution builds on the previous one – the latest start time for event 2 was day 3 therefore:

Activity	Preceding ET	–Duration	= Calulated ET
1 → 2	3	3	0
1 → 3	6	6	0
1 → 4	8	3	5

So, the latest start time for event 1 is day 0 (by this time, the minimum amount of remaining time is left to complete subsequent tasks).

Note that the latest time of event 1 must be zero (otherwise an error has occurred).

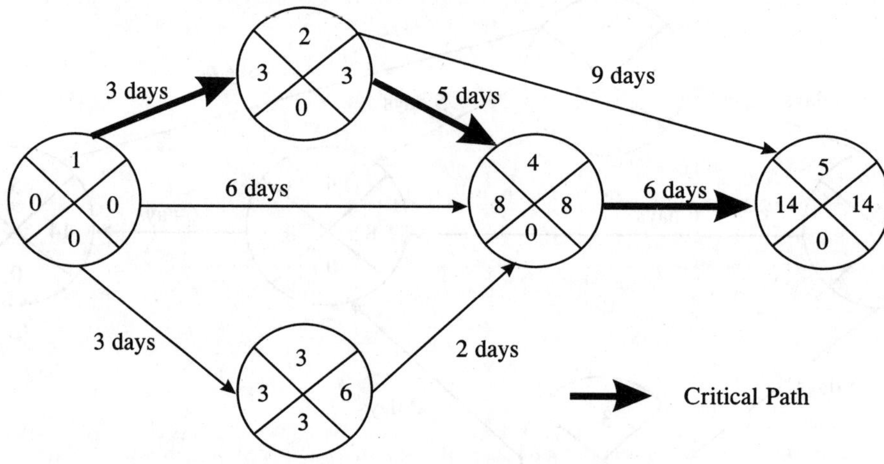

Figure 7.7 *Drawing the critical path*

7.9.1 Features of Critical Path Analysis

In project management, critical path analysis is the most effective tool for managing projects. Critical path analysis (CPA) has the following essential features:

- CPA puts in all individual activities for making up a larger project.
- CPA shows the way that activities need to be undertaken.
- CPA also explains the order of the activities, it shows which activities can take place once other activities are completed.
- CPA directs which activities can be done simultaneously, and in the process, can reduce the overall time for the completion of the total project.
- CPA also helps in just-in-time resource planning, thereby reducing unnecessary inventory holding.

- Along the critical path, nodes are numbered for identification of earliest start time (EST) of the activities and the latest finish time (LFT) for the immediate preceding activities.
- Along the critical path there must not be any crossing activities, which are very important among critical activities.
- Finally, CPA helps in time and resource optimization, and thereby minimizes the cost of project completion.

To compute the CPA, it is important to estimate the time elapsed for each activity, considering the time from commencement to completion. Some of the given constraining assumptions for CPA are:

- Availability of all resource inputs
- Availability of manpower
- Just-in-time availability of materials and other services
- Zero work disruption due to industrial relations problems
- Zero work disruption due to natural calamities.

With the identification of the critical path, through critical path analysis, we ensure zero float or slack through the critical path, resulting in no delay in the project execution. With zero float, the time along the critical path is the minimum time required for the completion of a project. To complete the activities along the critical path, it may be necessary to utilize extra manpower, incurring additional costs in terms of overtime costs, etc., but the overall time saving for project completion helps in neutralizing the extra cost burden.

7.9.2 Important Characteristics of a Critical Path

- Every network should have a critical path.
- A single network may have more than one critical path.
- A critical path is one of the connecting links (in a network, we may have more than one connecting link), between the initial and terminal activity.
- The number of activities in a critical path may be less than the activities in a non-critical path.
- A critical path may have dummy activity.
- A critical path determines project duration time.
- Activities on a critical path are, by nature, critical activities.
- If the project duration time needs to be shortened, then activities on the critical path need to be shortened.

7.9.3 How to arrive at the critical path in a network

- Draw the network enumerating all the paths.
- List the activities on each of these paths.
- Sum up the activities along each path.

- Identify the longest duration along each path. The longest duration is obviously the critical path in the network.

Let us now try this problem. In the table below, we have given optimistic (a), most likely (m) and pessimistic (p) time for the completion of a project. Compute the expected time of project completion and draw the network to show the critical path (please do the drawing part yourself)

Activity	Time			$Tie = a + 4m + b/6$	$oi = \frac{b-a}{6}$ (standard deviation of completetion time of an activity)	oi = variance of (completion time of an activity)
	a	m	b			
A 1–2	2	4	6	4	4/6	4/9
B 2–3	3	5	13	6	10/6	25/9
C 2–4	2	6	10	6	8/6	16/9
D 3–6	13	18	23	18	10/6	25/9
E 3–5	8	16	24	16	16/6	64/9
F 4–6	6	7	14	8	8/6	16/9
G 5–7	2	6	10	6	8/6	16/9
H 6–7	2	4	6	4	4/6	4/9
I 7–8	4	5	6	5	2/6	1/9

After you draw the network, check whether you are getting the critical path as 1–2–3–5–7–8 or A–B–E–G–I. Summing up the time, along the critical path, your expected time for project completion or project length would be 37 days.

Variance of the expected project length

$$= 4/9 + 25/9 + 64/9 + 16/9 + 1/9 = 110/9 \text{ days}$$

Standard deviation of expected project length

$$= /110/9 = 3.496 \text{ days}$$

7.9.4 Differences between PERT and CPM

Both PERT and CPM ultimately lead to the same end, the only difference is in their treatment of activity time. PERT considers activity time as a random variable. CPM, however, considers a single deterministic time value for the activities. Again, PERT focusses on an exclusive time variable, whereas CPM considers the trade-off between time and cost. CPM is applied for repeated projects, as leveraging our experience, we can understand the possible areas where we can reduce the time requirement. PERT, on the contrary, is for activity-wise first project time requirement analysis. Again, CPM considers, both the time and costs, while PERT considers only time requirements for the activities.

7.10 CRASHING OF A PROJECT

Project crashing refers to the reduction in the duration of any project activity, by allocating additional resources, which obviously incur higher cost. The process of crashing continues until the additional costs outweigh the benefits. The basic assumptions of CPM analysis are that the activities and functions of a project can be crashed to reduce the time required for project completion. However, crashing increases direct costs, due to the increase in man-hours (which in turn increases wage payment and wastage, like normal scrap-arising, etc.). Whether project crashing is beneficial or not, is weighed by finding out the difference between crash cost and normal cost. If crashing seems to be the better alternative, then the Critical Path is re-drawn by correspondingly reducing the time requirement. It is important to note that crashing will not eliminate the requirement of any activity, but it reduces the time requirement of any activity or activities.

7.10.1 Crashing of Project Time Requirements (AOA network example)

A company has made available the following information of a project. Apart from the above tabular information, the company has clarified that activity 7 cannot be started till the completion of activity 5.

Questions

1. Draw the network diagram.
2. Calculate the minimum overall project completion time.
3. Calculate the float time for each activity; identify the activities which are critical.

Activity	Start Node	End Node	Completion time (in weeks)
1	1	2	2
2	1	3	3
3	1	4	2
4	2	5	3
5	3	6	7
6	4	6	5
7	5	7	4
8	67	7	9
9		8	3

Solution

The network diagram is presented below:

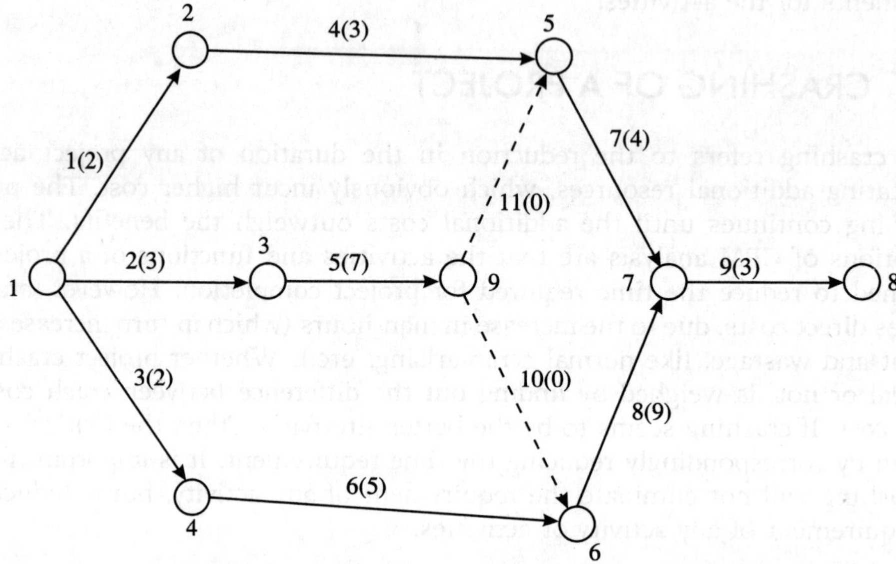

Observe: To complete the network diagram, we have introduced two dummy activities; these are 10 and 11 along with node 9. We can now calculate the earliest start times for the determination of the overall project completion time.

$E_1 = 0$ (by definition)

$E_2 = E_1 + T_{12} = 0 + 2 = 2$

$E_3 = E_1 + T_{13} = 0 + 3 = 3$

$E_4 = E_1 + T_{14} = 0 + 2 = 2$

$E_5 = \max [E_2 + T_{25}, E_9 + T_{95}]$

However, we are yet to calculate E_9. Also, we do not know the values of E_6, E_7 and E_8, till we calculate E_9.

$E_9 = E_3 + T_{39} = 3 + 7 = 10$

We can now calculate E_5 as we now know E_9.

$E_5 = \max [E_2 + T_{25}, E_9 + T_{95}] = \max [2 + 3, 10 + 0] = 10$

$E_6 = \max [E_4 + T_{46}, E_9 + T_{96}] = \max [2 + 5, 10 + 0] = 10$

$E_7 = \max [E_5 + T_{57}, E_6 + T_{67}] = \max [10 + 4, 10 + 9] = 19$

$E_8 = E_7 + T_{78} = 19 + 3 = 22$

The above calculations, therefore, authenticate that minimum overall project completion time is 22 weeks.

For the determination of the float times, that is, the process of identification of critical activities in the project, we need to calculate the latest start times as under:

$L_8 = 22$ (by definition)

$L_7 = L_8 - T_{78} = 22 - 3 = 19$

$L_6 = L_7 - T_{67} = 19 - 9 = 10$

$L_5 = L_7 - T_{57} = 19 - 4 = 15$

$L_9 = \min[L_5 - T_{95}, L_6 - T_{96}] = \min[15 - 0, 10 - 0] = 10$

$L_4 = L_6 - T_{46} = 10 - 5 = 5$

$L_3 = L_9 - T_{39} = 10 - 7 = 3$

$L_2 = L_5 - T_{25} = 15 - 3 = 12$

$L_1 = \min[L_2 - T_{12}, L_3 - T_{13}, L_4 - T_{14}] = \min[12 - 2, 3 - 3, 5 - 2] = 0$

Note that $L_1 = 0$ as required.

To calculate the float times, we use the equation $F_{ij} = L_j - E_i - T_{ij}$

Activity	i	j	L	E_i	T_{ij}	F_{ij}
1	1	2	12	0	2	10
2	1	3	3	0	3	0
3	1	4	5	0	2	3
4	2	5	15	2	3	10
5	3	9	10	3	7	0
6	4	6	10	2	5	3
7	5	7	19	10	4	5
8	6	7	19	10	9	0
9	7	8	22	19	3	0
10	9	6	10	10	0	0
11	9	5	15	10	0	5

Let us observe that all float times are = 0, as required. Hence, the critical activities are those with a float of zero, that is, activities 2, 5, 8, 9 and 10. Hence, these activities will form the critical path of the project, from the start node of 1 to the finish node of 8,

Note here that all float times are >= 0 as required. Hence, the critical activities (those with a float of zero) are 2,5,8,9 and 10, and these form the critical path from the start node (node 1) to the finish node (node 8) in the network.

7.10.1.1 *A Typical Activity on Node Network (AON Network)*

Consider the network below. Here, each node (circle) represents an activity, which is duly labelled by activity number and the time required for completion of the activity in parenthesis.

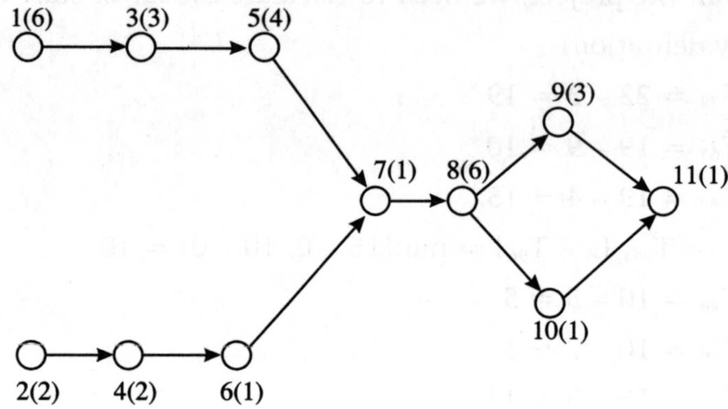

Figure 7.8 *Activity on node network*

To construct this network, we draw the node for each activity, add an arrow from one node to another, or one activity to another. Here, the arcs are arrows. Also, from the network, it is evident any activities which are not linked with precedence relationships can be done simultaneously.

7.10.1.2 *Network analysis – dynamic programming algorithm*

Let us draw the previous network diagram, introducing a dummy activity, with the completion time of zero.

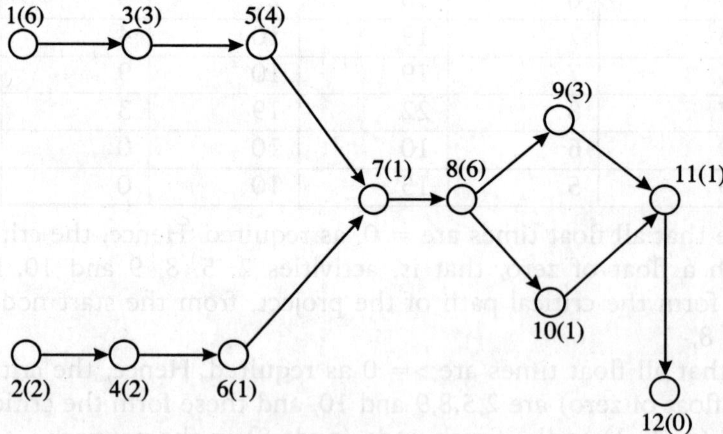

Figure 7.9 *Network with a dummy activity*

We first calculate, for each node (activity) in the network, the earliest start time to finish all the preceding activities.

7.10.1.3 *Earliest start time calculation*

In a network diagram, we can calculate earliest start time, moving from left to right. For ease of our calculation, let us follow the approaches of J.E. Beasley.

Assume *Ei* represents the earliest start time for activity *i*, where *i* running from 1, 2, 3, ...12. We need to calculate the values of *Ei* moving from left to right of the network diagram. Like *Ei*, to ease our calculation, we also consider *Ti*, i.e., the activity-wise completion time. For our given illustration in figure 7.9, we can then calculate the earliest start time as under:

$$E_1 = 0 \text{ (assume zero start time)}$$

$$E_2 = 0 \text{ (assume zero start time)}$$

$$E_3 = E_1 + T_1 = 0 + 6 = 6$$

$$E_4 = E_2 + T_2 = 0 + 2 = 2$$

$$E_5 = E_3 + T_3 = 6 + 3 = 9$$

$$E_6 = E_4 + T_4 = 2 + 2 = 4$$

$$E_7 = \max[E_5 + T_5, E_6 + T_6] = \max[9 + 4, 4 + 1] = 13$$

$$E_8 = E_7 + T_7 = 13 + 1 = 14$$

$$E_9 = E_8 + T_8 = 14 + 6 = 20$$

$$E_{10} = E_8 + T_8 = 14 + 6 = 20$$

$$E_{11} = \max[E_9 + T_9, E_{10} + T_{10}] = \max[20 + 3, 20 + 1] = 23$$

$$E_{12} = E_{11} + T_{11} = 23 + 1 = 24$$

Therefore, 24 weeks is considered to be the minimum time requirement to complete the activities, which we construe as project completion time. Hence, formal definition of earliest start time can be considered as:

$E_j = max[E_i + T_i j$: where *i* is one of the activities linked to *j* by the arc from *i* to *j*. A formal equation for E_j is the dynamic programming algorithm.

7.10.1.4 Latest start time calculation

From the above figure, we can also calculate the latest start time as under: We represent *Li* as the latest time, where *i* runs from 1, 2, 3 ....12. Unlike earliest start time calculation, here we move backward from right to left. Again referring to figure above, we get:

$L_{12} = 24$

$L_{11} = L_{12} - T_{11} = 24 - 1 = 23$

$L_{10} = L_{11} - T_{10} = 23 - 1 = 22$

$L_9 = L_{11} - T_9 = 23 - 3 = 20$

$L_8 = \min [L_9 - T_8, L_{10} - T_8] = \min [20 - 6, 22 - 6] = 14$

$L_7 = L_8 - T_7 = 14 - 1 = 13$

$L_6 = L_7 - T_6 = 13 - 1 = 12$

$L_5 = L_7 - T_5 = 13 - 4 = 9$

$L_4 = L_6 - T_4 = 12 - 2 = 10$

$L_3 = L_5 - T_3 = 9 - 3 = 6$

$L_2 = L_4 - T_2 = 10 - 2 = 8$

$L_1 = L_3 - T_1 = 6 - 6 = 0$

Therefore, the formal definition of the latest start time can be represented as:

$L_i = \min [L_j - T_i]$, where *jj* is linked to *i* by an arc running from *i* to *j*.

Important features of this calculation are:

- Latest start time must be ≥ 0
- At least one activity must have a latest start time of zero

Float

Once we know the activity-wise earliest start time E_i, and latest start time L_i, for each activity *i*, we can calculate the amount of slack or float time F_i, using the formula $F_i = L_i - E_i$. Float is the time by which we can increase the time for activity *i*, without, however, increasing the overall time for project completion. Using the table overleaf, we can calculate the float of a network diagram.

Activity	Li	Ei	Float Fi
1	0	0	0
2	8	0	8
3	6	6	0
4	10	2	8
5	9	9	0
6	12	4	8
7	13	13	0
8	14	14	0
9	20	20	0
10	22	20	2
11	23	23	0

It is important to note that any activity with zero float is critical in nature. Again, float values must be ≥ 0. In our above example, activities 2, 4, and 6 are non-critical in nature.

7.11 FREE AND INDEPENDENT FLOAT

We have two varieties of float for non-critical activities. These are free and independent float. In free float, delaying an activity is possible, when it begins at the earliest time, and so also other subsequent activities begin at the earliest time. On the contrary in independent float, delaying an activity is possible when all preceding activities start late, but the subsequent activities start at the earliest time. Free float affects the total float in the activity chain, while the independent float is activity specific and does not affect the activity chain.

The formulae for calculation of free and independent float are:

- For free float, for activity i = min[earliest start time for j, where j is an immediate successor of i] – earliest start time for i – completion time for i
- independent float, for activity i = min[earliest start time for j, where j is an immediate successor of i] – max[latest finish time for j, where j is an immediate predecessor of i] – completion time for i, where independent float is zero when calculation returns a negative number.

To calculate the free and independent float, based on the above table, at the outset, we have to calculate the latest finish, and the earliest finish. Latest finish = latest start + completion time, and earliest finish = earliest start + completion time). Accordingly, we have prepared the table below:

Activity	Latest start	Earliest start	Latest Finish	Earliest Finish	Completion Time
1	0	0	6	6	6
2	8	0	10	2	2
3	6	6	9	0	3
4	10	2	12	4	2
5	9	9	13	13	4
6	12	4	13	5	1
7	13	13	14	14	1
8	14	14	20	20	6
9	20	20	23	23	3
10	22	20	23	21	1
11	23	23	24	24	1

Now based on our network diagram, we can calculate the free and independent float as under:

Activity	Free Float	Independent Float
2	0	0
4	0	0
6	8	0
10	2	2

Here activity 10, which is a non-critical activity has both free and independent float of 2.

7.12 DEFINITION OF A PROJECT

The Project Management Institute, USA defined project as a "one-shot, time–limited, goal directed, major undertaking, requiring the commitment of varied skills and resources". It is also "a combination of human and non-human resources pooled together in a temporary organization to achieve a specific purpose". A project can be considered to be any series of activities and tasks that:

- Have a specific objective to be completed with certain specifications
- Have defined start and end dates
- Have funding limits (if applicable)
- Consume resources (money, people, equipment)

UNIDO defines a project as "a proposal for an investment to create and/or develop certain facilities in order to increase the production of goods and/or services in a community during a certain period of time". Baum and Tolbert defined a project as "a discrete package of investments, policy measures, and institutional and other actions designed to achieve a specific development objective (or set of objectives) within a designated period". James P. Lewis has defined a project as a "one time job that has defined starting and ending dates, a clearly specified objective or scope of work to be performed, a predefined budget, and usually a temporary organization that is dismantled once the project is completed."

7.12.1 Main Characteristics of a Project

The principle characteristics of a project are:

- It is an undertaking which has defined objectives, often including time, financial and technical performance goals.
- It has defined start and end points.
- It uses a wide variety of resources and skills and involves cost and time.
- It involves coordination across the organizational boundaries of groups and organizational units.
- It is an instrument of change and is unique.

Various works that are inter-related and are being performed to serve a common purpose can be grouped together and termed as a project.

In a project, there is a concept of wholeness despite diversities of work. Choudhury has explained the following features of a project. These are:

1. Set of objectives
2. It has a life span
3. Single entity
4. Team work
5. Life cycle – growth, maturity and decay
6. Uniqueness
7. Change – changes while project is on-going and may even change the entire character of the project
8. Successive principles – details get finalized
9. Made to order – customized
10. Unity in diversity
11. High level of sub-contracting
12. Risk and uncertainty

7.13 PROJECT LIFE CYCLE

By and large, all projects have to pass through the following five phases:

1. Conception phase: in this phase, the project idea germinates.
2. Definition phase: in this phase, a document is prepared based on an idea generated, covering the following aspects:

- raw materials
- plant size/capacity
- location and site
- technology/process selection
- project layout
- plant and machinery
- electrical and instrumentation work
- civil engineering works
- utilities – fuel, power and water
- manpower and organizational pattern
- financial patterns
- implementation schedule

3. Planning and organization phase: this is also known as the project execution plan and it incorporates:
   (a) project infrastructure and enabling phase
   (b) system design and basic engineering package
   (c) organization and manpower
   (d) schedules and budgets
   (e) licensing and governmental clearances
   (f) finance
   (g) systems and procedure
   (h) identification of a project manager
   (i) design basis, general conditions for purchase and contracts
   (j) site preparation and investigation
   (k) construction resources and materials
   (l) work packaging.

4. Implementation phase: 80% to 85% of the project work is done in this phase only.
5. Project Clean-up Phase: Drawings, documents, files, operation and maintenance manuals are catalogued and handed over to the customer. The customer has to be satisfied with guarantee test runs.

Any project, by definition, has a definite start and a finish. A project life cycle, therefore, follow basic sequential actions like start, plan, do, and finish. These are what we call the generic phases of a project. We do not have any consensus on different phases of a project life cycle. However, for production and operations management, as we usually refer to engineering or construction projects, we observe difference phases of the project life cycle as initiation, planning, implementation and commissioning. However, for a service project (like a software project), such phases change to inception, elaboration, construction and transition.

A typical project life cycle is illustrated below (Fig. 7.10):

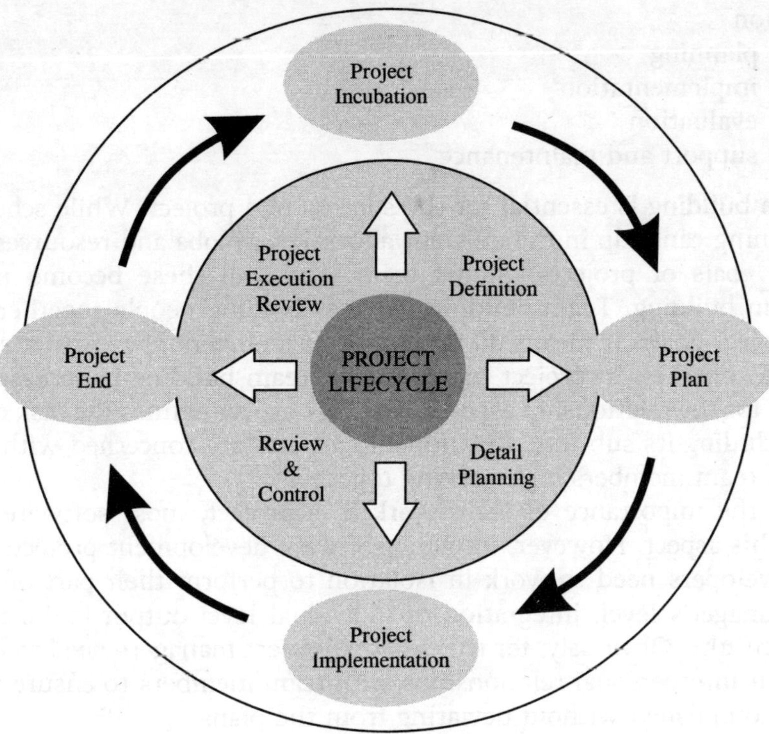

Figure 7.10 *Project life cycle*

Typically, in a project life cycle, we cannot cross the boundary of the plan, and the management of the project is highly dependent on the technology. Project life cycle therefore strictly conforms to hierarchical systems, which means, without the completion of the initial phase, it cannot proceed to the next phase or phases.

7.14 PROJECT MANAGEMENT

A project is a one-time activity to achieve some defined goals. It is different from a programme, which is an ongoing process like an inventory management programme, new product development programme, etc. From this perspective, a project is a sub-set of a programme, as a programme per se manages several projects at one point of time. Project management is a carefully crafted series of organized activities for the successful completion of a project. The various components of project management are: preparing a project plan with clear goals and objectives, identification of tasks for achieving goals and objectives, determining resource requirements, budgeting, and finally, deciding on the timeframe for accomplishing project goals. Successful project management requires strict enforcement of operational controls on project activities. Project management follows the cycle of activities as under:

- feasibility

- definition
- project planning
- project implementation
- project evaluation
- project support and maintenance

Project team building is essential for the success of a project. While scheduling and project planning can help in the efficient allocation of jobs and resources to achieve time-bound goals of projects, minus team work, all these become meaningless without team building. Team building requires binding people together to achieve common project goals. It means all project team members have to share a common goal to work together. In project management, team building is necessary both for the task and for the relationship aspects. The task aspect defines the task or the job to be done, including its sub-sets. Relationship aspects are concerned with interaction with project team members and working together.

Realizing the importance of team work in a project, most software companies emphasize this aspect. However, in many software development projects, individual software developers need to work in isolation to perform their part of the job. At a project manager's level, integration of individual level output is done to achieve the desired results. Obviously, for this reason, project managers need to interact and enhance their interpersonal relationships with team members to ensure that project goals are accomplished without deviating from the plans.

7.14.1 Project Planning Steps

Successful project management requires a project plan. Companies often consider this requirement redundant and directly engage in project activities, which often lead to multiple complications in project execution. Project planning is a prerequisite for successful project management. Some of the important steps of creating a project plan are:

Step 1: Project Goals The primary goal of a project plan is to meet the expectations of the direct and indirect stakeholders of a project. Therefore, to chalk out the project goals, at the outset it is important to understand who are the stakeholders, and how the project, directly or indirectly, exerts an impact on their interests. After the identification of the stakeholders, the next course of action is to understand their expectations. Through interviews, we need to assess their needs and relate the same to the project purpose. After the assessment of stakeholders' needs, we have to prioritize these needs, and select the goals in measurable terms. Such prioritized goals along with the measurement criteria have to be documented in the project plan.

Step 2: Project Deliverables After identification of measureable project goals, we have to focus on project deliverables. With the addition of the deliverables in the project plan, along with the estimated date of delivery, we then decide on project scheduling.

Step 3: Project Schedule At this stage, we create a list of tasks for each deliverable, duly identifying:

- the requirement to complete the task.
- the resource requirement to complete the task.
- people who are responsible to perform the task.

At this stage, companies may use readily available software packages, for example, *Microsoft* Project, or other established tools.

Step 4: Supporting Plans For successful project execution, apart from the project plan, we also have to create other supporting plans, to supplement the process. These are human resource plans, communication plans, risk management plans, etc. Human resource plans describe the people responsible for the project, their duties, responsibilities, roles, etc. Communication plans document the process of information sharing, feedback and control mechanism, etc. Risk management plans ensure systematic tracking of project risks, to ensure immediate correction of deviation from the project plans. Use of tracking signal discussed in Chapter 2 can be effective in this case.

Modern project management approach was developed in the early 1960s. Its first application was in the US Space programme. Tracing history, we find that project management goes back even further to the 19th century. Subsequently, it was felt that a more scientific approach to project management was necessary to reap the benefits of organized work around specific projects, coordination and the communication of project management-related work across departments or divisions of an organization.

Without seeking to arrive at a general definition of project management, let us first consider what the elements of project management are. The basic elements of project management are:

- Project management is a discontinuous process with definite beginning and end.
- Project management practices require the use of various tools to monitor and track the project. Some of the widely-used project management tools like Gantt charts and PERT have already been discussed in this chapter.
- Resource allocation to projects may not be fixed with the progress of work; it may require ad-hoc resource allocation.
- Risk and probability of failure in project management are considerably less, as it adopts more flexibility in managing the work. Such flexibility ensures lean management, which optimizes resources.
- Project management considers three most important factors: time, cost and scope.

Against this backdrop, we can define project management as follows:

Project management is the process of managing a discontinuous task or work within a budget and time constraint, achieving customers' satisfaction.

7.15 DUTIES AND RESPONSIBILITIES OF A PROJECT MANAGER

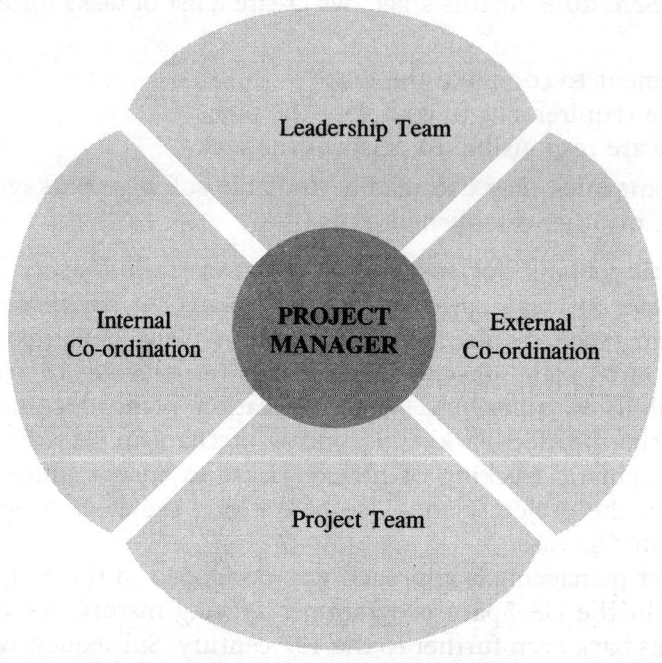

Figure 7.11 *Role of a Project Manager*

The successful management of a project requires the effective services of project manager, who manages the project. The job of a project manager now requires specialized knowledge and skill. The project manager has to be responsible for everything related to the project. Unlike other management roles, which are hierarchical, the project manager needs to manage the entire team's actions, both as a boss and as a team worker. His/her role even includes the control of contributions of seniors and peers. This requires managing upwards with an inverted hierarchy, as the role extends to even the project sponsor's actions, which need to be controlled for the ultimate success of the project Fig. 7.11. Coordination with other departments, contributions from other internal groups, coordination and cooperation of external agencies, and day-to-day monitoring of the tasks of the project group, to ensure on time deliverables, etc. are some of the important roles a project manager plays in an organization. Because of the multifarious role of project managers, we need to consider both technical and managerial competence.

SUMMARY

1. A project is a one-time activity to achieve some defined goals. It is different from a programme; which is an ongoing process; for example, an inventory management programme, new product development programme, etc. From this perspective, a project is a sub-set of a programme, as a programme per se manages several projects at one point of time. Project management is a carefully crafted series of organized activities for the successful completion of a project.
2. There are different forms of Network Analysis, which may be simple or complex, very generalized or exclusively designed for specific types of projects. PERT/PEP and CPM are the most widely used techniques used in Network Analysis.
3. A float is defined as the available time to delay an activity without, however, delaying the date of completion of a project. It means any possible delay in some activity or activities will not increase the duration of the project. However, it is important to understand that only non-critical activities can be delayed.
4. Programme evaluation and review technique (PERT), and critical path analysis (CPA) are two important project scheduling techniques which help in successful project planning.
5. Successful project management requires a project plan. Companies often consider this requirement redundant and directly engage in project activities, which often lead to multiple complications in project execution. Project planning is a prerequisite for successful project management.
6. Successful management of a project requires the effective services of a project manager, who manages the project. The job of a project manager requires specialized knowledge and skill. The project manager has to be responsible for everything related to the project.
7. A project life cycle follows certain basic sequential actions like: start, plan, do and finish. For production and operations management, we usually observe different phases of a project life cycle such as initiation, planning, implementation and commissioning. However, for a service project (like a software project), such phases change to inception, elaboration, construction and transition.

KEY WORDS

Lean Management Lean manufacturing or lean production systems originated from *Toyota* and have now become a widely acclaimed practice to achieve excellence in a competitive world. In a nutshell, lean practices enable an organization to achieve world class performance, world class practices (in methods and processes) and create a culture of relentless and continuous improvement (environment).

Index Method This method is applied to finite job loading cases. It is called finite because job loading is done according to the capacity of the machine. Under the Index

Method, the lowest time or cost required by a particular job–machine combination is taken as the base and the indices for the others are prepared based on the base variation.

Dynamic Slack/Remaining Operation (DS/RO) or Minimum Slack per Operation Method (MINSOP) In DS/RO we first calculate Dynamic Slack (DS), which is the difference between Due Time and Processing Time, and then divide this DS by the Remaining Operation (RO). Unless specified, RO will be assumed as one. The final scheduling of the job is done as per the ranking of DS/RO. Jobs with the lowest value are attended to first, a similar ranking is given in the order of the next lowest and so on

Johnson's Rule S.M. Johnson developed this sequencing process which helps to minimize idle time of different work centres by optimum job allocation. This is applied where a number of jobs have to be processed through different work centres.

Milestone Charts Milestones mark significant events in the life of a project, usually critical activities which must be achieved on time to avoid delay in the project. Milestones should be truly significant and be reasonable in terms of deadlines (avoid using intermediate stages).

Work Breakdown Structure (WBS) In order to identify individual tasks in a project, it is useful to create a Work Breakdown Structure. Get the team together and brainstorm all the tasks in the project, in no particular order. Write them down on sticky notes and put them on a whiteboard. Once everyone has thought of as many tasks as they can arrange, divide the sticky notes into groups, under the major areas of activity.

GENERAL REVIEW QUESTIONS

1. Explain the rules of network construction. Under what circumstances, can we think of using a dummy in a network?
2. Explain the concept of critical path. Why is a critical path drawn? What norms do we follow to draw a critical path?
3. Define project. Explain the important tools used to manage a project.
4. Short notes

   (a) Project Crashing
   (b) Project Life Cycle
   (c) Latest Start Time vis-a-vis Earliest Start Time
   (d) Critical Ratio
   (e) Job Lateness
   (f) Due Date

CRITICAL REVIEW QUESTIONS

Mono India has made available the following information about their activities.

Activity	Start Node	End Node	Completion Time (in weeks)
1	1	2	2
2	1	3	3
3	3	4	7
4	3	5	6
5	2	7	10
6	4	5	1
7	5	6	3
8	6	7	4
9	4	7	7
10	7	8	3

The company made it clear that activity 7 can be started only after the completion of activity 1. Similarly, activity 10 cannot be started until activity 7 is completed.

Based on the above information, the company wants you to draw a network diagram, compute the overall project completion time and the float time for each activity, and finally, draw the critical path for the project.

(Hints: overall project completion time is 21 weeks, Critical activities, that is, the activities with zero float are 2,3,6,7,8,10 and 13).

1. Interpret the network. Calculate the earliest start time for the determination of overall project completion time.

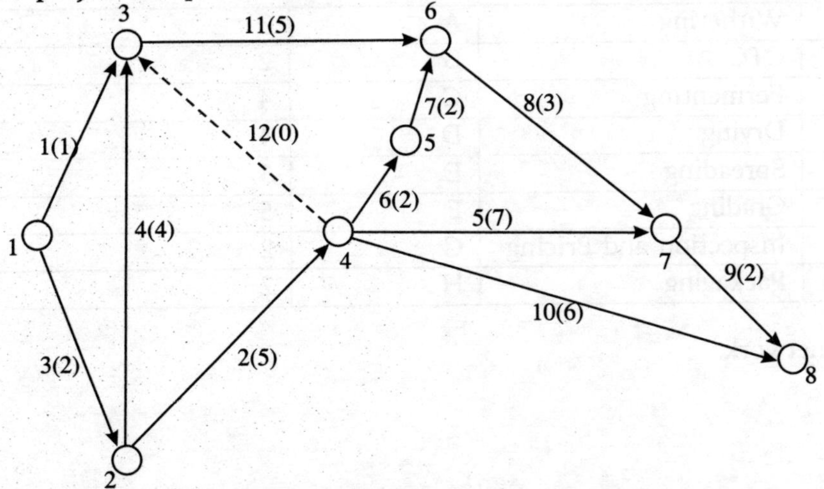

(Hint: critical activities with zero float are; 2,3,8,9,11 and 12).

2. *Sonajuli Tea Estate* is located in Assam. The company manufactures the finest CTC tea and sells the same in bulk, primarily, through the auction route. Fresh flushing of tea leaves start in *Sonajuli's* garden from end-October onwards, and during February, it reaches its peak. From February to end-April, the company runs its processing units round the clock. Green tea leaves after plucking have to be withered (normal drying), either in open or closed troughs. In open troughs, tea leafs have to be withered for 12–14 hours, while in closed troughs for such withering, as it is in a conditioned environment, 4–5 hours is considered adequate. After the withering, tea leaves go through the process of CTC operation through CTC machines. Crush, tear and curl (CTC) means forming tea globules, which still have moisture. After the CTC operations, it goes through the process of fermenting, again, in a closed environment, till a coppery colour appears. The fermenting time depends on ambient temperature, and takes roughly 2–3 hours. After this process, drying, grading, testing, pricing and packaging are done. Each production cycle takes 14 to 15 hours for completion. Tea processing operations, being time independent, and the time requirements for many activities vary due to reasons of environmental variation; it is difficult to reduce the cycle time. However in peak season, companies try to optimize the time for achieving higher production volume. *Sonajuli* has made available the following information on its tea processing activities with the precedence relationship between them, and the activity durations (di) in days.

Activities	**Descriptions**	**Predecessors**	**Activity durations (di) in days**
A	Plucking	None	2
B	Withering	A	3
C	CTC	B	2
D	Fermenting	C	4
E	Drying	D	4
F	Spreading	E	3
G	Grading	F	5
H	Inspection and Pricing	G	2
I	Packaging	H	2

Draw the network.

REFERENCES

1. Pritsker, A.A.B. 1966. *GERT: Graphical Evaluation and Review Technique*. Santa Monica, CA: Rand Corporation,
2. Beasley JE. OR-Notes. http://people.brunel.ac.uk/mastjjb/jeb/or/netaon.html, accessed on 9th March, 2012.
3. Baum, Warren, and Stokes, Tolbert. 1985. *Investing in Development*. New York: Oxford University Press.
4. S. Choudhury. 2004. *Project Management*. New Delhi: Tata McGraw-Hill.
5. James, P., Lewis. 1995. *Fundamentals of Project Management*. New York: AMACOM.

ADDITIONAL REFERENCES

1. Adams, J. R. and Barndt, S. E. 1983. Behavioral Implications of the Project Life Cycle. In *Project Management Handbook*, Cleland, D. I. and King, W. R. eds. New York: Van Nostrand Reinhold.
2. Burke, Rory. 1993. *Project Management: Planning and Control* 2nd ed. New York: John Wiley & Sons.
3. Cohen, M.A. 1997. *Manufacturing Automation*. Chicago: Irwin.
4. Gido, Jack. 1985. *An Introduction to Project Planning*. New York: Industrial Press Inc.
5. Konz. Stephen. 1983. *Work Design: Industrial Ergonomics*, 2nd ed. New York: John Wiley & Sons.
6. Lockyer, Keith and Gordon, James. 1996. *Project Management and Project Network Techniques*, 6th ed. London: Pitman Publishing.
7. Meredith, Jack R. and Mantel, Samuel J. 1995. *Project Management. A Managerial Approach*, 3rd. ed. New York: John Wiley & Sons Inc..
8. Richard, B., Chase, Nicholas, J., Aquilano, and F. Robert, Jacobs. 2002. *Operations Management for Competitive Advantage* New Delhi: Tata McGraw-Hill Publishing Company Limited.
9. Schmenner, R.W. 1995. *Service Operations Management*. Englewood Cliffs, N.J: Prentice Hall.
10. Wiest, J. D. and Levy, F. K. 1969. *A Management Guide to PERT/CPM*. Englewood Cliffs, NJ: Prentice-Hall.

CASE STUDY

Zenith India — the saga of a construction major

Time, cost and quality are the three important variables of a project. Effective project management, therefore, requires efficient management of these three variables. Identification of project activities along with project scheduling with appropriate techniques sets the process of project management. *Zenith India* is a well-known civil engineering companies, which simultaneously execute multiple projects in multiple locations. *Zenith*'s strength is its large pool of structural engineers, designers, soil engineers, piling specialists, civil engineers, etc. This knowledge pool undertakes civil project works throughout the world.

Apart from cross-cultural issues, the international project teams of *Zenith* face problems of delay in operation-level activities. For operational activities, *Zenith* has to hire from the local market on a project-to-project basis. Quite often, *Zenith* observed that low productivity on the part of locally hired workers was a major problem. *Zenith*'s project quotations are based on the work rate standards of Indian workers. An average Indian construction worker can carry a minimum of eight bricks, while in some of the foreign work sites, host country workers carry six bricks, resulting in 25% less productivity.

In a major bridge construction project in Norway, *Zenith* failed to assess the environmental impact, in accordance with the local environment regulations. This restriction forced *Zenith* to use more steel rather than cement concrete, requiring less machines and movement of trucks. Reducing the environmental impact caused a huge cost overrun, for which *Zenith* was not prepared.

In Mexico, *Zenith* faced the problem of poor motor skills of workers, resulting in increased cost of supervision and lower productivity. Likewise, it also faced problems of security and safety issues, workers' absenteeism and poor team work

All such lapses on the company's part can be attributed to poor project planning. Drawing a project plan without considering the planning premises, caused these problems.

Discussion Question

Read the case and suggest the approach that Zenith could have adopted to alleviate such project-related problems?

PROBLEMS AND EXERCISES ON NETWORK ANALYSIS

Network analysis – activity on node examples

The table below defines the activities of a project.

Activity	Completion Time (weeks)	Immediate Predecessor (activities)
A	2	-
B	3	-
C	4	A
D	3	B,A
E	8	D,C
F	3	C
G	2	E
H	3	F,G

Draw the network diagram.

Calculate the minimum overall project completion time and identify which activities are critical.

Find out the slack (float) time associated with each of the non-critical activities. Various options for completion time for activities C, D and E with associated costs is presented below:

Activity	Completion Time	Cost (Rs.'000)
C	4	3
	3	7
	2	10
	1	12
D	3	12
	2	16
	1	25
E	8	5
	7	6
	6	14

Formulate the problem to decide on the completion time for C, D and E, so that the project gets completed within 17 weeks.

Solution

The network diagram is drawn as under with dummy activity 1 (zero duration) to represent the end of the project.

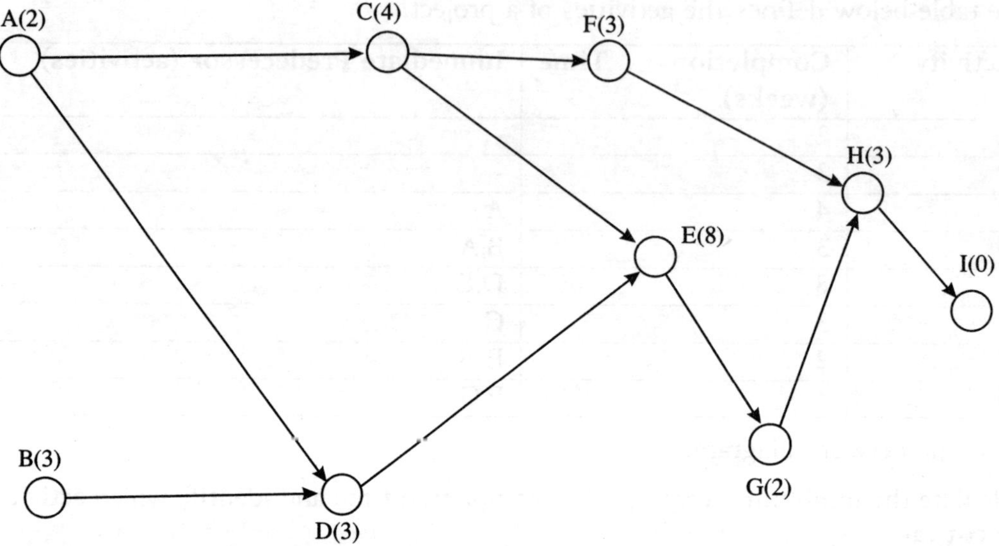

Let *Ei* represent the earliest start time for activity *i* such that all its preceding activities have been finished. We calculate the values of the E_i ($i = A, B, ..., I$) by going forward, from left to right, in the network diagram.

To ease the notation, let T_i be the activity completion time associated with activity i (e.g. TB = 3). Then E_i is given by:

$E_A = 0$ (assuming we start at time zero)
$E_B = 0$ (assuming we start at time zero)
$E_C = E_A + T_A = 0 + 2 = 2$
$E_D = \max [E_A + T_A, E_B + T_B] = \max [0 + 2, 0 + 3] = 3$
$E_E = \max [E_C + T_C, E_D + T_D] = \max [2 + 4, 3 + 3] = 6$
$E_F = E_C + T_C = 2 + 4 = 6$
$E_G = E_E + T_E = 6 + 8 = 14$
$E_H = \max [E_F + T_F, E_G + T_G] = \max [6 + 3, 14 + 2] = 16$
$E_I = E_H + T_H = 16 + 3 = 19$

Hence, the minimum possible completion time for completing all the activities of the project is 19 weeks.

We now need to calculate the latest times for each activity.
Let L_i represent the latest start time, when we can start activity i and still complete the project in the minimum overall completion time. We calculate the values of the L_i

(i = A,B,...,I) by going backward, from right to left, in the network diagram. Hence:

$L_I = 19$
$L_H = L_I - T_H = 19 - 3 = 16$
$L_G = L_H - T_G = 16 - 2 = 14$
$L_F = L_H - T_F = 16 - 3 = 13$
$L_E = L_G - T_E = 14 - 8 = 6$
$L_D = L_E - T_D = 6 - 3 = 3$
$L_C = \min[L_E - T_C, L_F - T_C] = \min[6 - 4, 13 - 4] = 2$
$L_B = L_D - T_B = 3 - 3 = 0$
$L_A = \min[L_C - T_A, L_D - T_A] = \min[2 - 2, 3 - 2] = 0$

All latest times are ≥ 0; at least one activity has a latest start time value of zero.

As we know, the earliest start time E_i, and latest start time L_i, for each activity i, it is clear that the amount of slack or float time F_i available is given by $F_i = L_i - E_i$ which is the amount by which we can increase the time taken to complete activity i without changing (increasing) the overall project completion time. Hence, we can form the table below:

Activity	L_i	E_i	**Float** F_i
A	0	0	0
B	0	0	0
C	2	2	0
D	3	3	0
E	6	6	0
F	13	6	7
G	14	14	0
H	16	16	0

Any activity with a float of zero is critical. All float values should be ≥ 0.

Hence, the critical activities are A,B,C,D, E,G and H and the float for the only non-critical activity F is 7 weeks.

In order to formulate the problem of deciding the completion time for C, D and E so as to ensure that the project is completed within 17 weeks, we make use of integer programming,

Let the x variables represent feasible start times for each activity (≥ 0 and integer). We consider feasible start times in formulating this programme rather than with the earliest start times.

Introduce zero-one variables
$C_i = 1$ if a completion time of i (i = 4,3,2,1) chosen for activity C, 0 otherwise
$D_i = 1$ if a completion time of i (i= 3,2,1) chosen for activity D, 0 otherwise

E_i = 1 if a completion time of i (i= 8,7,6) chosen for activity.

then the constraints relating to the choice of completion time are:

$C_4 + C_3 + C_2 + C_1 = 1$
$D_3 + D_2 + D_1 = 1$
$E_8 + E_7 + E_6 = 1$

exactly one completion time must be chosen for C, D and E respectively.

The constraints relating to the network logic are:

$x_A = x_B = 0$
$x_C \geq x_A + 2$
$x_D \geq x_B + 3$
$x_D \geq x_A + 2$
$x_E \geq x_C + 4C_4 + 3C_3 + 2C_2 + 1C_1$

where $4C_4 + 3C_3 + 2C_2 + 1C_1$ is the completion time for activity C (as C_4, C_3, C_2 and C_1 are zero-one variables).

$x_E \geq x_D + 3D_3 + 2D_2 + 1D_1$
$x_F \geq x_C + 4C_4 + 3C_3 + 2C_2 + 1C_1$
$x_G \geq x_E + 8E_8 + 7E_7 + 6E_6$
$x_H \geq x_F + 3$
$x_H \geq x_G + 2$
$x_H \geq 17 - 3$ (to complete in 17 weeks)

and the objective is

minimise $3C_4 + 7C_3 + 10C_2 + 15C_1 + 12D_3 + 16D_2 + 25D_1 + 5E_8 + 9E_7 + 14E_6$

Example – 2 Network diagram

A project consists of 8 activities. The activity completion times and the precedence relationships are as follows:

Activity	Completion Time (days)	Immediate Predecessor
A	5	-
B	7	-
C	6	-
D	3	A
E	4	B,C
F	2	C
G	6	A,D
H	5	E.F

1. Draw the network diagram.
2. Calculate the minimum overall project completion time and identify which activities are critical.
3. If activity E is delayed by 3 days, how is the project completion time affected?
4. If activity F is delayed by 3 days, how is the project completion time affected?

Solution

The network diagram is shown below. Dummy activity with zero time duration has been introduced to represent the end of the project.

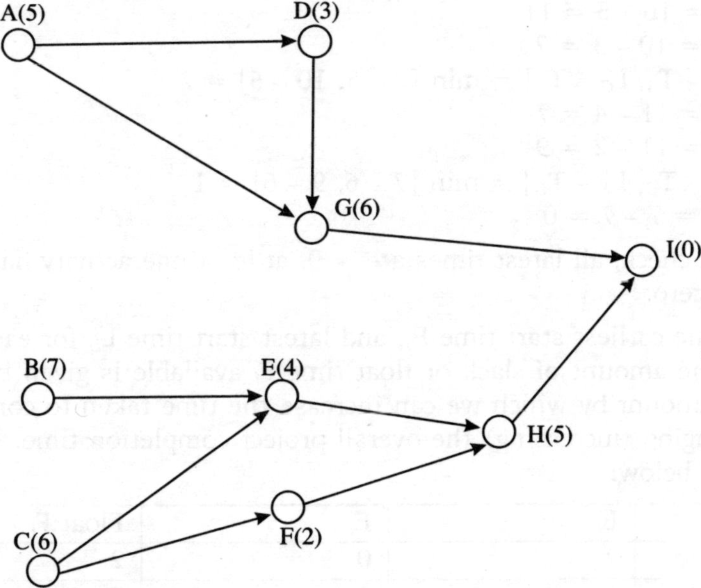

Let E_i represent the earliest start time for activity i such that all its preceding activities have been finished. We calculate the values of the E_i (i=A,B,...,I) by going forward, from left to right, in the network diagram.

To ease the notation let T_i be the activity completion time associated with activity i (e.g. $T_B = 7$). Then the E_i are given by:

$E_A = 0$ (assuming we start at time zero)
$E_B = 0$ (assuming we start at time zero)
$E_C = 0$ (assuming we start at time zero)
$E_D = E_A + T_A = 0 + 5 = 5$
$E_G = \max\, [E_A + T_A,\ E_D + T_D] = \max\, [0 + 5,\ 5 + 3] = 8$
$E_E = \max\, [E_B + T_B,\ E_C + T_C] = \max\, [0 + 7,\ 0 + 6] = 7$
$E_F = E_C + T_C = 0 + 6 = 6$
$E_H = \max\, [E_E + T_E,\ E_F + T_F] = \max\, [7 + 4,\ 6 + 2] = 11$

E_I = max [$E_G + T_G$, $E_H + T_H$] = max [8 + 6, 11 + 5] = 16

Hence, the minimum possible completion time for the entire project is 16 days, i.e. 16 days is the minimum time needed to complete all the activities. We now need to calculate the latest times for each activity.

Let L_i represent the latest start time we can start activity i and still complete the project in the minimum overall completion time. We calculate the values of the L_i (i = A,B,...,I) by going backward, from right to left, in the network diagram. Hence:

$L_I = 16$
$L_G = L_I - T_G = 16 - 6 = 10$
$L_H = L_I - T_H = 16 - 5 = 11$
$L_D = L_G - T_D = 10 - 3 = 7$
$L_A = \min[L_D - T_A, L_G - T_A] = \min[7 - 5, 10 - 5] = 2$
$L_E = L_H - T_E = 11 - 4 = 7$
$L_F = L_H - T_F = 11 - 2 = 9$
$L_C = \min[L_E - T_C, L_F - T_C] = \min[7 - 6, 9 - 6] = 1$
LB = LE – TB = 7 – 7 = 0

Note that as a check, all latest times are = 0, at least one activity has a latest start time value of zero.

As we know the earliest start time E_i, and latest start time L_i, for each activity i, it is clear that the amount of slack or float time F_i available is given by $F_i = L_i - E_i$ which is the amount by which we can increase the time taken to complete activity i without changing (increasing) the overall project completion time. Hence, we can form the table below:

Activity	L_i	E_i	Float F_i
A	2	0	2
B	0	0	0
C	1	0	1
D	7	5	2
E	7	7	0
F	9	6	2
G	10	8	2
H	11	11	0

Any activity with a float of zero is critical. Note here that, as a check, all float values should be ≥ 0.

Hence, the critical activities are B, E and H and the floats for the non-critical activities are given in the table above.

If activity E is delayed by 3 days, then as E is critical, the project completion time increases by exactly 3 days.

If activity F is delayed by 3 days, then as F has a float of 3 days, the project completion time is unaffected.

Network analysis example

A project consists of 8 activities named A to H. Construct a network so as to satisfy the scheduling requirements shown in the table below:

Activity	Completion Times (in days)	Immediate Predecessor activities
A	3	-
B	6	A
C	7	A
D	5	A
E	13	B,C
F	8	C,D,
G	11	D,E
H	6	G,E

Find the least time required to complete the entire project and identify the critical activities.

How is the project completion time affected if:

activity F is delayed by 3 days
activity E is delayed by 7 days
activity G is finished 7 days early

Solution

The network diagram is shown on page 244. Dummy activity 1 with duration of zero has been introduced to end the project.

Let E_i represent the earliest start time for activity i such that all its preceding activities have been finished. We calculate the values of the E_i (i=A,B,...,I) by going forward, from left to right, in the network diagram.

To ease the notation, let T_i be the activity completion time associated with activity i (e.g. $T_B = 7$). Then, the E_i are given by:

$E_A = 0$ (assuming the start time as zero)
$E_B = E_A + T_A = 0 + 3 = 3$
$E_C = E_A + T_A = 0 + 3 = 3$
$E_D = E_A + T_A = 0 + 3 = 3$

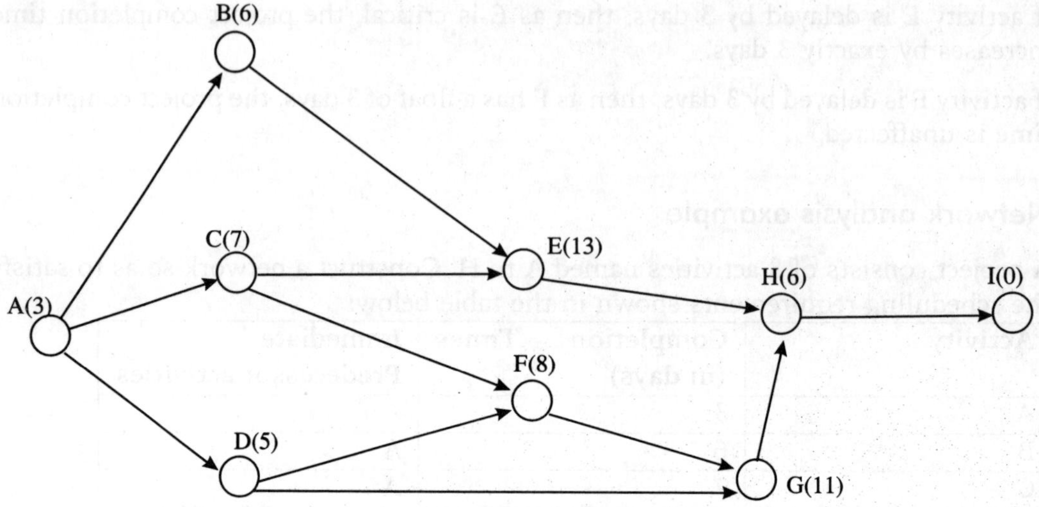

$E_E = \max[E_B + T_B, E_C + T_C] = \max[3 + 6, 3 + 7] = 10$
$E_F = \max[E_C + T_C, E_D + T_D] = \max[3 + 7, 3 + 5] = 10$
$E_G = \max[E_F + T_F, E_D + T_D] = \max[10 + 8, 3 + 5] = 18$
$E_H = \max[E_E + T_E, E_G + T_G] = \max[10 + 13, 18 + 11] = 29$
$E_I = E_H + T_H = 29 + 6 = 35$

Hence, the minimum possible completion time for the entire project is 35 days, this is the minimum time needed to complete all the activities.

We now need to calculate the latest times for each activity.

Let L_i represent the latest start time, we can start activity i and still complete the project in the minimum overall completion time. We calculate the values of the L_i (i=A,B,...,I) by going backward, from right to left, in the network diagram. Hence:

$L_I = 35$
$L_H = L_I - T_H = 35 - 6 = 29$
$L_G = L_H - T_G = 29 - 11 = 18$
$L_E = L_H - T_E = 29 - 13 = 16$
$L_F = L_G - T_F = 18 - 8 = 10$
$L_B = L_E - T_B = 16 - 6 = 10$
$L_C = \min[L_E - T_C, L_F - T_C] = \min[16 - 7, 10 - 7] = 3$
$L_D = \min[L_F - T_D, L_G - T_D] = \min[10 - 5, 18 - 5] = 5$
$L_A = \min[L_B - T_A, L_C - T_A, L_D - T_A] = \min[10 - 3, 3 - 3, 5 - 3] = 0$

As a check, all latest times are ≥ 0, at least one activity has a latest start time value of zero.

As we know, the earliest start time E_i, and latest start time L_i, for each activity i, it is clear that the amount of slack or float time F_i available is given by $F_i = L_i - E_i$, which is the amount by which we can increase the time taken to complete activity i without increasing the overall project completion time. Hence, we can form the table below:

Activity	L_i	E_i	Float F_i
A	0	0	0
B	10	3	7
C	3	3	0
D	5	3	2
E	16	10	6
F	10	10	0
G	18	18	0
H	29	29	0

Any activity with a float of zero is critical. Note here that, as a check, all float values should be ≥ 0.

Hence, the critical activities are A, C, F, G and H and the floats for the non-critical activities are given in the table above.

If activity F is delayed by 3 days, then as F is critical, the project completion time increases by exactly 3 days.

If activity E is delayed by 7 days, then as E has a float of 6 days,the project completion time is affected. The project completion time will increase by exactly (7–6) = 1 day to 36 days.

If activity G is finished 7 days early, then as G is a critical activity, the overall project completion time will (potentially) be reduced. To see the effect of this change, we need to redo the calculation for the earliest times given above, but with a completion time for G of 4 days. The only change is in the calculation of E_H and E_I and these now are:

$$E_H = \max[E_E + T_E, E_G + T_G] = \max[10 + 13, 18 + 4] = 23$$

$$E_I = E_H + T_H = 23 + 6 = 29$$

Hence, the overall project completion time falls to 29 days (a decrease of 6 days).

CHAPTER 8
Maintenance Management

LEARNING OBJECTIVES

After reading this chapter, you will be able to understand:

- Definition and Concept of Maintenance
- Different Types of Maintenance
- Total Productive Maintenance and Overall Equipment Effectiveness (OEE)
- Strategies of Maintenance Management
- Best Practice Maintenance Management
- Spare parts Planning and Maintenance
- Reliability and Solution to Various Maintenance-related Problems

Opening Vignette

Preventive Maintenance at Nippondenso, Japan

Nippondenso was the first company in the world to introduce plant-wide preventive maintenance in 1960. Preventive maintenance, per se, recognizes the need for a dedicated team of maintenance personnel, who systematically maintain machines. The company, however, subsequent to automation, found it difficult to sustain the requirement for an increased number of maintenance personnel. It was at the stage that it decided to integrate routine maintenance with the operations, requiring the operators to undertake repair work. This was the beginning of TPM or autonomous maintenance. TPM requires the maintenance group to undertake only essential repair work, while the operators look after routine maintenance. Operationally, TPM is the addition of preventive maintenance (performed by the maintenance group) to the autonomous maintenance (performed by the operators). The experience of *Nippondenso* has subsequently been replicated by other organizations across the world, and in the process, total productive maintenance (TPM) has been institutionalized as the best practice maintenance management. To increase the benefits of TPM, *Nippondenso* had embraced the practice of quality circles, to develop the culture of total employee involvement and has been recognized as a forerunner in TPM in the world.

8.1 INTRODUCTION

Maintenance can be defined as the operation of a pool of resources; this would consist of men, spares and tools, to control the level of availability and condition of the plant. Therefore, it means that the function of maintenance is to repair, replace, adjust or modify, as required, different parts of the plant to ensure its smooth operation and performance. This is done, using the resource pool of men, spares and tools. Maintenance ensures the flawless functionality of plant and machinery. It substantially reduces machine downtime, ensuring continuous production. With scientific back-up, maintenance support also contributes to the profitability of an organization, by substantially reducing costs.

In an organization, the task of maintenance is assigned to a separate technical team, known as the maintenance team or department. Those who work in the maintenance department are normally not assigned any job in the operations department. Their services are requisitioned on an as-and-when required basis, usually when a breakdown occurs. The problem of maintenance is that it is time independent, when it will occur is not known. Hence, planning for maintenance staff is difficult. So, every organization has to carry an inventory of maintenance manpower, whether they are required or not. For this reason, many organizations, to optimize maintenance costs, outsource this function. However, such outsourcing may not always be feasible, due to the criticality of maintenance jobs and high cost obligations for machine downtime.

Studies indicate that at least a third of maintenance cost is avoidable, with proper maintenance planning and control. Poor capacity utilization, decreased rate of output, quality failure, at least partially, can be attributed to the problem of maintenance. The problem of maintenance is a global issue, and in India, it is even more acute. Acute maintenance problems in India are due to factors like technology obsolescence, poor maintenance planning and more emphasis on breakdown maintenance.

The Total Quality Management (TQM) approach emphasizes maintenance management issues as well. Even to get ISO certification and sustain it, it has now become mandatory for organizations to restructure their maintenance function, to keep pace with the latest trends.

8.2 DIFFERENT TYPES OF MAINTENANCE

Maintenance functions can be classified into different types. Organizations select a specific type of maintenance, depending on their plans and programmes, and also their maintenance policies.

8.2.1 Breakdown Maintenance

This is a traditional form of maintenance, and it requires organizations to make available a separate maintenance team. The services of this maintenance team are called upon from time-to-time, whenever there is a machine breakdown. The frequency of such services or the problem of break-down occurrences depends on factors like the age of the machines and plant workload or defects in the system. To understand the trend, it therefore becomes necessary for every organization to maintain machine breakdown or failure statistics. By analyzing these, it is possible to understand three different kinds of probability distribution:

1. normal distribution
2. negative exponential distribution
3. hyper-exponential distribution

It is important to understand that maintenance problems do not follow any uniform defined distribution pattern. In fact, they vary from case to case. Breakdown maintenance work being time independent, it is often difficult for an organization to decide the optimal manpower requirement and requirement of other pools of resources, like spares and tools, for effectively carrying out maintenance work.

8.2.2 Preventive Maintenance

Normal wear and tear of machines can be avoided by adhering to a Preventive Maintenance Programme. According to BS (British Standards): 3811:1974, preventive maintenance has been defined as, "Maintenance carried out at pre-determined intervals, or to other prescribed criteria, and intended to reduce the likelihood of an item not meeting an acceptable condition."
Preventive maintenance activities involve:

- Periodic inspection to avert breakdowns and depreciation of plant
- Upkeep of plant by routine adjustment and repair

This helps to prolong the useful life of a plant by preventing breakdown and damage, thereby minimizing production interruptions.

The overall objective of the maintenance function is to support the operating department by keeping production equipment and facilities in proper running condition at the lowest possible cost. Preventive maintenance alone does not always prove adequate to achieve this. It also entails a huge cost and does not by itself facilitate actual investigation into the reasons for failure.

8.2.3 Corrective Maintenance

To compensate for the failings of Breakdown and Preventive Maintenance, a corrective maintenance policy is adopted. Corrective maintenance involves the study of equipment design and its improvement, like changes in design, substitution of more suitable components, or improved materials to eliminate or reduce the frequency of maintenance problems. Corrective maintenance tools in organizations are:

- Corrections: these are improvements in the maintenance pattern
- Redesign: which involves modifications in the existing design
- Substitution: which is the replacement of components with more improved versions
- Changes in material specifications

8.2.4 Predictive Maintenance

The predictive maintenance approach works on the prediction of likely failures of equipment and making a provision accordingly for maintenance activities ahead of the probable date of failure. For successful predictive maintenance, it is necessary:

- to monitor the condition of the equipment
- to analyze failure
- to collect statistical data

8.2.5 Total Productive Maintenance (TPM)

This kind of maintenance involves all the employees of an organization, through participation in small group activities. TPM was first introduced in *Nippondenso Co. Ltd.* of Japan in 1969, after they had experienced difficulty in the preventive maintenance activities of automated equipment (with a conventional maintenance crew). The important features of TPM are:

- activities to maximize equipment effectiveness
- autonomous maintenance by operators
- company-led small group activities

The TPM Programme organizes all employees from top management to production line workers in a company-wide maintenance system to support productive facilities. The dual goal of the programme is zero breakdowns and zero-defects. Its results are tremendous; there is obvious elimination of breakdowns and defects, improvement in operations, reduced costs; inventory can be minimized and productivity increased. In addition to tangible benefits, it also ensures intangible benefits, which the Japanese list as the five 'S's. These are:

i. *Seiri* (Orderliness)
ii. *Seiton* (Tidiness)
iii. *Seiso* (Purity)

iv. *Seiketsu* (Cleanliness)
v. *Shitsuke* (Discipline)

8.2.5.1 *Steps to Introduce TPM*

Some of the important steps to introduce TPM are:

Step-1: Preparatory stage This is the initial stage, when management announces the intent to introduce TPM in the organization. Such an announcement focusses on factors like employee awareness, management's commitment and involvement, etc. To increase the awareness, many organizations focus on workshops, seminars, training or mentoring.

Step-2: Setting up of committees TPM requires the active coordination of the activities of various departmental committees. The committees focus on aspects like improvement, autonomous maintenance and quality maintenance.

Step-3: Developing working systems and targets For effective TPM practices, it is necessary to establish a benchmark in each area and to set a target for the achievement for all the employees of the organization.

Step-4: Developing the Master Plan A master plan has to be developed to institutionalize TPM, and to make it a part of the culture of the organization.

Step-5: Introducing TPM At this stage, all stakeholders, including vendors or suppliers, are invited. The purposes, the benefits and quality output required are explained to them.

Step-6: Implementation This is the final stage of introducing TPM in the organization.

By following all the above steps, we can institutionalize the culture of TPM in the organization.

8.2.5.2 *Pillars of TPM*

Total productive maintenance is now acknowledged as one of the best maintenance management practices to achieve cost efficiency, quality improvement and customer satisfaction. To embrace this practice, it is essential for the organization to understand its processes and requirements.

A thorough understanding of TPM requires understanding its 'eight pillars', which are:

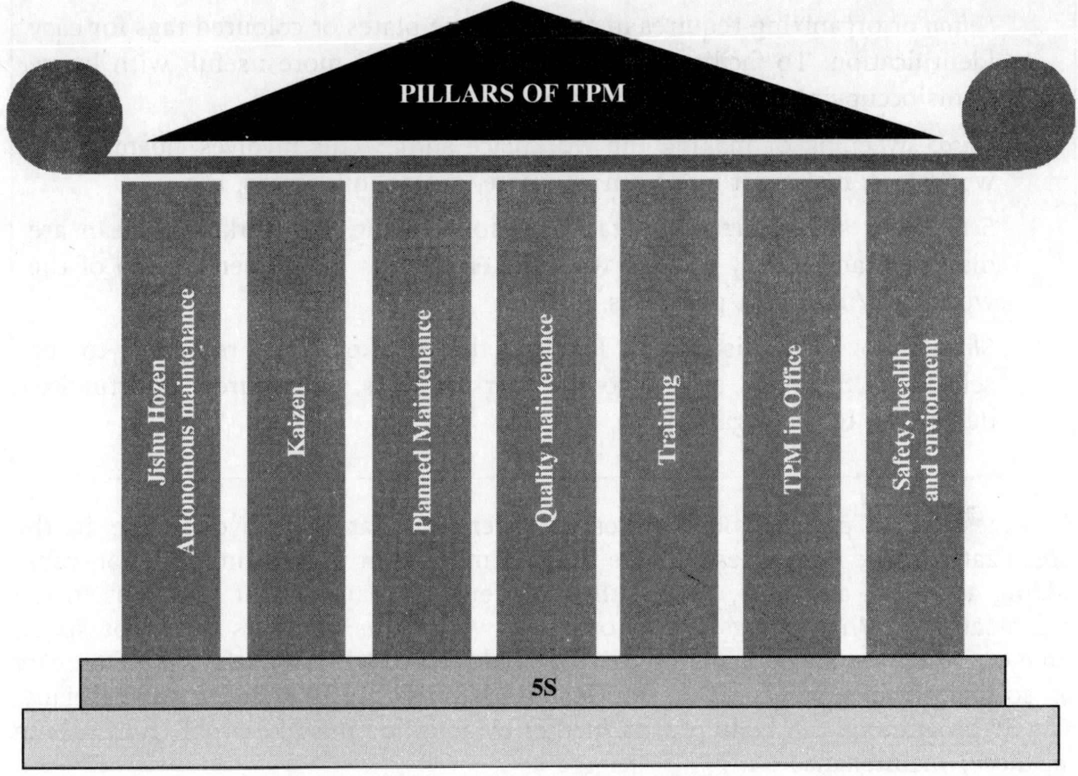

Figure 8.1 *TPM and its eight pillars*

Pillar 1 – 5S: An organized workplace is precondition for successful implementation of TPM. The 5S practices ensure an organized workplace. We have briefly introduced the concept in the foregoing paragraphs. However, for better understanding, more clarity is required. In table 8.1 below, the meaning and contexts of 5S are explained.

Table. 8.1 *The 5S concept*

Japanese 5 S
1. *Seiri* or sort out indicates organizing the items in an orderly manner; as critical, important, frequently-used items, useless items, etc. *Seiri* suggests that critical items must be made available in close proximity, so that it can be traced back, as and when required. Typically, priority for the arrangement of items may be low, average and high, depending on the frequency of use of the items.

2. *Seiton* or organizing requires items like name plates or coloured tags for easy identification. To facilitate this, vertical racks are more useful, with heavy items occupying the bottom position.
3. *Seiso*, sweeping or making the workplace shine: This involves cleaning the workplace, making it free from all waste, grease, oil, scraps, etc.
4. *Seiketsu* or standardization: Standards for keeping the workplace clean are discussed and jointly decided with the employees for proper upkeep of the workplace/machines/pathways, etc.
5. *Shitsuke* or self discipline: Finally, the workers are required to be self-disciplined, and adhere to the work process, procedures, punctuality, dedication to the organization, etc.

A successful 5S programme requires a leadership that can drive change in the organization. The uniqueness of this programme is that it can eliminate non-value adding activities, and thus, benefit the maintenance management functions in the organizations. When things are in order in workplaces, workers need not spend time on searching and organizing the materials. Also, with 5S, safety is taken care of, so maintenance work-related injuries and hazards can be reduced substantially. The 5S programme can be improved further by adopting mistake-proof (*poka yoke* in Japanese) maintenance.

Pillar 2: *Jishu Hozen* Autonomous Maintenance This pillar of TPM helps in developing operators, so that they can undertake minor maintenance work, to enable skilled maintenance team members to focus on more value-added maintenance tasks. The operators now feel responsible enough to take ownership of the equipment and machines that they use to produce goods, and prevent these from deterioration. Autonomous maintenance, therefore, ensures less work stoppage, eliminating defects at source through Total Employee Participation (TEI). It requires employee development, fixing of standards, general inspection, autonomous inspection and management.

Pillar-3 – *Kaizen* The word *Kaizen* means "change for the good or betterment". *Kaizen* helps in achieving minor improvements, but when used on a continuous basis, involving all cross sections of employees, it can bring in innovative changes and improve the efficiencies of workers in general. *Kaizen* requires practicing the concepts of zero losses in all spheres of activity, leading to cost minimization and overall effectiveness of plant maintenance.

Pillar 4 – Planned Maintenance This ensures flawless operation of machines and equipment, to churn out defect-free products for total customer satisfaction. The planned maintenance family of practices requires the practice of preventive maintenance, breakdown maintenance, corrective maintenance and maintenance prevention. The objective of planned maintenance is to the ensure the availability of operational machines and equipments, reduce unnecessary inventory holding and in the process, achieve the optimum cost of maintenance.

Pillar 5 – Quality Maintenance Its focus is to achieve customer satisfaction through defect-free quality manufacturing. In the process of performing these maintenance jobs, we understand which equipment affects product quality, this gradually improves our knowledge and also our attitude towards proactive maintenance, there is transcendence from quality control to quality assurance.

Pillar 6 – Training Training and developing employees is the most important pillar of TPM, as it helps in the process of multi-skill development of employees, who with improved morale, volunteer to perform all the required functions efficiently and effectively. Training focusses on overall improvement of knowledge, skills and abilities (KSA).

Pillar 7 – TPM in office TPM practices cascade to the office to improve the productivity and efficiency of administrative functions. This is facilitated by structured processes and procedures and through office automation. With the improvement in support functions (through TPM in office), the overall efficiency of the maintenance function also improves.

Pillar 8 – Safety, health and environment

This helps in developing a safe workplace. These eight pillars of TPM help organizations to achieve the following goals:

- Improvement of equipment effectiveness
- Improvement in maintenance effectiveness
- Improvement in maintenance prevention
- Improvement in the knowledge and skills of operators and maintenance crew members
- Improvement in the work of routine maintenance

Thus, reviewing our discussions on TPM, it is evident that starting from the approach of preventive maintenance in the 1950s, TPM focussed on productive maintenance, and from the 1970s onward, TPM has become a strategic choice to achieve productivity, quality and cost efficiency with minimum maintenance problems, through employee participation. TPM is a culture, a total concept and a revolution to optimize organizational resources.

8.3 TOTAL PRODUCTIVE MAINTENANCE (TPM) AND OVERALL EQUIPMENT EFFECTIVENESS (OEE)

The concept of Total Productive Maintenance (TPM) originated from the Japan Plant Maintenance Institute in 1972. TPM is a part of total quality control (TQC), and a management-led initiative for all cross-sections of workers (total employee involvement), to self-manage maintenance problems in the organization. Overall Equipment Effectiveness (OEE) is the key measure of the tangible benefits of TPM.

TPM discards the age-old view that maintenance is a standalone background function, rather it emphasizes that it is the joint responsibility of all supervisors, operators, and maintenance workers, so that plants, equipment and machines can run smoothly, and the performance of the organization as a whole improves. OEE ratio helps in the measurement of the goals of TPM. OEE ratio is calculated as follows:

OEE Ratio Calculation

OEE = availability × performance × quality rate.

Availability = Available time – downtime × 100

Downtime or machine downtime is computed by adding together loss of production time due to machine failure, so also for the set-up or machine adjustment time, and time wastage that might have caused loss of production.

Performance rate = ideal cycle time × processed quantity × 100.

Quality rate = processed quantity – defective quantity × 100

For better clarity, here again, we clarify OEE and its calculation.

Overall Equipment Effectiveness (OEE) metrics for the production is calculated using the following formula:

OEE = equipment availability × performance efficiency × first pass quality

World-class levels of OEE start at 85% based on the following values: 90% equipment availability × 95% performance efficiency × 99% rate of quality = OEE of 84.6%.

In OEE calculation, the first focus should be on major equipment effectiveness losses, because this is where the largest gains can be realized in the shortest time. There are 11 major areas of loss, and they fall within four broad categories.

8.3.1 Equipment Availability

1. Planned-shutdown losses
   (a) No production, breaks, and/or shift changes
   (b) Planned maintenance downtime losses
   (c) Equipment failure or breakdowns
2. Setups and changeovers
   (d) Tooling or part changes
   (e) Start-up and adjustment

3. Performance Efficiency:
   Performance efficiency losses
   (f) Minor stops (less than six minutes)
   (g) Reduced speed or cycle time
4. First Pass Quality
   (h) Quality losses
   (i) Scrap product/output
   (j) Defects or rework
   (k) Yield or process transition losses

Develop a vendor performance metric This metric is computed based on three considerations:

1. percentage of time vendor delivers in accordance with the agreed upon time,
2. percentage of time vendor delivers the wrong part, and
3. finally, the percentage of time vendor delivers wrong quantity of parts.

Summation of these three measurements equals the vendor performance metric. The standard should be 95%,

8.4 TPM AND TQM

TPM philosophy maintains that both operations and maintenance departments should feel responsible for the proper upkeep of plant and machinery. TPM is a maintenance function involving all the employees of the organization. TPM helps in avoiding wastage, reducing the cost of quality and solves the problem of poor productivity.

Both TPM and TQM (total quality management) have some similarity. Like TPM, TQM also requires commitment from the top, empowerment of employees and long-range perspectives. Some of the points of difference may be listed as in (Table 8.2):

Tabel 8.2 *Difference between TQM and TPM*

Category	TQM	TPM
Object	Quality (output and outcome)	Equipment (input and causes)
Means of attaining goal	Involves systematizing management and becoming software oriented	Involves employees' participation and becoming hardware oriented
Target	Quality for TPM	Elimination of losses and waste.

8.5 MAINTENANCE MANAGEMENT SYSTEMS AND STRATEGIES

Maintenance means the upkeep of plants, equipment and machines in operational condition, through repair, reconditioning, retro-fitting or reconfiguration. An extended life can be ensured for machines through repair. But again, repair alone may not always help. Companies cannot always afford to go in for replacement, due to the obvious need for additional capital investment. Thus, the primary objective of the maintenance function is to ensure that plants, equipment and machines are in operational condition, so that production systems can continue with their maximum possible utilization. This apart, through efficient maintenance management, companies also minimize the risk, by reducing the safety hazards for the operators. Whether it is the production or rendering of services, effective maintenance function is extremely important, as apart from cost-effective operations processes, this ensures uninterrupted services to customers. Obviously, for this reason, maintenance management is now a strategic function for organizations. Maintenance problems, by nature, are time independent. Hence, many organizations, unless it is strategically important, outsource this job, which substantially saves manpower costs. This may not be possible for highly specialized maintenance jobs, like aircraft maintenance, maintenance of defence items, etc.

Some of the strategic decisions on maintenance management, which any organization has to take, can be enumerated as under:

- breakdown/unplanned/ operate-to-failure maintenance
- preventive/planned or scheduled maintenance
- predictive or condition maintenance
- opportunity maintenance
- design out maintenance (design out maintenance focusses on those parts or spares which are costly and which are prone to more failure. This type of maintenance problem is more evident when the operation of equipments occurs outside the design specification, or when there are problems of inherently poor initial design. To address such maintenance problems, organizations first identify the high cost implications, and then adopt a suitable strategy to bring in suitable changes in design).

Breakdown maintenance strategy is adopted in those cases, where equipment and machines are not critical, and even in some cases, when companies have a stand-by arrangement. Breakdown maintenance, as the name goes, requires the companies to undertake the repair of a machine, when it actually breaks down, or becomes non-functional. Through repair, breakdown machines are put in order. On the contrary, companies have to go in for preventive or scheduled maintenance strategically at fixed time intervals, to avoid any possible dysfunction of equipments and machines. Preventive maintenance, done as a precaution, is more effective, particularly when machinery dysfunction can lead to accidents. Systematic lubrication of machines, overhauling, alignment and inspection are some examples of preventive maintenance.

Condition monitoring as a maintenance function can help the organization to detect and diagnose faults. Predictive maintenance strategy is usually adopted for very critical equipment and machinery, like aircraft maintenance, ship maintenance, maintenance of refineries, and bulk chemical manufacturing units, etc. Some of the techniques used in predictive maintenance are vibration, temperature, oil/lubricant analysis, etc. Opportunity maintenance strategy basically helps companies to decide on the timing of maintenance, so that it can minimize the effect of failures. The maintenance strategy that will work in a particular company depends on its maintenance policy, characteristics, cost and safety. Some of the new maintenance strategies are proactive maintenance, reliability-centred maintenance (RCM), total productive maintenance (TPM), etc.

1. Proactive maintenance identifies possible dysfunction of machines, monitoring the possible causes of failure. For example, a noisy sound on the roller may be a signal of dysfunction of bearings.
2. Proactive maintenance identifies possible dysfunction of machines, monitoring the possible causes of failure. For example, a noisy sound on the roller may be a signal of dysfunction of bearings.
3. RCM considers the reliability of the systems, based on its functions and possible failures. RCM strategy is more effective for critical systems like aircraft, nuclear power plants and in space.
4. TPM is a Japanese concept, and it requires total involvement/participation of all cross-sections of workers in the organization. The basic aim of TPM is to integrate maintenance functions with the operations, so that the operators themselves can ensure effective functioning of equipment and machines.

Indian Oil, the PSU (public sector unit) POL (Petroleum, Oil and Lubricant) major has introduced Turnaround Management Systems (TAMs) for the maintenance of its refineries. Maintenance of refineries requires plant shutdowns covering over 180 processes of the company. TAMs undertake the maintenance of all the process units, utilities and off-sites simultaneously. TAMs make use of resources with user-friendly multi-user software packages to coordinate all the maintenance jobs with stringent safety standards. Software like MS Project, Primavera, etc., is used extensively by the company to plan, schedule, and monitor and control maintenance activities. TAMs can provide daily status reports, exception reports, etc. on important maintenance criteria like activities due to start, activities due for finish, possible delay in completion of critical and non-critical activities, shutdown completion schedules, etc. It can create catch-up plans for any eventual delays or unanticipated work to meet the deadline for the completion of maintenance time.

8.6 ORGANIZATION AND FUNCTIONS OF MAINTENANCE

Maintenance functions optimize the ability of machines to function effectively through systematic upkeep. Based on organizational needs, maintenance functions can either be centralized or decentralized. A decentralized maintenance structure requires the integration of maintenance functions with shop floors, and therefore, it reduces the response time to maintenance problems. However, due to operational complexities, it may not always be feasible for companies to maintain a decentralized maintenance structure. It may not even be cost effective. With TPM, shop floor level maintenance tasks, to the extent possible, are given to the operators, after suitable training. Obviously, for these reasons, centralized maintenance functions are better chosen, so that a dedicated team of experts can undertake the maintenance work for the organization as a whole. Centralized maintenance can optimize the resources, but at times, lack efficiency and lead to a delayed response to shop floor problems. Hence, many organizations prefer to have a balance of both to ensure minimum machine down time, and an uninterrupted flow of production. Irrespective of the type of structure, a maintenance department makes use of three interdependent components – resources, administration and planning and control systems.

Some of the functions of the maintenance department are:

- maintenance of plants, equipments and machines, including facilities
- installation of equipments, machines and facilities
- preventive maintenance tasks
- condition monitoring tasks
- modifications
- inventory management
- supervision of maintenance crew
- maintaining maintenance records

8.7 ELEMENTS OF EFFECTIVE MAINTENANCE MANAGEMENT

Some of the elements of effective maintenance management functions are:

- documented maintenance policy
- materials control
- preventive maintenance
- condition monitoring
- maintenance work order
- maintenance job planning
- maintenance control
- maintenance data record keeping
- measurement of maintenance performance.

For assessing maintenance performance, an organization makes use of data on reliability, availability and maintainability (RAM). It requires the identification of specific parameters, against which the performance is measured.

With computer integrated maintenance management systems, organizations can monitor and assess performance. Software vendors like *Oracle, PeopleSoft, SAP*, etc. consolidate maintenance-related data, and generate reports for proper maintenance control. Such software packages are capable of performing the processing of work orders, asset management, preventive maintenance, inventory control and develop a maintenance score card, based on which companies can efficiently manage the maintenance function.

8.8 BEST PRACTICE MAINTENANCE MANAGEMENT

Overhauling and replacement of plants and machinery at fixed intervals has been the traditional approach to maintenance management. However, condition-based maintenance, reliability-centred maintenance, etc. are now gaining importance.

- A condition-based maintenance approach requires the maintenance department to focus on the consequences of failure. Such analysis of the consequences of failure helps the maintenance department to understand the need for and timing of maintenance.
- Reliability-centered Maintenance (RCM) is now considered more strategic. RCM originated in the airline industry in the 1960s. Subsequently, in 1978, it was institutionalized with the help of the US Department of Defense (with the support of *United Airlines*). The RCM process represents a complete change in management approach to maintenance strategies. The system requires empowerment and skill enhancement of the operators and the maintenance crew to integrate the culture of maintenance with the mainstream functions of the organization. The new version of RCM is RCM2, which requires the adoption of the following approaches for its implementation:

Step 1: Introduce the approach to the key decision-makers within the organization

Step 2: Select the appropriate equipment for initial analysis and estimate the potential benefits that would be gained from this analysis

Step 3: Select the appropriate team to conduct the analysis

Step 4: Train team members in the RCM2 approach

Step 5: Form a team and conduct the analysis

Step 6: Conduct a management and technical audit of the analysis

Step 7: Develop revised maintenance schedules

Step 8: Implement revised maintenance schedules

Step 9: Assess the benefits obtained

Step 10: Repeat steps 2 to 9, as desired.

The key consideration in the RCM2 approach is to analyse the potential consequences of failure of machines; these include looking into issues like consideration of machine downtime, loss of production, safety or environmental issues. Apart from consideration of the plant level data, it requires benchmarking with industry practices. The existing plant level data on the reliability of the machines, maintenance and operating costs have to be benchmarked. As it is a team-based maintenance management approach, it requires strategic team building. With RCM, and now RCM2, organizations can achieve sustainable improvements in machine performance.

8.9 MODELS OF MAINTENANCE ORGANIZATION STRUCTURE

Organizations can make use of a variety of maintenance structures, like the maintenance-centric model, the production-centric model and the engineering -centric model.

8.9.1 Maintenance-centric Model

In the maintenance-centric model, maintenance department reports to a plant or facilities manager, and simultaneously to the production manager. As the model suggests the use of cross-functional team work, it is more effective for start-ups.

8.9.2 Production-centric Model

In this structure, maintenance resources are made available to the production or operations managers. However, many them may not have the necessary technical skills to deploy maintenance resources, hence, it may fail to use the optimum level maintenance resources, and ultimately, reduce the maintenance function to a fire-fighting job. It is for this reason that a production-centric maintenance structure is considered ineffective, as it only helps to meet production targets without long-term sustainability.

8.9.3 Engineering-centric Model

In this structure, maintenance functions report to the engineering department, with common supervision. Since this structure is more feasible in the case of a project-based management approach, it may not work well for a stand-alone factory or manufacturing unit. In a project-based management system, performance measurement leans more on time-bound project completion than on sustainable maintenance practices. Operationally, in this structure, breakdown maintenance is more practiced than preventive and other types of maintenance. Which model is best suited where, depends on the organization's specific requirements.

8.10 ROLES AND RESPONSIBILITIES OF MAINTENANCE MANAGERS

Roles and responsibilities of maintenance managers vary depending on the nature of maintenance, and the type of organization, its plants, equipment and machines. However, based on industry practices, we can identify the following roles and responsibilities of maintenance managers:

- Directing the maintenance workers
- Ensuring that the maintenance job is executed in an effective and efficient manner
- Reviewing the work plan and scheduling work
- Ensuring quality of work
- Ensuring the availability of machines and equipment in working condition
- Ensuring security and safety while executing maintenance work
- Ensuring cost-effective maintenance work
- Promoting proactive maintenance, and developing maintenance personnel accordingly
- Monitoring the computerized maintenance management systems (CMMS)
- Implementing preventive and predictive maintenance for better efficiency
- Planning, scheduling and coordinating corrective and preventive maintenance activities
- Developing a maintenance schedule
- Assisting inventory management of spares, tools and other accessories, required for maintenance
- Ensuring maintenance cost control

8.11 NEED FOR MAINTENANCE POLICY

Every organization needs to adopt a Maintenance Policy based on the following factors to ensure an effective maintenance management programme:

- Establish a scheduled planned maintenance, based on predictive analysis or condition monitoring of equipment.
- Avoid unnecessary tampering with equipment.
- Liquidate breakdown problems, and deal immediately with equipment that may be affecting production, on a priority basis

Some organizations follow a work control system to organize maintenance activity, this involves:

1. Planning
2. Scheduling
3. Materials co-ordination
4. Maintenance contacts co-ordination

8.12 SPARES PARTS PLANNING AND CONTROL IN MAINTENANCE

Most organizations maintain a stock of spare parts for maintenance jobs. As this constitutes a major part of the inventory investment, proper planning and control of spare parts requirement is extremely important. Both for preventive and breakdown maintenance, we need to plan for spare parts. While preventive maintenance is planned and carried out at periodic intervals, breakdown maintenance problem is time independent. Even systematic preventive maintenance is not a guarantee that breakdown maintenance will be eliminated. Planning for spare parts depends on data analysis of failure patterns. Using these data, we decide on the service level or downtime/under-stocking cost, and accordingly, compute the number of spares to be stocked. However, the stocking policy depends on the nature of spares.

For regular spares, which are required in large numbers, breakdown occurs either as per normal distribution (normal wear-out) or as per Poisson distribution (for system overload). Service level in this case is computed by using the following formula:

$$\frac{K_u}{K_u + K_o}$$

where. K_u = opportunity cost for under-stock of one unit.

K_o = opportunity cost for over-stock of one unit.

This helps us to decide about regular and buffer stock. Usually, these are low-cost items.

For the insurance of spares, which are rarely required during the life span of equipment because of high reliability, we decide about procurement only when machine downtime cost is higher. For better approximation, we can use the following formula:

(Probability of failure) × *(Machine breakdown costs)*

These are usually high-cost items.

Capital spares are required in less quantity than regular spares. These are also expensive items and procurement decisions are taken on service level. Rotable spares arc rcpairablc and rc-usable. Here, we use a multi-channel single service queuing theory format to decide about the procurement of spares.

Example

A company is required to maintain an inventory of spares for breakdown maintenance. The failure pattern of this item shows a Poisson distribution trend. The mean breakdown rate is six items per month. Lead time for procuring this item is one month. The company wants to maintain a service level of 90%. Calculate the buffer stock requirement of spares.

Solution

This is a problem of regular spares requirement. Hence, we will use a fixed re-order system.

With mean breakdown rate of 6 (λ), the Poisson distribution table shows that the cumulative probability of X at 90% service level is 0.916. This is written as follows:

$$X = 9$$

Cumulative probability is 0.916
If we assume $X = 8$, Cumulative probability is 0.847, which, however, falls short of the 90% service level.

Thus, with a stock of 9 items (X), during lead time, we satisfy the requirement of maximum demand rate (D_{max}) corresponding to 90% service level. Buffer stock during lead time, therefore, would be the difference between D_{max} and λ (which is $D_{average}$).

$$X = (D_{max} - D_{average})$$

$$X = 9 - 6$$

$$X = 3$$

Therefore, the desired buffer stock would be three items only, during the lead time.

Let us now examine a problem on insurance spares. As explained earlier, insurance spares have high reliability and are expensive. Since such items are critical in nature, their non-availability may result in a huge downtime cost. Often, we have to decide whether we should procure these spares along with the equipment or not. We take such a procurement decision if:

(Probability of failure) $\times$ *(down time cost)* $\geq$ *Purchase Price*

Example

A critical spare used in a CNC Machining Centre has a very high reliability of 99%. The equipment is an imported one and its downtime cost in terms of lost sales (during the lead time of one month) is estimated at Rs. 3 crore. The cost of the spares is Rs. 15 lakh. The company would like to know whether they should procure the spares along with the machine or not.

Solution

(1) Calculate the probability of failure, which in our case is *(1 – Reliability, i.e., 1 – 0.990) 0.01*.
Compute the expected cost of downtime, which in our case is *(0.01 × Rs. 3 crore) Rs 3 lakh.*

Since the cost of procurement of spares is Rs. 15 lakh, which is much higher than the expected cost of procurement, it is not advisable to procure the spares along with the machines.

Capital spares are expensive (though less than insurance spares); for effective maintenance, it is desirable to hold the optimum number keeping in view the service level. We have explained the formula for its computation earlier. Here, we will examine a problem to understand its computation.

Example

A company has identified the probability of requirement of capital spares based on their historical data as under:

Requirement of Spares	Probability
0	0.05
1	0.05
2	0.05
3	0.10
4	0.15
5	0.20
6	0.15

The cost of machine downtime due to non-availability of spares has been estimated as Rs. 450/-. Each spare costs Rs. 150/- and failed spares have a salvage value of Rs. 20/-. The company would like to know the number of spares they should stock to maintain the service level.

Solution

(i) Compute the probability of **ith** (P_i)for the corresponding N (number of spares required). Corresponding N is determined averaging the spares requirement, which in our case is 21/7 = 3 (N). Cumulative probability (P_i)for N = 3 is 0.15 (0.05 + 0.05 + 0.05). For N – 1 (2) associated (P_i) is 0.10 (0.05 + 0.05).

(ii) Compute the associated probability for maintaining the service level. This is found by using following formula:

$C_s - C/C_s - S$, where, C_s = Cost of shortage per spare

C = Cost of each spare

S = Salvage value of each spare

In our case, it is therefore:

$$(450 - 150)/(450 - 20) = 300/430 = 0.69767$$

(iii) Now, compare this probability with the associated probability of N and N – 1 as found out in step (i). As per the formula, if associated probability for the service level (0.69767) is less than or equal to **N – 1** and **N**, we consider the corresponding N value as our optimal stock requirement. Hence, the company should maintain stock of a minimum of 3 spares to maintain the service level.

Rotable spares being repairable and re-usable, the multiple channel single service queuing theory is used, assuming defective equipments as 'arrivals' and spares as 'servers'. Service time here is the time taken to repair the spares. The utilization factor is computed first and then the cost implication for holding the different number of spares based on the data is assessed. The lowest cost for the corresponding spares becomes the basis for selection. Let us examine this problem using a live example.

Air India has hangers at Delhi Airport. These hangers are repair shops for *Boeing* planes. In one of their hangers, three *Boeing* planes arrive per week. The engines of these planes are repairable, and every time a *Boeing* is sent to the hangers for repair, the engines are thoroughly checked and overhauled. *Air India* has 20 *Boeings* and each *Boeing* has three engines. An engine costs Rs. 1.5 crore. To avoid downtime, engines are replaced from the stand-by spares, every time they are grounded for repairs. Their mean rate of repair/reconditioning is four engines per week. The cost of non-availability of engines to the company is Rs. 30 lakh per week and 25% is the capital cost of the engine to the company.

Assuming that breakdown and service rates follow a Poisson distribution, suggest what should be the optimum holding of spare engines.

Solution Hints

There are 20 *Boeings* with 3 engines each; hence, the total number of engines is 60. These being large in number, we will use infinite source assumption.

Mean arrival rate (λ) = 3 per week. Mean servicing rate (μ) = 4 per week.

Utilization factor (ρ) = λ / $S\mu$, where S is the number of spares. We analyse the problem for different values of S (i.e., Spare engines).

Assuming S = 2, we compute as under:

Utilization factor (ρ) = $\lambda/S\mu$ = 3/2(4) = 3/8 = 0.375

Likewise we have to find out the total cost and decide at which inventory level of spare engines, total cost will be at a minimum.

(Ans: 3 spare engines).

8.12.1 Assessment of Maintenance Capacity

It is necessary to compute the manpower requirement based on the maintenance load. This is illustrated below:

A company has given you the following information, based on which you have been asked to suggest the optimum number of workers.

A machine breaks down at a mean rate of 0.4 per day. A worker can repair one machine per day, i.e., u = 1. The machine is such that repair time is proportionately reduced with the increase in the number of workers. However, the number of workers cannot be increased beyond 3, as logistics support is inadequate. If at any point of time, the company desires to increase manpower beyond 3, it is required to develop a second line.

Maintenance workers are paid Rs. 300/- per day, while the machine's idle cost is Rs. 650/- per day. Consider the optimum number of workers assuming no other cost is involved.

Solution

Let us now compute the mean of the broken machine as follows:

$$\frac{\lambda}{\mu-\lambda} = \frac{0.4}{1-0.4} = 0.66$$

Total cost of a repair, assuming one worker is deployed, would then be:

$$1(300) + 0.66(650) = 300 + 429 = 729$$

Assuming two workers are deployed, the mean rate of failure would be:

$$0.4/(2-0.4) = 0.25$$

$$2(300) + 0.25(650) = 762.5$$

Assuming three workers are deployed, the mean rate of failure would be;

$$0.4/(3-0.4) = 0.15$$

$$3(300) + 0.15(650) = 997.5$$

From this problem, it can be seen clearly that the company benefits only when employing one worker, as the proportionate cost goes up with the increase in the number of workers. Hence, under the prevailing circumstances, the company should only use one worker for machine maintenance jobs.

8.12.2 Learning Curve

Discovered by T.P. Wright in 1936, the learning curve was used to analyse the factors affecting the cost of airplanes. Similarly, we can use the learning curve to assess manpower requirements, work scheduling, material requirement planning, etc.

An 80% learning curve means:

- The first unit takes 8 labour hours.
- The second unit takes 80% of 8 Hours, i.e., 6.4 hours.

Likewise, labour hours will proportionately decrease for subsequent units.

The usual learning curve model is $Y = ax^b$, where,

y = average time per unit of X units

a = time taken for the first unit

x = cumulative number of units

b = learning co-efficient

Like the learning curve, queueing theory can also be used in maintenance (See chapter-5).

Illustration

A company manufacturing TV sets has experienced an 85% learning curve. The company would like to compute the labour hours required to manufacture the 50th unit when it takes 3000 hours for manufacturing the first set.

Solution

$Y = 3000(50)^b$

'b' co-efficient is = – 0.23446, i.e. (log, 0.85/log,2 = –0.07058/0.30103)

Hence, $Y = 3000 \times 50^{-0.23446}$

Log 3000 – 0.23446(log 50) = 3.07878

Antilog of 3.07879 is 1198.8918 hours.

Hence, labour hours required for manufacturing the 50th unit would be 1199 hours, considering the learning curve rate of 85%.

Certain other maintenance problems like computation of failure rate, reliabilities, have also been illustrated through this problem for better appreciation of the subject.

Examples

Bearings used by Rollers of *Sonajuli Tea Co* go out of order frequently. The company maintains data for bearing failure. Data for the last 4 months has been given below:

Time to Failure	1st month	2nd month	3rd month	4th month
No. of Failure	50	30	20	18

From the above record, you have been asked to compute:
(a) Average time to failure
(b) Mean rate of failure
(c) Reliability of a bearing remaining in working condition for 4 months

Solution

Time	No. of failure at the end of the month	No. of bearings remain in working condition until the end of the month	Ratio of failure to surviving
1.	50	118	50/118 = 0.4237
2.	30	68 (118–50)	30/68 = 0.4411
3.	20	38 (68–30)	20/38 = 0.5263
4.	18	20 (38–20)	18/18 = 1.0

Average or Mean Time to Failure (MTTF)

$$1 * (50/118) + 2 * (30/68) + 3 * (20/38) + 4 * (18/20)$$
$$= 0.4237 + 0.8823 + 1.5789 + 3.6 = 6.4849 \text{ months}$$

Mean rate of failure

1 / 6.4849 = 0.1542 failures per month

8.12.3 Reliability

Reliability is the probability that a piece of equipment or component will perform its intended function satisfactorily for a prescribed time under stipulated environmental conditions. Unreliability is the probability of failure. Reliabilities are expressed either as decimals or percentages. The frequency at which malfunctions occur is called the failure rate, lamda (λ), and is measured by the number of failures for each hour of operation or number of operations. Five failures in 1,000 hours of operation would constitute a failure rate of 0.005 per hour. The reciprocal of the failure rate is the mean time between failures (MTBF). The mean time between failures for a failure rate of 0.005 per hour is 200 hours.

Reliability is defined as the probability that a particular item will perform under a given conditions for a defined time period. Reliability is expressed using the formula:

$$F(t) + R(t) = 1 \quad \text{or,} \quad F(t) = 1 - R(t)$$

Probability of survival $R(t)$ and probability of failure $F(t)$ are always unity.

For reliability computation, we consider information on availability, failure and maintainability. Availability is the probability of an item remaining functional, and therefore, usable. Failure indicates adverse effects on the system, and the failure criteria varies on a case to case basis, for example, it may be output failure, maintenance failure, etc. For failure analysis, we use the bathtub curve, explained later on in this chapter. Maintainability indicates the ease and the rapidity of restoring a system back to operation. Prima facie, it is the duration of maintenance.

In reliability computation, we make use of failure mode analysis. Failures occur independent of the reason for failure. For example, the failure rate during the early life period of a system can be calculated using the Weibull Distribution, as follows:

$$l(t) = lot - a$$

where $0 < a < 1$. $l(t)$ is usually expressed in percent failures per 1,000 hours.

Failure Modes and Effects Analysis (FMEA) helps to identify the modes of failure, assigning values in terms of unit cost and frequency, and then to rank the results in terms of significance of failures. Failure Modes, Effects and Criticality Analysis (FMECA) is the detailed version of FMEA, which examines the system as larger units, and then assigns criticality values to failures.

Mean Time between Failures (MTBF), Mean Time to Restore (MTTR), Root Cause Failure Analysis (RCFA), etc. are some of the techniques used to compute reliability.

8.12.3.1 Reliability System

We can develop a computerized reliability system using a block diagram (Fig. 8.2).

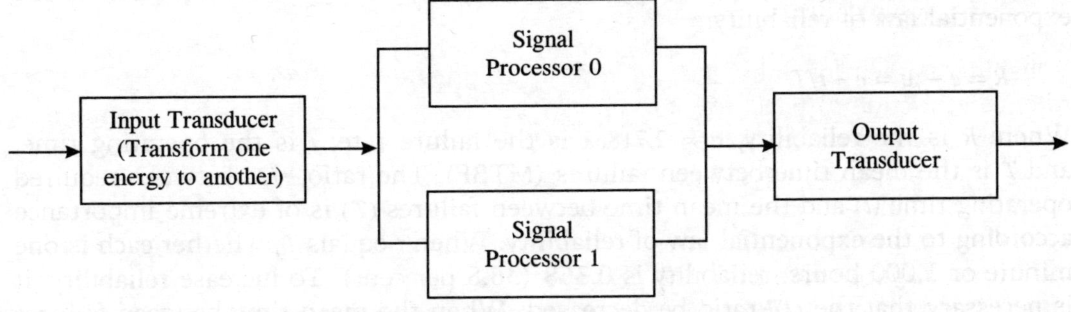

Figure 8.2 *Reliability system*

A reliability system consists of input which receives the signal and converts it to a data stream. The output transducer outputs the signal. Failure of input or output transducers ultimately indicates failure of the system.

With a reliability system in place, we can calculate the reliability of individual components as well.

8.12.4 Types of Failure

Equipment failures are of three types:

1. Early failures, which occur during the 'debugging' or 'burn-in' period due to poor assemblies or weak, sub-standard components that fail soon after start-up of a system. These are gradually eliminated leading to a decrease in the early failure rate until the overall failure rate reaches a fairly constant level. This fairly constant level is attributable to random failures.
2. Random or chance failures result from complex, uncontrollable, and sometimes unknown failures in the useful life of a component or system.
3. Wear-out failures begin when the components are past their useful life periods. The malfunction rate increases sharply due to old age and to some random failures.

Failure rates plotted against time for a large number of similar components produce the bathtub curve. Although reliability determinations are usually predicted on the useful or random failure period, the use of a constant failure rate concept is an over-simplification that has been undergoing modification lately.

According to the concept of constant failure rate, during the useful life of a large number of similar components, approximately the same number of failures will continue to occur in equal periods of time, if failed items are replaced continually. The constant failure rate can be described mathematically by an exponential function. When failed items are not replaced, the number of failures during any period will decrease since there are fewer remaining items than can fail. The mathematical expression, indicating the probability or reliability that components in a constant failure rate system will operate successfully to the end of a time period, is the exponential law of reliability:

$$R = e - \lambda t = e - t/T$$

Where R is the reliability, e = 2.718, λ is the failure rate, t is the operating time, and T is the mean time between failures (MTBF). The ratio, t/T, between required operating time (t) and the mean time between failures (T) is of extreme importance according to the exponential law of reliability. When t equals T, whether each is one minute or 1,000 hours, reliability is 0.368 (36.8 per cent). To increase reliability, it is necessary that the t/T ratio be decreased. When the mean time between failures is increased, the failure rate (which is its reciprocal) is also reduced.

The reliability of a complex system depends on the individual reliabilities of its components. If the operation of the system requires that all components operate satisfactorily at the same time, it is said to be a series system. In a series system, overall reliability is equal to the product of the individual reliabilities of the components.

System reliability, $Rs = R \times R \times R \times R \ldots$

This is called the Product Law of Reliability. In the event that each component of a six-component system has a reliability of 90%, the overall reliability is

Rs = 0.9 = 0.53 (53%).

Now, we can solve our earlier problem as follows:

No. of bearings surviving till the end of the 3rd month = 38, therefore, reliability for 3 months = 38/118 = 0.322, which we can assume as λ.

Using the negative exponential method, we can compute reliability more accurately.

Reliability $R - \lambda t$, where $\lambda t = 4 = e - (0.322 \times 4)$

Value of 'e' is constant, which is 2.7183.

We can solve this problem as follows:

1/2.7183 * 1.288 = 1/3.5011 = 0.2856

Hence, the reliability that bearings will perform satisfactorily for 4 months is 0.2856

Reliability is determined by the inherent merits of its design, and hence, reliability refers to the probability that a particular machine will perform its designed function satisfactorily.

By designing for RAM, that is, reliability, availability and maintainability, organizations can benefit significantly from improved performance of maintenance functions. Reliability is the probability of functionability of an asset under certain conditions over a specified period of time. Availability is the percentage of time an asset will function. Maintainability is the amount of effort needed to ensure that the asset remains in good condition to perform the desired jobs. Thus, reliability and maintainability together determine availability. With RAM, therefore, organizations can enhance their asset utilization rate, which is an indicator of efficiency for the maintenance function.

To manage reliability, we make use of Root Cause Analysis (RCA), and Reliability Centred Maintenance (RCM). The RCM approach is a structured decision-making process based on reliable historical failure data. However, even in the absence of such data, we can perform RCM analysis.

8.12.5 Bathtub Curves

This concept takes its terminology from life experiences like infant mortality, chance failures and wear-out period. Machines and equipment also experience this cycle. Tracking the trend of failure rates of machines and equipment, we can understand the root of the problem.

The bathtub curve represents three periods: an infant mortality period with a decreasing failure rate, followed by a normal life period with a low, relatively constant failure rate and finally, a wear-out period representing an increasing failure rate.

Using the analogy above, we can illustrate the bathtub curve (Fig. 8.3) as under:

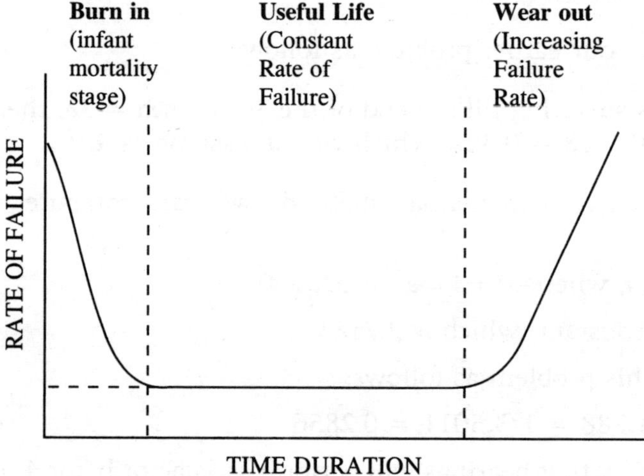

Figure 8.3 *The bathtub curve*

The curve in Fig. 8.3 is divided into three parts. The first part is the burn-in or infant mortality stage, which is characterized by failures due to inherent manufacturing defects. Often, we buy domestic durables, which we observe are non-functional right from the day of purchase or after a reasonable period of warranty. The second part witnesses the useful life stage, as it is characterized by a constant rate of failure. The third part of the picture is the wear-out phase, that is, the period when the machines and equipment witness an increasing failure rate from natural ageing and deterioration.

Thus, the bathtub curve is a typical visual model to represent the failure of machines and equipment. However, to frame this graph, it is necessary to have documented information on the plants and machines, in order to model a population of products with a calibrated bathtub curve.

8.12.6 Application of NPV Methods in Maintenance

Discounted cash flow method with the application of net present value (NPV) technique helps us understand the efficacy of our maintenance decisions. From the basic financial analogy, we know that a higher NPV is considered desirable, as it gives better return on investment. The NPV of a maintenance decision considers the time value of money, based on discounted cash flow, using the following formula:

$$NPV = \sum_{t=0}^{N} (C_t) \div (1 + r)^t$$

Where N = extended life of machines (in years) after maintenance;

t = timing of cash flow (year);

r = interest rate, or discount rate; and Ct = cash flow in year t.

The NPV, using the expected values (EV), helps us understand the need and justification of our maintenance decisions, as it facilitates a cost–benefit assessment of our maintenance investment. Through maintenance, we expect the life of machines or equipment to be extended. When the value of the extended life of machines (represented as NPV) is relatively less than the investments we make for maintenance, the decision for repair of the machines has to be dropped.

In the case of the EV of a failure event with uncertain outcomes, we compute the NPV using the following formula:

$$NPV = \sum_{t=0}^{N} (p_t \times C_t) \div (1 + r)^t$$

p_t = the probability of the event occurring at time t.

8.12.7 Descriptive Methods used in Maintenance Management

In maintenance, descriptive methods like simulation and replacements are used for the prediction of staff requirements. Already, we have mentioned that it is difficult to predict staff requirements in the maintenance department, as it is a time independent job. Globally, organizations optimize the maintenance cost, wherever it is possible, by outsourcing this function. Even to requisition the manpower requirement in such cases, simulation technique helps. The replacement method on the other hand helps us to take decisions on staff replacement, group or single replacement of items, and also, with regard to machines and equipment.

8.13 SIMULATION

In maintenance, we use simulation, a descriptive technique to examine the behaviour of the system. Using simulation, we can manipulate the variables and constants in an artificial environment, and then implement the same in a real life environment. In this process, we can avoid depending on our intuition and hunches and evaluate various alternatives to select the best course of action in predicting maintenance staff requirement in any organization. Thus, simulation helps us to estimate our action prior to implementation. There are four phases of simulation as under:

- definition of the problem and statement of objectives.
- construction of an appropriate model.
- experimentation with the model constructed and
- evaluation of the results of simulation.

8.13.1 Monte Carlo Simulation

The Monte Carlo or probabilistic simulation method is a numerical technique used to predict the behaviour of the system. The chance element is a very significant feature of Monte Carlo simulation and this approach can be used when the given process has a random or chance component.

Illustration

A power utility services company maintains a record of the maintenance staff requirements, to predict the requirement for different periods. The skills of the maintenance staff are interchangeable. The company, to ensure cost optimization outsourced their out-bound (at domestic customers' premises) maintenance staff requirement, and requisitions their requirement from a service provider on a daily basis. Information relating to the requirement for 200 days is as follows:

	Demand								Total
No. of staff	5	6	7	8	9	10	11	12	
No. of Days	4	10	16	50	62	38	12	8	200

Develop a simulation model to predict the demand of staff for a 10-day period.

Solution Steps

1. Derive the probability distribution of demand for the staff, expressing each of the frequencies in terms of proportions. This is done by dividing each of the values by 200, which is the total frequency. The resultant distribution would, therefore, be as follows:

No. of staff	5	6	7	8	9	10	11	12
No. of Days	0.02	0.05	0.08	0.25	0.31	0.19	0.06	0.04

2. Determine random numbers using any mechanism of a random number generator. There are various ways in which random numbers can be generated. These could be: result of some device, like a coin or die, a published table of random numbers etc. However, the most convenient method is to make use of the table of random numbers published by the Rand Corporation, USA.

3. Work out the assignment so that the interval of random numbers corresponds to the probability distribution. As the probabilities have been calculated to two decimal places, which add up to 1.00, we need 100 numbers of two digits to represent each point of probability. Thus, we take random numbers 00 through 99 to represent them. Now, as the probability of 5 staff is equal to 0.02, we assign two random numbers 00–01 to this demand level; the probability of 6 staff being equal to 0.05, the next five numbers, 02–06 would be assigned to this level. In a similar manner, each of the demand levels would be assigned appropriate intervals as seen below:

Demand (No. of staff)	Probability	Cumulative Probability	Random number Interval
5	0.02	0.02	00–01
6	0.05	0.07	02–06
7	0.08	0.15	07–14
8	0.25	0.40	15–39
9	0.31	0.71	40–70
10	0.19	0.90	71–89
11	0.06	0.96	90–95
12	0.04	1.00	96–99

The cumulative probabilities column analyzes the assigned numbers to correspond to the same probability range for each event.

4. Once the random number intervals are determined, we select a tracking pattern for drawing random numbers from the random number table. We may start with any column and row of the table and read the values in any set manner – horizontally, vertically or diagonally. Using the pattern, we draw the random numbers and match them with the assigned events.

Let us assume, for the purpose of this problem, we have decided to take every third value horizontally, starting with the fifth column and the fourth row of the table of random numbers. The random numbers, according to this pattern are 61, 74, 24,

03, 59, 16, 84, 92, 52, 07 .... etc. (for a 10-day demand period). We draw as many random numbers as the number of days for which demand was required to be simulated.

The first number – 61 – lies in the interval 40–70. This corresponds to the demand level of 9 staff. Thus, the simulated demand for the first day is 9 staff members. In a similar manner, we can obtain the demand for each day. For the 10-day period, we have the following demand:

Day	1	2	3	4	5	6	7	8	9	10
Number	61	74	24	03	59	16	84	92	52	07
Demand of staff	9	10	8	6	9	8	10	11	9	7

8.13.2 Advantages and Disadvantages of Simulation

Simulation techniques have many advantages and disadvantages too.
The major advantage of this technique is

1. Its capacity to lend itself to problems that are cumbersome, and even impossible to manage mathematically, using analytical methods.
2. Also, the technique allows us to experiment with the system behaviour without taking the risk of experimentation with the real system.
3. It also reduces the time taken for the manager to visualize the long-term effects in a quick manner.

The disadvantages are

1. It is not a derivation of the optimal solutions to a given problem; it merely characterizes the behaviour of the system in question for a given set of inputs.
2. Also, the approach is not precise, as it yields only estimates which are subject to sampling error.

However, the sampling error can be reduced by increasing the sample size. Also, it may not prove economical, as it requires greater effort to develop a suitable model. It is a tool of solution evaluation and does not generate problem solution. Therefore, it helps us to develop the proposed solution and then test the relative desirability of those solutions.

8.14 REPLACEMENT THEORY

A replacement is called for whenever new equipment offers more efficient or economical service than the old existing one. For example, the old equipment might fail and work no more, or is worn out and needs higher expenditure on its maintenance. The problem, in such situations, is to determine the best with respect to replacement of the equipment. The replacement theory provides an answer to this question in terms of an optimal replacement period.

We consider the question of replacement in the following situations:

- In respect of equipment/assets that deteriorate in performance over time and may be restored in whole or in part by expanding maintenance costs. Thus, the existing assets might be good technically, yet on economic considerations, it may not be worthwhile to continue with them, and hence, replacement may be called for. Machinery, equipment, and buildings fall in this category.
- In respect of units that perform adequately until sudden, complete failure. The length of their service until failure varies randomly over some predictable range. Car bulbs, tubes, some electronic components etc. are items that are in this category.
- In respect of replacement of the staff of an organization which diminishes gradually due to death, retirement, retrenchment and other reasons.

8.14.1 Staff Replacement

The staff of an organization calls for replacement because people leave the organization for several reasons. For planning a suitable recruitment policy, historical data are collected to estimate the likely stay of individuals with the organization through time. Here also, the stay of an individual employee may be a random variable, but the characteristics of the group of employees are likely to be fairly stable.

Example

Year	1	2	3	4	5	6	7	8	9	10	11	12
Percentage expected to leave by end of period	5	18	35	45	62	75	88	90	95	96	99	100

Using the above information, answer the following questions:

- What recruitment level per annum would be necessary to maintain this strength?
- If 15 of the sales persons are to be promoted to the next higher post, for what length of service in the organization is the primary criterion and at what average length of service can a new entrant expect to be promoted?

Answer

With an intake of 100 sales people every year, the distribution of the length of service of the sales force, when equilibrium has been reached shall be as follows:

Year	No. of people continuing
0	100
1	95
2	82
3	65
4	55
5	38
6	25
7	12
8	10
9	5
10	4
11	1
12	0
Total =492	

Recruitment of 100 sales people every year would thus give a total strength of 492. To maintain a staff strength of 80 sales persons, we need to recruit:

$$\frac{80 \times 100}{492} = 16.26 \text{ say } 16 \text{ persons}$$

With 80 persons in the sales team, the distribution of the completed length of service would be as follows:

Year	No. of Persons
0	16
1	15 (95%, of 16)
2	13 (82% of 16)
3	11 (65% of 16)
4	9 (55% of 16)
5	6 (38% of 16)
6	4 (25% of 16)
7	2 (12% of 16)
8	2 (10% of 16)
9	1 (5% of 16)
10	1 (4% of 16)
11	0
12	0

Since 15 sales persons are to be promoted and the promotion is to be on the basis of their length of service, the cumulative frequencies in this distribution reveals that a sales person can expect to be promoted after five years of service.

This is ascertained by counting backward, that is, from the 12th year onwards. After the fifth year, the total number of persons left is 16. Thus, promotion after the fifth year is considered to be better, if 15 people are required to be promoted based on length of service.

8.15 LEAN MAINTENANCE SYSTEM

Lean maintenance means aligning the processes and the organization of the maintenance functions in a way that productive equipment and machine time are not lost. It ensures zero maintenance time for optimum utilization of maintenance resources. The idea behind a maintenance value stream does not get disrupted and equipments and machines are productively used. However, zero maintenance time must not be misconstrued as making the maintenance functions altogether redundant.

Basically, the lean maintenance system follows a four-step process to transform the organization to a value stream-oriented maintenance organization that helps in achieving zero maintenance time. Such steps require systems prioritization, classification of the nature of maintenance, developing the concept, and finally, developing a lean organization.

System prioritization is done based on an assessment of each production sub-system for potential breakdown. These sub-systems are prioritized and dealt with. Some of the criteria for system prioritization are production system, value stream and the customers. Such categorization of systems prioritization subsequently helps in defining the recommended actions for the maintenance strategy. Systems which are critical are assigned the highest priority through detailed examination; for such systems, component-specific maintenance strategies are developed to optimize the maintenance resources to reach the goal of zero-maintenance time.

Through classification of the nature of maintenance, we develop a component-specific maintenance strategy. Basically, it helps in classifying the damage categories, and understands its potential effect on the systems. Along with such classification, we also develop the recommended courses of action for maintenance and ensure the availability of a stock of spare parts.

Concept development is done through a system-specific maintenance action plan, making a distinction between the critical and uncritical systems. Such an action plan is, by nature, a coordinated one and is capable of integrating the system priority, damage category priority and the maintenance work time.

Finally, a lean organization is developed to facilitate lean maintenance through well-defined actions and concepts. It requires the structuring of maintenance activities, calculation of man hour requirements for such activities, degree of centralization and decentralization of maintenance functions, etc.

The lean maintenance system organizes lean maintenance, assesses the potential operational capacities and achieves high systems availability, by following the basic principles of lean management, and using various lean tools. Lean management looks at the manufacturing of three primary processes that create value for consumers. These are product development, order to delivery and service through the products life cycle. It requires value creation from the standpoint of the customers, examining the current process and experimenting how it could perform better, understanding the requirement of the people and processes to support the value creation, and aligning the purpose, processes and people in search of the perfect process.

Lean is about removing waste from manufacturing processes. Lean maintenance therefore, is to provide maintenance services with the minimum possible waste of time to produce the desirable maintenance outcome.

Lean per se is the elimination of anything that stands as a stumbling block to a value stream, so that customers are satisfied. Some of the important core components of the maintenance value stream are work requisition, work order, job plans, coordination, scheduling, execution of jobs and its communication, etc. Other supplementary components to maintenance value stream are materials management functions, and also through 5S, Kaizen, value-stream mapping (scrutiny of the existing work process to eliminate the non-value adding activities). Through lean maintenance, we can standardize and fashion a mistake-proof (poka yoke) workflow process. Failure-modes-and-effects analysis, reliability-centered maintenance analysis and Hazops study also assist in implementing the lean maintenance plan. Hazops is the technique of studying the hazard and operability problems, so that through appropriate changes in the design, such issues can be taken care of.

SUMMARY

1. Traditionally, maintenance functions look after repair, replacement, adjustment or modification of plants, equipment and machinery to ensure the smooth running of production and operations activities of organizations.
2. Effective maintenance reduces machine downtime, ensuring continuous production. With scientific back-up maintenance support, organizations also reduce the cost of maintenance substantially.
3. Depending on the nature and type of organization, maintenance can be either breakdown, preventive, corrective, or predictive in approach. A recent trend is to focus on total productive maintenance (TPM). The effectiveness of a TPM programme can be accessed through OEE. OEE matrices are developed by considering equipment availability, first pass quality and vendor performance matrices. TPM also has a relationship with the TQM.
4. Maintenance management strategies help in the proper upkeep of plants and machines and ensure flawless operation through the extended life

of machines. Strategic maintenance deals with whether we need to consider breakdown (unplanned), preventive (planned), predictive or condition monitoring maintenance, opportunity or design out maintenance. All these have relative advantages and disadvantages. It is for the maintenance manager to consider these aspects.

5. Best Practice Maintenance Management now considers using condition-based maintenance, or reliability-centred maintenance. While condition-based maintenance focusses on the consequences of failure, reliability-centred maintenance emphasizes the creation of a culture of quality maintenance, empowering the employees and enhancing their skills.
6. Depending on the specific organizational needs, organizations adopt different varieties of maintenance structures or models, which can be either a maintenance-centric model, or a production-centric model, or even an engineering-centric model.
7. In this chapter, we have used various tools and techniques to assess maintenance functions and their effectiveness.

KEY WORDS

Breakdown Maintenance It is a traditional form of maintenance; it requires organizations to make available a separate maintenance team. The services of this maintenance team are called upon from time-to-time, whenever there is a machine breakdown.

Preventive Maintenance Normal wear and tear of machines can be avoided by adhering to a preventive maintenance programme. It includes periodic inspection to avert breakdowns and depreciation of plant, upkeep of plant by routine adjustment and repair.

Total Productive Maintenance (TPM) Maintenance of this kind involves all the employees of an organization through participation in small group activities. TPM was first introduced in *Nippondenso Co. Ltd.* of Japan, in 1969.

Learning Curve Discovered by T.P. Wright in 1936, the learning curve was used to analyze the factors affecting the cost of airplanes. Similarly, we can use the learning curve to assess manpower requirements, deal with work scheduling, material requirement planning, and even in the maintenance management function.

Bathtub Curve This curve explains the life cycle of machines and equipment, emulating our life experiences – the infant mortality, chance failures and wear-out period.

Production-centric Model This is a typical maintenance department structure where the maintenance functions and resources are made available to the production and operations managers. This structure may be ineffective, as it may emphasize production targets rather than the achievement of long-term sustainability.

GENERAL REVIEW QUESTIONS

1. Discuss the importance of the maintenance function. How does it differ from total productive maintenance?
2. In what way can we apply the Learning Curve Theory in maintenance management?
3. Draft a suitable maintenance policy for a company engaged in the generation and distribution of electricity to hande their customer complaints. Do you think in such cases, it is appropriate for them to sub-contract the maintenance function?
4. Briefly discuss how we can compute the reliability of a system. Is there any difference between the exponential law of reliability and the product law of reliability?
5. A company is engaged in producing different types of equipment for use in a steel plant. It has two different assembly lines to produce a particular equipment. The processing time for each assembly line is regarded as a random variable and is described by the following distributions:

Process Time (minutes)	Assembly – 1	Assembly – 2
10	0.10	0.20
11	0.15	0.40
12	0.40	0.20
13	0.25	0.15
14	0.10	0.05

Using the following random numbers, generate data on the process time for 15 units of the item and compute the expected process time for the product. For the purpose, read the numbers vertically taking the first two digits for the process time on assembly A1, and the last two digits for processing time on assembly A2.

4134	8343	3602	7505	7428
7476	1183	9445	0089	3424
4943	1915	5415	0880	9309

6. Consider that there is skill interchangeability, that is, the same workers can be used interchangeably in both the assembly lines. If the company is required to produce 500 units in a day, what would be the manpower requirement in an

8 hour working day with 20% fatigue allowance? Show your computation in terms of man-hours and man-day's also.

7. Short notes
   (a) Corrective Maintenance
   (b) Predictive Maintenance
   (c) Mean Rate of Failure
   (d) Systems Reliability

CRITICAL REVIEW QUESTIONS

1. Your company has recently introduced CNC (computer numeric control) machining centres, to replace the lathe machines. The existing lathe operators have been given skill change training and redeployed in other functions with proximity to their original job family. CNC operators are newly-recruited engineers who have vast experience in automated machines. To save the cost of maintenance, your company has gone in for TPM, requiring these newly-recruited operators to undertake general maintenance work along with their core responsibility of operations. For the maintenance of CNC machines, the company could not ensure the availability of a dedicated maintenance team; hence, it outsourced this job to vendors under an annual maintenance contract. Your decision to introduce TPM was resisted by the CNC operators, who allege that they are not paid for these additional job responsibilities. Draw a plan to convince them, so that TPM can be introduced successfully.

2. Your company wants you to introduce reliability-centred maintenance (RCM) management practices. Your company is engaged in the production of electronic security control systems. Elaborate your approach.

ADDITIONAL REFERENCES

1. Bhattacharyya, D.K. 2006, *Human Resource Planning*. New Delhi: Excel Books.
2. Jardine A. K. S. 1973. *Maintenance, Replacement and Reliability*. London: Pitman Publishing.
3. Hawkins, Bruce and Smith, Ricky. 2004. *Lean Maintenance*. Jordon Hill, Oxford: Elsevier Butterworth Heinemann.
4. Levitt, Joel. 2008. *Lean Maintenance*. New York, NY: Industrial Press.
5. Menipaz, E. 1984. *Essentials of Productions and Operations Management*. Englewood Cliffs, N.J: Prentice-Hall.
6. Nakajima S. 1988. *Introduction to TPM*. New York: Productivity Press.
7. Riggs, James, L. 1987. *Production Systemss: Planning, analysis and control*. New York: John Wiley & Sons.

8. Troyer, D. 2006. *Strategic Plant Reliability Management Course Book*. Tulsa, Oklahoma: Noria Publishing.

CASE STUDY

Clara India – the outsourced maintenance agent for the airlines

Effective maintenance management requires, at the outset, a ranking of the key assets based on risk. Risk is assessed based on vulnerability of machines and equipments, that is, on the degree or extent of effect, on the functioning of the plant as a whole, when such assets stop functioning. Based on the degree of risk, it is important to place orders for spares, when spares availability is vital for maintenance. Work orders for spares are also necessary for preventive maintenance work. At least for critical assets, it is necessary to prepare a documented corrective maintenance process, detailing the steps, labour hours required, machine drawings and the tools for repairing.

Clara India recently bagged orders for aircraft maintenance from two major airlines. To start with, the company prepared the overall equipment effectiveness metrics for the airline, and observed that in both cases, the metrics indicated a high degree of risk, leading to engines malfunction. While on the ground, the problem did not seem to impact the security and safety of passengers, on board, it could create problems. Every accident means payment of compensation to the passengers or their relatives, and litigation, causing loss of goodwill for the airlines.

Based on these results, *Clara* made the need for self checking, before the ground clearance on air worthiness, clear to the airlines. Both the airlines calculated that a single flight cancellation cost them Rs. 1.5 crore, while the eventual risk of engine failure on board would cost them not less than Rs. 10 crore. The overall equipment effectiveness (OEE) is the function of equipment availability, performance efficiency and first pass quality. Although the benchmarked OEE metrics is 85% (calculated based on 90% equipment availability, 95% performance efficiency and 99% rate of first pass quality), for the airlines, *Clara* had assumed 95% OEE, after studying the history of their aircraft. *Clara*'s insistence on 95% OEE ultimately resulted in the grounding of a minimum of two aircraft per week for both the airlines as the maintenance contract with *Clara* required them to compensate if the aircraft should crash.

Both the airlines are very critical about *Clara*'s OEE level, they felt it was too high and surpassed international standards. They urged *Clara* to reduce the OEE metrics to the international standard of 85%. *Clara* contended that most of the aircraft were old and required frequent repair, it is not advisable to urge them for reduced OEE metrics for their envisaged 90%. *Clara,* with its consistent track record of 95% vendor performance efficiency, felt that such a compromise would dilute their quality standards and would plunge them into a risk zone, which would result in subsequent loss of goodwill and business.

Discussion Questions

1. Do you agree with *Clara*? If yes, then as Clara's spokesperson how would you convince the airlines? If you do not agree, explain the reasons for your disagreement.
2. As the maintenance head for the airlines, what would be your argument to persuade *Clara* to reduce their OEE metrics.

CHAPTER 9
Quality Management Practices

LEARNING OBJECTIVES

After reading this chapter, you will be able to understand:

- The Basics of Quality Management Practices.
- Influence of Quality Management Practices on Organizational Improvement
- ISO Standards and Quality Systems Management
- Six-sigma and Innovation and Creativity
- Concept of Employee Empowerment, and Quality of Work-life (QWL)
- Concept of Quality Circles and its Relevance
- Quality Function Deployment
- Statistical Process Control

Opening Vignette

TVS's quality journey

The *TVS* group started its business in 1911 in Chennai, India. Beginning as a small transport company, they subsequently expanded into the manufacture of two wheelers, automotive components, spares, computer peripherals and subsequently, into financial services. *Sundaram Clayton Limited* (*SCL*), a flagship company of the group, started its business of manufacturing air braking systems for commercial vehicles in 1961. It later expanded its business to the manufacture of wheels and engines and various other specialty automobile spares for heavy and light commercial vehicles, and has now emerged a pioneer in the Indian automobile industry. For many Indian automobile companies like *Ashok Leyland, Tata Engineering and Locomotives, Hindustan Motors and Maruti Udyog, SCL* is the original equipment manufacturer (OEM). With more than 70% market share in the automotive air brake systems, *SCL* is now among the largest in India. Powered by its own full-fledged Research and Development Centre, *SCL* over the years has built world class facilities in design, development, simulation and the resting processes – it provides a range of expert services in vehicle testing like road trials, complete vehicle functions and process and test management. This process of indigenization put *SCL* on the world map as a quality manufacturer of automotive air brake systems. Even during the global slump in the automobile sector in the 1990s, *SCL* was able to achieve high business revenues. All these are attributed to its focus on quality.

SCL has institutionalized the core values of the *TVS* group, which are quality, reliability and service. To achieve these core values, every unit of the *TVS* group, including *SCL* follows company-wide quality control, encompassing product, systems, operations and processes. The company's quality management practices gained substantially in terms of employee participation in the quality mission, which ultimately helped the company achieve higher sales revenues and gain business success.

9.1 INTRODUCTION

Quality is defined as the totality of features and characteristics of products or services which satisfy the stated or implied needs of customers. It is now a must for the survival of an organization. Customers who buy our products or services have certain expectations. If the product or service meets or exceeds those expectations, time and again, then in the mind of the customer, it is a quality product or service. Quality provides a focus for all management concerns – cost reduction, productivity, team work, communication and training objectives like problem solving, decision making, organizational dynamics and interpersonal skills. These concerns acquire synergy and meaning only when aligned to organizational goals of quality and customer service. The responsibility for quality in manufacturing and services lies with the production and operations managers, who through various quality improvement initiatives, ensure the quality of products and services, and also facilitate developing the capability of the workers to troubleshoot problems of quality, and gradually, building a culture in the organization whereby quality is an in-built attribute of products and services. Such changes enhance the quality improvement programmes.

There is a paradigm shift from old to new realities with regard to quality, which encompasses the management culture in the organization. This is illustrated in table 9.1. Because of such a paradigm shift, it is now evident from the Mission Statement of most organizations that Quality issues are becoming increasingly focussed, so much so that quality is now an important competitive strategy.

The traditional focus on product quality has now been changed to Quality of Organization in the TQM era. Both for achieving internal efficiency and international acceptance, corporate houses are now getting ISO Certification to establish their quality identity.

Table 9.1 *The Paradigm Shift*

Old Realities	New Realities
Customer's freedom of choice is limited	Customer's freedom of choice is unlimited
Quality standards determined by seller	Quality standards determined by customer
Price is based on seller's cost plus profit margin requirement	Price is determined by what the customer is willing to pay
Marketing's role is to manipulate customers to buy. A one-way communication. Tell and sell.	Marketing's role is to add value and enhance customer satisfaction. A two-way communication.
Marketing is a distinct functional activity	Marketing is everything.
Marketing is solely responsible for achieving the company's primary objectives	Marketing is everyone's responsibility – from the worker on the shop floor to the Chairman
Focus on what is good for the company	Focus on what is good for the customer
Products are assets	Only brands are assets
Investment in plant and machinery gets top priority	Investment in building brand equity gets priority
Physical assets like land, building, machinery, people and money are viewed as real assets	Brands, corporate image, technology and skills are key assets
Manufacturing and maximizing production is a prime concern	Customization, meeting customer requirements is a prime consideration
Quality is the responsibility of the QC department	Quality is everyone's responsibility.

9.2 IMPORTANCE OF QUALITY IN AN ORGANIZATION

To sustain themselves in a competitive environment, organizations worldwide emphasize achieving quality, as it lowers costs, and at the same time, offers value for money to the customers. The mission statements of almost every organization declare that achieving quality is a priority to grow in a globally competitive market. The traditional focus on product quality has now been changed to Quality of Organization in the TQM era. Both for achieving internal efficiency and international acceptance, corporate houses are now getting ISO certification to establish their quality identity.

9.2.1 Cost of Quality

To appreciate the importance of quality, first it is necessary for the organization to understand the meaning of the term 'cost of quality'. Identification of cost of quality and the appropriate steps to reduce the same can help an organization in two ways – cost minimization and increased profitability. To analyze the cost of quality, it is necessary to first classify the nature of cost under three sub-headings as follows:

1. **Cost of failure** Quality may fail either internally – within the organization or externally – within the customer's premises. Therefore, the failure cost can be classified either as internal failure cost or external failure cost. Cost of re-work, cost of additional raw-materials, additional payments required to be made to workmen, eventual scrap arising etc. can be accounted for under internal failure cost. In the case of external failure, the cost incurred for re-transportation, re-packaging, servicing and handling of customer complaints and the cost of loss of goodwill will have to be considered, in addition to the cost to be incurred for internal failure. Experience shows that the cost of failure itself absorbs 70% of the total cost of quality.
2. **Cost of Appraisal** For verification of quality, the organization has to incur expenses towards inspection, for maintaining an inspection team. Also, for carrying out inspection, certain inspection gadgets and tools are required. All the expenses incurred toward this account are considered as cost of appraisal. On this account, usually an organization spends between 28%–29% of the total quality cost.
3. **Cost of Prevention** This type of quality cost is incurred to reduce the other two quality costs indicated above. Such expenses include the amount spent for Research and Development, and Human Resources Development. Expenses on this account normally vary from 1%–2%.

Although in Indian organizations, we are yet to make a serious study about computing the cost of quality, from an international perspective, it is seen that such costs, even though not accounted for under any separate head, are as high as 40% of the cost of production. In Indian organizations, we typically assume that in the normal manufacturing process, we are supposed to have some natural rejection, which may be as high as 22% (at least in some cases). We call this the Unavoidable Rejection Rate (UAR). On the other hand, in other developed countries, more particularly in Japan, organizations subscribe to the philosophy of zero defects.

Experience shows a mere 1%–2% more expenditure on cost of prevention, can substantially reduce the expenditure on the other two sub-heads of cost of quality. In fact, the rate of such incremental cost benefit is as high as 70%–80% for a mere additional 1%–2% expense on cost of prevention.

Thus, it is evident that cost of quality, even though not apparent from the books of accounts, is a significant but wasteful cost factor, which can be reduced substantially to increase the profitability of an organization. In fact, the ISO documentation process helps us prune the cost of quality and to augment the internal efficiency of an organization. It also helps to achieve Total Quality Management in a phased manner.

9.3 QUALITY TO QUALITY MANAGEMENT

With growing global competition, Quality Management is becoming increasingly important to the leadership and management of all organizations. Quality management principles provide an understanding of and guidance to the application of quality management. By applying the following quality management principles, organizations can produce benefits for customers, owners, people, suppliers and society at large.

Principle 1: Customer-focussed Organization Organizations depend on their customers, and therefore, should understand current and future customer needs, meet customer requirements and strive to exceed customer expectations.

Principle 2: Leadership Leaders establish unity of purpose and provide direction to an organization. They should create and maintain the internal environment in which people can become fully involved in achieving the organization's objectives.

Principle 3: Involvement of People People at all levels are the essence of an organization and their full involvement enables their abilities to be used for the organization's benefit.

Principle 4: Process Approach A desired result is achieved more efficiently when related resources and activities are managed as a process.

Principle 5: System Approach to Management Identifying, understanding and managing a system of interrelated processes for a given objective helps improve the organization's effectiveness and efficiency.

Principle 6: Continual Improvement Continual improvement should be a permanent objective of the organization.

Principle 7: Factual Approach to Decision Making Effective decisions and actions are based on the analysis of data and information.

Principle 8: Mutually Beneficial Supplier Relationships An organization and its suppliers are independent, and a mutually beneficial relationship enhances the ability to create value.

9.4 DEFINITION OF QUALITY MANAGEMENT PRINCIPLES

Quality Management is a comprehensive and fundamental rule or belief, for leading and operating an organization, it is aimed at continually improving performance over the long term, by focussing on customers, while addressing the needs of all stakeholders.

The ISO TC176 standard on Quality Management and Quality Assurance was developed through a consensus process. This standard provides a clear statement of the above-mentioned eight Quality Management Principles (QMP's) and places them in a business environment/framework. Also, this standard provides executive management with an understanding of the benefits for their organization of using the QMP's.

Successful Total Quality Management (TQM) requires both behavioural and cultural changes in the organization. Three management systems, which are aligned with the TQM initiative for any organization, are

- OM (organizational management system),
- HRM (human resource management systems) and
- TQM (total quality management).

For successful implementation of TQM in an organization, it is necessary to embrace both human resource development (HRD) and organizational development (OD) practices. From this perspective, we can define TQM as an organizational improvement strategy through the development of people. In simple terms, we can say HRD + OD = TQM.

9.5 ISO STANDARDS

Standards can be defined as documented agreements containing technical specifications and other precise criteria to be used consistently as rules, guidelines or definitions of characteristics, so as to ensure that materials, products, processes and services are fit for their purpose. The International Organization for Standardization (ISO) is a worldwide federation of national standards bodies from more than 140 countries, one from each country.

ISO is a non-governmental organization established in 1947. The ISO's mission is to promote the development of standardization and related activities in the world with a view to facilitate the international exchange of goods and services, and to develop cooperation in the spheres of intellectual, scientific, technological and economic activity.

ISO's work results in international agreements, which are published as International Standards.

In fact, 'ISO' is a word, derived from the Greek 'isos' meaning 'equal'. From 'equal' to 'standard', the line of thinking that led to the choice of 'ISO' as the name of the organization is easy to follow.

The name 'ISO' is used around the world to denote the organization, thus avoiding a plethora of acronyms resulting from the translation of 'International Organization for Standardization' into the different national languages of members, e.g. IOS in English, OIN in French.

9.5.1 ISO 9000:2000 Family of standards

The new ISO 9001:2000 is an integration of three familiar standards – ISO 9001, ISO 9002 and ISO 9003. ISO 9001:2000 specifies the requirements for a quality management system for any organization that needs to demonstrate its ability to consistently provide products that meet customer specifications and the applicable regulatory requirements. It aims to enhance customer satisfaction. ISO 9001:2000 has been organized in a user-friendly format with terms that are easily recognized by all business sectors. The standard is used for certification/registration and contractual purposes by organizations seeking recognition of their quality management system.

9.5.2 The ISO 9000 Family: Standards, Guidelines and Purpose

ISO 9000:2000, *Quality management systems – Fundamentals and vocabulary:* It establishes a starting point for understanding the standards and defines the fundamental terms and definitions used in the ISO 9000 family, which is needed, to avoid misunderstandings in use.

ISO 9001:2000, *Quality management systems – Requirements:* This is the requirement standard used to assess the ability to meet customer needs and applicable regulatory requirements and thereby address customer satisfaction. It is now the only standard in the ISO 9000 family against which third-party certification can be carried.

ISO 9004:2000, *Quality management systems – Guidelines for performance improvements:* This guideline standard provides guidance for continual improvement of the quality management system to benefit all parties through sustained customer satisfaction.

9.5.3 Examples of the ISO 9000 Standards in Use

If an organization is seeking to establish a management system that provides confidence that its product conforms to established or specified requirements, ISO 9001:2000 is used. It is now the only standard in the ISO 9000 family whose requirements of quality systems can be certified by an external agency. The standard recognizes that the word 'product' applies to services, processed material, hardware and software intended for, or required by, the customer.

There are five sections in the standard that specifies activities that need to be considered when implementing the ISO system. The first section describes the activities used to supply products. The other four sections are Quality Management

System; Management Responsibility; Resource Management and Measurement; Analysis and Improvement. These are relevant to all organizations, which need to demonstrate how they can apply them in their quality manuals or other documentation.

Together, the five sections of ISO 9001: 2000 define what we should do consistently to provide a product that meets customer and applicable statutory or regulatory requirements. In addition, it seeks to enhance customer satisfaction by improving an organization's quality management system.

9.5.4 ISO: 9001:2008

ISO 9001:2008 has been developed for better clarity of the requirements of ISO: 9001:2000, and also to ensure compatibility with ISO: 14001:2004. Hence, it does not introduce any new requirements and also does not change the intent of the ISO: 9001:2008 standards. Organizations use it for clarifications only as no new requirements have been spelt out in ISO: 9001: 2008.

9.5.5 COPC Inc. Standards

These standards are meant for the call centre industry, where customer contact services are involved. The standards provide a rigorous measurement system against global best practice benchmarks, and also suggest possible ways for enhancing service quality and customer satisfaction with a simultaneous lowering of costs. Industries that benefit from COPC include call centres, e-commerce, transaction processing operation centres, etc. Although COPC certification is not mandatory, service organizations do benefit in terms of increased efficiency and productivity. The COPC-2000 customer service provider (CSP) standard is aimed at improving performance metrics on customer satisfaction and services, inbound and outbound sales, dispatch, collections, retention and remittance processing.

The COPC-2000 VMO Standard is for Vendor Management. The COPC-2000 OSP Standard is designed to meet the unique requirements and constraints faced by Third-Party Outsource Service Providers. The COPC-2000§HSP Standard is applicable to the healthcare industry.

9.5.6 AGMARK Quality

AGMARK Agricultural Produce (Grading and Marketing) Act, 1937 (Agmark): The Directorate of Marketing and Inspection enforced this Act. This Act documents the Grade Standards for agricultural and allied commodities. These are known as 'Agmark' standards. The Ministry of Agriculture is vested with the responsibility to enforce and implement the provisions of this Act of 1937 (as amended in 1986). The Act outlines detailed procedures for licensing, setting up laboratories, consumer protection measures etc., applicable to all articles of agricultural and agricultural produce. The 'Agmark' label is an assurance of quality conformity of the items in terms of the provisions of the Act. 'Agmark' grading is a hallmark of quality in the case of agricultural and agricultural produce, both for the export and the domestic market; it is asked for by customers who always make an informed buying decision.

9.5.7 ISO 14000 Standards

The ISO 14000 family of standards covers various aspects of environmental management systems (EMS). The ISO 14001:2004 and ISO 14004:2004 are the core standards that deal with the EMS. ISO 14001:2004 provides the requirements for an EMS and ISO 14004:2004 gives general EMS guidelines. The other standards and guidelines in the family address specific environmental aspects, including labelling, performance evaluation, life cycle analysis, communication and auditing.

The core objectives of ISO 14001: 2004 can be listed as under:

- To identify and control the environmental impact of various activities, products or services
- To improve environmental performance continually
- To develop environmental objectives and targets
- To implement the identified environmental objectives and targets
- To demonstrate achievement of objectives and targets

The ISO 14004:2004 provides guidelines on the EMS, its implementation and the principal issues. In table (9.2), we have presented details of the ISO 14000 family of standards.

Table 9.2. *The ISO 14000 family of standards*

Standard	Title / Description
14000	Guide to Environmental Management Principles, Systems and Supporting Techniques
14001	Environmental Management Systems – Specification with Guidance for Use
14010	Guidelines for Environmental Auditing – General Principles of Environmental Auditing
14011	Guidelines for Environmental Auditing – Audit Procedures-Part 1: Auditing of Environmental Management Systems
14012	Guidelines for Environmental Auditing – Qualification Criteria for Environmental Auditors
14013/15	Guidelines for Environmental Auditing – Audit Programmes, Reviews and Assessments
14020/23	Environmental Labelling

Standard	Title / Description
14024	Environmental Labelling – Practitioner Programs – Guiding Principles, Practices and Certification Procedures of Multiple Criteria Programs
14031/32	Guidelines on Environmental Performance Evaluation
14040/43	Life Cycle Assessment – General Principles and Practices
14050	Glossary
14060	Guide for the Inclusion of Environmental Aspects in Product Standards

9.6 QUALITY GURUS AND THEIR CONTRIBUTION TO TQM PRACTICES

According to Phillip Crosby (1988), quality is conformance to the standards, which an organization expects to meet. The quality concept stems from the need for defect prevention, not defect correction. These can be achieved only through proper leadership, training, and discipline in work processes. Thus, adherence to quality ensures that an organization achieves defect-free performance standards. Any organization achieving quality, therefore, can save money by duly correcting poor workmanship; at the same time, it can emerge as a market leader by gaining customer confidence.

Philip Crosby is recognized throughout the world as a Quality Guru. Crosby's Quality Improvement Process is based on fourteen steps, by following these steps, an organization can endeavour to achieve quality improvement. These are:

1. Make management committed to quality.
2. Form cross-functional quality improvement teams.
3. Measure current processes and develop improved processes, duly identifying potential quality problems.
4. Evaluate the cost of quality and explain its use as a management tool.
5. Raise quality awareness and the personal concern of all employees.
6. Take action to correct problems identified through previous steps.
7. Establish progress monitoring for the improvement process.
8. Train supervisors to actively carry out their part of the quality improvement programme.
9. Hold a Zero Defects Day to let everyone realise that there has been a change and to reaffirm management commitment.
10. Encourage individuals to establish improvement goals for themselves and their groups.
11. Encourage employees to communicate to management the obstacles they face in attaining their goals for improvement.

12. Recognize and appreciate those who participate.
13. Establish quality councils to communicate on a regular basis.
14. Do it all over again to emphasize that the quality improvement programme never ends.

According to Crosby, to emerge as an 'Eternally Successful Organization', it is essential for an organization to understand and appreciate the following:

- People routinely do things right the first time.
- Change is anticipated and used to advantage.
- Growth is consistent and profitable.
- New products and services appear when needed.
- Everyone is happy to work there.

From the HRD point of view, it requires:

- participative management that ensures employee involvement in the decision-making process
- attitudinal change, which reflects through improved responsiveness to customer needs (both internal and external),
- effective communication (both internal and external)
- flexibility, which includes the willingness to accept changes.

In his explanation in 'Quality without tears', Crosby (1984) has exemplified the need for HRD by using figure 9.1 below:

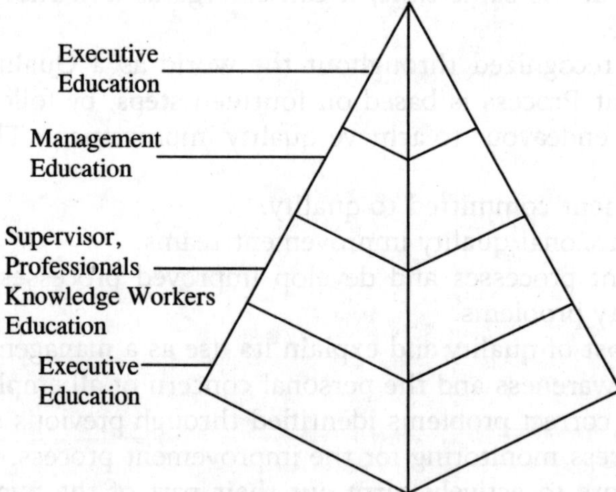

Figure 9.1 *Quality without tears (Crosby, 1984)*

9.6.1 Quality and HRD linkages

W Edwards Deming, another quality guru, developed six-fold productivity improvement programmes through quality improvement. Such productivity enhancement initiatives help an organization to reduce scrap and the need to rework the item involved. Extending Walter Andrew Shewhart's (1931) manufacturing approach to non-manufacturing and human variations, Deming suggested that managers should focus on variability and understand the difference between special and common causes. Special causes for quality variation prevent satisfactory performance. Special causes are easily assignable, and after their identification through Deming's statistical quality control methods, an organization can correct the situation through changes of operator, shift or procedure. Common causes are those which occur due to the design, or for the operation of the processes or systems. Common causes can be easily identified by the operators, but their elimination would be possible only by making use of management authority. Deming suggested a systematic approach to problem solving, using the PDCA (Plan, Do, Check, Action) cycle. This can lead to better results and efficiency for the organization. However, for practicing this, it is essential for the organization to ensure the capability development of its employees. Deming's PDCA Cycle can be illustrated as under (Fig. 9.2):

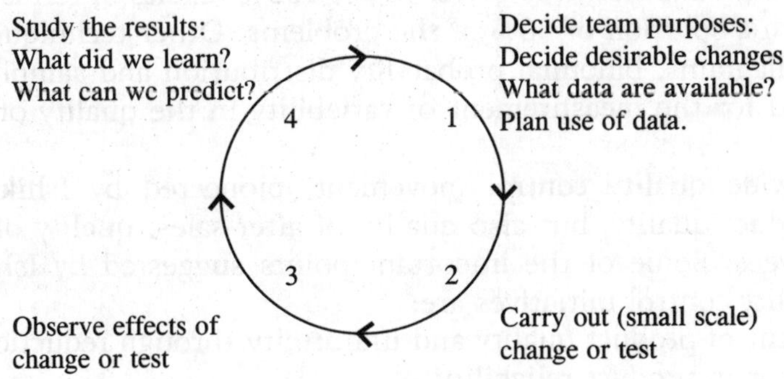

Figure 9.2 *Deming's PDCA cycle*

Like Deming, Dr Joseph Juran is also an expert in quality management practices. Along with Dr. Deming, he was invited to Japan by the Union of Japanese Scientists and Engineers (JUSE) in 1954. Juran focussed on planning, organizational issues and management's responsibility to quality improvement. Training and HRD activities can play a very crucial role in this regard.

Juran's 'Quality Planning Road Map' consists of the following steps:

- Identify the customers
- Determine the needs of those customers
- Translate those needs into our language
- Develop a product that can respond to those needs
- Optimize product features to meet our needs and customer needs
- Develop a process which is able to produce the product

- Optimize the process
- Prove that the process can produce the product under operating conditions
- Transfer the process to operations

Professor Kaoru Ishikawa, a Japanese quality guru, suggested the need for company-wide quality improvement initiatives through the quality circle movement. Both Ishikawa and Genichi Taguchi (another quality guru from Japan) emphasized the need for making effective use of technical, statistical techniques for quality improvement, simplifying it by the use of Pareto diagrams and cause-and-effect diagrams (also called Ishikawa or Fishbone diagrams).

Ishikawa's diagrams can find, sort and document the causes of quality variation through the participation of employees of the organization in quality circles or small-group activities. Similarly, Pareto graphs can plot quality variation, making use of frequency distribution and can then track how the elimination of problems can lead to changes in the quality level. The Pareto principle suggests that an organization should not try for 100% solution of problems, as there is obvious interdependence of one problem with another. It is better to get 100% results in terms of production and quality, with a solution of 80% of the problems. Other techniques like control charts, scatter diagrams, binomial probability distribution and sampling inspection can also be used for the measurement of variability in the quality of products and services.

A company-wide quality control movement, pioneered by Ishikawa not only emphasizes product quality, but also quality of after-sales, quality of management and the employees. Some of the important points suggested by Ishikawa, as the outcome of quality control initiatives are:

- Improvement of product quality and uniformity through reduction in defects
- Improvement in product reliability
- Reduction in costs
- Increase in production volume through rationalization in the production schedules
- Reduction in wasteful work and rework
- Improvement in production techniques
- Reduction in the cost of inspection and testing
- Rationalization of contracts between the vendor and vendee
- Enlargement of market
- Improved relationships between departments
- Reduction in false data and reports presentation
- More free and democratic discussions among organizational members
- Smooth conduct of meetings
- Rational repairs and installation of equipment and facilities
- Improved human relations

Quality circles were first started in the *Nippon Telegraph and Telephone Public Corporation* in 1962, and subsequently adopted by organizations throughout the world. The basic aims of quality circle activities are:

- Contribute to the improvement and development of the organization.
- Respect human relations and nurture healthy interpersonal relations, which create a culture of 'compelling workplace', which is one in which people feel like working.
- Full deployment of human capabilities and potential.

A model cause-and-effect diagram (Fig. 9.3) is presented below:

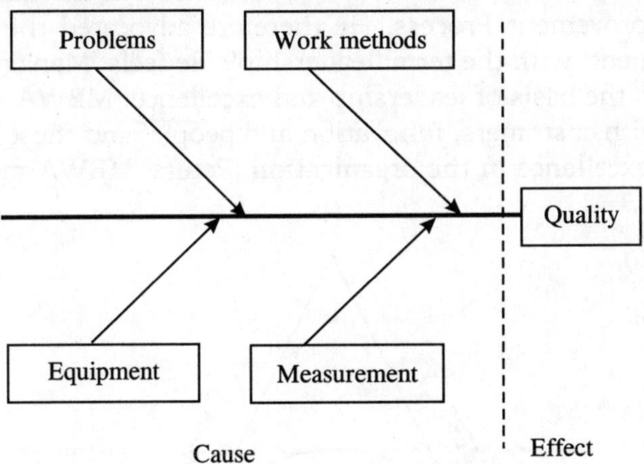

Figure 9.3 *Cause and Effect Diagram*

Using the above diagram, members of the quality circle team can identify quality-related workplace problems, issues pertaining to cost reduction, productivity improvement and workplace safety, and accordingly, can suggest on their own, ways to improve the same through mutual participation and cooperation.

For overall human resource development, therefore, an organization needs to master the seven tools outlined below, through continuous training and development functions. The seven tools are:

1. Pareto charts
2. Cause-and-effects diagrams
3. Stratification
4. Check sheets
5. Histograms
6. Scatter diagrams
7. Shewhart's control charts and graphs.

Taguchi methodology optimizes products and processes before manufacturing rather than achieving quality through inspection. Taguchi pushed back the concepts of quality and reliability to the design stage to develop an efficient and error-free manufacturing process. Taguchi methods, however, can also be used to troubleshoot critical manufacturing problems.

Shigeo Shingo, another quality guru revolutionized the manufacturing of goods; he suggested improvement principles, which help in achieving quality through drastic cost minimization. He has basically provided us with the strategy for continuous improvement through the creative involvement of all cross-sections of employees.

Tom Peters, an American management guru, based on his extensive research of successful American companies, evolved a system of quality improvement with a sales-orientated viewpoint. He had identified leadership as the factor that is central to the Quality Improvement Process. He therefore advocated the idea of replacing the term 'management' with the term 'leadership'. He feels 'Managing by Wandering About' (MBWA) is the basis of leadership and excellence. MBWA enables the leader to keep in touch with customers, innovation and people, and these three major areas help in achieving excellence in the organization. Peters' MBWA model is illustrated in Fig. 9.4 below:

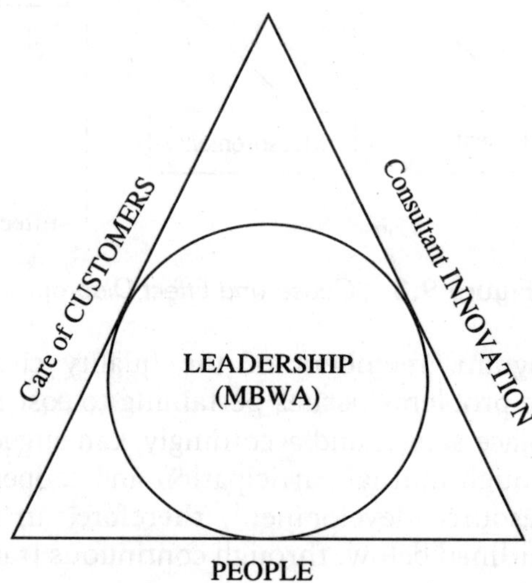

Figure 9.4 *The MBWA model*

Practicing MBWA, a leader can perform three major activities; these are:

- Listening – suggests caring.
- Teaching – values will be transmitted when the interaction is face-to- face.
- Facilitating – able to give on-the-spot help.

According to Peters, there are twelve traits which define successful quality improvement programmes. These traits are:

1. **Management's obsession with quality:** This emphasizes emotional commitment to quality, practising certain value systems like the abolition of rework mechanics in the organization in a phased manner, saying an absolute 'no' to shoddy goods, etc.

2. **Passionate systems:** A system without passion is 'no good' for achieving quality. Hence, the quality ideology should bind an organization.
3. **Measurement of quality:** Such criteria should be adequately displayed and transparent to all members of the organization.
4. **Quality is rewarded:** Quality achievement should be aligned with organizational compensation and reward systems.
5. **Everyone is trained for quality:** All members of the organization should be trained enough to understand quality imperatives. Training on quality is best possible through awareness of the cause-and-effect analysis, statistical process control, and the other seven tools, discussed earlier.
6. **Multi-function teams:** Quality achievement is best possible through the formation of cross-functional teams, small group activities like quality circles, value engineering team, total quality management teams, etc.
7. **Small is beautiful:** In quality improvement, even a small change can bring about big results.
8. **Create endless 'Hawthorne' effects:** (The'Hawthorne effect' indicates the propensity of people to work harder and perform better, when experiments are carried out on them). New goals, new themes, new events are the antidote; hence, continuous focus on change is necessary.
9. **Parallel organization structure devoted to quality improvement:** This requires the formation of shadow quality teams.
10. **Everyone is involved:** Suppliers, distributors and customers should all be a part of the organizational quality improvement process.
11. **When quality goes up, costs go down:** Quality improvement is the primary source of cost reduction.
12. **Quality improvement is a never-ending journey:** All quality is relative, hence, the every-day quality of a product or service either becomes better or worse, it never stands still. Therefore, organizations should pursue a continuous quality improvement programme.

Claus Moller (1988), the founder of 'Time Manager International' is the European quality management guru, who emphasized the need for improving the personal quality of employees to achieve quality in an organization. He developed the model of 'Putting People First'. Moller believed that the administrative process, and not the production process, offers more opportunity for overall productivity gains. Hence, to achieve quality, organizations must inspire people to do their best, and this is possible through the personal development of employees who can build the requisite competence in the three vital areas of productivity, relations and quality (Fig. 9.5).

Time Manager International (TMI), Moller's company, documented this model.

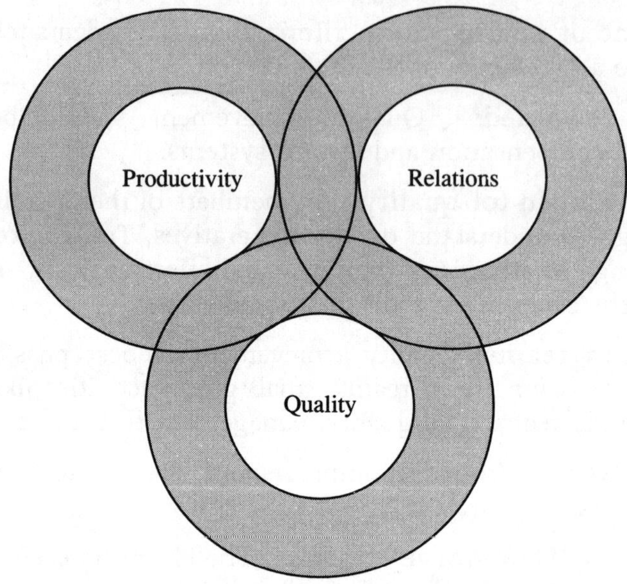

Figure 9.5 *Moller's Competency Model (TMI world - 1990)*

9.7 TEAMS AND TEAMWORK

When TQM is successful, employees at every level participate in decisions affecting their work. The most common vehicle for employee participation is a team. Teams range in scope and responsibility from problem-solving groups to self-managed work teams that schedule work, assign jobs, hire members, and set the standards and volume of output. A participative work culture is encouraged when quality becomes everybody's responsibility.

Employee-involvement practices in an organization may differ in terms of organizational policies and strategies. Common employment practices are:

- suggestion system
- survey feedback
- quality circles
- formation of a quality of work-life team
- job redesign
- formation of self-managed teams
- formation of a TQM team

Participative management is used as the most important approach for introducing TQM culture in any organization. A more organized or institutionalized approach to workers' participation in management dates back to 1920, when Mahatma Gandhi advocated the principles of trusteeship in industry. This idea was concretized during the Plan era through the enactment of various legislations and through policy decisions. Despite the benefits of participative management being successfully used for many years by organizations across the world, India was a little late in institutionalizing the approach. Statutory support has now made it mandatory for Indian industries to introduce this culture. Participation in some form or the other has now become virtually unavoidable for many organizations.

9.8 EMPLOYEE EMPOWERMENT

Employee empowerment is to confer legitimate rights to employees, irrespective of the nature of their job and their level in the hierarchy to make judgements, and to take decisions on their own. Hence, employee empowerment can facilitate the development of the problem-solving abilities of the employees. Operationally, in organizations, we empower employees first by developing their capabilities, and second, by being sufficiently indulgent to allow them to commit mistakes. Unlike other approaches to quality management, empowerment not only calls for employee participation in the operational area, but also allows them to participate in corporate level decision-making, so that they emerge as holistic individuals. An empowered employee, in other words, is not a mere seller of his time and labour for a contracted sum of money. The empowered employee acquires the necessary skill and authority to own. Employee empowerment, involvement and participative management, as important corporate practices, have been experimented with in several multinational and national organizations. In all these cases, it was identified that employee ownership and commitment (which is possible through employee empowerment) are the two ingredients that resulted in efficiency and productivity. Some organizations are even empowering their employees at the strategic level rather than confining their involvement only to limited operational activity.

9.9 QUALITY OF WORK-LIFE (QWL)

QWL is defined as those perceived important personal needs, which an individual tries to satisfy by working in an organization. Its conceptual foundations, though laid by a host of behavioural scientists, were in reality advocated by Chris Argyris (1975) in his famous work on *Personality and Organization*. The socio-technical systems theory, pioneered by the Tavistock Institute of Human Relations, London, in the 1960s is considered an important QWL construct. Growth and security are seen as important personal needs for an individual. The possibility of furthering one's career within the organization, has, therefore, been identified as an important QWL criterion. Although common QWL strategists emphasise more on job re-design, the formation of autonomous work groups and worker participation in management, there exist wide differences among the pioneers in this area regarding QWL factors. The process of QWL can be explained with the help of the following criteria:

- adequate and fair compensation
- safe and healthy working conditions
- immediate opportunity to use and develop human capacities
- future opportunity for continued growth and security
- social integration in the organization
- work and total life space
- social relevance of working life

From studies carried out, both in India and abroad, it is evident that the essence of QWL is the opportunity for employees, at all levels, to have substantial influence over their work environment. This is a result of their participating in the decision-making process relating to their work, thereby enhancing their self-esteem and the overall satisfaction from their work. Hence, QWL calls for an open style of management, which involves the sharing of information and genuinely encouraging efforts relating to the improvement of the organization. This makes it amply clear that QWL is an important managerial activity to develop the employees of an organization. The success of TQM programmes largely depend on appropriate HRD interventions like an emphasis on continuous training and development activity, encouraging participation in management through small group forums, increasing employees' motivation, looking after the career development of employees, employee empowerment, infusing attitudinal changes at the top (like accepting a more flat organization structure, following a democratic approach, becoming receptive to changes on a continuous basis, supporting group performance, etc.)

9.10 SIX SIGMA PRACTICES

To add economic value and practical utility to customers and organizations, globally, companies are now looking beyond total quality management practices. It is now well appreciated by the corporate world that customers have their rightful expectation to buy quality products at competitive prices. So, organizations should strive to improve the bottom line (profit). Synergy between these two can be achieved through Six Sigma practices.

Six Sigma as a business process allows organizations to improve their bottom line by designing and monitoring business activities in a way that minimizes waste and resources without, however, compromising on customer satisfaction. The Six Sigma process is broader than total quality management (TQM) programmes. While TQM focusses on detecting and correcting defects, Six-Sigma re-creates the processes to ensure that defects never arise right from the beginning. From the organization's point of view, it provides maximum value in the form of increased profits and from the customer's point of view, it provides maximum value in terms of high quality products and services at competitive costs.

Higher sigma values indicate better quality products and lower sigma values represent less quality products. At Six Sigma level, products are virtually defect-free – there are only 3.4 defects per million opportunities (DPMO).

Like TQM, Six Sigma also requires thorough changes in the culture and practices of the organization. Essentially, all the tools mentioned in the case of TQM are applicable to Six Sigma. However, additionally it requires the organization to make people more creative and innovative, as Six Sigma re-creates processes, to ensure defects never arise.

9.11 INNOVATION AND CREATIVITY

Innovation is a new technique or idea encompassing products/services, processes, managerial styles and even organizational structure. It may be technology-push or demand-pull or even a combination of both. The research and development (R&D) activities of an organization are examples of such innovation. In any organization, the need for innovation is primarily to keep pace with the competition. It has to be essentially customer-focussed, as this backward linkage facilitates process-centered innovative changes. Whether it is just-in-time (JIT) inventory control, supply chain management (SCM), business process outsourcing (BPO), flexible manufacturing systems (FMS), product/service customization, strategic backward or forward integration, synergy through merger or acquisition, alliances or collaboration, organizational re-engineering TQM or Six Sigma practices, new work culture as a facilitator of organizational change or any R&D initiative for value addition, which broadly encompasses innovation, all stem from customers' explicit or implicit needs.

Mapping customer needs and aligning them to initiatives in innovation is necessary to deal with competition. Innovation is enabled by pro-active organizational behaviour practices. It calls for creating a work environment that recognizes creativity, inter-organizational co-operation (rather than competition), working as cross-functional teams, productive meetings for innovative results, introduction of formal innovation programmes, and finally, the organization's receptivity to new ideas and perspectives. Fostering innovation requires a structured approach. It has to be broadly in the given context, leadership, values and culture. Contextual analysis helps in building the required innovation teams. Leaders facilitate the teams. Values enable the adoption of principles, which foster innovation, and finally, the culture provides the playing field.

At this stage, it is pertinent to define creativity, because innovation and creativity are often used interchangeably in the work place. The Webster's Dictionary defines creativity as "the ability or power to create, to bring into existence, to invest with a new form, to produce through imaginative skill, to make or bring into existence something new". Creativity is a core competency. It is the talent of the employees of an organization. Competitors can replicate the strategies of an organization, but not the creative talents of its employees. To encourage creativity, the organization first creates the right environment where employees feel safe even to come up with 'dumb' or 'crazy' ideas. Creativity is often punished in organizations, as creative people spend more time to get ready for action. They are also more difficult to manage. Organizations, therefore, often see them as major time- and money-wasters and inhibit their creative thoughts.

9.12 QUALITY CIRCLES AND TOTAL EMPLOYEE INVOLVEMENT

In the new economy, total participation of workers, as opposed to statutory participation, is a must. Participation may be through work committees, departmental councils and other representative forums. One way to enforce total participation is by forming quality circles (QC) or small group forums.

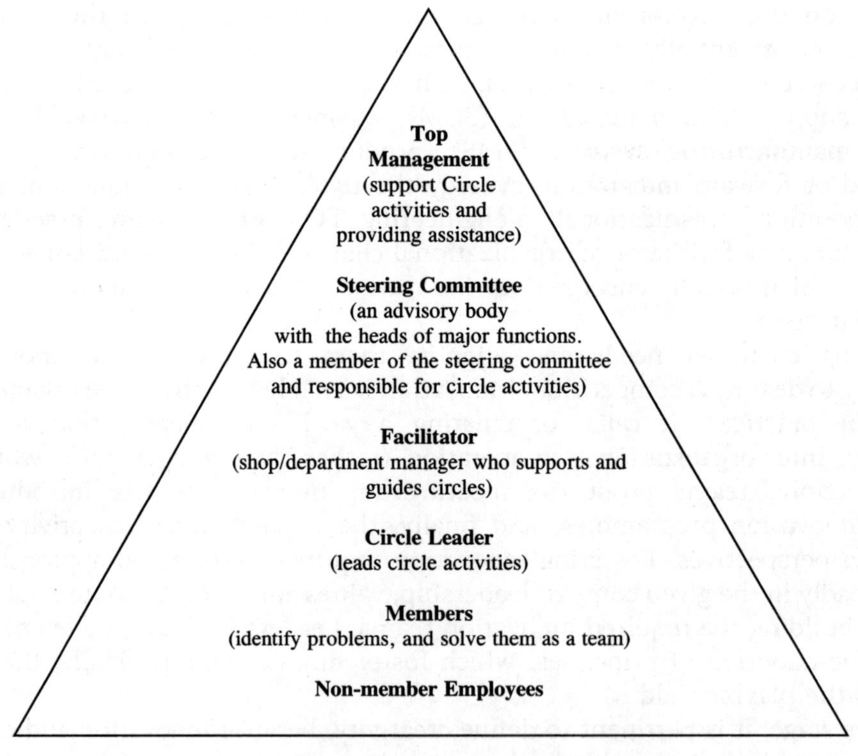

Figure 9.6. *Structure of a Quality Circle*

QC is an important managerial tool and can be related to increased employee motivation and productivity. Total knowledge, skill, creative abilities, talents and aptitude together with the values, attitudes and beliefs of the workers and/or individuals can represent an organization's effective human resource inventory. The total involvement of employees is ensured by QCs through a number of small group forums. Organizations have succeeded in improving their productivity by QC activities that increase employee motivation.

Organizations in India have now started training their workers and employees on QC concepts for its successful implementation. They are systematic about follow-up activity in connection with the setting up of QC forums involving all workers, forming homogeneous groups of 8–12 employees, who regularly meet once a week for at least an hour to deliberate on work-related problems and to identify possible solutions to those problems (Fig. 9.6). Many organizations have benefited from cost minimization, changing methods of production, work simplification, etc.

9.12.1 Seven Tools of Quality

The seven tools of quality were first advocated by Kaoru Ishikawa, who had pioneered the concept of quality circles. Although many contemporary quality gurus now mention some more tools for quality improvement in organizations, Ishikawa's concept is still considered to be generic. These seven tools are:

9.12.1.1 Cause-and-effect diagram

This consists basically of the fishbone chart, explained earlier. This chart helps in documenting the possible causes for an effect on quality problems by the quality circles' team members. By referring to this chart, we can identify the problems and also understand the perceived solution offered by team members. After the identification of possible causes for an effect or quality problem, through brainstorming among the members of quality circles, using this diagram, classification of the ideas into various useful categories is done. Moreover, it relieves the workers of the need to go in for an analytic presentation of the identified quality problems, as by referring to this diagram, all cross-sections of employees of the organizations can understand the quality scenario. The generic headings used for the purpose of this diagram are;

- methods
- machines (equipment)
- people (manpower)
- materials
- measurement
- environment

Quality-related problems are classified using the above categories through brainstorming. To get better insights into the problem, repeatedly in the brainstorming, we try to find an answer to the question, 'why does this happen?' A typical cause-and-effect diagram (Figure 9.7) is presented below:

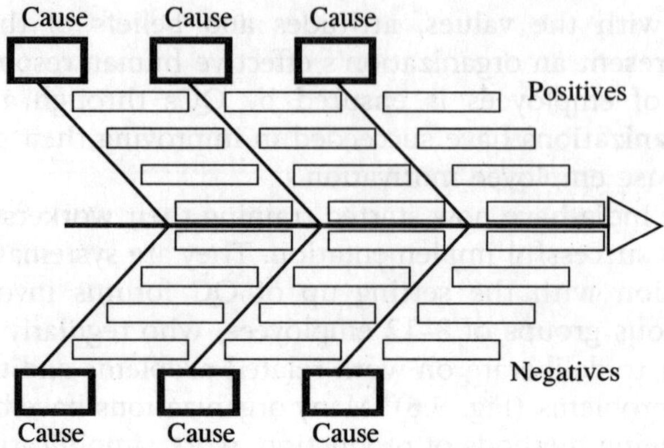

Figure 9.7 *Cause and effect diagram for quality control*

9.12.1.2 Check sheet

Check sheets help in collecting and analyzing data, and can be useful in documenting quality problems. It is also called a defect concentration diagram. Analyses of collected data are done using a structured check sheet or form. A check sheet is

CHECK SHEET

DATE ______________

NAME ______________

REF. ______________

PROBLEM	FREQUENCY
Measurement Categories	No. of times of occurrence
Problem - I	IIII
Problem - II	II
Problem - III	III
Problem - IV	I
Problem - V	IIII
Problem - VI	II
Problem - VII	IIII
Problem - VIII	II

Figure 9.8 *Check sheet to document quality issues*

useful, particularly when data are observed and collected at a particular place by the same person. The nature of data collected for the purpose of fitting to a check sheet are frequency or patterns of events, problems, defects and its causes and location, etc. It is for the person who collects data to decide on the type of data to be collected. Collected data are recorded by making check marks or cross marks or similar symbols. A typical check sheet is presented in Fig. 9.8.

9.12.1.3 Control charts

These charts illustrate how a process changes over time. A control chart is also known as a statistical process control chart. It is a graph to study how the process changes over time. A control chart is divided into three parts to study process quality. The central line (CL) for the average, the upper control limits (UCL) line above the CL, and lower control limit (LCL) below the CL. A typical control chart is illustrated in Fig. 9.9.

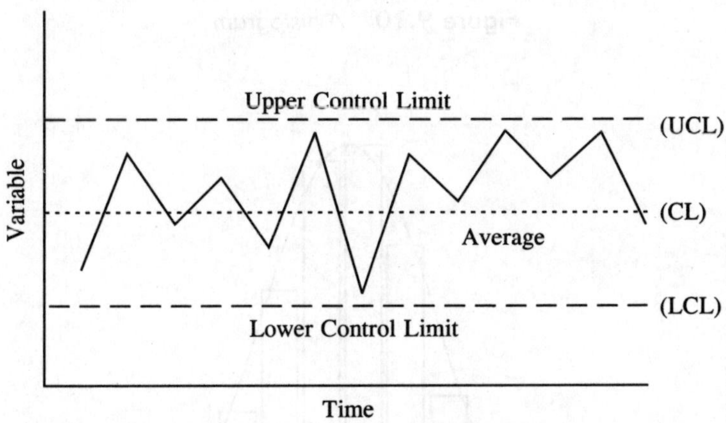

Figure 9.9 *A Control Chart*

9.12.1.4 Histogram

These graphs show the frequency distribution for a data set to explain the trend. It is basically used to explain the frequency of occurrence of different values in a set of data. Although typically, it resembles a bar chart, it is different. Frequency distribution helps us understand the shape of data distribution, particularly to understand whether the data are distributed normally. A typical histogram (Fig. 9.10) is presented in Fig. 9.10.

A histogram may have a normal or a skewed distribution trend, depending on symmetrical or asymmetrical data. A normal distribution histogram (Fig. 9.11) is presented in Fig. 9.11. A negatively skewed distribution (Fig. 9.12) is given overleaf.

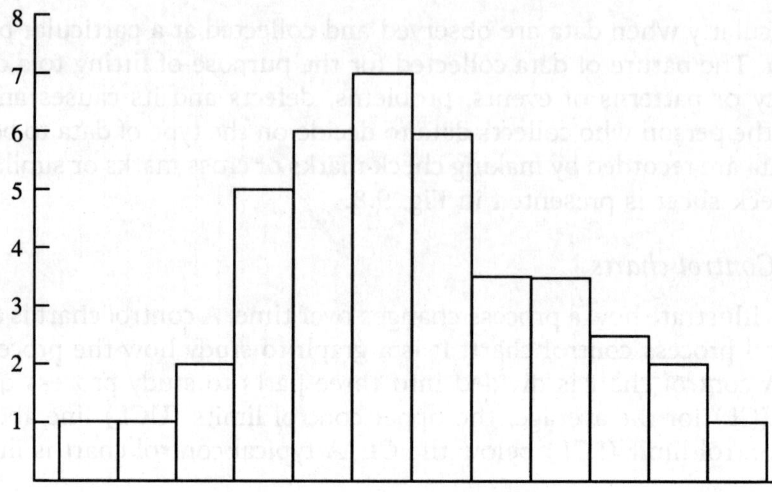

Figure 9.10 *A histogram*

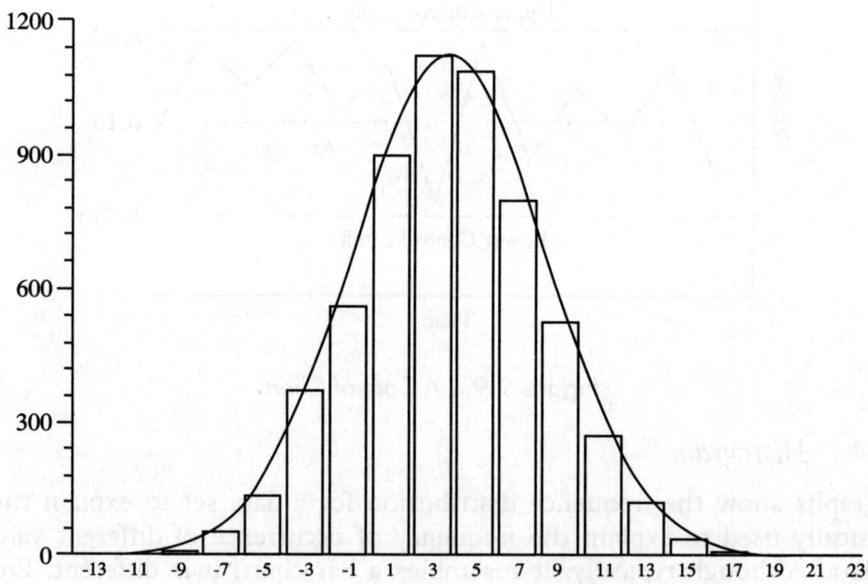

Figure 9.11 *A normal distribution histogram*

Depending on the nature of data and its occurrence, we may have double-peaked or bimodal distribution, plateaued distribution, edge peak distribution, comb distribution, truncated distribution, dog food distribution, etc.

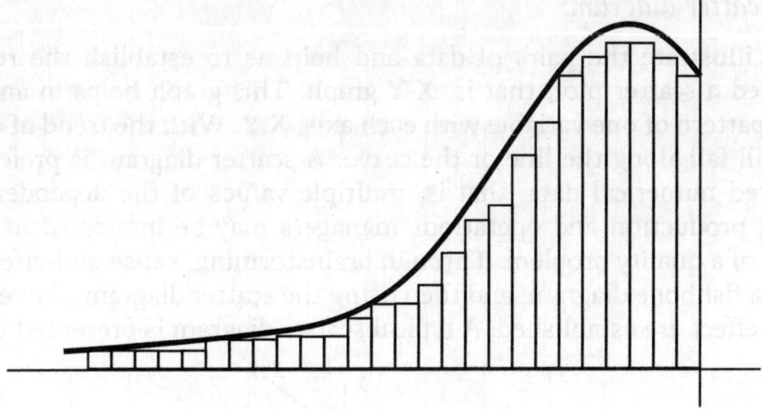

Figure 9.12 *A negatively-skewed distribution histogram*

9.12.1.5 Pareto chart

This is a bar graph to illustrate significant factors. It is also known as a Pareto diagram; it measures variations. It is like a bar graph, and the lengths of the bars represent frequency or cost, arranged with the longest bars on the left to the shortest bars on the right. As a result, referring to this chart or diagram, we can understand situations with varying levels of significances. Thus, the Pareto chart is used when we have to analyze data, with the degree of importance or significance, in the form of a frequency distribution. Production and operations managers can quickly understand the magnitude of the quality problem, by referring to this chart.

A typical Pareto chart (Fig 9.13) is presented below:

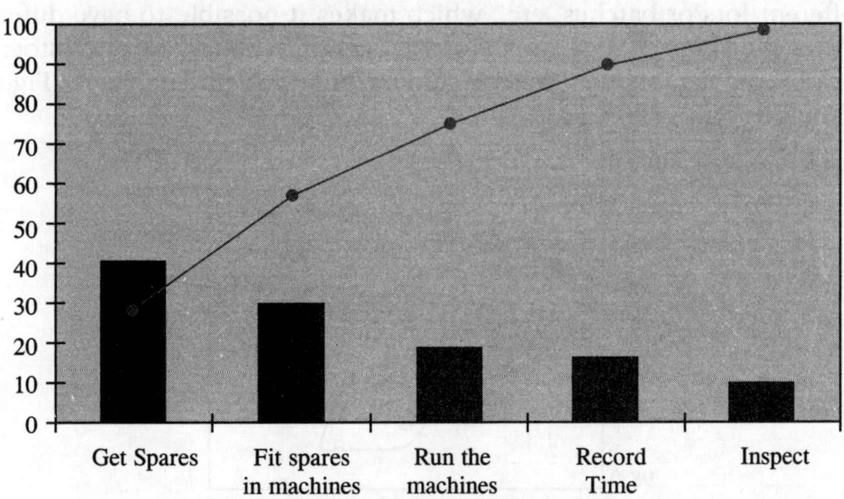

Figure 9.13 *A Pareto chart*

9.12.1.6 Scatter diagram:

Such graphs illustrate the pairs of data and help us to establish the relationship. It is also called a scatter plot, that is, X-Y graph. This graph helps in analyzing the relationship pattern of one variable with each axis, X,Y. With the trend of correlation, the points will fall along the line or the curve. A scatter diagram is preferred, when we have paired numerical data, that is, multiple values of the dependent variable. For example, production and operations managers may be interested in identifying the potential of a quality problem. Through brainstorming, cause-and-effects are first presented in a fishbone diagram, and then using the scatter diagram, the relationships of cause-and-effect are established. A typical scatter diagram is presented in Fig. 9.14.

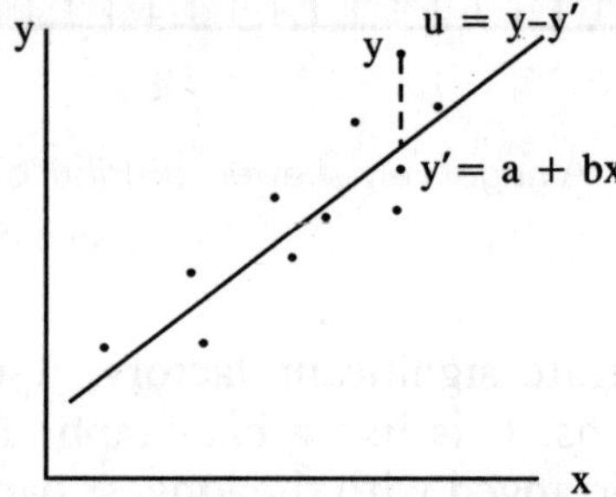

Figure 9.14 *Scatter diagram*

9.12.1.7 Stratification

This is a process of separation of a variety of data to study the problem. It is a combination technique; we use it in combination with other data analysis to study the patterns. For example, quality problems can be analysed by different shifts, different weeks, different lots or batches, etc., which makes it possible to have different sets of data. After plotting the data on a scatter diagram, control, chart, histogram, etc, we can stratify the data using different colours. A stratified data chart (Fig. 9.15) is presented below:

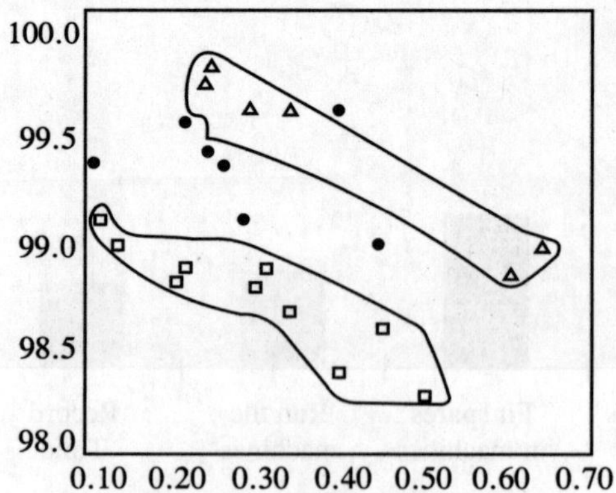

Figure 9.15 *Stratified data chart*

9.13 QUALITY FUNCTION DEPLOYMENT (QFD)

QFD was first conceptualized in 1966, and subsequently, was institutionalized as a total quality control tool by Shigeru Mizuno and Yoji Akao in 1972. QFD consolidates customer requirements, and then translates them to engineering specifications. In the process of doing so, QFD links customers, design engineers, competitors, and the process of manufacturing. Thus, QFD incubates the customers' perceived expectations, and helps in recreating the design and manufacturing process, new product development, etc. for overall improvement of production. Obviously, due to its ability to incorporate the customers' voice even in product design and development, it can help organizations to achieve customer satisfaction. To test the efficacy of the products to the customers, QFD helps, as it identifies product development plans integrating this with the technical abilities of the organization as a whole. By developing cost-effective, quality products in alignment with the customer's needs and expectations, organizations can gain a competitive edge. Customers want value for money.

QFD is defined as a structured approach to translate customers' needs and expectations into technical characteristics, and new design to churn out products and services that satisfy customers. QFD requires a cross-functional approach and teamwork. Apart from the key role of production and operations managers, in QFD, marketing, design engineering, quality assurance, marketing, human resources, finance, and planning and control departments are involved.

The scope of QFD is as follows:

- Product Planning: To translate customers' requirements into technical requirements of the product.
- Product Design: To translate technical requirements to the systems
- Process Planning: To identify key process operations essential to achieve the desired characteristics
- Process control: To establish process control, maintenance and training plans to enforce overall control of manufacturing operations.

To implement QFD, that is, to integrate the voice of the customers with the control process operations, we follow the steps as under:

- Understanding the elements.
- Understanding the voice of customers from market surveys, focus groups, unobtrusive observations, direct interviews, etc., including the customers' perceived rank order.
- Developing a chart to represent customers' issues.
- Conducting competitive analysis in relation to customers' requirements.
- Establishing a quality plan based on competitive analysis.

Following all the above, we develop the QFD chart focussing on the customers' perceived importance. Through QFD, therefore, we understand the demands of customers, design improvement requirements, process changes, product development, and finally, achieving customer satisfaction.

This QFD methodology flow is represented in Fig. 9.16. Another way of representing different phases of QFD is seen in Fig. 9.17.

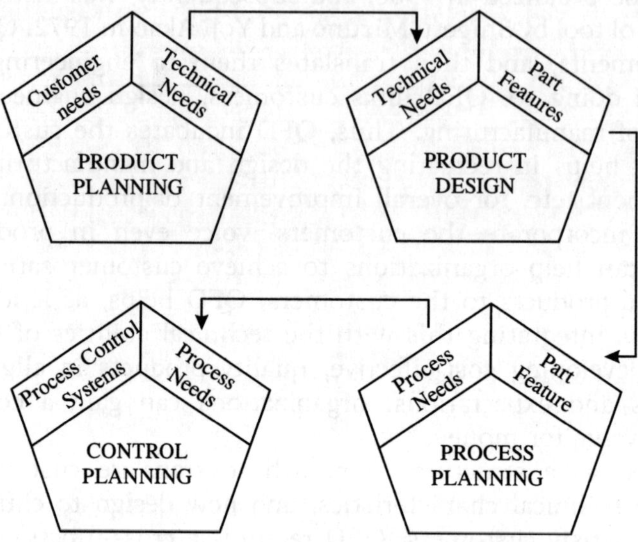

Figure 9.16 *QFD methodology flow*

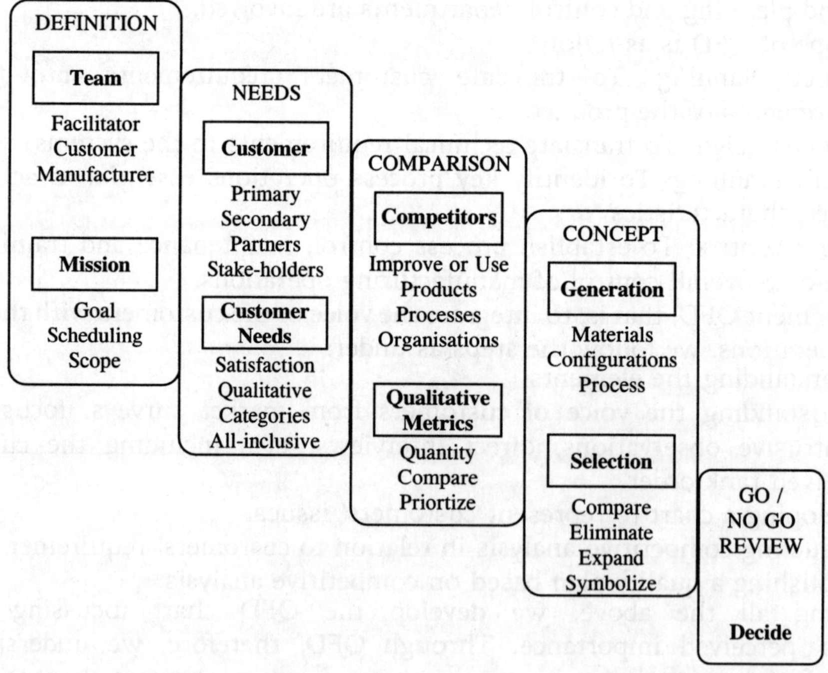

Figure 9.17 *QFD Flow*

9.13.1 QFD Process

After getting customer feedback, the process of QFD starts with product planning. After the plant's QFD team considers product and process designs, it decides on the process control, quality control and testing, maintenance of plants and equipment; the cycle ends with employee training. With such a process cycle, QFD requires the cross-functional participation of employees to look after the varied nature of activities. A cross-functional QFD team synergizes with the job of product development to reflect the needs of the customers. Therefore, it is a structured process for integrated product development, to ensure value for money for the customers. Planning and designing of activities is most crucial, and without a consensus, understanding and agreement on these two aspects, real product development cannot take place. Drawing lessons from corporate practices, some of the recommended lines of actions to facilitate QFD can be listed below:

- Get a commitment from management to introduce QFD.
- Develop clear objectives and goals for QFD, its scope, and the requirements of various actions. To start with, it is always desirable to begin with a small project, and then replicate the experience in a large project.
- Shortlist a multi-function team, and get a commitment from team members.
- Train QFD team members, and ensure that they understand the process. If required, initially, they may be helped by experienced mentors.
- Conduct regular meetings and monitor progress.
- Ensure that team members maintain their focus.
- Ascertain the needs of the customer from a bundle of exercises. There is no need to be completely scientific in understanding the customer's feelings. Rather, make use of intuition, and the use of unobtrusive observation.

Basically, QFD uses the systems engineering approach to manage the task of product development in line with customer requirements, and in the process, achieves tangible quality improvements

Among the benefits of QFD are that it is customer-centric and helps the organization to be more customer-focussed. Such organizational transformation helps companies to achieve sustainable competitive advantages. Also, QFD is essentially time-bound teamwork, primarily based on documentation.

Some of the tools used for QFD are affinity diagram, interrelationship graph, tree diagram, matrix diagram, etc.

Affinity diagram is a technique to document groups of ideas, process variables, concepts and opinions.

An interrelationship graph studies the cause and effect of the process improvement strategy.

A tree diagram documents (Fig. 9.18) all the possible outcomes of an event. A typical tree diagram is presented below:

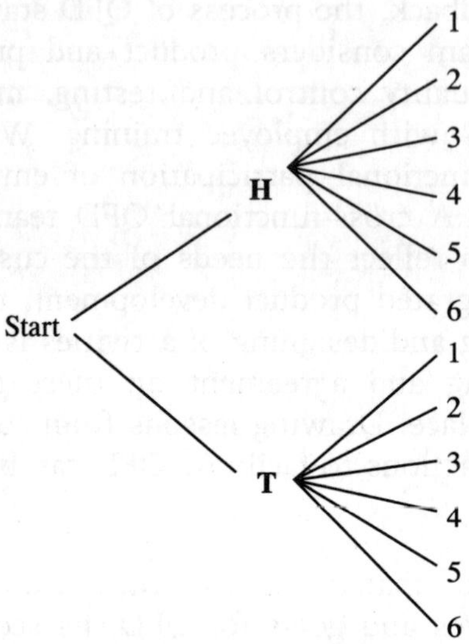

Figure 9.18 *Tree diagram*

A Matrix diagram helps us compare two or more groups of ideas, for determining relationship.

> ### *Failure Mode and Effects Analysis (FMEA)*
>
> FMEA is a step-by-step approach to identify all possible failures in newly-developed products or services, in designs and in the processes. The term 'failure mode' means the 'possibility of failures'. 'Effects' refers to the method used to study the consequences of failures. Using the FEMA technique, we prioritize failures in terms of gravity of consequences. The origin of FEMA was in the US Army in the 1940's. Thus, FMEA helps us analyze and prevent failures. Before introducing changes in the products and processes, FEMA helps us take preventive action to avoid failure, so that customers are assured of reliable and quality products. Depending on specific requirements, FEMA can be either process oriented or design oriented. Thus, it basically helps in taking corrective and/or preventive action to reduce or eliminate any potential failure that may affect product quality. FEMA documents the process and quantifies the risk of potential failure.
>
> FMEA is a two-phase process – identification of potential failure modes and implementation of corrective actions. Like QFD, FEMA also requires the participation of cross-functional team members. Some of the benefits of FEMA are:

- Determination of the best possible design for the quality and reliability of products.
- Understanding of potential failure modes and their potential effect on the reliability of manufactured products.
- Developing a documented process of improvements through corrective action.
- Providing useful information in developing the testing and monitoring criteria.
- Providing historical information to analyze potential product failure during the manufacturing process.
- Providing new ideas to improve designs or processes.

Thus, FEMA improves the quality, reliability and safety of products, services, machines and equipment, and the process of manufacturing. Also, FEMA provides sustainable competitive advantages to the organization, increases customer satisfaction, reduces product risk and enhances reliability.

FEMA can be used for process, design, concept development, equipment and services. In terms of the process, FEMA helps in analysis. In terms of design, FEMA analyzes the products. In the concepts area, FEMA helps in the analysis of systems and sub-systems. With regard to machines and equipment, it helps in understanding the design, and finally in services, FEMA helps in mapping the possible impact on the customers, before the development of new products.

9.13.2 Poka-yoke

Shigeo Shingo, an industrial engineer from *Toyota*, Japan introduced the concept of *poka-yoke* in the 1960's. The term means mistake-proofing or avoiding inadvertent errors. The method ensures availability of the appropriate situations, before an organization executes a step in the process; this prevents defects at the source. Thus, it requires that the process work starts the correct way, from the very beginning, which eliminates chances of error. Hence, *poka-yoke* eliminates defects in the process and products right from the beginning and substantially improves the quality and reliability of products. Because of this, it is often seen as an extension of the FEMA technique.

Poke-yoke is also used in line with the Six Sigma DMAIC (Define–Measure–Analyze–Improve–Control) cycle. As the name goes (mistake-proofing), *poke-yoke* can be used to fix the following types of errors:

- process operation
- set-up
- missing part
- improper part
- operations
- measurement

Primarily, therefore, *poka-yoke* is a prediction and detection method, which recognizes that a defect is about to occur or might have occurred. We have two types of *poke-yoke*: the control type and the warning type. Control *poka-yoke* prevents the starting or continuing of a process after the occurrence of an error. For example, a pirated CD or DVD may not work on a quality CD or DVD player, as it can sense the piracy and impurity of the products. The warning type of *poke-yoke* warns that an error has occurred; it cannot prevent the error, but stops the function, after the detection of an error.

Depending on the nature of the function, *poke-yoke* can use contact methods, fixed-value methods and motion-step methods. Contact methods sense defects in the shape and dimension of products. Using symmetrical designs, such defects can be prevented. Fixed-value methods are applied to those processes where the same activity is repeated, like the tightening of nuts and bolts. The motion-step method is used for processes that require the performance of activities in a sequence.

9.13.3 Genichi Taguchi's Quality Loss Function

The Quality Loss Function imputes a financial value to customer dissatisfaction, when product performance is below customer expectations. Likewise, when product performance exceeds customer expectations (target performance), it also imputes a financial value. The level of expectations of the customer or the target performance can be determined either based on intuition and hunches, or on customer surveys and feedback. Therefore, the quality loss function or Taguchi's technique helps the company take financial decisions, right at the design stage, on the cost of achieving the target performance. It is quality through robust design methodology.

Taguchi methods emphasize quality through robust design, and not quality through inspection. The methods break the design process into three stages – system, parameters and tolerance.

- System design creates the working prototypes.
- Parameter design experiments with the factors that influence the performance of a product.

- Tolerance design involves the setting of tight tolerance limits for the critical factors and loose tolerance limits of the non-critical factors. Through robust design methodology, designer experiments are carried out to determine the critical and non-critical factors of product performance.

The quality percepts of Taguchi stress the losses associated with a product. According to Taguchi, quality is the loss a product causes to society after being shipped, other than losses caused by its intrinsic functions. Taguchi restricts loss to two categories:

- loss due to functional variability and
- loss due to harmful side effects.

Based on this, Taguchi's definition of quality is the performance of intended functions without variability, with little or no harmful side effects. Based on his definition of quality, loss due to functional variability could be the loss of energy and time or money, while the losses attributed to harmful side effects could be a drop in market share. The focus of a company is to improve quality by minimizing possible losses to society. In the figure (Fig. 9.19), Taguchi's loss function is explained.

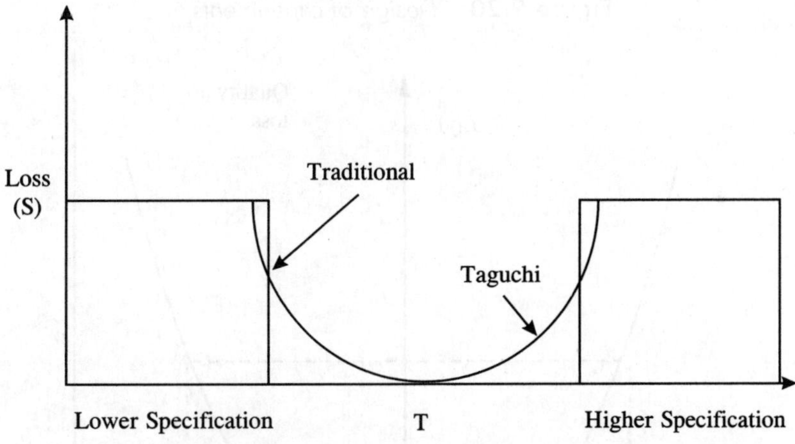

Figure 9.19 *Taguchi's loss function*

Here L(Y) is the expected loss associated with the specific value of Y. This equation explains that the loss is proportionate to the square of deviation of the measured value, that is, Y, from the targeted value, T. It implies that deviation from the targeted value can reduce customer satisfaction. Thus, conformance to specifications alone is not quality.

Taguchi has contributed significantly on the Design of Experiments (DOE). A typical DOE is illustrated in figure 9.20.

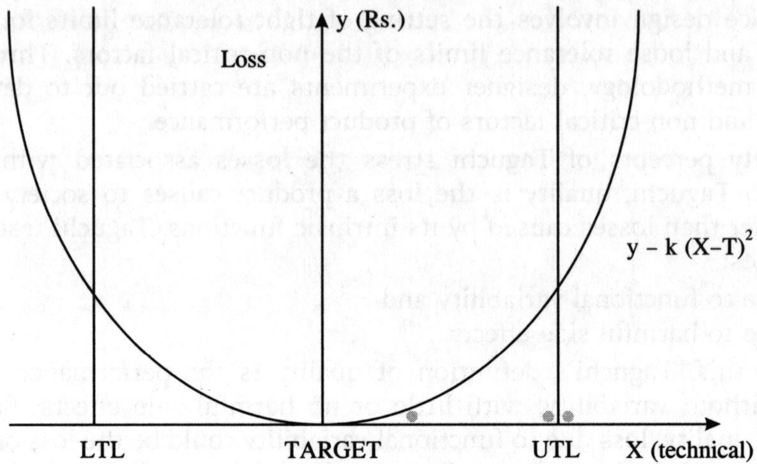

LTL : Lower Tolerance Limit
UTL : Upper Tolerance Limit

Figure 9.20 *Design of experiments*

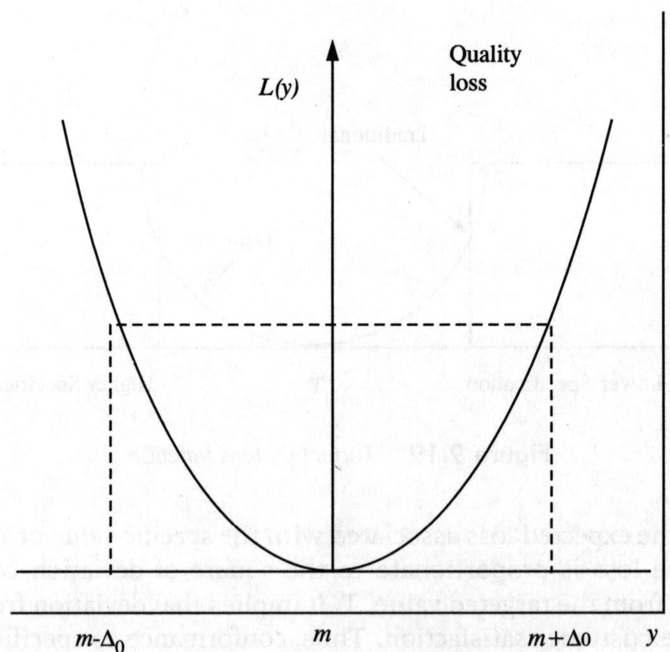

Figure 9.21. *Graphical presentation*

It suggests minimizing the loss; products must be produced ensuring minimum variation. Hence, quality has to be built into the product. Robust design here indicates, not a possible method to solve problems, but an approach to prevent quality failure.

Mathematically, the function may be expressed as:

$$L = k(y - m)^2$$

The graphical presentation for which is seen in Figure 9.21, where y represents the performance parameter of the system, m represents the target or the nominal value of y, L represents the quality loss, and k is a constant.

9.14 STATISTICAL PROCESS CONTROL (SPC)

SPC and the related control charts were developed by Dr Walter A Shewhart in the mid-1920s. Shewhart's main concern was to avoid tedious mathematical computation to ascertain quality problems and to identify a solution path. Two concepts are associated with SPC; these are 'in control' and 'out of control'. We ascertain these based on our interpretation of data in graphs or histograms. These help us understand the behaviour of variation of our observations. When we observe that the process is stable, we call it 'in-control'. But when the process is influenced by any exogenous factors, we call it 'out of control'. In other words, when the data distribution changes unpredictably over time, we consider the process as being 'out of control'. Shewhart's argument was that variation of any nature can be measured; he also observed that the manufacturing process differs in behaviour. Out of control variation can be further categorized into 'controlled variation' and 'uncontrolled variation'. Controlled variations are by nature stable, while uncontrolled variations are unstable. To measure the variation, Shewhart developed 'control charts'.

SPC guides us to initiate appropriate action to improve the process in three distinct phases – process stabilization through the identification and elimination of special causes, initiation of process improvement efforts tracking the common causes, and sustaining process improvement through systematic monitoring. Use of control charts, as a diagnostic tool, helps us in all these three cases.

SPC, therefore, helps organizations to quickly detect the occurrence of assignable cause or process shifts, to enable investigation into the process and to allow corrective action to be taken before any non-conforming units are manufactured. Assignable causes are those, which may occur due to improperly adjusted machines, operator errors and defective raw materials or other inputs. This causes some variability in the quality characteristics. A process that is operating under assignable causes over and above change causes is said to be out of control.

9.14.1 Differences between SPC and SQC

SPC is a method of monitoring the quality of products using statistical methods, so that through process improvement, quality can be further improved. SQC is also a statistical method used to analyze variations in the manufacturing process to access whether the products are acceptable or not. SQC works on data drawn from a specific sample size. With SQC, we can understand the acceptable limits on manufactured products. Thus, SQC is the use of statistical tools to analyze variations in the manufacturing process; SPC can be considered as a category of SQC to oversee and control the production process, to ensure the production of uniform products with less waste. SPC checks for process flaws, and uses the specific number of a sample to determine the acceptability of a product.

Statistical Process Control Terms

P	=	Fraction of defective units
np	=	Number of defective units
c	=	Number of defects
u	=	Number of defects per unit
n	=	sub-group size
k	=	Number of subgroups
X	=	Observation Value
R	=	Range

A_2, D_3, D_4, d_2, E_2 are all constants

9.14.2 Control Charts

Control charts are statistical tools for different applications. Primarily such charts are useful to monitor key product variables and process parameters. Control charts are used to enforce process control and to identify causes of variation. Let us now examine the control chart in Fig. 9.22.

Distributing the data, you can observe some values are either above the upper control limit (UCL) or below the lower control limit (LCL); while some values are distributed between the UCL and LCL. Values above the UCL and under the LCL are indicators of poor quality, they are a fall out of an 'out of control' process, while the values between the UCL and the LCL are considered indicators of acceptable quality, they are the fall out of an 'in-control' process.

Control charts are defined as process control tools, used primarily for the detection of assignable causes of quality variation. It is the graphical display of a sample quality measure (variables) versus sample number (or time). The centre line represents the average value of the quality characteristic corresponding to the in-control state. Proper understanding of the meaning of the chart is essential for its usage. The terms, 'control' and 'capability' are different. For example, a process in control may not be capable. Control means stability of the process, while capability means quality within the specification. Again, a control chart is not for a product but for a process. Therefore, a control chart should be viewed as a process improvement tool and not as a 'quality control' tool.

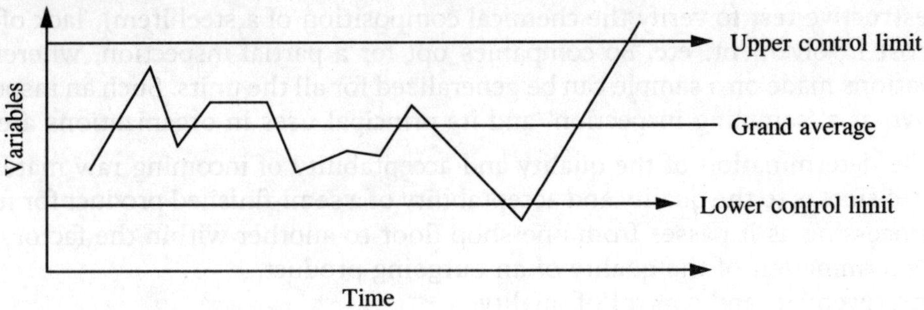

Figure 9.22. *A control chart*

9.15 DATA COLLECTION

Data are defined as 'known facts, which we use for drawing inference'. It can also be defined as the numerical facts of statistics. Data may be either in discrete (numerical), continuous (dimensional) or in attribute (descriptive) forms.

- Discrete variables being numerical can only be in particular numbers.
- Continuous variables, being dimensions can be in terms of length, volume, time, meters, liters, volts, etc.
- Attribute variables, being descriptive, can be in terms of present, absent, etc.

Irrespective of the forms of data, the data are collected in different phases, of which sampling is considered to be the best one. While collecting data through sampling, we need to understand the purpose or objective, the population or the sampling frame from which data are to be collected, the method of data collection, sample size, validation of the data, etc.

9.15.1 Sampling

For data collection, sampling is used as a method. The purpose of sampling is to ensure that data are collected in such a manner that sample data can represent the population, or the observations on sample, can hold good for the population. For the quality control function, sampling is very important. For example, to manufacture items, companies need to buy items, which are used in the form of inputs. The quality of end products largely depends on the quality of inputs. Hence, every company ensures the inspection of incoming or receiving items. Similarly for quality, there is inspection of in-process items and final inspection of finished items. We have to decide on the extent of inspection to be carried out. Obviously, it is not possible to go in for total enumeration in all cases. Through sampling, partial inspection is done.

Also, there are situations, where 100% inspection cannot be done for certain reasons like the absence of technical feasibility (like a life cycle test of an electric bulb or a destructive test to verify the chemical composition of a steel item), lack of time, huge cost involvement, etc. So companies opt for a partial inspection, wherein the observations made on a sample can be generalized for all the units. Such an inspection is known as a 'sampling inspection' and its principal uses in organizations are:

1. The determination of the quality and acceptability of incoming raw materials
2. Decision as to the quality and acceptability of a semi-finished product for further processing as it passes from one shop floor to another within the factory
3. Determination of the quality of an outgoing product
4. Improvement and control of quality

A sampling plan outlines the procedure to be followed for acceptance or rejection of products submitted for acceptance. The product is usually submitted in lots or consignments; the consumers accept lots of high quality and reject lots of low quality. Therefore, it is necessary to decide how the quality of a lot should be measured. There are several ways in which the quality of a lot can be described. It depends mainly on the following characteristics:

1. The proportion of defective items in the lot
2. The average number of defects per item or the constant area of the lot (defects per item)
3. The averages of an important measurable characteristic of the item in the lot, and the variability or dispersion among the items of the lot with respect to this characteristic (that is, the mean and standard deviation for the whole lot)

'Attribute sampling plans' are plans in which the item quality is defined by attributes and lot quality by fraction defective. Plans where item quality is an actual measurement and lot quality is specified by tolerances (mean dimension and dispersion) are called 'variable sampling plans'.

9.15.2 Various Methods of Sampling

For measuring quality characteristics, we use various types of sampling. The sampling method used, depends largely on factors like product characteristics, volume, feasibility, etc. Some common sampling methods are discussed below.

9.15.2.1 Random sampling

This is a common method, where sampling is done based on the lottery method. Each population at the outset is numbered, and then samples are drawn using the lottery method, so that every unit of population gets an equal opportunity of selection as a sample. As a result, observations on samples hold good for the population. Again, random sampling is of two kinds – simple random sampling and stratified random sampling. A simple random sampling is as the lottery method explained above. We follow this sampling approach, where there is homogeneity of population. However, in some cases we use stratified random sampling, to represent every cross-section of a population. For example, in cases, where we observe the phenomena of population, in terms of certain characteristics, say quality variation of tea in terms of section of garden from where the leafs were plucked, workers who were responsible for plucking, during or time of withering of plucked tea, etc., the population is divided into different strata, and then we draw samples from each such stratum, following the same approach, to ensure that each unit of the population stratum gets equal opportunity to be selected as a sample.

9.15.2.2 *Systematic Sampling*

This is another approach to sampling; it follows the 'constant skip method'. For example, after we allocate some numerical numbers to every unit of a population, we may consider every fifth item as sample. However, this can be applied when we have a large volume of data. A decision on the order of item to be selected as a sample depends on the percentage of the population to be selected as sample.

9.15.2.3 *Stratified Sampling*

The approach here is the same as for stratified random sampling – separating the population into strata, and ensuring proportional representation from each stratum.

Quota sampling, cluster sampling, multi-stage sampling are some other methods used to study quality characteristics.

Mystery shoppers

In market research, we use the 'mystery shoppers' method of sampling. This method helps us determine the quality of goods and services. Customer satisfaction mapping is a great task for the hospitality industry. Most of the approaches used by star-hotels only reveal half the truth. To understand customer feelings, often hotels conduct this experiment, by having their employees pose as customers. Such employees get a real feel of customer services. This method has now become popular in the service industries.

9.15.2.4 *Sequential or Double Sampling*

In quality control, sequential or double sampling methods are followed at times, depending on the nature of the investigation. Sequential samples are drawn one by one in groups and the results of the drawing at any stage decide whether sampling is to continue. Double sampling is a two-stage selection procedure where data are collected for a large sample (often by a low cost procedure such as a mail survey), and then a smaller sub-sample of the initial sample is selected for a second stage of data collection (often using a more expensive method of collecting data).

Depending on the nature of investigation, often it may be necessary to collect information by sampling, and then based on such information, draw the sub-sample for further investigation. This approach is known as double sampling, multi-stage sampling or sequential sampling. This is also used in stratified and cluster sampling. In stratified sampling, members of the population are assigned, at the outset, to a strata or groups, and then based on some characteristics, a sub-sample is drawn, keeping in view that they are mutually exclusive and collectively exhaustive. Bases of stratification, number of strata, and the sample size within the strata are decided based on the nature of the variable to be studied. For quality control, it can be used in cases where batch-wise bulk production is made, and acceptance or rejection decisions are taken based on random stratification of samples. Cluster sampling, on the other hand, is probability sampling. Cluster is ideally a mini-population with all the features of the population. This can also be used in quality control.

9.15.2.5 Operating Characteristic Curve

To judge the suitability of any sampling plan, we have to compare its performance, over a range of possible quality levels, of the submitted product. A comparison is provided by the Operating Characteristic Curve (OC Curve) of the plan. It shows clearly how a sampling plan discriminates lots of varying quality and evaluates the risks associated with any sampling plan. There are three important points that are often referred on the OC Curve. These are:

- Acceptable Quality Level (AQL)
- Lot Tolerance Percent/Fraction Defective (LTPD or LTFD)
- Point of Indifference

Acceptable Quality Level (AQL) or Average Acceptable Quality Level (AAQL) is the level that the consumer is willing to accept, all the time. But due to chance, variations in the batches may be rejected. Occasionally, rejections are possible even through the quality is better. The probability of such a chance is called 'Producer's Risk'.

A typical OC curve is reproduced in Fig. 9.23

Lot Tolerance Fraction Defective (LTFD) or Lot Tolerance Per Cent Defective is the level at which the consumer would like to reject, all the time. When it is expressed in terms of a percentage, it is called LTPD; when it is expressed in terms of a fraction it is called LTFD. The sampling plan involving some risk that will accept a lot with such a chance is called 'Consumer's Risk'.

Point of indifference is the point where the producer and the consumer take the same risk in the application of the plan. So, this is the point where the probability of acceptance and rejection of the lot are equal.

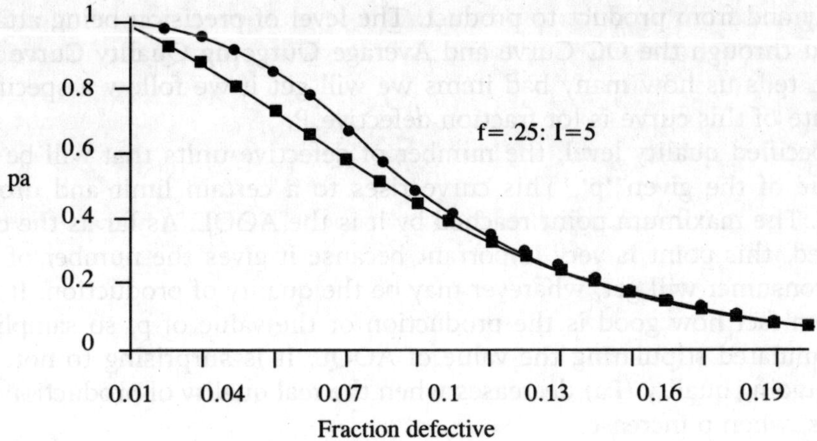

Figure 9.23. *An OC curve*

9.15.2.6 *Single Sampling Plan*

The simplest type of sampling plans are those in which the decision to accept or reject a lot is based upon a single sample. So from a homogeneous group, for this type of sampling plan, it is necessary to:

- Make a lot size of "N"
- Take a random sample size of "n"
- Inspect all the "n" units
- If the number of defective items is within "C" then accept the lot of size "N"
- If the number of defective items is outside the "C" limit, then reject the lot size of "N".
- "C" is called the acceptance number or critical number of the plan. If we consider an example with numerical values for the single sampling plan with:

  N = 10,000
  n = 300
  C = 5

  The process of operation is as follows:
  Make a homogenous lot of size 10,000. Out of this, choose a sample size of 300 randomly. If it is possible to use a random number table to select these 300 units, it is better. Otherwise, pick 300 units in an unbiased manner from the lot. Inspect all the 300 units. If the number of defective units is 0, 1, 2, 3, 4 or 5, accept the lot of 10,000 as good. If the number of defective units is more than 5, reject the entire lot of 10,000.

The selection of the plan for a quality control set-up depends upon the precision required, the economic aspect implied in the plan and the operational feasibility of the plan in the quality control set-up. Operational feasibility changes from company to company and from product to product. The level of precision being attained can be accessed through the OC Curve and Average Outgoing Quality Curve (AOQL). The AOQL tells us how many bad items we will get if we follow a specified plan. The ordinate of this curve is lot fraction defective P.

For a specified quality level, the number of defective units that will be accepted is the value of the given 'p'. This curve rises to a certain limit and drops down afterwards. The maximum point reached by it is the AOQL. As far as the consumer is concerned, this point is very important because it gives the number of defective units the consumer will get, whatever may be the quality of production. It is always an unknown fact how good is the production or the value of p, so sampling plans can be formulated stipulating the value of AOQL. It is surprising to note that the average outgoing quality (Pa) decreases when the real quality of production becomes bad, that is, when p increases.

9.15.3 Choice of Quality Characteristic

To begin with, a decision has to be made on the quality characteristic for which a control programme is to be derived. The characteristics affecting the performance of the product should normally be taken first. For example, these could be features of the materials, components or parts used, for the tensile strength of some steel item, thickness of some insulation, internal diameters of steel tubes, etc.

9.15.3.1 Choice of Control Station

In any manufacturing process, control charts are used at strategic points to conduct proper checks. To decide the ideal place for such controls, it is best to determine the areas of maximum potential for return in the form of direct profits – reduction in scrap, increase in production, etc. It is also worthwhile to study the production process to determine the nature and location of the causes that tend to give rise to deviations in the characteristic chosen.

9.15.3.2 Choice of Rational Sub-groups

When creating sub-groups, it is best to ensure against sub-groups consisting of items manufactured in different shifts, components obtained from different sources, from different production times, from different machines, moulds, operators, etc.

9.15.3.3 Frequency and Size of Samples

A number of practical considerations dictate the size and frequency of samples. Small samples taken at more frequent intervals will detect a large shift more quickly. Samples of size 4 or 5 should generally be used.

9.15.3.4 *Choice of the Type of Control Charts to be used*

When measuring quality characteristics, a pair of control charts – X-bar to control the average level of the process and the other R to control dispersion – is used. Many quality characteristics are not measured on a numerical scale. In such cases, each unit of the product should be judged, as either conforming or non-conforming, on the basis of whether or not it possesses certain attributes. We may count the number of non-conformities (defects) appearing on a unit of product. In such situations, control charts are used to count the number of defects or defective pieces.

As long as the points plot within the control limits, the process is assumed to be in control and no action is necessary. When a point plots outside of the control limits, it is interpreted as evidence that the process is out of control and investigative and corrective action is required, to find and eliminate the assignable cause or causes responsible for this behaviour.

9.15.4 Guidelines for Preparing Control Charts

Homogenization for dispersion: If the sample size chosen is less than 10 (usually the sample size is 4, 5 or 6), then for each of the samples in the set, the range (R) should be calculated and the average range ($\overline{R}$) computed. Depending upon the sample size, a suitable factor D should be read from the Table and if all the ranges are found to be less than or equal to the $\overline{DR}$, the initial data collected is deemed to be homogeneous and acceptable for the purpose of further calculation of control limits. In case one or more ranges are found to exceed the $\overline{DR}$, the observations in that (those) sub-group (s) will be discarded. For the remaining data, the above procedure is repeated (that is, the calculation of the new average range $\overline{R}$ and comparison of all the remaining ranges with $\overline{DR}$) till all the ranges are found to be within control.

If more than 25% of the samples are rejected for being out of control in this homogenization process, the entire data should be rejected and fresh data should be collected.

Homogenization for central tendency: Calculate the average of each sample ($\overline{\overline{X}}$) from the homogenized data. Then, calculate the average of these averages or the grand average ($\overline{\overline{X}}$) for all the samples. If any of the averages are found to be outside the interval $\overline{\overline{X}} \pm A_2 \overline{R}$ (where A is read from the Table value for the corresponding sample size), then the observations in the corresponding sub-groups should be discarded. From the remaining data, a fresh grand average should be computed and the above procedure repeated till all the average values are found to be within $\overline{\overline{X}} \pm A_2 \overline{X}$.

9.15.4.1 *Setting Up of Control Charts*

$\overline{X}$ and R charts: Suppose standard values of the process parameters (process mean) are 0 (process variability) are X and A respectively (when we do not compute the 0 value conventionally, by obtaining the square-root of variation). Then, the control limits on the $\overline{X}$ charts and R charts would be as follows:

For $\overline{X}$ chart

$$U.C.L. = \overline{\overline{X}} + A_2 \overline{R}$$
$$C.L. = \overline{\overline{X}}$$
$$L.C.L. = \overline{\overline{X}} - A_2 \overline{R}$$

For R-chart

$$U.C.L. = D_4 \overline{R}$$
$$C.L. = \overline{R}$$
$$L.C.L. = D_3 \overline{R}$$

P-chart or fraction defective chart:

The P-chart or fraction defective chart is defined as the ratio of the number of defective items in a population to the total number of items in that population. The sample fraction defective (p) is defined as the ratio of the number of defective units (d) in the sample to the sample size 'n', i.e., p = d/n. Suppose the standard value for process fraction defective (p) is p'. Then, the central line and control limits on the fraction defective chart would be:

$$U.C.L. = p' + 3 \sqrt{p' (1-p')/n}$$
$$C.L. = p'$$
$$L.C.L. = p' - 3 \sqrt{p' (1-p)/n}$$

where 'n' is a sub-group size. If L.C.L. is negative, it is taken as zero.

np-chart or chart for number of defectives: The number of defectives or np-chart is used when the sub-group size is constant. The central line and the control limits for the np-chart will be as follows:

$$U.C.L. = np + 3 \sqrt{np (1 - p)}$$
$$C.L. = np$$
$$L.C.L. = np - 3 \sqrt{np (1 - p)}$$

Number of defects or c – chart: A defective (or non-conforming) unit is a unit of product that does not satisfy one or more of the specifications. Each specific point at which a specification is not satisfied results in a defect or non-conformity. In this case, each sub-group consists of a single unit and 'c' would be the number of defects observed in one unit. It should be remembered that each inspection unit must always represent an identical 'area of opportunity' for the occurrence of defects. The control limits for the c-chart is given by:

$$U.C.L. = c' + 3 \sqrt{c'}$$

C.L. = c'
L.C.L. = $c - 3\sqrt{c'}$

where 'c' is the standard value for the average number of defects. If L.C.L. comes out negative, it is taken as zero.

9.15.4.2 Demerits of the Control Chart

A disadvantage of the Control Chart is that it gives equal importance to each class of defects. Different defects are unequal in their influence on costs. Some can be corrected by simple, inexpensive rework, others may require costly rework, and still others may require scrapping of the article inspected. A practical solution to this problem is to classify various defects into some broad categories, such as critical, major and minor defects, and then assign a different rating for each class of defects. The demerit score for each item is then calculated and can be plotted on the control chart.

Example

Tea produced in *Sonajuli* Tea Estate is subjected to moisture tests every day. Moisture formation occurs either due to improper drying operations or due to stockpiling continuously in bins for more than a week. Test checks are carried out, drawing at least five samples (at random) from each lot. On a particular day, the Factory Manager has drawn five samples (n) from 10 different lots and recorded his observation on moisture content as under:

Sample	Moisture content				
1	3.389	3.384	3.380	3.386	3.387
2	3.390	3.378	3.387	3.394	3.389
3	3.387	3.389	3.379	3.390	3.384
4	3.389	3.379	3.394	3.394	3.395
5	3.385	3.388	3.394	3.384	3.393
6	3.380	3.389	3.392	3.383	3.388
7	3.379	3.390	3.378	3.377	3.379
8	3.389	3.395	3.390	3.389	3.390
9	3.380	3.395	3.389	3.392	3.392
10	3.386	3.387	3.381	3.389	3.379

Design $\overline{X}$ and R charts with control limits at ± 3 Standard Deviations from the mean. Also suggest whether the process is in control.

Solution

Compute mean value and range of each sample. Range is the difference between the maximum and minimum values within a sample.

Sample No.	X	R
1	3.3852	0.009
2	3.3876	0.016
3	3.3856	0.011
4	3.3902	0.016
5	3.3888	0.010
6	3.3864	0.012
7	3.3806	0.011
8	3.3906	0.006
9	3.3896	0.015
10	3.3844	0.010
Total	33.8690	0.0116

Mean of Sample means $\bar{\bar{X}} = \dfrac{33.8690}{10} = 3.3864$

Mean of Ranges $\bar{R} = \dfrac{0.0116}{10}$

Instead of computing Standard Deviation conventionally, we can approximate this by referring to Table Value. Thus, the X chart and the R chart would be as under:

$\bar{X}$ Chart

$UCL = \bar{\bar{X}} + A_2 \bar{R}$

$LCL = \bar{\bar{X}} - A_2 \bar{R}$

R Chart

$UCL = D_4 \bar{R}$

$LCL = D_3 \bar{R}$

Table values of A, D for n of 5 are;

A = 0.577, D = 0, D = 2.115

Thus, the $\bar{X}$ Chart and R-chart would be as under:

For $\bar{X}$ Chart

UCL 3.3936

$\bar{\bar{X}}$ 3.3869

LCL 3.3802

For R-Chart

UCL 0.0245

$\bar{R}$ 0.0116

LCL 0.0000

Attribute Data Chart Formulas

Chart Type	Subgroup Size	Control Limits
p Chart Fraction Defective	Variable or Constant	Central Line: $\bar{p} = \sum np / \sum n$ $UCL = \bar{p} + 3\sqrt{(\bar{p}(1-\bar{p}))/n}$ $LCL = \bar{p} - 3\sqrt{(\bar{p}(1-\bar{p}))/n}$
np Chart Number Defective	Constant	Central Line: $n\bar{p} = \sum np / k$ $UCL = n\bar{p} + 3\sqrt{n\bar{p}(1-\bar{p})}$ $LCL = n\bar{p} - 3\sqrt{n\bar{p}(1-\bar{p})}$
c Chart Number of Defects	Constant	Central Line: $\bar{c} = \sum c / k$ $UCL = \bar{c} + 3\sqrt{\bar{c}}$ $LCL = \bar{c} - 3\sqrt{\bar{c}}$
u Chart Number of Defects Per Unit	Variable or Constant	Central Line: $\bar{u} = \sum c / \sum n$ $UCL = \bar{u} + 3\sqrt{\bar{u}/n}$ $LCL = \bar{u} - 3\sqrt{\bar{u}/n}$

Variable Data Charts

Chart Type	Subgroup Size	Control Limits
$\bar{X}$ and R Average and Range Chart	< 10 Usually 3-5	$\bar{X}$ Central Line: $\bar{\bar{X}} = \frac{(\bar{X}_1 + \bar{X}_2 + \ldots \bar{X}_k)}{k}$ $\bar{X}$ $UCL = \bar{\bar{X}} + A_2\bar{R}$ $\bar{X}$ $LCL = \bar{\bar{X}} - A_2\bar{R}$ R Central Line: $\bar{R} = \frac{(R_1 + R_2 + \ldots R_k)}{k}$ R $UCL = D_4\bar{R}$ R $LCL = D_3\bar{R}$
X and mR Individuals and Moving Range Chart Note: $\widetilde{mR}$ = Median Moving Range	1	X Central Line: $\bar{X} = \frac{(X_1 + X_2 + \ldots X_k)}{k}$ X $UCL = \bar{X} + (3.14 \times \widetilde{mR})$ X $LCL = \bar{X} - (3.14 \times \widetilde{mR})$ mR Central Line: Median Moving Range mR $UCL = 3.87 \times \widetilde{mR}$

9.15.4.3 Attributes of Control Charts

To classify or count observations, we use attribute data. Attribute data measures quality using control charts, which sort items into 'non-defective' and 'defective' types. Some examples of attribute data are: number of failures, proportion of malfunctioning items in a lot, etc. Attribute control charts that plot non-conformities are called c-charts (for count). Attribute control charts that deal with the proportion or fraction of defective products are called *p*-charts (for proportion). Another type of attribute control chart – the u-chart – handles defects per unit. In other words, this chart analyses the average number of non-conformities per unit of product.

Attribute control charts are different from variable control charts. In the case of attribute control charts, the unit of measurement used is a distinct value, while for variables, it is a computed measure of central tendency; that is, mean or range. The two types of attribute control charts are concerned with the percentage defective (*p*-chart) or with the defects per unit (*c*-chart).

These two charts, however, vary with respect to constant sample size and varying sample size. The other two attribute control charts are the *np*-chart, and the *u*-chart. Different attribute control charts are explained in the figure 9.24 below:

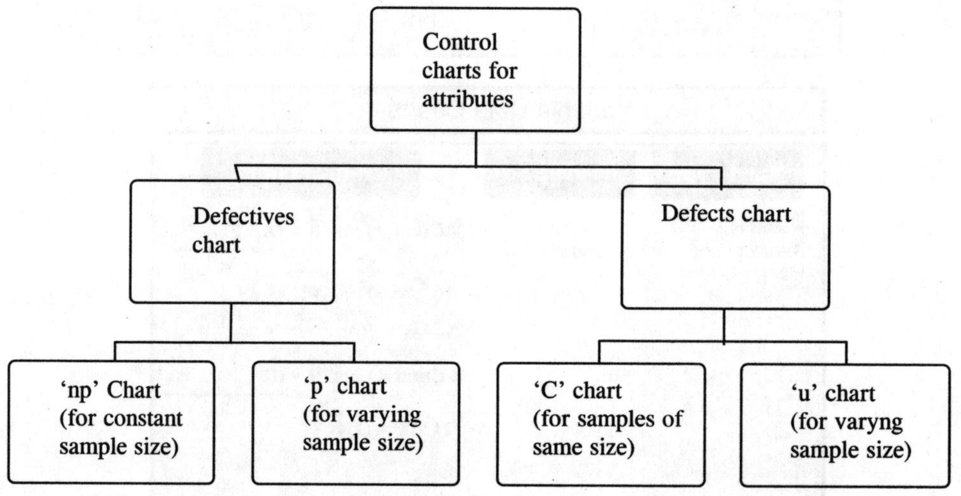

Figure 9.24: *Control Charts for attributes*

Percentage Defective Charts (p-chart)

Example

A retail mall systematically collects customer feedback every week using a structured questionnaire and interviewing about 100 randomly selected customers. The retail mall wishes to analyze the customer feedback using a control chart, and has documented the information from the consolidated survey data as follows:

	Week								
	1	2	3	4	5	6	7	8	Total
Number of customers who are dissatisfied	3	2	4	1	0	5	2	3	20
Fraction defective	0.03	0.02	0.04	0.01	0	0.05	0.02	0.03	0.2

Based on the above information indicate whether the nature of customer feedback is erratic or stable.

Steps:

1. First, calculate the fraction defective, which is 20/100 = 0.20.
2. Average defective percentage = 0.20/8 = 0.025.
3. Use the following formula:

$$\sqrt{\overline{p}(1-\frac{\overline{p}}{n})} = \frac{\sqrt{0.025(1-0.025)}}{100} = 0.156$$

4. Determine the control limits as under:

$$UCL_P = \overline{p} + 3\sqrt{\overline{p}(1-\frac{\overline{p}}{n})} = 0.25 + (0.0156) = 0.025 + 0.047 = 0.072$$

$$LCL_P = \overline{p} - 3\sqrt{\overline{p}(1-\frac{\overline{p}}{n})} = 0.25 - 3(0.0156) = 0.025 - 0.047 = 0$$

Based on the above results, we can conclude that the customer feedback pattern is stable.

Defects per Unit Charts (C-chart)

This chart is used when output defects can occur at different points; say in electronic equipment, textiles, for improper medications, etc. Here, the nature of failure approximates the Poisson distribution, and we use the $\overline{c}$ chart. To assess the average number of defects per unit of output, using three standard deviations, we determine the control limit as under:

$$UCL_c = \overline{c} + 3\sqrt{\overline{c}}$$

$$LCL_c = \overline{c} - 3\sqrt{\overline{c}}$$

The value of $\bar{c}$ is an estimate, as was $\bar{p}$; based on past accumulated data. The c-chart has many uses other than for quality purposes. Examples are found in the area of inventory control for controlling the number of stock-outs, in equipment maintenance for the number of breakdowns, and for accident statistics.

Example

The retail mall also receives customer complaints that range from issues pertaining to the bad behaviour of the counter salespersons, the queuing at cash counters, poor display of products making it difficult for the customers to make an informed choice, etc. The mall wants to construct a control chart for defects per unit, c-chart. The mall observed that 282 defects per sales counter occurred. Develop a control chart.

$$UCL_c = \bar{c} + 3\sqrt{\bar{c}} = 28.2 + 3\sqrt{28.2} = 44.13$$

$$LCL_c = \bar{c} - 3\sqrt{\bar{c}} = 28.2 - 3\sqrt{28.2} = 12.3$$

In the table below, we have explained various charts based on the count data.

Data characterized by Binomial model Area of opportunity = n		Data characterized by Poisson model Area of opportunity = a	
Constant n	Variable n	Constant a	Variable a
np-chart for counts	p-chart for proportions	c-chart for counts	u-chart for rates

9.15.5 Control Charts for Counts

Typical control charts for counts can be illustrated as in the figure overleaf

Example

The figure illustrates the number of defects in 20 samples, randomly drawn, containing 2000 items:

425, 430, 216, 341, 225, 322, 280, 306, 337, 305, 356, 402, 216, 264, 126, 409, 193, 280, 389, 326

Find out the values for the central line and control limits for p chart.

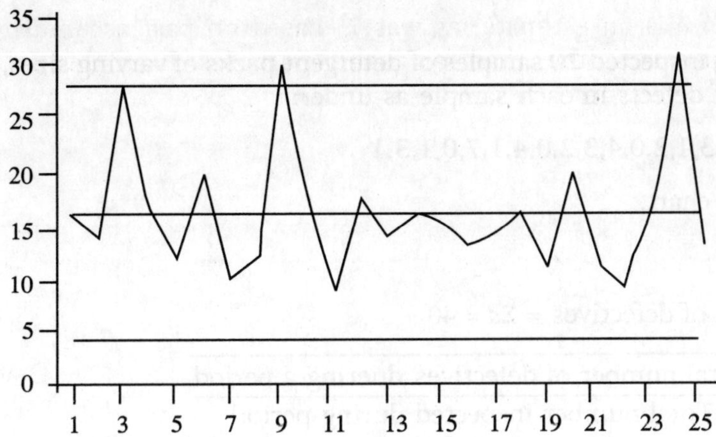

Solution

Total items = 20 ∗ 2000 = 40000 items

Total no. of defectives in 40000 items is $\Sigma d = 425 + 430 + 216 + \ldots.. + 326 = 6148$

$\overline{P} = 6148/40000 = 0.1537$

Therefore,

$$CL = \overline{P} = 0.1537$$

$$LCL = \overline{P} - 3\sqrt{\frac{\overline{p}(1-\overline{p})}{n}} = 0.1537 - 3\sqrt{\frac{0.1537(1-0.1537)}{2000}}$$

$$= 0.1537 - 0.0242 = 0.1295$$

$$UCL = \bar{p} + 3\sqrt{\frac{\overline{p}(1-\overline{p})}{n}} = 0.1537 + 0.0242 = \overline{0.1779}$$

'np' chart

The quantity 'np' is the number of units in the sub-group with some particular characteristic. For variable sub-group size, we use the fraction defective or 'p' chart, however, when the sub-group size is constant, we prepare an 'np' chart for the actual number of defectives. For 'np' chart calculations of the centerline, the control limits, etc. are the same as in a 'p' chart with constant sample sizes.

Center Line = $n\bar{p}$

$$UCL(np) = n\bar{p} + 3\sqrt{n\bar{p}(1-\bar{p})}$$

$$LCL(np) = n\bar{p} - 3\sqrt{n\bar{p}(1-\bar{p})}$$

In case the lower limit is negative, we use the value 0.0.

Example

The retail mall inspected 20 samples of detergent packs of varying sizes, and recorded the number of defects in each sample as under:

2,1,3,0,2,3,1,2,0,4,3,2,0,4,1,7,0,1,3,1

Draw the 'np' chart.

Solution

Total no. of defectives = $\Sigma d = 40$

$$\bar{p} = \sqrt{\frac{\text{Total number of defectives duering a period}}{\text{Total number inspected during period}}}$$

$$\bar{p} = \frac{40}{(20 * 100)} = \frac{40}{2000} = 0.02$$

Therefore an average of 2% defectives is present

$$n\bar{p} = \frac{\text{Total no. of defectives in all samples}}{\text{No. of samples}} = \frac{40}{20} = 2$$

Now,

$$UCL(np) = n\bar{p} + 3\sqrt{n\bar{p}(1-\bar{p})} = 2 + 3\sqrt{2(1-0.02)} = 6.2$$

$$LCL(np) = n\bar{p} - 3\sqrt{n\bar{p}(1-\bar{p})} = 2 - 3\sqrt{2(1-0.02)} = -2.2 \Rightarrow 0$$

$$CL_{(np)} = \mathbf{2}$$

'u' Charts

Plot the defects or errors in a sample of constant size. But sample characteristics may vary in terms of the length of pieces of materials or volume. Obviously, in such cases, we cannot use a 'c' chart. The 'u' chart is suitable to control this type of processes.

For a 'u' chart, we calculate the process average defect rate as follows:

$\bar{u}$ = Process average defects per unit.

= Total number of defects/Total number of samples inspected

$$= \frac{\Sigma x_i}{\Sigma n_i}$$

where 'x' is the number of defects in sample 'i'.

The u-chart, or the per unit defects, follow the Poisson distribution pattern.

Standard deviation is determined based on the square root of the process average. The control limits, therefore, lie at three standard errors on either side of the centre line for individual sample sub-group. The formulae, therefore, are:

$$LCL(u) = \bar{u} - 3\sqrt{\frac{\bar{u}}{n}}$$

$$UCL(u) = \bar{u} + 3\sqrt{\frac{\bar{u}}{n}}$$

When the lower control limit is negative, a value of 0.0 is used instead.

SUMMARY

1. Quality is the totality of features and characteristics of products or services which satisfy the stated or implied needs of customers. It is now a must for the survival of the organization. To sustain themselves in a competitive environment, organizations worldwide emphasize the importance of achieving quality, as it lowers the cost of production, and at the same time, offers value for money to the customers.
2. To appreciate the importance of quality, it is necessary for the organization to understand the meaning of the term, 'cost of quality'. The identification of the cost of quality and the appropriate steps to reduce the same can help an organization in two ways, in terms of cost minimization and increased profitability. Three important costs of quality are: cost of failure, cost of appraisal, and cost of prevention.
3. With growing global competition, Quality Management is becoming increasingly important to the leadership and management of all organizations. Quality Management Principles provide an understanding of and guidance on the application of Quality Management.
4. The ISO TC176 on Quality Management and Quality Assurance was developed through a consensus process. ISO standards are documented quality systems management guidelines.
5. Many quality gurus have contributed to the total quality management practices. Phillip Crosby said quality is conformance to standards, and it comes from defect prevention and defect correction.
6. W Edwards Deming developed six-fold productivity improvement programmes through quality improvement.
7. Dr Joseph Juran focussed on planning, organizational issues and management's responsibility with regard to quality improvement.
8. Professor Kaoru Ishikawa suggested the need for company-wide quality improvement initiatives through the quality circle movement.
9. Taguchi suggested optimisation of products and processes before manufacturing rather than achieving quality through inspection. Shigeo Shingo revolutionized

the manufacturing of goods, suggesting improvement principles, through the creative involvement of all cross-sections of employees.

10. Tom Peters evolved a system of quality improvement with a sales-orientated viewpoint. He identified leadership as the central factor to the Quality Improvement Process.
11. With successful quality management practices, organizations can involve all cross-sections of employees in their work-related decision making. Obviously, quality management practices encourage team work.
12. Employee empowerment through quality management facilitates the development of the problem-solving activities of employees.
13. Quality of work life, ensuring satisfaction of personal needs, also contributes to quality.
14. Six Sigma practices, reinforcing quality enhancement, add economic value and practical utility to the customers and the organizations as a whole.
15. Innovation and creativity ensure process-centered changes and improve the quality of products and services.
16. Statistical process control charts were developed by Dr Walter A Shewhart in the mid-1920s. Shewhart's chart avoids tedious mathematical computation to ascertain quality problems and identify a solution path.
17. An operating characteristic curve judges the suitability of a sampling plan.
18. In organizations, control charts are extensively used for mapping quality problems.

KEY WORDS

Employee Empowerment is to confer legitimate right to employees, irrespective of the nature of their job and their level in the hierarchy, to make judgments and to take decisions on their own. Hence, employee empowerment can facilitate the development of the problem-solving abilities of the employees. Operationally, in organizations, we empower employees first by developing their capabilities, and second, by being indulgent enough to allow them to commit mistakes.

Quality of work life (QWL) QWL is defined as those perceived important personal needs, which an individual tries to satisfy by working in an organization. Its conceptual foundations, though laid by a host of behavioural scientists, were in reality advocated by Chris Argyris (1975) in his famous work on 'Personality and Organization'.

Check sheet These help in collecting and analyzing data, and can be useful in documenting quality problems. It is also called a defect concentration diagram. Analyses of collected data are done using a structured check sheet or form. A check sheet is useful particularly when data are observed and collected at a particular place by the same person.

Pareto chart It is a bar graph used to illustrate significant factors. It is also known as a Pareto diagram and it measures variations. The lengths of the bars represent frequency or cost, arranged with the longest bars on the left to the shortest bars on the right. As a result, by referring to this chart or diagram, we can understand situations with varying levels of significance.

Stratification It is a process of separation of a variety of data to study the problem. It is a combination technique, which we use in combination with other forms of data analysis to study patterns.

Quality function deployment (QFD) QFD was first conceptualized in 1966, and subsequently, was institutionalized as a total quality control tool by Shigeru Mizuno and Yoji Akao in 1972. QFD consolidates customer requirements, and then translates these to engineering specifications. In the process of doing so, QFD links customers, design engineers, competitors and the process of manufacturing.

Failure mode and effects analysis (FMEA): FMEA is a step-by-step approach to identify all possible failures in newly developed products or services, in designs, and in the processes. The term failure modes means the 'possibility of failures'. Effects refers to the method of studying the consequences of failures. Using the FEMA technique, we prioritize the failures in terms of the gravity of consequences.

Poka-yoke Shigeo Shingo, an industrial engineer from Toyota, Japan introduced the concept of Poka-yoke in the 1960s. The term means mistake-proofing and avoiding inadvertent errors. The method ensures the availability of the appropriate situations, before an organization executes the process step, which means preventing defects at the source itself.

Genichi Taguchi's quality loss function The Quality Loss Function imputes a financial value to customers' dissatisfaction, when the product performance is below customer expectations. Likewise, when the product performance is better than customer expectations (target performance), it also imputes a financial value. Customer expectation levels or the target performance is determined based on intuition and hunches, or on customer surveys and feedback.

Statistical process control (SPC) SPC and the related control charts were developed by Dr Walter A Shewhart in the mid-1920s. Shewhart's main concern was to avoid tedious mathematical computation to ascertain the existence of quality problems and to identify a solution path. Two concepts are associated with the SPC, these are 'in control' and 'out of control'. We ascertain these based on our interpretation of data in graphs or histograms.

Control charts These are statistical tools for different applications. Primarily, however, such charts are useful to monitor key product variables and process parameters. Thus, to enforce process control and to identify causes of variation, control charts are very useful.

Stratified sampling The approach here is the same as for stratified random sampling, that is, separating the population into strata, and ensuring proportional representation from each stratum.

Operating characteristic curve: To judge the suitability of any sampling plan, we need to compare its performance over a range of possible quality. A comparison is provided by the Operating Characteristic Curve (or the OC Curve) of the Plan. It gives clearly how a sampling plan discriminates between lots of varying quality and evaluates the risks associated with any sampling plan.

Sequential or double sampling In quality control, sequential or double sampling methods are followed at times, depending on the nature of the investigation. Sequential Samples are drawn one by one in groups and the results of the drawing at any stage decide whether sampling is to continue. Double Sampling is a two-stage selection procedure where data are collected for a large sample (often by a low-cost procedure such as a mail survey), and then a smaller sub-sample of the initial sample is selected for a second stage of data collection (often using a more expensive method of collecting data).

GENERAL REVIEW QUESTIONS

1. What is the difference between the traditional quality concept and the modern quality concept?
2. How does the quality control approach differ with Total Quality Management philosophies?
3. Briefly discuss ISO Certification norms. In what way can it help an organization to improve their internal efficiency?
4. What is Statistical Process Control? How does it help an organization to improve Quality Control activities?
5. What is the role of the Quality Management Programme in developing human resources?
6. Explain the concepts of Employee Empowerment and Quality of Work-life (QWL). How can these two approaches help quality management function?
7. Explain the concept of the seven tools of quality control? How does a control chart help in improving the quality of an organization?
8. What is the Poke Yoke Method? How is it different from Quality Function Deployment? How can it be implemented in organizations?
9. Describe the characteristics of an OC curve. How does it help in the quality management function?
10. Explain the relevance of the quality control function?
11. Short notes

    (a) Quality Circles

(b) QWL
(c) Employee Empowerment
(d) Cost of Appraisal
(e) Stratification
(f) Six-Sigma

CRITICAL REVIEW QUESTIONS

1. Your company receives jute bags in lots for packing of tea. You have trained the storekeeper to carry out inspection at the receiving end, as any defective jute bag may ultimately affect the quality of tea at the users' end. Suggest what approach of quality control for effective receiving inspection would be suitable for the storekeeper?
2. Your company now carries out destructive tests for checking the quality of steel materials, etching the surface portion of steel and carrying out image testing. However, the company believes destructive tests on each and every item received from the vendors are not possible! Your company has asked you to carry out an effective sampling plan for quality checking. Suggest your line of action

REFERENCES

1. Argyris, Chris. 1975. *Personality and organizations*. New York: Harper.
2. Crosby, Philip. 1984. *Quality without Tears*. New York: McGraw-Hill.
3. Crosby, Philip. 1988. *The Eternally Successful Organization*. New York: McGraw-Hill
4. Moller, Claus. 1988. *Personal Quality: The Basis of All Other Quality*. New York: Time Manager International.
5. Paul, E. Plsek. 1997. *Creativity, Innovation and Quality*. New York: Quality Press.
6. Shewhart, Walter A. 1931. *Economic control of quality of manufactured product*. New York: D. Van Nostrand Company.

ADDITIONAL REFERENCES

1. Barker, T.B. 1986. Quality Engineering by Design: Taguchi's Philosophy. *Quality Progress* 19, no. 12, 32–42.
2. Bhattacharyya, D.K. 1995. Corporate Body Builder – The Emerging Role of the HRD Professional, A Prescriptive Model for Success. *Indian Journal for Training and Development*, New Delhi, April–June.
3. Bhattacharyya, D.K. 1995. Manpower Obsolescence – A study in *Indian Ordnance Factories, International Congress on Economic Transition with Human Face*; Indian Industrial Relations Association, New Delhi, September 3–6.

4. Bhattacharyya, D.K. 2000. Competency Mapping and Manpower Redundancy – Macro Level Study of India Organisations. *Management and Accounting Research* October–December, Volume 4, Issue-2, pp.97–105
5. Bhattacharyya, D.K. 2007. *Human Resource Research Methods*. New Delhi: Oxford University Press.
6. Phadke, M. S. 1989. *Quality Engineering Using Robust Design*. New York: Prentice Hall
7. Mizuno, Shigeru. 1979. *Management for Quality Improvement: The 7 New QC Tools*. Cambridge, MA: Productivity Press
8. Nancy R. Tague. 2004. *The Quality Toolbox*, 2nd ed, ASQ Quality Press
9. Nonka, Ikujoro and Takeuchi, Hikjiro 1995. *The Knowledge Creating Company*. Oxford University Press.
10. Pande, P.S. Neuman, R.P.; and Cavanaugh, R.R. 2002. *The six sigma way*. New York: McGraw-Hill
11. Daniel, Cuthburt. 1976. *Applications of Statistics to Industrial Experimentation*. New York: Wiley,
12. Deming, W. Edwards. 1993. *The New Economics*. Cambridge, MA: MIT Center for Advanced Engineering Study
13. Edward, E., Gordon. 2000. *Skill Wars, Winning the Battle for Productivity and Profit*. Boston: Butterworth-Heinemann.
14. Evans, James R., and William M. Lindsay. 2004. *The Management and Control of Quality*. South-Western Publishing
15. Farnum, Nicholas R. 1994. *Modern Statistical Quality Control and Improvement*. New York: Duxbury Press
16. Garvin, David A. 1988. *Managing Quality: The Strategic and Competitive Edge*. New York, NY: Free Press
17. Hamel, G. and Prahalad, C.K. 1990. The Core Competence of the Corporation. *Harvard Business Review*, Vol.68 No.8, May–June.
18. Hammer, Michael, and James Champy. 1993. *Reengineering the Corporation: A Manifesto for Business Revolution*. New York, NY: Harper Collins Publishers,
19. Ishikawa, Kaoru. 1982. *Guide to Quality Control*. Tokyo, Japan: Asian Productivity Organization
20. James, A., Christiansen 2000. *Competitive Innovation Management*. London: Macmillan Business.
21. Jonne, Cesrani and Peter Greatwood (2001), *Innovation and Creativity*. Crest Publishing House, New Delhi.
22. Juran, Joseph M., and Frank M. Gryna. 1988. *Juran's Quality Control Handbook*. New York, NY: McGraw-Hill,
23. Kackar, R. N. 1985. Off-Line Quality Control, Parameter Design, and the Taguchi Method. *Journal of Quality Technology* 17, no. 4: 176–88.

24. Stolovitch, H.D, and Maurice J.G. 1998. Calculating the Return on Investment in Training: A Critical Analysis and Case Study. *Performance Improvement*, Volume 37, Issue-8, pp. 9–20.

CASE STUDY

Myopia the leader in cardiac care

Myopia is a private hospital, specializing in cardiac treatment with a track record of more than 10,000 cases of successful heart operation. The company provides affordable cardiac care in Hyderabad. Patients come from all parts of India and abroad. The out-patient department is regularly visited by at least 1000 patients per week, of which at least 50% are for post-operative health care. At the time of discharge, *Myopia* issues an electronic card to each patient, containing his/her health data. At subsequent visits, this data are compared with the present state of health and abnormal variations, if any, are further investigated. Patients with normal variation are given medicines and immediately discharged. For this, the company makes use of control charts to assess the longitudinal health improvement (quality) indicators, and at the same time, to study the variation for relating the same to the post-operative treatment advice to the patients. Control charts are attached to the critical care and disease management systems, which provide immediate feedback on the variation in the health status. Guideline adherence increased in clinics that started using *Myopia*'s control charts, which are sensitive enough to detect changes in the health status of patients, both before and after operation.

Myopia's use of control charts as decision support systems gives them the ability to reduce the cycle time to advice patients. To extend the facility to patients, even when they live far away from Hyderabad, the company provides the opportunity to patients to send their data through electronic mail, this is automatically filled into the control charts and powered to give quick diagnostic advice The company feels that such decision-support facilitates quick response to patients' needs, and at the same time, provides quality healthcare support, which over the years, could make *Myopia* a trusted name in cardiac healthcare in India.

Myopia's analysis has indicated that even with such decision support systems, the chances of error are very significant. *Myopia* would like to introduce *poke yoke* along with their control charts to reinvent the process of healthcare.

Discussion Question

As a specialist in statistical process control, suggest approaches for introducing poke yoke at *Myopia*.

CHAPTER 10

Six Sigma in Production and Operations Management

LEARNING OBJECTIVES

After reading this chapter, you will be able to understand:

- Definitions and Concepts of Six Sigma
- Basic Characteristics of Six Sigma
- Six Sigma: Introduction in Organizations
- Steps in Six Sigma Implementation
- Calculation of Sigma Level
- Six Sigma and Culture, Quick Response Manufacturing and Lean Practices
- Six Sigma and HR Strategies

Opening Vignette

TVS Motors' pursuit of Six Sigma level Quality

Six Sigma involves a cultural transformation. Along with their Six Sigma initiative, *TVS Motors* has integrated Total Quality Management (TQM) practices, to encompass all their business practices. To ensure that TQM practices lead to improved performance, *TVS* introduced enterprise-wide performance management systems to track every employee's performance with their own metrics. This performance management system has Managing Points and Check Points (MPCP). With the help of the managing points, *TVS* measures its employees against certain performance metrics, and with the check points, the company ascertains the important enablers that help in achieving the managing points or performance targets. Thus, managing points are the performance metrics for those who work at the executive level, while the enablers of the check points are for employees in general, as they contribute to process compliance. Performance dashboards, like a balanced scorecard, help *TVS Motors* fine-tune their business strategy. *TVS* follows the participative process to fix targets. Through this process, *TVS* is gradually strengthening its Six Sigma level quality achievement.

10.1 INTRODUCTION

In a globally competitive market, organizations cannot sustain themselves without being price competitive and achieving excellence in quality. Achieving both these aspects require organizations to take a relook at their processes. By continuously improving and re-creating the process, organizations can achieve the highest level of quality, as new processes become error free. right from the beginning. Such organizational improvement strategies are known as the Six Sigma approach. Six Sigma (or zero defects) not only helps the organization to achieve excellence in quality, but also helps in the process of eliminating wastage and benefits the organization in terms of cost savings. Obviously, for this, organizations can also be price competitive, along with excellence in the quality of goods and services. Six Sigma is a learning continuum, and it can only be implemented by reinforcing the knowledge and competencies of people working with the organization. Among others, it requires embracing test practices, and processes in production and operations. Unlike the case in total quality management, which requires identification of problems, and then setting right the same to minimize the defects (without discarding the existing process), Six Sigma reinvents the process to make it defect free, so that problems never arise. Hence, it requires thorough understanding of the process, and developing and standardizing the defect free process for better quality and cost competitiveness. It benefits both the organization and the customers. While the organizations get the benefit of achieving defect free production of goods and services, and resultant cost savings, customers can get value for money in terms of quality and cost competitiveness.

Although the initial focus of Six Sigma was on production and operations, today it can be practiced for any business process improvement, including in the service industry. It is essentially a customer-centric top–down approach, requiring the involvement of all those who are engaged in the process.

10.2 DEFINITIONS AND CONCEPTS

According to the Greek alphabet, the etymological meaning of sigma is the standard deviation of a process. The concept was developed by *Motorola* in the mid-1980's and adopted by many major manufacturing organizations including *General Electric*. With *GE Capital*'s conformity to the Six Sigma level of quality in 1996, its scope has now been extended to any business process, including the service industry.

Six Sigma is defined as an error-free process improvement strategy to minimize waste and resources, to achieve customer satisfaction and achieve overall improvement of performance and profitability. The scope of Six Sigma is broader than Total Quality Management (TQM), as it goes beyond the detection and correction of defects, in that it leads to the development of a new defect-free process. Using our TQM knowledge as the base, we apply Six Sigma methodologies, and call it the statistical application of TQM.

TQM involves good quality management practices, but we cannot quantify the degree of quality achievement. Six Sigma, however, can quantify the degree of our quality level using the standard formula, which we will explain later. Thus, in terms of Six Sigma, we are able to measure overall business process improvement, using various process-centric metrics. It is, therefore, more strategic than TQM.

As a process, it requires the identification of objectives, collection of data, analysis of results, so that defects in the products and services are reduced, and gradually, companies can reach the stage of zero which is the highest sigma level. At the highest sigma level, that is, at the Six Sigma level, which we consider as the highest level of quality, we can only get 3.4 defects per million job opportunities.

10.2.1 Basic Characteristics

Based on our discussion above, we can outline the basic characteristics of Six Sigma as follows:

- Sigma denotes standard deviation of a process.
- *Motorola* developed it during the mid-1980's, and subsequently, *GE* also used it in their manufacturing.
- First adoption of Six Sigma in the service industry was at *GE Capital* in 1996.
- For the benefit of quantification, we call it statistical application of TQM.
- Sigma quality level denotes the output of a process.
- Six Sigma is a business improvement strategy; it includes waste minimization, quality improvement, cost reduction, cycle time improvement and achieves a higher level of customer satisfaction.
- It makes use of strategies, tools and statistical methodologies to improve customer satisfaction and the bottom line of these organizations.
- Sigma values indicate the degree of quality achievement. Higher sigma values indicate better quality, and lower sigma values represent poor quality of products and services.
- With Six Sigma level quality, we achieve virtually zero defects, as the allowable defects limit is only 3.4 per million job opportunity (DPMO). Such defects are known as allowable rejection for un-assignable causes.

10.3 INTRODUCTION OF SIX SIGMA IN ORGANIZATIONS

The achievement of Six Sigma level quality cannot be mandated by certification. It is a self-assessment tool for measuring process quality, which cascades to the quality of goods and services. As it involves a complex process of identification, development, and standardization, it cannot be achieved overnight. It requires the sustained efforts of the organization in selecting a particular process, and studying the same to develop it as an error-free one. After short-listing a process for Six Sigma compliance, organizations need to understand the critical to quality (CTQ) factors from the customers' perspectives, and then reinvent the process to achieve zero-defects or the highest level of quality. Some of the possible areas of Six Sigma application in organizations can be listed as follows:

- Processes
- Products and services
- Investor relationship
- Design
- Vendor relationship
- Recruitment
- Training and Development
- Performance Management, etc.

Some examples from the corporate world, can help us understand the process selection and critical to quality factors.

Asian Paints competes with *Berger Paints* in the domestic market. In the paint market, the availability of paint at the dealer's point is considered the most crucial strategic requirement, as the customer's choice of paint is time independent, and customers may not wait until the paint of their choice is available; they decide rather quickly to choose an alternative, taking price and quality considerations into account. To ensure real-time availability of paints, reducing the cycle time for order booking and delivery, *Asian Paints* has now made available a networked computer at the dealer's end to facilitate on-line order booking and processing, so it now takes 12 hours to reach the item to the dealer, so that customers do not opt for a competitor's products.

Exide enjoys the highest market share in automotive batteries. However, to esure that customers remain satisfied, it introduced Bat-mobile services – mobile vans that roam around cities receiving calls from the customers, and reaching them in less than half-an-hour to attend to the battery servicing. The defective battery is replaced with a stand-by; the defective one is sent for repair and subsequently delivered to the customer. This entire process ensures customer satisfaction and loyalty to the brand.

Likewise in manufacturing, machining jobs are now done using the services of a CNC Machining Centre, which has replaced conventional lathe machines. This process saves time and ensures accuracy and precision in machining jobs.

All these examples point out various options for cycle time reduction, which benefits the company immensely.

Six Sigma can also ensure valued-added products and services with substantial reduction in costs. Today, we observe various valued-added features in a mobile phone; for example, it can now function as a calculator, a calendar, an FM radio, provide e-mail services and many others functions, in addition to meeting the basic need for communication.

Let us consider a typical case of a multi-specialty hospital, which attends to the needs of terminally ill referral patients. Cycle time requirements from the reception desk to the bed, unless reduced significantly (as here, even a fraction of a second counts), patients may collapse even in the process of shifting. Through Six Sigma, we can identify the redundant activities in the process, and can improve cycle time significantly.

Likewise, Six Sigma can improve the activities of the entire organization through process improvement with a win–win approach, that is, through customer satisfaction and organizational bottom-line improvement.

A typical inverted relationship in Six Sigma breakthrough strategy (Fig. 10.1) would look like:

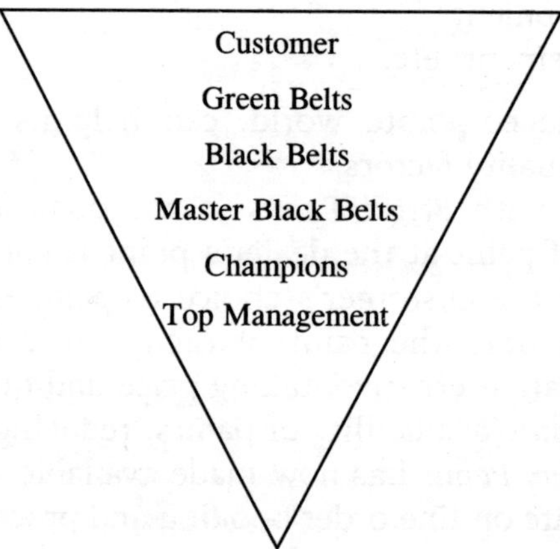

Figure 10.1 *Inverted pyramid relationship structure in Six Sigma*

At the bottom of the inverted pyramid is the top management. Top management supports and balances the Six Sigma implementation process in organizations. Top management selects the Champions (executive leaders), who in turn select the Master Black Belts, and facilitate the process of selection of Black Belts and Green Belts. The primary role of Champions is to select the leaders and connect them to Six Sigma. They activate the process improvement strategy. Master Black Belts sensitize people in the organization about the Six Sigma breakthrough strategy, and identify Six Sigma projects. Master Black Belts also train and develop Black

Belts and Green Belts to build their capabilities to handle Six Sigma projects. They also organize people, design cross-functional experiments, structure and co-ordinate projects and meetings, collect and organize information. Black Belts apply Six Sigma tools in identified projects. Green Belts are general workers, who are associated with the projects. They gradually embrace Six Sigma practices in their jobs. As Green Belts are operations level employees, who gradually introduce Six Sigma, without discarding their present activities, their involvement is only part of the Six Sigma implementation process, or else their regular scheduled jobs may suffer. Master Black Belts and Black Belts, however, put in 100% of their time for Six Sigma projects.

To successfully implement Six Sigma in organizations, we make use of statistical tools and techniques, and develop a culture of shared vision, to involve all cross-sections of employees and workers. This facilitates the proliferation of a culture of mutual cooperation and support, team-work, commitment from the people, which ultimately contributes to success.

To implement Six Sigma, Mikel Harry (2000) suggests intensive training for all members of the organization; this is to be followed by the identification of the Six Sigma catalysts. As it is a customer-centric and customer-driven approach to quality improvement, customers' expectations are made clear at the outset. Obviously, this requires an understanding of CTQs, that is, customer's perceived critical to quality factors.

10.4 STEPS FOR IMPLEMENTATION

Through Six Sigma, we strive to achieve zero defects in products and services, minimize the costs by waste elimination, optimize our resources, and in the process, we achieve the highest level of customer satisfaction and increase our profitability (bottom-line). For all these reasons, we call Six Sigma a break-through strategy. Six Sigma is important for production and operations management, as it can help in identifying issues pertaining to manufacturing and services, technology, quality, inventory management, designing and delivery systems.

For achieving Six Sigma level quality process that leads to defect free products and services, we follow eight steps. These steps are Recognize, Define, Measure, Analyze, Improve, Control, Standardize and Integrate. The eight steps are again broadly classified into four categories, as illustrated in Table 10.1.

At every step, we need to perform specific tasks for the implementation of Six Sigma. The identification phase identifies critical business processes in terms of their contribution to customers' satisfaction and organizational profitability. Through characterization, we consolidate the inputs for process improvement, understanding the quality gap, and aligning it with organizational goals and objectives. In the characterization process, Black Belts play a crucial role by listing the core product or service characteristics, and charting the process involved therein. Various tools like process control charts, different statistical tools, etc. are used for these jobs. In the analysis phase, a detailed study of the reasons for the quality problems in products and services are made, and the gravity of the quality problems is understood and categorized into technology- or process-related issues.

Table 10.1 *Six Sigma Steps*

	Stages	Strategy phase	Objectives	
B *R* *E* *A* *K*	Identification	Recognize and Define	To identify key business issues	
T *H* *R* *O*	Characterization	Measure and Analyze	To understand the level of current performance	*B* *L* *A*
U *G* *H* *S* *T*	Optimization	Improve and control	To initiate breakthrough improvement	*C* *K* *B* *E*
R *A* *T* *E* *G* *Y*	Institutionalization	Standardize and integrate	To transform day-to-day conduct of business	*L* *T* *S*

(*Source: D.K. Bhattacharyya (2010), Cross Cultural Management – Text and Cases, PHI Learning, New Delhi*)

The optimization phase is also known as the Design for Six Sigma (DFSS) stage. At this stage, we focus on reconfiguring products and services, to ensure that it conforms to Six Sigma level quality. In other words, at this stage, we develop a process to ensure zero defects in our products and services. This is the most crucial phase for achieving Six Sigma level quality. At the outset, problem-causing variables are identified, and products and services are designed eliminating such variables. In the optimization phase, strict monitoring and control is enforced to ensure non-recurrence of those problem-creating variables which were earlier identified as quality problem mediators for products and services. This, therefore, is the actual phase of process improvement that leads to customer satisfaction and bottom line improvement for the organizations.

With all these, we finally reach the stage of Six Sigma implementation. Through the process of institutionalization, standardization and integration, we ensure conformance to Six Sigma practices in the identified processes.

The stages of Six Sigma implementation explained above is also known as DMAIC, where:

D = Define
M = Measure
A = Analyze
I = Improve
C = Control

Along with DMAIC, we also use the term DMADV. Here, the only difference is, after the analyzing phase, the process is defined once again, and thereafter verified. Therefore, we can write DMADV as follows:

D = Define
M = Measure
A = Analyze
D = Define
V = Verify

Therefore, the purposes of DMAIC and DMADV are one and the same, only the approaches to achieve Six Sigma are different. Even then, we can differentiate between the two on the following grounds:

- The DMAIC methodology is used when a product or a process already exists in the company. DMADV, on the other hand, is used when the process or product is a new one.
- In DMAIC, the root cause of the defects is analyzed and determined. In DMADV, on the other hand, various process options are analyzed.

10.5 CALCULATING SIGMA LEVEL QUALITY

From the discussions above, it is clear that Six Sigma is an organizational improvement or break-through strategy to achieve the highest quality of products and services, and at the same time, customer satisfaction and profitability. Achieving Six Sigma right at the beginning is not possible. It requires sustained efforts from the production and operations managers to achieve the six sigma level. Initial efforts may partially ease the quality problems, which we can understand in terms of the achievement of the sigma level, using the standard formula. To calculate the sigma level, we use the Defects per Million Opportunities (DPMO) formula. To use this formula, we first need to identify and define critical to quality factors as perceived by customers. CTQs are opportunities for error. These apart, we need to have data on the following:

UNIT: Number of items produced or serviced
DEFECT: Number of defects
OPPORTUNITY: The chance for the occurrence of a defect

To illustrate, let us take the example of an FMCG company engaged in toothpaste manufacture. From the customer's point of view, a defect occurs, when the toothpaste fails to meet their expectations. Let us assume that there are two critical to quality (CTQ) factors from the point of view of the customers. These are less foam and hardness of the paste. These, therefore, are two areas which present opportunities for error. Once quantitative details about the number of units and defects are made available, we can use the following formula to calculate the sigma level:

$$\frac{\text{Number of Defects}}{\text{Number of Opportunities} \times \text{No. of Units for error}} X^{1,00,0000}$$

Suppose a manufacturer has sold 2500 tubes of toothpaste to customers, of which 10 were reported to have less foaming agents, and 5 were reported to be harder. The calculation, therefore, would be as follows:

$$\frac{15}{2 \times 2500} = X^{1,000,000} = 3000$$

3000 DPMO almost corresponds to 4.25 sigma level, which indicates, the hypothetical toothpaste manufacturer needs to further identify process flaws and improve the quality of the toothpaste. At the Six Sigma level, DPMO should be 3.4, or 3.4 defects per million. The number of opportunities for error in this case is two, as we have assumed two CTQs. Number of defects is 15 (10 + 5), which we obtain by adding the defects classified under two CTQs.

Now, of course, the Six Sigma calculation process has become easier with the availability of standard computer software. At the end of this chapter, we have appended a Six Sigma calculation table.

10.5.1 Six Sigma and Normal Distribution Curve

The normal distribution curve explains the frequency of an observed process value. We define a normal distribution curve by mean and standard deviation values. With mean, we measure the propensity of centralization of the curve. While with standard deviation, we explain the width or narrowness of the curve.

Let us observe the following curves (Fig 10.2):

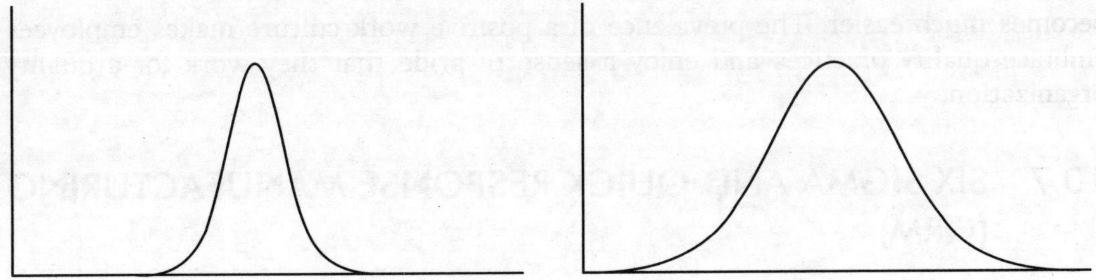

Figure 10.2 *Normal distribution curve*

The first curve has a propensity to centralization. While the second curve is wider; this indicates high standard deviation.

A Six Sigma curve can be graphically explained as in Fig.10.3:

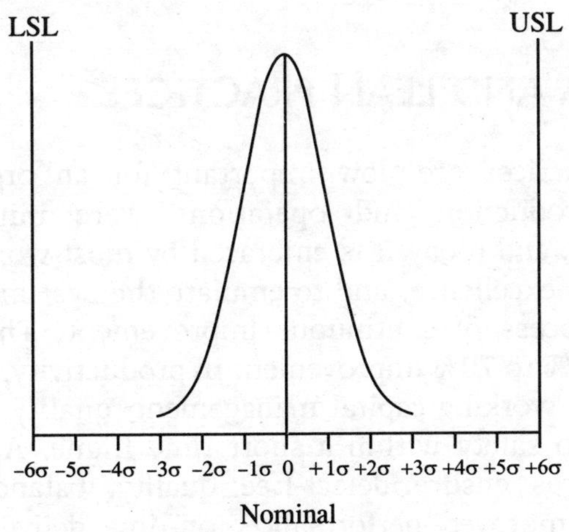

Figure 10.3 *A Six Sigma curve*

This curve indicates that the process has attained the Six Sigma level of quality.

10.6 SIX SIGMA AND ORGANIZATIONAL CULTURE

Although Six Sigma focusses on process improvement, because of its involvement of different cross-sections of people, it is highly dependent on the culture of the organization. Some important cultural constructs for Six Sigma implementation in organizations are team work, open communication, propensity of people to follow standard operating procedures, shared vision, organizational receptivity to employees' suggestions, culture of innovation and creativity, etc. When such cultural constructs are available in the organization, the process of Six Sigma implementation becomes much easier. The prevalence of a positive work culture makes employees embrace quality practices and enjoy a sense of pride that they work for a quality organization.

10.7 SIX SIGMA AND QUICK RESPONSE MANUFACTURING (QRM)

QRM is also another culture-dependent organizational strategy. Six Sigma facilitates QRM by reducing cycle time for processes, lead time for different activities, etc. The QRM process actually identifies the 'white spaces' in-between and within the processes and eliminates those that cause a time lag, to improve the operational efficiency. Like Six Sigma, QRM also focusses on continuous improvement in products and services, matching customer expectations, and helps in eliminating waste.

10.8 SIX SIGMA AND LEAN PRACTICES

Lean management practices are now important for an organization to survive competition. Lean production and operations were initially developed and implemented by *Toyota*, and today it is embraced by most world class organizations to achieve performance excellence, and to emulate the best methods and processes, which support the process of continuous improvement. Through lean practices, *Toyota* could achieve 50% to 70% improvement in productivity, efficient management of floor space, efficient working capital management, quality improvement and the highest conformance to safety within a short time frame. Apart from operational efficiency, lean practices ensure defect-free quality, balances the stakeholders' expectations through improved performance, on-time delivery to customers, and substantial cost savings for scalability of operations.

Six Sigma strengthens lean practices through the process of value stream analysis. Value stream analysis reduces the process delay, optimizes resources, achieves quality, and reduces costs.

Lean practices in manufacturing organizations create cells, and ensure zero or minimum work-in-process within cells, This is ensured by controlling the work-in-process within a cell using pull systems, like *Kanbans*. The literal meaning of *kanban* is a signboard or billboard. *Kanbans* facilitate just-in-time production. The system helps us to determine what to produce, when to produce and how much to produce. A pull system is a customer demand based process. With *kanbans* we can introduce the pull system in the production process. Pull systems are continuously developed to improve the value stream.

10.9 SIX SIGMA THROUGH STRATEGIC HR PRACTICES

Six Sigma is a learning continuum. Hence, to achieve the Six Sigma level, it is important for the organization to focus on strategic HR practices. In production and operations management, strategic HR practices, among others, require building the competencies of human resources, so that people can actively participate in Six Sigma projects to achieve excellence in products and services. For Six Sigma, strategic HR helps in the following ways:

- To make employees understand organizational values
- To develop a shared vision and mission to give a common direction to all employees
- To increase employees' commitment to quality
- To make employees multi-skilled
- To increase the motivation level of employees for Six Sigma level projects

10.9.1 Six Sigma Practices in India

In India, Six Sigma breakthrough strategies are now being practiced by many organizations. Among them, noted organizations like the *TVS* Group and the *Tata* Group. While the Six Sigma level is yet to be achieved, *TELCO* is reported to have achieved the 4.5 sigma level by reducing their defects per million opportunities. Incidentally, *TELCO* retained Japanese consultants for this project. Various other organizations are in different phases of implementation of the Six Sigma breakthrough strategy.

SUMMARY

1. This chapter discussed the concepts and processes of Six Sigma, highlighting its important characteristics, and its significance in a competitive, global market. The process of introduction of Six Sigma, detailing the various steps involved in it was explained.
2. A detailed discussion of sigma level computation is included. Six Sigma was related to organizational culture, quick response manufacturing and lean management practices.
3. Finally, HR strategies and how these can help Six Sigma achievement in organizations have also been discussed.

KEY WORDS

Six Sigma is a culture-based management philosophy. It emphasizes the setting of objectives, collection of data, and the analysis of results to reduce defects in products and services. It systematically measures the defects in a process, eliminates them, and in the process, tries to achieve zero defects. At Six Sigma level, which is the highest level of quality, we can only find 3.4 defects per million job opportunities.

Champions These are executive leaders who identify individual leaders to ensure that key functions are connected to Six Sigma. They are the grounding force to make the strategy work.

CTQs are opportunities for error. Since this is a quantitative measurement, we also need to have discrete information about units, number of defects, and opportunity for error to calculate CTQs.

Lean Practices These are characterized by world class performance (key measures), world class practices (methods and processes) and the culture of relentless continuous improvement (environment).

GENERAL REVIEW QUESTIONS

1. Define the concept of Six Sigma? How is it different from TQM?
2. What are the basic characteristics of Six Sigma?
3. How is Six Sigma introduced in an organization?
4. Describe the steps involved in Six Sigma implementation.
5. Discuss the relationship between Six Sigma and culture.
6. Elaborate on how lean management practices can facilitate Six Sigma implementation in an organization.
7. Short notes
   (a) Quick Response Manufacturing
   (b) DPMO
   (c) Critical to Quality factors
   (d) Breakthrough Strategy
   (e) Master Black Belt

CRITICAL REVIEW QUESTION

1. A well-known manufacturer of steel in India has requested advice on Six Sigma implementation. Suggest a possible course of action.

ADDITIONAL REFERENCES

1. Bhattacharyya, D.K. 2000. Competency Mapping and Manpower Redundancy – A Macro level study of Indian Organizations. *Management and Accounting Research,* October–December, Volume 4, Issue-2, pp. 97–105.
2. Bhattacharyya, D.K. 2002. Achieving Six Sigma through HR Strategy – A focus on Desired Organizational Practices. *The Chartered Accountant,* Vol. 51, No. 3, PP. 253–259.

3. Bhattacharyya, D.K. 2011. *Organizational Change and Development*. New Delhi: Oxford University Press.
4. Bhattacharyya, D.K. 2010. *Cross-cultural Management*. New Delhi: PHI Learning
5. Champy, J. 1995. *Reengineering Management*. New York: Harper Business Books
6. Davenport, Thomas, and Short, J. 1990. The New Industrial Engineering: Information Technology and Business Process Redesign. *Sloan Management Review*, Summer, pp 11–27
7. Davenport, Thomas. 1993. *Process Innovation: Reengineering work through information technology*. Boston: Harvard Business School Press
8. Drucker, Peter. 1972. Work and Tools, in *Technology and Culture* W. Kranzberg and W.H. Davenport eds. New York
9. Greenbaum, Joan. 1995. *Windows on the workplace*. Cornerstone
10. George, Eckes. 2001. The Six Sigma Revolution. New York: John Wiley and Sons, Inc.
11. Guha, S. Kettinger, W.J. and Teng, T.C. 1993. Business Process Reengineering: Building a Comprehensive Methodology. *Information Systems Management*, Summer
12. Hammer, Michael. 1990. Reengineering Work: Don't automate, obliterate. *Harvard Business Review*, Jul/Aug 1990, pp 104–112
13. Hammer, Michael and Champy, James. 1993. *Reengineering the Corporation: A Manifesto for Business Revolution*. New York: Harper Business Books.
14. Hammer, M. and Stanton, S. 1995. *The Reengineering Revolution*. London: Harper Collins.
15. Johansson, Henry J. et al. 1993. *Business Process Reengineering: Break Point Strategies for Market Dominance*. John Wiley & Sons
16. Kristine, Ellis. 2001. Mastering Six Sigma. *Training*, December, pp. 30–35
17. Leavitt, H.J. 1965. Applied Organizational Change in Industry: Structural, Technological and Humanistic Approaches in *Handbook of Organizations*, James March ed. Chicago: Rand McNally.
18. Mikel, Harry and Richard, Schroeder. 2000. *Six Sigma*. New York: Currency.
19. Richard, CH, Chua. 2001. Six Sigma: A Pursuit of Excellence and Dramatic Results. *Today's Manager*, August–September pp. 43–45

CASE STUDY

The language of quality in a cross-cultural set up: Lessons from *SKF*

SKF is an international giant in roller bearings. It is headquartered in Sweden and has manufacturing units in four countries – U.K., Germany, France and Italy. Cultural factors could make it difficult for *SKF* to adopt a unified policy with regard to Six Sigma and quality management factors, both of which are culture dependent.

Successful introduction of TQM and Six Sigma management practices requires a cultural transformation. Organizations with multiple locations across cultures obviously face this problem, as apart from organization-specific cultural constructs, national culture continues to influence employee beliefs and value systems. Quality management and Six Sigma practices require the adoption of a uniform concept for the entire organization, despite its presence in multiple locations, cutting across borders.

Quality management practices, in terms of cultural constructs, are influenced by power, distance, and uncertainty avoidance dimensions, according to Professor Geert Hofstede's model. Based on his *IBM* study in 72 different countries, Professor Geert Hofstede, came out with a cultural dimensions model with five different constructs. These are power and distance, collectivism and individualism, femininity versus masculinity, uncertainty avoidance, and long-term versus short-term orientation.

All the countries where *SKF* has its operations have one thing in common – they are 'individualist' in terms of culture. Except France, all the countries are 'masculine.' Again in terms of 'power–distance' construct of culture, France scores high, Italy scores moderate, while the UK and Germany score low. Similar differences are also observed for uncertainty avoidance. Except the UK, a high uncertainty avoidance syndrome is evident in all other countries.

In terms of cultural constructs, the quality perceptions of the countries are also different. For example, in the UK, quality is more of a compliance with specifications. In Germany, the main emphasis is on quality as pertaining to customer satisfaction. In France, the main aspect of quality is that it is global or total in nature. In Italy, the main view of quality is as an attitude.

SKF's products are of a very high quality, with relatively less customer complaints. Employees take genuine pride in their work with the company. Despite this, *SKF* had initial problems to introduce unified quality management and Six Sigma practices, due to lack of commitment for quality in the UK plants, due to rules and procedural formalities in Germany, due to communication problems in France and problems of attitude in Italy.

Appreciating all these as the inevitable outcome of culture, the company emphasized culture-specific values and systems and achieved a global cultural identity.

Discussion Question

Read the case study and document your understanding of the cultural influence on quality and Six Sigma management practices.

Six Sigma Chart

Defects per 100	Defects per 10,000	Defects per 1,000,000	Success rate	Sigma Value
93	**9,330**	**933,000**	**7%**	**0.0**
92	9,190	919,000	8%	0.1
90	9,030	903,000	10%	0.2
88	8,850	885,000	12%	0.3
86	8,640	864,000	14%	0.4
84	8,410	841,000	16%	0.5
82	8,160	816,000	18%	0.6
79	7,880	788,000	21%	0.7
76	7,580	758,000	24%	0.8
73	7,260	726,000	27%	0.9
69	**6,910**	**691,000**	**31%**	**1.0**
66	6,550	655,000	34%	1.1
62	6,180	618,000	38%	1.2
58	5,790	579,000	42%	1.3
54	5,400	540,000	46%	1.4
50	5,000	500,000	50%	1.5
46	4,600	460,000	54.0%	1.6
42	4,210	421,000	57.9%	1.7
38	3,820	382,000	61.8%	1.8
34	3,450	345,000	65.5%	1.9
31	**3,090**	**309,000**	**69.1%**	**2.0**
27	2,740	274,000	72.6%	2.1
24	2,420	242,000	75.8%	2.2
21	2,120	212,000	78.8%	2.3
18	1,840	184,000	81.6%	2.4
16	1,590	159,000	84.1%	2.5
14	1,360	136,000	86.4%	2.6
12	1,150	115,000	88.5%	2.7
10	968	96,800	90.32%	2.8
8	808	80,800	91.92%	2.9
7	**668**	**66,800**	**93.32%**	**3.0**
6	548	54,800	94.52%	3.1
5	446	44,600	95.54%	3.2
4	359	35,900	96.41%	3.3

3	287	28,700	97.13%	3.4
2	228	22,800	97.72%	3.5
2	179	17,900	98.21%	3.6
1	139	13,900	98.61%	3.7
1	107	10,700	98.93%	3.8
1	82	8,200	99.18%	3.9
1	**62**	**6,210**	**99.379%**	**4.0**
	47	4,660	99.534%	4.1
	35	3,470	99.653%	4.2
	26	2,560	99.744%	4.3
	19	1,870	99.813%	4.4
	14	1,350	99.865%	4.5
	10	968	99.903%	4.6
	7	687	99.931%	4.7
	5	483	99.952%	4.8
	3	337	99.966%	4.9
	2	**233**	**99.9767%**	**5.0**
	2	159	99.9841%	5.1
	1	108	99.9892%	5.2
	1	72	99.9928%	5.3
		48	99.9952%	5.4
		32	99.9968%	5.5
		21	99.9979%	5.6
		13	99.9987%	5.7
		9	99.9991%	5.8
		5	99.9995%	5.9
		3.4	**99.99966%**	**6.0**

CHAPTER 11

BPR, TQM, Cross-cultural Aspects and Models of Excellence

LEARNING OBJECTIVES

After reading this chapter, you will be able to understand:

- The Concept of Business Process Restructuring (BPR) and its Influence on Production and Operations Management (POM)
- Technology and the Influence of Culture on POM
- TQM and the Culture of Quality
- Cross-cultural Issues of POM Functions
- Pro-active and Re-active Culture
- Best Practice Models of POM
- Six Sigma Practices
- Lean, *Toyota* Production System (TPS) and Quick Response Manufacturing

Opening Vignette

Godrej – The Indian company that has always believed in staying ahead

In post-independence India, *Godrej*, like other Indian entrepreneurs had to tone down its change requirements at the organizational level, reflecting an obvious reluctance on the part of the nation, as a whole, to change. Customers had to accept the shoddy products and services offered by companies. Inertia at the national level, adversely affected the need for change at the individual or personal level. Organizations failed to promote the desired work culture to bring about change in the desired areas. However, *Godrej* from its inception had encouraged change. Some of the change tools used by *Godrej* are summarized as follows:

Godrej made extensive use of the *kaizen* systems and felt that this led to a significant increase in employee involvement and an improvement in their morale. By effecting substantial cost savings, the company became more flexible, and could increase its capability to adapt to the changing needs of the environment. In terms of quantitative achievement, it could reduce change over time on the shop-floors by more than 70%; increase the ability to pace its manufacturing to the needs of the market, yet enjoy the privilege of economies of scale. It could reduce inventory holding of finished products by over 40%, by developing a quick market response. With the introduction of Total Productive Maintenance, the company could reduce breakdowns and bring down the cost of spares and repairs to about 50% from the pre-introduction phase. The company even made one of its high pressure boilers in the Vikhroli factory redundant by achieving efficiency in energy consumption. Similarly, exercises in value analysis reduced the cost of materials, while enhancing the quality of output. As in manufacturing, the company could bring about positive changes in other functional areas like finance, marketing, HR, thereby promoting a culture of improvement. Today, at *Godrej*, employees look for opportunities to make improvements and savings.

11.1 INTRODUCTION

Effective POM functions require the systematic restructuring of organizations through business process restructuring (BPR), lean management and *Toyota* Production Systems (TPS) practices, Six Sigma, total quality management (TQM), and quick response manufacturing (QRM). These are considered the major drivers for organizational transformation. Along with the technicalities, practising these models require the organization to understand its own underlying culture. However, the most important part of an effective production and operations management function is to understand and manage technology.

BPR is essential to enable organizations to keep pace with global competition. It requires organizations to align with global change to redefine their missions, and if required, even refocus their business priorities. Two good examples of BPR are *Dell* and *IBM*. *Dell* reengineered from a computer renting business to a reseller with their K-12 workforce. Corporate circles were apprehensive and even skeptical about *Dell*'s attempt. However, today *Dell* is a success story. Similarly, *IBM* unable to sustain itself in price competition had to change its business focus from desktop manufacturing and selling to business process outsourcing (BPO) and other IT-enabled services (ITeS). Obviously, among others, BPR also requires production restructuring, redefining the processes and practices.

Similarly, lean management, TPS, TQM, Six Sigma, QRM, etc. require to be understood in terms of production and operations management functions.

Through the process of internationalization of production and operations management functions, globally, companies are now able to emulate best practice models, both in terms of theories and applications. In this chapter, we have also discussed some of these models, which can benefit organizations in terms of achieving quality and cost competitiveness. The appropriate mix of culture and practices for organizational advantages, particularly when organizations go global, has also been discussed.

11.2 BUSINESS PROCESS REENGINEERING – CONCEPTS AND DEFINITIONS

A process is theoretically understood as a certain structured, measured set of activities (Davenport 1993). Business process is defined as "logical tasks which are performed to achieve some defined business outcome" (Davenport and Short, 1990). Characteristically, we observe two important attributes of a project – customers and the cross-organizational aspect. Customers can be either internal or external, internal customers are the employees of the organization, while external customers are those who buy products and services from the companies, and other stakeholders like shareholders, suppliers, society; the cross-organizational factor indicates occurrences across or between organizational sub-units. Porter and Millar (1985) suggested understanding the business process of any organization in terms of an organizational value chain method. From the production and operations management point of view, every process has a process owner. These process owners develop new products, order goods from vendors, and even create the marketing plan. Therefore, the three dimensions of processes, according to Davenport and Short (1990), are:

- **Entities**: Processes take place between organizational entities. They could be inter-organizational, inter-functional or inter-personal.
- **Objects**: Processes result in the manipulation of objects. These objects could be physical or informational.
- **Activities**: Processes could involve two types of activities – managerial and operational.

Successful business process reengineering considers people-related issues as well. Employee empowerment, team work, developing communications, etc. are the people-related issues which are considered by the organization. According to Hammer and Champy (1993), introducing teamwork and empowerment of employees in any organization would not be possible unless these are done by addressing the culture of the organization. Therefore, through BPR, organizations create value-added jobs and structures, recognizing the values and beliefs systems.

Therefore, the restructuring of production and operations through BPR; particularly when organizations go global, needs to be thought of in the context of culture, which is a potential inhibitor and can act against the process of restructuring. Realizing the importance of culture-fit in the organizational restructuring process, Davenport (1993) considered organizational and human resource issues as being more important than technological issues in BPR. Davenport felt that culture exerts an effect, both on employee empowerment and control. Empowerment ensures participative management, open communications and greater employee satisfaction. People get actively involved in the BPR process, when they feel empowered. BPR in a control-oriented culture can work in a situation where the jobs are protocol-bound, and technology plays a more important role in achieving quality and effectiveness. However, absolute control may inhibit innovation and creativity, and may have an adverse effect on new design, and on new product development.

Culture of Control at *McDonald's*

Control fits in with *McDonald's culture*. Its core objective is to achieve the same quality and the same level of service worldwide. To ensure this, *McDonalds* has developed standard operating procedures (SOP), detailing each and every activity and sub-activity. Employees are supposed to perform their jobs in line with the SOP details, and cannot be innovative. It has to be understood that innovation-based BPR through employee empowerment cannot fit an organization of this type.

Thus, the effect of culture on BPR may vary, as culture can be an enabler, inhibitor or an outcome. Johansson et al (1983) had suggested that during the initial phase of BPR (the Discover phase), it is important to consider values and culture. In the next phase – the phase of Redesign – values and issues of culture are ignored, as it is at this stage that the organization systematizes processes. In the third phase – the Realize phase – issues of culture come up again. It is at this stage of BPR that organizations create a new corporate culture.

Andrews and Stalick (1994) have recognized that organizational culture is the "collective rules and beliefs, which become explicit through language, symbols, myths, and rituals... ". They believe that changing embedded corporate values is perhaps the most powerful change. In contrast to Johansson et al, Andrews and Stalick warn that leaders must not use negative reinforcement, but rather, encourage an environment which is:

1. reflective
2. open
3. problem solving
4. communicative
5. facilitating
6. packed with ideas
7. fun
8. learning
9. productive
10. quality-focussed and
11. customer-driven.

Obeng and Crainer (1994) highlighted the idea that cultural change precedes BPR. Hence, a given culture may decide the outcome of BPR. Their views of culture can be classified as an internal variable and enabler. Change addresses behaviour and values and the cultural type is task specific. This is why we say culture decides the way we do our work.

Leadership is primarily setting new behaviour patterns and also includes visioning and developing people and oneself. Vidgen et al (1994) see culture, or at least the neglect of people, as an inhibitor to effective implementation of BPR. They promote soft systems methodologies (SSM) that use "cultural stream analysis to establish which changes are 'culturally feasible". According to these authors "successful uses of the [SSM] methodology has been both participative and incremental in nature. Instrumentalism derives from its assumption that culture and politics are 'givens'."

The key aspect of BPR is that it defines completely new and radical ways of how an organization undertakes its activities. In this process, organizations often innovate, cutting across the organization and even outside it. Today, BPR is the strategic demand, and it cannot be differentiated from process improvements. Successful implementation of BPR brings order to organizations and provides business benefits.

BPR can be defined as the fundamental rethinking and redesign of the business processes of an organization, addressing technological, human and internal ways of functioning of the organization, keeping pace with the changes, to achieve success in critical performance areas like cost, quality, service and delivery. Strategy is at the core of BPR. The word BPR has now become so synonymous with manpower redundancy (although it is not), some scholars prefer to refer to it as Business Process Management (BPM).

11.3 IMPACT OF BPR ON ORGANIZATIONS

To assess the impact of BPR, McKinsey's 7s model is used. The 7s model is presented in Fig 11.1. McKinsey's 7-S framework identified seven independent organizational factors that have to be managed by today's managers.

1. Strategy: to determine the allocation of scarce resources and to commit the organization to a specific course of action.
2. Structure: to determine the number of levels (in a hierarchy) and authority centres.
3. Systems: to determine organizational processes, procedures, reports and routines.
4. Staff: to determine the key human resource groups in an organization and describe them demographically.
5. Style: to determine the manner in which managers should behave to achieve organizational goals.
6. Super-ordinate goals (shared vision): to determine the guiding concepts that an organization needs to instill in its members.

7. Skills: to determine the abilities of people in an organization.

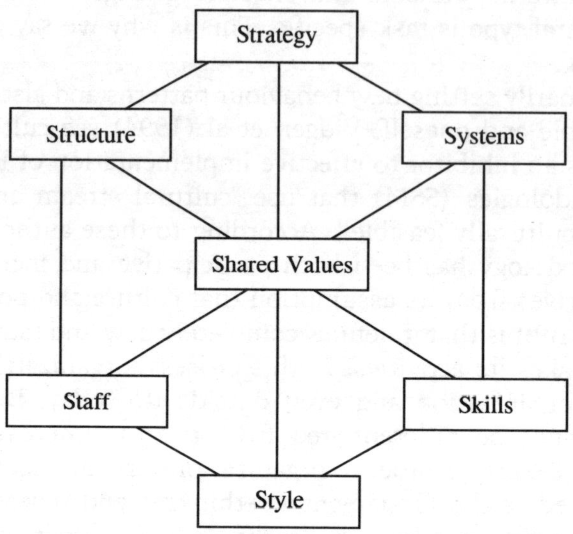

Figure 11.1 *McKinsey's 7-S diagram (Henley, 1991, p33)*

The 7-S framework suggests that any change in any S factor may result in an adjustment of other S factors. Now, however, the concept of 8-S has been introduced by adding one more S – streaming. Streaming includes those areas that either indirectly or directly influence or shape all the 7-Ss.

Peters and Waterman (1982) in their pioneering work, 'In search of Excellence' identified some common characteristics of excellent organizations. The characteristics have now become important management principles and also form the basis for BPR or BPM in organizations. The characteristics are:

- A bias for action – Excellent firms make things happen.
- Closeness to the customer – These firms know their customers and their needs.
- Autonomy and entrepreneurship – They value these in each employee.
- Productivity – They achieve this through people, based on trust.
- Hands-on, value-driven management – They make it mandatory.
- Stick to the knitting – They always deal from a position of strength.
- Simple form, lean staff – They develop cost-effective work teams.
- Simultaneous loose–tight properties – They decentralize many decisions, while at the same time, retaining tight overall control.

Global competition has also accentuated the need for enhancing quality and productivity. These two are the basic requirements to retain competitive advantage for any organization. Hence, management practices should focus on these by developing human resources to sustain their competitive advantage. But here again, we need to address the issues pertaining to culture, as in BPR.

That BPR can help organizations to achieve the goals is evident from the experience of *Proctor & Gamble*.

> *Procter and Gamble Corporation (P&G)*
>
> With 300 brands world-wide, *P&G* is now a global FMCG major. Being an innovation-driven organization, *P&G* cannot afford to stop increasing their brand portfolio, and hence, have reengineered their brand management activity introducing an 'innovating innovation' programme. Knowing well that innovation never dies, *P&G*, used a scorecard to evaluate which innovative idea can pay-off better. This approach helped *P&G* to introduce selectively, innovative brands to suit the market. This digital scorecard significantly improved the overall performance of *P&G*. Using this scorecard, *P&G* expects to perform 90% of its R&D in the virtual mode, and the residual 10% only for physical validation of results.

BPR, however, suffers from a limitation, as it succeeds in most cases when large-scale layoffs occur in organizations. These organizations, however, consider BPR as a manpower downsizing tool. Another reason for criticizing BPR is its overemphasis on technological aspects, rather than the people aspect. Despite all these criticisms, BPR benefits the production and operations management functions of an organization immensely.

11.3.1 Managing Change

BPR brings changes to the organization. It brings changes to the production and operations functions and also the restructuring process. Hence, the operating core faces the brunt of change, which requires specialized knowledge and skill for the production and operation managers to manage. The type of change that affects the operating core are mostly process centric. Process-centric changes require the production and operation managers to integrate the task and process parameters, ensuring minimum conflict with the operating core. This requires balancing the issues related to the external and internal environments, and also with those at the individual level, working at the operating core. While the external environmental factors that induce change at the operations level may be due to changes in the institutional rules and regulations (namely, pollution control norms, energy consumption, safety, occupational health issues, etc.), internal changes occur to adjust with the external environment-related changes. Such internal changes may be a change in the operating environment, a change in the behaviour of workers, etc. Individual level change issues may involve factors such as behavioural change, attitude to quality, skill and competency issues. Therefore, process-centric changes require the integration of organizational change issues with the operations and with those who are attached to the operational activities. Thus, for production and operations managers, optimizing employees' responses to process-centric organizational change is the biggest challenge. They need to understand how change in the process cascades down to the workers, and to manage the change to integrate, sharing information and making workers embrace the change voluntarily.

The introduction of new technology helps change to cascade down the operations; among others it requires cultural change, change in the design, quality management programmes, etc. Many Indian organizations fail utterly to manage technology-driven change.

11.4 TQM AND THE CULTURE OF QUALITY

The concept of TQM has been discussed in chapter 9. Here again, we reiterate that quality and TQM, is a culture. Particularly in the context of POM functions, organizations across the globe cannot sustain themselves unless they focus on quality. Therefore, commitment to quality has now become part of the core values of many organizations. Several organizations even endorse their commitment to quality in their mission statements. Organizations also consciously build up a culture of quality, so that the attitude and behaviour of its personnel are influenced and they nurture quality autonomously. Some of the steps undertaken by organizations to build up the culture of quality are:

- Determination of the meaning and significance of quality, specific to the organization.
- Analysis of the mission statement and espoused core values.
- Training of employees.
- Making employees responsible for aligning their behaviour with the quality programme.
- Making employees believe in the core values of the organization.
- Developing a compelling quality culture, so that employees understand and practice it, making effective use of quality tools, and also contribute to sustain the quality process in the organization.

If employees are expected to behave in accordance with quality programmes, organizations have to undertake an aggressive employee awareness programme, so that they understand the requirement of change to survive. They can identify the defects or errors and can fix the same immediately or report to the quality department for immediate intervention. As quality encompasses all functional areas, employees may be allowed to work in cross-functional teams to identify those solutions that exert an impact in various areas.

11.4.1 A Comparison of TQM and BPR

For effective POM functions, both TQM and BPR, as customer-oriented approaches, are adopted by organizations. Both are aimed at improving customer satisfaction through a process-oriented team approach. Despite such similarities, TQM and BPR can be differentiated in certain aspects. To appreciate those, let us first understand how these are practiced in organizations. BPR is essentially a top–down approach, and it could lead to resistance from employees. TQM, however, could be a top–down and a bottom–up approach. The difference between TQM and BPR can be better understood when we consider their respective contexts. TQM does not make the existing process redundant; rather, it tries to improve this, and hence, receives support from employees. BPR on the other hand, assumes that the existing system is redundant and therefore reinvents the process by reengineering an organizational restructuring. Similarly, TQM aims at incremental improvements, while BPR emphasizes radical changes and improvements.

Some of the other differences can be enumerated as under:

- TQM believes in total involvement, which even extends to all stakeholders, including customers and suppliers. It emphasizes the involvement of all functions of the organizations, for its obvious inter-relatedness. In contrast, BPR could be even without the participation of employees, as it is essentially a top–down approach to transform the organization. However, wherever required, it can involve people and functions on a small scale.
- Implementation of TQM in an organization is ensured through standardization of practices. This enables employees to achieve a consistent performance. But such documentation is not done in the case of BPR, which involves flexibility, and hence, makes standardization as low as possible.
- TQM makes use of statistical process control. BPR, however, does not require it. BPR only makes use of information technology.
- TQM is by nature a cultural issue. When TQM culture is built into an organization, TQM practices are automatically absorbed in the daily operations. BPR, however, is more like a project, which emphasizes achieving a time-bound target.
- BPR is used when organizations are in deep trouble, to overcome a crisis phase in the organization. In contrast, TQM is a consolidation approach, and it is always on-going to ensure continuous improvement.

11.5 CROSS-CULTURAL INFLUENCE AND TECHNOLOGY

Effective POM functions require the consideration of cross-cultural influences on technology, its selection and implementation. Before we start our discussion on this issue, it is appropriate at the outset, to resolve the debate on whether culture influences technology or technology influences culture!

We are increasingly getting things done through technology which, quite universally, shapes culture. On the other hand, technology is also influenced by our culture. For example, with a traditional blast furnace, the work culture is more rustic in a steel plant, as workers have to withstand the harsh temperatures on the shop floor, carefully drop the molten iron (manually) to segregate the impurities, and at times, feel agitated by frequent injuries due to sporadic sparking of impure items. But with modern, remote-controlled blast furnaces, this work culture is totally transformed, as technology supplements human labour to improve output. In this case technology, as a medium, influences the work culture. On the other hand, think of a mobile phone, or a digital diary, that reminds you when to contact whom, reminds you of your appointment schedules – there are many such features in a mobile phone or a digital diary. Making use of these features depends on our culture. Here, technology as content is influenced by our culture.

Quite often, we debate on how cross-cultural influences may persuade us to re-design our production processes. Technology and cultural issues have to be considered from different perspectives. Organization-wise, we can see variations in process design, how it is organized, and what equipment is used. However, culture-wise there hardly exists any variation in the areas like process monitoring and control, problem solving and product quality. Existing technology culture in an organization may drive discipline; it may be well planned and effective in problem solving and defect prevention. One culture may provide the optimum results and the highest probability of satisfied customers, while another may result in customer dissatisfaction. In the second case, dissatisfied customers then look for other suppliers or vendors, resulting in a drop in sales of the organization. Customers expect consistent results and performance from their suppliers. Two basic cultures, specific to technological issues are reactive technological culture and proactive technological culture. To determine the type of culture that exists in an organization or in a particular operation, we examine whether the organization monitors the process or the product. When the organization monitors the product, we understand that the culture is reactive in nature. Here, the emphasis is on finding the defects. In contrast, where the process is monitored in an organization, we call it a proactive culture, because such organizations focus on defect prevention, before the defect arises. A proactive technological culture can only be developed and sustained in an organization that addresses people-related issues.

11.6 PROACTIVE TECHNOLOGICAL CULTURE FOR POM

A proactive technological culture focusses on the prevention of defects before they happen. Second, proactive technological cultures never slow down process improvement efforts. For effective POM functions, organizations have to make their process improvement efforts continuous, considering quality and cycle time improvement as an unending journey. Obviously, such organizations need to focus on sustained human resource development activities, like

1. training in process development
2. statistics
3. problem solving
4. project management and
5. new product design.

These organizations consider customers as being inseparable from their operations and do their best for customer integration with their business and operational plans. Other characteristics of a proactive technological culture are:

- It invests in training its operators, supervisors, managers, engineers and technicians in Statistical Process Control (SPC), Design of Experiments (DOE), Design for Manufacturability (DFM), Problem Solving, etc.
- Proactive technological culture operation makes use of DOE to identify and quantify critical operating parameters or critical success factors (CSF), using statistical tools such as SPC to monitor the process.
- It monitors the process continuously to initiate corrective action.
- It monitors the process to prevent defects, and not to find defects that have already arisen.
- Proactive technological culture minimizes non-value added activity. One such non-value adding activity is process inspection.
- It is focussed on using timely data to drive continuous improvement.
- A proactive technological culture does not solve the same problems every day.
- A proactive technological culture involves all functions in the operation to brainstorm, evaluate and implement effective process improvements.

For all the reasons stated above, for effective POM functions, nurturing of proactive manufacturing culture is a must.

To understand whether an organization pursues a pro-active technological culture or not, or what exactly are the constructs of pro-activity can be based on the answers to the following questions:

1. To what extent does the organization focus on preventing defects or finding defects?
2. To what extent are the managers expert in preventing defects or finding defects?
3. Are the managers enforcing control over organizational processes or does the process control the managers?
4. Do the managers regularly discover the root cause of problems and initiate permanent corrective action?
5. Do the managers adopt a formal problem solutions approach by initiating defects prevention or do they try to escape from the customer after identifying the problem?

6. To what extent are managers required to do regular crisis management?
7. Are the nature of problems regular?
8. Do the managers 'train' and 'coach' operators, engineers, technicians, supervisors, etc. on understanding the entire process and how to identify and solve problems?
9. Do managers use formal statistical tools (DOE) to identify and quantify critical operating parameters?
10. To what extent do managers use formal problem solving tools to solve problems?
11. To what extent do managers institutionalize problem-solving and corrective action to ensure the perpetuation of such practices?
12. Do the managers seek and use all available information and inputs from all levels of the organization, including suppliers and customers, to develop the optimum solutions to problems?
13. Do the managers know how the process is performing at any particular point of time?
14. To what extent do managers remain busy to use formal tools in developing and implementing processes and solving problems?
15. How far is the manufacturing operation organized in the most efficient manner and how far does it provide the correct resources to meet the correct need in the shortest possible time?
16. Do organizations have both organizational and personal goals that aim at continuous improvement of the operation's performance and customer satisfaction?
17. Are these goals supported, coached and reviewed by management on a regular basis?
18. Are customer feedback and suggestions used to drive corrective actions and used in process improvement projects?
19. What does the customer want?
20. What makes the organization win over competition?
21. Do organizations have any specific detailed measurable process improvement goals, and the projects to achieve those goals?
22. Can the organization identify the most critical elements of business operation that must be evaluated and measured to ensure it is performing at an optimum level?
23. What are the standards (metrics) for evaluating the efficiency of a manufacturing operation?
24. On what basis do organizations decide and evaluate improvements and implement the same to provide the largest possible return?
25. Do organizations make use of information to create a culture of continuous improvement?

26. How do managers know if the improvement programmes that have been implemented are effective and can achieve the predicted results?
27. What do managers do to move to the next level of manufacturing operations performance?

Through a thorough study of existing manufacturing systems, we can transform an organization's culture from a reactive to a pro-active one. Other successive steps for technology transition, vis-à-vis changes in the production and operations management functions, are:

1. active management support and commitment
2. training
3. breaking down requirements into specific tasks
4. coaching
5. managing and executing transition plans, etc.

A study of manufacturing systems includes those factors which have the potential to exert an influence on the performance of an operation. Some of these factors are listed below:

1. Process Development
2. Process Control
3. Process Design
4. Process Layout
5. Process Flow
6. Process Line Balancing
7. Process Optimization Programme
8. Process Tooling and Fixtures
9. Process Technical Support
10. Process Documentation and Documentation Control
11. Process Capacity versus Required Capacity
12. Process Scheduling and Job Sequencing
13. Process Set Up and Change Over Procedure
14. Operator Responsibility, Training, and Efficiency
15. Relating Process Goals to Personal Goals
16. Management Process Support and Performance Review
17. Supplier Relationships
18. Material Control
19. Material Flow and Availability
20. Material Handling
21. Preventative Maintenance Program and Schedule
22. Calibration Control and Schedule
23. Continuous Improvement Programme and Goals
24. Industry and Process Benchmarking Programme

25. Product Design For Manufacturing Review Process
26. New Product Introduction Process
27. Model and Prototype Process and Scheduling
28. Engineering Change Order Process
29. Environmental Requirements and Control
30. Critical Process Parameter Development and Control

For production and operations management, manufacturing is a system. Conventionally, in organizations, the manufacturing function is organized with individual-centred responsibility. This leads to a conflict, without resolving which, the production and operations management function suffers.

Illustration

> We can illustrate such a situation in an organizational context. For example, those in marketing management may feel that maximum order booking will improve the profit performance of the organization. But there can always be a situation, when the manufacturing division fails to accommodate the increased order booking. This happens because job scheduling by production managers and order bookings marketing managers are done independently, without integrating both the functions with a system approach. The reverse may also occur in an organization – shop floors may remain idle due to the absence of production requisition by the marketing department.

Therefore, manufacturing improvement goals should be developed from a manufacturing systems perspective, integrating cross-functional areas to manufacturing.

It is now well recognized that culture and technology are interdependent. Culture forms an important aspect of technology design, development and utilization. Technological changes lead to adjustments at three levels: individual, social organization and of the cultural value system. Therefore, technology must be in congruence with the culture; it must complement the culture. Even sociologists consider technology as being a part of culture, considering it as inherited artefacts, goods, technical processes, ideas, habits and values. For example, reversed gripping demonstrated in Fig. 11.2 explains how cultural issues can influence technology.

11.6.1 Reversed gripping of share tools

According to Alrusheidat (2006), some of these culture-related ergonomic aspects are as follows:

1. **Interface design:** This relates to the use of human emotion in product design. It is concerned with factors like colour and shape. Culture-wise perceptions of colour differ. For example, red indicates danger in western countries, while it symbolizes happiness in China.
2. **Control/display compatibility**: It indicates spatial movement of control, and refers to the user's expectation of the stimulus–response relationship. A compatible system considers perceptual–motor behaviour, that is, differences in reading or scanning habits.
3. **Workplace design**: Suitable workplace design eliminates harmful posture and improves user performance; it has to take into account the user's biological needs, preferences and task requirements. Variations in preferred posture influence machine and workplace design. Therefore, it deserves improvement in the operator's efficiency and comfort.
4. **Design of protective equipment**: There exist both psychological and physical constraints with regard to wearing protective clothing. In some cultures, the use of helmets may be prohibited.

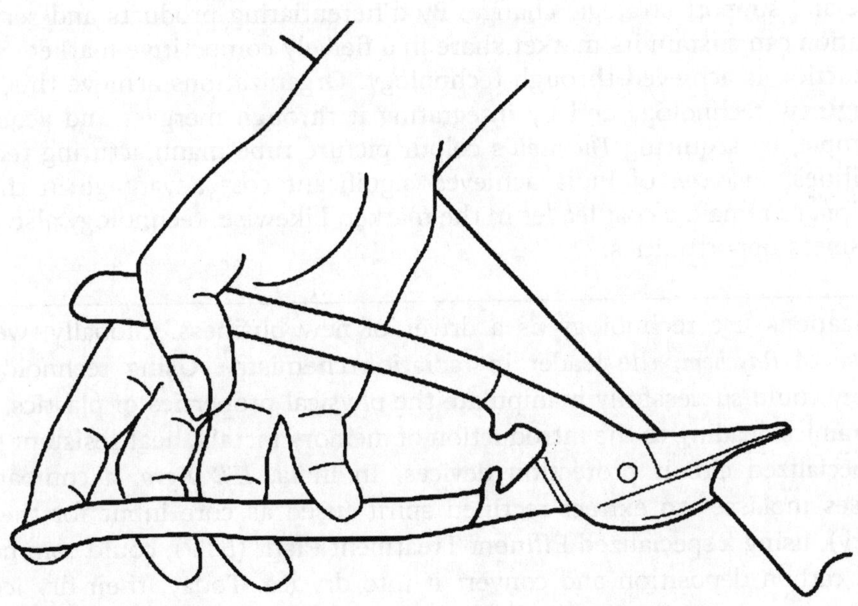

Figure 11.2 *Reversed gripping of share tools*

(*Source*: Alrusheidat, J. 2006. The impact of cultural dimensions on technology transfer in developing countries. *Journal of Food, Agriculture and Environment*, Volume 4, Issue 1, January, pp. 8–10.)

Similar culture-congruent ergonomic features, which influence the technology, could be selection of software systems, work organization and management, design of maintenance systems, design of shift work schedules, flexibility in work schedules, etc

In manufacturing, we assume that technology means high-end machinery and equipment, which substitute the traditional manual work process. Yet from another perspective, technology is a science and the outcome of research and development initiatives by firms. Chris Floyd in his 'Managing technology for corporate success' (1970), defined technology as the practical application of scientific or engineering knowledge to the conception, development or application of products or offerings, processes or operations. Floyd further argued that technology is important for two critical reasons:

(1) to achieve success in business, sustaining competitive position, and
(2) to promote a culture of innovation through technology for long-term sustainability.

By achieving the first objective, organizations can achieve product or service differentiation, reduce costs, develop new business opportunities, and finally, facilitate and support strategic change. By differentiating products and services, an organization can sustain its market share in a fiercely competitive market. Similarly, cost reduction is achieved through technology. Organizations achieve this, both by acquiring new technology and by integrating it through mergers and acquisitions. For example, by acquiring *Thomson*'s colour picture tube manufacturing technology and facilities, *Videocon* of India achieved significant cost advantage in their CTV production, to remain a cost leader in the market. Likewise, technology also provides new business opportunities.

Organizations use technology as a driver of new business. Globally, we know the case of *Raychem*, the leader in radiation chemistry. Using technology, the company could successfully manipulate the physical properties of plastics, metals and ceramics, leading to the introduction of memory metals, heat resistant plastics and specialized circuit protection devices. In India, *IFB Agro*, a company that processes molasses to extract rectified spirit (used as core input for the liquor industry), using a specialized Effluent Treatment Plant (ETP), could commercially exploit carbon deposition and convert it into dry ice. Today, their dry ice plant generates more revenue than their mother business of rectified spirit.

The second objective recommends the use of technology as a lever for strategic change. *Thomson*'s hiving off its colour picture tube manufacturing facilities to *Videocon* is basically a strategic move to LCD and plasma technology in TV manufacture.

Thus, using technology as a driver for organizational change, both for long-term and short-term objectives, is now more a strategic than just a technical issue. This *inter alia,* requires organizations to focus on people-related issues, considering technology as an ongoing process of change in an organization.

The advanced technologies, which particularly affect the areas of organizational operations, are:

- designs and engineering
- processing fabrication and assembly
- automated material handling
- inspection
- integration and control
- network communication

Advanced technologies, which are divided into the six major functional groups mentioned above, can be further categorized into specific areas of changes, which are brought in through technological inputs.

1. Design and Engineering Changes in the design and engineering function of an organization are enforced through the following methods of technological reinforcement:

- Computer-aided design/engineering (CAD/CAE)
- Computer-aided design/manufacturing (CAD/CAM)
- Modeling or simulation technologies

2. Processing Fabrication and Assembly In processing fabrication and assembly jobs, the following technological inputs are put into use:

- flexible manufacturing cells or systems (FMC/FMS)
- programmable logic control (PLC) machine/s or process/es
- lasers used in materials processing (including surface modification)
- Robot/s with sensing capabilities
- Robot/s without sensing capabilities

3. High Speed Machining For achieving operational efficiency, high-speed machining is now considered the most significant thrust area for an organization. High-speed machining is ensured through the following technologies:

- automated material handling
- part identification for manufacturing automation, like bar coding
- Automated storage and retrieval system (AS/RS)

4. Inspection Inspection and quality checks are essential for every organization to sustain its competitive strengths. Technologies, which facilitate this, are:

- automated vision-based systems used for inspection/testing of inputs and/or final products

- other automated sensor-based systems used for inspection/testing of inputs and/or final products

5. Integration and Control On the one hand, integration and control, facilitates alignment with the organizational business goals and objectives and, on the other hand, ensures timely intervention to correct any deviation from the plan. Integration and control functions are enforced through the following technologies:

- Manufacturing Resource Planning (MRP II/Enterprise Resource Planning (ERP))
- computer/s used for control on the factory floor
- computer integrated manufacturing (CIM)
- supervisory control and data acquisition (SCADA)
- Use of inspection data in manufacturing control
- Digital remote-controlled process plant control

6. Network Communications Effective network communications facilitate better coordination and enforce efficiency in organizational activities. Technologies, which are used in network communications, are:

- Local Area Network (LAN) for engineering/production
- Company-wide computer networks (including intranet and WAN)
- Inter-company computer networks (including extranet and EDI)

Thus, it is clear that technologies are not just limited to the production and operation function of an organization; they extend to all areas, including the managerial and strategic functions. Therefore, technology should be considered as an important driver for organizational growth and efficiency. And bringing in technological change would only be possible through the appropriate HR intervention.

How technology exerts an influence on the organization as a whole, including its design, can be understood in the context of the following models.

11.6.2 Thompson's Model

James Thompson (1967) developed three classifications for technology:
(1) intensive technology
(2) mediating technology and
(3) long-linked technology.

Intensive technology is developed, keeping in view, a high level of uncertainty. It helps to produce the desired outcomes, even in uncertain situations. Let us assume a particular organization makes use of traditional dedicated technology for producting certain items, say, long-playing record players. Suddenly, in the market, customers have changed their taste and preferences and switched to the use of CDs or DVDs. This will render long-playing records obsolete. The said organization will also suffer, as its earlier investments in technology cannot be salvaged. However, if the organization had made use of intensive technology (like flexible technology, CNC, etc.), this situation of technological obsolescence could have been avoided by the organization. Intensive technology also makes workers interdependent and creative. They become capable of solving their work-related problems. With intensive technology, organizations become flexible in decision making, rather than emphasizing on decisions which are SOP (standard operating procedure)-bound, and members resolve their work issues through mutual coordination.

Mediating technology brings together individuals and/or groups to seek a mutually beneficial exchange of values. This form of technological environment is more applicable in service industries, like banks, financial institutions, etc.

Long-linked technology is appropriate for mass-production processes, like an automobile assembly line. It depends on highly specialized tasks in a closely controlled sequence of activities to produce the final product.

Thompson's Model argues that each type of technology has specific bearings on the design and structure of organizations.

11.6.3 Woodward's Technologies

Joan Woodward (1965) with her team of researchers studied about 100 organizations in England in the 1960s, to establish the linkage between the size and the structure of organizations. However, they could not establish any such relationships. In their follow-up study, they could find some relationships between the structure and three basic forms of technology, which they categorized as small batch production technology, large batch or mass-production technology, and continuous process production technology.

1. *Small batch production technology* is suitable for the production of a few varieties of products, to meet the specific requirements of customers. Such customized production facilities are created by organizations to cater to specialized demands for the defence sector. In some cases, organizations demand initial technology development cost from the customers, as they decide that such investments are only for meeting customer-specific demands.
2. *Long-batch or mass production technology* is used for producing a large volume of standardized products to cater to the demand of a large market. Such organizations automate or mechanize their production facilities, where workers serve as complements to the equipment. This type of technology helps in handling large volume production of high quality goods, which may require dangerous or even monotonous operations. The technology used in an automobile assembly line is a good example.

3. *Continuous process production technology* is a complete mechanized production process, where machines undertake all the jobs, making people focus on quality inspection and adjustment, monitoring, etc. Most chemical processing units like petroleum refineries, chemical plants and nuclear power plants, make use of such technology, where production and processing continue uninterrupted.

Woodward and her associates referred to such differences in these three production technologies as technical complexity. From an organizational design point of view, differences in technology have different connotations. For example, more complex technology (like continuous process) creates tall organization structures, which require more supervision and coordination. Similarly, the span of management of lower level managers increases from small batch to mass production, while the technology level decreases from mass production to continuous process production. Similarly, with more technological complexity, support staff functions increase, and organizations become top-heavy (more managers).

11.7 BEST PRACTICE MODELS FOR EXCELLENCE IN POM FUNCTIONS

We have many best practice models for organizational excellence, and in all cases, we observe that production and operations management has been given the critical role to achieve organizational excellence. We will discuss some widely-used models.

11.7.1 EFQM Excellence Model

The EFQM Excellence Model was introduced in early 1992, as the framework for assessing applications for The European Quality Award. It is the most widely-used organizational effectiveness framework in Europe and has become the basis for most national and regional Quality Awards. The EFOM Model is a non-prescriptive framework that recognizes that there are many approaches to achieving sustainable excellence. Within this non-prescriptive approach, there are some fundamental concepts which underpin the EFQM.

The true measure of the EFQM Excellence Model's effectiveness is its widespread use as a management system, and the associated growth in the key management discipline of organizational self-assessment about its effectiveness and excellence. It helps the organization to understand whether it is on the path of excellence, duly identifying gaps and then stimulating solutions. The list of fundamental concepts is not exhaustive, but it can change or transform an organization to achieve excellence. A brief outline of the fundamental concepts is given below:

1. **Result Orientation:** Excellence is achieving results that delight the organization's stakeholders.

2. **Customer Focus:** Excellence is creating sustainable customer value
3. **Leadership and Constancy of Purpose:** Excellence is visionary and inspirational leadership, coupled with constancy of purpose
4. **Management by Processes and Facts:** Excellence is managing the organization through a set of interdependent and interrelated systems, processes and facts.
5. **People Development and Involvement:** Excellence is maximizing the contribution of employees through their development and involvement.
6. **Continuous Learning, Innovation and Improvement:** Excellence is challenging the status quo and effecting change by using learning to create innovation and improvement opportunities.
7. **Partnership Development:** Excellence is developing and maintaining value-adding partnerships.
8. **Corporate Social Responsibility:** Excellence is exceeding the minimum regulatory framework in which the organization operates and to strive to understand and respond to the expectations of their stakeholders in society

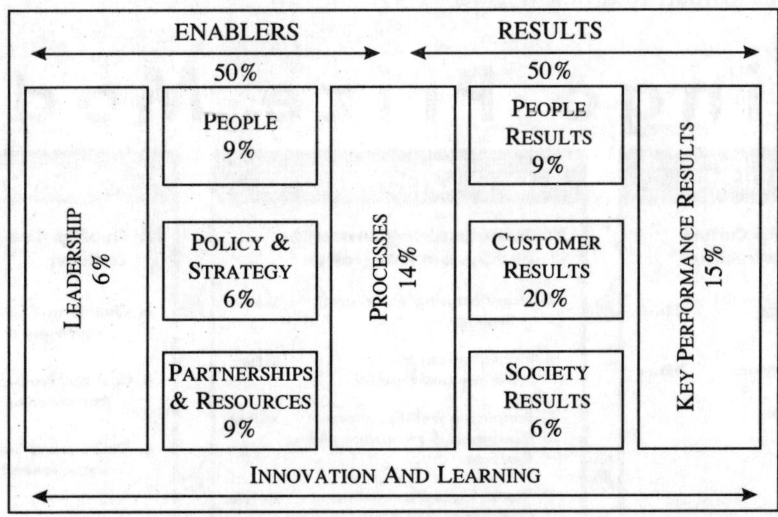

Figure 11.3 *EFQM Excellence Model*

The model is based on nine criteria. Five of these are 'enablers' and four are 'results'. The 'enabler' criteria cover what an organization does. The 'results' criteria cover what an organization achieves. 'Results' are caused by 'enablers' and feedback from 'results' helps to improve the 'enablers'.

11.7.2 Shingo Prize Model of Organizational Excellence

The Shingo Prize for Excellence in Manufacturing is named for the Japanese industrial engineer, Shigeo Shingo, who distinguished himself as one of the world's leading experts in improving manufacturing processes. Dr. Shingo has been described as an engineering genius who helped create and write about many aspects of the revolutionary manufacturing practices which comprise the renowned *Toyota* Production System.

The Prize was established in 1988 to promote awareness of Lean manufacturing concepts and recognize companies in the United States, Canada and Mexico that achieve world-class manufacturing status. The Shingo Prize philosophy is that world-class business performance may be achieved through focussed improvements in core manufacturing and business processes

The Shingo Prize Model includes 11 key elements of world-class manufacturing. These elements are grouped into five categories, signifying that it is necessary to integrate them into a complete system to achieve world-class results. The Shingo Prize criteria do not prescribe specific methods, techniques, practices or processes. Rather, for each element, the criteria lists practices and techniques that might be incorporated to achieve world-class quality, cost, delivery and business results.

The model is illustrated below (Fig 11.4):

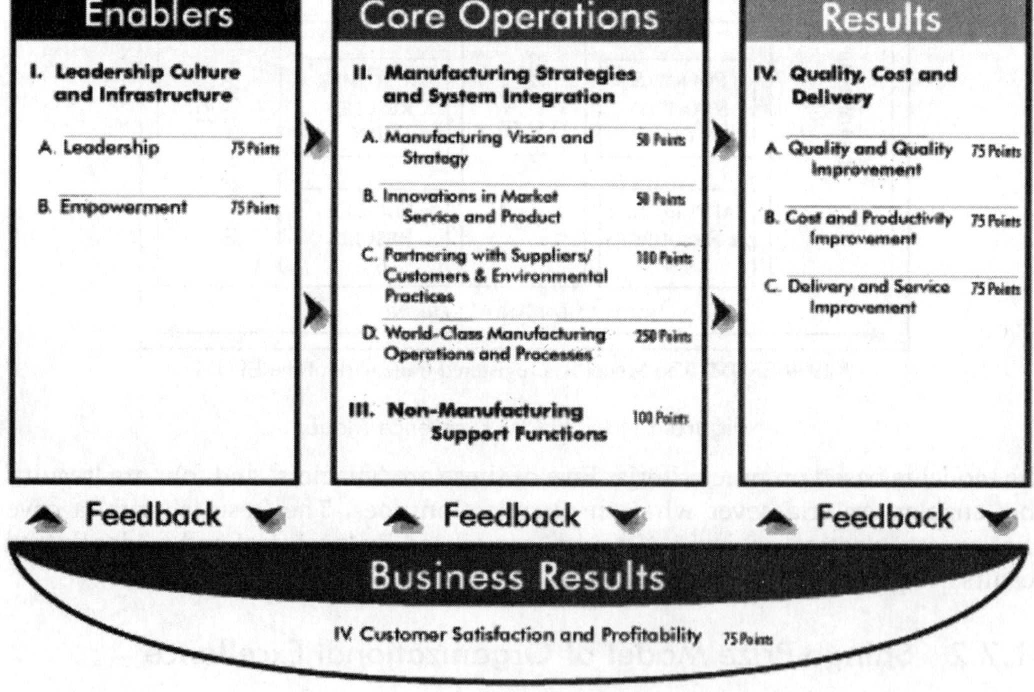

Figure 11.4 *The Shingo Prize Model*

11.7.3 Malcolm Baldrige Model for Organizational Excellence

In the form of a national quality award, the Malcolm Baldrige Model for organizational excellance was started in 1987 to recognise US companies for their achievements in quality and business performance, and to raise awareness about the importance of quality and performance excellence in gaining a competitive edge. The award is not given for specific products or services. Three awards may be given annually in each of these categories – manufacturing, services, small business, and, starting in 1999, education and healthcare.

The Baldrige performance excellence criteria are a framework, and any organization wanting to improve its overall performance can use such criteria as their basic guideline. There are seven categories that make up the award criteria:

- **Leadership:** It examines how senior executives guide the company and how the company addresses its responsibilities to the public and practices good corporate citizenship.
- **Strategic planning:** It examines how the company sets its strategic directions and how it determines key action plans.
- **Customer and market focus:** It examines how the company determines the requirements and expectations of customers and markets.
- **Information and analysis:** It examines the management, effective use, and analysis of data and information to support key company processes and the company's performance management system.
- **Human resource focus:** It examines how the company enables its workforce to develop its full potential and how the workforce is aligned with the company's objectives.
- **Process management:** It examines aspects of how key production/delivery and support processes are designed, managed and improved.
- **Business results:** It examines the company's performance and improvement in its key business areas:
  a) customer satisfaction b) financial and marketplace performance c) human resources d) supplier and partner performance and e) operational performance.

The category also examines how the company performs relative to competitors. The criteria are used by thousands of organizations of all kinds for self-assessment and training and as a tool to develop performance and business processes.

For many companies, using these criteria result in

1. better employee relations
2. higher productivity
3. greater customer satisfaction
4. increased market share and
5. improved profitability.

The Baldrige Award criteria is different from ISO 9000, as it focusses on results and continuous improvement, providing a framework for designing, implementing and assessing a process for managing all business operations. ISO 9000 is a series of five international standards published in 1987 by the International Organization for Standardization (ISO), Geneva, Switzerland. Companies can use the standards to help determine what is needed to maintain an efficient quality conformance system. ISO 9000 certification determines whether a company complies with its own quality system. It covers less than 10% of the Baldrige Award criteria.

Some of the important features of the Baldrige Model (Fig 11.5) are:

1. focus more on results and service
2. rely upon the involvement of many different professional and trade groups
3. provide special credits for innovative approaches to quality
4. include a strong customer and human resource focus, and
5. stress the importance of sharing information

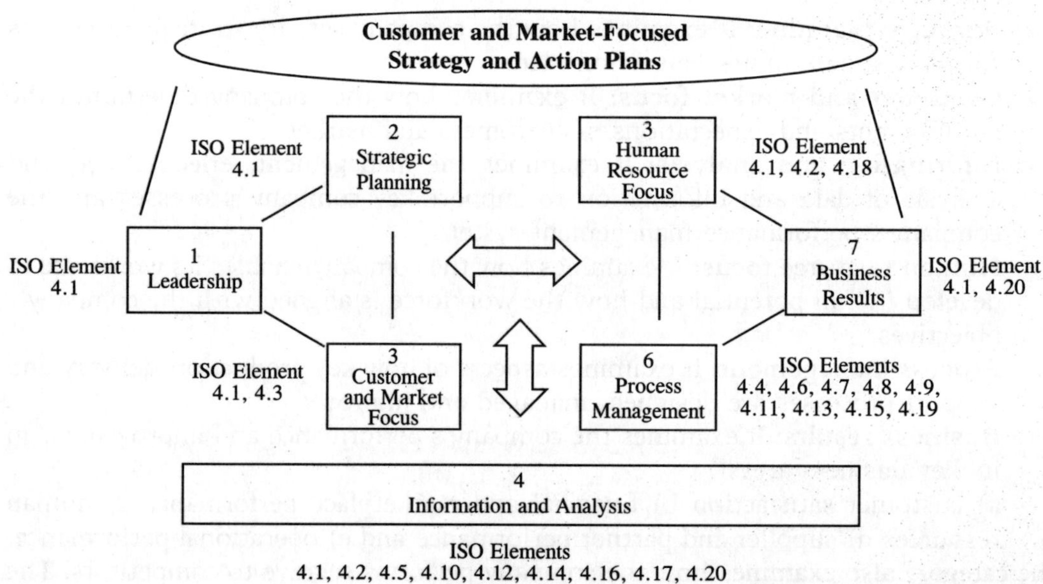

Figure 11.5 *Baldrige Criteria for Performance Excellence Framework vs. ISO 9001 Elements*

11.8 ORGANIZATIONAL CHANGE THROUGH SIX SIGMA

Six Sigma is a business process to improve the bottom line (profitability). This is done by designing and monitoring business activities in a way that minimizes waste and resources without, however, compromising customer satisfaction. Six Sigma process is broader than total quality management (TQM) programmes. While TQM focusses on detecting and correcting defects, Six Sigma re-creates the processes to ensure defects never arise, right from the beginning. From the organization's point of view, it provides maximum value in the form of increased profits and from the customer's point of view, it provides maximum value in terms of high quality products and services at competitive costs.

11.8.1 Basic Characteristics

- Sigma is a letter in the Greek alphabet and is used to denote the standard deviation of a process.
- First developed by *Motorola* from the mid-1980s and adopted by many major manufacturing organizations including *General Electric*. *GE Capital*, the world's first service transaction-based company introduced this in 1996.
- It is the statistical application of Total Quality Management.
- Sigma quality level describes the output of a process.
- It emphasizes business process improvement in general, which includes cost reduction, cycle-time improvement and increased customer satisfaction.
- It implies a whole culture of strategies, tools and statistical methodologies to improve the bottom line of companies.
- Higher sigma values indicate better quality products and lower sigma values represent less quality products. At six sigma level, products are virtually defect-free, that is, it allows for 3.4 defects per million opportunities (DPMO) only.

11.8.2 SIX SIGMA: INTRODUCTION IN ORGANIZATIONS

Six Sigma is a process of self-assessment of organizational quality. To adopt Six Sigma practices in organizations may not be an overnight exercise. At the outset, the intending organization needs to select a particular process, which it may like to recreate as an error-free one. Critical quality factors for the short-listed process also need to be identified from the customer's perspective, process recreation should start with continuous focus on quality improvement. Here, we are suggesting some areas of improvement, which six-sigma helps us to achieve.

- Improvement of process
- Improvement of products and services
- Improvement in investor relationship
- Improvement in designing
- Improvement in supplier relationship
- Improvement in training and recruitment.

For a discussion of typical inverted relationship in Six Sigma breakthrough strategy see Figure 10.1, in chapter 10.

11.8.3 Steps for Six Sigma

There are eight fundamental steps to achieve Six Sigma quality in the process division of an organization. These eight stages are:

1. Recognize
2. Define
3. Measure
4. Analyze
5. Improve
6. Control
7. Standardize and
8. Integrate.

These steps are explained in the in Chapter 10 (see Table 10.1) Six Sigma map.

1. In the identification phase, companies recognize in what way processes affect their profitability and what processes are critical to business.
2. The characterization phase helps to benchmark and provides the inputs to measure improvements. At this stage, an action plan is charted to close the gap between the current position and the future, matching the company's goals for product and services. It is at this stage that Black Belts select key characteristics of one or more products/services and develop a detailed description of each and every step in their processes. Using process control cards, Black Belts estimate the short-term and long-term process capability.
3. In the optimization phase, Design for Six Sigma (DFSS), is used to reconfigure products and services right from the beginning by discovering the key variables that lead to the problem and then designing the products and services eliminating such problem-generating variables. Proper control is ensured by strict monitoring of the processes to avoid recurrence of similar quality problems in products and services.
4. In the final stages of institutionalization, standardization and integration of Six Sigma practices are done to run the day-to-day business of an organization.

For calculating the sigma level, we use the Defects per Million Opportunities (DPMO) formula, duly defining the customers' perceived critical to quality (CTQ) factors. CTQs are opportunities for error. Since this is a quantitative measurement, we also need to have discrete information about the following items:

1. UNIT: The item produced or being serviced
2. DEFECT: Event that does not conform to customers' requirements
3. OPPORTUNITY: Chance for occurrence of a defect

Illustration

To illustrate, let us take the example of examination services of an educational institute. Students consider a defect in the system, when results are declared after three weeks. Let us assume students have four perceived CTQs, these are speed of delivery, correct transcript of marks, adequate information about incomplete or withheld results, and proper computation of grades. These, therefore, make four opportunities for error in discrete terms. Once quantitative details about the number of units and defects are made available, we can use the following formula to calculate the sigma level:

(Number of Defects ÷ {Number of Opportunities for error} × 1,00,0000)

Suppose in our case, we have 2500 results, of which 10 were late due to non-availability of assignment grades and 5 were bad due to improper computation of grades; the calculation, therefore, would be as under:

$$\frac{15}{2 \times 2500} X^{1,000,000}$$

$$= 3000$$

3000 DPMO almost corresponds to 4.25 sigma level, which indicates that the hypothetical institution needs to identify further the process flaws and improve upon the quality of service. At six sigma level, DPMO should be 3.4 or 3.4 defects per million.

Six Sigma is a learning continuum. It reinforces the intellectual capital to identify the best practices continually and standardize those within and across the business to create a win–win situation in a competitive world. Therefore, to achieve excellence in quality of products and services within a minimum time, organizations can adopt Six Sigma practices.

This requires foreseeing the future skill sets in terms of the changing technology or process. Similarly, regular competency mapping and a synergy between individual and organizational competencies need to be achieved through training and development intervention. Training employees on Six Sigma requires both technical and behavioural reinforcements. Any skill gap requires repeated training till all concerned are fit for the purpose. All employees cannot be black belts. It is also not required. But everyone should understand how important it is for them to improve their workmanship to produce defect-free products and services. Ranging from product to process familiarization, the training should focus on basic understanding of using statistical and analytical tools to help them measure the variability and attribute reasons for failure.

Similar importance to compensation planning, motivation and retention should be given to ensure commitment and loyalty to the organization. There are many ways to design compensation innovatively and also for employee retention. Six Sigma, even though a top–down approach, its success largely depends on the players, who are catalysts for such change. It makes no sense to engage a consultant and expect results, unless the initiatives are properly integrated with the HR strategy of the organization.

11.9 LEAN PRACTICES TO ACHIEVE ORGANIZATIONAL EXCELLECE

Lean production, lean management, lean thinking and lean excellence are organizational practices to achieve excellence and effectiveness in today's highly competitive environment. It was originally developed at *Toyota,* and is now embraced as a necessity for organizations to survive, particularly in a volatile market situation. Lean practices are characterized by world class performance (key measures), world class practices (methods and processes) and the culture of relentless continuous improvement (environment). Through lean practices, *Toyota's* Production System, has achieved a 50%–70% improvement in productivity, floor space, working capital, quality and safety in a 2–3 year time frame. The fundamental philosophy of lean practices focusses on a systematic shift in the expectations, measures, performance and vision (culture) of the company. These practices lead to operational excellence in terms of functional value, defect-free quality, outstanding delivery and compelling price.

The transformation of an organization through lean practices starts with the value stream concept. Value stream is the sequence of steps which an organization needs to perform to optimize its capital, material and labour costs to satisfy customer needs. With the change in value stream, it is possible to eliminate unnecessary activities that cause delays, and in the process, add value to customer satisfaction

Lean practices require the creation of cells and the determination of flow within the cells. The idea behind a cell is that there should have been hardly any work-in-process, which might otherwise deter the value-adding steps. Work-in-process within a cell is controlled via pull systems like *kanbans,* and production is managed through simple scheduling/replenishment systems. Pull systems are continuously developed to improve the value stream.

11.9.1 Important Factors of Consideration for Lean Management

Lean management and practices to achieve organizational excellence are not for every organization, as it requires thorough understanding of the processes and improving such processes at every stage, that is, of every cell, keeping in mind customer' perspectives of value addition. Some of the factors which directly affect the organizational ability to become lean can be listed are:

1. A strategic reason to pursue the lean path *(external and motivating)*

2. Active commitment of the top management team *(does your team understand the need to become lean?)*
3. Cost reduction opportunity *(will a decrease in labour cost and/or working capital affect your balance sheet?)*
4. Growth potential *(Will increasing market share improve your bottom line?)*
5. Committed owners of the company *(committed to providing tools, setting expectations, measuring performance and affecting change)*

11.10 QUICK RESPONSE MANUFACTURING (QRM)

Quick Response Manufacturing (QRM) is another culture-centric organizational strategy, which helps in reducing the lead times in all activities of organizations. The process identifies 'white spaces' within and between processes, and accordingly, eliminates those to shorten the time-to-market on products, and engineer-to-order product solutions. This approach also tries to achieve continuous improvement, creating customer-defined values in products and services, and in the process, also eliminates waste.

11.11 TOYOTA PRODUCTION SYSTEM (TPS)

TPS was developed in Japan by *Toyota Corporation*, led by Taiichi Ohno. It was based on two primary concepts – the manufacturing production system of Henry Ford and the Ford Motor Company, and the supermarket operations in the United States. Ohno visited the USA in 1956, and closely observed the functioning of the supermarket, where the supply of merchandise on every shelf was continuous, to ensure the availability of merchandise to the customers. Emulating this, TPS incorporated the Just-In-Time (JIT) production and *Jidoka* techniques to optimize time and human assets in the manufacturing environment. TPS later became the basis for lean production and the "lean enterprise" movements beginning in the early 1990s. Along with the TPS, we also have to explain the concepts of JIT and *Kaizen*, which are useful tools to support the TPS in any organization.

JIT system of production manufactures and delivers the required quantity just when it is needed. *Jidoka* practices ensure availability of machines and operators. *Jidoka* can detect the abnormal condition in the production systems, and can stop it immediately. It ensures in-built quality in each process and can separate men and machines to achieve better work efficiency.

Kaizen ensures continuous improvement of the entire value stream or an individual process, adding more value with less waste. System or flow *kaizen* focusses on the overall value stream, and process *kaizen* focusses on individual process. Both the levels of *kaizen* benefit the organization, achieving efficiency.

SUMMARY

1. BPR is the fundamental rethinking and radical redesign of a business process that requires dramatic improvements, especially in meeting customer needs and other external strategic demands. Like all other functions of management, BPR also affects production and operations management functions.
2. To be successful, business process reengineering projects need to be top–down, taking in the complete organization, and the full end-to-end processes. It needs to be supported by tools that make processes easy to track and analyze.
3. The effective implementation of technology is the key driver for the production and operations management function. Technology manifests into various economic and sociological issues. And all these issues deserve attention from managers.
4. Without proper technology management, organizational plans and programmes suffer. But technology alone cannot solve all problems. There must be a balance between technology and human intervention.
5. For achieving excellence in production and operations management functions, many organizations emulate best practice models like EFQM, Shingo Prize Model, Malcolm Baldrige Model of Excellence, etc. Production managers need to understand these models and its various components before implementation.
6. These apart, modern production and operations management also requires practice of TQM, lean management practices with *Toyota* Production Systems (TPS), Quick Response Manufacturing (QRM), etc.

KEY WORDS

Technology management It is the field of study which imparts skills and knowledge, designed to improve the entire process of technological change.

Designs and Engineering Brings changes to the designs and in the engineering function of an organization and is enforced through technological reinforcement.

Proactive technological culture A proactive technological culture focusses on the prevention of defects before they happen. Second, proactive technological cultures never slow down process improvement efforts. For effective POM functions, organizations need to make their process improvement efforts continuous, considering quality and cycle time improvement as an unending journey.

Quick Response Manufacturing (QRM) This is a culture-centric organizational strategy, which helps in reducing the lead times in all activities of the organization. The process identifies 'white spaces' within and between processes, and accordingly, eliminates those to shorten the time-to-market on products, and engineer-to-order product solutions.

Thompson's Model James Thompson (1967) developed three classifications for technology: (1)intensive technology (2) mediating technology and (3) long-linked technology. Intensive technology is developed keeping in view a high level of uncertainty. It helps to produce the desired outcomes, even in uncertain situations. **Woodward's Technologies** Joan Woodward (1965) with her team of researchers studied about 100 organizations in England in the 1960s, to establish the linkage between the size and the structure of these organizations. However, they could not establish any such relationships. In their follow-up study, they could find some relationships between the structure and the three basic forms of technology, which they categorized as small batch production technology, large batch or mass-production technology, and continuous process production technology.

GENERAL REVIEW QUESTIONS

1. Explain the concept of BPR. How is BPR different from TQM?
2. Can we consider TQM as a culture? Give your answer in the context of organizational examples
3. Explain how cross-cultural issues interfere with the technological change in any organization
4. What is pro-active technological culture? How is it different from a re-active technological culture? For production and operations management, which type of technological culture would you advocate and why?
5. Explain the EFQM model of excellence? Discuss how emulating these models can benefit organizations
6. Differentiate between the Singho Prize Model and the Malcolm Baldrige Model of Excellence. Explain how these two models benefit the production and operations management function of an organization
7. Explain the concept of six-sigma. How can six-sigma implementation benefit an organization?
8. In the context of *Toyota* Production Systems, explain the concept of lean management? Also discuss how lean management can improve the production and operations management function?
9. Explain how technology benefits an organization with some live case examples.
10. Short notes

    (a) Innovation
    (b) Technology Transfer
    (c) BPM
    (d) Reengineering
    (e) TPS

CRITICAL REVIEW QUESTIONS

1. Your organization is a well-known manufacturer of life saving drugs. For research inputs and trial data, your company has to depend on the research and development support of US-based research organizations. The same research organizations cater to many of your competitors. To maintain your uniqueness, you have decided to go in for investment in technology. However, you feel such an investment will put your organization in a financial crisis. Think of some other alternatives to resolve this issue
2. You have been asked to implement Six Sigma in production functions in a phased manner. Hypothetically, assume the nature of production and suggest your line of action.

REFERENCES

1. Andrews, D. C., Stalick, S. K. 1994. *Business Reengineering: The Survival Guide.* Englewood Cliffs, N.J: Prentice-Hall, Inc
2. Alrusheidat, J. 2006. The impact of cultural dimensions on technology transfer in developing countries. *Journal of Food, Agriculture and Environment* Volume 4, Issue 1, January, pp. 8–10.
3. Davenport, Thomas and Short, J. 1990. The New Industrial Engineering: Information Technology and Business Process Redesign. *Sloan Management Review*, Summer 1990, pp 11–27
4. Davenport, Thomas. 1993. *Process Innovation: Reengineering work through information technology*. Boston: Harvard Business School Press.
5. Davenport, Thomas 1995. Reengineering – The Fad That Forgot People. *Fast Company*, November.
6. Drucker, Peter. 1972.Work and Tools, in: W. Kranzberg and W.H. Davenport eds. *Technology and Culture*, New York
7. Floyd, Chris. 1970. *Managing Technology for Corporate Success*. London: Gower Publishing.
8. Johansson, Henry J. et al. 1983. *Business Process Reengineering: BreakPoint Strategies for Market Dominance*. John Wiley & Sons
9. Obeng, E, and Crainer, S., 1994. *Making Reengineering Happen*. London: Pitman Publishing.
10. Peters, Thomas J. and Waterman, Robert H. 1982. *In search of excellence*. New York: Harper and Row, Publishers
11. http://www.research.cornell.edu/cotaba.html accessed on 27th July, 2008.
12. Porter, Michael E and Millar, Victor E. 1985. How information gives you competitive advantage. *Harvard Business Review*.
13. Thompson, James. 1967. *Organizations in Action*. New York: McGraw-Hill.
14. Vidgen, R., Rose, J., Wood, J.R.G., Wood-Harper, A.T. 1994. Business process

reengineering: the need for a methodology to re-vision the organization. In: Glasson, B., ed. *Proceedings of IFIP TC8 on Business Process Re-Engineering:* Information System Opportunities & Challenges, May 8-11. Elsevier

15. Woodward, Joan. 1965. *Industrial Organization: Theory and Practice*. London: Oxford University Press

ADDITIONAL REFERENCES

1. Bhattacharyya, D.K. 2007. *Human Resource Research Methods.* New Delhi: Oxford University Press.
2. Castle, J.A. 1996. An integrated model in quality management, position TQM, BPR and ISO 9000. *The TQM Magazine,* Vol. 8 No. 5, pp. 7–13.
3. Champy, J. 1995. *Reengineering Management*. New York: Harper Business Books.
4. Daft, R.L. and Lewin, A.Y. 1990. Can organization studies begin to break out of the normal science straitjacket? An editorial essay. *Organization Science* 1, pp. 1–9
5. Greenbaum, Joan. 1995. *Windows on the workplace*. Cornerstone
6. Guha, S. Kettinger, W.J. & Teng, T.C. 1993. Business Process Reengineering: Building a Comprehensive Methodology. *Information Systems Management*, Summer
7. Hammer, Michael. 1990. Reengineering Work: Don't automate, obliterate. *Harvard Business Review*, Jul/Aug 1990, pp 104–112
8. Hammer, Michael and Champy, James. 1993. Reengineering the Corporation: A Manifesto for Business Revolution. *Harper Business* Chapter 1 excerpt
9. Hinnings, C.R., and Greenwood, R. 2002. Disconnects and consequences in organization theory. *Administrative Science Quarterly*, Vol. 47, Issue-3, pp. 411-421.
10. Kuhn, Thomas Samuel. 1996. *The Structure of Scientific Revolutions*, 3rd edition. University of Chicago Press.
11. Lewin, A.Y. and Stephens, C.U. 1994. CEO Attitudes as Determinants of Organizational Design: An Integrated Model. *Organization Studies* 15(2), p 183-212.
12. Leavitt, H.J. 1965. Applied Organizational Change in Industry: Structural, Technological and Humanistic Approaches, in: *Handbook of Organizations,* James March ed. Chicago: Rand McNally,
13. Loyd, Tom. 1994. Giants with Feet of Clay. *Financial Times,* Dec 5 1994, p 8
14. Malhotra, Yogesh. 1998. Business Process Redesign: An Overview. *IEEE Engineering Management*, Vol. 26.
15. Pettigrew, A.M., Whittington, R., Melin, L., Sanchez-Runde, C., Van den Bosch, F., Ruigrok, W. and Numagami, T. 2003. *Innovative forms of organizing, international perspectives*. London: Sage
16. Rogers, Everett. 2003. *Diffusion of Innovations,* 5th edition. New York: Free Press.

17. Roberts, Lon. 1994. *Process Reengineering: The Key To Achieving Breakthrough Success*. Milwaukee: Quality Press.
18. Taylor, Frederick. 1911.*The principles of scientific management*. New York: Harper & Row,
19. Vantrappen, H. 1992. Creating customer value by streamlining business processes, in *Organisational Transformation through Business Process Reengineering*, Sethi, V. and King, W.R. eds. Englewood Cliffs, NJ: Prentice Hall.
20. White, JB. 1996. *Wall Street Journal*. New York, N.Y.: Nov 26, 1996. pg. A.1
21. Weick, KE. 1999. Theory construction as disciplined reflexibility: Tradeoffs in the 90s. *Academy of Management Review*, Vol. 24, pp. 797–806

CASE STUDY

Strategic Technological Management to gain market share– *NEocast*'s experience

In the present business environment, technological change is taking place so fast that it has now become a moving target for organizations to chase. Captivating customers with brand value was all along the strategic focus of *NEocast*, the off-shoot of an Indian public sector bank, selling life insurance policies. The premium rate is not competitive, even then, people repose their trust in this company, as *NEocast* enjoys the highest brand value in India. Bank Assurance is the most convenient route to sell insurance policies. *NEocast* enjoys the highest customer conversion compared to competitors. However, business growth is still lagging behind.

Data mining with technology support is the biggest challenge for insurance companies. It is quite usual for the industry to track data using the opportunistic method, by interacting with suppliers of the competitors, attending trade shows of competitors, sales force meetings of the competitors, seminars and conferences of the competitors, and recruiting ex-employees of the competitors, discussion with shared distributors, social contacts with competitors, etc. Using professional telesales people, potential customers are tapped and then persuaded to buy the insurance policies. *NEocast*, however discarded this approach, and introduced a technology-intensive data tracking systems linking the large customer-base of its bank, with targeted potential customers. In addition, the systems also track those who file their tax returns through the bank's counters, but are not account holders of the bank.

In the next phase, the company installed free debit/credit card swiping machines at retail malls, large restaurants, hotels, air-line booking counters, railway ticket booking counters, etc. It is not so easy for the company to get permission to allow the free installation of machines. But with financial incentives, the move was successful to a large extent. Any credit and debit card swiped through these machines, automatically stores the information in the central database, which after careful study, is clustered into groups, and then used to market their product. The process helped them more than the sky-rocketing advertisement expenses of competing companies. Thus, the strategic use of technology could help the company gain a better marketing edge than its competitors.

Strategic technology management theoretically requires an organization to follow certain steps.

1. First, obviously, is to ensure selection of the right players.
2. The next is the understanding of the available infrastructure and its applications.
3. The third step is to evaluate current opportunities, and finally
4. The last step is to break the priority into a series of actionable tasks, to accomplish within a time-bound programme.

Accordingly, the company went in for the strategic management of technological change, breaking up their tasks into three distinct phases:

1. Market Entry Phase: for rapid market penetration to gain economies of scale.
2. Innovation Phase: to drive the change to achieve low cost, while ensuring value addition.
3. Commodity phase: to drive cost control to ensure the survival of the company.

In *NEOcast's* case, all these steps have been followed, and finally the above sequences of marketing were chalked out. The process worked well for *NEocast*, and today they enjoy the highest customer conversion rate.

NEocast is now more innovative in data mining to increase their customer-base. They have now introduced a customer referral scheme, which gives privileges to existing customers for every conversion of their referred customer. They call it the customer partnering model. But the tracking of potential customers is being done through internet scanning, introducing the latest e-mail management software of an internationally acclaimed vendor. The system efficiently tracks potential customers, by scanning the mails that they receive from their customers and people in general. As the volume of mail is quite large, the installed e-mail tracker segregates the mails and provides the list of potential customers, based on certain checks and balances.

Thus *NEocast* is a perfect example of the effective use of a technology-intensive marketing tool to sustain and grow in a competitive market.

Discussion Question

Read the above case. Study the technological change in any manufacturing industry and similarly frame your observation to transform their manufacturing process.

(*Hints* Change from mono-casting to continuous-casting, from conventional lathe to CNC lathe (for machining of jobs), from hot metal hardening process to cold-swaging process, etc.).

CHAPTER 12

Human Resources Management, Strategic Dimensions and POM

LEARNING OBJECTIVES

After reading this chapter, you will be able to understand:

- Meaning and Concept of Human Resource Management (HRM)
- Importance of HRM for POM
- History of HRM
- Various Functions of HRM
- HRM as a Strategic Function
- HRM as a Process
- Difference between Human Resource Management and Human Resource Development
- Various roles of HR Managers

Opening Vignette

Efficiency of POM through Comprehensive HRM Practices in Japan

Differences in HRM practices affect the performance and productivity of workers at the plant level. Japan is known for its comprehensive HRM practices, where the focus is on developing problem-solving teams, continuous worker development through training, absolute transparency through information sharing, job rotation, employment security, and profit sharing. In contrast, in the USA, at the plant level, comprehensive HRM practices largely centre on developing a problem-solving team and information sharing. This leads to relatively less efficiency at the plant level. We can understand this better when we benchmark the performance data of two plants engaged in the production of similar items: one in Japan and the other in the USA. Worker's participation in management cannot be ensured only by the formation of problem-solving teams.

It requires to be strengthened with employment security in line with the system in Japan. Without employment security, workers may fear that efforts to increase productivity will go against their interests. Similarly, job rotation practices require multi-skilled workers through continuous training. Thus, a comprehensive HRM practice plan in line with the Japanese model can contribute significantly to worker efficiency and to the efficiency of production and operations management functions in organizations.

12.1 INTRODUCTION

In production and operations management functions, workers' involvement in decision making and mutual discussions are necessary. Particularly in job scheduling and maintenance operations, these are essential. In service operations such requirements are even more, due to the need to interact with customers. When such decisions and interactions are not in conformity with requirements, organizational performance is affected. It is for this reason that production and operations managers need to understand the basics of human resource management functions. Through our opening case study, we have also tried to highlight the importance of human resource management issues for production and operations management. Today, many organizations train their line function staff on the basics of HRM, so that they can understand the human dynamics involved in the production and operations process.

12.2 HISTORY OF HRM

Before the industrial revolution, the status of labour was extremely low and the human relationships between the employers and the employees were characterized by slavery, serfdom and the Guild system. Slavery was based on a negative incentive system, while serfdom was based on a positive incentive system. The Guild System involving Master Craftsmen (the owner), the Journeyman (the traveling workers) and the Apprentice marked the beginning of Human Resource Management practices involving the selection, training and development of workers and the emergence of collective bargaining over wages and working conditions.

The industrial revolution followed the new economic doctrine of laissez-faire; new industrial organizations were characterized by a factory system (a change from the cottage system or home-centered production system; this caused a deterioration in the employer–employee relationship due to an unhealthy work environment, long working hours, fatigue, monotony, strain, increased likelihood of accidents, etc.).

Great thrust had been given to personnel management functions by business expansion, labour strategies and higher wage rates during World War I (1917). Before this, the thrust had been more on labour welfare to ensure that workers are not exploited in organizations. This was because social activists, political parties and trade unions of different countries were putting pressure on the governments of various countries to come out with legislations pertaining to labour, so that they are protected and given their due rights and privileges. Labour Welfare Officers were statutorily appointed to ensure that the interests of workers were safeguarded. Thus, many activities were initiated for welfare and paternalism. Labour Welfare Officers had no managerial role then. However, the devastating effect of the world war necessitated urgent reconstruction of the economy. At the organization level, there was immediate need to augment productivity. Labour Welfare Officers being more proximate to workers, were given the additional role of personnel management, so that they could effectively motivate people to contribute more towards enhancing productivity. The great depression of 1920–21, threw many personnel men out of jobs resulting in disillusionment in the profession. A number of literatures came up around the world during 1920–22, dealing with different areas of personnel administration and by 1923, the profession had reached a stage of maturity, as organizations started giving importance to this profession, recognizing its imperativeness like other core functions such as production and marketing.

12.3 DEFINITIONS AND CONCEPTS OF HRM

HRM is the management of an organization's human resources. This definition of HRM considers it from a normative perspective that focusses on the hard and soft dimensions of HRM. The hard dimension is the traditional approach that suggests linking of HRM functions (human resource planning, recruitment and selection, compensation, performance management issues, labour legislations, etc.) to organizational strategy. It conforms to the Harvard Model. The soft dimensions of HRM conforms to the Michigan Model, and it views HR as human capital, or as an asset, hence, it suggests managing this human capital by making use of organizational development, conflict management, leadership development, organizational culture, culture of collaboration, etc. Some of these definitions can be categorized under the normative category.

Boselie (2002) observes, "Human resource management involves management decisions related to policies and practices which together shape the employment relationship and are aimed at achieving individual, organizational, and societal goals." Schermerhorn (2001) considers HRM as the "process of attracting, developing and maintaining a talented and energetic workforce to support organizational mission, objectives, and strategies".

While Boselie's focus is on the achievement of social goals, meeting other stakeholders' requirements, Schermerhorn focussed on achieving organizational goals. Both the definitions consider HRM from the normative perspective. As per these two definitions, HRM function covers human resource planning (HRP), recruitment and selection, compensation management, training and development, performance management, motivation, organizational change and development, team development, work–life balance etc.

HRM can also be considered from the descriptive and conceptual perspectives. The descriptive perspective is concerned with getting facts right; while the conceptual aspect relates such facts to each other. Descriptive HRM, therefore, may not have any theoretical base. However, on the other hand, conceptual and normative perspectives require a sound theoretical foundation (Guest, 1997; Storey, 1992).

There are two more theoretical approaches to HRM; these are the Harvard model and the Michigan approach. The Michigan approach was developed by Fombrun and others (1984). Basically, it stems from the strategic orientation of traditional personnel management functions, like HRP, recruitment and selection, performance appraisals, rewards and compensation, and development. This approach argues that organizational policies in these areas will have an effect on the individual performance of its employees.

The Harvard model was developed and presented in Beer et al. (1984). The Harvard approach assumes that the interests of employees and other stakeholders, together with situational factors, have a direct influence on HRM policy choices (Boselie, 2002). The model recognizes that employees are not only resources for the production process, but also individuals in themselves. The Harvard model, therefore, stresses on the human factor in human resource management and emphasizes that the central objective of HRM should be to align employees with the organization and management. This requires the strategic vision of HR functions. The extent to which the HR of an organization nurtures strategic vision can be assessed by understanding the extent of integration of HRM practices with organizational policy.

The main distinction between the two approaches is while one limits the focus on the shareholders (Michigan), the other also includes social stakeholders (Harvard). Another possible distinction is that while the Harvard approach stresses the importance of the motivation of employees, the Michigan approach focusses on the ability of employees.

HRM can also be considered from the resource-based and behavioural perspectives. The resource-based view assumes that physical, organizational and human resource differences between companies lead to differences in their productive potential. Such heterogeneity in resources ultimately provides long-term competitiveness to the organization and differentiates one organization from another. The ultimate competitive advantages of an organization not only depend upon the differentiating resources but also on resources, which are sustainable and difficult to imitate (Prahalad and Hamel, 1990; Rangone, 1999). From this perspective, HR is the only sustainable competitive advantage factor for the organization. Organizations, therefore, try to stay competitive, by continuous development and renewal of the competencies of their human resources. Because of the importance of human resources, organizations have to adopt suitable HR strategies, keeping in view their objectives. In all HR functions, therefore, we frame strategies, which best align with organizational objectives.

The behavioural perspective on HRM focusses on the use of those HR practices as tools, which best shape, employee behaviour to achieve the desired goals and objectives of an organization (Naylor et al., 1980). The underlying assumptions are that different goals and objectives require different strategies and behaviours, and, therefore, different HRM practices (Snell, 1992). This obviously requires focussing on external fit, on contingency variables like size, technology, ownership, location etc. (Huselid, 1995; Legge, 1995; Delery and Doty, 1996). Based on this perspective, Schuler and Jackson (1987) tested Porter's three generic strategies (Porter, 1985) aligning different HRM practices. Their study suggested, if an organization selects HR policy and practices appropriate to particular generic strategies, they could experience higher work performance. Thus, the argument of fitting strategy and HRM practices is compelling.

12.4 HRM AND STRATEGY

HR Strategy is the pattern of decisions concerning policies and practices associated with the HR system. Each organizational system encompasses all the functional areas of an organization and thereby helps in the formulation of organization-wide strategies. Strategic Human Resource Management (SHRM) is a competency-based approach for the management of HR. It focusses on developing HR for sustainable competitive advantage.

There has been considerable debate about what 'Strategic Human Resource Management' (SHRM) actually means. There are many definitions, including:

- 'A human resource system that is tailored to the demands of the business strategy' (Miles and Snow 1984).
- 'The pattern of planned human resource activities intended to enable an organization to achieve its goals' (Wright and McMahan 1992).

Such definitions range from a portrayal of SHRM as a 'reactive' management field where human resource management is a tool with which to implement strategy, to a more proactive function in which HR activities can actually create and shape the business strategy (Sanz-Valle et al, 1998).

The range of activities and themes encompassed by SHRM can be seen, for example, in Mabey et al (1998), which looks at the subject from four perspectives:

1. The social and economic context of SHRM – including the internal (corporate) and external environments that influence the development and implementation of HR strategies.
2. The relationship between SHRM and business performance, emphasizing the measurement of performance.
3. Management style and the development of new forms of organization.
4. The relationship between SHRM and the development of organizational capability, including knowledge management.

Strategic HRM has been studied from three perspectives (Delery and Doty, 1996) – universalistic, contingency and configurational. The universalistic (or "best practices") studies look for particular policies or practices that are more effective than others and result in gains for all firms. Empirical studies from the universal perspective (Arthur, 1994; Huselid, 1995) have focussed on sets of "high performance work practices" that result in high levels of organizational outcomes but not necessarily outcomes directed at any particular strategy.

Both the contingency and configurational perspectives hold the idea that given a corporate strategy, certain HRM practices will support that strategy by shaping behaviours and outcomes. The contingency perspective links choices of practices within HRM systems to firm-level strategic positions (Schuler and Jackson, 1987). The empirical studies in this group (Begin, 1993; Gomez-Mejia and Balkin, 1992) have focussed on linking particular systems (for example, compensation systems) to a strategic model.

Configuration theorists take a more holistic approach by looking for ideal types and explicitly adopt a system assumption of equifinality (Doty, Glick and Huber, 1993). They examine how a pattern of several independent variables relates to a dependent variable. Wright and McMahan (1992) argued that to be effective, a firm's HRM systems must be aligned with the firm's strategy and with each other. Becker & Gerhart (1996) suggested that the architecture might be more important than specific practices. As an empirical example, Schuler and Harris (1991) demonstrated a specific configuration of HRM practices as highly aligned with an organization pursuing Deming-style quality as a corporate strategy.

There are a number of theories which define the role of HR Strategy. Behavioural role theory, pioneered by Katz and Khan (1978), Jackson and Schuler (1995), considers employee behaviour as key to successful strategy implementation. By aligning HR policies and practices with organization-wide strategy, employees can fulfill their role expectations within the organization. Resource-based theory, of Barney (1991) and Prahalad and Hamel (1990), suggests that HR has the sustainable competitive advantage for the organization. This is because HR is a characteristically rare, inimitable and non-substitutable resource for achieving competitive advantage. Other resources do not have such characteristic features. Becker's (1964) Human Capital Theory suggests that other economic assets such as knowledge, skills and abilities of the people are of strategic importance to HR and have economic values. This concept led to the development of human resource accounting by Flamholtz (1981) and others. Transaction cost theory of Williamson (1981) suggests that a Strategic HR approach can ensure cost minimization, as this will enhance periodic monitoring and governance. Eisenhardt's Agency Theory (1989) suggests that the strategic approach to HR aligns the interests of agents (employees) and principals (employers) and thereby ensures the streamlining of employment relations and systems within the organization.

All the above theories justify the alignment of HR with organization-wide strategy and therefore, they are grouped under Rational Choice Theories of HR. Institutional (Meyer and Rowen, 1977; Powell and DiMaggio, 1991) and dependency (Pfeffer and Salancik, 1977) theories on HR strategy, however, focus on constituency-based interest. This is because the strategic approach to HR is not empirically proved to be a contributor to organizational performance.

Prima facie, environmental, organizational, institutional and technological factors are potential influencers in strategy. The relative importance of each such factor will depend on organizational characteristics. However, for HRP, we need to give cognizance to each such factor, in order that it is a strategic decision for sustaining organizational growth and profitability. Any redundancy decision, without considering the possible reaction of unions may transpire as defeating. Similarly, for an FMCG organization, the product life-cycle is short, so employees with multiple skill-sets will always be better than those with specialized skill sets. In this chapter, we have discussed strategy as an organization-wide initiative with policies; procedures and examples of HR strategy have been provided, duly linking these with organizational strategy.

Strategic human resource management, therefore, requires the formulation of HR objectives, strategies and policies. These enable the provision of the skills and abilities needed to meet the requirements of an organization's overall objectives. In other words, they provide the framework, which ensures that in an organization, employee needs are met. In modern organizations, HR strategy is supported by information technology in the form of human resource information systems and workforce management systems.

Human resource management reflects an organization's strategy regarding people, profit and overall effectiveness. People are the greatest assets of an organization, because, through people all other resources are converted into utilities. However, the management of 'people resources' has always been a problem ever since the beginning of organized human activities. People can limit or enhance the strengths and weaknesses of an organization. Today, the changes experienced by organizations around the world include growing global competition, rapidly expanding technologies, increasing demand for individual and team responsibilities and competencies, increasing legal and compliance scrutiny and rising customer expectations. Changing markets and advances in communication technologies are paving the way to a new kind of working – in virtual teams. While virtual teams bring their share of opportunities, they also bring their share of challenges. They call for greater emphasis on communication and openness to a global community. As long as the benefits outweigh the challenges, virtual teaming enabled by technology will increasingly be the way organizations are going to work in the future. These changes combined with the realization that the performance of a firm's human assets must be managed, led and coached have resulted in the need for strategic planning and modern HRM practices. Because of the recognition of the crucial importance of people, HRM in an increasing number of organizations has become a major player in developing key plans. Today's HRM strategies must reflect clearly the organization's strategy regarding people, profit and overall effectiveness. HR professionals are expected to play a crucial role in improving the skills of employees and the firm's profitability. In essence, HRM is now viewed as a "profit centre" and not simply a "cost centre".

The HRM function, therefore, is strategically significant for organizational survival and prosperity For HR professionals, it is extremely important to understand the strategic manifestation of various HRM functions, including human resource planning. Some of the key concepts are:

- Analyzing and solving problems from a profit-oriented, not just service-oriented point of view
- Assessing and interpreting cost benefits of issues like performance, legal compliances, employee satisfaction, salaries and benefits, human resource planning, recruitment, training, absenteeism, turnover, training effectiveness, overseas relocations, layoffs, attitude surveys, accident rates and return on investments
- Using planning models that include realistic, challenging, specific and meaningful goals
- Preparing reports on HRM solutions to problems encountered by the firm.
- Training HR staff and emphasizing the strategic importance of HRM and its role in contributing to the firm's profits.

12.5 HR STRATEGY FACTORS

HR strategy factors encompass those areas, which are instrumental to the success of an organization. We can classify such factors (See Table 12.1).

The HRM function today is much more integrated and strategically involved. The importance of recruiting, selecting, training, developing, rewarding, compensating and motivating the workforce is recognized by managers in every unit and functional area of an institution. The increased strategic importance of HRM means that human resource specialists must show that they contribute to the goals and mission of the firm. The actions, language and performance of the HRM function must be measured, precisely communicated and evaluated.

Table 12.1 *HR strategy functions: A classification*

Recruitment and selection	Outsourcing or direct recruitment, contractual or on permanent payroll, multi-skill attributes or specialization are some of the issues considered at this level.
Career development	Career mapping, succession planning and management development, integrating career development with OD initiatives are the factors considered in this area
Performance appraisal	Designing appropriate tools and aligning such appraisal with training needs, promotion, transfer and relocation are the issues that deserve attention at this stage.
Training and development	Developing in house training, ROI models for evaluating training, training budgets, etc. are considered at this level.
Compensation designing	Designing compensation and incentive schemes, suitable to attract talent and retain them, NWLC aspects, etc. are the crucial factors.
Human Resource Planning (HRP)	Developing a Human Resource Information System, aligning HRP with corporate strategies, skill and competence mapping are important aspects of strategic HRP.

12.6 DIFFERENT SCHOOLS OF THOUGHT AND HRM

Despite our lengthy discussions delineating the HRM function from traditional personnel management and labour welfare, we still observe a reflection of traditional percepts of HRM practices. Often, they dilute the view that people are a resource and continue to treat people as a liability to the organization. Such paradoxical precepts can be better understood, when we see job advertisements for personnel managers or staff officers. Modern HR is more strategic, innovative and business integrated. However, without stretching the debate, we still find different schools of thoughts on HRM as under:

HRM is personnel management: It is argued that HRM is personnel management in a repackaged form. In fact, renaming personnel management and calling it HRM is a recognition of the profession in line with the other functional management areas, like marketing or finance.

HRM is strategic: For HRM functions, HR managers employ all the strategic management techniques, and even align HR functions with the business goals and strategies of the organizations.

HRM is managing people: HRM overviews all aspects of employee management, in tandem with the goals and objectives of the organization. It indicates HRM looks after all the operational aspects of people management issues.

Given all these approaches to HRM, Guest (1989) said HRM is a 'catch-all phrase'.

12.7 HUMAN RESOURCE MANAGEMENT AS A PROCESS

Tracing the process of development and growth of the world economy, we can summarize that the 80's were all about automation. The 90's, on the other hand, have been about people. Total Quality Management practices, to achieve organizational excellence throughout the 90's, focussed on people-related issues as key drivers for organizational change and transformation. Even the Six Sigma approach, developed subsequently, emphasizes people. Looking at some of the Excellence Models, like; EFQM (European Foundation of Quality Management), the Shingo Prize Model and the Malcolm Baldrige Model, it is evident that people-centred issues have received the highest attention, over technology and process. Before we proceed further, let us understand the people-centred definition of Total Quality Management (TQM).

The word TQM is defined in two parts. In the first part, we try to understand the definition of Total Quality, which is the quality of all people, at all levels, in all functional areas. In the second part, we try to understand TQM as a whole. TQM is organizational improvement strategy through TQ, or to be more specific TQM is organizational improvement strategy through the development of people. Among others, TQM focusses on:

- delegation
- involvement
- ownership of cross functional teamwork
- self-managed work teams

Six Sigma approach suggests recreating an existing process to make it error free. At Six Sigma level, we need to perform at 99.999666% of accuracy, or the natural occurrence of defects can only be 3.4 in one million jobs.

The EFQM, the Shingo Prize, Malcolm Baldrige and the Investor In People Models, consider HRM as a critical input to enhance business success. Some of the common HRM criteria considered by these models are:

- Planning, managing and improving human resources.
- Identifying, developing and sustaining people's knowledge and competencies.
- Involving and empowering people.

Thus, HRM inputs have a significant impact on the performance of the organization.

In the 90's, there was also discussion about business processes. Hammer and Champy (1993), while investigating and researching on business process architectures and models, classified the business process as under:

- manage processes
- operate processes and
- support processes

Within this architecture, HRM is classified as a support process, together with finance and IT. Therefore, there is a need to understand HRM as a business process in order to improve manufacturing performance. Considering HRM as a business process, Legge (1995) and Tyson (1995) developed HRM models. Legge has identified four HRM models:

- normative
- descriptive–functional
- descriptive–behavioural
- critical–evaluative.

Tyson has identified three HRM models:

- normative
- descriptive and
- analytical

Generally, in the literature, there is confusion with respect to the definitions of the normative model, descriptive model and analytical model. For example, the Harvard Model of HRM described by Torrington and Hall (1998) is analytical, while Pinnington and Edwards described the same model as normative. Actually, the Harvard model is made up of both prescriptive and analytical elements.

12.8 HRM AS A SYSTEM

Let us first understand the meaning and definitions of a system. A system is an entity, which maintains, exists and functions as a whole, interacting with its parts. Therefore, the behaviour of any system depends on how its parts are inter-related. Parts are the elements or components, but they have inter-connectivity. For example, Hay's performance evaluation system has several components. Sear's three C (compelling place to work, compelling place to shop and a compelling place to invest) has 74 elements or parts to evaluate a particular employee, how far he/she is meeting the three C requirements. The ISO 9000 Quality System has 20 elements or parts, which together make a Quality Assurance System. Individual elements of the ISO 9000 Quality System hardly have any significance, unless they are integrated with the total system. Therefore, the properties of a system are the properties of the whole.

When we consider HRM has a system, different elements or components of HRM like procurement (human resource planning and recruitment and selection function), maintenance (compensation, discipline, industrial relations) and development (performance appraisal and training and development), act as parts. Checkland (1984) used Systems Engineering principles, while categorizing HRM systems into hard and soft categories. A hard system approach deliberates on organizational requirements and identifies ways to meet such requirements. Thus, this approach, using well-defined systems formulate goals, identify problems, ascertain and evaluate options, and finally, select and implement rational plans to achieve the desired outcome. For these reasons, a hard system is considered a task-focussed approach. The soft systems approach, on the other hand, focusses on understanding what the purported HR system should do and how it should behave. More logically, it can be considered as an approach to refer to a problem situation with the intention of developing a conceptual model that defines how the system should operate.

12.9 HUMAN RESOURCE MANAGEMENT TECHNIQUES

A technique is a process, style and method of doing something. It might be the only way to do it, or it might be a version of the possible methods. A technique can be a very specific method set in stone, or more likely, it is a way of doing it that works. Human Resource Management techniques include:

- facilitating the implementation of team work
- assisting with annualized hours and shifts systems
- setting up and monitoring work organization projects
- training in a wide range of work study techniques

12.10 HRM FUNCTIONS

HRM Functions for any organization consider acquisition, maintenance and development of human resources. While the acquisition and maintenance functions of HR are concerned with manpower planning, recruitment, compensation design and discipline and industrial relations issues, the development functions concentrate more on performance management and training and development functions. The acquisition function of HR is known as the 'getting phase'. The maintenance function of HR is known as the 'keeping phase'. The development function of HR is known as the 'progressing phase'. We can list HRM functions as follows:

- manpower planning
- recruitment and selection
- compensation design and management
- employee motivation
- employee relations
- employee services
- employee performance management
- employee training and development

The functions of human resource management would be clearer from the changing expectations of the organizations from human resource managers. Let us review a job statement for HR managers from a diversified manufacturing group.

We expect our HR manager to:

- oversee the functioning of the HR department.
- arrange the systems for all the basic HR work.
- work with subordinates to recruit, train and dismiss employees.
- establish and maintain good relations with employees.

- plan and formulate HR policies.
- develop performance appraisal programmes.
- manage compensation schemes.
- coordinate with other managers.
- develop an efficient and motivated workforce.

Many organizations have renamed their HRM function to human resource development (HRD), though conventionally HRD is a sub-set of HRM. HRD percepts of HRM are based on the premise that organizations can achieve business results through their sustained focus on continuous development of human resources. Such efforts build the capabilities of employees and make them competent to cope with any eventualities in the future. Therefore, human resource management process should have more of a development focus.

12.11 ROLES, DUTIES AND RESPONSIBILITIES OF A HUMAN RESOURCE MANAGER

Traditionally, the role of the human resource management functions is to systematically monitor and comply with the people management issues in an organization. In such a traditional role, the HR department is viewed more as an impediment to achieving organizational objectives. The modern role of HR managers is, however, keeping pace with the changing needs of the organization on people management aspects. The test of efficiency of such a role for HR managers can be understood better, when organizations are able to become more adaptable, and respond quickly to customer requirements. This acknowledges HR's strategic role – acting to advocate and mentor change, facilitating employees.

HR managers constantly assess the effectiveness of HR functions, sponsor the change process, promote the overall success of their organizations, and champion the identification of the organizational mission, vision, goals, objectives and action plans. Finally, HR managers also determine the measures to assess organizational success.

Since HR managers are concerned with the management aspect of people-related issues, organization-wise their function varies. Thus, depending on the size of the organization, the HR manager has responsibility for all of the functions that deal with the needs and activities of the organization's people including the following areas of responsibility:

- human resource planning
- recruiting
- training
- developing organization structuring
- organization development
- communication

- performance management
- coaching/mentoring
- drafting HR Policies and recommending its implementation
- compensation management
- team building
- employee relations
- health and safety issues
- compliance with employment related laws
- leadership

With all of this in mind, in his book, *Human Resource Champion*, Dave Ulrich, among the best thinkers and writers in the HR field today, and a Professor at the University of Michigan, has recommended three additional roles for the HR manager.

1. Strategic Partner HR is now acknowledged as a strategic function. The HR manager's role as a strategic partner, requires effective contribution to the development and accomplishment of organization-wide business plans and objectives. The HR business objectives are to support the attainment of the overall strategic business plan and objectives. At the tactical level, HR managers design suitable work systems to support organizational strategies. People achieve success and develop their capability in line with the strategic intent of the organizations with the support of HR. Therefore, strategic partnership of HR has an impact on HR services like design of work systems, recruitment, compensation management, performance management, career development, etc.

2. Employee Advocate As a sponsor or advocate of people, HR managers play an integral role in achieving organizational success. The advocacy role requires expertise in nurturing a work environment that motivates people to spontaneously contribute to organizational needs. Employees, by developing their problem-solving skills, would feel responsible to set their own goals, achieve the same through self-empowerment and develop a sense of ownership of the organization. The scope of an employee advocacy role for HR managers, therefore, encompasses a wide range of issues concerning organizational culture and climate. Competency development, commitment to customers, employee development opportunities, employee assistance programmes, strategic compensation designing, organizational development, etc. are some of the initiatives taken by HR managers in this direction.

3. Change Champion Organizational change is a regular phenomenon. It can be either planned or routine. Planned changes are initiated in response to changes in the business environment, while routine changes are regular changes, more in the nature of periodic organizational restructuring. Both in the case of a planned change and routine change, HR managers play a crucial role. HR requires constantly evaluating the effectiveness of results and understanding the need for change, so that the organization can continue to grow. To champion the change, HR managers should have adequate knowledge and skill, not only to identify the change areas, but also to execute the change process, with the least amount of employee resistance and dissatisfaction. These apart, HR managers can play the role of business partners, policy formulators, internal consultants, service providers and monitors.

We can better appreciate the HR manager's role, by going through the following advertisement for a HR manager for a large organization.

Job Title: HR Manager
Responsible to (Line): General Manager
Responsible to (Function): HR Head
Responsible for (Line): Steel Manufacturing HR
Purpose/Role: Provide a professional, integrated HR service, aligned to the business strategy of the organization.

Key aims and objectives:

- Capable of using creative and innovative methods to harmonize diverse HR and business concepts and policies.
- Develop and implement integrated and coherent HR strategies to suit the local environment, aligning with organizational objectives.
- Optimize the deployment of human resources
- Frame suitable HR policies, procedures and systems in accordance with organizational HR values.
- Work within a budget.

Prime responsibilities and duties:

- To contribute and assist in the development and achievement of corporate objectives through support and advice to management on the optimum deployment of human resources, including the development of supporting strategies, policies and procedures
- Develop, introduce and maintain appropriate HR policies, procedures and systems, which are aligned with the needs of the organization.
- Assist in the expansion and enhancement of sustainable business
- To manage the implementation of the company's HR strategy
- Ensure business compliance with policies, procedures and legislations

- Develop and implement recruitment programmes which comply with all legal requirements, code of practice and organizational policy.
- Develop suitable remuneration packages for employees based upon sound market information
- Resource vacancies in a prompt, professional and cost effective manner
- Develop and manage budgets within the HR function
- Contribute to the development of HR strategy for the organization.
- Develop and progress appropriate resource strategies and plans with relevant line management
- Development and administration of policies for assigning staff away from their normal workplace
- Ensure effective implementation of health and safety policy

Allied occasional duties:

- Implementation of the company's disciplinary and grievance procedures
- Advising management on maintaining good employee relations
- Contribute to the development of manpower and succession plans
- Produce timely and accurate management information and reports on human resources
- Advise line management on appropriate labour law issues
- Work closely with other aspects of the operation to facilitate the development and harmonization of common areas.

Core competencies:

- Openness
- Safety, Health, Environmental
- Drive for Excellence
- Self-Motivation
- Flexibility
- Adaptability
- Perceptiveness
- Interpersonal awareness
- Communication
- Cross cultural awareness

- Business and commercial awareness
- Influencing leadership

12.12 HR MANAGER'S ROLE: CLARIFICATIONS

Using the table (12.2) below, we can understand how an organization can assign weights to different functional/competency areas of an HR manager. However, this varies from organization to organization. While in one organization, strategic perspective may get less weight, in another, it may receive the highest weightage.

Table 12.2 *Functional/competency areas of a HR manager*

Behaviour	Category	Definition
Strategic perspective	B	Focus on issues to support the broad organizational strategy. Maintain a broad view, and understand and consider the interests and aims of different stakeholders, both within and outside the organization.
Maximizing potential	A	Develop systems and strategies befitting the development of human resources at all levels of the organization. Create and nurture an environment that motivates people to achieve results.
Negotiation and influencing	A	Practice negotiation and influencing skills to persuade and exert influence over people, using logic and reason. Successfully sell the benefits of the ideas that provide acceptable solutions for all, both within and outside the organization.
Respect and value diversity	A	Understand the cross-cultural differences and be sensitive to social and racial differences. Ensure equal employment opportunity to all, irrespective of their social, cultural and racial differences.
Effective communication	B	Ensure transparency in communication (without compromising organizational confidentiality). Help people to understand organizational needs, instructions and decisions clearly. Make the communication style more adaptive to organizational needs and check the understanding of employees.

Planning and organizing	B	Effectively plan activities for self and others. Build milestones into plans, monitor progress and adjust plans to respond to changes. Make sure plans provide clear directions to people and ensure that they understand what is expected of them.
Personal responsibility	A	Be responsible for the actions of self and others. Manage situations and problems, leading by example, which demonstrates a commitment and determination to succeed. Focus on continuous learning and development.
Problem Solving	A	Develop problem-solving skills for self and others, applying different analytical techniques and understanding complex information issues.

12.13 HR ORGANIZATIONAL STRUCTURE

Organizing people is among the most challenging tasks of an organization. Through this division of work, individuals can become specialists at a specific job. Because a company usually has several employees – often at different locations – working towards a common objective, "there must be a plan showing how the work will be organized. The plan for the systematic arrangement of work is the *organization structure*. Organization structure is comprised of functions, relationships, responsibilities, authorities, and communications of individuals within each department" (Sexton, 1970). Child (1977) commented, "The design of its organization is one of management's major problems. This entails creating a structure which suits the need of the particular enterprise or institution, achieving consistency between the various aspects of the structure and adapting it over time to changing circumstances."

Mintzberg (1979) has developed four basic parts to illustrate the features of an organization structure. These include:

- foundation of organization (basic parts, coordinating mechanisms and the system of flow),
- design parameters,
- contingency factors and
- structural configurations.

Design parameters consider job specialization, behaviour formulation, training, unit grouping, planning and control systems, liaison devices, vertical decentralization and horizontal decentralization. Contingency factors consider age and size, technical system, environment and power. Structural configuration translates all the above stated factors into a simple structure, which includes machine structure, professional bureaucratic, divisional and adhocracy.

We depict the structure of an organization through a chart. This concept of structuring an organization through a chart has been in use since 1854 from Daniel McCallum, Superintendent of New York and Erie Railroad (Wren, 2004). The initial shape of the organization chart was more like a tree, where the roots represented the top hierarchy of management, the branches indicated departments and the leaves are the employees and the workers. Chandler (1988) improved the chart to establish the line of authority.

The organization structure of a HR Department depends on specific roles, which HR has to play in the organization. Following the basic principles of organizational structuring, the structure of the HR Department of TCS is reproduced below (Fig 12.1):

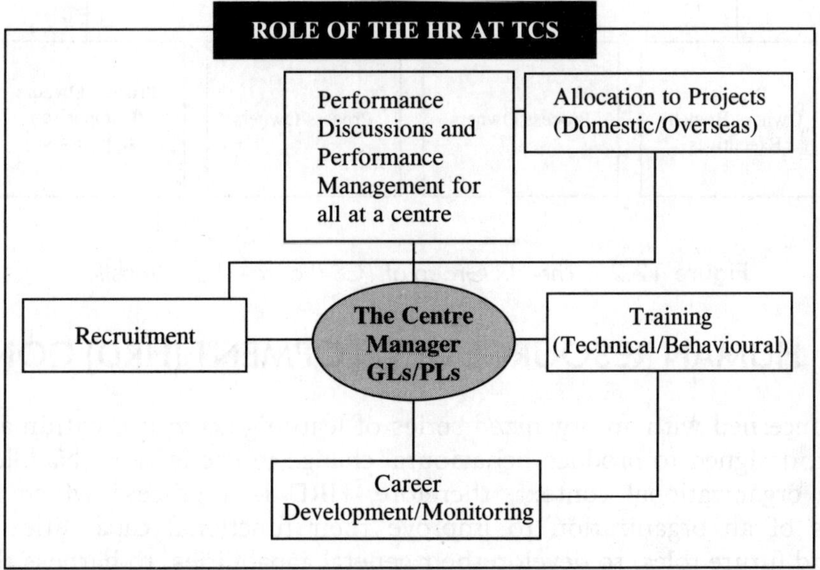

Figure 12.1 *Structure of the HR Department at TCS (Source: TCS website)*

The TCS-HR group operates with technical experts to create a synergy, which is enviable. HR evidently plays the role of a facilitator, a catalyst to initiate and institutionalize processes.

Figure 12.2 illustrates that the HR head at each region has a sufficient degree of authority to carry out relevant functions and yet is easily accessible for advice and guidance. Such a structure promotes sharing of best practices across regions and the institutionalization of the best across regions.

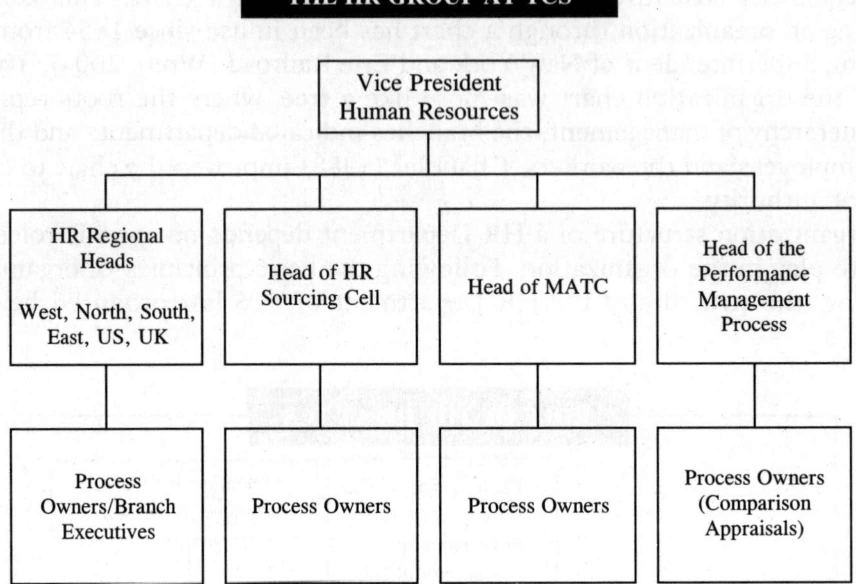

Figure 12.2 *The HR Group at TCS (Source: TCS Website)*

12.14 HUMAN RESOURCE DEVELOPMENT (HRD) CONCEPTS

HRD is concerned with an organized series of learning activities, within a specified time limit, designed to produce behavioural change in the learner (Naddler, 1969). From the organizational context, therefore, HRD is a process which helps the employees of an organization to improve their functional capabilities for their present and future roles, to develop their general capabilities, to harness their inner potential, both for self development and organizational development and to develop an organizational culture to sustain harmonious superior–subordinate relationships, teamwork, motivation, quality and a sense of belonging.

There are several misconceptions about training, education and development functions vis-à-vis HRD. Essentially, HRD activities are designed to make people effective in their present job position; this is a part of the training function. But when the focus is on a future identifiable job it becomes a part of the education function. For future unidentifiable jobs, that is, to develop capabilities for a future position or new activities within the organization, which are not very specific at the present stage, it becomes a part of the development function. Without precisely knowing the functions of training, education and development, it would be difficult for us to appreciate the objectives, roles and significance of HRD in an organization.

12.14.1 Role of HR Manager from a POM Perspective

It is apparent that the primary goal of HR is to increase worker productivity and the firm's profitability. The other goal is to prevent obsolescence at all levels. To achieve these two goals, the HR Manager of any organization plays the following important roles:

1. To assist people in obtaining the knowledge and skills they need for present and future jobs and to assist them in attaining their personal goals.
2. To play an 'enabling' role, providing the right context in which human performance occurs and the organization reaches its stated objectives.

12.14.1.1 Line Managers and HRD

Udai Pareek and T. V. Rao (1991) also emphasized the role of line managers in realizing the HR objective of an organization. Since line managers translate the objectives into action, they are responsible for developing and utilizing the manpower. In all the components of HRD – career planning, training, performance appraisal and organization development, line managers have certain specific responsibilities, which precede the development of certain congenial conditions for employees. Line managers need to ensure that they create such conditions in the work place which enable employees to:

- acquire and develop new capabilities;
- perceive the possible outcome of acquiring such new capabilities;
- assess self growth and
- enjoy the growth process.

Since line managers are in close proximity with the operations people, it is their responsibility to create and develop such conditions in the organization, which can then reinforce the HRD objectives of the organization as a whole. Creating the above conditions in the work place, is a pre-condition to realizing the HRD objectives by line managers, which, *inter alia,* also requires them to play a pro-active role.

Line managers need to define the capabilities of employees. By developing a capability profile of employees, they can facilitate skill and competency mapping for other strategic decisions of the organization, like HRP. This input also helps an organization to identify shortages in critical skill areas, and accordingly, an organization can initiate the required action plan through training and development programmes. Apart from the above strategic functions, it also helps in developing a skill inventory, deciding about redundancy, transfer, promotion, relocation, restructuring, redeployment, etc.

Line managers facilitate the identification of training needs. Because they are in close proximity to the operational people, they observe and understand the performance of employees better. This requirement is important even for the documentation of quality standards, i.e., ISO: 9000. All the ISO-certified organizations have documented systems in this respect.

Line managers play other developmental roles to motivate people to learn and take responsibility by continuous coaching and developing problem-solving skills, by recommending them for further training, etc. They encourage employees to promote Small Group Activities (like Quality Circles), TQM clubs, Value Engineering teams, etc. Many organizations prefer to involve line managers in in-house training programmes, rather than outsourcing training experts.

Line managers also play a role in the identification and clarification of Key resource Areas (KRAS)/Key Performance Areas (KPAs). Setting KRAs/KPAs alone cannot set the ball rolling. It requires the continuous support and sustaining of an environment of mutual trust and openness. Line managers by extending their help and support, enable the subordinates to realize their goals. This inculcates a sense of achievement, which has a tremendous motivational benefit.

In OD intervention also, line managers play an important role by identifying the required initiative, by participating in organizational diagnosis surveys, and finally, by implementing the suggested action plan.

Line managers also reinforce team-work and collaboration, suggest rewards for good performance and foster total participation culture by involving subordinates in decision making. These together reinforce the HRD climate in an organization.

Finally, in career planning and development also, line managers play a crucial role in the identification of career opportunities and encouraging subordinates to develop the required potential to grab such opportunities.

Internationally, it is now being debated whether HRM or HRD should continue as a separate support function or be integrated with line functions. Since the organizational structure is also changing (from a traditional functional system to strategic or independent business units), it is bound to get cognizance. HR as a core management knowledge is already recognized. However, for Indian organizations, this requires a major attitudinal change.

SUMMARY

1. The chapter highlights the importance of HRM for production and operations management functions. Although production and operations managers need not be HR specialists, it is necessary for them to understand the basics.
2. The Human Resource Management function in any organization is now recognized as an imperative to achieve organizational goals and objectives. In a competitive world, retaining the competitive advantage of an organization by anything other than human resources is not sustainable. Hence, HRM function has now transcended from mere operational issues to strategic aspects.
3. HRM, per se, cannot be understood without appreciating its process of development, suitably delineating it from traditional labour welfare and personnel management concepts. Even though we still have not found a suitable title for the profession, whether it should be called HRM or HRD and there

obviously exists a difference of opinion, we should leave it to the organizations concerned to name the function as they deem fit.

4. Whether it is utilization or development, strategic or operational, HRM and HRD cannot be separated as one reinforces the other. HRM is an integral part of HRD, and without successful HRM, organizations cannot remain competitive. HRP is an important strategic HRM function for any organization, and it begins with the process of acquisition of manpower.
5. HRM has an important role in Production and Operations Management since the primary goal of HR is to increase worker productivity and the firm's profitability. The other goal is to prevent obsolescence at all levels.
6. Line managers play a focal role in implementing HR practices from a POM perspective.

KEY WORDS

Personnel Management Managerial function focussing more on the operational issues of employee management.

Michigan Model Focus on strategic orientation of traditional personnel management functions, like recruitment and selection, performance appraisals, rewards and compensation, and development.

HRM or Human Resource Management The focus is more on the strategic aspects of people management.

Harvard model This model assumes that the interests of employees and other stakeholders, together with situational factors, have a direct influence on HRM policy choices. The model recognizes that employees are not only resources for the production process, but also individuals in themselves.

HRD Human Resource Development's focus is more on the continuous development of people in organizations.

Resource-based view of HRM It assumes that the ultimate competitive advantages of an organization not only depend upon the differentiating resources but also on resources, which are sustainable and difficult to imitate.

VRS Voluntary Retirement Scheme is adopted by organizations to rationalize their manpower.

Behavioural perspective of HRM It recommends the use of those HR practices as tools, which can best shape employee behaviour to achieve the desired goals and objectives of an organization.

TQM In Total Quality Management, the focus is on organizational improvement through the development of people.

EFQM European Foundation of Quality Management recommends a model incorporating people-centric issues to achieve organizational excellence.

T-Groups Training Groups focus more on sensitivity-training methodology.

Strategic Human Resource Management (SHRM) It is a competency-based approach for the management of HR. It focusses on developing HR for sustainable competitive advantage

GENERAL REVIEW QUESTIONS

1. Briefly discuss the history of development of the HRM function
2. Discuss the process of development of HRM, suitably delineating it from Labour Welfare and Personnel Management
3. Discuss why it is necessary for a Production and Operations Manager to understand HRM functions
4. What are the general functional areas of HRM? Answer this, keeping in view the HRM functions of any organization.
5. Do you think HRM and HRD are different functions? How did the concept of HRD develop in an organization?
6. Explain the role and significance of HRM. Do you think, in the present context in India, we really need HRM professionals in our organizations?
7. Outline the focus areas for designing an effective HRM system. Which area or areas do you consider to be more important than others?
8. What are the factors that should be considered while structuring the HRM unit of an organization? Illustrate your answer with an organization chart of the HR department of any organization.
9. Briefly discuss the principles for the functioning of the HRM system of an organization. What are the important roles of a HR Manger?
10. Explain the importance of human resource planning function for an organization. How is human resource planning strategically important for an organization?
11. Short notes
    (a) Structural change in employment
    (b) Kurt Lewin's contribution to the HR field
    (c) T-Groups
    (d) Competitive advantage
    (e) Human Resource Utilization (HRU)
    (f) Integrated HRM functions
    (g) Enabling organization
    (h) Harvard Model
    (i) Configurational School of Thought

(j) HR Manager as Change Champion
(h) HRM System

CRITICAL REVIEW QUESTION

1. Visit a manufacturing plant and critically evaluate its HR systems.

REFERENCES

1. Arthur, J. B. 1994. Effects of human resource systems on manufacturing performance and turnover. *Academy of Management Journal*, 37(3), 670–687
2. Barney, J. 1991. Firm resources and sustained competitive advantage. *Journal of Management*, 17: 99–120
3. Becker, G. 1964. *Human Capital*. Chicago: Chicago University Press
4. Becker, B. and Gerhart, B. 1996. The Impact of Human Resources Management on Organizational Performance: Progress and Prospects. *Academy of Management Journal*, 39: 779–802
5. Begin, J. P. 1993. Identifying Patterns in HRM Systems: Lessons from Organisational Theory. *Research in Personnel and Human Resources Management*, suppl. 3, pp. 3–20.
6. Bhattacharyya, Dipak Kumar. 2006. *Human Resource Management*, 2nd ed. New Delhi: Excel Books.
7. Bhattacharyya, Dipak Kumar. 2007. *Human Resource Research Methods*. New Delhi: Oxford University Press.
8. Bhattacharyya, Dipak Kumar. 2006. *Human Resource Planning*, 2nd ed. New Delhi: Excel Books.
9. Bhattacharyya, Dipak Kumar. 2009. *Organizational Behaviour – Concepts and Applications*. New Delhi: Oxford University Press.
10. Boselie, P. 2002. *Human resource management, work systems and performance: A theoretical–empirical approach*. Tinbergen Institute Research Series 274, Thela Thesis, Amsterdam.
11. Beer, M., B. Spector, P. Lawrence, D. Quinn Mills and R. Walton. 1984. *Managing Human Assets*. New York: Free Press.
12. Child, J. 1977. *Organizatikon*. New York: Harper & Row.
13. Chandler, Alfred D., Jr. 1988. Origins of the Organization Chart. *Harvard Business Review* 88:2, (March/April): p. 156
14. Delery, J. E. and Doty, D. H. 1996. Modes of Theorizing in Strategic Human Resource Management: Tests of Universalistic, Contingency and Configurational Performance Predictions. *Academy of Management Journal*, 39(4): 802–35

15. Doty, D. H., Glick, W. H., Huber, G. P. 1993. Fit, equifinality, and organizational effectiveness: A test of two configurational theories. *Academy of Management Journal*, 36:1196–1250.
16. Flamholtz, E. and Lacey, J. 1981. *Personnel management: Human capital theory and human resource accounting*. Los Angeles: Institute of Industrial Relations, UCLA.
17. Fombrun, Ch.J., N.M. Tichy and M.A. Devanna. 1984. *Strategic human resource management*. New York: Wiley.
18. Gomez-Meija, L.R. and Balkin, D.B. 1992. *Compensation, Organizational Strategy, and Firm Performance*. Cincinnati: South-Western.
19. Guest, D.E. 1997. Human Resource Management and Performance – A review and research agenda. *The Internal Journal of Human Resource Management*, 8(3).
20. Huselid, M.A. 1995. The impact of Human Resource Management Practices on Turnover, Productivity and Corporate Financial Performance. *Academy of Management Journal*, 38: 635–70.
21. Jackson, S.E. and Schuler, R.S. 1995. Understanding human resource management in the context of organizations and their environments. *Annual Review of Psychology*, 46, 237–264.
22. Katz, D., and Kahn, R. 1978. *The Social Psychology of Organizations*. New York: John Wiley & Sons
23. Legge, K. 1995. *Human Resource Management – Rhetoric and Realities*. London: Macmillan Business.
24. Miles, R.H., and Snow, C.C. 1984. Designing Strategic Human Resource Systems. *Organisational Dynamics*, 13(1), pp. 36–52.
25. Mintzberg, H. 1978. Patterns in Strategy Formulation. *Management Science*, 24, pp. 934–48.
26. Pareek, U and Rao, T.V. 1992. *Designing and Managing Human Resource Systems*. New Delhi : Oxford and IBM
27. Schemerhorn, J.R. 2001. *Management Update 2001*, 6th edition, New York: John Wiley and Sons.
28. Schuler, R. and Harris, D. 1991. Deming Quality Improvement: Implications for Human Resource Management as Illustrated in a Small Company. *Human Resource Planning*, 14(3): 191–207.
29. Schuler, R. and Jackson, S. 1987. 'Linking competitive strategies with HRM practices', *Academy of Management Executive*, 1: 207–219.
30. Snell, S. 1992. Control Theory in Strategic Human Resource Management: The Mediating Effect of Administrative Information. *Academy of Management Journal*, 35, 292–327.
31. Storey, J. 1992. *Development in the Management of Human Resources*. Oxford: Blackwell Publishing.
32. Pfeffer, Jeffrey, and Gerald R. Salancik. 1977. Administrator effectiveness: The effects of advocacy and information on achieving outcomes in an organizational context. *Human Relations*, 30: 641–656.

33. Prahalad, CK and Hamel, G. 1990. The core competence of the Corporation. *Harvard Business Review*. May/June
34. Porter, M. 1985. *Competitive advantage: Creating and sustaining superior performance.* New York: Free Press.
35. Powell, Walter W., and Paul J. DiMaggio eds. 1991. *The New Institutionalism in Organizational Analysis.* Chicago: University of Chicago Press.
36. Rangone, A. 1999 A resource based approach to strategy analysis in SMEs. *Small Business Economics,* 12 2: 233–248
37. Sanz-Valee, R., Sabater-Sanchez, R. and Aragon-Sanchez, A. 1999. Human resource management and business strategy links: An empirical study. *The International Journal of Human Resource Management* 10(4), 655–671.
38. Sexton, William P. 1970. "Organization Structure" In William P. Sexton, ed. *Organization Theories*. Columbus, OH: Charles E. Merrill.
39. Mabey, C., Skinner, D., Clark, T. eds. 1998. *Experiencing Human Resource Management*. London: Sage
40. Meyer, John W., and Brian Rowan. 1977. Institutionalized organizations: Formal structure as myth and ceremony. *American Journal of Sociology* 83:340–63
41. Nylor, J., R. Pritchard, and D. Ilgen. 1980. *A Theory of Behaviour in Organizations.* New York: Academic Press.
42. Torrington, D. and L. Hall, 1998. *Human Resource Management*. London: Prentice Hall
43. Tyson, S. 1995. *Human resource strategy*. London: Macmillan
44. Williamson, O. 1981. The Economics of Organization: The Transaction Cost Approach. *American Journal of Sociology*, 87(3): 548–577.
45. Wright, P.M., and McMahan, G.C. 1992. Theoretical Perspectives for Strategic Human Resource Management. *Journal of Management*, 18(2), 295.
46. Wren, Daniel A. 2004. *The Evolution of Management Thought*. New York, NY: John Wiley & Sons.

CASE STUDY

HR Objectives of ONGC

With a total manpower of 40,000, *ONGC* is among the most well-managed public sector units in India. Managing such a mammoth organization is possible only through plans, policies and strategies. *ONGC's* HR focus does not end with just recruitment; through systematic job rotation, it puts the right man in the right job. Sustained training and development efforts make *ONGC's* people motivated performers. In the hi-tech business of oil exploration, *ONGC* could successfully build its capabilities to create a niche for itself in the production of oil and gas-related oil field services. With an envious team of over 18,000 engineers and scientists of high calibre, *ONGC* can be proud of its competent pool of geologists, geophysicists, geochemists, drilling engineers, reservoir engineers, petroleum engineers, production engineers, engineering and technical service providers, financial and human resource experts, IT professionals, etc. *ONGC's* HR team focusses on achieving the following objectives for the company:

- Alignment of HR vision with corporate vision
- Shift from support group to strategic partner in business operations management.
- Enhance productivity and performance by developing employee competency and potential
- Developing professional attitude and approach

CHAPTER 13

Productivity, Incentives and POM

LEARNING OBJECTIVES

After reading this chapter, you will be able to understand:

- Concepts and Definitions of Productivity
- Process of Development of the Concept of Productivity
- Difference between Total Factor and Single Factor Productivity
- Important Drivers and Determinants of Productivity Growth
- Factors to Improve Productivity
- Misconceptions about Productivity
- Productivity Measurement
- Role of Trade Unions in Productivity Improvement
- Productivity-linked Incentives

Opening Vignette

IBM – Productivity-driven Business Growth

After its exit in the 1970s, *IBM* made its re-entry into India in 1992. Among the MNCs, *IBM* employs the highest number of employees in India. With a stupendous growth rate of 800% over a period of five years, it is among the most productive organizations in the country, with more than 1.5 lakh of employees on its payroll, It has about 50 branch offices in India. Its success is attributable to its high rate of productivity. *IBM* as a company always reinvents itself. Its new verticals for IT solutions for SMEs and MMEs (small manufacturing and medium scale manufacturing enterprises), started yielding results. So much so, *IBM* is no longer price prohibitive for small and medium scale enterprises. With such results, *IBM India* is expected to be the one of the largest MNCs in host countries. *IBM* believes that by respecting employees, organizations also receive respect, which cascades to employee sincerity and devotion, and ultimately improves the profit of the organization. Starting its journey in 1918, *IBM* is a class apart, as it could successfully withstand the turmoil of a series of economic recessions, global meltdowns, refocussing its strategies, changing its business focus, and building the capabilities of its employees. *IBM* emphasises improving customer satisfaction, sales and revenue growth, reducing costs, innovating processes, implementing technology and entering new markets. All these indices are positive for *IBM*, making it one of the most productive organizations in the country.

13.1 INTRODUCTION

Productivity is the major driver for effective POM functions. With improved productivity, companies can gain competitive advantages in terms of price efficiency. The concept of productivity received international attention with the declaration of the International Year of Productivity in 1982. Traditionally, productivity was considered an input–output relational measurement. Orthodox views attribute productivity to labour efficiency as output quantification can immediately be related to labour efficiency. However, this assumption suffers from a major lacuna, as many organizations, despite achieving high labour efficiency (measured in terms of value added in manufacturing), suffer from overall dysfunction and become sick.

Organizations operate on team effort, by distributing different functional areas to different departments; ultimate success depends on the effective joint efforts of different teams. A lapse in a single functional area or areas can offset the efficiency of another functional area or areas, so much so that it may ultimately affect corporate efficiency.

Even within the ambit of an input–output relationship, the concept of input has changed widely under the present circumstances. Inputs are no longer confined within the direct materials used for production, but also consider even supportive functions in a more abstract form. Thus knowledge, ideas, information, etc. have also been thought to be within the definitional context of inputs. In an organization, the production section in reality transforms physical inputs to outputs. But other functional departments, though not engaged in direct material transformation, provide supportive inputs to production departments for efficient functioning.

13.1.1 Process of Development

The concept of productivity was originally enunciated by classical economists like Adam Smith, David Ricardo, and J.S. Mill in the 18th and 19th centuries in the form of the law of diminishing return to all resources. However, in the 19th century, Frederick W. Taylor's thesis 'task study' gave a more reasonable slogan to the issue – human worth can be made infinitely more productive not by working harder but by working smarter. In India, the productivity movement and consciousness gained momentum with the establishment of the National Productivity Council (NPC) in 1958.

Tracing history, we find that productivity concepts originally emerged during the post-war period. After the Second World War, the war-ravaged economy in all countries needed urgent reconstruction, renovation and rationalisation. Growth was then everybody's concern and in such a milieu, growth theory was advocated by the economists.

The interest in economic growth and the focus on political, economic, social and cultural relations, anthropological, psychological, institutional, legal, managerial, and administrative and a host of other related aspects are instrumental in furthering economic growth.

The following basic economic factors have been unanimously recognized as crucial factors in economic growth:

- Capital formation for the present and to combat uncertainties in future,
- High productivity of all factors of production and inputs (including time and knowledge).

13.2 DEFINITION OF PRODUCTIVITY

From the introductory discussions, it is clear that productivity ranges from efficiency to effectiveness of the organization as a whole. The concept encompasses any form of output measures, be it the labour turnover and the rates of absenteeism, the measures of customer satisfaction, morale, employee loyalty, degree of job satisfaction, etc. Thus, the concept of productivity literally extends to any form of tangible or intangible outcome of individual or group efforts of employees, and the organization as a whole. This conceptual aspect of productivity, therefore, establishes the fact that productivity has both technical and managerial dimensions. Also, further conceptual analysis of productivity establishes that it has three distinct perspectives: economics, industrial engineering and administration. Because of the importance of productivity, from an organizational perspective, it needs to be defined and managed. Most appropriately, Krugman (1990) said "productivity isn't everything, but in the long run it is almost everything"

Iyaniwura and Osoba (1983); Antle and Capalbo (1988) defined productivity as the quantitative relationship between output and input. Likewise, Prokopenko, (1987); Eatwell and Newman (1991) defined productivity as a ratio of some measure of output to some index of input use. Put differently, productivity is nothing more than the arithmetical ratio between the amount produced and the amount of resources used in the course of production. This conception of productivity implies that it can indeed be perceived as the output per unit input, or the efficiency with which resources are utilized (Samuelson and Nordhaus, 1995). In simple terms, therefore, we can define:

Productivity = total output/total input

This, therefore, literally considers productivity as the efficient and effective utilization of the total resources of the organization and the achievement of organizational performance results. Olaoye (1985) defined the concept of productivity from two different dimensions, total factor productivity (TFP) and partial or labour productivity. TFP relates to the relationships between output produced and an index of composite inputs; meaning the sum of all the inputs of basic resources notably labour, capital goods and natural resources. Eatwell and Newman (1991) captioned total factor productivity as 'multi-factor productivity'. The 'multi-factor productivity' concept relates output to any factor of input. Thus, depending on the production process, as the nature of input varies, the definition of productivity also changes. For example in an organization, multi-factor productivity indices may be prepared for production, marketing, finance and HR functions. Again in each functional area, there may be multiple indices. In the production function we may have a raw material consumption index, energy consumption index, quality index, scrap arising index, etc. However, when output relates to per man-hour or per unit of labour, we consider this as partial factor productivity, and in this case, it is also known as labour productivity.

Partial factor productivity (which need not be always labour productivity) is considered as the average product. We can represent it symbolically as follows:

$$APF = Y/Fi,$$

where Y stands for output, and Fi for any individual factor.

APF here indicates the average product. Theoretically, it can only measure the change of per unit output over time, without considering the contributions from different factors, which is not a reality of the production process.

Labour productivity is the ratio of the physical amount of output achieved in a given period in relation to the labour inputs. Theoretically, therefore, labour productivity is the physical volume or value of output per worker or per man-hour. Here, we define labour more holistically, considering all cross-sections of people engaged in the production process, directly or indirectly. Any production process, by nature is the end result of all the activities of the organization, like direct labour hours spent, research and development inputs, managerial activities like planning, organizing, decision making, training, and so on. Labour inputs from all these areas, ultimately lead to achieving the output.

From the above discussions, therefore, we can define productivity as the rate, value, and the cost of producing results in accordance with the organizational objectives. Factors of productivity are the attributes or the property that directly or indirectly exert an influence on achieving results. Parameters are quantifiable factors of productivity. The metrics of productivity are the parameters that are observable and measurable. Machine productivity is the throughput process, while the human productivity is the response to the process to achieve the results.

From an economic point of view, productivity means the yield from:

- each factor of production (land, labour, capital and organization)
- each input (raw materials, fuel, information, time and knowledge)
- overall yield of the joint factors and resources enumerated above in combination.

From a common management perspective, productivity in its broadest sense is the quantitative relationship between what we produce and the resources that we use. There is a distinct difference between production and productivity. In simple terms, production means a process of transformation of raw materials and other inputs into finished goods or services. But productivity denotes surplus-generation. Productivity is defined in terms of an input–output relationship; while production is transforming inputs into output, by adding values, productivity is to get higher output over given input. The excess output, therefore, is tantamount to surplus generation. Productivity can be increased by interchanging the input ratios, while in such a changing process the output will proportionately increase more than the changes in input ratio.

We can therefore, holistically define productivity as the functional efficiency of all the factors of production and all other sub-systems. It is the index of organizational efficiency, as can be understood from the following:

Production	=	value addition to new materials
Productivity	=	efficiency of production
	=	*f* (surplus efficiency of all points)
	=	*f* (Men, Materials, Management)

13.3 KEY DRIVERS OR THE DETERMINANTS OF PRODUCTIVITY GROWTH

Reviewing the cross-country growth literature, Harris (1999) could identify three proximate drivers (the Big Three) of productivity growth. These are

1. investment in machinery and equipment
2. education, training and human capital and
3. openness to trade and investment

Harris further contends, an organization or a nation can move from the proximate determinants to the indirect linkages, and only then can understand how productivity is influenced by a large number of direct or indirect factors. Some of the indirect determinants of productivity as enunciated by Harris are:

1. innovation
2. technology diffusion
3. external economies of scale
4. managerial practices
5. institutional infrastructure

6. national income
7. fiscal policies
8. labour market flexibility
9. stability in exchange rate
10. rate of inflation, etc.

For ease in understanding such indirect linkages, we are explaining briefly how these can bring about changes in productivity.

1. Innovation can help in designing more efficient and effective new products, which can even give market leadership to the organization.
2. Technology diffusion can make the production process more efficient, giving cost and quality competitiveness to organizations.
3. External economies of scale can help in reducing the cost of production. Managerial practices exert a positive influence on productivity achievement.
4. Institutional or public infrastructure can help the organization in the efficient utilization of its resources.
5. Increase or decrease in national income can positively or negatively affect productivity.
6. Industry-friendly fiscal or taxation policy can bring about positive changes in the productivity rate.
7. Labour market flexibility eases the hiring and retention of labour.
8. Finally, a stable exchange and inflation rate can positively influence the rate of productivity.

Sharpe (1998) identifies the following seven determinants of productivity growth:

1. **The rate of technical progress** This can be understood in terms of the rate of new product development, process innovations, etc.
2. **Investment in physical capital** Physical capital is the plant and machineries, equipments and structures. In a physical capital-intensive production process, a worker produces more output than in manual production processes. Therefore, the investment in physical capital is essential for productivity growth.
3. **The quality of the workforce** It includes educational, training and experience levels. Literacy and numeracy skills as well as technical skills are essential to benefit the organization from technical advancement.
4. **The size and quality of the natural resource base** This can be explained with examples from iron-ore or coal mines. With high level deposits, the value addition potential of workers increased, which automatically increased the level of productivity.
5. **Industrial structure and inter-sectoral shifts** Aggregate labour productivity is the weighted average of industry labour productivity levels. Industry labour productivity depends on its structure and also on the inter-sectoral shifts.

6. **The macroeconomic environment or aggregate demand conditions** This is defined by the size of the output gap and the relationship between actual and potential output growth. Prolonged periods of insufficient demand can have a negative long-term effect on productivity growth.
7. **The microeconomic policy environment** This environment is broadly defined as the policies that affect behaviour at the firm level, including trade policy, tax policy, industrial policy, competition policy, and policies on privatization, intellectual property, regulation and foreign ownership.

There is still considerable uncertainty about the drivers of productivity. The relative and absolute contributions made by the different determinants may vary over time and across space. Many of the factors in productivity growth are interrelated and may act in synergy.

13.3.1 Productivity and Unemployment

Labour productivity is determined in terms of output and the number of people engaged for the output. From the macro perspective, therefore, such computation ignores the unemployed (even though they are in the employable age-group) and those who are not employable (being outside the employable age group). This technique of measurement, therefore, is not an efficient indicator of productivity measurement from the social perspective, as we cannot map the efficient allocation of labour forces from the macro or social perspective. Although the unemployment numbers may increase, labour productivity from the societal perspective may also increase.

Obviously, due to such discrepancies, we can consider developing a productivity measure, which considers an inclusive approach of considering unemployed and employed labour, as the labour input. This approach can truly establish a social relationship with labour and manpower availability, and truly reflect the labour productivity rate. Hence, traditional economic relationship established by measuring labour productivity only in terms of labour inputs utilized, may not reflect true productivity from a social perspective.

From a societal productivity perspective, economic downturns have a very negative effect on the overall productivity of the labour force.

13.4 FACTORS TO IMPROVE PRODUCTIVITY

Six important factors affect productivity in an organization. These factors are:

- **Nature and Quality of Raw Materials** This factor demands better methods to eliminate the awful waste which is evident in the use of natural resources and provide for efficient handling.
- **Basic Nature of Process Employed** Drive for better methods in using, what is possibly the most valuable of any nation's resources, demands that

technologies should be used to the best advantage in constantly improved processes. Scientific research should continuously try to improve processes and procedures.

- **Amount of Plant and Equipment Employed** In India, the physical effort of a workman is considerably less than in many others countries. Technically, it is highly uneconomical from a productivity point of view for a man to work manually, on work that could reasonably be done by mechanical equipment. Further, it is also counter-productive where a country's plants, equipment and buildings are obsolete and ill-designed. This is due to a failure to plough back enough capital for modern equipment for future profit. In India, this is particularly evident. Technological obsolescence is one of the most important factors for the non-achievement of productive efficiency by industries. Many industries are practically sluggish in growth and development and are becoming worse day by day. This virtually forces them to finally close down their operations. Thus, it is necessary to ensure that capital resources are used to the best advantage for productive efficiency. What should be a matching investment for plant and equipment, which also broadly includes periodic updating of existing technologies, varies from unit to unit.
- **Efficiency of Plant and Equipment Employed** This partly depends on the adequate supply of technologies, but it also demands eagerness and action at all levels in a company to obtain the best from existing resources. To make this eagerness effective, information on production, performance and cost must be made available to all concerned.
- **Volume Continuity and Uniformity of Production** Standardization of the product resulting in longer and more economical runs depends upon finding out the best and most simple products to fill the market needs and the best method of making them. Some customer education may be necessary, but this should not be difficult if the products offered are cheap and satisfying.
- **Utilization of Manpower** Manpower is a fundamental resource. There is a real need to see that both general planning and detailed methods of work are not wasteful and to avoid fatigue and frustration.

From the above discussion, we can see that productivity factors can be classified, broadly, into three types: general factors, organizational factors and human factors.

13.5 COMMON MISCONCEPTIONS ABOUT PRODUCTIVITY

Some of the common misconceptions about productivity are presented below:

1. Productivity is not only labour efficiency or labour productivity. It is the sum total efficiency of all the inputs utilized in the production process.
2. Productivity need not always be the increase in output or performance. This misconception is the result of confusion as observed by Sumanth (1984). Output

may increase without a corresponding increase in productivity, namely, output value for the same or even less volume of production may increase, which cannot be related to productivity enhancement.

3. Productivity and profitability for an organization may not be the same. Profitability is the function of the price realisation, which may be more, even when productivity is less.

Productivity need not always be about efficiency or effectiveness. Efficiency results in the production of high-quality goods, while effectiveness is the production of overall results. Scott (1983) observes that efficiency and effectiveness are actual measures of performance, while productivity is one of the measures of performance.

Therefore, productivity per se, is important for both the organization and national economic growth. By improving productivity, an organization can improve the performance, enrich the quality of work life of employees, make the employees innovative, and improve the bottomline. According to Lawlor (1985), productivity satisfies five arms: objectives, efficiency, effectiveness, comparability and progressive trends.

13.6 PRODUCTIVITY MEASUREMENT

Productivity measurement is possible indirectly, as we compute productivity, measuring other variables. Such difficulty in measurement of productivity is attributable to the difficulty in defining and quantifying inputs and outputs. Regardless of the approach taken by an organization in measuring its productivity, it should at least produce some indices, by referring to which we can understand the trend in productivity. For many organizations, productivity measures are used as a tool in evaluating and monitoring organizational performance. Proper productivity measures and the resultant indices enable managers to understand the trend, and also at the same time, enable them to take corrective action for bringing positive changes in the productivity indices. They can also establish the relationship of productivity measures with competitiveness, benchmarking the same with those of competitors. Foley (1962) argues productivity measurement can help in enforcing effective control, enabling the organization to initiate corrective action.

13.7 PRODUCTIVITY MEASUREMENTS–RATIO PROBLEM

Conventionally, productivity measurement is left to ratio analysis. Let us illustrate this with a small problem.

A company manufactures 50,000 scooters in a year. Each scooter sells at Rs.25000/-. The company spends Rs. 5000 per scooter in material inputs and 2,00,000 man-hours to make the scooters. Compute the following productivity ratios from the above problem:

- output/labour ratio
- output value/labour ratio
- value added/labour ratio

Solution

Output/labour ratio (in terms of man hours)

= 50,000 scooters/200,000 man hours = 0.25 scooter per man hour

Output value/labour ratio (50,000 scooters × 25,000 per scooter)/200000

Man-hours = Rs, 6250 per man hour

(a) **Value added/labour ratio**

This is computed by first computing the value added, which is

(Output value – material cost)

$= \{(50,000 \times 25,000)\text{-}(50,000 \times 5000) = 100,0000$

So value added/labour (in man hours) = 10,00,000/2,00,000 = Rs. 5 per man-hour.

But this approach to productivity measurement and linking it directly to wages will neither benefit the organization nor will it benefit the workers in the long run.

In today's complex production system, overall productivity being more important than labour productivity, for rational pricing of labour (that is, linking wages), the two following models can alternatively yield better results.

(b) Omni factor Model

This model gives a composite productivity index for all input and output costs of all the products. While input costs are taken for all, output costs are determined using the average marginal costs (AMC) method. Input costs are:

- raw material costs
- manpower costs
- capital costs, namely, depreciation, interest, stock investment, etc.
- indirect production costs
- cost of utilities
- output costs on AMC method worked out as under:

Assuming, we have three products, A, B and C.

Aggregate Output

$$= \text{Output A} + \text{Output B} \times \frac{(\text{AMC of B})}{\text{AMC of A}} + \text{Output C} \times \frac{(\text{AMC of C})}{\text{AMC of A}}$$

$$\text{Where, AMC percentage of A} = \frac{(\text{Total input costs of A})}{\text{Total output costs of A}} \times 100$$

Productivity = Aggregate output/Input costs

(C) Surrogate Models

This model primarily considers some qualitative factors to measure productivity. Factors like the satisfaction of investors, employees, customers and suppliers are considered in qualitative terms. The quantification of these qualitative terms is done as under:

Investors' satisfaction (S_i) = *Net Profit/Total Investment*

Employees' satisfaction (S_e) = *Total value added/Total number of man hours*

Customer satisfaction (S_c) = *Total Sales revenue/Total number of customers*

Supplier satisfaction (S_s) = *Total purchases/Total number of Suppliers*

Composite Productivity Index, therefore,

$$A.S_i + B.S_e + C.S_c + D.S_s$$

A, B, C and D are constants, which indicate the relative weightage of the four parameters.

Linking wages to productivity, based on these two models, yield better results as organizations can objectively price the labour, and also, labour could get their legitimate share of productivity gain.

13.7.1 Productivity Measurement Difficulty for Knowledge Workers

Measuring productivity for the number of units produced by a worker using a machine is not difficult for the obvious ease of quantification. But the productivity of knowledge workers is difficult to measure. This is primarily because of the difficulty in relating cost of input in measurement. Other difficulties can be related to the following factors:

1. The effects of strategic decisions, both positive and negative, may not be immediately evident. Such a time lag is therefore difficult to relate to a particular

time period. Moreover, we cannot directly relate every strategic decision to an individual's efficiency or inefficiency. The outcome of some strategic decisions may depend on various external factors, which may be beyond the control of managers.

2. Knowledge workers often extend services to other units of an organization, which may have some effects on final output but it is difficult to quantify. For example, an Advertising Manager's efforts in increasing sales are difficult to measure.
3. Knowledge workers often contribute indirectly to the achievement of the end result, which is difficult to measure. For example, a knowledge worker's contribution, towards design and development, may not directly be attributable to the final output, yet his efforts are all the more important.

Due to such difficulties, Total Factor Productivity (TFP) is a better approach, as it considers the functional efficiency/performance of all departments of an organization at the aggregate level, without bothering about individual productivity. We have already discussed this at length.

13.8 PRODUCTIVITY AND QUALITY

When quality increases productivity also improves. This is because waste and rework are reduced and inputs are optimally utilized. Higher productivity enables an organization to reduce price and gain a competitive advantage both in terms of price and quality. Customers also feel happy as they get value for their money. Since the organization's bottom line improves, it raises the satisfaction level of all stakeholders, including employees. The significance of cost of quality has been discussed, while explaining ISO certification requirements. Saving the cost of quality will have an immediate effect on the enhanced productivity of an organization. All these establish that quality and productivity are indirectly related.

Thus, productivity should not be misconstrued as labour performance alone. It is sum total efficiency, and therefore, linking productivity to wages should be objectively done to create a win–win situation.

In table 13.1, we have explained human development progress in India and adjoining countries. The human development index (HDI) and the human performance index (HPI).

In Table 13.2, we have explained the organizational level labour productivity data of leading steel manufacturers in some countries, which indicate year-wise variation of labour productivity. HRD activities in different steel plants played a very significant role in labour productivity.

Table 13.1 *Human Development Progress*

Country	HDI rank	HPI rank
Sri Lanka	23	22
China	29	18
Maldives	..	..
Myanmar	43	40
India	49	47
Pakistan	50	64
Bangladesh	54	67
Nepal	..	..
Bhutan	63	62

Note: HDI and HPI ranks have been recalculated for 78 countries.

Table. 13.2 *Labour Productivity Index (Per Tonne per employee)*

Company	1981-82	1986-87	1987-88	1990-91	1994
BSL	71	61	66	98	108
DSP	38	39	41	45	45
RSP	47	44	47	56	56
IISCO	34	29	31	24	29
SAIL	55	51	56	70	78
TISCO	64	74	74	72	72

Irrespective of the steel industries data, India ranks the lowest in labour productivity, as well as, overall productivity data. According to the analysis of the Associated Chambers of Commerce and Industry in 2001, India is the lowest, at the 49th position in the world, with labour productivity per person employed per hour valued at $2.42 and overall productivity valued at $5,452 as against Luxembourg that tops the list with labour productivity valued at $41.90 and the overall productivity at $73,999. The prescriptive model for the correction of the situation is the adoption of a flexible work culture and the extensive adoption of human resource development activities.

13.8.1 Productivity Index

Productivity is a relative measure. For this, it is always appropriate to compare it to something. For example, it may be necessary for the organization to compare the productivity values with their competitors, or even internally across departments, across employees, and even across machines, for different time periods. Such efforts can help them to successfully understand the trends in productivity improvement over a time period, the impact of the measures undertaken by the organization in the form of new decisions, introduction of new processes, equipment, and any other initiatives, that are, directly or indirectly, related to the change in productivity. To have the values for comparison, organizations develop a productivity index.

A productivity index can be defined as the ratio of productivity measured in a certain time period to the productivity measured in a base period. For example, if the base period's productivity is calculated to be 1.78 and the following period's productivity is calculated to 1.89, the resulting productivity index would be 1.78/1.89 = 0.9417989. This indicates that organizational productivity has decreased by 6% over the base period. Therefore, the productivity index provides valuable quantitative data for managers to enable them to evaluate the results of all the organizational measures leading to the improvement in performance.

13.8.2 Productivity and Production

The term 'productivity' must not be confused with 'production'. Productivity is a ratio, while production relates to a volume. Increased production does not necessarily mean an increase in productivity. If the input of resources goes up in direct proportion to the increase in output, productivity will remain the same. And if input increases by a greater percentage than output, higher production will be achieved at the expense of a reduction in productivity.

13.9 ROLE OF TRADE UNIONS IN PRODUCTIVITY IMPROVEMENT

Productivity improvement at the national and organizational level is most important for long-term sustainability. Improved productivity, in reality, enhances the welfare of the employees of an organization, and the nation as a whole. From this perspective, a trade union has a very important role in improving productivity, be it for the nation, or for the organization. Any productivity-deterrent actions can ultimately affect the common interest of all of us. Hence, instead of opposing managerial actions for productivity improvement, trade unions need to cooperate. Organizations should also place the emphasis on taking the trade unions into confidence, by making productivity improvement initiatives participative. To make our country and the organizations globally competitive, today, a partnership approach to productivity improvement, involving the trade unions, is necessary. The national conference on the role of trade unions in productivity improvement, organized by the National Productivity Council during February, 1990 in collaboration the with Ministry of Labour, Government of India, and the International Labour Organization at New Delhi had emphasized the important role of trade unions in productivity improvement, to enhance the quality of work life of all cross-sections of people.

13.10 PRODUCTIVITY-LINKED INCENTIVE DETERMINATION

Performance- or productivity-linked incentive determination is now a common organizational practice. Organizations can optimize their compensation cost, linking incentives to the productivity level of individual workers, teams, and even to the overall performance of the organization. Some of the widely-used compensation methods are enumerated below.

13.10.1 Straight Piece-rate Method

This method considers a fixed rate per piece, which remains constant for different output levels. Under this system, workers are paid strictly according to their output. Most organizations follow this method as a substitute for the time rate. The major difficulty in this system is that workers do not get any guaranteed payment for their work, excepting some basic hourly rate, which again depends on achieving some fixed level of output. We can illustrate this using the following formula:

Work piece rate = Adjusted hourly rate/Average production per hour

Using this formula, let us consider the day's earning of a particular worker in the following case:

Example

A company pays a worker for a given job as follows:

Basic hourly rate	Rs. 6
Increase on rate	25%
Standard hourly output level for the job	800 Units

Suppose the worker in a particular day of 8-hour work produced 7000 units. Compute the day's earning for the worker:

Solution

Basic hourly rate : Rs. 6
Increase on rate : 25%
Adjusted hourly rate : $1.25 \times 6 =$ Rs. 7.50
Average output per hour : 800 Units
Therefore, hourly work
Piece rate = Adjusted hourly rate/Average output per hour
= $7.50/800 = 7.50 \times 8^{-3}$

Hence, for producing 7000 units in an 8 hour work day, the worker will receive:

Day	Day's Production	Work Piece Rate	Day's Earnings
1	7000	7.50×8^{-3}	Rs. 65.63

13.10.2 Differential Piece Rate Methods

13.10.2.1 Taylor's Method

There is no guarantee of minimum wage. Workers are required to produce at 100% level of efficiency as specified by established standard time. There are two-piece rates specified for each job. A lower piece rate is applicable for performance below the standard level and a higher piece rate is applicable for performance higher than the standard level. Let us examine the following problem:

Example

A company using time study fixed the standard output level per hour for a given job as 125 units. Hourly labour rate is Rs. 7. The company applies two differential rates for determining the earnings of a worker. Workers get 80% of the standard piece rate for below standard level of performance and 120% of the standard piece rate for above standard level of performance. Calculate the earnings of a worker in the two following cases for two different days:

1. In an 8-hour work day when the worker produces 900 units
2. In an 8-hour work day when the worker produces 1200 units

Solution

Standard output per hour	125 unit
Labour rate per hour	Rs. 7
Standard piece rate	7/125 = 0.056
Lower Piece rate	0.056 × 0.8 = 0.045
Higher Piece Rate	0.056 × 1.20 = 0.067
Earning of the worker in day 1	900 × 0.045 = Rs. 40.5
Earning of the worker in day 2	1200 × 0.067 = Rs. 80.4

Notice in day 1 the worker produced less than the standard level. With 125 units per hour, the standard output level for 8-hour work in a day should have been 1000 units.

13.10.2.2 Merrick Differential Piece Rate

Here too, there is no guaranteed minimum wage. A standard time is established for each job and workers are paid following differential rates.

Example

In a particular week, a worker has produced one item as under:

Day	Quantity Produced
1	120
2	185
3	210
4	195
5	220
6	198

Standard output per day of 8 hours work is 190 units and hourly rate is Rs. 5. Calculate the earnings of the worker for different days of the week using Merrick's Differential Piece Rate Method.

Solution

Standard output per day of 8 hours work	190 Units
Hourly rate	Rs. 5/-
Rate differentials For output up to 83%: Basic Rate For output above 83% and up to 100%: Basic Piece Rate + 10 Rs. of hourly rate as bonus For output above 100%: Basic Piece rate + 20% of hourly rate as bonus.	
Standard output per hour	190/8 = 24 units
Basic Rate per piece	5/24 = Rs. 0.21

We can now tabulate the earnings of the worker for the entire week as under:

Day	Standard output	Actual output	Output performance	Rate applicable	Day's earning (quantity × rate) (in Rupees)
1	190	170	89%	BR + 20%	170×1.10×0.21= 9.27
2	190	185	97%	- do -	185×1.10×0.21 = 42.74
3	190	210	111%	- do -	210×1.20×0.21 = 52.92
4	190	195	103%	- do -	195×1.20×0.21 = 49.14
5	190	220	116%	- do -	220×1.20×0.21 = 55.44
6	190	198	104%	- do -	198×1.20×0.21 = 49.90

13.10.2.3 *Gantt Task System*

The only difference between this system and earlier systems is that it provides minimum guaranteed wage even if the performance is below the standard level. Let us examine the following problem:

Example

The hourly wage rate for a worker is fixed at Rs. 5/-. The standard time set for the job is 10 minutes per unit. High rate for the job (above the standard level) is Rs. 1.70 per unit. Assume the worker has produced output for the entire week as per the figure given in the 'Actual output column' in the table. Compute day-wise earnings of the worker for the week.

Solution

Standard output per day = Standard time per unit × 8 hours (assuming 8 hours work per day)

Standard time per unit = 12 minutes

Standard output per hour = 60/12 = 5 Units

Standard output per day = 5 × 8 = 40 Units

Day-wise earnings of the worker

Day	Actual Output	Actual output as percentage of standard	Payment Rate	Day's earnings (in rupees)
1	36	90	Day wages	5 × 8 = 40
2	44	110	High piece rate	44 × 1.70 = 75
3	56	140	- do -	56 × 1.70 = 95
4	50	125	- do -	50 × 1.70 = 85
5	40	100	Day wages + 20% Bonus	1.20 × 5 × 8 = 48
6	50	125	High Piece rate	50 × 1.70 = 85

13.10.2.4 *Emerson's Efficiency Plan*

Under this plan, efficient workers are rewarded at a rate that increases with the increase of their performance, measured in terms of saving of time. The main features of the plan are:

- Guaranteed day wages are paid irrespective of performance.

- Standard output is determined based on past performance, which is taken at 100% efficiency.

Performance of the workers is measured in terms of the efficiency achieved, comparing actual output with the standard output, using the following formula:

Efficiency percentage = (Actual Output/Standard Output) × 100

Incentive bonus is paid if the worker's efficiency exceeds two thirds (66.67%) of the standard performance (taken as 100%). Incentive rates vary with the increase of performance beyond two thirds (66.77%), at an increasing rate.

Efficiency Rate	Remuneration
Below 66.67%	No incentive bonus, only time wages
Over 66.67% but up to 100%	Time wages + proportionate bonus for incremental output percentages, rising up to 20% at 100% level of efficiency
Over 100%	Time wages + 20% bonus + 1% bonus for each 1% increase in efficiency beyond 100%.

The worker is assigned different jobs in a day, and for each job unit, the company has fixed a standard time. Based on the tabulated information, compute the total earnings for the day.

Job code	Quantity Produced	Standard time set per unit (in hours)	Time taken (in hours)
A-1	2	1/2	1.25
B-3	4	1/2	1.75
C-1	20	1/3	5.00

Solution

Bonus for each job has to be computed separately. The calculation can be tabulated as under:

Job Code	Standard time for the job (in hours) – Qty. × Standard time per unit	Time taken (in hours) in Rupees	Bonus earned, if any (50% of time saved)
A-1	2 × 1/2 = 1 hour	1.25	Nil
B-3	4 × 1/2 = 2 hour	1.75	0.625
C-1	20 × 1/3 = 6.67 hour	5.00	4.175
		Total	Rs. 4.8

Total earnings for the day = (8 × 5) + 4.8 = Rs. 44.8

13.10.2.5 *Halsey Premium Plan*

Halsey Premium Plan is the core incentive model, where the worker is paid a time rate, when the actual time is equal to standard time. The worker, however, faces a penalty when he/she exceeds the standard time requirement for doing the job. However, when the worker is able to complete the job in less than the pre-determined standard time, he/she gets a bonus at 50% of the time saved.

13.10.2.6 *Rowan Premium Plan*

Rowan Premium Plan is different from the Halsey Premium Plan in respect of computation of incentive bonus payable to a worker. Incentive bonus here is not calculated at a fixed percentage of time saved. It is the ratio of the actual time taken to the standard time for the job. Therefore, incentive bonus is computed using the following formula:

$$\frac{T}{S}(S - T) \times R$$

where T = Actual time taken by the worker
S = Standard time set for the job
$(S - T)$ = Difference between standard and actual time
R = Hourly rate of wages

Let us examine this plan using following example:

Example

In a factory, standard time set for a job is 8 hours and the basic wage rate is Rs. 3 per hour. The workers receive normal wages for their actual work and an incentive bonus at a fixed proportion of the time saved. Compute incentive bonus payable to workers for different levels of actual time, as mentioned in the 'actual time' column

Actual time Taken (T)	Standard time (S)	Time Saved (S – T)	Incentive earned $[\frac{T}{S}(S - T) \times R]$
8	8	0	0
7	8	1	2.625
6	8	2	4,5
5	8	3	5.625
4	8	4	6.0
3	8	5	5.625
2	8	6	4.5
1	8	7	2.625

It is evident from the table that when time saved is beyond 50% of the standard time, workers get bonus at a diminishing rate. This is the major defect of the scheme, as it discourages workers to save more than 50% of the standard time.

13.10.2.7 *The Scanlon Plan*

It is a popular group incentive scheme, which relates labour cost ratio to the total sales value to measure labour effectiveness. Incentive bonus is paid to the workers based on the percentage reduction in the labour to sales ratio, comparing the base period with the assessment period. The formula for computing percentage reduction in the labour index is as follows:

$$\frac{\frac{L_b}{R_b} - \frac{L_a}{R_a}}{\frac{L_b}{R_b}} \times 100$$

Where; L_b = Total labour cost for the base month

R_b = Total sales value for the base month

L_a = Total labour cost for the assessment month

R_a = Total sales value for the assessment month

$\frac{L_b}{R_b}$ = Standard labour to sales ratio for the base month

$\frac{L_a}{R_a}$ = Actual labour to sales ratio for the assessment month.

Example

A company employs 150 workers. Sales during the base month were Rs. 15 lakh. For the same period, labour cost was Rs. 2.5 lakh. Compute the group incentives payable, if any, to the workers in the following situations:

1. Sales value is Rs. 16 lakh against a labour cost of Rs. 2.25 lakh.
2. Sales value is Rs. 16 lakh against a labour cost of Rs. 2.8 lakh.

Solution

(a) Labour cost during the base month (L_b) = Rs. 2.5 lakh

Sales value during the base month (R_b) = Rs. 15 lakh

Standard labour to sales ratio $\frac{L_b}{R_b}$ = $L_b/R_b \times 100$

= $2.5/15 \times 100$

= 16.67%

Labour cost for the assessment month (L_a) = Rs. 2.25 lakh

Sales value for the assessment month R_a = Rs. 16 lakh

Actual labour to sales ratio during the
Assessment month = $L_a/R_a \times 100$
= $2.25/16 \times 100 = 14.06\%$

Here, the actual labour to sales ratio is lower than the standard labour to sales ratio. Therefore, employees would be entitled to receive an incentive bonus as follows:

$$\frac{\frac{L_b}{R_b} - \frac{L_a}{R_a}}{\frac{L_b}{R_b}} \times 100$$

$= 16.57 - 14.06/16.67 \times 100$

$= 2.61/16.67 \times 100 = 15.66\%$ (approximately).

(b) In situation (b), this would be as under:

L_a = Rs.2.8 lakh

R_a = Rs. 16 lakh

$L_a/R_a \times 100 = Rs.17.5\%$

In this case, since actual labour to sales ratio is higher than the standard labour to sales ratio, workers would not be entitled to receive any incentive bonus. Hence, their wages would be restricted to a fixed rate.

13.10.2.8 The Bedeaux Point Plan

Under this plan, a minute is considered as a time unit. For each job, standard time in minutes is determined. The unit of measurement under the Bedeaux point plan is named *B*. Therefore, if standard time for a job is 6 hours, it is expressed as 360 *Bs*. If the workers fail to complete a job within the standard time or just finish the same within the standard time they are paid just the normal time rate. If, however, they can complete their work earlier, they receive an incentive bonus equal to the wages for the time saved, measured in terms of excess of *B* points over the actual time taken. Incentive bonus is paid to the workers normally at 75% of the time saved. The remaining 25% goes to the supervisors.

Let us explain the plan using the following illustration:

Hourly rate for workers (R) = Rs. 6
Standard time for the job (S) = 360 Bs (6 hours)
Actual time taken by the workers
for the job (T) = 300 Bs (5 hours)
Value of time saved = 360–300/60 × 6 = Rs. 6

Total wages payable	=	$S \times R$ + 75% of the value of time saved
	=	$6 \times 6 + (75/100 \times 6)$
	=	$36 + (0.75 \times 6)$
	=	36 + 4.5 = Rs. 40.5

13.10.2.9 Priestman Production Plan

This is also a popular group incentive plan, where employees are paid a guaranteed time wage and an incentive bonus for an increase in productivity in proportion to the increase in per-capita output. Under the scheme, a standard output level is determined on mutual agreement between the employer and the employees. Then, actual output is compared with the standard output to decide about incentive bonus. The percentage of productivity bonus payable to each employee is determined as per the following formula:

$$\frac{\frac{P_a}{W_a} - \frac{P_a}{W_b}}{\frac{P_a}{W_a}} \times 100$$

Where, P_a	=	Actual production during the assessment month
W_a	=	Number of workers in employment during the assessment month
P_b	=	Standard production in the base month
W_b	=	Number of workers in employment during the base month
P_a/W_a	=	Actual production per worker during the assessment month
P_b/W_b	=	Standard production per workers during the base month

Let us illustrate this using the following example:

A steel plant employs 500 workers. Standard output of steel is fixed at 1000 tonne per month. As per the agreement, each worker is entitled to get productivity bonus for the percentage increase in production over the standard output level. Compute bonus payable, if any, to workers in the following two situations:

1. Output has increased to 1200 tonnes, but the number of workers engaged during the corresponding period increased to 550.
2. Output is 1100 tonnes, workers engaged is 520.

Solution

Standard output in the base month (P_b)1000 Tonne

Standard output per employee $P_b/W_b = 1000/500 = 2$ Tonne

(a) Output during the assessment month (P_a) = 1200 Tonne

Number of employees during the assessment month (W_a) = 550

Output per employee during the assessment month (P_a/W_a) = 1200/550 = 2.182

Percentage increase in production per employee

$$\frac{\frac{P_a}{W_a} - \frac{P_b}{W_b}}{\frac{P_a}{W_a}} \times 100 = (2.182 - 2)/2.182 \times 100 = 8.34\%$$

Hence, in this case, all workers would receive a productivity-linked bonus of 8.34% over their basic pay.

(b) In situation (b), output per employee during the assessment month P_a/W_a is 1100/520 = 2.12

Percentage increase in production per employee = (2.12 – 2)/2.12 × 100 = 5.66%

13.10.2.10 Some Incentive Payment Practices in Organizations

Payment of group incentives, as a practice, is followed by many organizations, based on their self-designed formula. Here, we are illustrating one such practice, which designs productivity-linked incentive as follows:

This is for a plant manufacturing wheels and axles for the Railways.

1.	Define the Plant capacity and standard man hours: Plant capacity for Wheels = 8800/month Plant capacity for Axles= 4500/month Standard Man-hours: - Wheel shops = 87,414 - Axle shops = 41,724	
2.	No bonus up to 83% plant capacity.	
3.	Incentive rates based on the minimum of the pay scale - Wheel shops = Rs.0.55/wheel - Axle shops = Rs.1.07/axle	Incentive for wheel shop = (0.55 × Eligible production in the month/base output) × (100 – Actual Absenteeism % in the month)/84. Incentive for axle shop = (1.07 × Eligible production in the month/base output) × (100 – Actual Absenteeism % in the month)/84.

13.11 ECONOMIC VALUE ADDED (EVA)

EVA is a much-discussed issue now in the corporate world. EVA measures internal and external company operating performance, funds the credit initiative, and deals with the constraints and challenges. It can be tied to evaluating employee performance and success by developing a goal-oriented compensation package based on an incentive reward system that links cause and effect accountability. The EVA results should be made available to all managers and employees to be used as a performance measurement and management that is directly calculated and applied. Earnings, operations performance, return on capital invested are measured and compared to profits. They are then compared with the cost of debt and equity to fund operations.

EVA = Net Operating Profit after tax (NOPAT) – Capital Charge (Invested Debt and Equity * Weighted Average Cost of Capital(WACC)
NOPAT = Operating Income – Operating Expenses + Interest Expense + Taxes
WACC = Cost of Equity (Equity) + Cost of Debt (Debt)) i.e. the cost of capital

The excess EVA equals profit. The initial implementation of EVA values current operations, then subsequent new projects are measured with a decision being made on whether the accounting numbers are justified to go forward with the project. If the cost of the project exceeds the value added, the project should not go forward, since adding shareholder value is the bottom line goal of the company.

EVA was originated by the Stern Stewart company in 1982. The Stern Stewart "Four Ms"are:

- Measurement: designing a measure of value creation that best reflects economic reality in a particular industry.
- Management: developing policies, procedures and tools, which link decision-making to the measure of value-creation.
- Motivation: establishing incentive plans that simulate ownership by giving managers a share of value created.
- Mindset: increasing the business literacy of employees through training and communications.

Therefore, EVA measures the change in financial worth performance through operating performance, focussing at the unit management level, and at an employee level. The main drivers of EVA are operating revenues, operating expenses and capital charges. EVA-based compensation aligns the interests of management and employees with the shareholders.

13.12 ORGANIZATIONAL SICKNESS AND PRODUCTIVITY

Productivity is now considered as the effect of sum-total efficiency of each and every functional area. Hence, organizational sickness can be directly studied in depth by using total factor productivity indices. In that respect, organizational sickness has a direct relationship with the productivity achievement figures of the company and the total factor productivity indices also help us to study the industrial sickness at the macro level.

Among other things, industrial sickness in most cases is attributed to

- quality of management
- impractical planning
- lack of financial control
- diversion of resources
- inadequate attention to research and development
- technological obsolescence and
- poor industrial relations.

In fact, taking into account the above management-related causes, when the sickness trend is analyzed, it transpires that over 95% of the total causes of sickness can be directly attributed to such reasons, which are more internal than external.

All such reasons being internal in nature can be considerably averted, provided early detection of such causes or reasons through analysis of total factor productivity indices is initiated on time. This is possible when such monitoring at the corporate level is done on a continuous basis. Since total factor productivity analysis enables us to quickly identify the weak operational areas, immediate intervention can help in avoiding the situation, the culmination of which can otherwise prompt sickness for the unit.

Although an organizational level study to relate sickness to total factor productivity indices has not been initiated in India, such exercises to identify corporate dysfunction have already been initiated in many industrially advanced countries. Such a study acts as an early signal to locate weak operational areas and it helps the industries to adopt quick remedial measures. Thus, instead of fully relying on financial performance indicators to understand the viability or otherwise of a sample organization, it is more appropriate to consider the productivity trend to study corporate health.

In the context of recent changes in the Indian economy, productivity analyses have assumed greater importance. The Board for Industrial and Financial Reconstruction (BIFR), to understand the viability prospect of sick industries, to a great extent relies on productivity indices. On such analyses, if BIFR finds that a particular industry has become sick due to inefficient operations in a number of cases and that mere pumping of credit simply cannot help in averting such lapses, it recommends winding up.

SUMMARY

1. For any production process, productivity is the index or the ratio of relationship between the output of goods and services and the inputs of resources, human and non-human.
2. Any increase in the ratio of outputs to inputs for the organization and also for the nation as a whole, is the indicator for positive changes in the productivity rate.
3. Therefore, productivity is a key indicator for efficiency and progress. Productivity is an overall measure of the ability to produce a good or service. More specifically, productivity is the measure of how specified resources are managed to accomplish timely objectives as stated in terms of quantity and quality. A productivity index or ratio may be computed for a single operation, a department, a facility, an organization, or even an entire country. Being an objective concept, organizations can monitor productivity for any strategic decisions.

KEY WORDS

Emerson's Efficiency Plan Under this plan, efficient workers are rewarded at an increasing rate with the increase of their performance, measured in terms of saving of time.

Priestman Production Plan This is also a popular group incentive plan, where employees are paid a guaranteed time wage and incentive bonus for an increase in productivity in proportion to the increase in per-capita output. Under the scheme, a standard output level is determined on mutual agreement between the employer and the employees. Then, actual output is compared with the standard output to decide about incentive bonus. The percentage of productivity bonus payable to each employee is determined as per formula

Straight Piece rate Methods This method considers a fixed rate per piece, which remains constant for different output levels. Under this system, workers get paid strictly as per their output. Most organizations follow this method as a substitute for time rate. The major difficulty in this system is that workers do not get any guaranteed payment for their work, excepting some basic hourly rate, which again depends on achieving some fixed level of output.

Productivity index can be defined as the ratio of productivity measured in a certain time period to the productivity measured in a base period. For example, if the base period's productivity is calculated to be 1.78 and the following period's productivity is calculated to be 1.89, the resulting productivity index would be 1.78/1.89 = 0.9417989. This indicates that organizational productivity has decreased by 6% over the base period. Therefore, the productivity index is valuable quantitative data for the managers to evaluate the results of all the organizational measures leading to the improvement in performance.

Omni factor Model This model gives a composite productivity index for all input and output costs of all the products. While input costs are taken for all, output costs are determined on the average marginal costs (AMC) method.

Surrogate Model This model primarily considers some qualitative factors to measure productivity. Factors like satisfaction of investors, employees, customers and suppliers are considered in qualitative terms.

GENERAL REVIEW QUESTIONS

1. Explain the concept of productivity. Also, discuss how the concept of productivity has gained worldwide attention.
2. Discuss the difference between total factor and single factor productivity. Can these two productivity concepts also be considered as multi-factor and labour productivity?
3. What are the important drivers and determinants of productivity growth?
4. From an organizational perspective, which are the factors that can improve productivity?
5. What are the misconceptions about productivity?
6. Discuss the concept of productivity measurement. Why is it difficult to measure the productivity of knowledge workers?
7. Discuss the role of trade unions in increasing productivity levels at the national and organizational level.
8. Discuss some of the important productivity-linked incentives?
9. Short notes
   (a) Productivity and unemployment
   (b) Productivity and production
   (c) Productivity and quality
   (d) Multi-factor productivity

CRITICAL REVIEW QUESTIONS

Productivity Game

In the table overleaf, we have presented the indices of Partial Labour Productivity, Partial Capital Productivity and Total Factor Productivity for the years 1985–86 to 1988–89, which are taken from the published documents (1997) of the Indian Labour Year Book, 1995, Labour Bureau, Shimla.

Base 1970 – 71 = 100

S. No	Industry Type	Partial Labour Productivity Indices				Partial Capital Productivity Indices				Total Factor Productivity Indices			
		85-86	**86-87**	**87-88**	**88-89**	**85-86**	**86-87**	**87-88**	**88-89**	**85-86**	**86-87**	**87-88**	**88-89**
1.	Hydrogenated oils (vanaspati)	380	423	532	252	298	280	376	286	338	343	447	267
2.	Edible oils (other vanaspati)	286	167	261	332	186	104	167	130	222	126	201	180
3.	Tea Processing	219	210	300	230	316	285	422	311	269	250	361	272
4.	Cotton Textiles	130	135	278	90	130	142	336	122	130	137	288	90
5.	Tyres and Tubes	223	240	249	279	190	222	322	540	201	228	289	396
6.	Petroleum Refineries	1566	1386	1094	908	989	832	620	590	1090	922	696	646
7.	Chemicals and Chemical Products	476	520	562	619	393	350	385	444	420	400	439	500
8.	Cement Lime and Plaster	207	188	305	430	167	112	179	253	182	136	218	310
9.	Iron and Steel	197	169	227	304	177	147	193	290	193	165	221	302
10.	Ship Building and Repairing	142	160	171	156	103	102	105	96	139	154	166	151

Study the productivity trends under each category in the table and argue whether different productivity measures have any inter-relationship.

REFERENCES

1. Antle, M. J. and Capalbo, S.M. 1988. "An Introduction to Recent Development in Production Theory and Productivity Measurement" in Capalbo, S.M. and Antle, M.J. '*Agricultural Productivity: Measurement and Explanation*', Resources for the Future, Inc., Washington, DC.
2. Eatwell, J.M. and Newman, P. 1991. *The New Palgrave: A Dictionary of Economics* vols. 3, 4 .and 12. Tokyo: Macmillan.
3. Foley, G.N. 1962. *Planning for Increased Productivity in Industries*. Sydney, London: Butterworths.
4. Harris, R.G. 1999. "Determinants of Canadian Productivity Growth: Issues and Prospects." Discussion paper #8. Ottawa: Industry Canada.
5. Iyaniwura, O. and Osoba, A.M. 1983. Measuring Productivity; Conceptual and Statistical Problems: Improvement of Statistics in *'Productivity in Nigeria. Proceedings of a National Conference.'* Osoba A.M. ed. Ibadan: NISER.
6. Krugman, P. 1990. *The Age of Diminished Expectations*. Cambridge, Mass: MIT Press.,
7. Lawlor, A. 1985. "*Productivity Improvement Manual*". United Kingdom: Aldershot.
8. Olaoye, A. O. 1985. "Total Factor Productivity Trends in Nigerian Manufacturing" *Nigerian Journal of Economic and Social Studies*, vol. 27, no. 3, pp.317–345.
9. Prokopenko, J. 1987. *Productivity Management: A Practical Handbook*. Geneva: International Labour Organization.
10. Samuelson, P.A. and Nordhaus, W. D. 1995. *Economics*, 15th ed. USA: McGraw-Hill.
11. Scott, S. 1983. Much Ado About Productivity: Where Do We Go From Here? *Industrial Engineering*, vol. 15, no. 10, October.
12. Sharpe, A. 1998. *Productivity: Key to Economic Success*. Centre for the Study of Living Standards for the Atlantic Canada Opportunities Agency. Ottawa and Moncton, NB: CSLS and ACOA. Available: www.csls.ca
13. Sumanth, D. J. 1984. *Productivity Engineering and Management*. New York: McGraw-Hill.

ADDITIONAL REFERENCES

1. Ahluwalia I. J. 1991. *Productivity and Growth in Indian Manufacturing*. Centre for Policy Research, New Delhi: Oxford University Press.
2. Bhattacharyya, Dipak Kumar. 2006. *Human Resource Management*. New Delhi: Excel Books.

3. Diewert, W. E (1985) *Productivity Management: Planning, Measurement and Evaluation, Control and Improvement*. New York: John Wiley and Sons.
4. Grosskopf, S. 1993. Efficiency and Productivity in *The Measurement of Production Efficiency: Techniques and Applications*, Fried, H.O, Lovell, C.A.K. Schimidt, SS eds. UK: Oxford University Press.
5. Knox, C. L. L. and Shelton, S. S. 1993. *The Measurement of Productive Efficiency: Techniques and Applications*. New York: Oxford University Press, pp.160–194.
6. Klitgaard, R. 1989. Incentive Myopia in *World Development*, vol. 17, no. 4 pp. 477–459.
7. Solow, R. 1957. Technical Change and the Aggregate Production Function. *Review of Economics and Statistics* 39(3):pp. 312–20.
8. Wonnacott, P. and Wonnacott, R. 1986. *Economics* 3rd edition. New York: McGraw-Hill Book Company.

CASE STUDY

Value-added operations management of *Premier Steel*

The cold rolling and galvanizing shop is a profit centre for *Premier Steel*. In galvanizing sheets, the company enjoys the highest market share. To retain the market share, the company often requires to compromise with the vital efficiency measures, like cost control, manpower optimization and after-sales customer services. Although all these aspects are an important part of the productivity indices of the organization.

Recently, the company started observing certain dysfunctional syndromes, which slowly started reducing the market share. Some of the indicators were slow improvement of key parameters, an unstructured problem-solving approach, uncontrolled consumption of raw materials, ineffective resource utilization, lack of reliability, etc.

All these had a cascading effect, and started affecting the company's productivity as a whole. At the individual level, workers were achieving their performance targets; executives and managers were delivering results. A high-powered committee at *Premier Steel* could attribute this to the market leadership status of the company; however, it was apprehensive that this leadership could not be sustained in the long run.

To ease such organizational productivity problems, the company adopted a multi-pronged approach which involved:

1. Identification of key value drivers
2. Introduction of six-sigma in a phased manner in key areas
3. Introduction of total productive maintenance training to all operators
4. Reframing of Standard Operation Procedures (SOP) for protocol-bound jobs
5. Installing automatic customers' complaint tracking software.
6. Inventory control through the introduction of a raw material consumption index, etc.

All the above steps ultimately led to the achievement of significant cost saving and increased revenue, optimization of raw materials consumption, energy efficiency, significant reduction in the inventory holding and in the cycle time to respond to customer complaints, etc.

On achieving success, the company feels, all the results are not the outcome of the efforts of people, rather these are the outcome of organizational effectiveness practices. Hence, despite the prevalence of existing systems of factoring productivity-linked incentives on organizational performance achievement, the company decided to keep such achievement results outside the purview. Employees and workers did not consider this wrong. However, they all started establishing their stake, when the company paid 10% more annual productivity incentives to managers and executives. They demanded a similar increase in their annual performance incentives; else, they threatened to go on indefinite strike. The company's rough estimate indicates that payment of 10% more to employees and workers as an annual performance incentive will outweigh the benefits accrued for the recent effectiveness measures.

Discussion Question

Premier is literally in a fix now. Suggest your action plan to overcome this impasse.

CHAPTER 14

Materials Management and Inventory Control

LEARNING OBJECTIVES

After reading this chapter, you will be able to understand:

- Definitions and Concepts of Materials Management and Inventory Control.
- Various Activities Involved in Materials Management.
- Selective Inventory Control Through Various Techniques.
- Concept and Theories of Economic Ordering Quantity.
- Supply Chain Management and Inventory Control.

Opening Vignette

JIT Inventory

To economize the cost of inventory holding, many organizations practice Just-in-time (JIT) inventory control, which also facilitates the introduction of lean manufacturing practices. JIT inventory control is usually implemented as a cost-cutting mechanism. The reduction of waste is imperative as an organizational goal. For an organization to reduce waste, it is necessary to continually monitor excessive waste of time for inventory which occurs when procurement requires a huge lead time and also the flow of materials from the stores to the shop floors is time consuming, there are inflated inventories, unnecessary movement of people or material, unnecessary processing steps, etc. All these together are termed as non-value added activities. JIT inventory control makes the production and operations management function more efficient, and cost effective. With JIT inventory control, organizations can purchase and receive components only when they are needed, thus eliminating the need for unnecessary inventory holding. Many organizations develop vendors who can supply items on an as-and-when required basis, within a minimum lead time. However, with a weak supply chain, lean or JIT inventory control practices may be difficult.

To make JIT inventory management practices successful, most of the retail chains maintain a vendor-managed inventory (VMI).This process requires the supplier to manage the inventory levels. Vendor-managed inventory reduces internal costs associated with planning and procuring materials and enables the vendor to better manage the inventory through higher visibility to the supply chain. A vendor-managed inventory may be owned by the vendor (consignment inventory) or the customer.

14.1 INTRODUCTION

Materials are a vital resource input in any production process. Conventionally, for any organization, the five M's in terms of resource inputs are vital. The five M's are Men, Machines, Materials, Money and Management. In today's business context, however, information and knowledge are also construed as vital resource inputs. The relative importance of such resource inputs, however, varies from organization to organization. However, materials as resource inputs are almost always considered the most vital, for any industry or business. This does not, however, mean that making available plenty of material resources would be the answer for any organization for its smooth functioning. Holding materials involve costs.

For any organization, the prime objective is to maximize its ROI (rate of return). ROI is judged with respect to the ratio arrived at by dividing the profit by capital employed (investment). While profit is the total receipt minus total expenditure, capital investment is the aggregate of fixed assets and current assets. ROI for any organization can be maximized by increasing total receipts, reducing total expenditure, reducing investments in fixed assets, and also by reducing investments in current assets. Materials costs are incurred in two ways: cost of materials and the cost of holding the materials. Materials are part of the current assets, and around 40% of the current assets are made up by inventories of raw materials, consumables, work-in-progress materials (that is, materials at different stages of production), and finished goods. Therefore, to maximize ROI, efficient management of materials assumes importance. It means the organization's profitability can increase substantially with proper materials and inventory control.

In many manufacturing organizations, the cost of materials alone range from 40% to 60% of the total expenditure. Obviously, better management of material is expected to ensure reduction in overall cost of operation and a smooth supply of inputs. This requires a well-coordinated approach towards various issues involving decision making with respect to materials. All materials-related activities, such as material planning and indenting, purchase systems and procedure, variety reduction through standardization and rationalization, reducing uncertainties in demand and supply, handling and transportation, inspection, proper storage and issue of materials to the internal customers, inventory management, vendor management, and finally, disposal of obsolete, surplus and scrap materials. All this taken together is termed integrated materials management.

14.2 DEFINITION AND CONCEPTS OF MATERIALS MANAGEMENT

Materials Management essentially involves short-term decisions on supplies, inventories, production levels, staffing patterns, schedules and distribution. Therefore, it involves tactical rather than strategic decisions. It has strong relations with production, inventory control and supply chain management. It is a dynamic process to establish and operate an efficient and effective method which ensures the supply and use of the required quantity and quality of material at the right time, at the right place and for the purpose for which it is needed. It is concerned with planning, organization and control of the flow of materials, from the initial purchase through internal operations to the distribution/delivery or to the service points.

Materials management can be defined as a joint action of various materials activities directed towards a common goal, which is to achieve an integrated management approach to planning, acquiring, processing and distributing production materials from the raw material state to the finished product state.

Materials Management is a key business function that is responsible for the co-ordination of planning, sourcing, purchasing, moving, storing and controlling materials in an optimum manner, so as to provide a pre-decided service to the customer at a minimum cost.

In the process of managing materials, we consider many sub-fields like

1. inventory management
2. value analysis
3. receiving
4. stores and management of obsolete, slow moving and non moving materials.

The scope of materials management is vast. Its sub-functions include materials planning and control, purchasing, stores and inventory management besides others. The various activities represent these four functions:

- Planning and control of materials
- Purchasing of materials
- Value analysis of materials
- Physical distribution of materials

It is an approach for planning, organizing and controlling all those activities principally concerned with the flow of materials into an organization. The scope of materials management varies greatly from company to company and may include materials planning and control, production planning, purchasing, inventory control and stores, in-plant materials movement, and waste management. The main issues in materials management are:

- Value added Manufacturing
- Creating competitive operating environment
- Developing competitive lead time and manufacturing strategies
- Clarifying organizational role in materials management
- Recognizing the Supply Chain and Concepts of Supply Chain Management
- Describing Characteristics of Manufacturing Processes

Thus, materials management involves short-time horizon decisions on supplies, inventories, production levels, staffing patterns, schedules and distribution. Typically, materials management decisions are tactical and not strategic, detailed and not aggregate. Inventories are items of potential economic value, which are held ahead of demand. Inventory control in any organization become necessary for avoiding the diminishing of economic value of inventory holding due to deterioration, obsolescence and pilferage. Moreover, excess inventory holdings unnecessarily block the capital of the organization, which cannot be utilized for other purposes, as it creates a problem of liquidity (cash availability) for the organization.

On the other hand, inventory management becomes necessary for an organization to meet an unpredictable demand, to hedge against poor quality, to guard against supply uncertainty and to avail of economies of bulk purchase.

Depending on the nature of the organization and its areas of activity, the type of inventory holding varies. However, most general types of inventory relate to raw materials, consumables, spare parts, etc. Organizations, whose production plans are independent of market demand also hold finished inventory for subsequent sales in the market. The cost of raw materials for many manufacturing organizations varies between 35% and 40% in India. Taking into consideration other costs like general consumables, spare parts and even finished goods, the inventory holding costs of many Indian organizations rises to a very alarming level of 30% to 35%. In many world class organizations, with the introduction of Just-in-Time (JIT) inventory control systems, inventory holding costs have been reduced to minimum. Therefore, we can understand the importance of inventory control and management function in any organization. The benefits of inventory management are to optimize the time and place utilities of stock and also to optimize investment in inventory.

In Fig. 14.1, we have explained the various stages of the material cycle, to illustrate that inventory control functions encompass all these areas.

The planning function involves determination of the categories of stock based on future demand. Future demand depends on past consumption, changing clientele and the priorities of organizational activities. While planning, the organization also requires specifying the quality and the quantity to be procured.

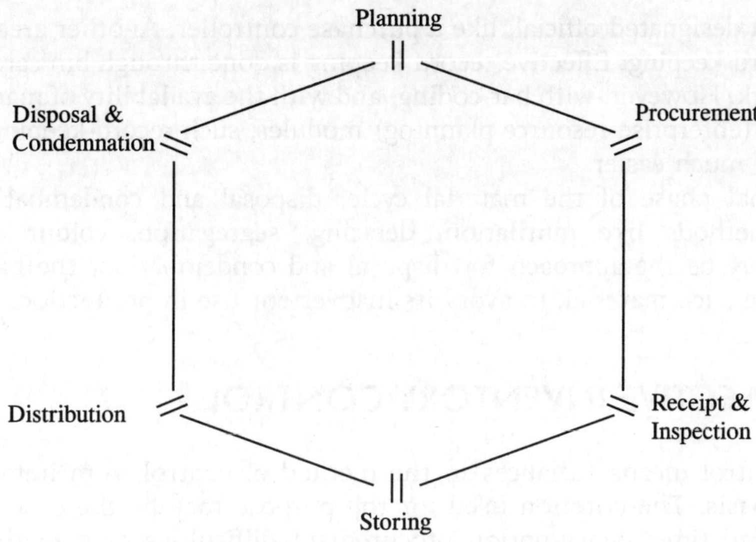

Figure 14.1 *The Material Cycle*

In the procurement phasc of inventory control, the organization requires to ensure right quality, right quantity, right price, right time and the right source of supply. Decision-making areas consider issues like vendor development, vendor evaluation, rate contract decisions and the distribution of financial authority of procurement. At the receipt and inspection stage of inventory control, the organization quantity, physical condition and chemical testing (to verify the physical and chemical properties of the materials received). However, in all cases, chemical testing need not be necessary.

At the storage stage, areas like location, preservation, layout and materials issues are taken into consideration. Location means the exact place where the stock piling is done to store the inventory. In some organizations, a centralized storage space is used, and all departments draw their requirements from this centralized store. However, for certain items, storage in the specific departments, where the production is being done, is considered more appropriate, either because of the size of the item, as the lifting of a heavy item may create problems in moving it from one place to another, or because of preservation problems. For example, the storage of certain items requires environmental conditioning. Hence, the preservation issue is also considered while storing the materials or the inventory. Layout is the physical arrangement of storage space. For quick retrieval, it is necessary to store the materials in such a way, so that that retrieval and supply can be done with ease and speed.

The other important area of material storage is to determine the system to be used for the issue of material. In many organizations, it is issued against the standard intends duly signed by the authorized representatives of the user section. However, where organizations are centrally controlled, such material issue may require the approval of a designated official, like a purchase controller. Another area of material issue is record keeping. Effective record keeping is done through bin card posting by the store clerk. However, with bar-coding, and with the availability of many inventory control ERP (enterprise resource planning) modules, such record-keeping tasks have now become much easier.

In the final phase of the material cycle, disposal and condemnation is done following methods like mutilation, defacing, segregation, colour coding, etc. Whatever may be the approach for disposal and condemnation, the basic purpose is to separate such material, to avoid its inadvertent use in production.

14.3 SELECTIVE INVENTORY CONTROL

Selective control means variances in the method of control from item to item on a selective basis. The criterion used for the purpose may be the cost of the item, criticality, lead time, consumption procurement difficulties or something else. In order to control the area of operations for good performance, time, money and effort are required.

Therefore, to achieve their objective, they must control only that area of operation, which is not controlled and is likely to cause damage. It involves selecting the area of control so that the required objective is achieved quickly without any loss of time which would happen if the entire operations were covered. Focussing on a selected area of control, leads to:

- minimum loss of energy and efforts
- at minimum cost without loss of time.

14.3.1 Deterministic and Probabilistic Model of Inventory Control

Organizations now spend more than 60% of their annual production costs on materials and other inventories; efficient inventory management can optimize inventory costs, and eventually make organizations more cost effective and competitive. The pattern of inventory management largely depends on the specific nature of activities of the organization and the complexity of its operations. Therefore, the selection of inventory models is very organization specific. Deterministic and probabilistic models of inventory control are used to forecast optimum inventory. The deterministic model helps in the estimation of inventory reserves based on the available data and information. We can define it as a method of determining the optimal inventory of a single item when demand is incomprehensible. This model assumes that inventory is built up at a constant rate to meet the determined and accepted demand. Let us explain this through a specific problem in an organization. A particular organization received an order in April to produce 1000 heavy trucks, the delivery mandate for which is on the completion of

10 months. This means the organization has to produce at the rate of 100 heavy trucks per month, to build up inventory in order to complete this order successfully.

The probabilistic inventory control model, on the other hand, makes use of known economic and engineering data and information to estimate the stock reserve and related probabilities. Using this approach, inventory control can be better modelled, as probability values lie within a bandwidth.

A deterministic model assumes that the situation is certain to occur; hence, the parameters can be taken into consideration with confidence. In a real life business situation, however, this condition rarely exists, as there is always an element of uncertainty in the business environment. The probabilistic model is also used considering the situation of uncertainty, but as it prototypes probabilistic demand and supply, the application of this model in inventory control become much more reliable. However, it is important to remember that the primary purpose of inventory control is to optimize the cost of inventory by controlling the cost of inventory holding, be it of raw materials or finished inventories.

14.3.1.1 Deterministic Inventory Model Example

1. Maximum Inventory Level (s)

   Optimum value of $S = S*$

   $S* = \sqrt{(2DCo/Cc)(Cs/Cc + Cs)}$

2. Time between receipt of orders, which also indicates when to order:

   $t* = Q*/D = \sqrt{2Co/DCo(Cs + Cc/Cs)}$

3. Optimal total inventory cost:

   $(TC*) = \sqrt{2DCoCc(Cs/Cs + Cc)}$

4. Reorder Level, $(R) = Q* - S*$

   $= Q*(1 - Cs/Cc + Cs)$

   where, Q = Quantity ordered each time

   $Q*$ = Optimum quantity of inventory ordered for minimum total cost

   D = Annual demand of parts (in units)

   C = Cost of inventory per unit of the item

   Cc = Carrying cost per unit of an individual item, expressed as a percentage of unit cost

   Co = Ordering, set-up or procurement cost per order

   R = Reorder point

T_C = Total annual costs

T_L = Lead time

C_S = Cost of shortages due to non-availability of inventory.

Therefore,

TC = (Ordering Cost) (Number of Orders placed in a year) + (Carrying cost per unit) (Average inventory level during year)

Number of orders to be placed in a year = Demand in a year/ Quantity ordered each time = D/Q

Average inventory carried during the year = $Q + O/2 = Q/2$

This is because the inventory level decreases uniformly from Q to zero.

Hence,

$$TC = C_O(D/Q) + C_cQ/2$$

Important Assumptions of the Model:

For this model, we make following important assumptions:

- Inventory demand is known with certainty.
- Inventory demand rate is constant
- Orders are placed in a single lot.
- No back orders are considered.
- Per unit purchase cost is fixed, as no discount is allowed.
- Lead time is constant and independent of demand.
- Inventory control is done from one point.

14.3.1.2 Probabilistic Model Example

Using a probabilistic model of inventory control, we can take vital inventory management decisions. Let us assume, for a given item, the important factors involved in determining C_1 and C_2 are:

Unit selling price (S)

Unit purchase cost (C)

Carrying cost for the entire period (Ch)

Salvage value (V)

Shortage penalty cost (Cs)

The unit costs of over-ordering and under-stocking are then

$$C1 = C + Ch - V$$

$C2 = S - C + Ch/2 + Cs$

Example

A company needs to stockpile some products, sourcing it in bulk from abroad. The company can import the item only once a year, in the month of April. The cost of each item is Rs. 25/-, which the company can sell at Rs. 50/- each. Being known in the market as the only quality importer, failure to make the item available in the market in times of demand results in a goodwill cost to the company of Rs. 15 per unit. Due to its limited life cycle, the company has to sell the items within 12 months of its import. However, any item remaining unsold is given a salvage value of Rs. 10 per unit. Inventory holding cost is 10% of the price. With the following probability distribution of demand, estimate the optimum number of items to be stocked.

Units in stock	2	3	4	5	9
Probability of Demand p(D=Q)	0.35	0.25	0.20	0.15	0.05

Solution

Given S = Rs. 50, C = Rs. 25, C_h = 0.10 × 25 = 2.5, V = Rs. 10, C_s = 15.
The probability distribution of demand is given in the following table.

Units Stocked	Probability of Demand p (D = Q)	Cumulative probability of P(D = Q)
2	0.35	0.35
3	0.25	0.60
4	0.20	0.80
5	0.15	0.95
6	0.05	1.00

$C_1 = 25 + 2.5 - 10 = 17.5$

$C_2 = 50 - 25 - (2.5/2) + 15 = 38.75$

The ratio, $\dfrac{C_2}{C_1 + C_2} = \dfrac{38.75}{17.5 + 38.75} = 0.69$

The observed ratio (0.69) lies between cumulative probabilities of 0.60 and 0.80, which in turn reflect the values of Q as 3 and 4, that is, $P(D < 3) = 0.60 < 0.69 < 0.80 = P(D < 4)$. Therefore, the optimal number of units to stock is 4 units.

14.4 SELECTIVE INVENTORY CONTROL THROUGH VARIOUS TECHNIQUES

Depending on the objective of materials management, there are various techniques of selective control. These are listed below:

- ABC analysis
- HML analysis
- VED analysis
- SDE analysis
- GOLF analysis
- SOS analysis
- FSN analysis
- XYZ analysis

14.4.1 ABC Analysis

ABC analysis is a selective control technique which is required to be applied when we want to control the value of consumption of an item in rupees; obviously, in such cases, we must select those materials whose consumption is very high.

In any manufacturing company, the number of items which are consumed or traded may run into thousands. It has been found after a number of studies for different companies that

Value of consumption of items (value in Rs).	No. Of items	Grade
70% of consumption	10% of no. of items	A
20% of consumption	15% of no. of items	B
10% of consumption	75% of no. of items	C

On the basis of the above analysis, these items are termed as ABC items as detailed below:

A-items: these are items which form hardly 5%–10% of the total, but their consumption may amount 70%–75% of the total money spent on materials.

B-items: these are items which are generally 10%–15% of the total items, and their consumption amounts to 10%–15% of the money spent on materials.

C-items: these are a large number of items which are cheap and inexpensive, and hence, insignificant. They are large in numbers and account for hardly 5%–10% of the total money spent on materials.

Based on the above analysis, decisions can then be taken to control the consumption, so as to optimize inventory costs.

A graphical presentation of the ABC Model (Fig. 14.2) is given on page 469.

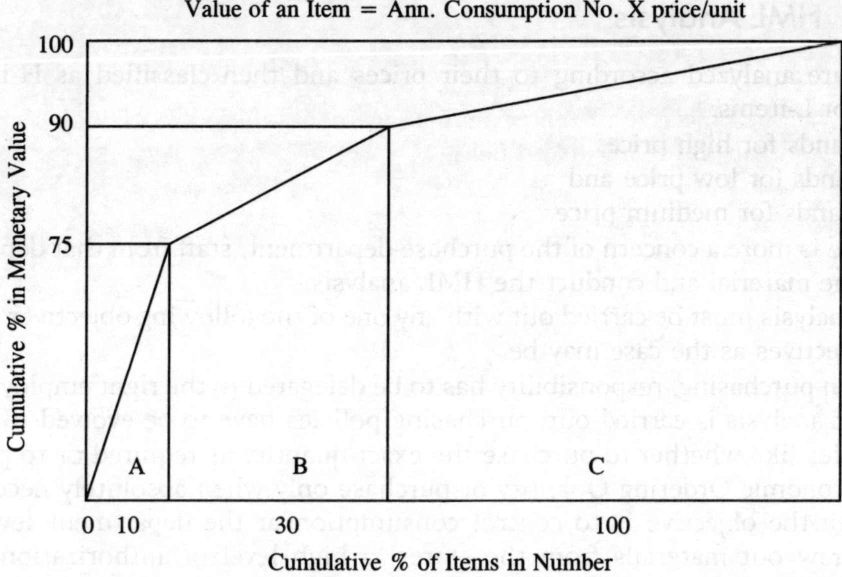

Figure 14.2 *ABC Classification*

A-items: A senior level executive must be made responsible for regularly reviewing the consumption of overseas items; up-to-date and accurate records should be maintained for these items. The inventory of these items must be at a minimum and orders for these items should be staggered, so that the timely arrival of these items is ensured. Attempts must be made to reduce the internal and external lead-time of this item. Safety stocks of these items should be kept to a minimum because if the frequency of ordering of these items is kept high, the price discount for these items cannot be given, because physical ordering is very frequent.

B-items: These items should be kept under normal control and a report of the goods must be maintained. Safety stock of these items can be moderate. Safety stock level is maintained to guard against demand variability. This stock level is determined based on the occurrence of demand variability. Price discount can be given and physical stocktaking can also be moderate.

C-items: Little control is required for c-items and the job of controlling should be left to those at a junior level, such as those in charge of stores. A large quantity of inventories can be maintained for this stock because it is cheap. To avoid a stock-out situation, these items should not be kept under lock and key and must be kept at convenient places, open to all users. Price discount can be given for purchases in bulk. Physical checking of the stock can be done once in six months.

14.4.2 HML Analysis

Material are analyzed according to their prices and then classified as H-items or M-items or L-items.

- H stands for high price,
- L stands for low price and
- M stands for medium price.

Since price is more a concern of the purchase department, staff from that department analyze the material and conduct the HML analysis.

HML analysis must be carried out with any one of the following objectives or some of the objectives as the case may be.

- When purchasing, responsibility has to be delegated to the right employee level.
- HML analysis is carried out; purchasing policies have to be evolved to address queries like whether to purchase the exact quantity as required or to purchase in Economic Ordering Quantity or purchase only when absolutely necessary
- When the objective is to control consumption at the department level, then to draw out materials from the stores, a high level of authorization will be given to H items, a low level authorization for L items and a medium level of authorization for M items.
- The frequency of stock taking is very frequent for H category, very rarely for L category and of average frequency for M category items.
- With regard to security arrangements, H items are kept under lock and key, L items are kept on the shop floor and M items are used under supervision.

14.4.3 VED Analysis

VED analysis is carried out to control situations that are critical. In VED analysis, we try to identify material according to their criticality to the production; this means those materials, without which production will come to a halt. From this point of view, material can be classified into three categories.

- V – vital
- E – essential
- D – desirable

Vital categories of items are those for the want of which production will stop. For example, power in the factory. An essential group of items are those items, which if non-available will result in very high stockout costs. In the case of the desirable group of items, non-availability will not lead to an immediate loss of production and stock cost is very limited, but it may cause a minor disruption in production for a short time. Any item may be vital for a number of reasons or can cause the following problems:

- Serious production losses
- The lead-time of procurement may be very large.
- It could be a non-standard item which is difficult to procure.

- An item with only one source of supply which is located far away from the production site.

How to conduct VED analysis?

Steps: 1 Identify the factors that you have to consider for VED analysis. This may be as below:

FACTOR	1st DEGREE	2nd DEGREE	3rd DEGREE
Stock out case	Below Rs. X	Between Rs. X and Y	Above Rs Y
Lead time	1–4 week	4–8 week	Above 8 week
Nature of item	Commercial std item	Non-stock item according to supplier standards	Totally non-std item.
Source of supply	Local	Out station	Imported

Step: 2 Assign points or weightage to these factors according to the importance they have to the company as shown above.

Step: 3 Divide each factor into 3 degrees and allocate points to each degree.

Step: 4 Prepare a categorization plan to provide a basis for the evolution of items as shown below

Categorization plan.	
Points	**Classification**
100–160	D
161–230	E
231–300	V

Step: 5 Specify the degree and allocate weights to all the factors.

Step: 6 Evaluate and find the final score for every item and specify the type of item.

14.4.4 SDE Analysis

SDE analysis is carried out so as to take care of various purchasing problems that normally come on a day-to-day basis. Various purchasing problems that come on a day-to-day basis are as follows:

(1) Non-availability
(2) Scarcity
(3) Longer lead-time
(3) Geographically scattered

(4) Unreliable sources or supply

Therefore, it would be better for managers to identify the materials that pose problems peculiar to them and then allot these items for procurement purposes to those subordinates who can handle this judiciously. And therefore from this point of view, materials are classified into three categories namely:

- S – Scarce materials are those materials, which are hardly available.
- D – Difficult materials are those materials, which are available with difficulty.
- E – Easy materials are those materials, which are available easily.

Scarce Materials These materials are normally in short supply. They can be imported material or have to be procured through government agencies or authorities. Therefore, such materials have to be procured less often, say once a year, because it involves substantial effort and expenditure to procure.

Difficult Materials These are materials which are not easy to procure, but are available indigenously, or those materials, which have to come from far-off places, and for which there are no reliable sources of procurement. These items require sufficient notice in advance for their procurement.

Easy Materials These are those materials, which are readily available and are also standard materials; in their case, the supply or availability is much more than the demand in the market. These are also available in the local market.

Once SDE analysis is carried out and the items are identified, decisions can be made regarding which subordinate should purchase which materials on a regular basis. SDE analysis also helps to decide purchasing policies. For example, for scarce materials, forward purchasing policies can be adopted. For difficult materials, schedule-purchasing policies can be adopted and for easy group of items, contract-purchasing policies can be adopted.

14.4.5 GOLF Analysis

This analysis is similar to SDE analysis and is based upon the nature of the suppliers and the type of market from where the purchases are made, because they determine what they supply, the lead-time, the payment terms, consistency and continuity of service and administrative procedures. Therefore, it becomes necessary to identify separately, different groups of suppliers having these variations; accordingly, the suppliers can be classified into four groups

- G for government suppliers
- O for ordinary or non government suppliers
- L for local suppliers
- F for foreign suppliers

All these suppliers have their own peculiarities and payment terms, their own administrative procedures and so on.

For example, if the supplies are sourced from government suppliers such as the STC or DGTD or public sector corporations, then transactions to these types of suppliers may require the payment of an advance, caution money deposit, security deposit, long lead time and so on. On the other hand, transactions with ordinary suppliers may require moderate delivery times, credit facility and so on. Similarly, local suppliers normally accept cash purchases, they may even offer delivery at the manufacturing site, but sourcing foreign suppliers requires administrative or procedural work, such as obtaining bills of lading licenses, import and export formalities, opening letters of credit with the banks and shipping, packing and forwarding procedures.

Therefore, a purchase manager if he/she wants to run his department efficiently and control his department properly, must identify purchases according to the category of supplier and allot experts in these areas to conduct such purchases. Training must also be offered from time to time to train employees in these areas, so that purchasing become efficient and smooth.

14.4.6 SOS Analysis

SOS Analysis is based upon seasonal availability of an item. Depending upon this, purchasing problems and workload may vary, and therefore, the purchasing function must be organized to deal with such products or materials.

Thus, items are classified into two groups:

- S stands for seasonal items
- OS stands for non-seasonal items.

Seasonal items can be classified into two groups

1. Those seasonal items which are available only for a limited period. For example, agricultural products such as mangoes or raw material for a cigarette factory or raw materials for the paper industry are available for a limited time during a particular season. Therefore, the purchasing department is expected to procure its full year's consumption quota during this period. This could lead to problems of storage space, compounded by the perishable nature of these items; the objective will be to get the materials at a discount, disregarding the application of the economic order quantity concept.
2. These are seasonal items but they are available throughout the year, for example, apples and all other food grains. These items are cheap during season at the lowest price, but they are made available to the customer throughout the year. Such items have to be purchased in bulk, taking advantage of the discount, but at the same time, care should be taken ensure that savings due to price discounts are not offset by holding or carrying cost of inventory.
3. Non-seasonal items are those, which are available throughout the year, without any appreciable price variation. Items like salt fall under this category. These

items are purchased taking into consideration the normal purchasing problems, and involve using the normal purchasing procedures

Once the organization ascertains the category of the items being purchased, purchasing work will be organized accordingly.

14.4.7 FSN Analysis

This type of analysis is done from the point of view of movement of the item or issue of the item.

'F' items are those that are fast moving i.e. in a given period of time, say a month or a year, a large number of these may have been issued. However, fast moving does not necessarily mean that these items are consumed in large quantities.

'S' items are those items that are slow moving in the sense that in a given period of time, they would have been issued very few times.

'N' or non-moving items are those, which have not been issued at all for a considerable period of time.

Thus, the stores department concerned with the movement of items should know and classify the items stored in one of these categories, so that they can manage, operate and plan their stores activity accordingly. For example, for efficient operations it is necessary that fast-moving items as far as possible should be stored as close as possible to the point of issue, so that it can be issued with a minimum of handling. Also, such items must be stored at the floor level. Avoid storing them at higher levels.

Similarly, if the items are slow moving or issued once in a while in a given period of time, they can be stored in the interior of the stores, and even at higher levels, because the handling of these items is very rare.

Further, it is necessary for the stores-in-charge to know about non-moving items for the following reasons:

- They mean unnecessary locking up of finances and thereby affect the rate of returns of the company.
- They also occupy valuable space in the stores without any usefulness, and therefore, it becomes necessary to identify these items and delve into the reasons for their non-movement, and if justified, recommend to top management for their speedy disposal, so that the company's operations are performed efficiently.
- Also, inventory control to some extent, can also be exercised on the basis of FSN analysis. For example, fast-moving items can be controlled more severely, particularly when their value is also high. Similarly, slow-moving items may not be controlled and reviewed very frequently, since their consumption may not be frequent and their value may not be high.

14.4.8 XYZ Analysis

This type of analysis is carried out from time to time, from the point of view of the value of balance stocks lying in the stores and all the items are classified as:

'X 'items are those whose value of balance stocks are very high.

'Y' items are those items whose value of balance stock is moderate.

'Z' items are those items whose value of balance stock is very low.

Following this type of classification, action can be taken to control the situation as shown below:

1. From the security point of view, high-value items must be stored and kept under lock and key, or if this is not possible, they should be kept in such a way that they are always under supervision. Similarly, arrangement can be made for y and z items accordingly.
2. From the inventory control point of view, the reasons for the high inventory for x items should be identified. Inventory control procedures should be reviewed for each and every high item, because stock should be maintained to take care of lead-time consumption and also to provide safety stocks. For high-value items lying in stores, we should review the reasons for the long lead-time, as well as demand variations, and see whether lead time consumption and safety stocks can be reduced. Proper inventory control procedures can be developed on the basis of an XYZ analysis.

Thus, proper selective control methods should be selected to control the supply of materials, to prevent a loss of profit for the company.

14.5 ECONOMIC ORDERING QUANTITY

The economic order quantity (EOQ) is the order quantity that minimizes total holding and ordering costs for the year. Even if all the assumptions do not hold exactly, the EOQ gives us a good indication of whether or not, current order quantities are reasonable.

Economic order quantity is the level of inventory that minimizes the total inventory holding costs and ordering costs. The framework used to determine this order quantity is also known as the Wilson EOQ Model. The model was developed by F. W. Harris in 1913. But still R. H. Wilson is given credit for his early in-depth analysis of the model.

Some of the assumptions of the EOQ are:

- Constant cost of ordering
- Constant rate of demand
- Fixed lead time

- Constant purchase price with zero discount
- Stock replenishment is instant

EOQ is arrived at by ensuring minimum ordering and inventory carrying costs, EOQ variables are:

- Q = Order quantity
- Q* = Optimal order quantity
- D = Annual demand
- P = Per unit cost of purchase
- C = Fixed cost per order
- H = Annual holding cost per unit

(Source: http://en.wikipedia.org/wiki/Economic_order_quantity)

14.5.1 The Total Cost Function

The single-item EOQ formula finds the minimum point of the following cost function: EOQ is the level of the inventory, where ordering cost and carrying cost remains equal.

Total cost = purchase cost + ordering cost + holding cost.

1. Purchase cost: This is the variable cost of goods; purchase unit price × annual demand quantity. This is P×D
2. Ordering cost: This is the cost of placing orders; each order has a fixed cost C, and we need to order D/Q times per year. This is C × D/Q
3. Holding cost: the average quantity in stock (between fully replenished and empty) is Q/2, so this cost is H × Q/2

In order to determine the minimum point of the total cost curve, set its derivative as being equal to zero. The result of this derivation is:

Solving for Q gives Q* (the optimal order quantity):

Therefore, Q* is independent of P, it is a function of only C, D, H.

14.5.2 Extensions of the EOQ Model

From the core EOQ model, we can have several extensions. These are backordering costs, interval between economic order, economic production quantity, etc. At times we find goals and strategies of the companies also conflict with EOQ. In many cases, by making EOQ a performance criterion, organizations suffer from the increased cost of operations. Despite this, EOQ is still used essentially as an accounting formula to optimize the cost of ordering and inventory carrying.

Inventory control in any organization is of prime importance. It helps in time and cost savings. Balanced inventory holding helps avoid unnecessary inventory holding costs, and also benefits the organization by not exposing it to the problem of obsolescence. Problems of obsolescence may even force an organization into bankruptcy. The EOQ model ensures a trade-off between the cost of holding inventory and the costs of re-ordering inventory, and in the process, minimizes the total cost of inventory. Important inventory costs are the costs of ordering, costs related to placing an order, costs of inventory holding or carrying. All these costs are considered in the EOQ model. It is important to understand that all these costs are variable in nature. Purchasing cost, which is constant, is not considered in this model. Let us now understand the various cost components.

Annual Usage/Demand This cost is expressed in terms of units, i.e., the forecasted annual demand or usage. In an EOQ equation, this cost aspect can be easily determined, once we arrive at the annual forecasted demand.

Order Cost This is the purchase cost or set up cost, and it is arrived at by summing up the fixed costs that are incurred by the organization every time the order is placed. To be more specific, this cost relates to the cost incurred for the activities involved in processing the order, like costs for placing purchase order or requisition, costs for purchase approval, costs to process the receipt of the purchase items, incoming inspection, invoice processing and vendor payment, and in some cases, a portion of the inbound freight may also be included in the order cost. Hence, these costs depend on the order frequency, and not really on the quantities ordered. For placing any order, organizations need to spend time. Such time costs are included in the order costs. A tentative detail of time costs is given below:

Type of Time spent	Reasons for time spent
For checking the receipt, entering the receipt and for doing other related paper work.	It is important to match the receipt with the order and to maintain proper records, as these are essential documents for future audits.
Time spent repacking materials, unloading trucks and delivery to other departments.	Some organizations also factor in such time loss in cost of ordering, while others do not consider these costs. However, it is more a convention not to consider these costs, as these are incurred only after the placement of the order.

Type of Time spent	Reasons for time spent
Time spent to inspect a fixed quantity per receipt, and its repacking is included.	However, time spent for quality inspection in conformity with the technical specifications and processes is not considered, as these costs are included in the cost of inspection.
Time spent to prepare the purchase order, to get it approved, to contact and negotiate with suppliers or vendors, to expedite vendors for timely delivery, to review the order reports and forecasts, etc. are included in the order costs. associated with creating the purchase order, approval steps, contacting the vendor, expediting and reviewing order reports; you would not include time spent reviewing forecasts, sourcing, getting quotes (unless you get quotes each time you order), and setting up a new item	In some cases, organizations get a quote every time they order, as such costs for ordering are very negligible, organizations as a convention, exclude this.
Time spent to deal with vendor invoices.	Vendors or suppliers send their invoices along with every supply, which requires verification and subsequent matching with the receipt.

Inventory Carrying Costs (Inventory Holding Costs) These costs are apportioned on the carrying of inventory from the suppliers or vendors, and also the costs for upkeep of the inventory, i.e., the storage cost. In EOQ calculation, such costs are considered as constant per inventory unit. Some of the components of inventory carrying costs are:

- *Interest costs*: As we spend money for the inventory (whether it is borrowed or from own funds), we apportion the cost of levying interest on the amount spent. The logic behind levying interest also on money spent on inventory is that we could have earned a return had this money been invested for some alternative gain.
- *Insurance costs*: To ensure risk-free inventory holding, we also need to insure it. Such insurance costs are directly attributed to the inventory value, and hence, apportioned as part of the inventory carrying costs.
- *Taxes:* Also, we need to pay taxes on the inventory that we buy. Such taxes are also charged on the cost of inventory.
- *Storage Costs*: These costs are what we attribute to the warehouse for stockpiling

the inventory. For EOQ calculation, we divide the total cost of warehousing by average inventory holding. We do it even though such costs may not be directly attributable to inventory levels, and may not even be representative of the actual utilization of the storage space. For EOQ calculation, ideally, we need to consider those costs that vary with inventory levels.

14.5.3 Graphical Solution

If we minimize the sum of the ordering and carrying costs, we are also minimizing the total costs. To help visualize this, we can graph the ordering cost and the holding cost as shown in the chart (Fig.14.3).

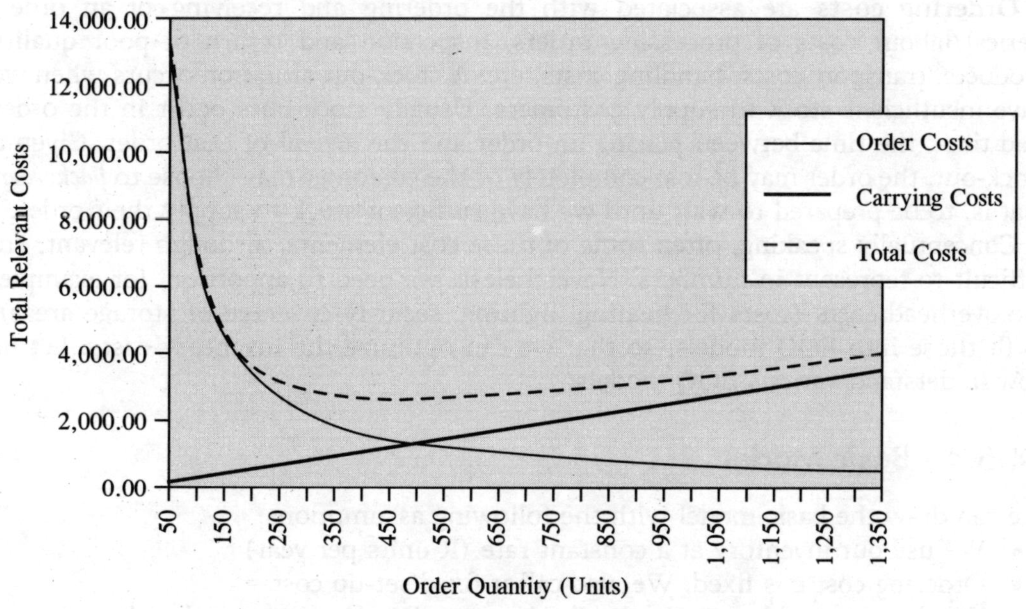

Figure 14.3 *Economic Order Quantity*

This chart shows costs on the vertical axis or Y-axis and the order quantity on the horizontal or X-axis. The straight line which commences at the origin is the carrying cost curve, the total cost of carrying units of inventory. As expected, as we order more on the X-axis, the carrying cost line increases in a proportionate manner. The downward sloping curve which commences high on the Y-axis and decreases as it approaches the X-axis and moves to the right is the ordering cost curve. This curve represents the total ordering cost depending on the size of the order quantity. Obviously, the ordering cost will decrease as the order quantity is increased, thereby resulting in fewer orders which need to be placed in any particular period of time.

The point at which these two curves intersect is the same point which is the minimum of the curve which represents the total cost for the inventory system. Thus, the sum of the carrying cost curve and the ordering cost curve is represented by the total cost curve and the minimum point of the total cost curve corresponds to the same point where the carrying cost curve and the ordering cost curve intersect.

The costs that we need to consider so that we can decide the amount of stock to have can be divided into stock *holding* costs and stock *ordering* (and receiving) costs as below.

Stockholding costs are incurred while keeping the stock over time. Other costs are already indicated above are storage costs, rent/depreciation, labour, overheads (like heating, lighting, and security), costs for money being tied-up, that is, loss of interest, opportunity cost, costs of obsolescence, stock deterioration (loss if product deteriorates whilst being held), theft/insurance, etc.

Ordering costs are associated with the ordering and receiving of an order, clerical/labour costs of processing orders, inspection and return of poor quality products, transport costs, handling costs, etc. A stock-out situation occurs when we have insufficient stock to supply customers. Usually stock-outs occur in the order lead time, the time between placing an order and the arrival of that order. Given a stock-out, the order may be lost completely or the customer may choose to *backorder*, that is, to be prepared to wait until we have sufficient stock to supply their order.

Conceptually speaking, often some of these cost elements, although relevant, are difficult to represent in numbers. Nevertheless, we need to apportion, for example, the overhead costs (costs for heating, lighting, security coverage of storage areas), to fit those into EOQ models, so that we can optimize the inventory costs. Let us now understand various EOQ models.

14.5.4 Basic Model

We can draw the basic model with the following assumptions:

- We use our inventory at a constant rate (R units per year)
- Ordering cost c is fixed. We also call it fixed set-up cost
- We do not consider any lead time, i.e., the time lag between the placement of order and the receipt of the items.
- Variable inventory holding cost c is assumed to be per unit per year. Then we need to decide Q, the amount to order each time, often called the batch (or lot) size.

Based on the above assumptions, we can represent graphically the stock level as in Fig 14.4.

The diagram represents a constant inventory level at Q/2 over time. Hence, we get:

- Annual holding cost = ch(Q/2)
- where Q/2 is the average (constant) inventory level
- Annual order cost = co(R/Q)
- where (R/Q) is the number of orders per year (R used, Q each order)

- So, total annual cost = ch(Q/2) + co(R/Q)

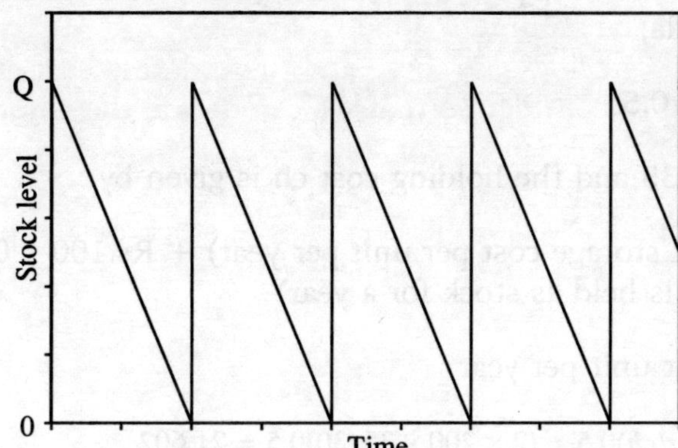

Figure 14.4 *Graph of stock level over time*

We try to minimize the annual cost by choosing the appropriate value of Q. Using the diagram (Fig. 14.5), we can illustrate the total annual cost curve. As could be seen from the diagram, with the change in Q, the other two costs, that is., annual holding costs and annual ordering costs also change. However, Q corresponds to the minimum total costs, at the point where it cuts the ordering and holding costs line.

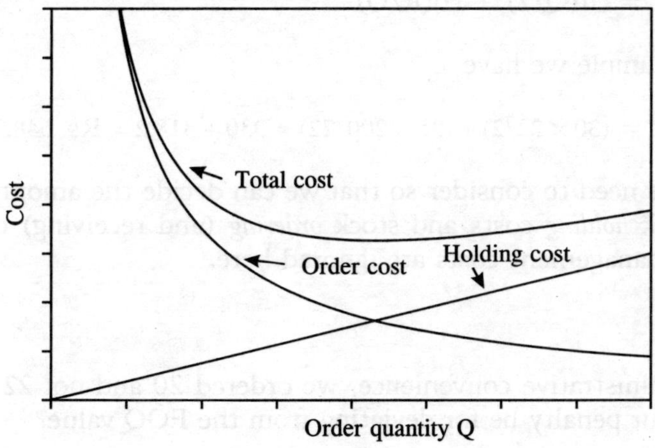

Figure 14.5 Total Annual Cost Curve

Example

A retailer expects to sell about 200 units of a product per year. The storage space taken up in his premises, by one unit of this product, costs Rs.20 per year. If the cost associated with ordering is Rs 35 per order, what is the economic order quantity with a given interest rate of 10% per year and the total cost of one unit is Rs. 100. We use the EOQ formula,

EOQ = (2Rco/ch) 0.5

Here, R=200, co=35 and the holding cost ch is given by

ch = Rs. 20 (direct storage cost per unit per year) + Rs.100 × 0.10 (this is the interest lost if one unit is held as stock for a year)

i.e. ch = Rs. 30 per unit per year

Hence $EOQ = (2Rco/ch)0.5 = (2 \times 200 \times 35/30)0.5 = 21.602$

But as we must order a whole number of units we have

EOQ = 22

We can illustrate this calculation by reference to the diagram (Fig 14.6) which shows order cost, holding cost and total cost for this example.

With this EOQ, we can calculate our total annual cost from the equation

Total annual cost = ch(Q/2) + co(R/Q)

Hence for this example we have

Total annual cost $= (30 \times 22/2) + (35 \times 200/22) = 330 + 318.2 =$ Rs 648.2

The costs that we need to consider so that we can decide the amount of stock to be divided into stock *holding* costs and stock *ordering* (and receiving) costs. Note that conventionally, management costs are ignored here.

Example

Suppose, for administrative convenience, we ordered 20 and not 22 at each order – what would be our penalty be for deviating from the EOQ value?

With a Q of 20, we look at the total annual cost

$= (c_h Q/2) + (c_o R/Q)$

$= (30 \times 20)/2 + (35 \times 200/20) = 300 + 350 =$ Rs.650

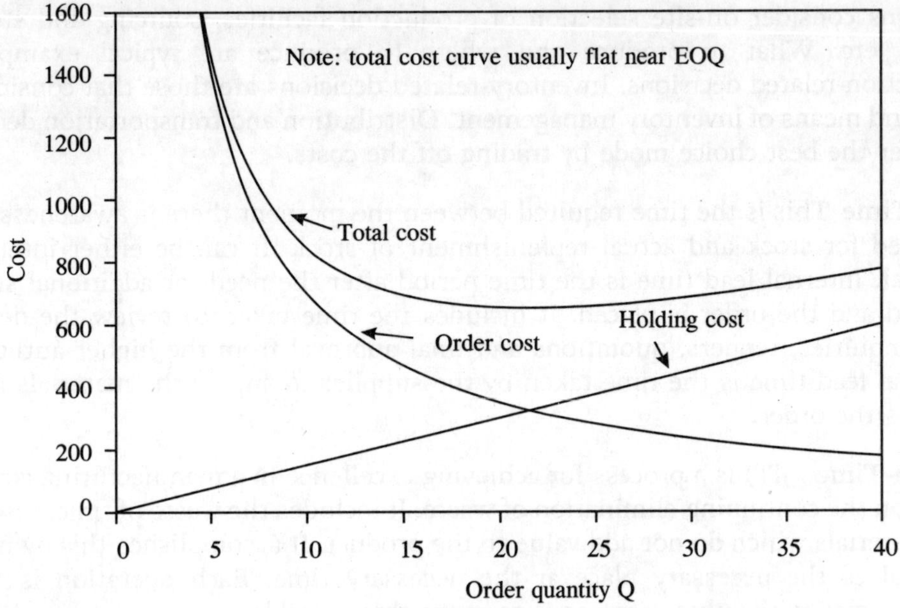

Figure 14.6 *Diagram showing order cost, holding cost and total cost*

Hence, the penalty for deviating from the EOQ-derived value of 22 and ordering 20 on each order is Rs 650 – Rs 648.2 = Rs 1.80

14.6 SUPPLY CHAIN MANAGEMENT AND INVENTORY CONTROL

Supply chain is an integrated term, encompassing procurement, transformation and distribution of produced goods to customers. Supply chain concepts now even extend to service organizations. Its scope, however, varies from organization to organization. In a multi-product organization, shared supply chains, in terms of shared utilization of all facilities, like components, facilities and capacities may exist. Efficient supply chain management requires the integration of marketing, sales and distribution, and purchasing functions. Integrated supply chain management can benefit the organization both in terms of cost optimization and value-added products and services to the customers. Integrated supply chain ensures proper coordination among various players in the chain, and helps them to work as a balanced relay team (Cooper and Ellram, 1993).

Supply chain decisions can be either strategic or operational. Strategic supply chain decisions are linked with the strategy of the organizations; hence, encompass issues related to policies, and design. Operational supply chain management issues cover location, manufacturing, inventory and distribution (transportation). Location decisions consider on-site selection of production facilities, sourcing and stocking points, etc. What to produce and where to produce are typical examples of production-related decisions. Inventory-related decisions are those that consider the ways and means of inventory management. Distribution and transportation decisions consider the best choice mode by trading off the costs.

Lead Time This is the time required between the moment there is awareness about the need for stock and actual replenishment of stock. It can be either internal or external. Internal lead time is the time period after the need for additional stock is realized and the order is placed. It includes the time taken to review the demand, trade inquiries, tenders, quotations and final approval from the higher authorities. External lead time is the time taken by the supplier to supply the materials after it receives the order.

Just-in-Time (JIT) is a process for achieving excellence in a manufacturing company based on the continuing elimination of waste. It includes the waste of time, resources and materials which do not add value to the product. It accomplishes this by moving material to the necessary place at the necessary time. Each operation is closely synchronized with subsequent ones to make this possible.

JIT is actually a quality initiative with the goal of eliminating wasted steps, wasted labour and wasted cost. EOQ is one of the tools to achieve just-in-time. Thus, EOQ is used to determine which components fit into the JIT model and the level of JIT that is economically advantageous for the operation of the organization.

Inventory Control is the activities, techniques and methods of maintaining an accurate stock of items at a desired level. The stocks may be of finished goods, parts, work in progress or raw materials.

There are three phases to the flow of goods:

- Raw materials flow into the manufacturing company from a physical supply system.
- The raw materials are processed by manufacturing into finished goods.
- The finished goods are distributed to the customer through a distribution system.

SUMMARY

1. Materials are one of the vital resource inputs in any production process.
2. Conventionally for any organization, the five M's of resource inputs are vital. These are Men, Machines, Materials, Money and Management.
3. In today's business context, in many manufacturing organizations, the cost of materials alone ranges from 40% to 60% of the total expenditure. Obviously, better management of material is essential to achieve organizational success.

4. This chapter discussed various activities involved in materials management. For example, how to plan and control materials, how to purchase materials, how to conduct a value analysis of materials and the process of physical distribution of materials. Selective inventory control techniques like ABC Analysis, SDE Analysis, GOLF Analysis, SOS Analysis, FSN Analysis, XYZ Analysis, etc. have been explained with suitable examples. Various EOQ techniques and their applicability in different situations have also been explained.
5. Finally, supply chain management and inventory control have also been discussed.

KEY WORDS

Selective Inventory Control It refers to variances in the method of control from item to item on a selective basis. The criterion used may be the cost of the item, its criticality, lead time, consumption procurement difficulties or other factors.

Order Cost This is the purchase cost or set up cost, and is arrived at by summing up the fixed costs incurred by the organization every time an order is placed

Inventory Carrying Cost (inventory holding costs) Also called holding cost, carrying cost is the cost associated with having an inventory on hand. It is primarily made up of the costs associated with the investment in inventory and storage costs.

Stock holding costs are incurred while keeping the stock over time. Other costs are storage costs, rent/depreciation, labour, overheads (like heating, lighting and security), cost of money being tied-up, i.e., loss of interest, opportunity cost, costs of obsolescence, stock deterioration (loss if product deteriorates whilst being held), theft/insurance, etc.

Supply chain A supply chain is a network of facilities and distribution options that performs the functions of procurement of materials, transformation of these materials into intermediate and finished products, and the distribution of these finished products to customers. Supply chains exist in both service and manufacturing organizations, although the complexity of the chain may vary greatly from industry to industry and firm to firm

Supply chain decisions We classify the decisions for supply chain management into two broad categories – strategic and operational. As the term implies, strategic decisions are made typically over a longer time horizon. These are closely linked to the corporate strategy, and guide supply chain policies from a design perspective. On the other hand, operational decisions are short term, and focus on activities on a day-to-day basis. The effort in these types of decisions is to effectively and efficiently manage the product flow in the "strategically" planned supply chain.

There are four major decision areas in supply chain management: 1) location 2) production 3) inventory and 4) transportation (distribution), and there are both strategic and operational elements in each of these decision areas.

Lead time This is the time required between the moment you are aware about the need for stock and its actual replenishment. It can be either internal or external. Internal lead time is the time period after the need for additional stock is realized and the order is placed. It includes the time taken to review the demand, trade inquiries, tenders, quotations and the obtaining of final approval from the higher authorities. External lead time is the time taken by the supplier to supply the materials after it receives the order.

Just-in-time (JIT) is a process for achieving excellence in a manufacturing company, based on the continuous elimination of waste. Waste does not add value to the product. It is accomplished by moving material to the required place at the required time. Each operation is closely synchronized with subsequent ones to make it possible.

JIT is actually a quality initiative with the goal of eliminating wasted steps, wasted labour, and wasted cost. EOQ is a tool to achieve JIT. Thus, EOQ is used to determine which components fit into the JIT model and the level of JIT that is economically advantageous for the organization.

GENERAL REVIEW QUESTIONS

1. Explain the concept of materials management function. What are the activities involved in materials management?
2. Explain how inventory control relates to the materials management function?
3. What is selective inventory control? How is such control ensured?
4. For a steel manufacturing organization, suggest some selective inventory control measures.
5. Explain the concept of supply chain management. How does it relate to inventory control?
6. Short notes
   (a) ABC Analysis
   (b) SDE Analysis
   (c) GOLF Analysis
   (d) SOS Analysis
   (e) FSN Analysis
   (f) XYZ Analysis
   (g) EOQ Variables

ADDITIONAL REFERENCES

1. Cohen, M.A. 1997. *Manufacturing Automation*. Chicago: Irwin.
2. Konz. Stephen. 1983. *Work Design: Industrial Ergonomics*, 2nd ed. New York: John Wiley and Sons.
3. Richard, B., Chase, Nicholas, J, Aquilano., and F. Robert, Jacobs. 2002. *Operations Management for Competitive Advantage*. New Delhi: Tata McGraw-Hill Publishing Company Limited.
4. Schmenner, R.W. 1995. *Service Operations Management*. Englewood Cliffs, N.J: Prentice Hall.
5. Ballou, R. H. 1992. *Business Logistics Management*, 3rd ed. Englewood Cliffs, NJ: Prentice Hall .
6. Cohen, M. A. and H. L. Lee. 1988. Strategic Analysis of Integrated Production-Distribution Systems: Models and Methods. *Operations Research*, 36, 2, 216–228.
7. Cohen, M. A. and H. L. Lee. 1989. Resource Deployment Analysis of Global Manufacturing and Distribution Networks. *Journal of Manufacturing and Operations Management*, 81–104.
8. Cooper, M. C., and L. M. Ellram. 1993. Characteristics of Supply Chain Management and the Implications for Purchasing and Logistics Strategy. *The International Journal of Logistics Management*, 4, 2, 13–24.
9. Lee, H. L., and C. Billington. 1993. Material Management in Decentralized Supply Chains. *Operations Research*, 41, 5, 835–47.

CASE STUDY

Building organizational capabilities – *Dell*'s supply chain management

To build supply chain capabilities, organizations need to redraw their business model. Supply chain management (SCM) requires new strategies, and even changes in terms of in-customer operations, channel strategy, core operations capabilities and organizational structure. The focus of SCM is more on revenue increase rather than on cost control, as a well-structured SCM model can increase the market spread for the company. It is possible for the company to enhance its market share to the extent of 35%. Despite such potential benefits from SCM, organizations traditionally look for operational cost control.

Till 1994, *Dell Computers* was a tier-II PC manufacturer. *Dell* used to order components from vendors in advance, manufacture computers and stockpile these as finished inventory. With SCM, *Dell* could convert its operations to a build-to-order model. This helped the company to introduce just-in-time inventory, and also JIT philosophy became a part of their business practices. Today *Dell* sells its computers directly to customers.

With its new SCM capabilities, *Dell* has been able to achieve efficiency and productivity, making a trade-off with the other functional activities of the organization. Theoretically, SCM requires changes in the following critical areas:

1. Account selection
2. In-customer operations
3. Channel strategy
4. Core operations capabilities
5. Management/organization structure

In all these areas, *Dell* has carefully crafted its SCM strategy, to ensure business growth. Accounts selection was done by targeting corporate customers with predictable, budgeted needs. Obviously, these customers are kept outside the SCM loop. An in-customer operation means the ability to operate within the customers' organizations. *Dell* could differentiate the corporate market (for institutional sales) through customer-specific intranet websites. Such dedicated websites could facilitate the provision of real-time solutions of customer needs. Effective channel strategy ensures less access of important target accounts and market segments to competitors. *Dell* could strengthen its channel strategy through in-customer operations, ensuring direct distribution to high-end customers. A similar focus on core operations capabilities, going beyond the achievement of overall operating efficiency, ensured that *Dell* could strengthen its supply chain model. Some of the areas of emphasis in enhancing operations capabilities are flawless make-to-order systems, just-in-time operations, following the philosophy of 'sell what you have', product life cycle management, etc.

CHAPTER 15

Supply Chain Management

LEARNING OBJECTIVES

After reading this chapter, you will be able to understand:

- Definitions and Concepts of Supply Chain Management (SCM)
- Process of SCM
- Selection of Channel Strategy
- Core Operations Capabilities
- Supply Chain Management Decisions
- Supply Chain Management Models

Opening Vignette

The success of a supply chain depends on the efficient and effective flow of materials. Hence, it involves suppliers, assemblers or manufacturers, distributors, retailers and customers. For many organizations, the supply chain model is simple, as they make use of single or captive suppliers or vendors. However, in some organizations, the same component may be routed through multiple suppliers or vendors, where each vendor or supplier performs some specific tasks on the same component. In such cases, the supply chain model is complex. The supply chain model requires synchronization with just-in time (JIT) processes to reduce the cycle time for procurement, and at the same, to reduce inventory holding costs. Minimization of costs of transportation, inventory holding, and set-up costs need to be ensured for effective supply chain management. In the service industry, for example in retailing, supply chain management, requires effective coordination with vendors, production and distribution units, and inventory management systems for better customer service.

15.1 INTRODUCTION

Supply chain management is a comparatively new discipline, which integrates the knowledge of management and engineering to develop some optimized solutions for cost effective, value added and quality services to the customers. It has gained popularity since the 1980's, when organizations worldwide realised that to compete in the market they had to sustain collaborative relationships with different entities in the chain that ultimately ensures sales and services to the customers. For many companies, some of these entities are outside their organizations. Hence, integrating with such entities through effective supply chain systems results in better services to the customers, and at the same time, companies can achieve cost optimization.

Even with economies of scale, organizations cannot remain price competitive, unless they focus on other cost minimization techniques. Effective supply chain management can help an organization to achieve such goals. Through vendor development and effective logistics management, organizations are now developing supply chains for the increased satisfaction of customers. An effective supply chain ensures value-added services to customers. However, to make the supply chain effective, it is necessary for organizations to take a relook at their strategy, as supply chain capabilities, among others, require organizations to align their activities in terms of new strategies, that is, they involve the alignment of those activities that help in building supply chain capabilities with areas like in-customer operations, channel strategy, core operations capabilities and the management of organization structure. An effective supply chain need not focus on cost control alone; in fact, it can be an independent revenue centre for organizations.

Internationally, it is observed that effective supply chain management can contribute to at least 35 percent of the market share of any organization. Thus, with the focus on operational efficiency, effective and efficient supply chain management (SCM) can contribute significantly to organizational success.

15.2 DEFINITIONS AND CONCEPTS

A supply chain results in value addition to any manufactured product. The process of value addition in manufacturing begins with the supply of raw materials and various components, packaging, transportation, warehousing, logistics, and finally, delivery to the customers.

SCM has gained importance over the years due to the increase in international competitiveness, the need for customized products and services, and the need for value creation outside the boundary of organizations. All these have created a compelling pressure on organizations to design a collaborative structure of operations to balance the needs between production and consumption. Lamming (1996) considered SCM an extension of logistics. However, subsequent researchers like Tan et al.(1999, 2002), and Akkermans et al. (1999) recognized the need for aligning customers in the SCM. SCM, therefore, ensures the smooth flow of goods and information between organizations, from procurement of raw materials to the end users. Effective SCM establishes inter-organizational linkages and a profitable business process.

Thus, SCM is defined as an approach to design, implement and evaluate the flow of information, materials and products (both finished and semi-finished) among suppliers or vendors, manufacturers, distributors, retailers, and even to customers or end users. Thus, the supply chain encompasses those business processes, which involve procurement, production and delivery of goods and services. Organizations are now required to manage their supply chains innovatively.

The Stanford University's Global Supply Chain Management Forum emphasizes flexibility and agility within the supply chain for gaining competitive advantage. The model helps in streamlining operations, increasing delivery reliability, and at the same time, maximizing profitability. The forum partners with 20 global organizations, and continuously researches the best practices to come out with innovative supply chain strategies for a globally competitive market. The model suggests cross-functional integration of key business processes within the organization and also across the network, which are part of the supply chain entities. Such integration can help in leveraging the relationship to achieve improved business performance.

American Productivity and Quality Centre Process Classification Framework pioneered the SCOR model. Although we have many computer-enabled models for managing supply chains, SCOR (Supply Chain Operations Reference) is considered to be the best in this regard. SCOR is very user friendly and it provides a pre-defined set of business activities integrated with different phases of supply chain processes. To manage the supply chain with SCOR requires primary understanding of the various configurations and their contributions to the supply chain process. The pre-defined process of SCOR, among others, considers the following aspects:

- The receipt of an order
- Supply of sub-assemblies
- Channels between suppliers and manufacturers
- Production, stocking, routing and shipment of purchased items
- Delivery of final products, meeting contractual obligations

However, operationally, SCOR cannot quantify performance, and therefore, may be less effective in addressing capacity planning issues.

15.3 PROCESS OF SCM

From our introductory discussions, it is evident that SCM represents certain activities involving the design of products and services, raw material procurement and transforming the raw materials into semi-finished or finished products. The scope of SCM even extends to the end-users or customers. It is known as an end-to-end process, as it starts right from product design to shipment to the customers for their consumption. The complete supply chain process therefore, covers all those activities that involve product design, planning, procurement, forecasting, production, distribution, fulfillment, after-sales support and disposal at the customers' end.

Considering the above issues, the SCM process can be classified into two broad categories: configuration, and coordination.

1. The process of **configuration** involves mainly the design aspects, involving manipulation of the core infrastructure, on which the SCM can ultimately be operational. This means that designing something which cannot be accommodated within the available constrained infrastructure of the company must not be considered. To be more specific, the configuration aspect focusses on designing the supply chain network to serve the needs of a specific market, within the given constraints of warehouses, retail outlets, vendors or supply sources, and the location and capacity aspects of the manufacturing facilities. Designing the supply chain considering all these aspects ensures cost optimized services to the customers.
2. **Coordination** issues are those which facilitate execution of the supply chain.

Broadly, in configuration issues, we also consider decisions pertaining to procurement and vendor or supplier selection, decisions pertaining to production, distribution and information support. In procurement-related decisions, we consider the process of selection of suppliers, make-or-buy decisions including outsourcing, and procurement systems, including contractual issues.

Production-related decisions consider developing a manufacturing network, selection of manufacturing sites at different locations, including overseas, decisions on the installed capacity of production, product types, product lines and product mix, and flexibility of product customization.

Distribution-related decisions consider the channels of distribution and mode of transportation. Decisions on Information Support involve the selection of appropriate ERP (enterprise resource planning) software – standard or customized.

Coordination issues in SCM primarily involve decisions on material flow. Here again, the main focus is on inventory management. Inventory management broadly encompasses the pattern of inventory holding, decisions on vendor-managed inventory holding, just-in-time inventory management systems, etc. Decisions on information flow under coordination issues involve the degree of electronic interface with the supply chain process. Also, under this category, the company decides on cash flow parameters from the suppliers' perspective; these include payment schedule to suppliers, price negotiation and cost reduction.

Thus, the process of SCM cuts across several functional areas with the involvement of different intermediaries and in-house resources. It often requires addressing conflicting issues, and dealing with situations of clash of interests.

SCM of *Dell Computer*

Till 1994, *Dell* was known as a tier-II desktop manufacturer. Like any company, it used to order its components to manufacture computers and hold the same as finished inventory, till it was sold in the market. Huge cost overruns for stockpiling of inventory put *Dell* in a relatively disadvantageous position in terms of price competition. To remove this bottleneck, the company changed to a build-to-order process of operations, introducing a just-in-time inventory management system and direct selling to customers. By integrating such new supply chain capabilities with their strategy, *Dell* could achieve efficiency and a competitive market position. To do this, *Dell* segregated customers into institutional and retail. Institutional buyers, who buy in bulk from *Dell*, have a relatively stable and predictable demand. Among retail customers, *Dell* could identify some repeat customers. *Dell* produces in advance to meet such predictable patterns of needs. For other buyers, whose demand pattern is unpredictable, *Dell* has introduced build-to-order systems with just-in-time inventory management.

15.4 SELECTION OF CHANNEL STRATEGY

In SCM, channels are defined as the conduits that companies use for the distribution of their products and services to their customers. Companies select such channels strategically, to ensure cost optimized and value added quality sales and services to the customers

Selection of appropriate channel strategy is a pre-condition for effective SCM. Companies select a channel strategy which restricts competitors' access to the accounts of important customers, or even market segments. The other important aspect of channel strategy is to enforce price control, so that customers are not put to unnecessary pressure to pay more than the company's mandated price. For example, *Dell*'s direct-to-customer channel strategy was revolutionary, as it enabled the company to sustain its high-end customer market.

Some of the advantages of an effective channel strategy are:

- Direct control over customer feedback and the market situation
- Flexibility in pricing and sales incentives
- Understanding the product life cycle and determining the need for product replacement
- Quick replenishment of old stocks, offering price incentives.

15.5 CORE OPERATIONS CAPABILITIES

To increase the operating efficiency of a supply chain, organizations need to emphasize building operations capabilities. It may even require re-creating (new) operations capabilities. It requires effective partnerships with all agencies involved in the supply chain process. This helps organizations to achieve more profit than the traditional means of minimization of operations cost. For building new operations capabilities, organizations need to focus on the following aspects:

1. Creation of an effective build-to-order system.
2. Integrate build-to-order system with the business model.
3. Introduce an effective supplier or vendor management system to reduce the cycle time of procurement and achieve the desired quality standards.
4. Develop a system of sell what you have, balancing supply and demand.
5. Manage product life cycle, both for cost efficiency and strategic advantages.
6. Collaborate with suppliers, and extend the same spirit of collaboration to all agents in the supply chain process.
7. Focus on IT-integrated supply chain management systems.
8. Adopt scientific outsourcing programmes.

15.6 SCM DECISIONS

In SCM, decisions are categorized into two types – strategic and operational.

1. Strategic decisions are aligned with the strategy of the organization and focus on the design aspect of the supply chain. Strategic decisions are usually taken from a long-term perspective.
2. Operational decisions, on the other hand, are those that support the strategic decisions of supply chain, managing the flow of materials and products on a day-to-day basis.

Irrespective of strategic and operational decisions of supply chain, we observe four major types of decision making in SCM. These are decisions on location, production, inventory and distribution (including transportation).

1. Decisions about location help in identifying production facilities, storage or warehousing points, etc. Obviously, facilities location decisions require long-term resource commitment. Location decisions have strategic significance as they have a significant impact on cost, customer and other services, and on overall profitability. Location decisions also exert an influence on operation-level issues of SCM.
2. Production decisions consider issues like what to produce, and where (in which location) to produce, which supplier or vendor to be allocated to which location,

and which market segment to be covered from which location. Like the decision on location, production decisions also have an impact on costs, customer services and profitability. Production decisions in SCM also consider issues pertaining to degree of capacity building, production scheduling and integration with the mainstream activities of the organization.

3. Inventory decisions encompass inventories of raw materials, semi-finished or finished goods. Optimization of inventory holding costs, holding of inventories for critical items to ensure the smooth flow of production, ordering and re-ordering points, maintaining safety stock positions, etc. are all crucial areas of inventory-related decisions.
4. Decisions on transportation and distribution require trading-off the cost–benefit of the mode of transport. It is closely linked with inventory decisions.

15.7 SCM MODELS

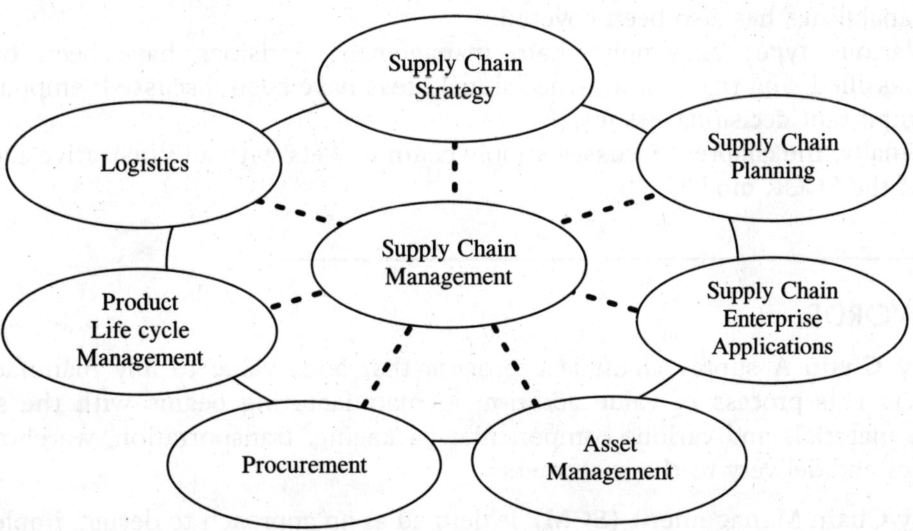

Figure 15.1 *SCOR model*

An effective supply chain model can be developed broadly within the ambit of strategic and operational level decisions. SCM models can be based on network design, rough-cut methods (rough cut methods of SCM focus on operational and tactical decisions. The thrust of rough cut methods is on the design of inventory control policies considering multi-level services to customers. *IBM* follows this approach for their spare parts inventory control. To ensure customer services, finished inventories are maintained at several levels to achieve proper integration of SCM. This ensures minimum lead time to customers' services), and simulation.

Network models are normative and encompass the above four decisions. Such models focus primarily on the design aspects of the supply chain.

The rough cut model suggests policy guidelines for decision making. This model primarily suits single site facilities. Simulation models are comprehensive, as they combine both strategic and operational decision-making issues. However, such a model is more evaluative in nature, that is, it cannot suggest the best supply chain process. The SCOR model of SCM is presented in Fig. 15.1. As can be seen from the model, it covers all constituent functions of the SCM.

SUMMARY

1. The chapter introduces the concept of supply chain management and explains its importance in the present competitive business era.
2. Subsequently, it takes us through the process of supply chain management, duly focussing on various activities involved in an effective supply chain.
3. The process of selection of channel strategy and building of core operations capabilities has also been covered.
4. Various types of supply chain management decisions have been broadly classified, and then, various decisional areas have been discussed, emphasizing important decisional issues.
5. Finally, the chapter discusses supply chain models with an illustrative example of the SCOR model.

KEY WORDS

Supply Chain A supply chain is a process that adds value to any manufactured product. This process of value addition in manufacturing begins with the supply of raw materials and various components, packaging, transportation, warehousing, logistics and delivery to the customers

Supply Chain Management (SCM) is defined as an approach to design, implement and evaluate the flow of information, materials and products (both finished and semi-finished) among suppliers or vendors, manufacturers, distributors, retailers, and even to customers or end users. Thus, the supply chain encompasses those business processes, which involve procurement, production and delivery of goods and services.

Supply Chain Process The supply chain process covers all those activities that involve product design, planning, procurement, forecasting, production, distribution, fulfillment, after-sales support and disposal at the customer's end.

Rough cut Model The rough cut model suggests policy guidelines for decision making. This model suits single site facilities.

Simulation models are comprehensive, as they combine both strategic and operational decision-making issues. However, such a model is more evaluative in nature, that is, it cannot suggest the best supply chain process.

GENERAL REVIEW QUESTIONS

1. Define the concept of supply chain management. Why is it important in today's organizations?
2. Discuss the process of supply chain management.
3. Explain how an organization selects its channel strategy
4. Discuss the core operations capabilities of an organization.
5. Discuss how supply chain management decisions are taken
6. Explain the basic elements of the SCOR Model.
7. Short notes
   (a) Configuration process of supply chain
   (b) Coordination issues in SCM
   (c) Strategic SCM Decisions
   (d) Just-in-time

CRITICAL REVIEW QUESTION

1. *Wal-Mart* is considered an efficient company which has gained substantially through effective supply chain management. Study the available web-based information on this company and discuss its SCM practices.

REFERENCES

1. Akkermans, H., Bogerd, P., Vos, B. 1999. Virtuous and vicious cycles on the road towards international supply chain management. *International Journal of Operations & Production Management*, Vol. 19 No.5/6, pp.565–82.
2. Lamming, R. 1996. Squaring lean supply with supply chain management. *International Journal of Operations & Production Management*, Vol. 16 No.2, pp.183–96.
3. Tan, K., Choon, L., Steven, B., Wisner, J.D. 2002. Supply chain management: a strategic perspective. *International Journal of Operations & Production Management*, Vol. 22 No.5/6, pp.614.
4. Tan, K.C., Kannan, V.R., Handfield, R.B., Ghosh, S. 1999. Supply chain management: an empirical study of its impact on performance. *International Journal of Operations & Production Management*, Vol. 19 No.10, pp.1034–52.

ADDITIONAL REFERENCE

1. Cachon, G. 2003. Supply chain coordination with contracts. *Supply Chain Management – Handbook in OR/MS,* Vol. 11. S. Graves, T. de Kok, eds. North-Holland, Amsterdam, The Netherlands.

CASE STUDY

IBM's Technology-enabled Supply Chain Management Systems

IBM, in 1994, reengineered its global supply chain to increase the cycle time to respond to customer needs with minimum inventory holding. *IBM* could facilitate this by using a self-developed Asset Management Tool (AMT). *IBM*'s AMT can integrate the process through graphical modelling, and can perform a host of other activities like performance optimization, activity costing, enterprise wide database connectivity, etc. to perform quantitative analysis of extended supply chains.

With AMT, *IBM* performs inventory planning and budgeting, customer services, new-product development, etc. Extending the AMT to all business units and the channel partners, *IBM* could benefit by $750 million in terms of material cost-saving help *IBM* manage its supply chain activities effectively. For this, *IBM* had to focus on the following activities.

- Designing methods for reducing inventory
- Developing alternatives for achieving inventory
- Development and implementation of a consistent process to manage inventory and customer-service targets
- Tool deployment
- Evaluation of assets as service parts, production materials and finished goods in the global supply network
- Evaluation of cross-brand products and unit synergy to improve the management of inventory and risk.

With such a focus, AMT has now become a strategic decision support tool for *IBM*.

Discussion Question

Visit any large manufacturing organization. Study their supply chain management systems and critically evaluate the same.

CHAPTER 16

Ethics, Corporate Social Responsibility and Environment Management in Production and Operations Management

LEARNING OBJECTIVES

After reading this chapter, you will be able to understand:

- The Basics of Production and Operations Ethics
- Code of Ethics in Manufacturing
- Environmental Issues in Production and Operations
- Pollution Concepts and Definition
- Waste Management Strategies
- Environment Management and ISO Standards
- Corporate Social Responsibility and Environmental Issues
- Workplace Environment
- Fatigue at the Workplace
- Legal Provisions for Occupational Health and Safety
- Managing Stress in Organizations

Opening Vignette

Production Ethics – Follow the Leader 'Kellogs'

The ethical issues of production and operations management focus on a company's products and the processes of production. The primary emphasis is on the philosophy that these should not cause any harm to the users of these products and to society at large. Although most companies try to adopt their own code of ethics to ensure that their production and operations processes are ethics complaint, we have a number of cases globally, involving world-renowned organizations, where such violations have happened, leading to legal action and causing much harm to the reputation of these companies. Some of these cases relating to the *Ford* Pinto scandal (a compact car introduced in 1971, it became a major scandal when it was realized that its fuel tank exploded and lead to fires when there were any rear-end collisions. The company was aware of this but did not redesign the car, leading to 27 deaths and several lawsuits), *Peanut Corporation of America*(dead rodents, rodent faces, and bird feathers were found, causing an outbreak of salmonella, leading to several deaths) *Union Carbide* (Bhopal Gas Tragedy in India), etc. The use of preventive technology, not conforming to the use of harmful chemicals within the defined degree of permissibility, selling defective items to customers, carbon emission through the manufacturing process, etc. are some instances of ethical violations in production and operations.

Ethical problems in production and operations management are observed in industries like the genetically-modified food industry, the mobile phone industry (radiation effect), automobile, cement, oil refineries, steel plants, thermal power generation, etc. Companies violate animal rights in the name of products testing.

The *Kellogg's Cornflake Company*, Michigan, U.S.A. is the leader in breakfast cereals; it operates out of 19 countries, and has spread its market to 160 countries. The company is now world renowned, primarily for its strict conformance to quality.

16.1 INTRODUCTION

Ethics are the norms for conduct that distinguish between acceptable and unacceptable behaviour. In many countries, there are legal norms and standards to regulate production and operations management functions. Such legal issues are more in the form of standards, which we often construe as being synonymous with ethics, despite the fact that there is a basic difference between ethics and laws. Ethical standards promote the values that are essential to production and operations work, such as trust, accountability, mutual respect and fairness. Ethics in production and operations promote a variety of other important moral and social values like social responsibility, human rights and animal welfare, compliance with the law, and health and safety.

Production and Operations Managers are required to operate in a competitive environment; hence, their basic focus is on cost effectiveness, quality and on-time delivery. As a result, ethical issues take the backseat, and many production and operations people are not even aware about their ramifications. If we browse through the vision and mission statements of companies, in most cases, we may not find anything mentioned about production or operations or manufacturing ethics. Ethics is not something which can always be embedded in the products we manufacture. It is the behavioural and decision-making variables that go into the production and delivery of goods and services. With ethical manufacturing, it is possible for the company to conduct their business in such a way that it can elicit respect from employees, customers, suppliers and society as a whole.

Ethical considerations in production and operations functions are of recent origin. Ethical issues encompassing operations management are related to:

- products and service design
- layout, production process
- use of technology
- job design
- planning and control
- inventory management
- supply chain management issues
- focus on quality, etc.

These apart, production ethics also encompass a company's commitment to the recycling of waste, and compliance with environment and pollution control requirements.

In production, managers often face the dilemma of competitive pressure to reduce the cost of production. In the process of achieving cost efficiency, managers often compromise with quality, forgetting the ethical commitment to their customers and other stakeholders. For example, over-burnt or under-burnt made tea, instead of being segregated from the market lot, is blended by tea manufacturing companies to increase sales. Globally, we have many cases of manufacturers who have had to recall their products due to inherent manufacturing defects, which pose security and safety hazards for users.

The dilemma for production and operations managers, therefore, is whether or not to compromise on ethical issues pertaining to production, like the degree of permissibility of the use of harmful chemicals or other agents in the production process, production at the cost of the safety of workers, etc.

16.2 DEFINITION AND CONCEPTS

Ethics are moral principles (about what is good, defensible and right). Although operationally, ethics need to be integrated with our behaviour and actions, often we treat ethics as an afterthought. Ethics and ethical reflection need to be integrated into all organizational practices. A common philosophical definition of ethics is "the science of conduct or values of management". Moral values such as respect, honesty, fairness and responsibility are important constructs of ethics. Organizations, by adopting a code of ethics, ensure the application of ethics. Thus, ethics include the fundamental ground rules whereby organizations give their employees the opportunity to make an informed choice and to understand whether something is right or wrong and then take decisions making the right choice. Ethics, therefore, is the framework of values for moral behaviour. It is a social glue to ensure that an organized society prospers and everybody's interest is served.

The Ten Commandments of the *Old Testament* or the teachings of the *Bhagwad Gita* are sources of direction for ethical behaviour in life. Today, we are concerned with the issue of ethics in two aspects of life, namely in business and in various professions. Business represents entrepreneurs, while profession represents those who are employed in an organization or work for an employer. In other words, ethics are equally applicable to the employers and the employees.

In India, we find several references to ethics in the *Bhagwad Gita*. Our traditional Guild systems laid down the ethics of a business or a profession. The *Gita* emphasizes the need for the internalization of the ethical codes by individuals, so that they can reflect the same through their behaviour. Organizations benefit when they make their employees internalize ethical codes and values. Bad workmanship was construed as violation of ethics, and workers used to face strict disciplinary action in the skill- or crafts-based social systems in India. Now, external forces also compel organizations to comply with ethical issues. These external forces need not always be the regulatory authorities, they could even be stakeholders, whose changing expectations require organizations to step up their ethical standards and conduct. In the case of a profession, it could be the professional association or the Guild, and in the case of a society where there is a government, it is the government agency, which ensures that the laws are obeyed. In fact, in a secular society, it is the law that lays down what is acceptable conduct and what is not. Acceptable conduct is encouraged and unexpected conduct is considered illegal and punishment is meted out.

When production and operations management practices are abused in an organization, we call it a violation of ethics. It not only speaks of poor corporate governance, but also creates an unhealthy work environment, where every employee feels demoralized. Reduced focus on quality, compromising with security and safety norms, flouting environmental issues, etc., weaken organizational competitive strength.

16.3 THE CODE OF ETHICS IN MANUFACTURING

Many companies have their own defined code of ethics for manufacturing. Operations executives are taken through such a code of ethics through formal training, and their compliance in the workplace is closely monitored. Some of the important areas which figure in such a documented code of ethics are:

- Commitment to manufacture and deliver quality products, complying with safety and security issues, etc
- Making customers aware of the use of the products, their benefits and effects, etc. either through the sales store or through community outreach programmes.
- Investment in research and development to ensure customers' value for money

- Design new products to match customer expectations
- Strict compliance with the standards, rules and regulations, social norms in production
- Implementation of code of ethics in the workplace

After a consensus decision to document the code of ethics in production and operations management function, necessary steps are taken to introduce the same.

The Institute of Business Ethics recommends these general steps to be followed in the initial planning phase:

Step 1 Find a champion—preferably a very senior level management person.
Step 2 Get endorsements from the chairman and the board.
Step 3 Find out what bothers people—talk to both, the employees and the management, to find out sensitive issues or those that require guidance.
Step 4 Pick a well-tested model, looking to other organizations' codes to develop ideas and to understand what is appropriate for meeting the company's own organizational needs.
Step 5 Develop your own organization's code of conduct, document it, with due care given to customization to deal with the problems that are likely to arise in all areas of organizational relations.
Step 6 Pilot test it, both within and outside the organization, to understand its suitability.
Step 7 Issue the code—publish the code and make sure it is sent directly to all employees, shareholders, suppliers and customers. It is also a good idea to post it on the company's website.
Step 8 Introduce examples of the code in action into the company's training programmes.
Step 9 Enforce the code and regularly review it, and assess whether it continues to remain a good fit for your needs.

Ben and Jerry's code (1978) begins with a mission statement. The code goes on to state the company's mission, relating it to its product quality, economic mission and social mission. Similarly, *Gap Inc*'s code (1998) contains specific statements for each group with whom the company has a relationship, namely, 'commitment to ethical sourcing', 'code of vendor conduct', 'code for global compliance team', etc. Such elaborate codes for specific groups, the company feels, are necessary because of its globally expanded operations, including outsourcing from factories located in Malaysia, Guatemala and Italy. The company has even developed codes for many of its internal activities such as training, etc.

Some of the usual practices to introduce a code of ethics in the production and operations management function are training the existing workers, induction training for new workers, customization of examples of ethical problems in production, recognition and rewards to workers who are totally ethics compliant, corrective measures for those workers who violate ethics, etc. With such a structured approach, it is possible to implement ethics in the production and operations management functions.

United Technologies Corporation (UTC)

UTC is a global conglomerate with multiple business units like *Carrier Corporation, Hamilton Sundstrand, Otis Elevators, Pratt & Whitney, Sikorsky, UTC Power,* and *Chubb*. With more than 2.5 lakh employees, *UTC* has a presence in 4000 locations, spread across 62 countries. *UTC*'s most challenging role is to orient its new recruits about its global ethics programme. Integrating the global ethics programme in cross-cultural and cross-country work environments has made *UTC* design a programme that conforms to the global workplace. Most of *UTC*'s business units are almost a century old. *UTC*'s businesses range from aircraft engines, helicopters, security and fire protection, air control systems, detector locks, machine tools, etc. Compliance with ethical issues is especially important, as many regulatory norms are applicable to *UTC*'s manufacturing ventures. As a major vendor to the US Government's Department of Defense in the 80's, there was serious allegation of ethical violation in one of its units, which had made a super-normal profit on defence contracts.

All this prompted *UTC* to increase a self-regulating system through a formal Code of Ethics, which it adopted in 1990. This code articulates the standards of conduct, which surpass even legal requirements. *UTC* could successfully embrace the Code of Ethics and has made it a part of its corporate culture and business practices.

16.4 ENVIRONMENTAL ISSUES IN PRODUCTION AND OPERATIONS

Environment relates to the surroundings; the impact of an organization on its surroundings can be either detrimental or positive. Organizations being a part of society, complex external environmental factors exert an influence on them. The term, 'environment', is considered a super-set, of which an organization as a system is a sub-set. Environment, per se is an object or action that consists of the substances, circumstances, objects, or conditions by which it is surrounded or in which it occurs. However, some scholars prefer to use the environment, either as a prefix or suffix to an object, circumstances, conditions or substances, like 'work environment', 'political environment', 'social environment', etc. From this perspective, we can define the environment as the circumstances, influences and stresses, competitive, cultural, demographic, economic, natural, political, regulatory and technological factors.

In the environmental domain, environmental engineering improves the environment through the application of science and engineering. Today, for engineers, the study of environmental engineering has become necessary to successfully develop the capabilities of the organization to respond to environmental factors. Environmental engineering not only helps organizations in terms of tackling issues pertaining to the environment, but also helps in terms of identifying suitable anti-pollution measures, like the installation of effluent treatment plants, etc. Organizations, in the process of their operations, may pollute the environment by discharging chemical, biological, thermal, radioactive or even mechanical solid wastes. Without pollution control measures, organizations can violate regulatory norms. With inputs from civil engineering, chemical engineering, public health, mechanical engineering, chemistry, biology and geology, such norms can be satisfied by adopting suitable pollution control measures. The proper identification of effluent treatment plants helps organizations get the benefits of synergy, in the form of new business avenues, based on by-products or joint products. The scope of environmental engineering encompasses the following areas:

1. Environmental impact assessment and mitigation
2. Water supply and treatment.
3. Waste water recycling and treatment.
4. Air quality management.

Production and operations managers with knowledge of environment engineering can do justice to their profession, making companies responsive to environmental issues.

16.5 POLLUTION CONCEPTS AND DEFINITIONS

Organizations through their activities contaminate the environment. Such contamination causes pollution. The manufacturing and production process is considered to be responsible for pollution. The effect of pollution due to the production and operations functions may not be always immediate, for example, nitrogen oxide discharge; prima facie as a substance it may not be harmful, but it may adversely affect the solar system by resulting in smog. Industrial pollution is now a global issue, as industrial activities in one country may pollute the environment of another country (for example, radioactivity for nuclear testing). Major local pollution issues are fly ash from thermal power stations, harmful gas emissions from chemical units, pollution caused by cement and steel plants, noise pollution, etc. Irrespective of the reasons for pollution, it is the responsibility of the organization to adopt immediate preventive measures, which may require the installation of effluent treatment plants, waste recycling, introducing new manufacturing processes using improved technology, etc. Today, pollution issues are integrated with good corporate governance practices. Apart from the mandated clearance from the Pollution Control Board, it is necessary for organizations to comply with ISO certification requirements.

16.5.1 Pollution Control Measures

Pollution control is not only a regulatory requirement; it is a part of an organization's corporate social responsibilities. Every organization has to address pollution issues by adopting various measures. It is also important to understand that industry is an important beneficiary of pollution control measures. Let us now examine some pollution control measures.

16.5.1.1 Energy Conservation

Efficient use of energy helps its conservation, and stems the depletion of resources (like coal) from which we get energy. Energy conservation through efficient energy use is possible by reducing the dependence on non-renewable sources of power generation like coal, crude oil, natural gas, etc., and exploring the possibility of power generation through renewable resources like wind power, hydro-power, solar power, etc.

Other prescriptive measures for energy conservation are:

- Replacing incandescent lights with compact fluorescent lights (CFL), leading to the saving of electricity to the extent of 80%.
- Putting-off lights and fans when not in use.
- Promoting captive power generation from industrial waste materials. This requires Government to persuade industries to make use of their own wastes for power generation. For example, paper factories can have their captive power plants (own power unit), which can generate power, by recycling their bamboo wastes.
- Ensuring systematic energy audit to rationalize the use of energy both for cost-effectiveness and energy conservation.

16.5.2 Waste Management Strategies

The basic focus of waste management strategies is to reduce waste and make effective use of it through recycling in an environment-friendly manner. Often, for the typical process of production, waste arising is substantial. A good example is the conventional blast furnace, where the melting process is manual, so the waste arising is more. Hence, waste management practices are basically an innovative approach for effective minimization of waste, and proper recycling of waste, using an environment-friendly approach. Automated cutting of fabric patterns can reduce the wastage of cloth, and can also ensure the use of such waste (in pieces) in ready-to-use garments.

16.5.2.1 *Extended Producer Responsibility*

Another approach to waste management is the extended producer responsibility (EPR), which requires the producer to feel responsible for the waste products associated with production. The producer has to feel responsible for environmental hazards and provide services to society through actions like providing for carbon deposits, forestation measures, proper disposal of industrial wastes, etc.

16.5.2.2 *Product Stewardship*

Product stewardship is another waste management strategy, which has some similarity with the EPR concept. Here, the responsibility of the producer extends beyond product manufacturing to the supply chain, which even encompasses government, consumers, recyclers, etc. For example, the packaging materials used by manufacturers should be environment friendly, to reduce hazards and facilitate recycling.

This processing may be to reduce the hazard of the waste, recover material for recycling, produce energy from the waste, or reduce it in volume for more efficient disposal. Packaging materials, unless recycled, can generate solid waste, and occupy huge space for its disposal. These may even cause pollution. Disposal by land filling is possible only when land is available; otherwise, such wastes have to be incinerated (process of destroying waste material by burning). In both cases, it may cause environmental pollution. For such reasons, more innovative and environment-friendly packaging materials are now available.

16.5.2.3 *Managing Organic Solid Waste*

Managing organic solid waste by composting and digestion is another strategic approach to efficient waste management. After killing the harmful pathogens, such solid wastes can be recycled and used for agriculture and landscaping purposes. Similarly, the process of gasification by incineration (thermal treatment) in a closed vessel can generate energy. This provides an opportunity to the industry to generate power in a more cost-effective and environment-friendly manner. The solid waste residue, after incineration, is rich with carbon and presents an opportunity to the organization to explore a new business line like dry ice and carbon for industrial use.

16.5.3 Other Environmental Issues

Pollution caused by companies due to their production and manufacturing processes is one way of looking at environmental issues. But there are other environmental issues, which also influence the production and operations management functions.

16.5.3.1 Work environment

The work environment is the working conditions that exert an influence on work. Again, working conditions encompass general, physical, social, psychological and environmental conditions. We can assess the work environment by analyzing the lighting, temperature, noise level, etc. A positive work environment can increase the productivity of workers.

16.5.3.2 Organizational Environment

This consists of administrative, technological, political, economic and socio-cultural factors (Lusthaus, Anderson and Murphy, 1995). Using various strategic tools, we can measure the organizational environment, and accordingly, develop an organizational response mechanism in the form of strategies. Organizations now diagnose environmental issues using tools, and accordingly, develop the capabilities to adapt to environmental changes. Environmental issues may be extra-institutional, but have a potential adverse effect on the overall performance of the organization. Such environmental issues may be specific or general. Specific issues exert a direct influence on achieving organizational goals. General environmental issues are, however, broad external issues like economic, political, legal, technological, socio-cultural, demographic, or even the global environment per se, that affect the organization.

Socio-cultural, political and legal, technological, economic and global influences are external or indirect environmental forces that organizations need to manage. For organizations, socio-cultural dimensions, rather than societal values, influence their offering of goods and services. This dimension largely depends on the demographics and values of the customer base. Demographics are the characteristics of the people and social groups, that is, the age, gender, income, etc. Values are the beliefs of the people, which shape their behaviour in choosing the products and services offered by organizations. The political and legal dimensions are the regulatory frameworks within the ambit of which organizations need to work. Among others, such regulatory norms influence policies on taxation, trade regulations, minimum wage legislation etc. Technological dimensions are the scientific processes that change the inputs and the production processes of organizations for more cost-effective quality output. The economic dimensions encompass interest rates, inflation, unemployment rates, gross national product and the value of the currencies with respect to internationally tradable currencies like the US dollars, pound sterling, etc. The global dimensions of the environment refer to the factors that affect an organization, despite its origin in countries other than those where they operate. Trade globalization has resulted in increased competition for domestic organizations.

Various pressure groups like consumer forums, *Greenpeace*, etc. through regulatory norms and corporate social responsibilities, try to ease organizational environment issues, but in reality, for dealing with environmental issues, organizational voluntariness is important. Organizations have to be self conscious, and can, only then, successfully build the capabilities necessary to cope with environmental issues.

16.6 ENVIRONMENT MANAGEMENT AND ISO STANDARDS

The International Organization for Standardization (ISO) set up in Geneva, Switzerland in 1947 to facilitate the promotion of international trade with common quality systems and standards, represented by more than 150 countries of the world, now also provides guidelines for efficient environment management practices. ISO 14001:2004 provides detailed guidelines on environmental management systems. Organizations following such guidelines can successfully address environmental management issues, ensuring protection of the environment, prevention of pollution and improvement of overall environmental performance. Today, ISO 14001certification authenticates organizational adherence to an environmental management system (EMS), and makes them globally acceptable trading partners. ISO 14000 series of standards cover the following:

- Environmental management systems
- Environmental auditing
- Eco-labelling
- Life cycle assessment
- Environmental aspects in product standards
- Environmental performance evaluation
- Certification for quality practices in EMS; this is given under ISO 14001, we call it ISO 14001 certification.

ISO 14000 comprises a series of standards and documents. The following is a brief introduction to those standards which directly relate to environment management.

ISO 14001 This is the main specification document that describes the required elements to be satisfied by an organization for certification.

ISO 14002 This specification provides guidance to small and medium-sized organizations that intend to implement ISO 14001.

ISO 14004 This specification provides guidelines with examples to implement and enhance the EMS.

ISO 19011 This specification provides comprehensive guidelines for quality audit of EMS. This specification has been introduced replacing ISO 14011 and ISO 14012, which are two old specifications.

ISO 14020 This specification guides the goals and the principles to frame environment management programmes and efforts.

ISO 14021 It offers guidance on the terminology, symbols, testing and verification methodologies to be used by an organization for self-declaration of environmental aspects.

ISO 14024 Provides guidelines for the principles and protocols for third-party practitioners.

ISO 14031 This specification provides guidelines for the design and use of environmental performance evaluation and the process of identification of environmental performance indicators.

Other miscellaneous specifications for environment management systems (EMS) are:

ISO 14040 – ISO 14043: Life Cycle Assessment

ISO 14050 – Terms and Definitions.

16.7 CORPORATE SOCIAL RESPONSIBILITY AND ENVIRONMENTAL ISSUES

Intertwined with the concept of environment is 'Corporate social responsibility', which refers to the deliberate, socially responsible behaviour of an organization. Even though globally, we have many corporate governance mandates, both in terms of business norms and legislation, we find that many organizations fail to integrate social responsibility with their business practices. It is important to understand that only complying with the legislative requirements of corporate social responsibility is not enough, organizations have to make it their deliberate choice. Much of an organization's carbon discharge into the environment during the process of manufacturing may not attract pollution control norms, but the installation of an effluent treatment plant to arrest carbon deposition, for its subsequent economic use, may be a deliberate choice and the fulfillment of organizational social responsibility. Similarly, organizational social audit may not be a statutory requirement, but voluntary social audit and its disclosure helps create a better image and reflects a high degree of social responsiveness by the organization. So too, waste recycling, adherence to pollution control norms, correct financial results disclosure, compliance with labour laws, etc. are good examples of organizational responses to social norms.

> In India, we have a good role model in the *Tata* organizations, whose care for social responsibility goes beyond fulfilling statutory requirements, creating a win–win situation; so much so, that today *Tata Steel* enjoys a substantial cost–benefit advantage by sourcing materials from their Community Development Centres. Similarly, the *Murugappa Group*, based in the southern part of India enjoys social prestige due to their obvious care for society. Organizational investment in their employees' quality of work-life also adds value to society.

Quality of work-life can be defined as the "perceived personal needs of the employees, which they try to satisfy while they work for the organization. Among others, employees always look for social integration with their work organizations, and relate society with their working life. Important constituents of social responsibility, from an organization's point of view encompass all the stakeholders for the organization." Schermerhorn (1989) suggests eight important areas of organizational social responsibility. These are:

1. ecology and environmental quality, which covers pollution control, dispersion of industry, and effective land use, including beautification.
2. consumerism, that is, truth in lending, advertising and in business.
3. community needs, meeting educational and health requirements, effective solution of local problems and voluntary participation in community development work
4. government relations
5. cognizance of minorities and disadvantaged persons.
6. labour relations
7. shareholder relations
8. philanthropy, that is, financial support to the promotion of art and culture, offering scholarships for education and financial support to charities.

Environment, caution, ethics-compliant facilities and operations of *Exxon Mobil*

Exxon Mobil is the US-based international oil and gas company which is more than 125 years old and is the leader in the energy industry. The company has a vibrant presence in the petroleum and petrochemical industries. It integrates environmental concerns and regulatory requirements right from the project design process, duly analyzing potential risks. In 2010, the company implemented Project Environmental Standards to establish a consistent approach across all activities. Each business is expected to develop, maintain, and consistently apply Project Environmental Standards applicable to the specific risks of that business. These Project Environmental Standards include:

- air emissions (sulfur dioxide (SO_2), volatile organic compounds (VOCs) and particulate matter)
- nitrogen oxides (NOx) emissions
- drill cuttings discharge, water management, waste management and land use
- flare and venting
- energy efficiency and greenhouse gases (GHGs)
- marine geophysical operations and
- socio-economic impact.

This initiative has improved the quality of the company's activities, and has made them widely acclaimed as an environmentally cautious, ethical operations management practitioner in the apparently risk-prone business of hazardous chemicals.

16.8 WORKPLACE ENVIRONMENT

The term, 'work environment', has two dimensions: the task environment and the mega environment. The task environment is internal to an organization, while the mega environment is exogenous to organizations, yet they influence the task or internal environment. We can clarify the issue through an example. Change of work process through organizational re-engineering, is a construct of task or the internal work environment. On the other hand, an increase in global competition is a component of mega environmental issues. Both have a strong influence on changing the organizational work environment. However, in this chapter, we are more concerned with internal or task environmental issues, which have a strong linkage to human resource management issues.

Globally, the work environment is undergoing constant change. In factories, manufacturing units and production houses, the work scenario and working conditions are changing. Some changes like prolonged working hours, specialization of job profiles, technical complexities of jobs, increase in work pressure, etc are globally visible. Organizations are required to manage all such changes to survive in a competitive business. Achieving increased production, maintaining quality requirements, by ensuring long working hours, managing the safety and welfare of employees, reducing fatigue, have now become almost essential business imperatives to stay ahead in competition. Some aspects of the work environment can exert a positive effect on the working capacity of employees, while others may have a negative effect. A better working environment, for example, may exert a positive influence. But an unhygienic physical environment may exert a negative influence on employees.

16.8.1 Internal Task Environment Issues

Some internal or task environment issues are discussed below.

16.8.1.1 Hours of work and its effect on production

It is our general belief that by increasing the working hours, organizations can achieve increased production. But this may not always be true. Even by analyzing the ratio of total working hours and the total production, either in value or volume terms, we cannot establish this. This is because of the difference between the real working hours and nominal working hours. The working capacity of employees is limited to the real working hours, stretching the working hours (nominal), may require employees to contribute more, but with reduced work energy, change in production values and volume. Therefore, increasing working hours may not always be the right choice. During the extended working hour period, employees' unproductive working time, rest pauses and work pace change significantly. Hence, it creates a difference between actual hours of work and nominal hours of work. For industrial workers, the payment of overtime is a statutory obligation. Many organizations, to keep pace with their increased production plan, often feel compelled to retain such workers on overtime. However, globally, it has been established that during the overtime period, production is actually reduced.

Various psychological studies conducted in industrial organizations suggest that breaks or work pauses during work time enhance the working capacity of employees and assist in increasing production. Hence, HR managers need to study the implications of the length and frequencies of the breaks, particularly its impact on the performance of employees. For example, in call centers, tele-callers cannot leave their workstations. Thus, the system of giving just one break in eight working hours may not be the right approach. Rather, they should be given staggered breaks, batch-wise, every two hours or so, to ensure that workstations are manned, limiting the total time allotted to breaks as per organizational policies. This renews the work energy of workers, reducing their work-related fatigue. Thus, regular rest pauses to employees decreases fatigue or monotony, enhances production and productivity, and also, results in the development of a good corporate image. The type and nature of work determines the duration and the frequencies of the rest pauses. Organizations should ensure that during the rest period, employees are allowed to change their posture, for example, if the work requires being seated, then during the rest period, employees should be allowed to stand and walk around or vice-versa. This will help decrease the level of fatigue.

Prolonged working hours also increase absenteeism; increased absenteeism affects the level of production. Although there are many other reasons for absenteeism, work-related fatigue due to prolonged working hours can be construed as an important cause.

There are many other physical work environment-related factors that affect production. These are illumination, ventilation, the amount of noise, temperature of the work environment, etc. When we make the work environment employee friendly, we can achieve success in making the workplace a compelling one. Employees will then volunteer to come regularly, and with the enhanced quality of work life, they will become more productive. Use of various colour schemes on walls, ergonomically-designed machines, chairs, benches and rest rooms, music at the workplace exert a positive influence on the mind-set of workers, which by default increases the total output of production.

16.8.1.2 Music at work

Music at work is a popular work environment change. However, a decision on its intensity and variety is crucial. Instrumental, classical, jazz and pop are examples of variety, while volume is an example of intensity. During the lunch break in industrial production units, playing of pop songs with increased intensity is a normal practice. Jazz and instrumental music with low intensity during working hours is a popular practice, both in offices and factories. HR managers must ensure that music should not conflict with the work efficiency of employees, by diverting their attention. Some organizations instead of playing music uniformly throughout the working time, may play it at synchronized intervals, may be 10 minutes, after each hour, strategically, to use it as a fatigue buster. In complex jobs, the use of music may often be counter-productive. Hence, a decision on exerting positive work environment changes through music at work should be taken very carefully. Psychological research on music at work suggests using the rhythm of music, to keep pace with the work rhythm.

16.8.1.3 Noise level at work

Any sound that is unpleasant to the ears is considered as noise. Noise is generally an annoying sound, which distracts our attention, and interferes with our work. In some workplaces, machine operation-related noises are steady in nature and may even exceed the required 65-decibel limit. A good example is a jute mill. In such cases, workers adapt themselves to the noise level. Since they become used to it, barring their impaired hearing, it may not interfere with their work efficiency. But intermittent noise may act as a distracter and interfere with work efficiency. In a steady-noise work environment, sudden silence at the workplace may be a distracter. In such an environment, if the noise level exceeds the permissible limit, employees should be protected with earplugs or earmuffs, to protect their hearing capacity.

16.8.1.4 Illumination

Illumination involves maintaining daylight or daylight-equivalent brightness in the workplace. Actual daylight is the best source of illumination for work. However, at all workplaces, natural daylight may not be available. This may be for reasons like the nature of work (which may require to be done in a closed environment), night-work, or even the particular layout of the office or the production unit. Wherever artificial lighting is required, the organization should ensure that it is more proximate to daylight, both in colour and composition. While installing the lighting system in the workplace, it is important to emphasize factors like distribution, location and the glare of the lights, so that it illuminates the workplace properly. To the extent possible, illumination should combine daylight and artificial light. Artificial light should be free from colours. However, where it is difficult to avoid colourful lights, Mazda or yellow light is the best choice. Unbalanced or unmatched colour creates hinderances in the workplace. Again, artificial lighting should have adequate property of diffusion, that is, it should have minimum glare. Excessive brightness leads to visual discomfort. To avoid this, proper lighting accessories like translucent bowls, etc. should be used, so that light is directed to the ceiling and is then reflected to the work areas. This process ensures better transmission of light downward and serves the purpose of both direct and indirect lighting.

16.8.1.5 Miscellaneous Factors

To make the work environment free from dullness and monotony and free from physical discomfort, some other measures can also be taken. One such is building cafeterias, which provides an opportunity to employees, not only to feel relaxed, but also to further their thought processes, either through discussions with other team members or in isolation over a cup of tea or coffee. Earlier, the cafeteria concept was more evident in IT or software development organizations, but now, manufacturing and processing organizations have also started setting up cafeterias, which are different from conventional canteens. A conventional canteen serves food and functions only during lunch breaks, while cafeterias remain open throughout and can serve tea, coffee, soft drinks or snacks. However, management has to be on guard as the cafeteria often becomes a center for criticism. To avoid administrative hassles, often organizations may not provide food or snacks directly; they may outsource this, either by installing self-service vending machines or by bringing in a professional canteen service provider. In some organizations (depending on their area of location), the system of giving food coupons to employees exists. In such cases, employees use their food coupons to buy food or snacks from nearby restaurants.

Another important aspect of the work environment is the availability of a proper rest room. Also, hygienic sanitary facilities, appropriate temperature and humidity level, ventilation, etc. contribute significantly towards inculcating a positive attitude among workers and improve overall productivity and efficiency at the workplace. Therefore, organizations should not limit their focus on those workplace environment aspects, which are statutorily required, but should provide more facilities, to develop the workplace, into a compelling one to the employees.

16.9 FATIGUE AT THE WORKPLACE

Managing stress and fatigue at the workplace has now become an important organizational issue from the operations management point of view. Operations managers today focus on various innovative steps, like appropriate design of machines, processes, layout, working pauses, etc. to address the problem of fatigue and stress at the workplace. However, for efficient management of fatigue and stress, workers also need to take initiatives. Again, the nature and problems of fatigue are very job specific. For sales and marketing professionals, it may be due to frequent travel. On the other hand, for operation level workers, it may be due to shift duty, overwork, inappropriate layout or machine design, frequent movement of vulnerable body parts, etc. It is necessary to identify the causes of fatigue and stress at the outset, and then work out action plans, involving the workers also, so that they can equally feel responsible for managing this problem. The terms, stress and fatigue, are used interchangeably, as fatigue can be the cause of stress, and stress can be the causes of fatigue.

From a medical perspective, fatigue can be defined as physical and mental exhaustion, which can be caused by stress, or some mental or physical ailment. Building/work-related fatigue may have a variety of causes. It may be due to work-related stress or ergonomic concerns such as working at a computer/computer terminal for extended periods of time. There is no doubt that the strain of working at a computer 4–8 hours a day can result in headache and fatigue, which is particularly noticeable late in the day. Work-related stress may also cause late afternoon fatigue and headache. It is not unusual for office workers to experience fatigue as early as 10 o'clock in the morning. Such fatigue is not likely to be work-induced. There could be some other cause. In most cases, such symptoms appear to be related to ventilation deficiencies. Buildings have to be ventilated to remove the contaminants that we ourselves produce. These contaminants are referred to as bio-effluents. They include carbon dioxide (CO_2), acetone, ammonia, methane, a large number of volatile fatty acids, solvents previously inhaled, etc. These bio-effluents are not believed to be individually harmful. However, as bio-effluent levels increase (as determined from CO_2 concentrations), building occupants increasingly begin to complain of unpleasant human odour, stale, unpleasant air, lack of air movement, and fatigue and headache.

16.9.1 Causes of Fatigue

The ranges of causes that can trigger fatigue include:

- undiagnosed medical conditions
- unhealthy lifestyle choices
- workplace issues
- emotional concerns and stress.

Fatigue can be caused by a number of factors working in combination.

16.9.1.1 Medical Causes

Many diseases and disorders can trigger fatigue. From the Operations Manager's point of view, such medical causes of fatigue are difficult to measure. However, by keeping track of the medical status of individual employees, managers can ascertain a possible link between employee fatigue and medical reasons. Some of the diseases, which are known to create an effect on employee fatigue, are listed in table 16.1. However, the list is not exhaustive.

16.9.2 Diagnosis of Fatigue

Since fatigue can present a vast range of symptoms and be caused by many different factors working in combination, diagnosis can be difficult. It may be diagnosed using a number of tests including:

- Medical history: Recent events such as childbirth, medication, surgery or bereavement may contribute to fatigue.

- Physical examination: Ensures identification of signs of illness or disease. The doctor may also ask detailed questions about diet, lifestyle and life events.
- Tests: This may include blood tests, urine tests, x-rays and other investigations. The idea is to rule out any physical causes, such as anemia, infection or hormonal problems.

Table 16.1 *Diseases that cause fatigue*

Flu	Tuberculosis
Glandular fever	Chronic pain
Anemia	Coeliac disease
Sleep disorders, such as sleep apnea or restless leg syndrome	Addison's disease
CFS/ME (formerly known as chronic fatigue syndrome or myalgic encephalopathy)	Parkinson's disease
Hypothyroidism	Heart problems
Hepatitis	HIV
	Cancer
	Certain medications

16.9.3 Workplace-related Causes of Fatigue

Common workplace issues that can cause fatigue include:

- **Shift work**: The human body is designed to sleep at night. This pattern is set by a small part of the brain known as the circadian clock. Shift workers confuse their circadian clock by working when their body is programmed to be asleep. Sleeping during the day is usually difficult, because the person's brain chemicals (neurotransmitters) are naturally set to 'wakefulness' mode.
- **Poor workplace practices**: These can add to the level of fatigue. These may include long work hours, hard physical labour, irregular working hours (such as rotating shifts), stressful work environment (such as excessive noise or temperature extremes), boredom, working alone with little or no interaction with others, or fixed concentration on a repetitive task.
- **Workplace stress**: This can be caused by a wide range of factors including job dissatisfaction, heavy workload, conflicts with bosses or colleagues, bullying, constant change, or threats to job security.
- **Burnout**: This is the result of striving too hard in one area of life, neglecting everything else. 'Workaholics', for example, put all their energies into their career, which puts their family life, social life and personal interests out of balance.

- **Unemployment**: The financial pressures, feelings of failure or guilt, and the emotional exhaustion of prolonged job hunting can lead to stress, anxiety, depression and fatigue.

16.9.4 Psychological Causes

Studies suggest that psychological factors are responsible in at least 50% of fatigue cases. These may include:

1. **Depression**: This illness is characterized by severe and prolonged feelings of sadness, dejection and hopelessness. Those who are depressed may experience chronic tiredness.
2. **Anxiety and stress**: Those who are chronically anxious or stressed keep their body in overdrive. The constant flooding of adrenaline exhausts the body, and fatigue sets in.
3. **Grief**: Losing a loved one causes a wide range of emotions including shock, guilt, depression, despair and loneliness.

16.9.5 Implications of Fatigue

In workplaces, fatigue is a critical safety issue, which has a detrimental impact on employee performance. Often, misconceptions prevent us from implementing suitable programmes for fatigue management. Even government regulations fail to relate fatigue with workplace safety issues. Apart from physical fatigue, which is more prevalent among workers, cognitive fatigue may also be experienced by managers and executives. Cognitive fatigue degrades the individual's capacity for decision-making, reasoning and judgmental power. Workplace boredom adds to the problem of fatigue as it leads to the perception of employees that they are working in a dull, tedious and stimulation-less work environment. Boredom at the workplace can be effectively managed through job enrichment and job enlargement programmes. Measures such as participative decision making, allowing workers to follow creative pursuits, etc., can effectively reduce boredom. In a typical assembly line production system, boredom and fatigue can adversely affect the performance of workers, resulting in serious quality problems.

Workplace hazards significantly affect the performance of workers and are a potential source of human injury, ill health or disease. Such hazards could be physical, psychological or social. Physical hazards are readily identifiable, as these could result in physical injuries. Social and psychological hazards stem from an individual employee's perceived feelings. While problems concerning physical hazards can be managed through proper layout and design, physical and social hazards are managed through transparent communication, participative work culture, collaborative work environment through teamwork, and by quickly responding to staff issues. To ensure systematic intervention from the managers, many organizations have introduced the concept of a hazard audit; this is a formal examination and documentation of the hazards identified and the control measures selected. A small team of suitable staff should undertake the hazard audit.

16.10 LEGAL PROVISIONS FOR OCCUPATIONAL HEALTH AND SAFETY

Workplace safety has an impact on employee motivation and morale and so too on productivity. With poor safety management, organizations not only suffer financial loss, but are also deprived of the benefits of an increase in productivity. Thus, safety issues are now a voluntary and strategic initiative of an organization. However, Indian organizations are still lagging behind with regard to safety initiatives. Indian labour laws have laid down certain provisions, requiring organizations to comply with these provisions to ensure a safe workplace, free from occupational health hazards. The Factories Act, 1948, gave effect to some of the ILO's conventions and recommendations in its 1976 amendment, and made it compulsory to appoint a safety officer. Such stringent requirements were further reinforced with the 1987 amendment of the Factories Act, extending the safety issues outside the organizational boundary. All organizations are now bound to disclose information about their safety preparedness to the statutory authorities.

Similarly, the Mines Act, 1952 also spelt out occupational health and safety issues. Likewise, The Dock Workers (Safety, Health and Welfare) Act, 1986; The Plantations Labour Act, 1951; The Shop and Establishments Act; The Explosives Act, 1884; The Petroleum Act, 1934; The Insecticides Act, 1968; Indian Boilers Act, 1923; The Dangerous Machines (Regulation) Act, 1983; The Environment (Protection) Act, 1986; The Indian Atomic Energy Act, 1962, etc. have some provisions or the other concerning occupational health and safety issues in organizations.

Translating commitment to practice – *Tata Iron and Steel*

Tata Iron and Steel has always believed that the complete cooperation and participation of its employees could only improve efficiencies and churn out better quality products. The company has emphasized the culture of self-policing, and has shown its concern for environmental and ethical issues, and also broad-based corporate governance issues. Such concerns of the company were also recognized by the Ministry of Finance, Government of India with a National Award for corporate excellence in 2000. The company was also recognized for its quality initiatives through the prestigious Golden Peacock Award in 2002. *Tata Steel* has a multi-pronged governance structure that provides for checks and balances throughout its operations. The first layer of this structure is the law of the land.

16.11 MANAGING STRESS IN ORGANIZATIONS

Apart from fatigue, boredom and safety issues, workplace stress is another important area of concern for Production and Operations Managers. While stress may be due to job pressure, typical systems of production are also instrumental in causing workplace stress, which is defined as the physical, mental or emotional response to events that causes bodily or mental tension. Physical stress is caused by the fear of something dangerous, emotional stress is due to mental worries, while mental stress is caused primarily by cognitive dissonance. In the workplace, however, stress primarily develops due to fatigue and overwork.

To manage stress at work, a leading Japanese collaboration company engaged in producing industrial chemicals, spelt out its policy, delineating the responsibilities of managers, individual employees and the organization. The main thrust of the policy was to adopt a proactive approach in matters of stress management, rather than waiting for problems to arise. The policy document explained that management of stress in the workplace is inseparable from the duties and the job roles of managers and supervisors. Being in the business of hazardous chemicals, stress in the workplace also occurs due to occupational health hazards, in addition to work-related stress. To guide managers and supervisors, the policy document has categorized the possible reasons for stress as:

- culture
- demands
- control
- relationships
- change
- role
- support

After categorization of possible stress issues that are likely to occur or have occurred, through brainstorming, managers and supervisors decide on a possible course of action and recommend the same to the top management, who after review, recommend its implementation within a day or two. Reviewing the initial pilot testing report on the suggestive approach to stress management, managers and supervisors, streamlined the policy documents. To help the workers to self-manage workplace stress, and as stress may be exogenous to the organization, a detailed FAQ (frequently asked questions) list was made and prominently displayed in canteens, shop floors, etc.

This approach to stress management helped the company reduce workplace stress significantly. Backup support through counselling also helped the company to reduce stress exogenous to the organization, like family matters, relationship problems, etc.

SUMMARY

1. Production and Operations Managers operate in a competitive environment. Along with their basic functional domains like manufacturing, cost competitiveness, quality, and effective supply chain management, they must also give due cognizance to ethical and environmental issues.
2. Ethical issues encompass products and service design, layout, production processes, use of technology, job design, planning and control, inventory management, supply chain management issues, focus on quality, etc. These apart, production ethics also encompass companies' commitment to recycling of waste, and compliance with environment and pollution control norms.
3. Today's organizations, to ensure their commitment to ethical issues in manufacturing, adopt their own code of ethics, ensure that their employees understand the same through formal training, and monitor their compliance with such ethics, while they do their work.
4. Like ethics, environmental issues are also important for production and operations management. Environmental factors exert an influence on the organization. From the operations managers' point of view, the environment has to be understood as the circumstances, influences and stresses, competitive, cultural, demographic, economic, natural, political, regulatory and technological factors.
5. Pollution control is a major area of responsibility for production managers. With the selection of the appropriate process and technology for production, managers can significantly reduce the pollution level. We have discussed some pollution control measures with examples from industry.
6. Other areas like waste management, corporate social responsibilities, workplace environment, fatigue, occupational health, safety, hazards management and managing stress, also requires consideration from the operations managers' point of view.

In this chapter, we have focussed on a number of corporate practices for better understanding of the theoretical inputs.

KEY WORDS

Code of ethics This specifies the ethical standards that a group (for example, staff or a professional group) should follow in order to remain a member of the group. The code is generally formally stated and members are required to accept them as part of their membership of the group, while accepting employment.

Energy Conservation The efficient use of energy helps its conservation, and helps save depleting resources (for example, coal), from which we get energy. Energy conservation through efficient energy use is possible by reducing dependence on non-renewable sources of power generation like coal, crude oil, natural gas, etc., and exploring the possibility of power generation through renewable resources, like wind power, hydro-power, solar power, etc.

Ethical culture The ethical environment of an organization, which influences the ethical or unethical behaviour of the members of an organization.

Waste Management Strategies The basic focus of waste management strategies is to reduce waste and make effective use of the waste through recycling in an environment-friendly manner.

Work environment Work environment per se is the working conditions that exert an influence on work. Again, working conditions encompass the general, physical, social, psychological and environmental conditions. We can assess the work environment by analyzing the lighting, temperature, noise level, etc. A positive work environment can increase the productivity of workers.

Fatigue at workplace Fatigue is physical and/or mental exhaustion that can be triggered by stress, medication, overwork, or mental and physical illness or disease.

Stress Workplace stress is an important area of concern for production and operations managers. While stress may prima facie be the reason for job pressure, typical systems of production are also instrumental in igniting workplace stress. Stress is defined as our physical, mental, or emotional response to events that causes bodily or mental tension.

Ethics Ethical issues encompassing operations management are related to products and service design, layout, production process, use of technology, job design, planning and control, inventory management, supply chain management issues, focus on quality, etc. These apart, production ethics also encompass companies' commitment to the recycling of waste, and compliance with environment and pollution control norms.

Corporate Governance This refers to the deliberate socially responsible behaviour of an organization. Waste recycling, adherence to pollution control norms, correct financial results disclosure, compliance with labour laws, etc. are good examples of corporate social responsibilities

GENERAL REVIEW QUESTIONS

1. Explain the meaning and importance of corporate ethics. Do you think compliance with ethics will deter an organization from achieving its business goals? Justify your answer.
2. In designing ethical guidelines for managing the production and operations management functions of an organization, what are the important areas one should consider? Illustrate your answer, selecting an area (like discipline,

promotion, transfer, etc.), with a suitable description of the concerned ethical issues.
3. Explain how ethical cultures can be built in organizations.
4. Discuss the various environmental issues that concern organizations.
5. Explain the concept of pollution. What are the causes of pollution and how can it be controlled by an organization?
6. Explain the waste management strategies that organizations must adopt for suitable management of environment issues.
7. Explain the significance of ISO: 14000 standards for environment management systems.
8. Discuss the rationale behind an organization's responsibility towards society?
9. What are the mega and task environment issues that affect an organization?
10. What advantages and disadvantages do organizations experience as they become socially responsive?
11. Write short notes on the following:
    a) Code of Ethics
    b) Ethical Decision Making
    c) International Business Ethics
    d) Ethics in Production
    e) Incineration
    f) Technological factors
    g) Task Environment

CRITICAL REVIEW QUESTIONS

1. Visit some recent press reports on ethical violations in organizations. Critically examine those and suggest what could be the possible course of action for your chosen organization to avoid such ethical violations.
2. Study the ethical compliance report of an Indian organization. Relate their degree of compliance with their business achievements. Give your comments and observations.
3. Visit any organization in your locality and study their internal work environment. Relate your identified work environment issues as per our given list and suggest possible remedial action to the organization.

REFERENCES

1. Charles Lusthaus, Gary Anderson, and Elaine Murphy. 1995, *A Framework for Strengthening Organizational Capacity for IDRC's Research Partners*, Ottawa, ON, Canada: IDRC
2. Gap Inc's Code of Ethics. 1978. Source: www.gapinc.com. (Accessed 7th July, 2007).

ADDITIONAL REFERENCES

1. Andrews, K. R. 1989. Ethics in Practice. *Harvard Business Review,* vol.67 no.,5 pp. Sept–Oct, 99–104
2. Badenhorst, J. A. 1994. Unethical Behaviour in Procurement: A Perspective on Causes and Solutions. *Journal of Business Ethics,* vol. 13, pp. 739–45.
3. Bhattacharyya, Dipak Kumar. 2010. *Cross-cultural Management – Text and Cases.* New Delhi: PHI Learning.
4. Bhattacharyya, Dipak Kumar. 2010. *Industrial Management*. New Delhi: Vikas Publishing,.
5. Bhattacharyya, Dipak Kumar. 2009. *Organizational Behaviour – Concepts and Applications*. New Delhi: Oxford University Press,.
6. Chen, A. Y. S., Sawyer, R. B., Williams, P. F. 1997. Reinforcing Ethical Decisions through Corporate Culture. *Journal of Business Ethics,* vol.16, pp. 855–865.
7. Drucker, P. F. 1954. *The Practice of Management*. New York: Harper.
8. George, C. S., Jr. 1972. *The History of Management Thought*. Englewood Cliffs, N.J: Prentice-Hall, Inc.,
9. Hegarty,W. H., and Sims, Jr. H. P. 1978. Some Determinants of Unethical Behaviour: An Experiment. *Journal of Applied Psychology,* vol.63, no. 4, pp. 451–457.
10. International Organization for Standardization (ISO). 2009. Social Responsibility-ISO 26000. Website: http://www.iso.or/sr.
11. Jerry, White. 1978. *Honesty, Morality and Conscience*. Colorado Springs, Colorado:Nav Press.
12. Klassen, R. and C. McLaughlin. 1996. The Impact of Environmental Management on Firm Performance. *Management Science,* 42, 1199–1214.
13. Lawrance, Himan. 1964. *Immanuel Kant: The Ethics of Duty*. Oxford: Clarendon Press.
14. Madsen, P. and Shafritz, J. M., eds. 1990. *Essentials of Business Ethics*. New York: Penguin Books.
15. McNulty, T. and Pettigrew, A. 1999. Strategists on the board. *Long Range Planning,* Vol. 20 No. 1, pp. 47–74
16. Norman Bowie. 1982. *Business ethics*. Englewood Cliffs, N.J: Prentice–Hall, Inc.,
17. Pastin, M. 1986. *The Hard Problems of Management: Gaining the Ethics Edge*. San Francisco: Jossey-Bass.
18. Vincent Barry. 1979. Moral Issues in Business. Belmont, California: Wadsworth Publ. Co. pp. 84–97.
19. Webley, S. 2003. *Developing a code of ethics.* London: IBE.
20. Wood, D. 1991. Corporate Social Performance Revisited. *Academy of Management Review,* Vol.4, pp. 691–718.

CASE STUDY

Haglöfs – an ethics-compliant world renowned manufacturer

Haglöfs, a Sweden-based company, specializing in footwear and other outdoor dress materials preferred by tourists and adventurists, follows strict production ethics. The company ensures that its products are manufactured conforming to ethical standards and in an environmentally sustainable manner, duly recognizing the fact that their business activities have both negative and positive effects on their surroundings. Conforming to production ethics minimizes the negative influence on society. The company uses the term 'sustainability' in conformance with the European Unions' (EU) definition. EU defines sustainability as the voluntary integration of ethical and environmental considerations in business operations. *Haglöfs*'s commitment to sustainability harmonizes ethical and environmental issues with its profitability and growth.

Such integration of sustainability percolates down to the company's day-to-day activities, and forms an essential part of their core business philosophy, strategies and planning. The vision statement of the company espouses the philosophy of sustainability. The company's policy of sustainability requires a mutual sharing of the following values by the management and the employees of the company:

- respect for human rights and healthy working conditions
- consideration and respect for the global environment
- rejection of corruption
- compliance with legislation and regulations.

The scope of sustainability not only influences the company's business activities, it even extends to transportation, office activities and warehousing. To offset the negative impact of the company's business activities; *Haglöfs* produces high quality products with timeless design and a long life cycle, its designers have to undergo sustainability training.

Since H*aglöfs*' products are meant for outdoor usage, they have to be chemically treated to ensure conformance to water-repellent, waterproof and breathing standards. The company thus requires full control of the chemicals used in manufacture and post-production treatment. They even debar suppliers from using prohibited chemicals in fabrics and accessories.

Such commitment to ethical production standards conforming to the EU's concept of sustainability is evident from the following actions taken by the company:

1. Systematic measurement of greenhouse gas emissions, and attempts made to reduce the emissions through a carbon offsets programme
2. Restriction of CO_2 emissions from the company's vehicles
3. Reduction of energy consumption
4. Scientific waste disposal
5. Participation in national recycling programmes
6. Serving organic food, tea and coffee in all offices, etc.

Discussion Question

Read the case and compare similar initiatives of any Indian textile manufacturer (Hint: visit *Grasim*'s website).

CHAPTER 17

Production and Operations Management Research

LEARNING OBJECTIVES

After reading this chapter, you will be able to understand:

- Concepts of Production and Operations Management Research
- Production and Operations Management Models
- Use of Linear Programming Model for Production and Operations Management Research
- Use of Network Analysis for POM research
- Use of Transportation Models for POM research
- Use of Game Theory for POM research

Opening Vignette

Dabur getting younger over the years

From a small pharmacy in 1884 in the then British India capital – Calcutta, today, *Dabur India Limited (DIL)* is the third largest FMCG Company with a turnover of more than Rs. 2,233 crore. It has a Consumer Care Division (CCD), Consumer Healthcare Division (CHD) and Dabur Foods Limited. In July 2007, *Dabur* announced the de-merger of *DFL* from *DIL*. *Dabur* had popularized ayurvedic medicines in India at a time when it was the only option to treat diseases like malaria, plague and cholera. Through sustained efforts over a century, *Dabur* is now a household name in India. This century-old journey was not at all smooth. Scientific testing of medicines before their positioning in the market, computerization of operations in 1957, etc. could help the company achieve excellence in operations. Gradually, with the entry of *HLL, P&G, Marico, Himalaya* and *ITC, Dabur* faced a stupendous challenge. With a large array of products, *Dabur*'s supply chain was gradually becoming more and more complex.

Moreover, the company used to be perceived as a herbal products company, and hence, it was preferred by the older generation. A brand rejuvenation programme with celebrities, helped *Dabur* overcome this problem. Along with these initiatives, it revamped its operations and management practices, to emerge as a company that appealed to young Indians as well.

17.1 INTRODUCTION

Production and operations management research helps us to understand the prevailing systems in the organization and to identify the appropriate approach to modify prevalent practices for better results. Also, through POM research we try to build theories. Let us first understand the various definitions of research. Research is "Systematic investigation towards increasing the sum of knowledge" (Chambers 20th Century Dictionary). "An evaluation to discover new or collate old facts, etc. by the scientific study of a subject or by a course of critical investigation" (The Concise Oxford Dictionary). Thus, there is general agreement that research is a systematic and methodical process of inquiry and investigation that increases knowledge and/or solves a particular problem. From the production and operations management point of view, the purpose of research is to review and synthesise existing knowledge, investigating the existing situation or problems and developing suitable solutions to avoid the recurrence of such problems in future. POM research helps us develop new systems and procedures for achieving efficiency and effectiveness in POM functions. Like other research, POM research is also a rigorous scientific activity. It is the systematic development and acquisition of knowledge and is tailored to specific organizational needs to answer specific questions within a given timeframe. It is now a subject of study, to understand how organizations are structured and function; the practices of decision-making; the factors that affect organizational operations, the strategies that contribute to the enhancement of the strategic advantages of an organization.

In POM research, we make use of operations research (OR) tools as it helps in informed decision making. OR also helps in the application of information technology. The basic premise of OR is optimum resource allocation to maximize profit and minimize costs. Various analytical and numerical techniques are used in OR. Manipulating various mathematical models, we take decisions. Thus, OR is an analytical method of problem solving and decision making, necessary to manage an organization. For the purpose of managers, OR is applied to decision making through linear programming, network or scheduling, transportation and assignment problems, game theory. In this chapter, the usage of certain decisional tools for POM research has been discussed. Production and operations managers need to use such quantitative decisional tools to understand the efficacy of the prevalent systems and the possible ways of improving it.

17.2 DIFFERENT APPROACHES TO POM RESEARCH

While the process of production and operations follows a typical structure, approaches may be different and vary from situation to situation. It may be purely academic or theoretical or action oriented. But the approach that is appropriate to a given situation largely depends on the specific need of the researcher. We find five types of POM research. These are:

1. **Pure basic research** This research intends to develop a basic discipline by resolving, illuminating and exemplifying a theoretical issue. Therefore, its basic purpose is to enhance knowledge and understanding. The results of such research become the source of knowledge for practising managers. Most of the core POM concepts are developed from pure basic research.
2. **Objective research** The focus is on how to overcome a general problem in the application of established knowledge. It is, however, not intended to solve a specific POM problem. For such research, the researcher frames certain clear objectives and hypotheses and then tests the validity of established knowledge in a given situation.
3. **Evaluative research** This research, in contrast, assesses some aspects of the operations function by analysing the effectiveness of a given problem, like the effects of incentives on worker productivity, technology transfer and the corresponding change in the process, total productive maintenance and workers' level of commitment, etc. This type of research is most common as it helps practising managers develop 'scientific neutrality' to look into some issues and develop a framework for future POM functions.
4. **Applied research** This type of research is more specific; it is used to solve a particular problem within an organization by the application of appropriate knowledge. To illustrate, we may apply our existing knowledge on job scheduling to identify the most appropriate approach for customer satisfaction, suitably changing our existing style. Many companies who cannot afford independent research embrace best management practices to benchmark their systems with others.
5. **Action research** In this type of research, action (solution of a problem) is both an outcome and a part of the research process. Its main purpose is to improve the stock of knowledge by tackling a problem, which has relevance to theory. However, the researcher in such a case changes the research during the process, the outcome, it is often alleged, cannot be replicated, which is a constraint to testing the validity of the research in another situation. Thus, it may prevent the development of general knowledge.

Through POM research, we also try to build models to represent cause, effect and other relationships. The model basically refers to a dynamic framework or scheme to portray the key concepts, propositions, etc. of a theory. It is a representation of a process or a system and it shows the most important variables in the system in such a way that analysis of these variables leads to insights into the system. However, it must be understood that a model is not an explanation; it is only the structure or functions, some aspect of a system or the system as a whole. It may be highly conceptual or theoretical (theory itself being a model), developed at the start of a research and then tested through the process of data gathering, analysis and reasoning. Although we have different types of models, for POM research, we make use of mathematical models to show the functional relationships between different variables. Mathematical models may be either optimization models or heuristic models. Optimization models help us to analyse problems and suggest solutions. Heuristic models, on the other hand, are some established decision-making procedures to solve a problem.

17.3 LINEAR PROGRAMMING (LP)

Linear programming is a mathematical technique to select an optimum plan. It helps in getting the best solution to a decisional problem with many interactive variables. Through linear programming, we try to maximize the profit or contribution margin, and minimize the costs. We always try to achieve the optimum objective (which could be profit maximization or cost minimization). Like any other decisional problem, in linear programming, we have various constraints, restrictions and possible decisional alternatives. Such constraints describe availability, limitations, and the relationships of resources to alternatives. Some of the characteristic features of linear programming can be listed as follows:

1. Contribution margin or the cost associated with one unit of product or activity is the same for all identical units.
2. Resource input per unit of activity is considered to be the same for all units.
3. All factors and relationships are deterministic.
4. Some inherent constraints in terms of capacity of machine, labour availability, time availability, capital availability, etc. must exist.
5. With the data fitting in equations, the linear programming can be solved graphically.
6. With more than two variables, linear programming problems are solved using the simplex method.

Example

Your Company produces three products: A, B, C. The contribution margin for each product is as follows:

Product	Contribution Margin (Rs.)
A	2
B	5
C	4

The production requirement of your company along with the information pertaining to departmental capacities is as follows:

Department	**Production (hours)**	**Requirement**	**By**	**Product/Departmental Capacity (in hours)**
	A	B	C	
Assembling	2	3	2	30,000
Painting	1	2	2	38,000
Finishing	2	3	1	28,000

Formulate the objective function and the constraints.

Solution

Objective:

$$CM = 2a + 5b + 4c$$

Constraints:

Assembling: $2a + 3b + 2c \leq 30,000$

Painting: $1a + 2b + 2c \leq 38,000$

Finishing: $2a + 3b + 1c \leq 28,000$

QUESTION

Formulate the problem with the objective and constraints as under:

- Your company seeks to minimize the total cost of materials A and B.
- The cost per kg. of A is Rs. 25 and B is Rs. 10.
- Combining products A and B, we get materials which weigh 50 kg.
- At least 20 kg of A and not more than 40 kg of B can be used.

Solution

$$C = 25a + 10b$$

Subject to: $a + b = 50; a \geq 20; b \leq 40$

Linear Programming Problem Formulation:

Minimize

$$180x + 160y$$

Subject to:

$$6x + y \geq 12$$

$$3x + y \geq 8$$

$$4x + 6y \geq 24$$

$$x \leq 5$$

$$y \leq 5$$

$$x, y \geq 0$$

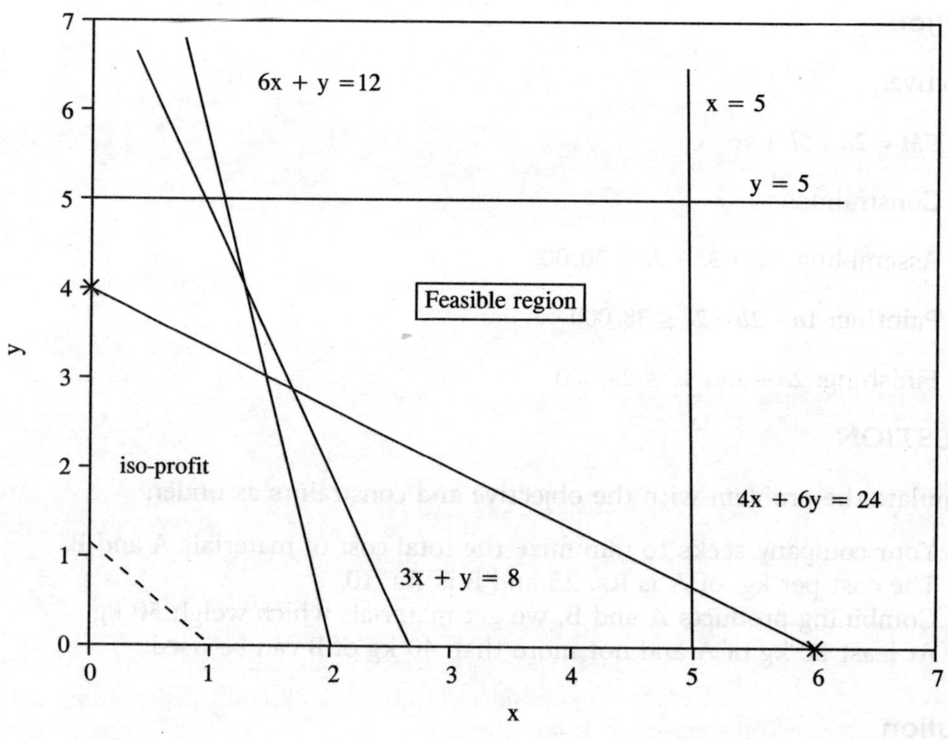

Figure 17.1 *Graphical representation of an LP problem*

Here, we have only two variables. The graphical representation of the LP problem, clearly demonstrating the feasible region of solutions, within the given constraints can be presented as in Fig. 17.1.

Here, we have turned all inequality constraints into equalities, drawing the corresponding lines on the graph (constraint $6x+y \geq 12$ becomes the line $6x+y = 12$ on the graph). After drawing the line, we can work out which side of the line corresponds to feasible solutions to the original inequality constraint (Here, all feasible solutions to $6x + y \geq 12$ lie to the right of the line $6x + y = 12$).

The optimal solution to the LP problem can be determined by plotting $(180x + 160y) = K$(K constant) for varying K values (iso-profit lines). One such line $(180x + 160y = 180)$ is shown as dotted on the diagram. The smallest value of K (considering a minimisation problem), i.e., $180x + 160y = K$ goes through a point in the feasible region is the value of the optimal solution. The optimal solution to the LP, therefore, occurs at the vertex of the feasible region formed by the intersection of $3x + y = 8$ and $4x + 6y = 24$. It is important to understand that values of x and y need to be determined through simultaneous equations, and not from the graph. The equations here:

$$3x + y = 8$$

$$4x + 6y = 24$$

to get $x = 12/7 = 1.71$ and $y = 20/7 = 2.86$ and hence the value of the objective function is given by $180x + 160y = 180(12/7) + 160(20/7) =$ Rs. 765.71

Hence, the optimal solution has a cost of Rs. 765.71

Again, graphical approach to solve LPs can be relevant only in cases where we have two variables. But in cases, where we have more than two variables, we use the simplex method to solve the problem.

17.3.1 Simplex Method

With more than two variables, we use the simplex algorithm. In this case, the optimal solution to LP occurred at a vertex (corner) of the feasible region. This is the key to the simplex algorithm for solving LP's. It starts at one vertex of the feasible region and moves to another vertex, until it reaches the optimal solution. Thus, the simplex method is an iterative process which approaches an optimum solution in such a way that an objective function of maximization or minimization is fully reached. Iteration in this process reduces the distance (mathematically and graphically) from the objective function. Iteration is the application of a function repeatedly, that is, from the output of one iteration to the input of another iteration. In other words, we can also call it the approximate numerical solution to certain mathematical problems. In the simplex method, the steps to solve the problem of cost minimization are similar to those steps taken in the contribution margin and maximization margin. Using slack variables, at the outset, we try to arrive at the first feasible solution. Apart from slack variables we also make use of artificial variables with two restrictions or constraints, that is, equal-to-type and greater-than-or-equal-to-type. Artificial variables are of value only as computational devices in maximization and minimization problems. In this minimization problem, an artificial variable, a1, is introduced in the first constraint, which is of the equal-to type. Thus, the simplex method is an iterative step-wise process to achieve an optimum solution to reach the objective function of maximization or minimization. A problem formulation of the simplex method can be written as follows:

maximize $x1 + 3x2 - 3x3$

subject to $3x1 - x2 - 2x3 \leq 7$

$2x1 - 4x2 + 4x3 \leq 3$

$x1 - 2x3 \leq 4$

$2x1 + 2x2 + x3 \leq 8$

$3x1 \leq 5$

$x1; x2; x3 \geq 0$:

From the above discussions, we can summarize the essential components of the simplex method as under:

- The objective row indicates coefficients of the objective function.
- The variable row, including the slack variables, indicates variables of the problem.
- The problem row indicates the variables constraints within one row.
- Variables which are not included in the constraint are assigned zero coefficients.

17.3.2 Linear Programming Problems and Solutions

Example 1

Your company regularly needs to transport manufactured products to different destinations. You have a strong Logistics and Supply Chain department, which always tries to optimize the cost of transportation to gain substantially in terms of economic value addition. Although you have your own fleet, at times, you also outsource. Your trucks can take a load of 60 metric tonnes. Trucks are of two types: type-A and type-B. Type-A trucks are divided into two parts; refrigerated and non-refrigerated; 20 metric tonnes can be transported in a refrigerated condition and the remaining

40 metric tonnes can be transported in a non-refrigerated condition. In Type B trucks, the space is equally divided into two parts. On a particular day, your company has to transport 3000 metric tonnes of refrigerated items and 4000 metric tonnes of non-refrigerated items. The per kilometer transportation cost for a Type-A truck is Rs. 30, while for a Type-B truck, it is Rs. 40. Your company wants to understand which type of trucks should be used, and in what ratio, to minimize the cost of transportation.

Solution

Step-1

Understand the unknowns.

X = Type-A

Y = Type-B

Step-2

Write the objective function

$$F(x, y) = 30x + 40y$$

Step-3

Write the constraints (keeping in mind the system of inequalities)

	A	B	Total
Refrigerated	20	30	3000
Non-Refrigerated	40	30	4000

$20x + 30y \geq 3000$

$40x + 30y \geq 4000$

$x \geq 0$

$y \geq 0$

Step-4

Find the set of feasible solutions and graphically represent the constraints (Fig. 17.2).

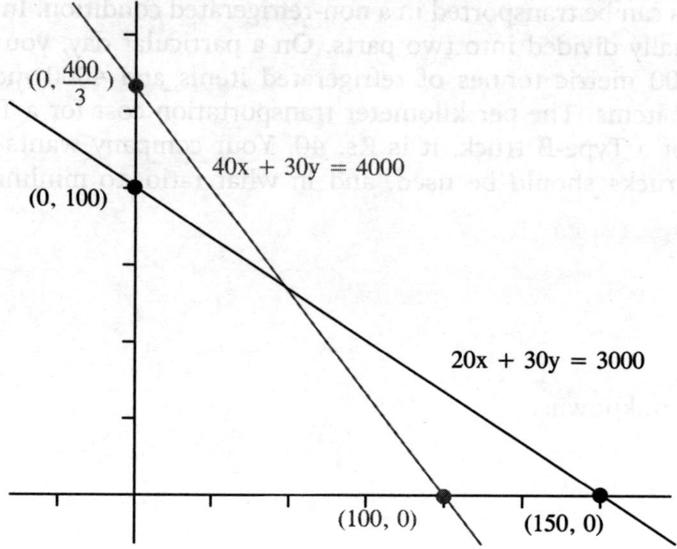

Figure 17.2 *Coordinates represented graphically*

Step-5

Calculate the coordinates of the vertices from the compound feasible solutions (Fig.17.3).

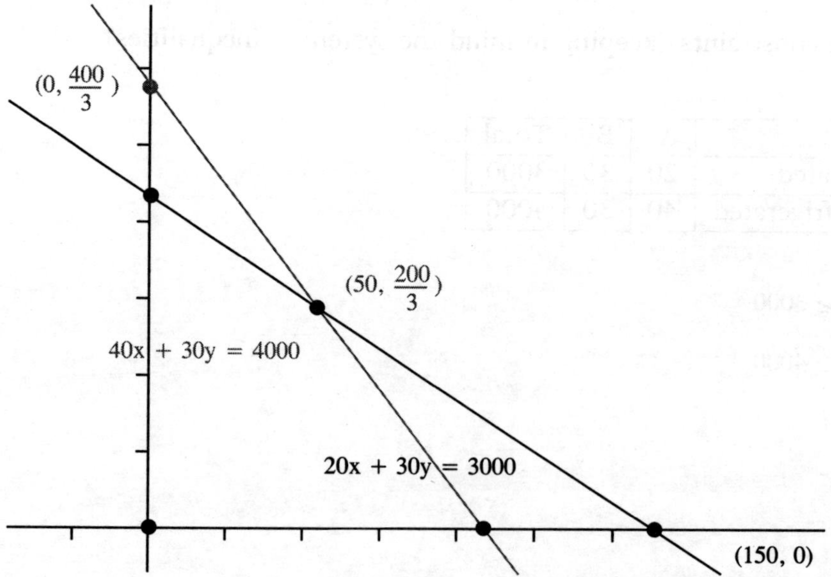

Figure 17.3 *Graph to calculate coordinates of the vertices*

Step-6

Calculate the value of the objective function at each of the vertices to determine which of them has the maximum or minimum values.

$$f(0, 400/3) = 30.0 + 40.400/3 = 5,333.332$$

$$f(150, 0) = 30.150 + 40.0 = 4,500$$

As x and y must be natural numbers, round off the value of y, solving the equation in step-3 ($x = 50, y = 67$), we can write:

$$f(50, 67) = 30.50 + 40.67 = \text{Rs. } 4,180 \text{ Minimum}$$

The minimum cost is Rs. 4,180. To achieve this, 50 trucks of Type A and 67 trucks of Type B are needed.

Example - 2

Your company, according to the terms of its employment contract, has to provide pick up and drop services to its 400 employees. Your company wants to outsource this to a renowned transporter. The transporter can provide 10 luxury buses of 50 seats each and 8 deluxe buses of 40 seats each. However, only 9 drivers are available. The per day hiring charges for a 50-seater bus is Rs. 800 and for a 40-seater bus it is Rs. 600. The company wants you to calculate the least possible cost of such hiring of buses. Also suggest how many buses of each type should be hired.

Solution

x = small buses

y = big buses

$$f(x, y) = 600x + 800y$$

$$40x + 50y \geq 400$$

$$x + y \leq 9$$

$$x \geq 0$$

$$y \geq 0$$

Calculation of maximum or minimum values (Fig. 17.4)

$$f(0, 8) = 600.0 + 800.8 = \text{Rs. } 6,400$$

$$f(0, 9) = 600.0 + 800.9 = \text{Rs. } 7,200$$

$$f(5, 4) = 600.5 + 800.4 = \text{Rs. } 6,200 \quad \text{Minimum}$$

The minimum cost is Rs. 6,200. This is achieved with 4 luxury and 5 deluxe buses.

More Linear programming examples

XYZ Ltd., makes products, X and Y, with two machines, A and B. The production of each unit of X requires use of machine A for 50 minutes and 30 minutes machine time on machine B, while product Y time requires 24 and 33 minutes respectively on these machines.

XYZ Limited starts with an existing stock of 30 units of X and 90 units of Y. However, the company needs to produce more to further build up stocks of products X and Y, despite the constraint of 40 hours being available on machine A, and 35 hours on machine B. The company assesses the present demand for X at 75 units and for Y at 95 units. Suggest how the company can maximize the combined sum of products X and Y.

Solution

Let x be the number of units of X produced

y be the number of units of Y produced

The constraints are, therefore;

$50x + 24y \leq 40(60)$ machine A time

$30x + 33y \leq 35(60)$ machine B time

$x \geq 75 - 30$

i.e. $x \geq 45$ so production of $x \geq$ demand (75) – initial stock (30), which ensures we meet demand

$y \geq 95 - 90$

that is, $y \geq 5$ so production of $y \geq$ demand (95) – initial stock (90), which ensures we meet demand.

The objective is to maximise $(x+30-75)+(y+90-95) = (x+y-50)$, that is, to maximise the number of units in stock.

It is evident from the graph (Fig 17.5) that the maximum occurs at the intersection of $x = 45$ and $50x + 24y = 2400$. With simultaneous solutions (rather than values from the graph), we get $x = 45$ and $y = 6.25$ with the value of the objective function being 1.25.

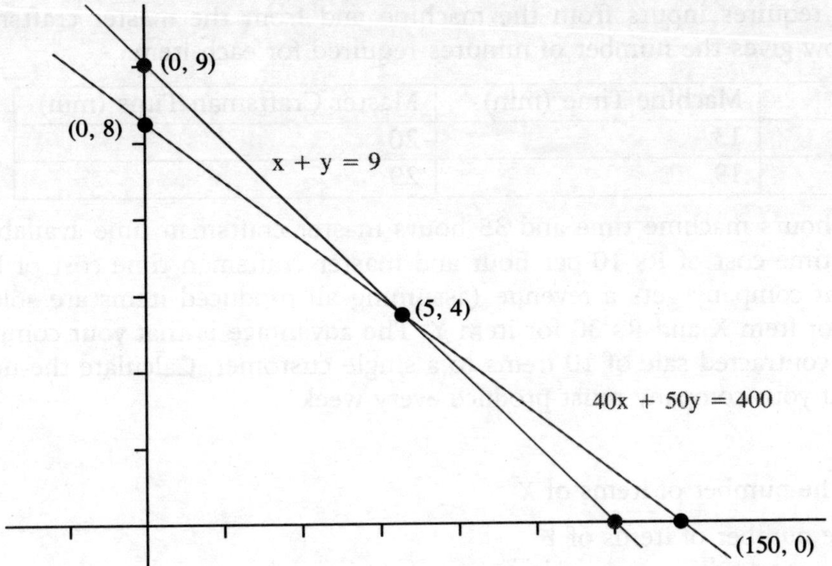

Figure 17.4 *Graph*

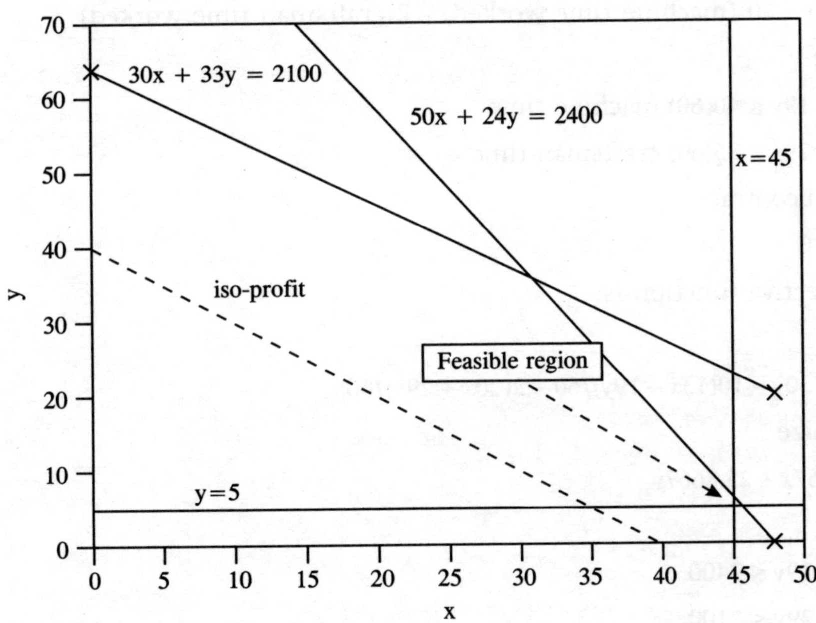

Figure 17.5 *Graph showing maximum production*

Linear programming example

Your company produces two items, *X* and *Y*. For producing these items, your company requires inputs from the machine and from the master craftsman. The table below gives the number of minutes required for each item:

Item	Machine Time (min)	Master Craftsman Time (min)
X	13	20
Y	19	29

With 40 hours machine time and 35 hours master craftsman time available, and a machine time cost of Rs 10 per hour and master craftsman time cost of Rs. 2 per hour, your company gets a revenue (assuming all produced items are sold) of Rs. 20 each for item X and Rs 30 for item Y. The advantage is that your company gets a weekly contracted sale of 10 items to a single customer. Calculate the number of items that your company must produce every week.

Solution

Let x be the number of items of X

y be the number of items of Y

then the LP is:

maximize

$20x + 30y - 10$ (machine time worked) - 2(craftsman time worked)

subject to:

$13x + 19y \leq 40(60)$ machine time

$20x + 29y \leq 35(60)$ craftsman time

$x \geq 10$ contract

$x, y \geq 0$

so the objective function is:

maximize

$$20x + 30y - 10(13x + 19y)/60 - 2(20x + 29y)/60$$

i.e. maximize

$$17.1667x + 25.8667y$$

subject to:

$$13x + 19y \leq 2400$$

$$20x + 29y \leq 2100$$

$$x \geq 10$$

$$xy \geq 0$$

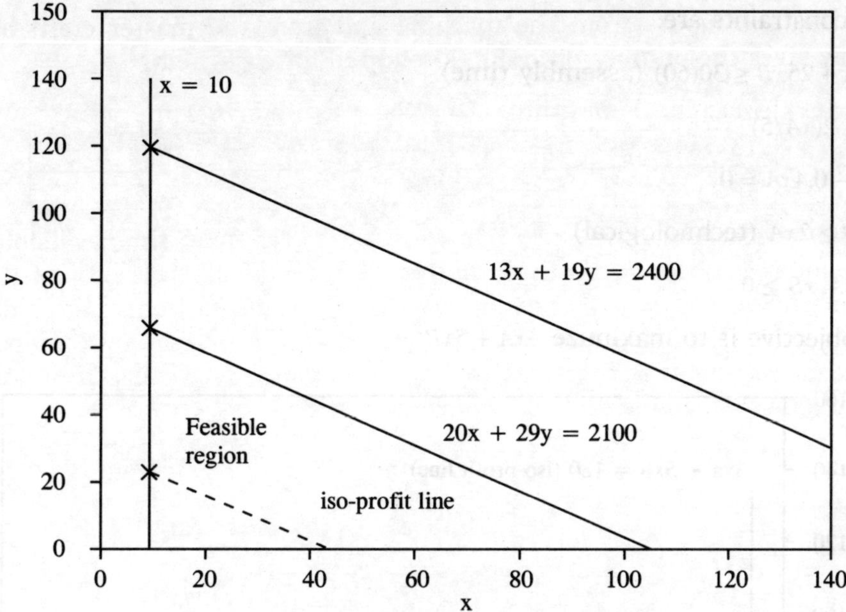

Figure 17.6 *Linear programming*

As evident from the graphical presentation (17.6) above, the maximum occurs at the intersection of $x = 10$ and $20x + 29y \leq 2100$. Simultaneous solution (without reading the values of the graph) gives us $x = 10$ and $y = 65.53$ with the value of the objective function at Rs. 1866.5.

Linear programming example

ABC company manufactures two products (A and B) and gets a profit from per unit sold at Rs.3 and Rs. 5 respectively. Both the products need to be produced using a particular machine. For every unit of product A and B, machine time requirement is 12 and 25 minutes respectively. ABC company has the constraint of machine time availability of 30 hours per week. Technically, ABC can produce 2 units of product B against 5 units of product A.

Using linear programming, suggest the appropriate quantity of items to be produced by ABC to maximize their gain. Also assume if machine time hiring is allowed, what should be the maximum payment that your company can afford towards hiring charges per week.

Solution

Let

xA = number of units of A produced

xB = number of units of B produced

then the constraints are:

$12xA + 25xB \leq 30(60)$ (assembly time)

$xB \geq 2(xA/5)$

i.e. $xB - 0.4xA = 0$

i.e. $5xB \geq 2xA$ (technological)

where $xA, xB \geq 0$

and the objective is to maximize $3xA + 5xB$

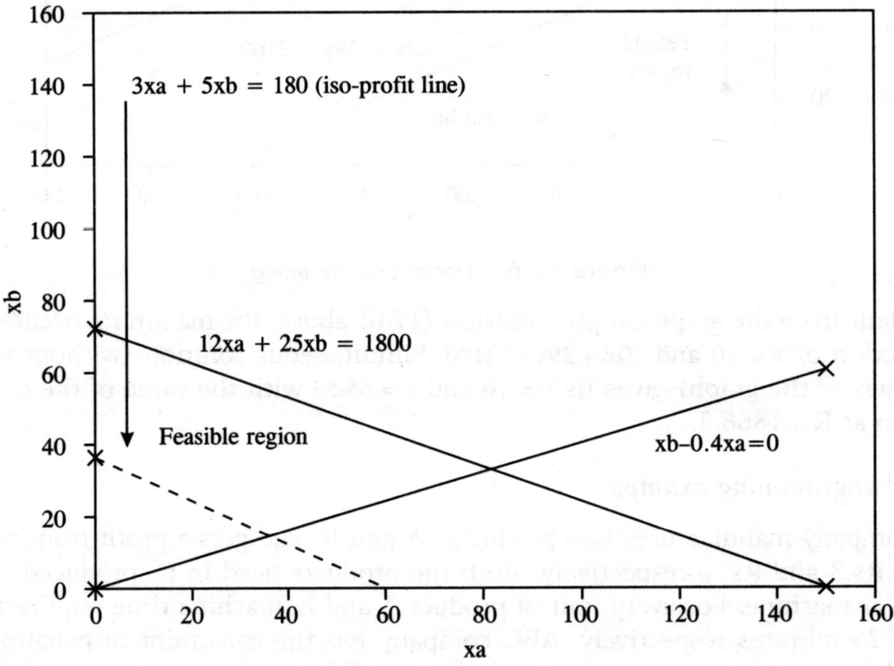

Figure 17.7 *Graphical presentation*

As evident from the graphical presentation above (Fig. 17.7), maximum occurs at the intersection of $12xA + 25xB = 1800$ and $xB - 0.4xA = 0$. However, simultaneous solution indicates:

$xA = (1800/22) = 81.8$

$xB = 0.4xA = 32.7$

with the value of the objective function at Rs. 408.9.

By doubling the machine time availability, existing constraints of $12xA + 25xB \leq 1800$

become $12xA + 25xB = 2(1800)$. The optimal solution, therefore can be obtained from the intersection of $12xA + 25xB = 3600$ and $xB - 0.4xA = 0$

i.e. at $xA = (3600/22) = 163.6$

$xB = 0.4xA = 65.4$

with the value of the objective function being Rs.817.8

Hence, ABC can make an additional profit of Rs. 408.9(817.8 – 408.9), and only this amount can be paid by them toward hiring a machine to double the rate of production.

17.4 NETWORK ANALYSIS

Network analysis – activity on node examples
The table below defines the activities of a project.

Activity	Completion Time (weeks)	Immediate Predecessor (activities)
A	2	-
B	3	-
C	4	A
D	3	B,A
E	8	D,C
F	3	C
G	2	E
H	3	F,G

Draw the network diagram.

Calculate the minimum overall project completion time and identify which activities are critical. Find out the slack (float) time associated with each of the non-critical activities. Various options for completion time for activities C, D and E with associated costs is presented below:

Activity	Completion Time	Cost (Rs.'000)
C	4	3
	3	7
	2	10
	1	12
D	3	12
	2	16
	1	25

E	8	5
	7	6
	6	14

Formulate the problem to decide on the completion time for C, D and E, so that the project is completed within 17 weeks.

Solution

The network diagram (Fig.17.8) is drawn as follows with dummy activity 1 (zero duration) to represent the end of the project.

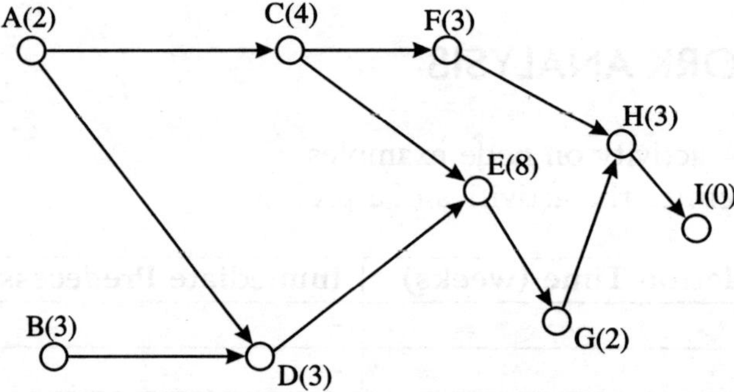

Figure 17.8 *Network diagram*

Let *Ei* represent the earliest start time for activity i, such that all its preceding activities have been finished. We calculate the values of $Ei(i = A, B, ..., I)$, by going forward, from left to right, in the network diagram.

To ease the notation, let Ti be the activity completion time associated with activity i (for example, TB = 3). Then, the Ei are given by:

EA = 0 (assuming we start at time zero)

EB = 0 (assuming we start at time zero)

EC = EA + TA = 0 + 2 =2

ED = max [EA + TA, EB + TB] = max [0 + 2, 0 + 3] = 3

EE = max [EC + TC, ED + TD] = max [2 + 4, 3 + 3] = 6

EF = EC + TC = 2 + 4 = 6

EG = EE + TE = 6 + 8 = 14

EH = max [EF + TF, EG + TG] = max [6 + 3, 14 + 2] = 16

EI = EH + TH = 16 + 3 = 19

Hence, the minimum possible completion time for completing all the activities of the project is 19 weeks.

We now need to calculate the latest time for each activity.

Let *Li* represent the latest start time, that is, we can start activity i and still complete the project in the minimum overall completion time. We calculate the values of the Li (i=A,B,...,I) by going backward, from right to left, in the network diagram. Hence:

LI = 19

LH= LI – TH = 19 – 3 = 16

LG = LH – TG = 16 – 2 = 14

LF = LH – TF = 16 – 3 = 13

LE = LG – TE = 14 – 8 = 6

LD = LE – TD = 6 – 3 = 3

LC = min[LE – TC, LF – TC] = min[6 – 4, 13 – 4] = 2

LB = LD – TB = 3 – 3 = 0

LA = min[LC – TA, LD – TA] = min[2 – 2, 3 – 2] = 0

All latest times are = 0; at least one activity has a latest start time value of zero.

As we know the earliest start time *Ei,* and the latest start time *Li,* for each activity *i*, it is clear that the amount of slack or float time Fi available is given by $Fi = Li - Ei$ which is the amount by which we can increase the time taken to complete activity *i* without changing (increasing) the overall project completion time. Hence, we can form a table:

Activity	Li	Ei	Float Fi
A	0	0	0
B	0	0	0
C	2	2	0
D	3	3	0
E	6	6	0
F	13	6	7
G	14	14	0
H	16	16	0

Any activity with a float of zero is critical. All float values should be ≥ 0.

Hence, the critical activities are A, B, C, D, E,G and H and the float for the only non-critical activity F is 7 weeks.

In order to formulate the problem of deciding the completion time for C, D and

E, so as to ensure that the project is completed within 17 weeks, we make use of integer programming,

Let the x variables represent feasible start times for each activity (≥ 0 and integer). We consider feasible start times in formulating this programme rather than the with earliest start times.

Introduce zero-one variables

$Ci = 1$ if a completion time of $i(I = 4, 3, 2, 1)$ chosen for activity C, 0 otherwise

$Di = 1$ if a completion time of $i(i = 3, 2, 1)$ chosen for activity D, 0 otherwise

$Ei = 1$ if a completion time of $i(i = 8, 7, 6)$ chosen for activity E, 0 otherwise

then the constraints relating to the choice of completion time are:

$$C4 + C3 + C2 + C1 = 1$$

$$D3 + D2 + D1 = 1$$

$$E8 + E7 + E6 = 1$$

In other words, exactly one completion time must be chosen for C, D and E respectively.

The constraints relating to the network logic are:

$$xA = xB = 0$$

$$xC \geq xA + 2$$

$$xD \geq xB + 3$$

$$xD \geq xA + 2$$

$$xE \geq xC + 4C4 + 3C3 + 2C2 + 1C1$$

where 4C4 + 3C3 + 2C2 +1C1 is the completion time for activity C (as C4, C3, C2 and C1 are zero-one variables).

$$xE \geq xD + 3D3 + 2D2 + 1D1$$

$$xF \geq xC + 4C4 + 3C3 + 2C2 + 1C1$$

$$xG \geq xE + 8E8 + 7E7 + 6E6$$

$$xH \geq xF + 3$$

$$xH \geq xG + 2$$

$$xH \leq 17 - 3 \text{ (to complete in 17 weeks)}$$

and the objective is

$$\text{minimize } 3C4 + 7C3 + 10C2 + 15C1 + 12D3 + 16D2 + 25D1 + 5E8 + 9E7 + 14E6$$

Example 2

Network diagram

A project consists of 8 activities. The activity completion times and the precedence relationships are as follows:

Activity	Completion Time (days)	Immediate Predecessor
A	5	-
B	7	-
C	6	-
D	3	A
E	4	B,C
F	2	C
G	6	A,D
H	5	E.F

Draw the network diagram.

Calculate the minimum overall project completion time and identify which activities are critical.

If activity E is delayed by 3 days, how is the project completion time affected?

If activity F is delayed by 3 days, how is the project completion time affected?

Solution

The network diagram (Fig. 17.9) is shown below. Dummy activity with zero time duration has been introduced to represent the end of the project.

Let *Ei* represent the earliest start time for activity i such that all its preceding activities have been finished. We calculate the values of the $Ei(i = A, B, ..., I)$ by going forward, from left to right, in the network diagram.

To ease the notation, let Ti be the activity completion time associated with activity i (for example, TB = 7). Then the Ei are given by:

EA = 0 (assuming we start at time zero)

EB = 0 (assuming we start at time zero)

EC = 0 (assuming we start at time zero)

ED = EA + TA = 0 + 5 = 5

EG = max [EA + TA, ED + TD] = max [0 + 5, 5 + 3] = 8

EE = max [EB + TB, EC + TC] = max [0 + 7, 0 + 6] = 7

EF = EC + TC = 0 + 6 = 6

EH = max [EE + TE, EF + TF] = max [7 + 4, 6 + 2] = 11

EI = max [EG + TG, EH + TH] = max [8 + 6, 11 + 5] = 16

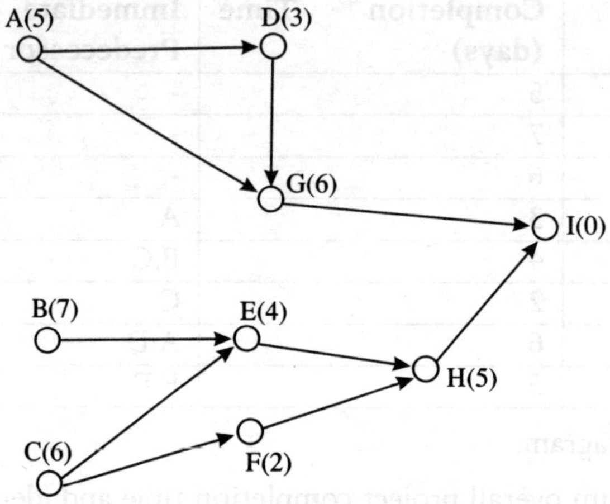

Figure 17.9 *Network diagram*

Hence, the minimum possible completion time for the entire project is 16 days, or 16 days is the minimum time needed to complete all the activities. We now need to calculate the latest times for each activity.

Let Li represent the latest start time we can start activity i and still complete the project in the minimum overall completion time. We calculate the values of the Li (i=A, B,...,I) by going backward, from right to left, in the network diagram. Hence:

LI = 16

LG = LI – TG = 16 – 6 = 10

LH = LI – TH = 16 – 5 = 11

LD = LG – TD = 10 – 3 = 7

LA = min [LD – TA, LG -- TA] = min [7 – 5, 10 – 5] = 2

LE = LH – TE = 11 – 4 = 7

LF = LH – TF = 11 – 2 = 9

LC = min [LE – TC, LF – TC] = min [7 – 6, 9 – 6] = 1

LB = LE – TB = 7 – 7 = 0

Note that as a check, all latest times are ≥ 0, at least one activity has a latest start time value of zero.

As we know the earliest start time Ei, and latest start time Li, for each activity i, it is clear that the amount of slack or float time Fi available is given by Fi = Li -- Ei which is the amount by which we can increase the time taken to complete activity i without changing (increasing) the overall project completion time. Hence, we can form the table below:

Activity	Li	Ei	Float Fi
A	2	0	2
B	0	0	0
C	1	0	1
D	7	5	2
E	7	7	0
F	9	6	2
G	10	8	2
H	11	11	0

Any activity with a float of zero is critical. Note here that, as a check, all float values should be = 0.

Hence, the critical activities are B, E and H and the floats for the non-critical activities are given in the table above.

If activity E is delayed by 3 days, then as E is critical, the project completion time increases by exactly 3 days.

If activity F is delayed by 3 days, then as F has a float of 3 days the project completion time is unaffected.

Network analysis example

A project consists of 8 activities named A to H. Construct a network so as to satisfy the scheduling requirements shown in the table below:

Activity	Completion Times (in days)	Immediate Predecessor activities
A	3	-
B	6	A
C	7	A
D	5	A
E	13	B,C
F	8	C,D,
G	11	D,E
H	6	G,E

Find the least time required to complete the entire project and identify the critical activities.

How is the project completion time affected if:
activity F is delayed by 3 days
activity E is delayed by 7 days
activity G is finished 7 days early

Solution

The network diagram (Fig. 17.10) is shown. Dummy activity 1 with duration of zero has been introduced to end the project.

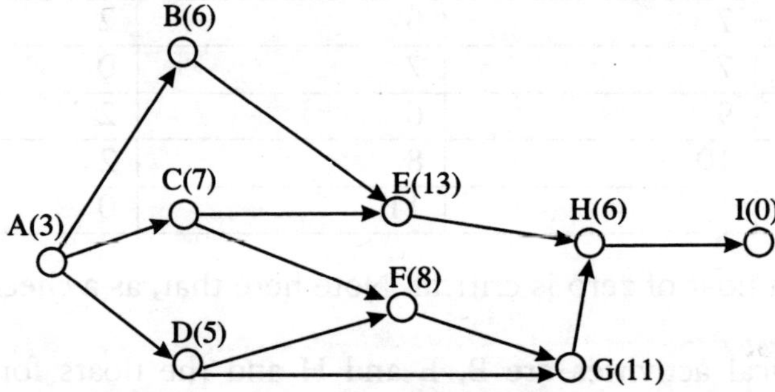

Figure 17.10 *Network diagram*

Let Ei represent the earliest start time for activity i such that all its preceding activities have been finished. We calculate the values of the Ei (i=A,B,...,I) by going forward, from left to right, in the network diagram.

To ease the notation, let Ti be the activity completion time associated with activity i (for example, TB = 7). Then the Ei are given by:

EA = 0 (assuming the start time as zero)

EB = EA + TA = 0 + 3 = 3

EC = EA + TA = 0 + 3 = 3

ED = EA + TA = 0 + 3 = 3

EE = max[EB + TB, EC + TC] = max[3 + 6, 3 + 7] = 10

EF = max[EC + TC, ED + TD] = max[3 + 7, 3 + 5] = 10

EG = max[EF + TF, ED + TD] = max[10 + 8, 3 + 5] = 18

EH = max[EE + TE, EG + TG] = max[10 + 13, 18 + 11] = 29

EI = EH + TH = 29 + 6 = 35

Hence, the minimum possible completion time for the entire project is 35 days, or 35 days is the minimum time needed to complete all the activities.

We now need to calculate the latest times for each activity.

Let Li represent the latest start time we can start activity i and still complete the project in the minimum overall completion time. We calculate the values of Li (i=A,B,...,I), by going backward, from right to left, in the network diagram. Hence:

LI = 35

LH = LI – TH = 35 – 6 = 29

LG = LH – TG = 29 – 11 = 18

LE = LH – TE = 29 – 13 = 16

LF = LG – TF = 18 – 8 = 10

LB = LE – TB = 16 – 6 = 10

LC = min[LE – TC, LF – TC] = min[16 – 7, 10 – 7] = 3

LD = min[LF – TD, LG – TD] = min[10 – 5, 18 – 5] = 5

LA = min[LB – TA, LC – TA, LD – TA] = min[10 – 3, 3 – 3, 5 – 3] = 0

As a check all latest times are ≥ 0, at least one activity has a latest start time value of zero.

As we know the earliest start time Ei, and latest start time Li, for each activity *i*, it is clear that the amount of slack or float time Fi available is given by Fi = Li – Ei which is the amount by which we can increase the time taken to complete activity i without increasing the overall project completion time. Hence, we can form the table below:

Activity	Li	Ei	Float Fi
A	0	0	0
B	10	3	7
C	3	3	0
D	5	3	2
E	16	10	6
F	10	10	0
G	18	18	0
H	29	29	0

Any activity with a float of zero is critical. Note here that, as a check, all float values should be ≥ 0.

Hence, the critical activities are A, C, F, G and H and the floats for the non-critical activities are given in the table above.

If activity F is delayed by 3 days, then as F is critical, the project completion time increases by exactly 3 days.

If activity E is delayed by 7 days, then as E has a float of 6 days, the project completion time is affected. The project completion time will increase by exactly (7–6) = 1 day to 36 days.

If activity G is finished 7 days early, then as G is a critical activity the overall project completion time will (potentially) be reduced. To see the effect of this change, we need to redo the calculation for the earliest times given above, but with a completion time for G of 4 days. The only change is in the calculation of EH and EI, and these now are:

$$EH = \max\ [EE + TE, EG + TG] = \max[10 + 13, 18 + 4] = 23$$

$$EI = EH + TH = 23 + 6 = 29$$

Hence, the overall project completion time falls to 29 days (a decrease of 6 days).

17.4.1 Network analysis–activity on node

Each node (circle) in the network diagram (Fig 17.11) represents an activity. Hence, nodes are labelled for activity identification with the completion time. Let us consider the following activity on node (AON) network.

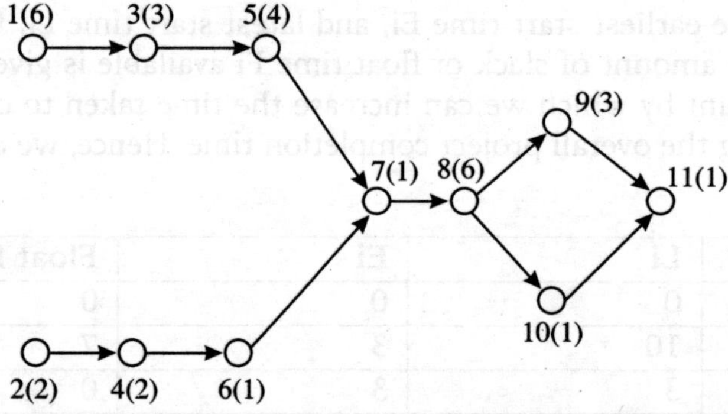

Figure 17.11 *Network diagram showing activity on node*

Here we have considered a node for each activity. With an arrow from activity node *i* to activity node *j*, we indicate the direction or the flow of the project. Observe that the project flows from the left to right. After we draw the network diagram, it is possible for us to analyse it using the algorithm. Wherever activities are not linked by any precedence relationships, it can be simultaneously done, which can facilitate the reduction of the project duration time.

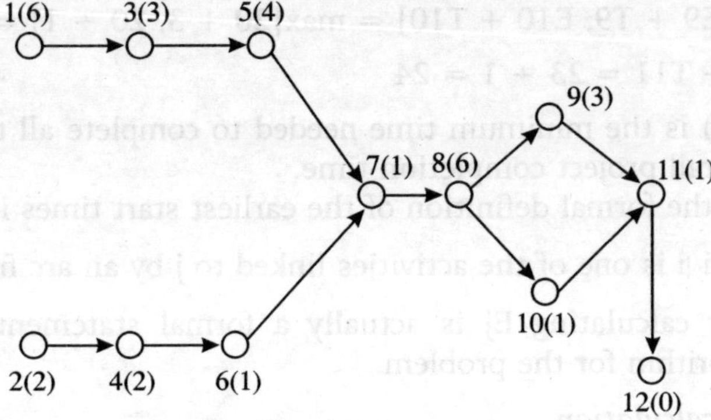

Figure 17.12 *Network diagram*

17.4.2 Network analysis - dynamic programming algorithm

Let us draw the previous network diagram (Fig. 17.12) introducing a dummy activity with the completion time of zero.

We first calculate, for each node (activity) in the network, the earliest start time to finish all the preceding activities.

Earliest start time calculation

Let Ei represent the earliest start time for activity i, such that all its preceding activities have been finished. We calculate the values of the Ei (i=1,2,...,12) by going forward, from left to right, in the network diagram..

To ease the notation, let Ti be the activity completion time associated with activity i (for example, T5 = 4). Then, the Ei are given by:

E1 = 0 (assuming we start at time zero)

E2 = 0 (assuming we start at time zero)

E3 = E1 + T1 = 0 + 6 = 6

E4 = E2 + T2 = 0 + 2 = 2

E5 = E3 + T3 = 6 + 3 = 9

E6 = E4 + T4 = 2 + 2 = 4

E7 = max[E5 + T5, E6 + T6] = max[9 + 4, 4 + 1] = 13

E8 = E7 + T7 = 13 + 1 = 14

E9 = E8 + T8 = 14 + 6 = 20

E10 = E8 + T8 = 14 + 6 = 20

$E11 = \max[E9 + T9, E10 + T10] = \max[20 + 3, 20 + 1] = 23$

$E12 = E11 + T11 = 23 + 1 = 24$

Hence, 24 (weeks) is the minimum time needed to complete all the activities; it is the minimum overall project completion time.

Note here that the formal definition of the earliest start times is given by:

$Ej = \max\ [Ei + Ti \mid i$ is one of the activities linked to j by an arc from i to j]

This equation for calculating Ej is actually a formal statement of the dynamic programming algorithm for the problem.

Latest start time calculation

Let Li represent the latest time we can start activity i and still complete the project in the minimum overall completion time. We calculate the values of the Li (i=1,2,...,12) by going backward, from right to left, in the network diagram. Hence:

$L12 = 24$

$L11 = L12 - T11 = 24 - 1 = 23$

$L10 = L11 - T10 = 23 - 1 = 22$

$L9 = L11 - T9 = 23 - 3 = 20$

$L8 = \min[L9 - T8, L10 - T8] = \min[20 - 6, 22 - 6] = 14$

$L7 = L8 - T7 = 14 - 1 = 13$

$L6 = L7 - T6 = 13 - 1 = 12$

$L5 = L7 - T5 = 13 - 4 = 9$

$L4 = L6 - T4 = 12 - 2 = 10$

$L3 = L5 - T3 = 9 - 3 = 6$

$L2 = L4 - T2 = 10 - 2 = 8$

$L1 = L3 - T1 = 6 - 6 = 0$

The formal definition of the latest start times is given by:

$Li = \min[Lj - Ti \mid j$ one of the activities linked to i by an arc from i to j]

Note that as a check that we have done both the earliest start times and latest start times calculations correctly we have:

all latest start times must be ≥ 0

at least one activity must have a latest start time of zero

17.4.3 Float

As we know the earliest start time Ei, and latest start time Li, for each activity i, it is clear that the amount of slack or float time Fi available is given by Fi = Li – Ei, which is the amount by which we can increase the time taken to complete activity i without changing (increasing) the overall project completion time. Hence, we can form the table below:

Activity	Li	Ei	Float Fi
1	0	0	0
2	8	0	8
3	6	6	0
4	10	2	8
5	9	9	0
6	12	4	8
7	13	13	0
8	14	14	0
9	20	20	0
10	22	20	2
11	23	23	0

Any activity with a float of zero is critical. Note here that, as a check, all float values should be ≥ 0 and that these float values are the same as those derived by the package. The float figures derived are known as total float. As in the above example, a "chain" of successive activities (in this case 2, 4 and 6) share the same float and this is common with total float.

17.4.4 Free and independent float

Two other varieties of float (for non-critical activities) are also conventionally distinguished:

1. **Free float:** The delay possible for an activity if all preceding activities start as early as possible while all subsequent activities start at their earliest time. An equivalent (and easier) definition is the delay possible in an activity if it starts at its earliest time and all subsequent activities start at their earliest time
2. **Independent float:** The delay possible for an activity if all preceding activities start as late as possible, while all subsequent activities start at their earliest time, where here by delay, we strictly mean "the increase in completion time".

The effect of the free float calculation is to "push" the total float associated with a chain of successive non-critical activities onto the last activity in the chain. The significance of an independent float is that it is associated solely with one activity and not with a chain of two or more activities.

With regard to calculating free and independent float, convenient formulae are: free float for activity i = min[earliest start time for j |j is an immediate successor of i] – earliest start time for i – completion time for i

independent float for activity i = min[earliest start time for j

|j an immediate successor of i] – max[latest finish time for j

|j an immediate predecessor of i] – completion time for i,

where independent float is taken to be zero, if this calculation returns a negative number

Recalling the table we calculated above (and adding latest finish = latest start + completion time, and earliest finish = earliest start + completion time) we have:

Activity	Latest start	Earliest start	Latest Finish	Earliest Finish	Completion Time
1	0	0	6	6	6
2	8	0	10	2	2
3	6	6	9	0	3
4	10	2	12	4	2
5	9	9	13	13	4
6	12	4	13	5	1
7	13	13	14	14	1
8	14	14	20	20	6
9	20	20	23	23	3
10	22	20	23	21	1
11	23	23	24	24	1

and recalling the network diagram (Fig. 17.13)

we have that free and independent float (for the non-critical activities) are:

Activity	Free Float	Independent Float
2	0	0
4	0	0
6	8	0
10	2	2

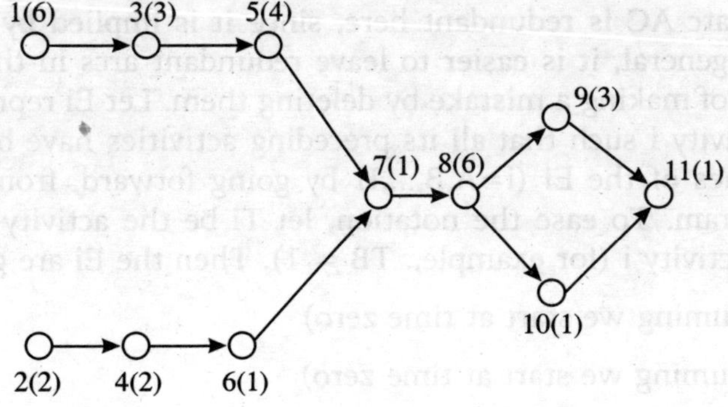

Figure 17.13 *Network diagram*

As observed before, free float pushes the total float associated with a chain of successive activities onto the last activity in the chain. Activity 10, as it is by itself and not in a chain of non-critical activities, has a free float of 2 (= its previously calculated total float), as well as an independent float of 2.

Network analysis example

The table below defines the activities within a small project.

Activity	Completion Time	Immediate predecessor activities
A	3	-
B	1	A
C	2	B,A
D	7	-
E	8	D,A
F	3	B
G	1	E,F
H	2	D

Draw the network diagram.

Calculate the minimum overall project completion time and identify which activities are critical.

What is the slack (float) time associated with each of the non-critical activities.

Solution

The network diagram (Fig 17.14) is shown overleaf. Note the introduction of a dummy activity 1 with duration of zero to represent the end of the project.

Note that the arc AC is redundant here, since it is implied by the arcs AB and BC. However, in general, it is easier to leave redundant arcs in the network rather than run the risk of making a mistake by deleting them. Let Ei represent the earliest start time for activity i such that all its preceding activities have been finished. We calculate the values of the Ei (i=A,B,...,I) by going forward, from left to right, in the network diagram. To ease the notation, let Ti be the activity completion time associated with activity i (for example,. TB = 1). Then the Ei are given by:

EA = 0 (assuming we start at time zero)

ED = 0 (assuming we start at time zero)

EB = EA + TA = 0 + 3 = 3

EH = ED + TD = 0 + 7 = 7

EC = max[EA + TA, EB + TB] = max[0 + 3, 3 + 1] = 4

EE = max[EA + TA, ED + TD] = max[0 + 3, 0 + 7] = 7

EF = EB + TB = 3+ 1 = 4

EG = max[EF + TF, EE + TE] = max[4 + 3, 7 + 8] = 15

EI = max[EC + TC, EG + TG, EH + TH] = max[4 + 2, 15 + 1, 7 + 2] = 16

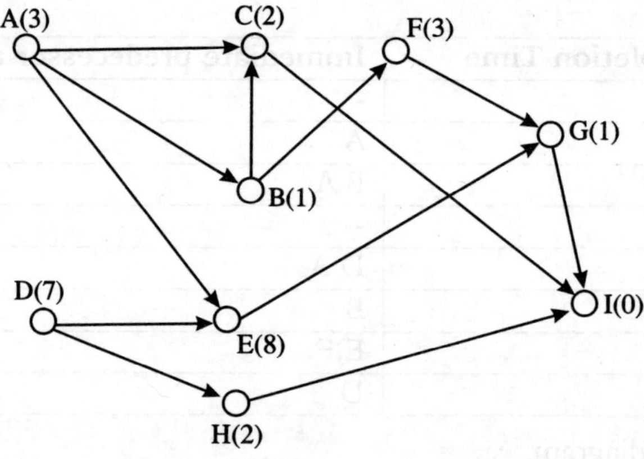

Figure 17.14 *Network diagram*

Hence, the minimum possible completion time for the entire project is 16 weeks. In other words, 16 (weeks) is the minimum time needed to complete all the activities. We now need to calculate the latest times for each activity. Let Li represent the latest start time we can start activity i and still complete the project in the minimum overall completion time. We calculate the values of the Li (i=A,B,...,I) by going backward, from right to left, in the network diagram. Hence:

LI = 16

LG= LI – TG = 16 – 1 = 15

LC = LI – TC = 16 – 2 = 14

LH = LI – TH = 16 – 2 = 14

LF = LG – TF = 15 – 3 = 12

LE = LG – TE = 15 – 8 = 7

LB = min[LC – TB, LF – TB] = min[14 – 1, 12 – 1] = 11

LA = min[LC – TA, LB – TA, LE – TA] = min[14 – 3, 11 – 3, 7 – 3] = 4

LD = min[LE – TD, LH – TD] = min[7 – 7, 14 – 7] = 0

Note that as a check all latest times are ≥, at least one activity has a latest start time value of zero.

As we know the earliest start time Ei, and latest start time Li, for each activity i, it is clear that the amount of slack or float time Fi available is given by Fi = Li – Ei which is the amount by which we can increase the time taken to complete activity i without changing (increasing) the overall project completion time. Hence, we can form the table below:

Activity	Li	Ei	Float Fi
A	4	0	4
B	11	3	8
C	14	4	10
D	0	0	0
E	7	7	0
F	12	4	8
G	15	15	0
H	14	7	7

Any activity with a float of zero is critical. Note here that, as a check, all float values should be ≥ 0.

Hence, the critical activities are D, E and G and the floats for the non-critical activities are given in the table above.

17.5 TRANSPORTATION AND ASSIGNMENT TECHNIQUES

Transportation and assignment techniques are special-purpose algorithms to solve different types of linear programming problems. North-west corner Rule, Vogel's approximation method, least cost entry method are some of the known techniques used in solving transportation and assignment problems. A specific allocation m+n–1 is used to solve the problems, where m=number of rows and n=number of columns.

In transportation problems, the initial allocation through the assignment technique is used. Let us assume a situation where the data constitute selling price, cost of production and shipping costs. To maximize or minimize, each data can be construed separately as a transportation problem, that is, maximize selling price, minimize cost of production and minimize transportation costs. When the selling price and the cost of production are uniform to each column and row, and the transportation costs is different, we can show that the solution obtained for the allocation of the transportation cost individually will also be the solution for the selling price as well as cost of production, taken independently or collectively, that is, selling price minus cost of production. This is because of the fact that application of the assignment technique in case of selling price minus cost of production results in a constant difference and ultimately will lead to zero in the case of each cell. When all the cells are zero, we can have any number of solutions. Transportation problems involve determination of how to transport goods optimally. Assignment problems are primarily concerned with assignment of people for the jobs.

Features of transportation problems

1. Aggregate supplies exceed aggregate demand; hence, each supply from the sources represents maximum supplies that can be distributed from the source.
2. In situations when aggregate supplies are less than the sum of the demands, destination-wise demand represents the maximum amount that can be received at a specific destination.
3. Each destination or receiving point, has both the minimum and maximum demand, hence, any amount between these two values can be received.
4. Source–destination combinations cannot be used for distributing or transporting units.
5. The objective is to maximize the total profit with the distribution of units rather than minimization of the total cost.

Keeping in view all the above features, we formulate and reformulate the problem to make it the right fit for a specific transportation problem.

Thus, Transportation and Assignment problems deal with assigning sources and jobs to destinations and machines. Suppose a company has *m* factories where it manufactures its product and *n* outlets from where the product is sold. Transporting the product from a factory to an outlet costs a certain amount of money which depends on several factors and varies for each choice of factory and outlet. The total amount of the product a particular factory makes is fixed, and so is the total amount a particular outlet can store. The problem is to decide how much of the product should be supplied from each factory to each outlet so that the total cost is at a minimum.

Let us consider an example.

Suppose a CTV assembler has three assembly centres in cities A, B and C and two major distribution centers in D and E, the monthly capacities of the three assembly centres are 1000, 1500 and 1200 CTVs. The monthly demands of the two distribution centers are 2300 and 1400 CTVs respectively. The transportation costs between the plants and the distribution centers can be represented as under:

Cost Table	**Dist. Centre D**	**Dist. Centre E**
Assembly Centre-A	80	215
Assembly Centre-B	100	108
Assembly Centre-C	102	68

Which assembly centre should supply how many CTVs to which outlet so that the total cost is at a minimum?

The problem can be formulated as an LP model:

Let xij be the amount of CTVs to be transported from source i to destination j. Then, the objective is to minimize the total cost which is $80 \times 11 + 215 \times 12 + 100 \times 21 + 108 \times 22 + 102 \times 31 + 68 \times 32$. The constraints are the ones imposed by the amount of CTVs to be transported from each Assembly Centre, and the availability of CTVs in the service centres.

The entire model is:

Minimize $z = 80 \times 11 + 215 \times 12 + 100 \times 21 + 108 \times 22 + 102 \times 31 + 68 \times 32$

subject to,

$$x11 + x12 = 1000$$

$$x21 + x22 = 1500$$

$$x31 + x32 = 1200$$

$$x11 + x21 + x31 = 2300$$

$$x12 + x22 + x32 = 1400$$

$x_{ij} \geq 0$ and integer, $i = 1, 2, 3, j = 1, 2.$

The problem can be solved using the simplex method.

Hence, the transportation problem is another important decisional issue, solved through linear programming. It involves maximization of profit through transportation from the sources or service centres to destinations. Apart from the transportation problems, we also optimize the quantity to be transported from different service centres or sources of a company. Thus, the main issues involved in transportation are decisions on the transportation of commodities from different sources (as a company may have multiple service centres, or warehouses, or factories) to each destination (the customers' places), keeping profit maximization in mind.

For example, *Unilever* has multiple production facilities and warehouses throughout the country. It also caters to market requirements across the country. By making use of transportation solutions, *Unilever* can optimize the cost and the finished inventory holding. This can be done by formulating the transportation problem in terms of linear programming. The following mathematical formulation can clarify our understanding.

For *Unilever*, let us consider the m-plant locations (origins) as $O_1, O_2, \ldots, O_m$
The company has n-retail shops (destination) as $D_1, D_2, \ldots.., D_n$ respectively.
Let $a_i \geq 0, i = 1, 2, \ldots.m$, be the amount available at the ith plant O_i.
Let the amount required at the jth shop D_j be $b_j \geq 0, j = 1, 2, \ldots.n$.
The cost of transporting one unit of *Unilever*'s product from ith origin to *jth* destination be $C_{ij}, i = 1, 2, \ldots.m, j = 1, 2, \ldots.n$. I
$fx_{ij} \geq 0$ be the amount of products to be transported from i^{th} origin to *jth* destination, then the problem is to determine x_{ij} so as to minimize
Subject to the constraint

$$\sum_{j=1}^{n} x_{ij} \sum_{i=1}^{n} x_{ij} \sum_{j=1}^{n} x_{ij} = a_i, i = 1, 2, ...m$$

$$\sum_{i=1}^{m} x_{ij} = b_j, j = 1, 2, ...n.$$

and $x_{ij} \geq 0$, for all *i* and *j*.

For a feasible solution to the transportation problem, a necessary and sufficient condition is that:

$$\sum_{i=1}^{m} a_i = \sum_{j=1}^{n} b_j$$

The set of constraints are;

$$\sum_{i=1}^{m} x_{ij} = b_j \text{ and } \sum_{j=1}^{n} x_{ij} = a_i$$

Here, we represent $m + n$ equations in mn non-negative variables, and each variable xij appears in exactly two constraints, one is associated with the origin and the other is associated with the destination. When we put this in the matrix form (Fig 17.15), the elements of A are either 0 or 1.

For a feasible solution to a transportation problem, we find an initial basic feasible solution as under:

1. The North-West corner rule
2. Vogel's Approximation method.

17.5.1 The North-West Corner Rule

We call it the North-West Corner Rule, as we start the assignment in the cell which occupies the upper left-hand (north-west) corner of the transportation table. The minimum feasible amount is allocated, i.e., $x_{11} = min(a_1, b_1)$.

D_1	D_2	. . .		D_n	supply
O_1	C_2	C_{12}	. . .	C_{1n}	a_1
O_2 O_m	C_{21} C_{m1}	C_{22} C_{m2}	. . . . . .	C_{2n} C_{mn}	a_1 a_m

Figure 17.15 *The Transportation Matrix*

	D_1	D_2	D_3	D_4	Availability
O_1	6	4	1	5	14
O_2	8	9	2	7	16
O_3	4	3	6	2	5
Requirement	6	10	15	4	

Solution to the above problem is

6 6	8 4	1	5
8	2 9	14 2	7
2 4	3	1 6	2

Figure 17.16 *North-West corner rule*

When $b_1 > a_1$, the capacity of origin O_1 is exhausted even though the requirement at D_1 is not satisfied. Hence, we move down to the second row, and make the second allocation:

$x_{21} = min(a_2, b_1 - x_{11})$ in the cell (2,1).

If $a_1 > b_1$, allocate $x_{12} = min(a_1 - x_{11}, b_2)$ in the cell (1,2).

Likewise, we continue this until all the requirements and supplies are satisfied.

Example

Let us determine an initial basic feasible solution to the following transportation problem using the North-West corner rule (Fig 17.16):

Now we have satisfied all the requirements; hence, we can get the initial basic feasible solution. The total cost of transportation with such an allocation is:

$$Z = 6 * 6 + 4 * 8 + 2 * 9 + 14 * 2 + 1 * 6 + 4 * 2 = \text{Rs.}128.$$

17.5.2 Vogel's Approximation Method (VAM)

We use the following steps to solve transportation problem using this type of solution.

1. For every row of the transportation table, we identify the smallest and the next to smallest costs. We then determine the row-wise difference between them. Next, we display them in respective rows alongside the transportation table in parenthesis. Likewise, we also compute the differences for each column.
2. We then identify the row or column with the largest difference among all the rows and columns. When a tie occurs, we use any arbitrary tie-breaking choice. The greatest difference corresponds to i^{th} row and the minimum cost is C_{ij}. Allocate a maximum feasible amount

   $x_{ij} = min(a_i, b_j)$ in the $(i, j)^{th}$ cell, and cross off the ith row or j^{th} column.
3. Continue the re-computation of the column and row differences for the reduced transportation table and go to step 2. Repeat the procedure until all the requirements are satisfied.

With this, we get the initial basic feasible solution, which is close to the optimum solution.

Problem

Obtain an initial basic feasible solution to the following transportation problem using Vogel's approximation method (Fig. 17.17)

	I	II	III	IV	
A	5	1	3	3	34
B	3	3	5	4	15
C	6	4	4	3	12
D	4	–1	4	2	19
	21	25	17	17	

Figure 17.17 *Vogel's approximation method*

Assignment Problem

Assignment problems can also be used when we have n-jobs with n-machines in a plant. A job $i (i = 1, 2, \ldots n)$ when processed by machine $j (j = 1, 2, \ldots n)$ is assumed to incur a cost c_{ij}. The job assignment is done in such a way that each job can associate with one machine and can minimize the overall costs.

Mathematical formulation of Assignment Problems

We can define;

$x_{ij} = 0$, if the ith job not assigned to jth machine.

= 1, if the ith job is assigned to jth machine.

We can assign one job to each machine,

$$\sum_{i=1}^{n} x_{ij} = 1, \text{ and } \sum_{j=1}^{n} x_{ij} = 1$$

The total assignment cost is given by

$$z = \sum_{j=1}^{n} \sum_{i=1}^{n} c_{ij} x_{ij}$$

Transportation and Assignment Problems - Examples

Assign three jobs on three machines based on the following cost matrix. :

Jobs	Machines		
	M1	M2	M3
J1	Rs. 14	Rs.12	Rs.16
J2	Rs.11	Rs.17	Rs.21
J3	Rs.20	Rs. 8	Rs. 7

Solution

Step 1:

Subtract minimum entry in each column from all the entries on that column and develop a job-opportunity–cost matrix.

Step 2:

Subtract the minimum entry in each row of job-opportunity–cost matrix from all the entries of that row. This is a total opportunity cost matrix:

		Machine		
		M1	M2	M3
Jobs	J1	0	1	6
	J2	0	9	14
	J3	9	0	0

Figure 17.18 *Total opportunity cost matrix*

Step 3 - Check for Optimality

Draw minimum number of horizontal and vertical lines to cover all zeros. This can be done in 2 lines, which is one less than the number of rows (which is 3). Thus, the solution is not yet final. Hence, go to step 4.

Step 4:

From the uncovered entries, the minimum is 1. Thus, subtract 1 from all entries, which are uncovered. Add one at junction of lines, i.e., at J3-M1. We get the following matrix now (Fig 17.20), as the received opportunity cost matrix.

Now, go to step 3 to check the optimality. We can cover all zeros of the above matrix by at least three lines (which is also equal to the number of rows). Hence, the solution above may be used for optimal assignment.

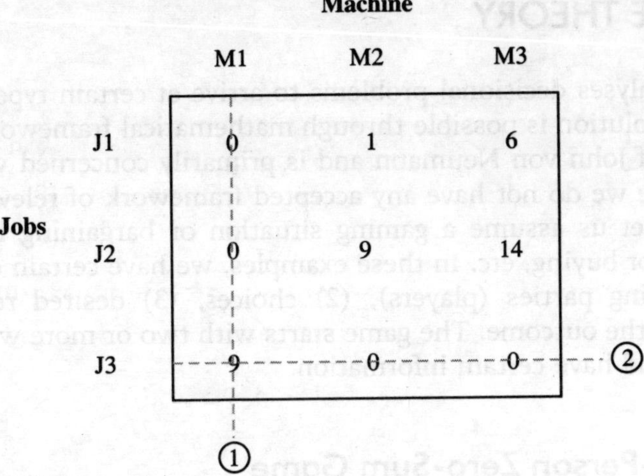

Figure 17.19 *Check for optimality*

Machine

Jobs	M1	M2	M3
J1	0	0	5
J2	0	9	14
J3	10	0	0

Figure 17.20 *Revised total opportunity cost matrix*

Step 5: Assignment Scheme

Refer to the revised total opportunity cost matrix. Row J2 has only one zero at M1 column. Hence, assign J2 to M1. Remove row J2 and column M1.

Column M3 of the remainder matrix has one zero at J3 row. Assign J3 to M3. The last assignment is the remaining job J1 to M2. Thus, the final assignment is:

Job	Machine	Cost
J1	M2	Rs.12
J2	M1	Rs.11
J3	M3	Rs. 7

Total Cost Rs.30

17.6 GAME THEORY

Game theory analyses decisional problems to arrive at certain types of conclusions. A game theory solution is possible through mathematical frameworks. Game theory is the creation of John von Neumann and is primarily concerned with area–conflict situations, where we do not have any accepted framework of relevant evidence and interpretation. Let us assume a gaming situation or bargaining like chess, which involves selling or buying, etc. In these examples, we have certain common features like (1) conflicting parties (players), (2) choices, (3) desired results, results of choices, and (6) the outcome. The game starts with two or more who have a certain set of choices, and have certain information.

17.6.1 Two-Person Zero-Sum Game

In a two-person zero-sum game, two players (Player A and Player B) play, and one player's loss equals the other player's gain (zero-sum). The outcome of the game is called the payoff. A positive payoff indicates a win for Player A, a negative payoff indicates a win for Player B, and zero indicates a draw.

When Player A has m moves to choose from and Player B has n, we can represent the game using a payoff matrix, the m × n matrix showing the payoff resulting from each possible pair of choices of moves. We call player A the row player, and player B the column player.

17.6.2 Game Theory – Mathematical Solution

Example

Suppose you want to buy an old refrigerator and you have also a seller. Your offer of Rs. 3000 for the old refrigerator can only be deemed fit by the seller, if its value is less than Rs. 3000 to him. You feel that all values between Rs. 1000 and Rs. 3000 are equally likely, and the refrigerator you want to buy can have an expected value of Rs. 2000. When you increase the average value by a third, the refrigerator will be worth Rs. $2,667[(4/3) \times Rs.2000]$. Hence, your offer of Rs. 3000 to close the deal will cause you to lose in value. With your offer of Rs. 1000/-, the expected value of the refrigerator will be (1000 + O) / 2 (considering o is the amount offered). The refrigerator may be worth an additional 1/3, when you can successfully repair it. This will result in an increase of the expected value that you can win as:

$$(4/3) \times (1000 + O)/2 = (2/3) \times (1000 + O)$$

It is always important to remember, that to win in this deal, your offer (o) should always be less than the expected value.

$(2/3) \times (1000 + 0) > O$

$= (2/3)1000 > (1/3)O = 2000 > O$

Thus, if your offer is above 2000, it will lead to an expected loss, with less than Rs. 2000 offer, you can gain. When you want to gain through this deal, you need to revise your bid.

SUMMARY

1. Production and operations managers play a crucial role in managing the most critical functions of any organization.
2. Understanding the processes and techniques are essential to manage these functions, at times, production and operations managers also need to carry out research to understand a particular process, situation or to simply state a problem. So, it is essential for managers to understand the tools and techniques of research.
3. In this chapter, we have introduced certain quantitative tools, which can be used for carrying out production and operations management research.

KEY WORDS

Evaluative research This research assesses some aspects of the operations function by analysing the effectiveness of a given problem, like the effect of incentives on worker productivity, technology transfer and a corresponding change in the process, total productive maintenance and workers' level of commitment, etc

Action research In this type of research, action (that is, the solution of a problem) is both an outcome and a part of the research process. Its main purpose is to improve the stock of knowledge by tackling a problem, which has relevance to theory.

Linear programming It is a mathematical technique to select an optimum plan. It helps in getting the best solution to a decisional problem with many interactive variables.

Free float It indicates the delay possible for an activity if all preceding activities start as early as possible, while all subsequent activities start at their earliest time.

Independent float It indicates the delay possible for an activity if all preceding activities start as late as possible, while all subsequent activities start at their earliest time.

The North-West Corner Rule It is called the North-West Corner Rule, as we start the assignment in the cell which occupies the upper left-hand (north-west) corner of the transportation table.

GENERAL REVIEW QUESTIONS

1. Explain the concept of Production and Operations Management Research. Why is it important for production and operations managers?
2. What is the significance of models in production and operations management research?
3. Explain how linear programming helps in POM research. What are the limitations of linear programming?
4. Network and transportation are two important tools for POM research! Do you agree with this statement? Justify your answer.
5. Explain the significance of game theory in POM research
6. Short notes
   (a) Applied research
   (b) Simplex Method
   (c) Activity on node
   (d) Dynamic programming algorithm
   (e) Two-Person Zero-Sum Game

CRITICAL REVIEW QUESTIONS

1. Your company would like to introduce supply chain management systems. Suggest the possible line of actions, duly stating your company's hypothetical activities, customers, market spread, vendors, etc.
2. You always observe your competitors reactions to your new product development initiatives prevents you from creating a niche in the market. As a production and operations manager suggest an action plan to stop such damages.

ADDITIONAL REFERENCES

1. Anderson, David R., Dennis J. Sweeney, and Thomas A. Williams. 2000. *An Introduction to Management Science: Quantitative Approaches to Decision Making*, 9th ed. Cincinnati, OH: South-Western College Publishing,
2. Banks J., Carson II J., and Nelson B. 1995. *Discrete-Event System Simulation*. Prentice-Hall,
3. Bhattacharyya, Dipak Kumar. 2002. *Effective Human Resource Planning Using Quantitative Tools – A Suggestive Approach*. Gurgaon: Vision, MDI , January – June, PP. 33–40.
4. Bhattacharyya, D.K. 2007. *Human Resource Management Research*. New Delhi: Oxford University Press.
5. Camm, Jeffrey D., and James R. Evans. 2000. *Management Science and Decision Technology*. Cincinnati, OH: South-Western College Publishing,
6. Gibbons, M. et al.1994. *The New Production of Knowledge*. London: Sage.

7. Huff, A. S. 2000. Changes in Organizational Knowledge Production. *Academy of Management Review* 25(2) pp. 288–293.
8. Hillier, F.S. and Liberman, G.J. 2005. *Introduction to Operations Research*. New York, NY: McGraw-Hill Higher Education.
9. Johnson, P. and Duberley, J. 2000. *Understanding Management Research: an introduction to epistemology*. London: Sage.
10. Murty, K.G. 1995. *Operations Research Deterministic Optimization Models*. Englewood Cliffs, NJ: Prentice Hall.
11. Pannell, David J. 1996. *Introduction to Practical Linear Programming*. New York: John Wiley & Sons,
12. Rardin, R.L., 1998. *Optimization in Operations Research*. Englewood Cliffs: Prentice Hall,
13. Taha, H.A., 2002. *Operations Research: An Introduction*. Englewood Cliffs: Prentice Hall.
14. Voss, C., Tsikriktsis, N. and Frohlich, M., 2002. Case research in operations management. *Inter. J. of Operations and Production Management*, 22, 2, 195–219,
15. Ward, D., Bechet, T.P. and Tripp, R. eds. 1994. *Human resource forecasting and modelling*. New York: The Human Resources Planning Society.

CASE STUDY

Market Driven Operations Management

Most international car manufacturers were apprehensive about China's emergence as a powerhouse in the global automobile market. To understand the direction of Chinese progress in the automobile arena, many Indian automobile companies started thinking positive, based on their research observations. A research team formed by an Indian automobile major found that the Chinese automotive businesses, in the long-term, would have to depend on Indian automobile companies for sourcing their assemblies. Moreover, India would have to lend support in automobile design, and in matching the taste and preferences of Asian countries. Armed with such findings, the automobile majors of India, as a part of their backward integration programme acquired a series of small-scale automobile spare manufacturers. These small scale units were later invested with the facility of modular production, resulting in the production of need-specific automobile modules. This approach, it is believed, will help to position products in the global market, without much of an adverse effect from developments in China.

Discussion Question

As a Production and operations manager, develop your own research guidelines for such research.

CHAPTER 18
International Production and Operations Management

LEARNING OBJECTIVES

After reading this chapter, you will be able to understand:

- The Meaning and Context of International POM
- Globalization and its Impact on International POM
- Advantages and Disadvantages of International POM
- Strategic Issues in International POM
- Network Strategy
- Organizational Practices in International POM

Opening Vignette

Ford's Production Systems

Henry Ford established *Ford Motors* in 1903, with an initial focus on craft manufacturing systems, that is, a job shop production system to facilitate the customization of cars according to the choice of the customers. While the chassis and engine remained the same, the designs were flexible, depending on the customer's choice and preferences. Customizing cars did not give cost efficiency to *Ford*, moreover, it restricted the market to certain privileged customers (niche market), who could afford an increased price. In 1908, *Ford* for the first time introduced a mass-production system, standardizing parts and gauging systems. The fitter-assemblers at *Ford*, who were earlier performing multiple tasks, were then required to focus on specific tasks, using standardized parts and gauges. Mass production systems gradually ensured uniformity in quality and features, and at the same time, resulted in cost effectiveness.

In 1913, *Ford* could introduce assembly line manufacturing, for the first time in the world, in automobile manufacturing. Since then, the company has continued its efforts to innovate its manufacturing processes, introducing 3-D tools like computer-aided design (CAD), computer-aided manufacturing (CAM), etc. From the mid-1990s onwards *Ford* focussed on greater flexibility in manufacturing through reengineering, which we know as the *Ford* Production Systems (FPS). Although FPS is, by and large, modelled on the *Toyota* Production Systems (TPS), FPS is unique in terms of its lean management practices. The uniqueness of FPS lies in its greater focus on the human aspects, in terms of work groups, teams, empowerment and decentralized decision making. With FPS, *Ford* gained in terms of increased productivity and improved financial results across all its plants, dispersed throughout the world.

18.1 INTRODUCTION

In a globalized economy, the pace of change is now exerting an influence on the production and operations management function. The advancement of technology, falling trade barriers, emergence of 'new economy' countries, geographical dispersion of customers and suppliers, have together, changed the process of production and services. Such internationalization of the production and operations function, requires companies to train and develop their managers so that they can understand the realities of developing their operations on a global scale. Production and operations management is primarily concerned with the efficient and effective process of manufacturing and servicing to support organizational strategic goals. These apart, operations management is also concerned with the design and operations of systems; this encompasses planning, scheduling and controlling the activities that transform inputs (raw materials and labour) into outputs (finished goods and services). All these are also relevant for international production and operations management functions.

In a globalized era, operations management needs to be considered from an international perspective, as it involves a comparison of production and operations in various countries. Some of the variables that affect international production and operations management functions are economic, cultural, legal or political. Some of the issues that deserve attention are the dimensions of the changes in the new economy and its effect on the production and operations management functions.

International production and operations management requires network-based manufacturing. Such network-based models of business are not new in the corporate world. Companies like *Avon* and *Tupperware* have an expertise in network-based marketing. *Toyota Motors* of Japan maintains a well-knit network of suppliers across the world to get the most cost-effective and quality items for assembling their finest cars. Network-based business, therefore, now generates a competitive advantage equally in production, supply chain and also in services.

With state-of-the-art information and telecommunications technology, companies now design and develop products and processes that can match the quality expectations of their customers, and are also affordable. Technology-intensive organizations like *AT&T* and *IBM* could build their business empires across the globe, because of their sincere efforts in building capabilities to leverage global expertise.

Like domestic production and operations management, international production and operations management requires the same activities, but the relative importance assigned by companies to such activities differs from organization to organization.

Reviewing the literature, it is evident that the following activities are critical determinants for companies to expand their production and operations across the border

Performance evaluation and productivity	26%
Product development and process selection	23%
Work organization and reward systems	23%
Production scheduling	20%
Operations strategy and competitiveness	20%
Inventory management	17%
Location	17%
Ethics and the environment	17%

On the other hand, just-in-time (6%), lean production (6%), theory of constraints (6%), maintenance and reliability (6%), and project management (6%) received the least priority for companies' cross-border operations.

Some of the specific areas, related to the factors mentioned above, are based on the practices of the organization, and can be explained as follows:

1. Under 'Performance evaluation and productivity', companies try to gain through cross-border operations; specific methods to evaluate performance effectiveness, particularly in service operations; mechanism to trade-off between profit and human values, etc.
2. Under 'Product development and process selection', companies try to gain through the process of co-designing, technology-based product development, knowledge management practices, process of developing virtual service networks, introduction of modular system supply networks, innovation and creativity, etc.
3. In production scheduling, companies try to emulate modular production systems. In operations strategy and competitiveness, companies make an effort to learn the process of network building, alignment of markets with operations and services, the process of evaluation of strategic impact on production and operations, reliability and flexibility in production and operations, etc.
4. In inventory management, companies emulate best practice models and supply chains. Finally, in ethics and the environment, companies learn about compliance issues, its relationship with technologies, work ethics issues, and the process of building ethical values in production and operations management functions.

Although it does not figure in global studies as a significant factor, international production and operations management functions benefit companies in supply chain management in terms of

1. RFID technology
2. collaborative planning
3. network building
4. cross cultural issues
5. 'make-or-buy' decisions
6. reliability and risk factors in virtual supply chains
7. process of building value chains, etc.

Similarly, global producion and operations facilitate process management through tele-work and effective demand forecasting (for an increase in the market spread). Global exposure to production and operations, developing knowledge and intellectual capital, gradually become the most important competitive advantage for the company. Expansion of service networks not only helps in increasing market spread, but helps in real-time customer services.

To understand international POM, we need to understand the issues pertaining to the internationalization of POM functions which prima facie indicate an international network of manufacturing facilities of the companies, their vendors, markets, supply chain, human resources, technology and information. Companies like *BMW, McDonalds, Benetton,* etc. have extensively internationalized their operations. While for *BMW,* the efficiency in production allocation between multi-locational plants is the ultimate determinant of success of international POM, for *McDonalds,* it depends on sustaining global standards, irrespective of the location of their outlets. On the other hand, *Benetton*'s success in maintaining their operations in more than 120 countries depends on efficient supply chain and logistics management. *Ford Motors* strategizes their international POM, locating their technology development centres across the world to support their manufacturing processes.

Other factors for international POM are

- country-specific exchange rates
- tariffs
- resource availability
- state of the economy
- opportunity to learn and grow
- infrastructural support
- laws and regulations and
- culture.

To address these issues, companies prepare country-specific benchmark indices, and then take decisions on internationalization. India has recently allowed 100% foreign direct investment (FDI) in a number of production activities. One such area is pharmaceutical research. Obviously, this has prompted many global pharmaceutical companies to base their research and development wing in India, due to the availability of competent employees, at a relatively cheaper cost.

18.1.1 Need and Importance of International POM

Globalization has increased the spate of competition on the one hand, and the spread of market opportunities across the border, on the other. Many companies, in order to increase their market share beyond their country of origin, try to be more proximate, basing their production and manufacturing facilities close to the market. Many Indian companies like *Dabur, Asian Paints, Videocon,* etc. have production facilities in multiple locations across the world. For *Asian Paints,* apart from new market opportunities, manufacturing sites are based abroad primarily to save on logistics costs, and for maintaining the quality of paints. For *Dabur,* it is to gain a market advantage. For *Videocon,* it is for better forward and backward linkages.

International POM requires managers and executives not only to understand country-specific business needs, but also the culture and social systems, without balancing which they cannot survive.

18.2 IMPACT OF GLOBALIZATION

Globalization has played a crucial role in the internationalization of the production and operations management function. Globalization has changed business practices, and so we interpret globalization as a process. The ramifications of globalization can be understood in terms of expansion of international trade, cross-border labour migration, flow of investments, cross-cultural impact, restructuring of business processes, increased spate of technology transfer and so on. Obviously, globalization has necessitated the internationalization of production and operations management functions as well. The free flow of goods and people from one country to another, and increased network development, has enabled companies to gain competitive strength through cross-border collaboration and partnership. Such internationalization of POM has become a necessity in the post-globalization era, because of the complexities of technology and the process of manufacturing and services, and the ever-changing expectations of customers in terms of quality and price competitiveness.

Thus, the cascading effect of globalization even transcends the task or the operational environment of business organizations. Changes in the operational environment not only require focus on new products or service development, but also on skill and competency sets, attitudes, values and culture of people. Such changes are primarily attributable to the shift in expectations of customers and the behaviour of competitors.

In India also, globalization has made it necessary for the government to bring in many institutional changes to encourage Indian organizations to compete globally.

Such institutional changes encourage foreign investments, lead to the removal of trade restrictions, etc. Although many Indian organizations (which are reluctant to change) are now exposed to intense completion, many more benefit in terms of a level playing field. Thus, restructuring of the production process, based on technological dynamism in an organization, has become imperative.

Economic restructuring at the macro-level has an inevitable impact on the production process in an organization at the micro-level. Restructuring of a production process, as a natural consequence of economic restructuring, necessitates restructuring of manpower in an organization.

18.3 ADVANTAGES AND DISADVANTAGES OF THE INTERNATIONALIZATION OF POM

Some of the advantages of the internationalization of POM are:

1. With more investment, companies can generate new employment, create new production facilities and can bring about positive changes in the economy.
2. By setting up manufacturing facilities abroad, companies can help the country to improve its balance of payments; in import substitution and in export promotion.
3. With the transfer of technology and consequent changes in the process, the efficiency and effectiveness of the factors of production increase, which can benefit the country as a whole.
4. It helps in generating revenue, both for the company and for the government (in terms of tax pay-outs).
5. It saves precious foreign exchange.

Internationalization of POM functions also has certain disadvantages:

- Political and economic uncertainty: This can even lead to the withdrawal of business, which may create an imbalance in the host country's economy.
- Control: Often, companies can exert control over the host country's government, both economically and politically, which may be detrimental to the interest of the nation as a whole.
- Transfer Pricing: By lowering the internal price structure, companies can reduce their profits, and in the process, can deprive the host country of their legitimate tax pay-outs.
- Environmental imbalance: At times, companies can create environmental imbalances by extracting natural resources, and polluting the environment of the host countries.
- Killing domestic producers: Companies which compete with local firms can substantially weaken the competitive strength of the local organizations.

18.4 INTERNATIONAL POM STRATEGY

Companies, while taking decisions on the globalization of their production and operations functions, have to consider certain strategic intents, most important among which is competitiveness. The strategic dimension of manufacturing activities was first discussed by Skinner (1969; 1974) of Harvard University. International production and operations strategy, at the outset, focusses on designing and managing networks. Such networks not only help to churn out tangible products, but also abstract services. It can be called offering the best package to the customers.

Apart from the conventional 'top-down' approach of strategy formulation, in international POM, strategy can also be framed using a 'bottom–up' approach. Following this approach, companies adopt a resource-based strategy to leverage knowledge-intensive assets for better economy of operations. Conventionally, we adopt POM strategy for making a trade-off between the cost and the benefit. International POM strategy emphasizes the learning aspect, like the concept of dynamic capabilities. Similarly, in contrast to conventional POM strategy, international POM strategy emphasizes the possibility of cooperation with competitors. By cooperating with competitors, companies can protect their market share. Such cooperation is often in the form of 'anti-poaching' agreements between IT majors to prevent job hopping, or a strategic collaboration, like the one between *IBM* and *PWC*, to compete in an exclusive market.

International POM strategy even emphasizes mutual information-sharing, which increases the agility of companies in responding to change. A similar strategic focus is seen in product development and process selection to offer a value package to customers; building up supply chain capabilities, quality management, inclusive decision making, production planning and scheduling, and project management.

Some of the important strategic roles of production and operations managers in a globalized economy can be drawn after Mark Davis, Nicolas Aquilano and Richard Chase (1999). Such roles can be listed as follows:

- To reduce the cycle time for the development and manufacture of new goods and services.
- To achieve and sustain world class quality, duly enforcing cost control.
- To integrate new technologies and control systems with current processes.
- To source, train and retain talented workers, employees and managers.
- To effectively coordinate work with other business functions to accomplish the goals of the organization.
- To integrate multi-locational production and operations activities.
- To develop vendors and a customer base.
- To partner with other organizations through strategic alliances.

The internationalization of production and operations management functions, therefore, require companies to move beyond traditional stand-alone tasks and processes, to elevate it and invest it with the strategic drive necessary to achieve business goals and objectives.

Globalization at *IKEA*

IKEA is a Swedish furniture manufacturer with globalized operations. This goes against our conventional beliefs that furniture, due to its bulkiness and high cost of transportation, cannot be produced and marketed across the world. The uniqueness of *IKEA*'s internationalization of production and operations primarily rests on their business practice of supplying furniture in an unassembled condition. This facilitates easy shipment of items, optimizing the cost of transportation. What is more interesting is that *IKEA* has reduced its costs further by integrating customers into the value chain! Using *IKEA*'s illustrative guidelines, customers can assemble their own furniture. Although such a move is praiseworthy from a strategic perspective, in some markets (like in the USA), *IKEA* is facing the brunt of competition, as customers now prefer customized furniture. Many attribute this to *IKEA*'s culture, with its emphasis on frugality which runs counter to the USA's culture of extravagance.

Strategic international production and operations management function, therefore, provides both competitive and comparative advantages to the organization. Competitive advantages are reaped by companies leveraging the global network to facilitate production of cost-effective quality goods and services on a sustained basis. Comparative advantages are gained in terms of factor endowments (land, labour, resources, etc.). As per the theory of comparative advantage, factor endowments suggest producing those goods, for which the required factors are available in abundance.

Another example is *Philips,* which pursues a multi-domestic strategy to promote innovation. This helps the company achieve cost efficiency and quality. *Matsushita,* the Japanese company followed a global strategy through their global distribution network. *Matsushita* with its strong global distribution network, successfully practices international POM. *Whirlpool*'s mass customization strategy, on the other hand, provides cost competitiveness through economies of scale.

18.5 NETWORK STRATEGY OF INTERNATIONAL POM

The global operations of MNCs are increasing in complexity. Basing production facilities in one country and then selling the products globally is no longer the only option that can ensure cost competitiveness and quality. This argument is even valid for low technology items. Producing a remote-controlled toy car in China is no longer a cost-effective and quality conscious option. At best, China can now be the site for final assembly. The components for the car may come from different countries, depending on country-specific specialized skills and economic advantage. For example, Malaysia is now known for specializing in the production of the plastic body for these toy cars, while Taiwan is known for its computer chips. Without such quality inputs, a remote-controlled toy car made in China cannot compete globally, in terms of price and quality. Thus, it is important to decide on country-specific production activity, depending on the expertise and the economy of advantage.

Thus, managing an international production network requires strategic decisions on the global spread of production facilities, outsourcing and supply chain management. Individual companies can gain a competitive advantage through effective management of their global production network. Strategic decisions on the global network of production facilities are primarily based on network theory pioneered by Ghosal and Bartlett (1990), evolutionary theory (Zander and Kogut, 1993), learning organization and knowledge management (Grantt, 1996). All these theoretical connotations have established that the global production decisions of a multinational organization are a web of inter- and intra-organizational relationships. MNCs can greatly benefit from the transfer of resources and the sharing of knowledge and competencies, rather than remaining in the cobweb of their individual capabilities. The spread of manufacturing networks (Shi and Gregory, 1998) has been further accentuated due to the advancement of information and communication technologies. It has now become less difficult to mutually leverage the capabilities of one organization by another, irrespective of their country of operation.

To build global production networks, companies can adopt either the 'footloose' or the 'deep roots' models. Those who pursue a 'footloose' model; always look for a better site for moving their production facilities, regardless of whether it is within or outside their country of origin. Those who pursue the 'deep roots' model, believe in long term commitment in developing resources and capabilities in their product sites, and remain dedicated to the same; these companies usually do not like to spread their manufacturing facilities globally. Both models have advantages and disadvantages. A company with a high degree of agility can pursue a 'footloose' network strategy. But obviously, uncertainty and volatility make such decisions more risk-prone. On the other hand, companies that prefer stability develop unique production facilities, following the 'deep roots' strategy. Characteristically, the first category of companies always prefers to leverage the capabilities or production facilities of others, focussing on design and marketing. The second category, on the other hand, always believes in leveraging its own manufacturing and distribution capabilities.

In many cases, we find companies shifting between these models, primarily to gain incremental benefits. Such decisions may or may not benefit the company. We can understand such decisional dichotomy from the strategies of two multinationals with regard to their global operations. For example, *Phillips*, the Dutch electronics major globally hived off a third of its factories (at present it has 150 plants). *Samsung*, on the other hand, continues to build factories across the world to strengthen its presence in the global market. Both models, therefore, can be successful or otherwise. *IKEA* has succeeded with the footloose model and *Intel* with the deep roots model.

Footloose Strategy at *IKEA*

IKEA, the Swedish furniture manufacturer maintains possibly the largest network of 1300 suppliers in 53 countries. It has a product range of almost 9500. With its philosophy of simplicity, *IKEA* always pursues a strategy of lower prices. The company always looks for lower cost suppliers with matching capabilities. Vendor selection and businesses with the vendors are established through a trial-and-error process. Europe and Asia are the primary regions for *IKEA*'s vendor selection. Constant addition of new suppliers, while sustaining the relationships with the present ones, helps *IKEA* cope with market volatility due to political and economic upheavals. *IKEA*'s vendors, therefore, are *IKEA*'s extended manufacturing hubs. Each vendor supplies particular modules and makes available the supplies in separate boxes straight to *IKEA*'s customers, who assemble these parts to get the complete furniture. While this ensures cost effectiveness, *IKEA* ensures vendors' quality through a stringent quality monitoring system. *IKEA* is a typical illustration of a company with a 'footloose' manufacturing strategy.

In contrast to *IKEA's* footloose strategy of manufacturing, *Intel* pursues a deep roots manufacturing strategy.

Deep rooted Strategy at *Intel*

Experts at *Intel*'s in-house team were aware from the beginning that the requirement of components would vary over the years, and the cost of manufacturing would double every four years. Faced with such a situation, any company would like to pursue a footloose strategy, rather than investing in manufacturing. However, *Intel* pursued the deep rooted strategy of manufacturing, building capabilities at its existing factories through investment in plant and machinery and by adopting a value-added strategy. *Intel*'s strategy is to retrofit old plants, rather than closing them down. Today, *Intel* maintains a network of 15 manufacturing hubs across the world.

Footloose manufacturing network is often criticized as an aphorism. Without raising the internal production capabilities, many companies now go in for contract manufacturing to fill the present gap in production capacity. In fact, this is also a typical footloose manufacturing strategy. The primary motive behind such a strategy is attributable to reduced cost of production, lowering of investment in manufacturing, and improving the return on investment (ROI). Instead of investment in building manufacturing capabilities, many companies adopt this strategy, to make available more resources for brand building in order to get a competitive market edge. *Nike* is a good example, which thrives on contract manufacturing. While there may be individual cases of success, its long-term sustainability is still a matter of debate.

Many companies, instead of building their own production capabilities across borders, prefer to adopt the strategy of developing network manufacturing, collaborating with their vendors, as in the case of *IKEA*. However, maintaining skeletal manufacturing facilities, and leveraging on one's own design and research and development capabilities is always preferable.

18.6 OUTSOURCING

Outsourcing in production and operations management has assumed importance subsequent to globalization. As a result of globalization, competition has increased, and at the same time, it has created new market opportunities for manufacturing and service organizations. With IT support, production and operations managers now outsource jobs to any location in the world, where they feel it is cost competitive, and at the same time, matches quality requirements. Outsourcing has significantly influenced the production and operations strategies of firms. It not only requires effort to identify proper outsourcing vendors, but also logistics and supply chain management on a global scale. Obviously, today's production and operations managers need to understand the technicalities of outsourcing, acquire negotiation skills, and develop skills with regard to cross-cultural issues. Some emerging economies like China, Brazil, Russia, and even India, are favourite destinations for the international outsourcing of jobs. From manufacturing and services, the scope of outsourcing has expanded to medical research. Many global pharmaceutical companies have located their research and development divisions in India. Such opportunities have created tremendous scope to get the services of best research talents at competitive costs. In India, much of the international outsourcing business comes from the information technology sector. In China, however, international outsourcing in manufacturing is more.

Some of the reasons for choosing Indian outsourcing companies are their cost effective services, increased productivity and efficiency, significant reduction in operations costs, and achievement of highest quality. This is particularly true in the case of IT jobs that are outsourced to India. These reasons can be listed as follows:

- Availability of quality and cost-effective services
- Availability of high-end technology and infrastructure support
- Availability of skilled and talented professionals of international standards
- Availability of a wide portfolio of services
- Political stability
- Quick services

Apart from the outsourcing of international jobs to India, domestic manufacturers and service providers also outsource their jobs to outsourcing vendors within the country, to meet their increased market commitment. In this process, domestic companies gain a competitive advantage.

SUMMARY

1. In a globalized economy, the pace of change is now exerting an influence on the production and operations management function. The internationalization of the production and operations functions requires companies to train and develop their managers so that they can understand the realities of developing their operations on a global scale.
2. International production and operations management requires network-based manufacturing and the ability to deal with its corresponding effects. Lessons on network-based models of business have been drawn in line with world class organizations, like *Avon, Tupperware, Toyota, Ford, BMW,* etc. Network-based business, generates competitive advantages equally in production, supply chain and in services.
3. With state-of-the-art information and telecommunication technology, companies through internationalization, now design and develop products and processes that match the quality expectations of customers, and also their ability to pay.
4. Many Indian companies like *Dabur, Asian Paints, Videocon,* etc. have their own production facilities in multiple locations across the world. For *Asian Paints,* apart from new market opportunities, the manufacturing sites are based abroad primarily to save on logistics costs and for maintaining the quality of paints. For *Dabur,* it is for gaining market advantages. For *Videocon,* it is for better forward and backward linkages.
5. International POM requires managers and executives not only to understand country-specific business needs, but the culture and social systems, without balancing which they cannot survive.
6. Companies, while taking decisions on globalization of their production and operations functions think about certain strategic intents, the most important among which is competitiveness. This apart, international production and operations strategy, at the outset, focusses on designing and managing networks.

KEY WORDS

International POM Internationalization of POM functions prima facie indicates that the company has an international network of manufacturing facilities with vendors, markets, supply chain, human resources, technology and information.

Globalization has changed business practices, and so we interpret globalization as a process. The ramifications of globalization can be understood in terms of expansion of international trade, cross-border labour migration, flow of investments, cross-cultural impact, restructuring of business processes, increased spate of technology transfer and so on. Obviously, globalization has necessitated the internationalization of the production and operations management functions as well.

International POM strategy International production and operations strategy, at the outset, focusses on designing and managing networks. Such networks not only help in churning out tangible products but also in terms of abstract services, offering the best package to customers. Apart from the conventional 'top–down' approach of strategy formulation; in international POM, strategy can also be framed following a 'bottom–up' approach.

Comparative advantages These are gained in terms of factor endowments (land, labour, resources, etc.). As per the theory of comparative advantage, factor endowments suggest producing those goods, for which the required factors are available in abundance.

Network strategy of International POM In the international production and operations management function, it is important to decide country-specific production activity, depending on the expertise and the economy of advantage. To manage an international production network requires strategic decisions on the global spread of production facilities, outsourcing and supply chain management. Individual companies can gain a competitive advantage for the effective management of their global production network.

Transfer pricing By lowering the internal price structure, companies can reduce their profits and in the process can deprive the host country of legitimate tax pay-outs.

GENERAL REVIEW QUESTIONS

1. Explain the concept of international production and operations management. Discuss how it benefits the organization.
2. Discuss how globalization has influenced the production and operations management function
3. What are the strategic issues of international production and operations management? Discuss the different types of strategies in international POM functions.
4. What are the advantages and disadvantages of international POM functions?
5. What is network strategy of international POM? How does it benefit an organization?
6. Short notes
   (a) Footloose strategy
   (b) Deep-rooted strategy
   (c) Network-based manufacturing
   (d) Internationalization

(e) Environmental imbalance

CRITICAL REVIEW QUESTIONS

1. An Indian furniture manufacturer with the largest market share in the domestic market would now like to expand its business abroad. The furniture manufacturer specializes in wooden furniture only. For its global market development, the company has chosen Germany, Italy and France as its initial target markets. These three countries have specific tastes and preferences. Suggest, as an expert, how the company can develop a network for market development in these countries?
2. *Dabur* is of late experiencing difficulty in their international operations. As an expert suggest whether the company should focus on deep-rooted strategy, or focus on their present footloose strategy?

REFERENCES

1. Davis, Mark M., Nicholas J. Aquilano, and Richard B. Chase. 1999. *Fundamentals of Operations Management*. 3rd ed. Boston: Irwin McGraw-Hill,
2. Ghoshal, S., and C.A. Bartlett. 1990. The multinational corporation as an interorganizational network. *Academy of Management Review* 15, pp. 603–625.
3. Grant, R.M. 1996. Towards a knowledge-based theory of the firm. *Strategic Management Journal,* 17, pp. 109–122
4. Heizer, Jay; Render, Barry. 2008. *Operations Management*. 9th ed. New Jersey: Prentice-Hall.
5. Krajewski, Lee J., Ritzman, Larry P. 2004. *Operations Management*. Reading: Addison Wesley.
6. Rainbird, Mark. 2004. A Framework for Operations Management: The Value Chain. *International Journal of Operations and Production Management,* 34, no. 3/4: 337–345.
7. Sahiman, W. 1999. The new economy is stronger than you think. *Harvard Business Review,* Vol. 77, No, 7, November–December, pp. 99–106.
8. Shi, Y. and Gregory, M. 1998. International Manufacturing Networks: To Develop Global Competitive Capabilities. *Journal of Operations Management,* Vol. 16, pp. 195–214.
9. Zander, U. and Kogut, B. 1995. Knowledge and the speed of the transfer and imitation of organizational capabilities: an empirical test. *Organization Science,* 6: 76–92

ADDITIONAL REFERENCES

1. Bartlett, C. A.; Ghoshal, S. 1992. *Transnational Management: Text, Cases and Readings in Cross-Border Management*. Irwin: McGraw-Hill.
2. Chase, Richard B., Jacobs, F. Roberts; Aquilano, Nicholas J. 2006. *Operations Management for Competitive Advantage,* 11th ed. Boston: McGraw-Hill Irwin.
3. Corrêa, H. L. 2008. Changes in the Role of Production and Operations Management in the New Economy. *Journal of Operations and Supply Chain Management* 1(1), pp.1-11,
4. Dilworth, James B. 2000. *Operations Management: Providing Value in Goods and Services*, 3rd Ed. Fort Worth: Dryden Press.
5. Finch, Byron. 2006. *Operations Now*. 2nd ed., Boston: McGraw-Hill Irwin.
6. Farrell, Diana. 2003. The Real New Economy. *Harvard Business Review*. October. pp. 105–112.
7. Fisher, Marshall. 1997. What is the right supply chain for your product? *Harvard Business Review*. March–April, pp. 105–116.
8. Friedman, Thomas L. 2005. *The World is Flat: A Brief History of the 21st Century*. New York: Farrar
9. Karlsson, C. 2003. The development of industrial networks: Challenges to operations management in an enterprise. *International Journal of Operations and Production Management,* 19–1, pp. 44–61.
10. Straus and Giroux. Gaither, N., Frazier, G. 2002. *Operations Management*. 9th. ed. Cincinnati: South-Western.
11. Hayes, Robert H. 2002. Challenges posed to operations management by the new economy. *Production and Operations Management*. Vol. 11, No. 1, Spring, pp. 21–32.
12. Hayes, Robert H.; Wheelwright, Steven C. 1984. *Restoring our competitive edge*. New York: The Free Press.
13. McGee, John; Bonnici, T.A.S. 2002., Network Industries in the New Economy. *European Business Journal*. Vol. 14, pp. 116–132.
14. Melnyk, Steven A.; Denzler, David R. 1996. *Operations Management: A Value-Driven Approach*. New York: Irwin McGraw-Hill.
15. Raturi, Amitabh, and James R. Evans. 2005. *Principles of Operations Management*, Mason, OH: Thomson Southwestern,
16. Reid Dan R., Sanders, Nada R. 2002. *Operations Management*, New York: John Wiley and Sons.
17. Russell, Roberta S.; Taylor III, Bernard W. 2000. *Operations Management*, 3rd Ed. New Jersey: Prentice Hall.
18. Sahlman, William A. 1999. The New Economy is Stronger than You Think. *Harvard Business Review*, Vol 77, No. 6. November–December, 99–106.
19. Starr, Martin K. 2004. *Production and Operations Management*. Cincinnati: Atomic Dog Publishing.

20. Stevenson, Willian J. 2005. *Operations Management*, 8th ed. New York: Mcgraw-Hill Irwin.
21. Walker, D.L. 1999. *Operations Management*. London: Thomson Business Press International.
22. Wild, Ray. 1995. *Production and Operations Management*, 5th ed. London: Thomson Learning.

CASE STUDY

Asian Paints to restructure international operations news

Asian Paints has a vibrant presence across the globe and almost 30% of its sales revenue comes from its international operations spread across 22 countries. With the acquisition of Singapore based *Berger International*, the company has now become more global. To become a major player in the decorative paints business, the company focussed on the emerging markets, subsequent to the acquisition of *Berger International* and *SCIB Chemical S.A.E.* of Egypt. These two successive acquisitions could make *Asian Paints* one of the top ten decorative paint manufacturers of the world. Strategically, the company focussed on emerging markets for international business, as these markets itself share more than 50% of the world's population.

Business expansion, be it in the domestic market or abroad is not possible without a strong supply chain. *Asian Paints'* supply chain management is adjudged the best in the country. A network of 14,500 dealers, 2500 stockists, is efficiently managed by the company from 70 sales locations through their supply chain management systems. Further, with increased focus on cost issues, and improved working capital management, the company could also achieve cost efficiency.

Global expansion of business is not just possible with internal efficiency; it also requires product innovation, and new product development. Realizing this as important, the company focussed on improving their operational activities, side by side with their focus on sustained research and development activities. Leveraging the expertise of *Berger International* and *SCIB Chemicals*, the company could come out with new products, considering country-specific requirements.

Today, *Asian Paints* operates in 24 countries and all its 27 production facilities constantly endeavour to achieve efficiencies in operations, production, distribution and new product development.

Discussion Question

Visit the website of *Asian Paints,* read the information and list their priorities in international operations. Critically evaluate whether such focus can help the company to achieve excellence in global business exposure

Index